M000248767

REFRAMING FINANCIAL REGULATION

REFRAMING FINANCIAL REGULATION
Enhancing Stability and Protecting Consumers

EDITED BY HESTER PEIRCE AND BENJAMIN KLUTSEY

MERCATUS CENTER
George Mason University

Arlington, Virginia

About the Mercatus Center at George Mason University

The Mercatus Center at George Mason University is the world's premier university source for market-oriented ideas—bridging the gap between academic ideas and real-world problems.

A university-based research center, Mercatus advances knowledge about how markets work to improve people's lives by training graduate students, conducting research, and applying economics to offer solutions to society's most pressing problems.

Our mission is to generate knowledge and understanding of the institutions that affect the freedom to prosper and to find sustainable solutions that overcome the barriers preventing individuals from living free, prosperous, and peaceful lives.

Founded in 1980, the Mercatus Center is located on George Mason University's Arlington and Fairfax campuses.

Mercatus Center at George Mason University
3434 Washington Blvd., 4th Floor
Arlington, VA 22201
www.mercatus.org
703-993-4930

© 2016 by the Mercatus Center at George Mason University. All rights reserved.

ISBN-13: 978-1-942951-30-8 paperback
ISBN-13: 978-1-942951-31-5 Kindle e-book

Cover design by Studio Gearbox, Sisters, OR
Editing and composition by Westchester Publishing Services, Danbury, CT

Printed in the United States of America

CONTENTS

Part 3: Regulating Securities and Derivatives Markets

Part 4: Regulating Consumer Finance

Part 5: Facilitating Innovation

Part 6: Improving the Regulatory Process

FOREWORD

JAMES M. KILTS
Centerview Capital

This book's solutions embody one of the key lessons I learned on the job: Accountability for consequences belongs with the people who make the decisions. It is time to remake the financial regulatory framework so that companies, not regulators, are making decisions and are on the hook for the bad ones.

The challenges of successfully running a large company are best learned by doing. Even top-notch instruction in the business school classroom cannot prepare people for the real-world scenarios they will face in the boardroom. A competing cascade of difficult decisions, promising opportunities, and unanticipated roadblocks draws on every strand of a management team's mental and physical strength. A company's management team has to collaborate in establishing the company's fundamentals, deciding what and whom to pay attention to and what to ignore, choosing among radically different strategies for growth, and determining whether to cut the company's losses or instead to pour more money into a project. Often these decisions have to be made quickly and without all of the relevant information. And all of these decisions are made against the backdrop of a changing world.

My on-the-job learning came in the consumer products industry at the helm of some of America's best-loved companies, including Kraft Foods, Nabisco, and The Gillette Company. Leading these American icons was a privilege, but it required a lot of intense work to outperform the public's high expectations. In the competitive consumer products industry, even well-known companies must constantly strive to serve customers' needs better than their rivals do. There is no time to sit back and enjoy a product's success, and new products must be consistently high quality in order not to damage the company's brand. Dependable excellence is essential.

The consumer marketplace is far from static. Consumers' desires and competitors' strategies for meeting them are constantly changing. Only a company that is willing to embrace the market's dynamism can thrive. Companies that stop pushing to be the best lose their edge quickly. A winning product, whether it is a razor, a battery-powered toothbrush, or a frozen pizza, comes only through knowing your customers, anticipating their needs and budget constraints, and understanding what appeals to them. The successful company takes seriously the task of collecting, processing, and responding to feedback from customers, suppliers, and distributors. The discipline of having to compete for customer loyalty is intensely rigorous and shows no mercy for a company that stops striving for excellence. In short, consumers—through their pocketbooks—hold companies accountable for their performance.

Although financial products and services are very different from the consumer products that were the focus of most of my career, accountability is key in this industry, too. Financial-services companies face similar challenges to other companies seeking to anticipate and meet the needs of their customers. The CEO of a bank or an asset manager has to think about how her company can stand out in a competitive landscape, just as her peers in the consumer products industry must do. In financial services as in consumer products, complacency means that rivals will woo customers with offerings that better meet customer needs. Customers can and do reward financial-services companies that serve them well and abandon others that don't measure up.

As this book demonstrates, however, the current approach to financial regulation is changing the way the financial industry works and thinks. An ever-thickening layer of regulations has added to the already-difficult job of running banks, brokerages, and insurance companies. Every decision is colored by—and increasingly driven by—regulatory considerations. The needs of customers are taking a back seat, and some companies enjoy regulation-induced competitive advantages over other companies. The result is an industry that is increasingly distracted from the needs of the individuals and companies it is supposed to serve. The stakes are high; without a properly accountable financial industry, this country's economic prosperity will suffer.

There is a better way. This book sets forth some creative solutions to the financial regulatory questions of our day. Is there a way to address consumer protection and systemic risk concerns without fundamentally changing the incentives and competitive market dynamics that encourage individuals and companies to provide excellent products and services? This book says yes.

The book contains regulatory approaches that build on the fundamental market forces that should remain the backbone of our economy. It offers solutions that recognize that users of the financial system—consumers, investors, and companies—should select its winners and losers. The book recognizes the importance of allowing the people who run financial companies to make decisions without having constantly to seek regulatory permission. It also underscores the importance of competition in ensuring that consumers have access to high-quality, appropriately tailored, safe products and services. The contributors to this book are not proposing a regulation-free financial system, but they are outlining more effective ways to achieve the important regulatory objectives of protecting consumers, ensuring financial stability, and enhancing economic growth.

This book doesn't purport to have all the answers, but it is a good place for policymakers to start in crafting a better, safer, and more customer-oriented financial regulatory system.

ACRONYMS AND ABBREVIATIONS

AA	agency algorithms
AFSA	American Financial Services Association
AIG	American International Group
AIM	Alternative Investment Market (of the London Stock Exchange)
AML/KYC	Anti-money Laundering/Know Your Customer
APR	annual percentage rate
ASI	American Share Insurance
ATS	Alternative Trading Systems
BHC	bank holding company
BSA	Bank Secrecy Act
CARD Act	Credit Card Accountability Responsibility and Disclosure Act
CCP	central counterparty
CDARS	Certificate of Deposit Account Registry Service
CDIC	Canadian Deposit Insurance Corporation
CDO	collateralized debt obligation
CDS	credit default swap
CEA	Commodity Exchange Act
CFED	Consumer Federation of America
CFPB	Bureau of Consumer Financial Protection
CFSA	Community Financial Services Association of America
CFTC	US Commodity Futures Trading Commission
CLOB	central limit order book
coco	contingent convertible bond
CPMI	Committee on Payments and Market Infrastructures
CPSS	Committee on Payment and Settlement Systems
CRD	Central Registration Depository
DCM	Designated Contract Market
DCO	Derivatives Clearing Organization
DIDMCA	Depository Institutions Deregulation and Monetary Control Act
DIF	Deposit Insurance Fund
EFTA	Electronic Fund Transfer Act
EMV	Europay, MasterCard, and Visa (standard)
ERISA	Employee Retirement Income Security Act

FASB	Financial Accounting Standards Board
FCM	Futures Commission Merchant
FDIC	Federal Deposit Insurance Corporation
FDICIA	Federal Deposit Insurance Corporation Improvement Act
FHA	Federal Housing Administration
FinCEN	Financial Crimes Enforcement Network
FINRA	Financial Industry Regulatory Authority
fintech	financial technology
FMU	Financial Market Utility
FSLIC	Federal Savings and Loan Insurance Corporation
FSOC	Financial Stability Oversight Council
FTC	Federal Trade Commission
FTT	financial transaction tax
G10	Group of Ten
G20	Group of Twenty
GAAP	generally accepted accounting principles
GFE	good faith estimate
GPR	general-purpose reloadable
G-SIB	global systemically important bank
HFT	high-frequency trading
HUD	Department of Housing and Urban Development
IB	Introducing Broker
IMF	International Monetary Fund
IOSCO	International Organization of Securities Commissions
IPO	initial public offering
IRA	Individual Retirement Account
ISDA	International Swaps and Derivatives Association
JOBS Act	Jumpstart Our Business Startups Act of 2012
LLC	limited liability company
MAT	Made Available to Trade
MBS	mortgage-backed security
MLP	master limited partnership
MSP	major swap participant
MSRB	Municipal Securities Rulemaking Board
NAAG	National Association of Attorneys General
NASD	National Association of Securities Dealers

NCCF	National Commission on Consumer Finance
NCUA	National Credit Union Administration
NCUSIF	National Credit Union Share Insurance Fund
NFA	National Futures Association
NILA	National Installment Lenders Association
NMS	National Market System
NOW	negotiable order of withdrawal
NSMIA	National Securities Markets Improvement Act
NYSE	New York Stock Exchange
ODGF	Ohio Deposit Guarantee Fund
OIRA	Office of Information and Regulatory Affairs
OLA	Orderly Liquidation Authority
OMB	Office of Management and Budget
OTC	over-the-counter
OTF	Organized Trading Facility
PAT	proprietary algorithmic trading
PCA	prompt corrective action
PCAOB	Public Company Accounting Oversight Board
RESPA	Real Estate Settlement Procedures Act
RFQ	request for quote
RIA	regulatory impact analysis
SCI	Systems Compliance and Integrity
SD	swap dealer
SDR	swap data repository
SEC	US Securities and Exchange Commission
SEF	swap execution facility
SIFI	systemically important financial institution
SIFMA	Securities Industry and Financial Markets Association
SIP	Securities Information Processor
SIPA	Securities Investor Protection Act
SIPC	Securities Investor Protection Corporation
S&L	savings and loan
SPOE	single point of entry
SRO	self-regulatory organization
TARP	Troubled Asset Relief Program
TBTF	too big to fail

TILA	Truth in Lending Act
VaR	value at risk
VCBA	Virtual Currency Business Activity
WaMu	Washington Mutual
YSP	yield spread premium

INTRODUCTION
Market-Based Financial
Regulation

HESTER PEIRCE AND BENJAMIN KLUTSEY
Mercatus Center at George Mason University

The financial system exists to facilitate the transfer of capital from savers and investors to people and companies in want of capital and to spread risks among individuals and entities with varying appetites for risk taking. The financial markets are the main channel for providing access to capital, which in turn fuels economic activity. However, our current regulatory system does not improve market functioning. A better approach is possible, but it requires a willingness to revisit our current regulatory models and ask whether they are working as intended to foster financial stability, support economic growth, and protect consumers.

A regulatory approach that relies on—rather than represses—the market's inherent dynamism, competition, and sensitivity to customer demand offers great promise and is the subject of this book. Financial markets transmit abundant amounts of information containing valuable signals to providers and consumers of financial products and services. Market participants glean this information as they go about their day-to-day business. The late economist Friedrich A. Hayek calls this "the knowledge of the particular circumstances of time and place."[1] This book's underlying theme is that the knowledge of the particular circumstances of time and place is essential to effective financial regulation. It is not government regulators who possess this knowledge, but private market participants. Accordingly, regulation that takes that knowledge into account must come from the bottom-up, not the top-down. For instance, the knowledge of intelligent, well-intentioned government regulators cannot determine what financial products or services are appropriate for different types of consumers, the interest rates lenders should charge on various loan products, which financial technologies best address customers' needs, or which investments should populate investor portfolios. Consumers respond to firms' offers by buying or refusing to buy, and firms take into account market participants' needs in the design of products and services. This dynamic feedback process provides discipline as customers move away from options that do not serve them well and firms cut back on products their customers do not like.

THE ROLE OF FINANCIAL MARKETS

Allen and Yago have pointed out that in ancient societies "access to capital . . . was limited to rulers, priests, craftsmen, and merchants."[2] Because of market competition and entrepreneurial innovations, our modern financial system has evolved to provide capital access to people from all walks of life, and it is still evolving to further expand access. This transformation of the financial system, in conjunction with technological change, has meaningfully affected people's lives. Individuals conduct banking transactions, obtain mortgages, and finance small businesses online. Face-to-face is giving way to the mobile interface, a development that further democratizes capital access.

By expanding access to capital, financial markets foster economic growth. As technological and societal barriers fall, capital increasingly can flow to its highest and best use. Based on an edited compilation of research across many countries, Demirgüç-Kunt and Levine conclude that "overall financial development tends to accelerate economic growth, facilitate new firm formation, ease firm access to external financing, and boost firm growth."[3] Other analyses also show that economic growth tends to follow the development of a robust financial market system, fueled by a strong legal and institutional infrastructure.[4] However, ill-considered financial regulation creates new barriers that prevent individuals and businesses from obtaining the capital they need and thus stands in the way of individual prosperity and economic growth.

FINANCIAL REGULATIONS

The United States has a long history of banking and financial crises. Over the past 180 years we have had at least fourteen severe banking crises.[5] The legacy of these crises is an ever-growing rulebook. Hence, contrary to popular narratives, the financial services industry is among the most regulated areas of our economy. Prior to the last financial crisis, total regulatory restrictions related to the financial services sector had expanded annually from 1999 to 2008 for a total increase of 23 percent.[6] Since the crisis, the regulatory framework has grown even larger and more complex, especially with the passage of the Dodd-Frank Wall Street Reform and Consumer Protection Act in July 2010 (Dodd-Frank).[7] Using the Mercatus Center's online dataset, our colleagues Patrick A. McLaughlin and Oliver Sherouse show that the scale of new rules promulgated under Dodd-Frank substantially exceeds any previous set of regulations governing financial markets.[8] According to McLaughlin and Sherouse, Dodd-Frank adds a total of nearly 28,000 new restrictions to the body of US financial regulations.

Many of these postcrisis regulations rely on the limited knowledge and interventionist hand of financial regulators. Regulators who are situated outside the markets are unable to collect and analyze the "knowledge of the particular circumstances of time and place" with the necessary speed and completeness to carry out the obligations with which Congress has charged them. Regulators—suffering from their innately constrained view of the financial system—were not able to anticipate and react to the events that led to the crisis.[9] Indeed, their actions may have inadvertently made the crisis worse. In addition to placing impossible expectations on regulators, as this book explains, the bulked-up financial regulatory structure provides a false sense of security, distorts competition, and impedes capital flows.

THE MUDDLED OBJECTIVES OF FINANCIAL REGULATION

Financial regulation suffers from the unclear objectives that guide it. Sound financial regulation provides the framework within which a healthy financial system can thrive and change to effectively meet the needs of individuals, corporations, governments, and the economy as a whole. Today's financial regulators seem to be striving for multiple amorphous goals, including eliminating risk, creating a failure-free financial system, and directing capital to satisfy noneconomic objectives.

Risk taking must be part of the financial system. As former US Securities and Exchange Commission (SEC) member and contributor to this volume Daniel M. Gallagher noted in a 2014 speech before the Institute of International Bankers, "In the capital markets, there is no opportunity without risk—and that means real risk, with a real potential for losses."[10] Thus, people who provide capital to an enterprise sign on to sharing in the potential gains and losses, and the regulatory framework should not stand in the way.

Market discipline is a missing ingredient in the regulation of the financial system. Financial institutions and products must be allowed to disappear when they do not meet the needs of their customers. Failure, perhaps counterintuitively, can enhance the long-term health of the financial system.[11] A well-regulated but competitive financial system manages failure to minimize devastating consequences to households and the economy, while bidding an unsentimental farewell to failed firms and welcoming in their place new entrants with products and services that meet customer needs.

Attempts to eliminate failure also deprive individuals, firms, and markets of the valuable lessons in failure.[12] Citing Milton Friedman, Russell Roberts notes that capitalism is a profit and loss system where "profits encourage risk taking [and] losses encourage prudence."[13] When this risk-reward calculus is appropriately incorporated in decision-making, firms and investors effectively learn lessons from previous actions. In their research, Bouwman and Malmendier explore "whether a bank's capitalization and risk appetite are affected by the economic environment and outcomes it has faced, and survived, in the past."[14] In a nutshell, their research shows that "past macroeconomic and bank-specific shocks experienced (and survived) by a financial institution appear to affect its capitalization and risk taking, suggesting that experiences propagate into the future and generate some form of institutional memory."[15] Institutions and their managers who have been through crises tend to learn from them and benefit from these lessons by exhibiting more careful lending behavior and becoming more capitalized, which makes them resilient in the next crisis.

The financial regulatory framework should not be used to direct capital toward favored causes or away from disfavored ones. Financial regulators now actively craft macroprudential strategies for the whole financial system that override the decision-making of individual institutions. Whether it is providing incentives to make mortgage loans that a lender would not otherwise make, discouraging the provision of financial services to certain types of businesses, or subsidizing economically unsound lending to politically favored industries, financial regulation and regulators affect how capital is allocated in our economy. A properly designed regulatory system allows capital to flow to its highest and best use, as determined by market participants' expressions of value.

Our financial regulatory system needs to be reoriented to meet the objective of providing the framework within which individuals and institutions come together freely to engage in mutually beneficial financial transactions. This book offers market-oriented ideas to allow financial markets to flourish as they dynamically supply capital to meet the constantly changing needs of consumers, investors, and businesses. Each chapter raises concerns about the existing regulatory framework and offers substantive reform ideas. The book is not intended to be a comprehensive plan for replacing our current top-down regulatory apparatus. Rather, we intend to ignite a conversation about reimagining the existing framework and replacing it with a more effective organic approach to regulation. Consistent with the goal of inspiring debate over these important issues, the book offers a variety of viewpoints and different ideas about how to reform the regulatory structure.

Part 1 deals with bank capital and deposit insurance, two tools used to foster prudence and financial stability. In chapter 1, Mercatus Center–senior affiliated scholar Arnold Kling discusses the introduction of risk-based capital in the United States, identifies the weaknesses in this approach, then discusses alternative ideas to improve financial regulations, including reducing the tax advantage of debt and incentivizing managers to make prudent choices. In chapter 2, Mercatus Center Senior Research Fellow Stephen Matteo Miller reviews the effectiveness of capital regulations in US banking history and looks at alternative, simpler capital requirement proposals instead of a capital regime that focuses on risk weights. Thomas Hogan and Kristine Johnson focus on deposit insurance in chapter 3 and make the case that government-provided deposit insurance fosters moral hazard by eliminating the incentives for depositors to monitor bank activities. They consider alternatives, including private forms of deposit insurance.

Part 2 presents a diverse set of views on addressing failure at large financial institutions in a way that minimizes disruption to the overall financial system and does not rely on taxpayer bailouts. Pointing out the persistence of the too big to fail (TBTF) problem and the flaws in Dodd-Frank's Orderly Liquidition Authority provisions, American Enterprise Institute Fellow Peter Wallison argues in chapter 4 that traditional bankruptcy mechanisms work and carefully monitored, adequate capital levels are the best way to address TBTF. Alternatively, in chapter 5, Garett Jones, Associate Professor of Economics and BB&T Professor for the Study of Capitalism at the Mercatus Center, George Mason University, notes the strong political temptation to bail out failing firms during crises and argues for precrisis commitments to "nonutopian alternatives to 100 percent bailouts." These alternatives include the bail-ins Jones has discussed in prior work.

Part 3 discusses the securities and derivatives markets. In chapter 6, the Honorable Daniel M. Gallagher surveys the federal oversight regime governing the operations and conduct of broker-dealers. Highlighting that the regime is comparatively more market-oriented than some other areas of the financial system, he recommends conducting economic analysis of proposed new regulatory burdens and a return to truly self-regulatory organizations. In chapter 7, J. Christopher Giancarlo, a commissioner of the US Commodity Futures Trading Commission (CFTC), reviews the requirement under Dodd-Frank that swaps be executed on regulated trading platforms. This chapter analyzes the flaws in the CFTC's implementation of the swaps trading regulatory framework and proposes a more effective, less top-down alternative that better aligns regulatory oversight with inherent swaps market dynamics.

In chapter 8, Hester Peirce and Vera Soliman of the Mercatus Center look at the new regulations that require mandatory clearing of over-the-counter derivatives through central counterparties (CCPs). They suggest that regulatory reforms have unintentionally destabilized the financial markets and outline an alternative regulatory model that would allow the derivatives markets to develop through market mechanisms complemented by principles-based regulation and robust reporting. Chapter 9 gives a historical account of the evolution of stock exchanges and trading platforms; Edward Stringham, Kathryn Wasserman Davis Professor of Economic Organizations and Innovation and Deputy Director of the Shelby Cullom Davis Endowment at Trinity College, uses lessons from history to show that the rules and regulations of private exchanges can effectively reduce fraud and facilitate financial transactions.

In chapter 10, Holly A. Bell, Associate Professor of General Business at the University of Alaska Anchorage, discusses the concerns regulators have about algorithmic trading and outlines cooperative solutions for addressing human and technology errors. In particular, she proposes confidential self-reporting to learn how technology errors occur, how they affect markets, and how they can be addressed. Bell also suggests that regulators allow for the emergence of competing trading venues, platforms, and software to provide different (and potentially superior) services to investors. Chapter 11 examines the law and economics of securities offerings and mandatory disclosure requirements. In this chapter, David Burton, Heritage Foundation Senior Fellow in Economic Policy, questions how well the existing system works and suggests reforms to enhance the ability of the securities markets to serve investors and issuers.

Dodd-Frank substantially changed consumer finance regulation by introducing a new federal regulator and reopening debates that have played out at the state level for the past century. Given these changes, part 4 discusses the current consumer finance regulatory regime and offers market-based ways to think about fostering effective, dynamic, consumer-centric markets. In chapter 12, Todd Zywicki, Foundation Professor of Law and Executive Director of the Law & Economics Center at George Mason University's Antonin Scalia Law School, distinguishes between market-reinforcing regulations and market-replacing regulations and argues that the latter approach limits choice and competition. In chapter 13, Thomas W. Miller Jr., Professor of Finance and Jack R. Lee Chair of Financial Institutions and Consumer Finance at Mississippi State University's College of Business, and Harold A. Black, Professor Emeritus at the University of Tennessee, Knoxville, argue that interest rate caps limit consumer choice and thus harm the consumers they are supposed to help. They propose four concrete actions for policymakers and academics seeking to improve consumer well-being.

Over the past few decades we have seen a plethora of welfare-enhancing innovations in the financial markets. Part 5 looks at some of these innovations and provides a way forward that allows beneficial financial innovation to occur. In chapter 14, William Luther, Assistant Professor of Economics at Kenyon College, considers the popular justifications for regulating Bitcoin and offers simple guidelines for regulators to keep in mind. In chapter 15, Houman Shadab, Professor of Law and Co-Director, Center for Business and Financial

Law at New York Law School, reviews new technologies that foster improved access to capital, facilitate consumer payments, and simplify personal finance. Shadab outlines principles for fostering a pro-innovation, pro-consumer regulatory approach. In chapter 16, J. W. Verret, Associate Professor of Law at George Mason University's Antonin Scalia Law School and Mercatus senior scholar, argues against the excessive federalization of corporate governance and proposes to allow states and municipalities greater latitude to experiment with different approaches.

Finally, part 6 concludes with a chapter that examines whether there is a role for economic analysis in financial regulations. For the past several years there has been vigorous debate, with some skeptics arguing that the unique nature of financial markets means that economic analysis of financial regulations is either impossible or must at least be conducted much differently than for other types of regulations. In chapter 17, Senior Research Fellow Jerry Ellig and Vera Soliman of the Mercatus Center explain why economic analysis is not only possible but important in financial regulation.

One notable omission from this book is an alternative to the broken housing finance system that relies so heavily on the notoriously troubled government-sponsored entities. The late Dwight Jaffee of University of California, Berkeley, who was working on exactly such a piece, passed away during the drafting of this book. We will greatly miss Jaffee's careful and creative approach to these matters. The Mercatus Center at George Mason University will continue to investigate market-based regulatory approaches in housing finance and other areas that did not make it into this book.

NOTES

1. Hayek, "Use of Knowledge in Society."

2. Allen and Yago, *Financing the Future*, 10.

3. Demirgüç-Kunt and Levine, *Financial Structure and Economic Growth*, 11.

4. See Shin, "Financial Markets."

5. Calomiris and Haber, *Fragile by Design*, 5; Jalil, "New History of Banking Panics."

6. McLaughlin and Greene, "Did Deregulation Cause the Financial Crisis?"

7. Pub. L. No. 111–203, 124 Stat. 1376 (2010).

8. McLaughlin and Sherouse, "Dodd-Frank Wall Street Reform."

9. See, for example, Barth, Caprio, and Levine, *Guardians of Finance*; Roberts, "Gambling with Other People's Money"; and Kling, *Not What They Had in Mind*.

10. Commissioner Daniel M. Gallagher, Remarks Given at the Institute of International Bankers Twenty-fifth Annual Washington Conference, March 3, 2014.

11. For a discussion of the value of systems that thrive on failure, see Taleb, *Antifragile*.

12. For a discussion of the salutary role that failure can play, see McArdle, *Up Side of Down*.

13. Roberts, "Gambling with Other People's Money," 6.

14. Bouwman and Malmendier, "Does a Bank's History Affect Its Risk-Taking?"

15. Ibid., 5.

REFERENCES

Allen, Franklin, and Glenn Yago. *Financing the Future: Market-Based Innovations for Growth.* Upper Saddle River, NJ: Pearson Prentice Hall, March 2010.

Barth, James, Gerard Caprio Jr., and Ross Levine. *Guardians of Finance: Making Regulators Work for Us.* Cambridge, MA: MIT Press, 2010.

Bouwman, Christa H. S., and Ulrike Malmendier. "Does a Bank's History Affect Its Risk-Taking?" *American Economic Review: Papers & Proceedings 2015*, 105, no. 5 (May 2015): 1–7.

Calomiris, Charles W., and Stephen H. Haber. *Fragile by Design: The Political Origins of Banking Crises and Scarce Credit.* Princeton, NJ: Princeton University Press, 2014.

Demirgüç-Kunt, Asli, and Ross Levine, eds. *Financial Structure and Economic Growth: A Cross-Country Comparison of Banks, Markets, and Development.* Cambridge, MA: MIT Press, 2001.

Hayek, Friedrich A. "The Use of Knowledge in Society." *American Economic Review* 35 (1945): 519–30.

Jalil, Andrew J. "A New History of Banking Panics in the United States, 1825–1929: Construction and Implications." *American Economic Journal: Macroeconomics* 7, no. 3 (2015): 295–330.

Kling, Arnold. *Not What They Had in Mind: A History of Policies That Produced the Financial Crisis of 2008.* Washington, DC: Mercatus Center at George Mason University, September 2009.

McArdle, Megan. *The Up Side of Down: Why Failing Well Is the Key to Success.* New York: Penguin Books, 2014.

McLaughlin, Patrick, and Robert Greene. "Did Deregulation Cause the Financial Crisis? Examining a Common Justification for Dodd-Frank." Mercatus Center at George Mason University, July 19, 2013.

McLaughlin, Patrick, and Oliver Sherouse. "The Dodd-Frank Wall Street Reform and Consumer Protection Act May Be the Biggest Law Ever." Mercatus Center at George Mason University, July 20, 2015.

Roberts, Russell. "Gambling with Other People's Money: How Perverted Incentives Caused the Financial Crisis." Mercatus Center at George Mason University, May 2010.

Shin, Yongseok. "Financial Markets: An Engine for Economic Growth." *The Regional Economist*, Federal Reserve Bank of St. Louis, July 2013.

Taleb, Nassim Nicholas. *Antifragile: Things That Gain from Disorder.* New York: Random House, 2012.

PART 1

REGULATING LOSS ABSORPTION

CHAPTER 1
Risk-Based Capital Rules

ARNOLD KLING
Mercatus Center at George Mason University

The reality of financial regulation is that new rules open new avenues for regulatory arbitrage, as institutions find loopholes in regulations. That in turn forces authorities to institute new regulations in an ongoing cat-and-mouse game (between a very adroit mouse and a less nimble cat). Staying away from dark corners will require continuous effort, not one-shot regulation.

—Olivier Blanchard[1]

If federal regulators are thought to have better judgment about risk than the bankers themselves (due to the bankers' presumed moral-hazard problems), then there really is no reason to allow private banking to continue.

—Jeffrey Friedman and Wladimir Kraus[2]

Financial instability has vexed policymakers for generations. Many well-intentioned efforts have so far not been able to insulate modern economies from banking crises. One of those efforts, undertaken in the 1980s and still included in the structure of bank regulation, is to impose minimum capital requirements on banks that vary according to regulatory measures of risk. These risk-based capital rules are the subject of this chapter.

Risk-based capital rules were first issued in the United States as part of the international bank regulation agreement known as the Basel Accords, which were adopted in the 1980s in the aftermath of the US Savings and Loan Crisis. Subsequently, they have been modified several times. "The History of Risk-Based Capital Regulations" section of this chapter reviews the history of these rules.

The original rules, known as Basel I, and one of the modifications, known as the Recourse Rule, played a role in steering mortgage lending in the United States away from the "originate to hold" model for acquiring mortgage assets. These rules instead encouraged banks to obtain highly rated tranches of securities backed by mortgages. As a result, risk-based capital rules contributed to financial instability, quite the opposite of their intended objective. This is explained in "Risk Buckets, Securitization, and the Financial Crisis."

During the crisis itself, banks came under pressure to sell mortgage securities in order to comply with capital rules. That in turn drove prices for securities lower, which worsened the balance-sheet conditions of other financial institutions. Thus, in the context of a crisis, risk-based capital rules were revealed to be procyclical, which is undesirable from the perspective of financial stability. "Procyclical in a Crisis" looks at this issue.

Risk-based capital rules dramatically affect the rate of return banks earn from holding different types of assets. Regardless of the intent of these rules, they strongly influence capital allocation in the economy. They substitute even crude regulatory judgment for individual bank discretion and market mechanisms. As Friedman and Kraus point out, these rules impose on bank managers the regulators' judgment about the riskiness of different asset classes. These judgments override both the local knowledge of the individual bank manager and the evolutionary learning that comes from success and failure in the market. This aspect of the risk-based capital approach is discussed in "The Regulators' Calculation Problem."

What is the public policy rationale for risk-based capital rules? In "Managers, Risks, and Incentives," I argue that the motivation for risk-based capital rules is to try to increase the incentives for bank managers to make prudent decisions with respect to portfolio selection (operating leverage) and capital structure (financial leverage). In part, the government is trying to offset adverse incentives created elsewhere by government policy. The three government policies that encourage risk taking are the tax advantage of debt finance, the explicit guarantee of deposits through deposit insurance, and the implicit guarantee of bank debt that derives from policymakers' reluctance to permit bankruptcy of large financial firms ("too big to fail").

In "Alternatives to Capital Rules," I argue that risk-based capital rules are a misguided attempt to enhance bank soundness. The regulators' risk buckets effectively determine the prices of different types of assets. Because the regulators are far from omniscient as price-setters, the regulations are more likely to exacerbate than to reduce financial instability.

Instead, banking policy should focus more on the overall incentives for bank managers to act prudently. One option is to reduce the tax advantage associated with debt finance. Another option is to limit the total dollar amount of government-guaranteed deposits that a single institution can have in its liabilities. A third option is to use holistic audits of banks to evaluate their risk management, rather than relying on a simple formula. A final option is to enact legislation that puts some of the compensation of bank management at risk should the bank fail.

THE HISTORY OF RISK-BASED CAPITAL REGULATIONS[3]

In 1974, the central bankers of the Group of Ten (G10) countries established what became the Basel Committee on Banking Supervision to enable bank regulators in these countries to communicate and coordinate with one another.[4]

As recently as 1980, the Federal Deposit Insurance Corporation (FDIC) and the Federal Savings and Loan Insurance Corporation (FSLIC) had no formal numerical rules or guidelines concerning bank capital. Instead, capital was one of the factors included in a judgmental approach to evaluating bank risk. Altogether, the factors were capital adequacy, asset quality, management, earnings, and liquidity, producing the acronym CAMEL. In 1995, another factor was added, representing sensitivity to market risk, leading to the acronym CAMELS.

The year 1981 saw the FDIC introduce the first numerical capital standards applicable to all banks. However, the standards differed slightly by type of institution. Community banks were given a standard ratio of capital to assets of 6 percent, while large regional institutions were assigned a standard of 5 percent.

In 1985, US regulators abolished the differences by type of bank in favor of a uniform standard of 5.5 percent. Regulators also made it clear that banks whose ratio of capital to assets fell below 3 percent would face enforcement actions.

Meanwhile, regulatory agencies in the United States and the Basel Committee were considering two important issues with regard to capital regulation. One issue was how to include off-balance-sheet items, such as loan guarantees. Another issue was how to adjust capital standards for the risk of the bank's asset portfolio.

In July 1988, the Basel Committee issued its first important recommendations (Basel I), which bank regulators agreed to implement by 1992. Basel I included two definitions of capital. Tier 1 capital, or core capital, consisted only of common stockholders' equity, noncumulative perpetual preferred stock, and minority interests in equity accounts of consolidated subsidiaries (minus goodwill), plus disclosed reserves. Tier 2 capital, or supplementary capital, consisted of allowance for loan and lease losses (up to 1.25 percent of risk-weighted assets), perpetual preferred stock, hybrid capital instruments and mandatory convertible debt securities, term subordinated debt, and intermediate-term preferred stock. The amount of term subordinated debt plus intermediate-term preferred stock that could count as supplementary capital could not exceed 50 percent of core capital.

Total capital consisted of Tier 1 capital plus Tier 2 capital. Basel I called for a minimum ratio of total capital to risk-weighted assets of 8 percent. Also, at least half of this total capital had to be Tier 1 capital, which meant that the minimum ratio of core capital to total assets was 4 percent.

Basel I called for risk-weighted assets to be computed using four risk buckets, with national banking regulators having some discretion to assign asset classes to each bucket. The risk buckets were defined as 100 percent, 50 percent, 20 percent, and 0 percent, with each number representing a percentage of the highest risk class. Thus, if all of a bank's assets were in the 100 percent risk bucket, the bank would be required to have a minimum ratio of total capital to assets of 8 percent (including at least 4 percent Tier 1 capital). If all the bank's assets were in the 20 percent risk bucket, then the minimum capital ratio would be just 1.6 percent (including at least 0.8 percent Tier 1 capital).

If a bank's assets consisted of $50 in the 100 percent bucket and $50 in the 20 percent bucket, then its risk-weighted assets would be $50 + $10 = $60, and its total capital requirement would be 8 percent of that, or $4.80, with at least half of that consisting of Tier 1 capital.

In the United States, the risk buckets were specified as follows:

0 percent (not requiring any capital): Cash, balances due from Federal Reserve banks and Organisation for Economic Co-operation and Development (OECD) central banks, US Treasuries, gold.

20 percent: Cash items in the process of collection; all claims on, and the portions of claims guaranteed by, US depository institutions and OECD banks; all short-term claims on, and the portions of short-term claims guaranteed by, non-OECD banks; the portions of claims that are conditionally guaranteed by the central governments of OECD countries and US government agencies; claims on, and the portions of claims guaranteed by, US government-sponsored agencies; general obligation claims on, and the portions of claims that are guaranteed by the full faith and credit of, local governments and political subdivisions of the United States and other OECD local governments; claims on, and the portions of claims that are guaranteed by, official multilateral lending institutions or regional development banks; the portions of claims that are collateralized by securities issued or guaranteed by the US Treasury, the central governments of other OECD countries, US government agencies, US government-sponsored agencies, or by cash on deposit in the bank; the portions of claims that are collateralized by securities issued by official multilateral lending institutions or regional development banks; certain privately issued securities representing indirect ownership of mortgage-backed US government agency or US government-sponsored agency securities; investment in shares of a fund whose portfolio is permitted to hold only securities that would qualify for the 0 or 20 percent risk categories.

Note that government-sponsored agency securities includes securities issued by Freddie Mac and Fannie Mae.

50 percent: Loans secured by first liens on one to four family residential properties; revenue bonds or similar claims that are obligations of US state or local governments, or other OECD local governments, but for which

17

the government entity is committed to repay the debt only out of revenues from the facilities financed; credit equivalent amounts of interest rate and foreign exchange rate related contracts, except for those assigned to a lower risk category.

100 percent: All other claims on private obligors.

US regulators finalized their Basel I rules in 1989, with requirements phased in through the end of 1992.

The regulators also arrived at a classification scheme (table 1) for bank capital adequacy.

Regulatory policies for addressing a bank that failed to maintain at least adequate capital were known as prompt corrective action. These included:

- An institution deemed below adequately capitalized must file a written restoration plan within forty-five days of notification. The regulatory agency must decide on approval within sixty days. If a plan is not approved, not submitted, or not implemented, the institution is immediately subject to "significantly undercapitalized" conditions.

- Immediately upon being deemed undercapitalized, significantly undercapitalized, or critically undercapitalized, the institution is subject to:
  (i)   Restricting payment of distributions and management fees;
  (ii) Requiring that the agency monitor the condition of the institution;
  (iii) Requiring submission of a capital restoration plan;
  (iv) Restricting the growth of the bank's assets; and
  (v)   Requiring prior approval of certain expansion proposals.

- Significantly and critically undercapitalized institutions are immediately subject to an additional provision that restricts compensation paid to senior executive officers of the institution.

Critically undercapitalized institutions were immediately subject to additional provisions that varied by regulator. In fact, the expectation was that the agency insuring the depositors of the institution would either take over or arrange a merger of that institution within ninety days of it being deemed critically undercapitalized.

In the mid-1990s, the Basel Committee began wrestling with the concept of market risk. Prior to this, the risk buckets were based solely on credit

Table 1. Basel I Bank Capital Adequacy Classification Scheme

Category	Ratio of Total Capital to Risk-Weighted Assets	Ratio of Tier 1 Capital to Risk-Weighted Assets
Well capitalized	10 percent or greater	6 percent or greater
Adequately capitalized	8 percent or greater	4 percent or greater
Undercapitalized*	Less than 8 percent	Less than 4 percent
Significantly undercapitalized*	Less than 6 percent	Less than 3 percent
Critically undercapitalized		Less than 2 percent

Falls into this category if either ratio falls below the threshold.

risk. However, banks also risked taking losses from changes in interest rates, exchange rates, or other factors. In 1996, the Committee formally recommended addressing market risk using an approach known as a value at risk (VaR). These topics are outside of the scope of this chapter.

Starting in 1995, US bank regulators tried to address transactions in which the risk of an asset and the ownership of the asset were separated. The issue first arose in the form of a bank selling a loan but giving the buyer "recourse" to put the loan back to the bank in the case of default. Hence, this regulatory issue became known as the Recourse Rule.

By the time that the Recourse Rule was finalized by the Federal Reserve Board, the Office of the Comptroller of the Currency, and the FDIC in 2001, the main issue to address was asset-backed securities, which were being sliced into tranches with different levels of risk. The regulators had to develop a policy for assigning risk weights to the different tranches. They settled on using ratings by Nationally Recognized Statistical Rating Organizations (NRSROs). Securities rated AAA or AA were given a risk weight of 20 percent. A security rated A would be assigned a risk weight of 50 percent. A security rated BBB (the lowest investment grade) was assigned a weight of 100 percent, and securities rated BB (below investment grade) were assigned a risk weight of 200 percent.

In 2004, the Basel Committee put out a new paper of recommendations that became known as Basel II. Basel II included using NRSRO ratings for corporate bonds. It also allowed for models-based risk calculations, similar to VaR, for credit risk. In the United States, rules for implementation of Basel II were published at the end of 2007, but implementation was superseded by the financial crisis and subsequent Dodd-Frank legislation. The approach to be implemented in the near future precludes regulators from using NRSRO ratings for security tranches. Among other changes, it raises the minimum Tier 1 capital requirement to 6 percent and also allows for an additional countercyclical capital buffer of up to 2.5 percent to be applied to large banks at regulators' discretion during a period of high credit growth.

RISK BUCKETS, SECURITIZATION, AND THE FINANCIAL CRISIS

By the mid-1980s, policymakers had experienced the Savings and Loan Crisis, which affected the thrift industry in the United States, and the Latin American debt crisis, which affected large commercial banks in many countries. They decided that one of the issues that needed to be addressed was the need to adjust minimum capital requirements for the risk of a bank's asset portfolio. In the absence of any adjustment, a bank could meet the minimum capital requirement while acquiring a portfolio of risky assets for which the required regulatory capital provided insufficient protection.

Regulators were particularly concerned about the potential impact of cross-country differences in the regulatory treatment of assets. Suppose that there is a low-yielding, low-risk asset, Z, and there are two risky assets, X and Y. If one country discouraged banks from holding risky asset X but not risky asset Y, while another country discouraged banks from holding Y but not X, then each country's banks could end up holding nothing but risky assets, with all banks spurning the low-risk asset, Z.

The approach adopted in 1988, known as Basel I, classified different types of assets into "risk buckets." The riskiest assets, commercial loans, had a weight of 1.0. If the capital requirement was 8 percent, then each additional $100 in commercial loans required the bank to raise an additional $8 in capital. On the other hand, government debt had a weight of zero, so that a bank could increase its holdings of government debt without raising any additional capital. (Note that even default-free government debt carries risk, in that long-term bonds can change in value as interest rates change.) The securities of government-sponsored enterprises, including Fannie Mae and Freddie Mac, were given a weight of 0.2, meaning that if the capital requirement was 8 percent, each additional $100 in Freddie or Fannie securities required only $1.60 in additional capital.

In 2001, an important modification to the risk buckets was incorporated in what was called the Recourse Rule.[5] The original purpose of the rule was to deal with assets that were off of a bank's books but for which the bank remains exposed from a risk perspective. For example, if a bank has sold a loan to another institution with recourse, that means that in the event the loan defaults, the other institution can force the bank to repurchase the loan at par. Thus, although the loan is off the books, the bank is still liable for the risk. The Recourse Rule required the bank to hold capital against such a loan, just as if it held that loan in portfolio.

Along with the Recourse Rule, the regulators changed their approach to assigning risk weights to tranches of asset-backed securities. The new approach was based on risk ratings by NRSROs. This reduced the risk-weight for AAA-rated and AA-rated securities backed by mortgages to just 20 percent. As Friedman and Kraus pointed out, this provision stimulated very rapid growth in the issuance of private mortgage-backed securities, meaning securities that were not issued by Freddie Mac or Fannie Mae. Because Wall Street underwriters could fashion large tranches of AAA-rated and AA-rated securities (these were known as "senior" tranches) even when the underlying mortgages were subprime loans, this in turn created the financial fuel for the boom in subprime lending and the housing bubble.

To understand the power of the risk buckets to influence bank behavior, consider a hypothetical example. Suppose that a bank faces a capital requirement of 8 percent of risk-weighted assets, and it is trying to choose from among deploying its capital to make commercial loans, mortgage loans that it originates and holds, or highly rated mortgage securities backed by loans originated by other lenders. Each $8 in capital can support either $100 in commercial loans, $200 in mortgage loans originated to hold or AA-rated mortgage-backed securities, or $500 in AAA-rated mortgage-backed securities.

Bank regulators, by establishing low-risk weights on mortgages and especially on mortgage-backed securities, exerted a powerful influence on the allocation of capital not only in the United States but throughout the world. Trillions of dollars of the world's savings were directed toward an expansion of mortgage credit to American households.

If the intent of the regulators was to reduce systemic financial risk, they did not succeed. It turned out that there were several flaws in the risk buckets:

1. The task of assigning ratings to mortgage securities was given to credit rating agencies, primarily Moody's, Standard and Poor's, and Fitch. To maintain its market share, each rating agency had the incentive to find ways to generously rate the security structures produced by Wall Street firms. Because the ratings were used primarily for regulatory purposes, the rating agencies had relatively little incentive to please investors by producing ratings on securities that were as conservative as those on corporate bonds.

2. Among regulators, investors, and rating agency analysts, the assumption was widespread that any decline in house prices would be concentrated in local markets. Under this assumption, geographic diversification could serve to ensure the safety of senior tranches of mortgage-backed securities. In fact, the house price declines that took place were more widespread than had been allowed for in the statistical models used to rate the securities.

3. Regulators, investors, and rating agency analysts paid insufficient attention to the deterioration in the quality of the underlying mortgage loans. Increasingly, borrowers lacked the means to meet the payments on loans. The only way that they could avoid default was to take out a new loan to pay off their mortgages. This refinancing process in turn required continual appreciation of home values in order to support rolling over mortgage loans in this way. Because of the fragile financial situations of so many borrowers, when house prices stopped rising the default rates were higher than would have been the case with loans that met more traditional, conservative underwriting standards.

PROCYCLICAL IN A CRISIS

The intent of capital requirements is to prevent financial crises by ensuring that banks hold sufficient capital to cover their risks. However, an unintended side effect of capital requirements is that they are procyclical. That is, they encourage banks to expand when times are good, and they amplify bank contraction when times are bad. During a crisis, this can create a particularly rapid vicious cycle.

During good times, the market value of bank assets may increase. That is, a loan that was made last year and appeared to be risky now seems safe because of good economic conditions (perhaps an increase in home prices has reduced the risk of a mortgage loan). This increase in value adds to the equity of the bank, providing it with more capital. The bank may choose to expand lending, and as banks do so, this may feed the process of economic expansion, raising the value of bank assets even further.

During bad times, the process reverses. The value of bank assets falls, and capital ratios start to fall. To restore capital ratios, banks will contract lending or sell assets. This in turn will reduce the market value of other bank loans, causing capital ratios to fall further.

The typical bank asset is a loan, the value of which can fall farther and faster than it can rise. That is because the value of a loan depends on the probability that it will be repaid, which tends to be high to begin with. If the probability of repayment is 95 percent, then the most that the probability can increase is 5 percent, which will only increase the value of the loan by a small amount. However, the probability of repayment can decrease by 95 percent, which would lower the value of the loan considerably.

During a crisis, the procyclical characteristic of capital requirements becomes quite pronounced. The value of bank assets declines sharply, forcing banks to rapidly sell off assets, reducing their market values even further.

Risk-based capital regulations proved to be particularly procyclical during the financial crisis of 2008. During the crisis, the rating agencies downgraded the ratings of mortgage-backed securities. Not only did the market value of these assets fall, but the downgrades moved these securities into higher risk buckets, requiring banks to hold more capital against these assets.

Market-value accounting, which requires banks to value their assets at market prices, plays a role in this procyclical behavior. Prior to the 1980s, regulators allowed banks to carry assets at book value, which means that changes in market conditions do not require banks to revalue their assets. During a downturn, therefore, the decline in the market value of assets does not affect capital requirements.

During the Savings and Loan Crisis, book-value accounting made it very difficult for regulators to identify and resolve troubled institutions in a timely manner. Thrifts held mortgages that had been originated at low interest rates, and the market value of these assets had fallen considerably as rates rose. However, the loans were still carried at book value, so the firms could insist that they were sound when in fact they were insolvent. This historical cost accounting was widely criticized. For example, in 1991, Richard Breeden, then chairman of the US Securities and Exchange Commission, wrote,

> The nation's experience with the savings and loan industry demonstrates the substantial danger of a reporting system for financial institutions that is premised on historical cost accounting principles. Because [generally accepted accounting principles (GAAP)] failed to reflect massive unrealized losses in savings and loan portfolios, institutions that were deeply insolvent on an economic basis continued to operate and to report a positive net worth. Besides tending to legitimize a policy of regulatory forbearance, the absence of adequate market-based information made it difficult for investors to make a meaningful assessment of the real economic value and risk exposure of a depository institution. We should therefore explore the extent to which the relevance and credibility of bank and thrift financial statements can be enhanced by a broader application of market value accounting.[6]

Market-value accounting gives regulators a more accurate assessment of the financial condition of a bank. Returning to book-value accounting would reduce the procyclical responses of banks, but at the cost of making it much more difficult for regulators to distinguish troubled banks from sound ones.

Rather than abandon market-value accounting in the hope of mitigating procyclical bank behavior during a crisis, regulators would do better to focus on making capital requirements less procyclical. For example, as an economic expansion matures, the basic capital requirement might be raised, say, from 8 percent to 10 percent. In a crisis situation, regulators might temporarily lower the capital requirement, thereby reducing banks' need to rapidly sell assets in order to remain in compliance.[7]

THE REGULATORS' CALCULATION PROBLEM

Many decades ago, Ludwig von Mises and F. A. Hayek pointed out that social-ist central planners would face a computational challenge in deciding how to allocate resources. In a market system, prices work as signals to indicate scarcity or surplus. In the absence of such signals, a central planning body would have to substitute its own judgment in deciding where production should be increased or decreased. This is known as the socialist calculation problem.[8]

Regulators face a similar calculation problem. For example, in deciding whether to require that a safety device, such as an air bag, be installed in cars, the regulator must make a benefit-cost calculation. However, in such relatively narrow regulatory decisions, the regulator can rely on a relatively clear set of facts and assumptions.

In the case of risk-based capital requirements, the regulator is affecting the relative returns of an enormous range of investments. Instead of leaving it up to the bank to determine the relative risk of mortgage loans, asset-backed securities, or commercial loans, the regulatory body is taking upon itself the task of setting relative prices for these asset classes.

One disadvantage that regulators have in setting relative prices among asset classes is a lack of specific information. When a bank chooses to make a loan, it can examine the specific characteristics of the borrower, the purpose of the loan, and any collateral against which the loan will be made. The regulatory body ignores all of this specific information in setting up its arbitrary risk buckets.

As noted earlier, the consequences of ignoring specific information can be considerable. On its own, a bank likely would have paid close attention to the fragile financial condition of borrowers who were applying for mortgage loans in the latter years of the housing boom. The regulators gave this issue no consideration in putting highly rated mortgage-backed securities into a low-risk bucket. Moreover, the rating agencies to which regulators delegated the authority to assign AA and AAA ratings also paid little or no attention to the specific characteristics of the mortgages or borrowers involved.

Risk-based capital requirements serve to centralize the process of assessing the relative risk of different investments. This necessarily reduces the amount of local, specific information that is incorporated in decision-making. Because such information can be very important in the context of lending, the adverse consequences can be quite severe. As Andrew Haldane, executive director of the Bank of England, put it,

> Hayek titled his 1974 Nobel address "The Pretence of Knowledge." In it, he highlighted the pitfalls of seeking precisely measurable answers to questions about the dynamics of complex systems. Subsequent research on complex systems has confirmed Hayek's hunch. Policy predicated on over-precision risks catastrophic error. Complexity in risk models may have perpetuated Hayek's pretence in the minds of risk managers and regulators.[9]

Another, more subtle effect of centralized risk assessment is that it chokes off the market's evolutionary learning process. With decentralized risk assessment, each bank's underwriting policies and procedures represent an experiment. Those policies and procedures that work well will be maintained and emulated. Those that work poorly will be modified or driven from the market altogether.

In contrast, with risk assessment concentrated in the hands of a single regulatory body, there is no such process of experimentation, evaluation, and evolution. The regulator's learning process is likely to be much slower and the regulator's mistakes, rather than being limited in scope to a few institutions, will be systemic.

MANAGERS, RISKS, AND INCENTIVES

Banks, like all firms, face two broad decisions with respect to risk. One decision concerns *financial leverage*, which is the ratio of debt to equity. The other decision concerns *operating leverage*, which is the choice between high-risk investments and low-risk investments.

An individual firm's managers make these decisions in the context of a capital market in which investors have the opportunity to alter their own risk profiles. This ability of individual investors to make their own portfolio choices plays an important role in modern corporate finance.

For example, there is the Modigliani-Miller theorem,[10] which in its most basic form says that in the absence of tax distortions and bankruptcy costs, investors are indifferent with respect to financial leverage. If, as an investor,

I am uncomfortable with the ratio of debt to equity at a given firm, I can dial up the leverage by buying shares on margin or dial down the leverage by holding shares in combination with risk-free short-term bonds.

Next, there is modern portfolio theory as first articulated by Sharpe,[11] which says that as an investor, I can use diversification across firms to mitigate the operating leverage of the individual firms. Only to the extent that returns on investment projects are correlated across firms am I unable to diversify away risk. From the point of view of an investor in a broad market portfolio, the risk of an individual investment project is not its overall variability but only that portion of variability that is not diversifiable.

The Modigliani-Miller theorem would suggest that investors might not care about capital ratios at banks. If a bank has "excess" capital, an investor can take a levered position in that bank. If a bank has a thin capital margin, an investor can compensate for this by purchasing risk-free securities.

Portfolio theory would suggest that investors would not care about whether banks choose high-risk or low-risk assets. Instead, an investor would evaluate one bank's assets in terms of how much risk they add in the context of the investor's entire portfolio, taking into account diversification.

In fact, as Modigliani, Miller, and others recognized, tax distortions and bankruptcy costs are important. Because interest expenses are deductible from corporate income taxes, while dividend payments are not, the most tax-efficient capital structure is one with the highest ratio of debt to equity. Working against this is the fact that there are costs of going through bankruptcy. Legal expenses are incurred in undertaking reorganization under bankruptcy. Even more important are the costs associated with damage to the firm's reputation with counterparties and creditors. Becoming insolvent costs a firm in terms of lost "franchise value."

A firm's managers may attach more significance than its shareholders to franchise value. While shareholders may be diversified, managers are likely to have a large share of their financial wealth and human capital tied to the specific firm. Relative to shareholders, managers may prefer to run the firm with less operating leverage and also less financial leverage.

Under a partnership structure, as opposed to a public corporation, managers have an especially large share of their financial wealth tied up with the firm. This tends to make managers more attuned to franchise value and more risk-averse in a partnership structure.

For a bank, franchise value is particularly important. Bank customers place a high value on the liquidity and safety of their funds on deposit. A bank with a strong reputation will be able to attract deposits at a much lower interest rate than a bank that is considered weak.

One component of franchise value that has been important in banking is charter value, which is the value of the legal right to engage in banking. Historically, governments have made bank charters difficult to obtain. When a charter is difficult to obtain, competition is restricted and profits are high. Shareholders and managers have an incentive not to take risks that could lead to bankruptcy and loss of the charter.

As of 1970, competition in banking in the United States was limited by restrictions on branch banking, ceilings on deposit interest rates, and the legal separation of investment banking from commercial banking. These restrictions on competition made charters for banks and savings and loans relatively valuable, and this may have contributed to conservative management.[12]

Over the next two decades, these regulations were gradually eliminated. In addition to these policy changes, high inflation in the 1970s interacted with Regulation Q ceilings on interest rates on deposits to cause consumers to seek higher yields outside of banks and thrifts. Higher interest rates also undermined the value of savings and loan charters by increasing the risk associated with using deposits to fund mortgage loans. Innovations such as the money market fund reduced the value of bank charters by giving investment banks a tool to compete against bank deposits for short-term liquid funds.

All of these developments in the 1970s and 1980s reduced charter value for banks and savings and loans, which may have made management less conservative and may account for the crises of those decades that in turn led policymakers to develop the Basel Accords.

Government guarantees tend to increase the incentive for bank managers to take risks. Deposit insurance and the implicit guarantee of too big to fail (TBTF) reduce the cost of debt finance. This encourages more financial leverage by lowering the cost of debt relative to equity. It also encourages operating leverage, because shareholders retain the upside while the cost of adverse results is shifted in part to taxpayers.

Economists see government guarantees as creating moral hazard at banks. That is, managers have an incentive to take more risk than otherwise would be prudent. This in turn implies a need for regulators to try to limit risk taking.

Note, however, that as Friedman and Kraus point out, before the financial crisis, most banks were *not* taking the maximum amount of operating risk or regulatory risk allowed under the Basel Accords. This suggests that the capital requirements may not have been the binding constraint on bank risk taking. Instead, banks used less financial leverage and invested more safely than was required by regulation. Perhaps franchise value dictated even less risk-taking than was tolerated by regulatory capital requirements.

ALTERNATIVES TO CAPITAL RULES

In postmortems written in the wake of the 2008 financial crisis, risk-based capital rules have come in for considerable criticism. For example, the Bank of England's Andrew Haldane wrote,

> [C]onsider the experience of a panel of 33 large international banks during the crisis. This panel conveniently partitions itself into banks subject to government intervention in the form of capital or guarantees ("crisis banks") and those free from such intervention ("no crisis banks"). . . .
> [T]he reported capital ratios [just prior to the crisis] of the two sets of banks are largely indistinguishable. If anything, the crisis banks looked slightly stronger pre-crisis on regulatory solvency measures. Second, regulatory capital ratios offer, on average, little if any advance warning of impending problems.[13]

Acharya, Schnabl, and Suarez wrote,

> Securitization was traditionally meant to transfer risks from the banking sector to outside investors and thereby disperse financial risks across the economy. Since the risks were meant to be transferred, securitization allowed banks to reduce regulatory capital. However, in the period leading up to the financial crisis of 2007–09, banks increasingly devised securitization methods that allowed them to retain risks on their balance sheets and yet receive a reduction in

regulatory capital, a practice that eventually led to the largest
banking crisis since the Great Depression.[14]

Capital rules have not worked well as a tool for promoting prudence and
financial stability in the banking system. In hindsight, it is easy to see why.

A simple capital rule, which sets a minimum ratio of capital to total assets,
only affects financial leverage. It does not affect operating leverage. A bank
could meet the requirement of a simple capital rule while taking inordinate
risks simply by investing in risky assets.

The fact that a simple capital rule can be undermined using operating leverage is what gives rise to the alternative of risk-based capital rules. However,
risk-based capital rules are problematic in that they substitute the crude, distant
judgment of regulators for the refined, local knowledge of bank management in
determining the relative risk of different types of assets.

Policymakers should consider alternative ways to influence bank managers to take less risk. Financial leverage could be reduced by increasing the cost
of debt relative to equity. Financial leverage and operating leverage could be
reduced by making franchise value more salient to managers.

Steps that would bring the cost of debt more in line with equity could include:

- Lowering the corporate income tax rate, which in turn would reduce
  the tax advantage of debt.

- Limiting the deductibility of interest on debt, particularly for financial firms. For example, the tax laws could be changed so that beyond
  the first $100 million in interest expense, only 80 percent of interest
  expense is deductible from corporate income tax.

- Limiting the amount of government-insured deposits available to any
  one financial institution. If this limit were below the level of deposits
  currently held at the nation's largest banks, the result would be to shrink
  the largest banks and reduce concentration in banking. That in turn could
  reduce the "too big to fail" subsidy for risk taking at the largest banks.

- Limiting the aggregate amount of insured deposits. This could be done
  through a voucher system. If the FDIC were to insure $1 trillion in
  the aggregate, then it would auction vouchers for $1 trillion in deposit
  insurance.[15] These vouchers would then trade in a secondary market.

The cost of the vouchers would add to the interest expense that banks pay on deposits. That in turn would reduce the incentive of bank managers to add deposits and thereby increase financial leverage.

Steps that would make franchise value more salient would include:

- Holistic audits of bank management practices. Audits could cover a range of issues, including the way that compensation incentives align with risk management, the way that training programs align with risk management, the responsibilities assigned to key executives for risk management, the formal risk management policies of the organization and the methods used to ensure internal compliance, and so on. Adverse audit findings can be used to compel banks to make changes to management practices or face penalties, such as suspension of dividend payments and executive bonuses.

- Having bank managers paid in part in deferred compensation, with the deferred compensation a junior liability of the bank. In the event that the bank has to be rescued or put through bankruptcy, the deferred compensation is forfeited. This would increase the managers' incentive to treat franchise value as important.

- Deliberately increasing the barriers to competition in banking. In theory, this would make banking more profitable and thereby increase charter value. This may have been the effect of banking laws that existed from the mid-1930s through the mid-1970s. However, these regulations kept small depositors from earning fair market returns on their funds. Also, financial institutions were driven to innovate in ways to evade such regulations, and these regulations did not succeed in preventing the Savings and Loan Crisis. Indeed, they likely contributed to it. Thus, as a policy option, raising barriers to entry may have too many drawbacks to be a viable option.

CONCLUSION

Risk-based capital rules put the wrong agents in charge of assessing the relative risk of different assets. Bank regulators do not possess the information, particularly at a detailed level, that is needed for this task. However, for many reasons, particularly the existence of explicit and implicit government guarantees of bank creditors, the public has an interest in seeing that bank managers have an incentive to behave prudently. One approach for doing this is to decrease the incentive for high financial leverage by raising the relative cost of debt finance. Another option is to limit the total dollar amount of government-guaranteed deposits that a single institution can have in its liabilities. A final option might be to increase the personal liability of bank management in the event of failure.

NOTES

1. Blanchard, "Where Danger Lurks."

2. Friedman and Kraus, *Engineering the Financial Crisis*, 61.

3. The information in this section was collated from a variety of sources, including the FDIC, "First Fifty Years." I would like to thank Kristine Johnson for research assistance.

4. Bank for International Settlements, "History of the Basel Committee."

5. Board of Governors of the Federal Reserve System et al., "Agencies Adopt Recourse."

6. Breeden, "Thumbs on the Scale."

7. A somewhat more complex and flexible scheme was proposed under Basel III. See Bank for International Settlements, "Guidance for National Authorities."

8. Key articles on this topic include Mises, "Economic Calculation"; and Hayek, "Use of Knowledge in Society."

9. Haldane, "Capital Discipline," 6.

10. Modigliani and Miller, "Cost of Capital."

11. Sharpe, "Capital Asset Prices."

12. See Salter, "Robust Political Economy"; Gorton, *Slapped by the Invisible Hand*, 54–58.

13. Haldane, "Capital Discipline."

14. Acharya, Schnabl, and Suarez, "Securitization without Risk Transfer."

15. Along these lines, Tuckman ("Federal Liquidity Options," 25), suggested that one "approach could be to determine an appropriate total quantity of deposit insurance to be outstanding at any time and to auction that quantity to eligible banks."

REFERENCES

Acharya, Viral V., Philipp Schnabl, and Gustavo Suarez. "Securitization without Risk Transfer." *Journal of Financial Economics* 107, no. 3 (2013): 515–36.

Bank for International Settlements. "Guidance for National Authorities Operating the Countercyclical Capital Buffer." December 2010. http://www.bis.org/publ/bcbs187.htm.

———. "History of the Basel Committee." Last updated October 1, 2015. http://www.bis.org/bcbs /history.htm.

Basel Committee on Banking Supervision. "Basel Committee on Banking Supervision Reforms—Basel III." http://www.bis.org/bcbs/basel3/b3summarytable.pdf.

———. "International Convergence of Capital Measurement and Capital Standards." July 1988. http://www.bis.org/publ/bcbs04a.pdf.

———. "Basle Capital Accord: Treatment of Potential Exposure for Off-balance-sheet Items." April 1995. http://www.bis.org/publ/bcbs18.pdf.

———. "Amendment to the Capital Accord to Incorporate Market Risks." January 1996. http://www .bis.org/publ/bcbs24.pdf.

———. "Modification of the Basle Capital Accord of July 1988, as Amended in January 1996." Press Release. http://www.bis.org/press/p970918a.htm.

———. "A New Capital Adequacy Framework." 1999. http://www.bis.org/publ/bcbs50.pdf.

———. "Overview of the New Basel Capital Accord." January 2001. http://www.bis.org/publ /bcbsca02.pdf.

———. "Revisions to the Basel II Market Risk Framework." July 2009. http://www.bis.org/publ /bcbs158.pdf.

———. "Basel III: International Framework for Liquidity Risk Measurement, Standards and Monitoring." December 2010. http://www.bis.org/publ/bcbs188.pdf.

Blanchard, Olivier. "Where Danger Lurks." *International Monetary Fund Finance and Development* 51, no. 3 (September 2014): 28–31.

Board of Governors of the Federal Reserve System. "Federal Reserve Board Approves Final Rule to Help Ensure Banks Maintain Strong Capital Positions." Press Release, July 2, 2013. http:// www.federalreserve.gov/newsevents/press/bcreg/20130702a.htm.

Board of Governors of the Federal Reserve System, Federal Deposit Insurance Corporation, Office of the Comptroller of the Currency, and Office of Thrift Supervision. "Agencies Adopt Recourse, Direct Credit Substitutes, and Residual Interests Final Rule." Joint Press Release, November 29, 2001. http://www.federalreserve.gov/boarddocs/press/boardacts/2001 /20011129/.

Breeden, Richard. "Thumbs on the Scale: The Role That Accounting Practices Played in the Savings and Loan Crisis." *Fordham Law Review* 59, no. 6 (1991): S71–S91.

Federal Deposit Insurance Corporation (FDIC). "Annual Report of the Federal Deposit Insurance Corporation for the Year Ending December 21, 1934." August 15, 1935.

———. "Basel and the Evolution of Capital Regulation: Moving Forward and Looking Back." January 14, 2003. https://www.fdic.gov/bank/analytical/fyi/2003/011403fyi.html.

———. "The First Fifty Years: A History of the FDIC 1933–1983." Last updated July 24, 2016. https://www.fdic.gov/bank/analytical/firstfifty/.

Friedman, Jeffrey, and Wladimir Kraus. *Engineering the Financial Crisis*. Philadelphia: University of Pennsylvania Press, 2011.

Getter, Darryl E. "US Implementation of the Basel Capital Regulatory Framework." Congressional Research Service, Library of Congress, November 14, 2012. http://fpc.state.gov/documents /organization/201108.pdf.

Gorton, Gary. *Slapped by the Invisible Hand: The Panic of 2007*. New York: Oxford University Press, 2010.

Haldane, Andrew G. "Capital Discipline." Speech given to the American Economic Association, Denver, CO, January 9, 2011. http://www.bankofengland.co.uk/archive/Documents /historicpubs/speeches/2011/speech484.pdf.

Hayek, Friedrich A. "The Use of Knowledge in Society." *American Economic Review* 35, no. 4 (1945): 519–30.

Kapstein, Ethan B. *Supervising International Banks: Origins and Implications of the Basle Accord.* Princeton, NJ: Princeton University Press, 1991.

Mises, Ludwig von. "Economic Calculation in the Socialist Commonwealth." In *Collectivist Economic Planning*, translated by F. A. Hayek, 87–130. London: George Routledge and Sons, 1935.

Modigliani, Franco, and Merton Miller. "The Cost of Capital, Corporation Finance, and the Theory of Investment." *American Economic Review* 48, no. 3 (1958): 261–97.

Salter, Alexander William. "Robust Political Economy and the Lender of Last Resort." *Journal of Financial Services Research* 50, no. 1 (August 2016): 21–22.

Sharpe, William F. "Capital Asset Prices: A Theory of Market Equilibrium under Conditions of Risk." *Journal of Finance* 19, no. 3 (1964): 425–42.

Tuckman, Bruce. "Federal Liquidity Options: Containing Runs on Deposit-Like Assets without Bailouts and Moral Hazard." Center for Financial Stability Policy Paper, January 24, 2012.

CHAPTER 2
On Simpler, Higher Capital Requirements

STEPHEN MATTEO MILLER
Mercatus Center at George Mason University

I n the aftermath of the recent crisis, bank regulators in the United States and abroad have sought to increase bank capital requirements as a way to reduce the likelihood of a banking crisis. To understand why, one way to think about capital is that it reflects a bank's net worth, measuring the difference between bank assets and liabilities; greater net worth, as reflected by a larger value of the bank's equity, means the bank is farther from experiencing the risk of default. Elliott[1] points out, there are three key features of effective bank capital: (1) it requires no repayment to any party, (2) it requires no interest or dividend payment to any party, and (3) in the event of bankruptcy this group of claimants would be among the last to receive proceeds from a liquidation.

To better understand the role of bank capital, consider a bank operating in a hypothetical unregulated market for banking services that takes in deposits from customers and sells equity shares (or perhaps even long-term bonds) to investors. Bank staff use those funds to originate a variety of loans to businesses and households, or buy a variety of securities. Crouhy and Galai[2] point out that in such a market, no optimal capital structure reflecting the bank's funding mix between its deposits and equity would exist for the bank. In contrast, the US banking industry has historically been highly regulated and a key aspect of that regulation has concerned capital adequacy.

As Miller[3] suggests, regulatory capital requirements, including those discussed here, will not stop people in banks from misappropriating funds, but they can provide one way regulators might address two key problems that arise in regulated markets for banking services. First, bank deposits tend to have a shorter-term maturity than the assets on the balance sheet, and banks with more capital rely less on the shorter-term funding. Second, as Cochrane,[4] among many others, points out, bank deposit redemption occurs on a "first come, first served" basis. These features of deposits could invite bank runs if depositors catch on to default risks lurking on bank balance sheets. A well-capitalized bank, however, would be much less prone to bank runs because it would be farther from experiencing insolvency, as the most effective forms of capital need not be repaid in the event of an insolvency.

In addition, Black and others[5] discuss how by offering deposit insurance, the government essentially becomes a lender to the bank. Like a typical lender, the government then has concerns over the value of a bank's assets relative to deposits, as well as the riskiness of bank assets. Capital adequacy offers a low-cost method of controlling the risk of bank insolvency, as relatively higher bank capital means there would be relatively less for the government to insure. Of course, as Thomas Hogan and Kristine Johnson (in chapter 3 in this volume) point out, alternatives—such as private deposit insurance— exist too, which would change the story. In any case, any change in bank capital requirements could have benefits and costs that must be weighed against each other.

A full benefit-cost analysis remains beyond the scope here, but the benefit of higher capital might be measured as the reduction, or perhaps elimination, of the economic effects of banking crises. To see how capital might do that, Gornall and Strebulaev[6] developed a framework that explains why banking corporations have much higher leverage than nonbanking corporations and predicts that merely doubling bank equity capital requirements from 8 to 16 percent would reduce failure rates among banks by 92 percent. To the extent that banking crises adversely affect the formation of an economy's real capital stock (e.g., plant and equipment), increasing bank capital could reduce the loss of gross domestic product (GDP) arising from banking crises.

The cost might be measured as the reduction in GDP arising from the extent to which higher bank capital requirements translate into a higher cost of capital that gets passed on to borrowers, which in turn might lower formation of the economy's real capital stock and GDP. Some view the costs, among other drawbacks, as important (see, for instance, Elliott[7]), while others claim that higher capital involves no increase in costs (see Admati et al.).

Miles and others[8] developed a framework linking the benefits of higher capital requirements to the costs of higher capital applied to the six largest banks in the United Kingdom. They show that higher capital requirements transmit only partially, rather than fully, to the return on equity, which in turn increases the cost of capital slightly, resulting in lower firm capital accumulation and output. Based on these costs and the benefits of eliminating crises, they find the optimal capital ratio for the United Kingdom lies in the range of 16 to 20 percent of risk-weighted assets, which as Hogan and Manish[9] explain, down-weights total assets according to any weighting factors used to calculate Basel-type regulatory capital. Cline[10] applies a similar exercise and finds that the optimal capital ratio for US banks to be roughly 12 to 14 percent of risk-weighted assets. The use of risk-weighted assets, which reduces the amount of assets for which banks have to have capital, may create other undesirable outcomes that I will discuss, but so far, the evidence does not suggest lowering capital requirements would be desirable.

In what follows, I discuss several proposals for simpler, higher bank capital requirements as a way to reduce the harmful economic effects of banking crises. Simpler capital requirements imply returning to a flat capital-to-asset or capital-to-liability ratio and limiting the definition of bank capital to equity and possibly long-term debt. Higher capital requirements mean increasing capital relative to total assets or liabilities, well above existing levels. To motivate the discussion of simpler, higher capital requirements for US banks, I explain how in a hypothetical unregulated market a bank's capital structure relates to the interest rates it offers, then contrast that with the US historical experience with regulatory capital, and then end with proposals going forward.

BANK CAPITAL STRUCTURE IN A HYPOTHETICAL UNREGULATED MARKET

Crouhy and Galai[11] observe that bank capital, in particular equity capital, functions in a much different way than regulatory capital measures, such as the book equity to book asset ratio constructed by accountants. In an unregulated world, the equity-to-asset ratio would be measured at market value and would be constant, since any reduction in asset values would result in a reduction in the value of the bank's equity, at least until the bank became insolvent. In this sense, equity capital does not provide a buffer to protect depositors, but would reflect whether the bank is solvent.

The capital structure would be reflected by the interest rates offered by banks, though. Banks would pay interest rates to depositors that varied with the riskiness of the loans and securities on its balance sheet, as well as the fraction of assets funded with equity. For instance, banks that had riskier loans for a given equity-to-asset ratio would offer higher interest rates to depositors to compensate them for the risks. Similarly, banks that had a low equity-to-asset ratio, because they depended more on depositors to fund their loans and investment purchases, would also have to compensate depositors for the greater potential risk of insolvency. Here, just as bank assets reflect a risk-reward tradeoff, bank liabilities pay risk-adjusted rewards to investors and depositors. This discussion of bank capital structure in a hypothetical unregulated market for banking services contrasts sharply with how bank capital structure has been affected by the US bank regulatory framework over time.

HISTORICAL PERSPECTIVES ON US BANK CAPITAL STRUCTURE AND REGULATION

The Very Long Road to Basel

Mengle[12] points out that banks in the United States have always been subject to a mix of primarily state but also federal regulation. Calomiris and Haber[13] and Bordo and others[14] observe that US banks historically were weakened by state-based, interstate banking and branching restrictions that made bank assets less diversified than they might be without those restrictions. In addition, Gorton[15] observes that banks sometimes had requirements to hold state bonds, which subjected banks to state default risk, as when nine states defaulted on their debt during the period between 1837 and 1843. Rather than fostering stability, bank regulations exposed US banks to regional shocks that could result in bank failures and runs, so the United States experienced frequent crises.

While challenges exist in identifying earlier crises, Jalil[16] finds that between 1825 and 1929, the United States experienced major banking crises in 1833, 1837, 1839, 1857, 1873, 1893, and 1907, in addition to twenty minor banking crises. After that, the United States experienced a major banking crisis during the Great Depression from 1930 to 1933, during the Savings and Loan (S&L)

Figure 1. Total Number of US Banks, 1834–2014

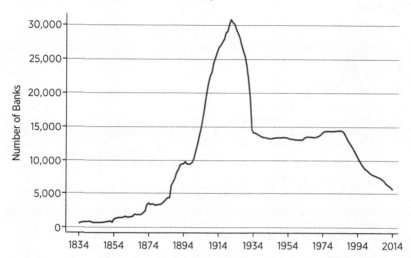

Note: Data from 1834 to 1933 are from the 1957 Historical Abstract of the United States, series N-19, 262–263, http://www2.census.gov
/prod2/statcomp/documents/HistoricalStatisticsoftheUnitedStates1789-1945.pdf. Data after 1933 are from table CB01, https://www5
.fdic.gov/hsob/SelectRpt.asp?EntryTyp=10&Header=1.

Crisis from 1987 to 1989, and then again during the most recent crisis from
2007 to 2009. That means the United States has experienced at least ten major
crises and twenty minor crises since 1825 alone. A related and peculiar feature
of the US banking landscape is the dramatic rise and subsequent decline in the
number of banks.

Figure 1 shows the number of banks in the United States from 1834 to 2014.
Changes in the number of banks reflect new entrants, bank failures, and mergers. The number of banks increased rapidly toward the end of the nineteenth
century, surpassing 10,000 (10,382) in 1900 and peaking at 30,812 in 1921.
The number of banks has fallen since 1921. Mengle[17] and Walter[18] suggest that
one reason for the increase in the number of banks was the decline in minimum capital required to enter the industry, particularly after 1900 (which will
become apparent in figure 3). A recent study by Adams and Gramlich shows
that state-based capital requirements for new bank charters still exist.[19]

Walter also describes how the large number of small bank failures during the 1920s suggested to regulators that barriers to entry should protect

Figure 2. Total Bank Capital as a Fraction of Total Bank Assets, 1834–2014

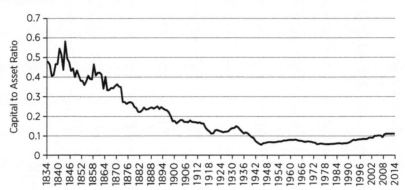

Source: Graph shown is updated from Allen Berger, Richard Herring, and Giorgio Szego, "The Role of Capital in Financial Institutions," Journal of Banking and Finance 19 (June 1995), 393–430.

Note: Data from 1834 to1933 are computed by dividing series N-24 (Capital, Surplus, and Net Undivided Profit) by N-20 (Total Assets or Liabilities), as reported in the Historical Abstract of the United States 1789–1945, 262–263, http://www2.census.gov/prod2/statcomp /documents/HistoricalStatisticsoftheUnitedStates1789-1945.pdf. Data after 1933 are computed by dividing Total Equity Capital by Total Liabilities by Equity Capital from table CB14, https://www5.fdic.gov/hsob/SelectRpt.asp?EntryTyp=10&Header=1.

incumbents, since new entrants, rather than the small size and small number of branches, were seen to be the cause of the problem of bank failures. This seems consistent with the relatively flat trend in the number of banks after the establishment of the Federal Deposit Insurance Corporation (FDIC) in 1934.

Finally, during the last thirty years or so, much consolidation has taken hold in the US banking system, just as regulators have sought to increase bank capital requirements. Bank consolidation through interstate banking began to take hold, first at the state level in the 1970s.[20] Interstate banking at the federal level became official with the passage of the Riegle-Neal Interstate Banking and Branching Efficiency Act of 1994.[21]

Figure 2 depicts the historical record of total bank capital to total bank assets for the US banking system. The ratio peaked in 1843 at just over 58 percent and declined steadily after that. Lowering the minimum capital requirement would expand the pool of potential entrants to the banking market. The steady decline through the 1920s captures observations about the reduction in minimum bank capital requirements, which both Mengle and Walter suggest[22] explains the dramatic growth in the number of banks between 1900 and 1921 (observed in figure 1).

Figure 3. Number of Banks Depicted against Total Bank Capital to Total Bank Assets, 1834–2014

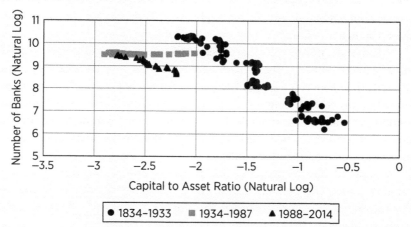

Note: *The source of the data for the number of banks is as reported in the note under figure 1, while source of the data for the capital ratio is as reported in the note under figure 2.*

Figure 3 depicts the natural log of the number of banks against the natural log of the total bank capital to total bank asset ratio for all banks in the United States during three "regimes": (1) the pre-FDIC era from 1834 to 1933, when bank capital served as a barrier to entry;[23] (2) the FDIC era prior to Basel from 1934 to 1987, when regulators sought to limit entry by other means; and (3) the Basel era from 1988 to 2014, when capital adequacy has been viewed as a way to foster bank safety. The inverse relationship between the number of banks in the pre-FDIC era seems consistent with observations by Mengle and, later, Walter, about capital serving as a barrier to entry.[24] Figure 3 also helps understand the relationship between capital adequacy and banking crises, and in particular why so many banks failed throughout US history, even though capital requirements had been high.

For instance, the frequent crises observed during the pre-FDIC era may have occurred because banks were too small,[25] even though they had histori-cally high levels of capital. In more recent times, just as the number of banks has been declining, bank capital has been relatively low by historical standards. One implication could be that bank capital alone cannot ensure stability of the banking system if regulations, such as interstate banking and branching restrictions, interfere with bank size as driven by market demands for banking services. With no geographical limits on where banks can operate and with higher capital requirements, banks might diversify their risks while increasing their distance to default.

To elaborate, Bordo and others discuss how Canadian banks never experienced a major banking crisis since Confederation in 1867 because they could diversify their loan risks and pool deposits from across Canada.[26] Interestingly, some late-nineteenth-century US policymakers understood why Canadian banks were relatively more stable than US banks, but also understood that the political forces driving banking laws and regulations at the time would prevent change toward a more stable model.[27]

With the establishment of the FDIC, regulators moved away from minimum capital requirements as a way to limit entry.[28] This may be reflected by the fact that the inverse relationship between the number of banks and the capital ratio vanishes during the FDIC era from 1934 to 1987.

Finally, during the Basel era, a negative relationship again exists between the number of banks and the capital ratio. This finding likely reflects the fact that the number of banks in the United States has been declining for other reasons, including bank consolidation following the growth in interstate banking activity, while at the same time regulators sought to increase bank capital requirements.

The impetus for the increase in capital requirements was the International Lending Supervision Act of 1983 in the aftermath of the 1982 Latin American Debt Crisis.[29] The new legislation called on bank regulators to find a multilateral, rather than unilateral, way to raise bank capital requirements so that US banks would not find themselves at a competitive disadvantage with their foreign competitors. Ethan Kapstein[30] (1994) describes how those events culminated in the Basel capital adequacy standards.

Capital Adequacy Standards since Basel

US bank supervisors offered the finalized version of their Basel capital adequacy rulings in 1989.[31] Under the original "standard approach," banks would classify assets by simple risk buckets. After the Market Risk Amendment originally proposed in 1996, Basel guidelines would eventually suggest how banks could apply an "advanced approach" by measuring the credit risk on their

Figure 4. A Stylized Bank Balance Sheet under Precrisis Basel Guidelines

	Assets	Liabilities	
0%	Reserves Some Treasury bonds; some agency MBS tranches	Demand Deposits NOW Accounts	
20%	Some agency MBS tranches; some municipal bonds; AAA- & AA-rated private label MBS & CDO tranches (starting in Q4 2001)	Savings Deposits	
50%	Mortgages; A-rated private label MBS & CDO tranches (starting in Q4 2001)	Time Deposits	
100%	Commercial Loans	Subordinated Debt	Tier 2 Capital
		Tangible Equity	Tier 1 Capital
	Franchise Value/Intangible Assets	Total Equity	

Source: Adapted from Suresh Sundaresan and Zhenyu Wang, "Bank Liability Structure," 2014 (unpublished manuscript).

balance sheet continuously, using internal risk-based models, instead of discretely as with the risk buckets.[32]

Figure 4 depicts a stylized bank balance sheet to help visualize capital requirements by asset class under the "standard approach" and how they link to the capital and liability side of the balance sheet. The balance sheet entries are measured at historical book value, rather than market value. As under the original Basel guidelines, on the asset side, I categorize assets according to 0 percent, 20 percent, 50 percent, and 100 percent risk-weight classifications, which incur capital requirements of 0 percent, 1.6 percent, 4 percent, and 8 percent. Hogan and Manish[33] discuss the components of these categories in more detail, but the stylized presentation serves to motivate the discussion that follows. On the liability side, I list a variety of deposits as classified by US bank regulators, as well as Tier 1 capital, including common equity and tangible common equity, and Tier 2 capital such as subordinated debt.

On the asset side of the balance sheet, a bank has reserves as required by law to cover *expected withdrawals* from depositors. In addition, some of the asset categories I include, such as tranches of private label mortgage-backed securities (MBS) and collateralized debt obligations (CDOs), lay at the heart of the recent crisis. Erel and others[34] point out that the Recourse Rule, finalized by banking regulators on November 29, 2001, reclassified the highly rated, private label tranches from 50 percent risk bucket assets or higher to 20 percent if they were AAA- or AA-rated and 50 percent if they were A-rated.[35] While not depicted, even higher risk weights of 200 percent were applied to some assets with ratings of BB or lower after the Recourse Rule.

On the liability (and capital) side, the entries near the top reflect sources of bank funding. Along with the introduction of risk buckets, Basel capital adequacy standards also widened the scope for alternative forms of capital beyond common equity, such as preferred stock, disclosed reserves, and published retained earnings. For the capital entries near the bottom, Tier 1 capital includes tangible equity, while franchise value reflects the present value of the bank's future earnings. Tangible capital would go toward covering *unexpected losses* in asset values, as a result of nonperforming loans and defaults.[36] However, Miller observes that no financial intermediaries could expect to survive in a competitive banking system by relying on some components included in regulatory capital requirements.[37] For instance, as Elliott notes, the franchise value/intangible asset component of common equity would not easily convert to cash during a crisis.[38] The remaining types of capital fall under Tier 2, which includes subordinated debt and loan loss reserves.

To put this balance sheet in operational perspective, figure 5 depicts the average fraction of bank assets allocated to assets in each risk bucket across all US bank holding companies from Q1 2000 to Q1 2015, when the Federal Reserve collected the series. The figure shows that, on average, 100 percent risk bucket assets tend to dominate bank balance sheets, although this would tend to be true for smaller holding companies, not the largest. The 20 percent and 50 percent risk bucket asset categories make up the next largest balance sheet items, respectively. Lastly, the 0 percent risk bucket category makes up the smallest item on balance sheets, although larger banks tend to have a higher fraction allocated to this risk bucket. Holdings in this bucket would lower their risk-weighted assets, which could help make a bank's capital to risk-weighted assets ratio appear higher.

Figure 6 depicts the average ratio of demand deposits, savings accounts, negotiable orders of withdrawal (NOW) accounts, and time deposits to total assets for commercial bank subsidiaries across all bank holding companies in the United States from Q1 1985 through Q1 2015. Figure 6 also depicts the average book equity to total asset ratio for the holding company. The figure shows that both the fraction of bank funding coming from savings accounts

Figure 5. Average Fraction of Holding Company Assets by Risk Bucket across All Bank Holding Companies, Q1 2000–Q1 2015

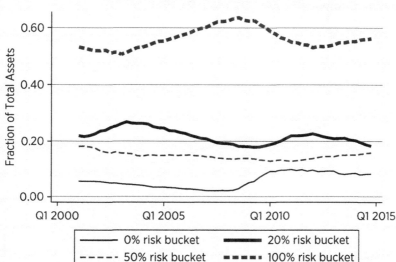

Note: The series measures the average across all reporting bank holding company corporations with total assets greater than $1 billion recorded in the Chicago Fed Call Report Y-9C forms, available from https://wrds-web.wharton.upenn.edu/wrds/. The Call Report variables are included in the following description to facilitate replication. To compute the 0% risk bucket asset share, I divide total assets in the 0% risk bucket, bhc02170, by total assets, bhck2170. To compute the 20% risk bucket asset share, I divide total assets in the 20% risk bucket, bhc22170, by total assets, bhck2170. To compute the 50% risk bucket asset share, I divide total assets in the 50% risk bucket, bhc52170, by total assets, bhck2170. Finally, to compute the 100% risk bucket asset share, I divide total assets in the 100% risk bucket, bhc92170, by total assets, bhck2170.

and equity capital increased throughout the sample. Time deposits of at least $100,000 increased slightly as a fraction of bank liabilities from 1994 through 2006. They have since fallen back to the 1980s level and now make up a share roughly equal to that for time deposits smaller than $100,000, which have fallen since the 1980s. Demand deposits fell throughout the sample period before reversing in 2009. NOW accounts provide a small fraction of funding.

I also depict book value of equity to book value of assets against other measures of regulatory capital in figure 7, including the key regulatory measures of Tier 1 to risk-weighted assets, Tier 1 and Tier 2 capital relative to risk-weighted assets, and the market value of bank equity relative to book value of assets. The data indicate that while book equity tends to be the lowest measure, it is fairly stable. In contrast, the market value of equity to book value of assets ratio can fluctuate significantly, reflecting a source of market discipline via falling share

Figure 6. Average Holding Company Book Equity Capital and Deposit Liabilities of Commercial Bank Subsidiaries as a Fraction of Total Holding Company Assets, Q1 1985–Q1 2015

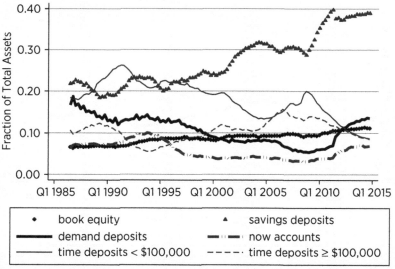

Note: The equity series measures the average across all reporting bank holding company corporations with total assets greater than $1 billion, while the deposit series are measured for the commercial bank subsidiaries of those bank holding companies recorded in the Chicago Fed Call Report Y-9C forms, available from https://wrds-web.wharton.upenn.edu/wrds/. The Call Report variables are included in the following description to facilitate replication. To compute book equity to assets, I divide total equity capital, bhck3210, by total assets, bhck2170. To compute total savings accounts to assets, I divide nontransaction savings deposits, bhcb2389, by total assets, bhck2170. To compute total demand deposits to assets, I divide total demand deposits, bhcb2210, by total assets, bhck2170. To compute total NOW accounts to assets, I divide total NOW accounts subject to Automatic Transfers from Savings (ATS), and other transaction accounts in domestic offices of commercial banks, bhcb3187, by total assets, bhck2170. To compute total time deposits less than $100,000 to assets, I divide total time deposits less than $100,000, bhcb6648, by total assets, bhck2170. To compute total time deposits of at least $100,000 to assets, I divide total time deposits of $100,000 or more, bhcb2604, by total assets, bhck2170.

prices. The volatility of the market value of equity to book value of assets ratio does not violate Crouhy and Galai's claim[39] that in an unregulated market the equity-to-asset ratio would remain fixed, since the ratio combines market values that can vary significantly with book values that may not. Finally, one drawback of using the Tier 1 and Tier 2 capital to risk-weighted asset ratios is that it creates incentives for banks to tilt their portfolios toward certain asset classes.

Arnold Kling (see chapter 1 in this volume) and Hogan and Manish[40] explain that regulatory arbitrage began in earnest following the adoption of Basel Accord capital adequacy standards after 1988. By 2001, federal regulators had finalized the Recourse Rule.

Figure 7. Alternative Measures of Capital, Q3 1998–Q3 2014

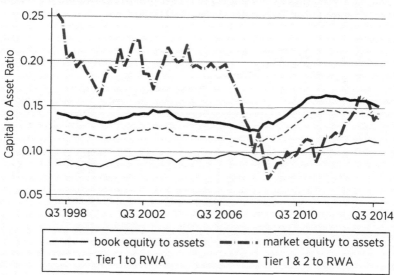

Note: The series measures the average across all reporting bank holding company corporations with total assets greater than $1 bil-
lion recorded in the Chicago Fed Call Report Y-9C forms, available from https://wrds-web.wharton.upenn.edu/wrds/. The Call Report
variables are included in the following description to facilitate replication. To compute book equity to assets, I divide total equity capital,
bhck3210, by total assets, bhck2170. To compute market equity to total assets, I divide the end of quarter market value of each bank
holding company's shares (market price multiplied by number of shares), taken from the Center for Research in Securities Prices (CRSP)
database, available from https://wrds-web.wharton.upenn.edu/wrds/, by total assets, bhck2170. To merge the CRSP data to the Call
Report data, I use the Federal Reserve Bank of New York's 2014-3 "CRSP-FRB Link", available from https://www.newyorkfed.org
/research/banking_research/datasets.html. To compute Tier 1 capital to risk-weighted assets, I divide Tier 1 capital allowable under risk-
based capital guidelines, bhck8274, by risk-weighted assets (net of allowances and other deductions), bhck2170. To compute Tier 1 and 2
to risk-weighted assets, I divide the sum of Tier 1 capital allowable under risk-based capital guidelines, bhck8274, and Tier 2 capital
allowable under risk-based capital guidelines, bhck8275, by risk-weighted assets (net of allowances and other deductions), bhck2170.

Determining the effects these rule changes had on bank balance sheets
proves challenging, because bank regulators did not require holding companies to report much detail about private label MBS holdings and did not ask for
CDO holdings until after the crisis began to unfold. That said, it is possible to
infer some of that activity by comparing average bank holdings of 20 percent
or 50 percent risk-weighted assets as a fraction of total assets, conditional
on whether banks hold positive amounts of the private label MBS tranche
holdings, as depicted in figure 8. The highly rated tranches can be estimated,
using the method of Erel, Nadauld, and Stulz,[41] by computing the residual of
20 percent and 50 percent risk bucket balance sheet and trading assets that

Figure 8. Average Holdings of 20 Percent and 50 Percent Risk Bucket Assets as a Fraction of Total Assets Conditioned on Holdings of Highly Rated, Private Label Tranches, Q4 2001–Q1 2009

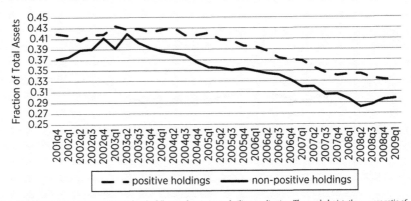

Note: The Call Report variables are included in the following description to facilitate replication. The graph depicts the average ratio of the quantity of the sum of 20 percent risk bucket assets, bhc22170, and 50 percent risk bucket assets, bhc52170, divided by total assets, bhck2170, for all reporting bank holding company corporations with total assets, bhck2170, greater than $1 billion recorded in the Chicago Fed Call Report Y-9C forms, available from https://wrds-web.wharton.upenn.edu/wrds/. The graph conditions on whether banks hold positive holdings of estimated highly rated, private label tranches after Q4 2001. To estimate these holdings, Erel et al. (2014) suggest adding held-to-maturity securities in the 20 percent and 50 percent risk buckets, bhc21754 and bhc51754, available-for-sale securities in the 20 percent and 50 percent risk buckets, bhc21773 and bhc51773, and trading assets—all other mortgage-backed securities, bhck3536. From this total, they subtract amortized cost of held-to-maturity US government agency and corporation obligations issued by US government-sponsored agencies, bhck1294; amortized cost of available-for-sale US government agency and corporation obligations issued by US government-sponsored agencies, bhck1297; amortized cost of held-to-maturity mortgage pass-through securities issued by Fannie Mae and Freddie Mac, bhck1703; amortized cost of available-for-sale mortgage pass-through securities issued by Fannie Mae and Freddie Mac, bhck1706; amortized cost of held-to-maturity mortgage-backed securities issued or guaranteed by Fannie Mae, Freddie Mac, or Ginnie Mae, bhck1714; amortized cost of available-for-sale mortgage-backed securities issued or guaranteed by Fannie Mae, Freddie Mac, or Ginnie Mae, bhck1716; amortized cost of other held-to-maturity mortgage-backed securities collateralized by MBS issued or guaranteed by Fannie Mae, Freddie Mace, or Ginnie Mae, bhck1718; amortized cost of other available-for-sale mortgage-backed securities collateralized by MBS issued or guaranteed by Fannie Mae, Freddie Mac, or Ginnie Mae, bhck1731; amortized cost of held-to-maturity securities issued by states and political subdivisions in the United States, bhck8496; and amortized cost of available-for-sale securities issued by states and political subdivisions in the US, bhck8498.

are neither US federal government, nor US agency securities, nor municipal securities. They show that the measure offers insights that are consistent with other measures that include CDOs, even though CDO holdings are not explicitly recorded in the data.

Figure 8 shows that after the rule change in Q4 2001, banks with positive holdings of highly rated tranches had more than 3 percent higher average holdings of 20 percent and 50 percent risk bucket assets. While not shown, these higher holdings initially came at the expense of fewer 0 percent risk bucket assets, and later at the expense of 100 percent risk bucket assets.

If the regulatory capital requirements created incentives for banks to tilt their portfolios toward some of the assets that experienced distress during the crisis, the question still remains: How could such small changes in holdings lead to bank distress? To see how, Erel and others[42] estimate that at the end of 2006 the average bank holding company had about 1 percent of its total assets allocated to the highly rated tranches. The largest trading banks had 5 percent of total assets allocated to the highly rated tranches, or 6.6 percent if off-balance-sheet items were included in the calculation. However, some banks had even larger exposures. For instance, Citigroup had 10.7 percent of total assets in the form of private label MBS and Structured Finance (SF) CDOs. At the same time Citigroup had only 6.3 percent common equity to cover its assets. With those values, write-downs of just under 60 percent would have wiped out common equity, exposing Citigroup to insolvency risk.

While 60 percent write-downs might seem extreme, Larry Cordell and others[43] estimate that SF CDO write-downs between 1999 and 2007 averaged 65 percent; write-downs on tranches originated in 2006 and 2007 were on average even higher. Losses of this magnitude help explain why a few large banks like Citigroup faced distress during the recent crisis. If the collapse of the SF CDO helps explain why there was a crisis, in principle, a simple way to address the problem is to introduce simpler, higher capital requirements.

DODD-FRANK AND SIMPLER, HIGHER CAPITAL REQUIREMENTS

In the aftermath of the crisis, Congress enacted the Dodd-Frank Wall Street Reform and Consumer Protection Act of 2010 (Dodd-Frank).[44] Much of Dodd-Frank concerns issues far-removed from capital adequacy, but it does push capital adequacy in the same direction as the proposals I present here. For instance, Title VI Sections 606 and 607 call for changing the language in the US Code of Federal Regulations from "adequately capitalized" to "well capitalized." Also, Title IX Section 939 calls for removing statutory references to credit ratings. To the extent that Dodd-Frank calls for higher capital requirements that make no reference to credit ratings, the proposals that I discuss next are consistent with those legislative objectives.

Figure 9. Admati and Hellwig's Proposal

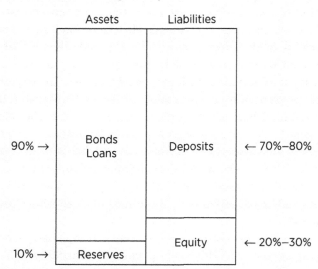

Source: Anat Admati and Martin Hellwig, The Bankers' New Clothes *(Princeton, NJ: Princeton University Press, 2013).*

Simpler capital requirements imply returning to pre-Basel capital adequacy standards by eliminating the risk-weighting of assets and using a flat leverage ratio and by limiting what capital consists of to equity and possibly long-term debt. *Higher* capital requirements imply increasing banks' distance to default. I begin by reviewing Admati and Hellwig's proposal for higher capital requirements using their stylized balance sheet, shown in figure 9.

They focus primarily on the liabilities side of the story, but assume here that loans and investments make up 90 percent of assets while reserves make up the remaining 10 percent. On the liabilities side, Admati and Hellwig[45] suggest having equity in the range of 20 to 30 percent of total assets, which means a bank might have to fund the remaining 70 to 80 percent of its asset purchases with deposits. The range of values draws from pre-FDIC evidence,[46] as depicted in figure 2.

Alternatively, while capital adequacy standards tend to focus on the asset side of the balance sheet, figure 10 depicts Black's suggestion, which is to have equity and/or long-term debt equal to at least 100 percent of deposits.[47] That

Figure 10. Black's Dollar-for-Dollar Proposal

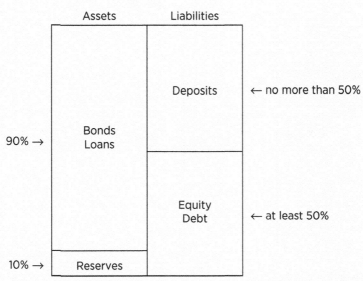

Source: Fischer Black, "Bank Funds Management in an Efficient Market," Journal of Financial Economics 2, no. 4 (1975): 323–39.

implies a dollar-for-dollar rule whereby for every dollar of funds the bank obtains from depositors, the bank must find at least another dollar of equity or bond funding. While banks may not reduce capital when deposits decrease, they would have to increase capital when deposits increase. In such a world, any form of deposit insurance, public or private, might prove unnecessary, since investors would bear the loss of asset values.

In some ways, Cochrane[48] takes Black's proposal even further. Cochrane's solutions aim to eliminate all "run-prone" debt, including demand deposits. Among other proposals, he considers the possibility of eliminating deposits altogether by having banks fully fund their safe asset purchases, like US Treasury bonds, with floating value equity. Miller[49] had also suggested this possibility in passing and, like Cochrane, observed that it would stop runs. In essence, banks might look somewhat like US Treasury bond exchange-traded funds, whose liabilities (shares) float in line with the value of the underlying assets. In terms of a balance sheet, that might look something like figure 11.

Figure 11. Cochrane's Proposal without Deposits

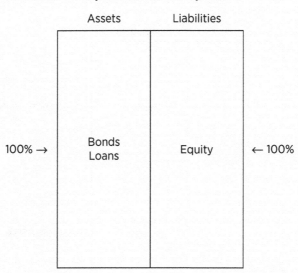

Alternatively, Cochrane[50] suggests that if deposits continue to exist, then they would be backed by US Treasuries, while riskier investments of any kind would be backed 100 percent by equity. I depict this stylized bank balance sheet in figure 12—which resembles the long-standing "Chicago" plan for banks following the Great Depression.

Cochrane proposes this solution because he argues that the current sentiment focusing regulation on bank assets is a hopeless enterprise. Interestingly, commenting about trends in the late 1970s, Black, Miller, and Posner reflect positively on the fact that banking regulation had turned its focus from "exclusive preoccupation with bank-asset safety and toward greater awareness of the benefits of competition."[51] In that sense, bank regulation unfortunately has come full circle.

Cochrane's suggestion[52] would require substantial changes in the way transactions get settled as well. He imagines individuals in this system would settle payments by exchanging their equity claims, thereby eliminating any incentives to run. In spite of the merits, the financial system in this world might prove problematic in less secure transaction environments, and many individuals would still choose to be unbanked. Unlike the proposals of Admati and

Figure 12. Cochrane's Proposal with Deposits and Equity

Assets	Liabilities
Treasuries	Deposits
Riskier Investments	Equity

Source: John Cochrane, "Toward a Run-free Financial System," in Across the Great Divide, ed. Martin Neil Baily and John B. Taylor (Stanford, CA, and Washington, DC: Hoover Institution Press and Brookings Institution, 2014), 197–249.

Hellwig or Black,[53] this proposal would not only require rethinking financial intermediaries, but also the payments system, although innovations in financial technology may ultimately render this obstacle obsolete.

ADDITIONAL ISSUES CONCERNING IMPLEMENTATION

Additional issues arise if simpler, higher capital requirements like the proposals discussed here are applied at the bank holding company level. They include the treatment of off-balance-sheet items, whether to measure capital at book or market value, and whether capital requirements should vary by bank size or complexity.

Off-Balance-Sheet Items

Black[54] observes that while bank regulation imposes costs on banks, banks have every incentive to find ways to get around those regulations, and those that do will be more profitable than those that do not. Off-balance-sheet assets and liabilities may not ordinarily appear on a bank's balance sheet but would, under certain contingent events, be specified in the terms of the individual transactions and thus have a chance to dramatically change a bank's balance sheet, for better or for worse. Off-balance-sheet items therefore create uncertainty about a bank's capital adequacy, whereas simpler, higher capital requirements are intended to reduce that uncertainty. Therefore, as Admati and Hellwig and Admati and others suggest,[55] simpler capital requirements would also mean giving off-balance-sheet items the same treatment as on-balance-sheet items.

Measuring Capital at Market or Book Value

A second issue concerns whether capital should be measured using book values or market values. Black[56] suggests that capital, whether debt or equity, should be measured at market value, since he imagines capital backing deposits rather than assets. In principle, bank stock and bond prices would reflect asset values, while the dollar-for-dollar funding constraint could induce bank staff to take less risk to eliminate the risk of not meeting the constraint.

In practice, in the United States, one difficulty arising from measuring capital at market value is that while holding company shares are traded, many banks' shares do not trade. This poses a challenge to the idea of using market values, since Kupiec[57] observes that 85 percent of all US banks are owned by holding companies. Moreover, Kupiec and Black and others[58] suggest that capital requirements of the bank subsidiary, rather than at the holding company level, make more sense for maintaining bank solvency.

In the current banking landscape dominated by the holding company, measuring capital at market value may not work. However, the fact that the holding company regulatory framework is becoming more onerous could eventually make the holding company an inefficient organizational form relative to a bank, especially since restrictions on branching and interstate banking have fallen.[59] A prerequisite for measuring capital at market value would entail having banks sell tradable bonds and shares of stock.

Bank-Size Adjustments

Finally, some debate has centered on whether larger or more complex banks should have higher capital requirements.[60] Focusing on size and complexity creates new reasons for banks to arbitrage around the regulation. For instance, with capital requirements differentiated according to whether a bank has

$250 billion in assets, banks may take otherwise unnecessary actions to avoid crossing the threshold. Similarly, the idea of applying different capital charges for more complex banks does not account for the fact that some banks may become complex to skirt the complex regulatory framework. In short, complex regulations breed complex banks. Therefore, no differentiation based on size or complexity seems necessary if all banks have higher capital requirements.

CONCLUSION

Discussions concerning the future of banking regulation tend to focus on whether the banking system should be regulated or deregulated, which detracts from the historical reality that the US market for banking services has always functioned within a highly regulated landscape. A more promising avenue for discussions concerning bank regulation may rest with comparing the costs and benefits of regulation. Bank capital adequacy regulations have relatively low enforcement costs and tie directly to bank solvency. To enable these regulations to serve their intended purpose, the key challenges are preventing capital adequacy regulations from being weakened by exemptions on assets through risk-weighting and ensuring that the definition of capital does not include sources of funding that cannot be used in a time of distress.

NOTES

1. Elliott, "Primer on Bank Capital."
2. Crouhy and Galai, "Economic Assessment of Capital Requirements."
3. Miller, "Do the M&M Propositions Apply to Banks?"
4. Cochrane, "Toward a Run-free Financial System."
5. Black, Miller, and Posner, "Approach to the Regulation of Bank Holding Companies."
6. Gornall and Strebulaev, "Financing as a Supply Chain."
7. Elliott, "Higher Bank Capital Requirements."
8. Miles, Yang, and Marcheggiano, "Optimal Bank Capital."
9. Hogan and Manish, "Banking Regulation and Knowledge Problems."
10. Cline, "Benefits and Costs."
11. Crouhy and Galai, "Economic Assessment of Capital Requirements."
12. Mengle, "Case for Interstate Banking."
13. Calomiris and Haber, *Fragile by Design*.

14. Bordo, Redish, and Rockoff, "Why Didn't Canada Have a Banking Crisis?"

15. Gorton, *Misunderstanding Financial Crises*.

16. Jalil, "New History of Banking Panics."

17. Mengle, "Case for Interstate Banking."

18. Walter, "3-6-3 Rule."

19. Adams and Gramlich, "Where Are All the New Banks?"

20. See Mengle, "Case for Interstate Banking"; Walter, "3-6-3 Rule"; Kroszner and Strahan, "What Drives Bank Deregulation?"; and Calomiris and Haber, *Fragile by Design*.

21. Pub. L. No. 103-328, 108 Stat. 2338 (1994).

22. Mengle, "Case for Interstate Banking"; and Walter, "3-6-3 Rule."

23. This is the argument made by Mengle, "Case for Interstate Banking," and by Walter, "3-6-3 Rule."

24. Ibid.

25. See Calomiris and Haber, *Fragile by Design*; Bordo, Redish, and Rockoff, "Why Didn't Canada Have a Banking Crisis?"

26. Bordo, Redish, and Rockoff, "Why Didn't Canada Have a Banking Crisis?"

27. Ibid.

28. Bank supervisors relied more on discretionary judgment than quantitative measures of capital adequacy. See FDIC, "Basel and the Evolution of Capital Regulation."

29. See International Lending Supervision Act of 1983, S. 695, 98th Cong. (1983); and Kapstein, *Governing the Global Economy*.

30. Kapstein, *Governing the Global Economy*.

31. Hogan and Manish, "Banking Regulation and Knowledge Problems."

32. See Basel Committee on Banking Supervision, "Amendment to the Capital Accord," for the original proposal, which took considerable time to finalize.

33. Hogan and Manish, "Banking Regulation and Knowledge Problems."

34. Erel, Nadauld, and Stulz, "Why Did Holdings?"

35. See 66 Fed. Reg. (November 29, 2001): 59614.

36. See Elliott, "Primer on Bank Capital"; Sundaresan and Wang, "Bank Liability Structure."

37. Miller, "Do the M&M Propositions Apply to Banks?"

38. Elliott, "Primer on Bank Capital."

39. Crouhy and Galai, "Economic Assessment of Capital Requirements."

40. Hogan and Manish, "Banking Regulation and Knowledge Problems."

41. Erel, Nadauld, and Stulz, "Why Did Holdings?"

42. Ibid.

43. Cordell, Huang, and Williams, "Collateral Damage."

44. Pub. L. 111-203; 124 Stat. 1376 (2010).

45. Admati and Hellwig, *Bankers' New Clothes*, 189.

46. Berger, Herring, and Szego, "Role of Capital in Financial Institutions."

47. Black, "Bank Funds Management."

48. Cochrane, "Toward a Run-free Financial System."

49. Miller, "Do the M&M Propositions Apply to Banks?"

50. Cochrane, "Toward a Run-free Financial System."

51. Black, Miller, and Posner, "Approach to the Regulation of Bank Holding Companies," 383.

52. Cochrane, "Toward a Run-free Financial System."

53. See Admati and Hellwig, *Bankers' New Clothes*; Black, "Bank Funds Management."

54. Black, "Bank Funds Management."

55. Admati and Hellwig, *Bankers' New Clothes*; and Admati, DeMarzo, Hellwig, and Pfleiderer, "Fallacies, Irrelevant Facts."

56. Black, "Bank Funds Management."

57. Kupiec, "Title II."

58. Black, Miller, and Posner, "Approach to the Regulation of Bank Holding Companies."

59. See Miller, "TLAC," for an elaboration on this point.

60. Banking politics aside, Black ("Bank Funds Management") suggests the opposite: requiring small banks the shares of which are not traded to have twice or three times as much capital as deposits, to reflect the difficulty of measuring market value.

REFERENCES

Adams, Robert, and Jacob Gramlich. "Where Are All the New Banks? The Role of Regulatory Burden in New Bank Formation." *Review of Industrial Organization* 48 (2016): 181–208.

Admati, Anat, Peter DeMarzo, Martin Hellwig, and Paul Pfleiderer. "Fallacies, Irrelevant Facts, and Myths in the Discussion of Capital Regulation: Why Bank Equity is Not Socially Expensive." October 22, 2013. Max Planck Institute for Research on Collective Goods 2013/23; Rock Center for Corporate Governance at Stanford University, Working Paper 161; Stanford University Graduate School of Business Research Paper 13-7.

Admati, Anat, and Martin Hellwig. *The Bankers' New Clothes*. Princeton, NJ: Princeton University Press, 2013.

Basel Committee on Banking Supervision. "Amendment to the Capital Accord to Incorporate Market Risks." January 1996. http://www.bis.org/publ/bcbs24.pdf.

Berger, Allen, Richard Herring, and Giorgio Szego. "The Role of Capital in Financial Institutions." *Journal of Banking and Finance* 19 (June 1995): 393–430.

Black, Fischer. "Bank Funds Management in an Efficient Market." *Journal of Financial Economics* 2, no. 4 (1975): 323–39.

Black, Fischer, Merton Miller, and Richard Posner. "An Approach to the Regulation of Bank Holding Companies." *Journal of Business* 51 (July 1978): 379–411.

Bordo, Michael, Angela Redish, and Hugh Rockoff. "Why Didn't Canada Have a Banking Crisis in 2008 (or in 1930, or 1907, or . . .)?" *Economic History Review* 68 (February 2015): 218–43.

Calomiris, Charles, and Stephen Haber. *Fragile by Design: The Political Origins of Banking Crises and Scarce Credit.* Princeton, NJ: Princeton University Press, 2014.

Cline, William. "Benefits and Costs of Higher Capital Requirements for Banks." Working Paper 16-6, Peterson Institute for International Economics, Washington, DC, 2016.

Cochrane, John. "Toward a Run-free Financial System." In *Across the Great Divide,* edited by Martin Neil Baily and John B. Taylor, 197–249. The Hoover Institution Press and Brookings Institution, 2014.

Cordell, Larry, Yilin Huang, and Meredith Williams. "Collateral Damage: Sizing and Assessing the Subprime CDO Crisis." Working Paper 11-30, Philadelphia Federal Reserve Bank, 2012.

Crouhy, Michel, and Dan Galai. "An Economic Assessment of Capital Requirements in the Banking Industry." *Journal of Banking and Finance* 10 (February 1986): 231–41.

Elliott, Douglas. "A Primer on Bank Capital." Brookings Institution, Washington, DC, January 28, 2010. http://www.brookings.edu/~/media/research/files/papers/2010/1/29-capital-elliott /0129_capital_primer_elliott.pdf.

———. "Higher Bank Capital Requirements Would Come at a Price." Brookings Institution, Washington, DC, 2013. http://www.brookings.edu/research/papers/2013/02/20-bank-capital -requirements-elliott.

Erel, Isil, Taylor Nadauld, and Rene Stulz. "Why Did Holdings of Highly Rated Securitization Tranches Differ So Much across Banks?" *Review of Financial Studies* 27 (2014): 404–53.

Federal Deposit Insurance Corporation (FDIC). "Basel and the Evolution of Capital Regulation: Moving Forward, Looking Back." January 14, 2003. https://www.fdic.gov/bank/analytical /fyi/2003/011403fyi.html.

Gornall, Will, and Ilya Strebulaev. "Financing as a Supply Chain: The Capital Structure of Banks and Borrowers." Unpublished manuscript, 2014.

Gorton, Gary. *Misunderstanding Financial Crises: Why We Don't See Them Coming.* Oxford: Oxford University Press, 2012.

Hogan, Thomas, and G. P. Manish. "Banking Regulation and Knowledge Problems." In *Studies in Austrian Macroeconomics (Advances in Austrian Economics, Volume 20),* edited by Steven Horwitz, 213–34. Bingley, UK: Emerald Group Publishing Limited, 2016.

Jalil, Andrew. "A New History of Banking Panics in the United States, 1825–1929: Construction and Implications." *American Economic Journal: Macroeconomics* 7 (July 2014): 295–330.

Kapstein, Ethan. *Governing the Global Economy.* Cambridge, MA: Harvard University Press, 1994.

Kroszner, Randall, and Philip Strahan. "What Drives Bank Deregulation? Economics and Politics of Relaxation of Bank Branching Restrictions." *Quarterly Journal of Economics* 114 (1999): 1437–67.

Kupiec, Paul. "Title II: Is Orderly Liquidation Authority Necessary to Fix 'Too Big to Fail'?" In *The Case against Dodd-Frank: How the "Consumer Protection" Law Endangers Americans,* edited by Norbert Michel, 55–85. Washington, DC: Heritage Foundation, 2016.

Mengle, David. "The Case for Interstate Banking." *Federal Reserve Bank of Richmond Economic Review* (November/December 1990): 1–17.

Miles, David, Jing Yang, and Gilberto Marcheggiano. "Optimal Bank Capital." *Economic Journal* 123 (March 2013): 1–37.

Miller, Merton. "Do the M&M Propositions Apply to Banks?" *Journal of Banking and Finance* 19 (1995): 483–89.

Miller, Stephen Matteo. "TLAC: Off to a Good Start but Still Lacking." Public Interest Comment. Mercatus Center at George Mason University, Arlington, VA, January 29, 2016.

Sundaresan, Suresh, and Zhenyu Wang. "Bank Liability Structure." 2014. https://www0.gsb .columbia.edu/mygsb/faculty/research/pubfiles/6375/BankLiabilitySW.pdf.

Walter, John. "The 3-6-3 Rule: An Urban Myth?" *Federal Reserve Bank of Richmond Economic Quarterly* 92 (Winter 2006): 51–78.

CHAPTER 3
Alternatives to the Federal Deposit Insurance Corporation

THOMAS L. HOGAN*
Johnson Center for Political Economy, Troy University

KRISTINE JOHNSON*
Mercatus Center MA Fellow at George Mason University (Alumna)

T he financial crisis of 2008 has caused economists to reexamine the
forces that stabilize (or destabilize) the financial system in the United
States and around the world. Despite much debate, there remains serious disagreement as to the root causes of the crisis and hence the best solutions for preventing future crises. Some studies claim the crisis was caused by
deregulation in the financial sector,[1] but the quantity and complexity of financial regulations had in fact increased significantly in the decades leading up to
the crisis. Other studies, by contrast, argue that poor or misguided financial
regulations were themselves a major cause of the crisis.[2] The form of potentially misguided financial regulation that we focus on here is government-
administered deposit insurance, managed in the United States by the Federal
Deposit Insurance Corporation (FDIC). This chapter discusses the evidence
from US history and around the world that government deposit insurance

*The authors are currently committee staff members in the US Senate. The views presented here are those of the authors alone and do not necessarily represent the views of any senator or committee.

leads to more bank failures and financial crises. We consider changes that might be made to the FDIC and the US deposit insurance system to help stabilize the banking system and prevent future financial crises.

Many people are unaware that deposit insurance can reduce stability in the banking system. The literature in support of deposit insurance is largely based on theoretical models.[3] This line of research assumes banking is inherently unstable and that the government has special powers or privileges that enable it to prevent bank runs when private actors cannot. Deposit insurance is often modeled as an idealized and actuarially fair system that prevents crises without creating any harm to the economy.[4] More realistic models, however, include the disadvantages of deposit insurance, such as the problems of moral hazard and increased risk taking that occur when depositors' funds are guaranteed since the depositors no longer have strong incentives to monitor banks' risk-taking activities. From theory alone, it is unclear whether government deposit insurance should be expected to reduce the number of bank failures by preventing runs or to increase the number of bank failures because of moral hazard. We must therefore turn to the empirical studies that analyze the effects of deposit insurance in the real world.

Despite the common perception among both laymen and economists that deposit insurance helps stabilize the banking system, most empirical studies find that introducing deposit insurance decreases stability. After briefly discussing the history of the FDIC, we analyze two strands of the empirical literature. First, international studies of deposit insurance systems around the world indicate that countries with higher levels of deposit insurance coverage and countries with more government involvement in the administration of deposit insurance tend to have higher numbers of bank failures and more frequent financial crises. Second, studies of the banking system in the United States prior to the establishment of the FDIC show similar results. Many US states established their own deposit insurance systems through public or private means, especially prior to the nationalization of the US banking system during the Civil War. Other states evolved competing private systems of insurance or functioned efficiently with no deposit insurance system at all. These private, pre-FDIC systems were effective at regulating the financial system, bailing out troubled banks, and preventing contagious bank runs that can lead to financial crises. Overall, the evidence indicates that reducing the FDIC's role in deposit insurance is likely to increase stability in the US banking system.

Given this evidence, we next consider three potential changes to the FDIC system. First, the administrative side of deposit insurance can be improved by replacing the FDIC with a privately managed organization, as is the case in most developed nations. Second, the mandated level of FDIC coverage could be reduced, allowing private suppliers to make up the difference. Third, the system could be privatized entirely by eliminating mandated coverage and allowing insurance to be provided privately rather than through the FDIC. Absent the FDIC, private institutions similar to those that existed before the FDIC would likely evolve to provide deposit insurance, consumer protection, and banking stability, although the political reaction to such a transition remains unclear.

Reducing or eliminating FDIC deposit insurance would be an important step toward restoring financial stability in the United States, but would not put an end to banks' lobbying for bailouts and subsidies. Banks always have and always will attempt to gain special privileges. However, reducing the level of FDIC insurance and reducing the government's involvement in the deposit insurance system would reduce the risk of bank failures and financial crises, making the need for future bailouts less likely. Similar deregulations have proven greatly successful in banking and other industries. The suggested changes would reduce the problems with government deposit insurance, especially moral hazard, and would help stabilize the US banking system.[5]

STUDIES OF DEPOSIT INSURANCE

Deposit insurance creates two conflicting forces that influence bank failures. On one hand, it removes the incentive for depositors to run on the bank, so banks are less likely to fail from nonfundamental causes. On the other hand, it creates moral hazard by decreasing the relative cost of taking risk, so banks are more likely to fail from fundamental causes. It is impossible to know in theory which of these effects will be greater, so we must look to the empirical literature—including literature on the history of the FDIC and international studies comparing deposit insurance systems around the world and deposit insurance in the United States prior to the FDIC—to find out whether deposit insurance makes banks more or less likely to fail in the real world. The evidence strongly indicates systems with higher levels of deposit insurance and more government involvement are subject to higher instances of bank failures and financial crises.

The FDIC

The FDIC was established to stabilize the banking system and protect individual depositors in response to the banking panics of the early 1930s that largely contributed to the Great Depression in the United States.[6] Although the FDIC is commonly credited with stemming bank runs,[7] deposit insurance has also increased the number of bank failures due to moral hazard. Many studies find that deposit insurance played an important role in contributing to the 2008 financial crisis, and the Federal Savings and Loan Insurance Corporation (FSLIC) that is now a part of the FDIC did the same in the savings and loan (S&L) crisis of the 1980s.

A series of bank failures during the early years of the Great Depression paved the way for the adoption of federal deposit insurance.[8] In 1931, the rate of bank failures and losses to depositors skyrocketed as the Federal Reserve failed to abate the shortage of liquidity in the banking system.[9] In January 1932, a federal lending agency called the Reconstruction Finance Corporation was created, and by the end of the year it had "authorized almost $900 million in loans to assist over 4,000 banks striving to remain open."[10] Nevertheless, deteriorating conditions led to a nationwide bank holiday and, after much deliberation and debate, the FDIC was established in the Banking Act of 1933.[11] The act provided the Temporary Deposit Insurance Fund, which began coverage on January 1, 1934, and a permanent plan that was to take effect on July 1, 1934, but was later delayed to July 1, 1935.[12] There was strong opposition to federal deposit insurance, even by President Franklin Roosevelt and others in the administration,[13] but sentiments began to shift in 1934 as the rate of bank failures declined.[14] The Temporary Deposit Insurance Fund was, at the time, seen as a major contributing factor in stopping bank failures, so the opposition to it mostly faded. Thus, the perception that FDIC insurance stabilizes the banking system has been perpetuated to the present day, despite much evidence to the contrary.

The FDIC's scope, coverage, and costs have greatly expanded over time and no longer resemble its original purpose. The initial coverage level of $2,500 per depositor was increased to $5,000 within just six months of adoption.[15] Since permanent FDIC insurance took effect in 1935, the maximum coverage amount has been increased six times, most recently in 2008 when it was increased to $250,000, where it stands today. "Since its inception, the real scope of federal deposit insurance . . . has increased by roughly 514 percent," outpacing growth in total deposits and income per capita.[16]

Despite the early perception that the FDIC reduced the frequency of bank failures, most evidence suggests it actually did the opposite. As Calomiris and Haber point out, "Although the civics textbooks used by just about every American high school portray deposit insurance as a necessary step to save the banking system, all the evidence indicates otherwise: it was a product of lobbying by unit bankers who wanted to stifle the growth of branch banking."[17] Many studies find that political support for the FDIC was driven by special interests, mostly to benefit small country banks and unit banking states at the expense of big city banks and branch banking states.[18] Calomiris and White explain that "the branch-banking movement of the early twentieth century created profound differences across states in the propensity for failure, which encouraged high-risk unit-banking states to attempt to free ride on the stability of branch-banking states through the establishment of national deposit insurance."[19] As a result, the states hit by the agricultural banking crisis of the 1920s became the staunchest advocates of deposit insurance legislation.

Empirical studies of FDIC insurance suggest the effects of moral hazard are present and possibly strong. Cebula and Belton find that federal deposit insurance coverage increased the rate of commercial bank failures,[20] and Shiers indicates that "higher levels of deposit insurance are positively and significantly associated with increased riskiness of commercial banks."[21] Saltz examines the link between the level of FDIC coverage and the frequency rate of bank failures and finds "strong evidence of a cointegrating relationship between the bank failure rate and the extent of central government-provided deposit insurance,"[22] indicating that "federal deposit insurance very likely induced bank failures."[23]

Evidence also indicates federal deposit insurance was a major cause of the S&L crisis of the 1980s. At the time of the crisis, deposit insurance for these institutions was provided through the FSLIC. Like the FDIC, the FSLIC served the same function and suffered from the same destabilizing moral hazard effects. Both the FSLIC and FDIC guaranteed deposits up to $100,000 per account, after being increased from $40,000 in 1980.[24] In the 1980s, the S&L industry experienced widespread failures, resulting in the largest collapse of financial institutions since the Great Depression.[25] Over the course of the crisis, 525 insolvent institutions were liquidated or sold, and another 517 institutions were insolvent but still operating at the end of the decade.[26] The FSLIC was insolvent by 1986, and taxpayers were forced to cover the excess losses. In 1989, it was abolished and its functions moved under the FDIC, where they reside today.[27] A study by the FDIC estimates the total cost of the crisis at $153 billion, of which $124 billion was contributed by taxpayers and only $29 billion by the S&L industry.[28] Many studies find the high levels of risk taken by the S&Ls were primarily the result of moral hazard created by deposit insurance.[29] A study by Dotsey and Kuprianov attributes the magnitude and costs of the crisis to "the blanket guarantees provided by deposit insurance, which permitted insolvent institutions to continue attracting deposits and to engage in high-risk activities that ultimately resulted in heavy losses."[30]

Following the crisis, proposals called for terminating government deposit insurance, rolling back deregulation, and implementing "narrow" banking, among other things.[31] Not wanting to enact radical change, Congress opted for a more "politically feasible, quickly implementable" solution, which took form in the Federal Deposit Insurance Corporation Improvement Act (FDICIA) of 1991.[32] The main pillars of FDICIA were prompt corrective action (PCA) and least-cost resolution (LCR). Prompt corrective action established fixed capital adequacy categories, such as well capitalized, adequately capitalized, and undercapitalized, based on a bank's capital ratio and a set of resolution procedures that were to take effect once a bank fell below a certain level. However, the thresholds determining when corrective action was necessary were set so low as to not be effective.[33] Balla, Prescott, and Walter examine banks from the crisis in the late 1980s and the financial crisis of 2008, finding that "despite the implementation of PCA, the FDIC's losses on failed banks over the period 2007–13 were significantly higher."[34] They claim that "one purpose of PCA was to shut down a failing bank before its losses got too big, and on this dimension it failed."[35] They argue that "PCA was doomed to fail because . . . 1) When a bank fails, the market value of its assets is significantly less than its book value; 2) PCA triggers were set at levels such that capital levels of a bank on the path to failure were only a few hundred basis points higher than pre-PCA."[36] Kaufman also finds that FDIC losses have increased in the post-FDICIA era.[37]

FDIC insurance also appears to have contributed to the financial crisis of 2008. Admati and Hellwig argue that by removing depositors' incentives to monitor banks' risk-taking activities, deposit insurance reduces the cost of debt for the largest US banks and encourages them to use much higher leverage. "In effect, taxpayers subsidize the use of borrowing by banks."[38] Higher leverage magnified banks' losses during the crisis, putting the largest banks at risk and increasing financial contagion. Admati and Hellwig also explain how flaws in the "self-financing" of FDIC can exacerbate the crisis. "For close to a decade, until 2006, the FDIC did not charge any deposit insurance premium at all . . . as a result . . . the FDIC is short of funds when default rates are unexpectedly high."[39] The successive events, which culminated in the bailouts of a number of US banks and other financial firms by the Federal Reserve and the US Treasury, were, according to Admati and Hellwig, driven by misguided regulations, including FDIC deposit insurance.[40]

This discussion by Admati and Hellwig is analogous to Hogan and Luther's description of the FDIC's Deposit Insurance Fund (DIF) as a rainy-day fund rather than a true insurance program. Once the DIF is fully funded, banks are charged only a minimal fee to maintain the fund rather than an actuarially fair assessment rate that would reflect their risk-taking activities. "For example, an actuarially fair rate would have been high in 2006 with risk building up in the banking system, but the actual assessment rate was only $0.0005 [per $100 in deposits], the lowest rate in FDIC history!"[41] The poor incentives in the current system could be largely avoided if, rather than being managed as a rainy-day fund, US deposit insurance providers bore some risk of losses on the assets they insured, such as in the private insurance providers and privately administered national deposit insurance systems (discussed later in "Alternatives to the FDIC System").

International Studies

Unlike the FDIC in the United States, most developed nations have systems of deposit insurance that are either partly or fully privatized. Many studies compare across countries the different types of deposit insurance systems and levels of deposit insurance coverage. They consistently find that higher levels of deposit insurance and more government involvement in the deposit insurance system lead to more bank failures and financial crises.

In a sixty-one-country study over the period from 1980 to 1997, Demirgüç-Kunt and Detragiache examine various coverage aspects, such as level of insured deposits, presence of a coverage limit, and share of deposits covered; and the "results uniformly suggest that explicit deposit insurance tends to increase bank fragility, and the more so the more extensive is the coverage."[42] Using a similar database of surveys from 107 countries, Barth, Caprio, and Levine show that "[t]he relationship between deposit insurance and bank fragility is economically large."[43] A bank-level dataset of thirty countries from 1990 to 1997 also indicates that "explicit deposit insurance is found to reduce market discipline" and that "a higher coverage limit significantly reduces interest rates [paid on deposits] and weakens market discipline."[44]

International studies also reveal that the adverse effects of deposit insurance are stronger where government has greater involvement in the deposit insurance system. Demirgüç-Kunt and Detragiache find "the adverse impact of deposit insurance on bank stability tends to be stronger . . . where it is run by the government rather than the private sector."[45] Demirgüç-Kunt and Kane show that "deposit insurance schemes that involve the private sector in their day-to-day management control moral hazard and financial fragility more effectively."[46] Demirgüç-Kunt and Huizinga conclude that publicly managed systems "tend to reduce market discipline (and increase moral hazard)."[47] Specifically, schemes funded only by the government have the most significant decline in interest rates and the largest reductions in market discipline, whereas private and joint management tend to improve market discipline.

Deposit insurance also appears to increase the probability of financial crises. Demirgüç-Kunt and Detragiache analyze the causes of banking crises in developed and developing countries from 1980 through 1994 and find that "[c]ountries with an explicit deposit insurance scheme were particularly at risk."[48] Based on research in another study, they argue that "explicit deposit insurance tends to increase the likelihood of banking crises."[49] Demirgüç-Kunt and Kane demonstrate that "explicit insurance makes banking crises more likely" and that "the countries with highest coverage limits in the sample . . . are five times more fragile than the countries that impose the lowest coverage limits."[50] Barth, Caprio, and Levine find "deposit insurance generosity is positively associated with the likelihood of a crisis."[51] In an analysis of the costs of crises under different institutional regimes, Hohohan and Klingebiel assert that unlimited deposit insurance guarantees "add greatly to the fiscal cost of banking crises."[52] Demirgüç-Kunt and Kane conclude that "[p]olicymakers should view the positive correlation between poorly designed deposit insurance and banking crises as a wakeup call."[53]

Because deposit insurance decreases financial stability, it has been found to have negative effects on economic development and long-run economic growth. Using a cross-sectional dataset of forty-nine countries, Cecchetti and Krause show "that countries with explicit deposit insurance and a high degree of state-owned bank assets have smaller equity markets, a lower number of publicly traded firms, and a smaller amount of bank credit to the private sector."[54] Similarly, Cull, Senbet, and Sorge find that in countries with less-developed legal and regulatory regimes, "[g]enerous government-funded deposit insurance tends to have a negative effect on financial development and growth. . . ."[55] Demirgüç-Kunt and Kane review the literature on deposit insurance and conclude that although government backing might be helpful in specific instances, "[o]ver longer periods, it is more likely to undermine market discipline in ways that reduce bank solvency, destroy real economic capital, increase financial fragility and deter financial development."[56]

Studies of individual countries also show the adverse effects of expansive government deposit insurance. Carr, Mathewson, and Quigley examine the stability of the Canadian banking system prior to and since the adoption of federal deposit insurance in 1967. They find that insolvencies have increased since the establishment of the Canadian Deposit Insurance Corporation (CDIC) in 1967 and argue that the absence of deposit insurance "provided incentives for both prudence on the part of bank management and monitoring by depositors and bank regulators."[57] Similarly, Mondschean and Opiela find evidence of decreased market discipline in Poland following an increase in coverage as "bank specific variables became less important in explaining differences in deposit interest rates."[58] Chernykh and Cole indicate that "financial risk and, to a lesser degree, operating risk increase[d] following implementation" of Russian federal deposit insurance in 2004.[59] From 1975 to 1998, the deposit insurance scheme set up by German banks was completely private in funding and management. Examining this period, Beck finds that "German banks take very low risks compared to other countries and do not seem able to extract a net subsidy from the financial safety net."[60]

It is clear that substantial empirical evidence supports the claim that deposit insurance increases bank failure rates, and a further look at the varying schemes in other countries provides policy implications for the United States. The findings suggest the negative effects of deposit insurance are stronger where coverage is higher and when deposit insurance is administered by the government. Although most examples are of increased government involvement in deposit insurance, with only a few cases of deregulation (such as the case of New Zealand, discussed later in greater detail), the evidence clearly indicates that private deposit insurance systems or systems with private involvement empirically tend to do a better job at combating the harmful effects of moral hazard. These alternatives may provide guidance for improving the deposit insurance system in the United States.

Pre-FDIC Insurance

Prior to the establishment of the FDIC, deposit insurance in the United States was administered at the state level through public or private mechanisms. Many states had either legally mandated or government-run deposit insurance systems. Other states had fully privatized systems of coinsurance administered by a clearinghouse or banking organization. Studies of pre-FDIC deposit insurance find that higher state involvement leads to a higher number of bank failures.

Comparisons of state-level deposit insurance systems demonstrate that government involvement in deposit insurance tends to decrease stability. Calomiris shows that "in both the antebellum period and in the 1920s, insurance systems that relied on self-regulation, made credible by mutual liability, were successful, while compulsory state systems were not."[61] Thies and Gerlowski also examine the state-sponsored systems in the nineteenth and twentieth centuries, finding that "other things equal, state banks in states with guaranty funds failed at a higher rate than state banks in states without guaranty funds."[62] Weber compares state-run funds of the pre–Civil War era to mutual guarantee systems and concludes that "the schemes that provided the most control of moral hazard were those that had a high degree of mutuality of losses borne by all banks participating in the scheme."[63]

Among the pre–Civil War deposit insurance systems, Indiana, Iowa, and Ohio were mutual guarantee systems with small numbers of banks that had strong incentives to police one another, and these programs appear to have been successful at preventing bank failures. By contrast, systems in Michigan,

New York, and Vermont "were much more like later deposit insurance systems, including the federal system," and were not successful because they "produced very large bank failures, sufficiently large to bankrupt the insurance fund."[64] For example, New York's fund, established in 1829, continued to suffer losses until 1842, when "it ceased to be able to repay losses of failed banks and thus ceased to provide protection to the payments system."[65] The Indiana, Iowa, and Ohio systems experienced few to no failures, mostly avoided suspension of convertibility, and enabled banks to maintain operations. While Indiana's scheme was in place from 1834 to 1865, no insured bank failed. Both Iowa's (1858–1866) and Ohio's (1845–1866) schemes had similar results.[66] These systems "were brought to an end not by insolvency, but by federal taxation of bank notes designed to promote the National Banking System."[67]

Studies using individual bank data find similar results. Dehejia and Lleras-Muney examine state-chartered banks from 1900 to 1940 and conclude that "the overall effect of deposit insurance was negative. And these negative effects, when significant, are sizable."[68] Hooks and Robinson use data from Texas state-chartered banks over the period from 1919 to 1926 and find "the existence of deposit insurance for state-chartered banks increased their likelihood of failure."[69] Several studies examine the voluntary state insurance program in Kansas in the 1920s[70] and assert that "insured banks were more likely to fail than non-insured banks."[71] According to one study, "The uninsured banks, in fact, were generally stronger institutions that exhibited higher capital ratios, fewer real estate lending problems, and far less need for public assistance."[72]

In the absence of deposit insurance, other mechanisms served to maintain stability and limit bank failures. Banks often formed clearinghouses to coordinate the exchange of banknotes, but "during banking panics the clearinghouse united banks into an organization resembling a single firm which produced deposit insurance."[73] Prior to the establishment of the FDIC, bank shareholders faced double or even triple liability for their equity investments and were therefore responsible for a portion of the bank's losses after insolvency. Macey and Miller indicate that "double liability was an effective regulatory system" and that, "unlike deposit insurance, the threat of double liability appears to have induced caution on the part of bank managers in their use of depositors' funds."[74] As Dowd[75] notes, a bank can also maintain depositor confidence and thus stability in other ways, such as hiring an independent auditor to evaluate its soundness, developing reliable accounting standards, publishing its financial data, and maintaining adequate capital.

Overall, studies of pre-FDIC deposit insurance in the United States find state-run systems were largely unsuccessful and increased bank failures and that self-regulating systems privately managed by banks that bore a portion of liability were the most successful. Based on these studies, it seems reasonable to conclude that moving in the direction of decentralized administration and privatization of losses would improve the current US deposit insurance system.

ALTERNATIVES TO THE FDIC SYSTEM

This section proposes three potential changes that might be made to the current system of deposit insurance managed by the FDIC. First, international studies find that private or semi-privately managed deposit insurance systems tend to outperform public systems. The FDIC might therefore be partly or fully privatized in a manner similar to most European deposit insurance systems. Second, the evidence shows that lower levels of mandated deposit insurance coverage tend to increase stability in the banking system. The current maximum level of $250,000 in mandated FDIC deposit insurance coverage can be greatly reduced without endangering the vast majority of depositors, a change that is likely to benefit smaller depositors by increasing stability and reducing costs. Finally, we propose that mandated insurance could be eliminated and the FDIC be privatized or abolished altogether. Historical evidence of deposit insurance prior to the FDIC indicates that private mechanisms such as clearinghouses, coinsurance programs, and systems of self-regulation are likely to emerge to stem bank risk. The empirical evidence indicates that these proposals are likely to increase efficiency and stability in the US banking system.

Private Administration of Deposit Insurance

The United States could maintain a government mandate on deposit insurance but allow the system to be privately administered. As mentioned earlier, private management tends to reduce bank risk and the rate of bank failures. Many developed countries around the world currently use such models. Thirteen countries have privately administered schemes and many others have joint public-private administration, as defined by the World Bank.[76] New Zealand has no deposit insurance but instead employs a system for resolving insolvent banks. This section discusses the examples of privately administered systems in Switzerland and Italy, the special case of a private system in Germany, and the bank resolution system used in New Zealand. Belgium, Brazil, Denmark, Finland, France, Japan, Luxembourg, Norway, Spain, and many other countries have privately administered systems similar to the ones discussed here.[77]

Switzerland and Italy are examples of countries with deposit insurance systems that are mandated by law but privately administered by organizations of member banks. The scheme in Switzerland, *esisuisse*, is identified as "self-regulation."[78] The Swiss Federal Law on Banks and Savings Banks requires that depositors be insured up to 100,000 Swiss francs but calls for a self-regulating organization approved by the Swiss Financial Market Supervisory Authority (FINMA) to insure deposits.[79] All deposit banks in Switzerland are required to be members of esisuisse and are subject to its regulations. Administrative functions, such as setting annual member contributions, are carried out internally by esisuisse.[80] When a bank becomes insolvent, FINMA holds the authority to trigger deposit protection, at which time all other banks in esisuisse must supply the necessary funding within twenty days.[81] Dirk Cupei, Managing Director of Financial Market Stability and Deposit Protection for the Association of German Banks, notes of the Swiss scheme, "[T]he central principles are set down in legislation, but most things are left for the financial services industry to regulate itself." He claims that this lean model "works very well" and that "[i]t is right that the funds of an insolvent institution should first be used to cover client credit balances. This rule not only makes deposit protection more efficient, it also means that in many cases banks can be wound up without having to use money from the deposit protection scheme."[82] According to an esisuisse annual report, "The esisuisse depositor protection scheme in Switzerland is unique: a self-regulated model with joint and several liabilities that has proven its ability to work on more than one occasion since 2007."[83]

In Italy, the Interbank Deposit Protection Fund was established in 1987 as a voluntary consortium, "but has since become a mandatory fund."[84] All Italian banks except mutual banks are members of the fund.[85] Although the Protection Fund is private, with statutes and bylaws adopted by a general meeting of members, the Italian central bank, the Bank of Italy, has full powers in supervising and coordinating the Fund's activities.[86] Italian law dictates maximum coverage of 100,000 euro.[87] Once the Bank of Italy initiates compulsory administrative liquidation of the bank, the Deposit Protection Fund has twenty days to provide funds for reimbursement. The Fund's board determines the procedures and schedule for the reimbursement of depositors. Major administrative decisions are made at the general meeting, such as determining member contributions, electing officials, and approving the balance sheet.[88]

In Germany, the Association of German Banks established its private deposit insurance scheme, the Deposit Protection Fund, in 1975. Beck describes Germany's model as "a club that provides a nonrival, but excludable good for its members" and notes that the scheme's structure resembles the successful historical schemes in the United States.[89] The Deposit Protection Committee, whose members are elected from the Association of German Banks, manages the fund.[90] While the Deposit Protection Fund is voluntary and emerged absent a statutory mandate, a new statutory scheme, the Compensation Scheme of German Banks (EdB), was introduced in 1998 in response to a European Union (EU) mandate for compulsory deposit insurance schemes. As required by the EU mandate, the EdB set a minimum coverage level of 20,000 euro per depositor, but the level has since increased to 100,000 euro per depositor.[91] The EdB is also privately managed and shares features of the voluntary scheme, but is under regulation and supervision of the Federal Banking and Supervisory Office. The Ministry of Finance sets the premiums for the statutory system.[92]

These privately managed deposit insurance systems might serve as a guide for a privately administered program in the United States. As discussed, many developed nations have systems in which banks work together to administer and manage deposit insurance. One potential option for administering deposit insurance through private banking organizations might be to give responsibility to the regional Federal Reserve Banks. The structure of the US Federal Reserve System closely resembles some of the privately administered deposit insurance schemes in place around the world. Each of the twelve regional Reserve Banks has a board of directors intended to reflect the diverse interests of the districts and convey a private-sector perspective. All member banks hold stock in their Reserve Bank and may receive dividends. Administering deposit insurance through the regional Reserve Banks might combine the federal oversight desired by regulators with the private incentives needed to create stability. We leave it to further studies to explore whether such a change would indeed be possible in practice.

New Zealand does not currently have a government deposit insurance program at all. The government introduced a system of deposit insurance during the financial crisis of 2008 but has since allowed its temporary program to expire. "Following the closure of the Retail Deposit Guarantee Scheme on 31 December 2011, there was not a case to introduce a deposit insurance scheme on its own."[93] As a substitute, its Open Bank Resolution (OBR) tool is aimed at maintaining operations in the event of a bank failure rather than providing a deposit insurance safety net. If a bank fails, a portion of its liabilities are frozen to allow the bank to continue operations until it is acquired by another bank or resolved completely. If the bank is resolved, the priority of creditors is maintained such that shareholders bear the first losses, followed by subordinated debt holders, and then by depositors last. However, only a portion of depositors' funds are frozen for use against the bank's losses, and the rest of the unfrozen funds become available the next day, allowing depositors to conduct transactions. "While the initial portion of the creditors' claims that are frozen puts a ceiling on their final losses, their actual losses may be less than this if it turns out that the estimate of the losses was too conservative . . . creditors could well regain access to much of their frozen funds once the bank's losses are determined."[94] Unfrozen liabilities are ultimately funded through liquidation of assets, takeover, or restructuring. As Toby Fiennes of the Reserve Bank of New Zealand says, "[OBR] does not change the fact that depositors' and other creditors' funds are at risk."[95] The OBR scheme reduces moral hazard while enabling the financial system to continue to function during a crisis.

Reducing the Level of FDIC Coverage

The provision of deposit insurance can be improved by privatizing administration, but it might also be beneficial to improve the consumer side by lowering the mandated level of coverage. This change would have benefits that are attractive to both supporters and opponents of the current FDIC system. Supporters argue that deposit insurance requires government support to backstop the banking system in the event of a financial crisis. Opponents would prefer that individuals be allowed to choose how much of their deposits, if any, they would like to insure rather than be required to purchase deposit insurance for up to $250,000 in deposits. Reducing the mandated level of deposit insurance coverage would maintain a backstop for the banking system while creating benefits to any consumer who might prefer to opt out of the currently mandated system of deposit insurance, especially low-income consumers who might have trouble affording a bank account under the current system.

Two arguments are often given in favor of government deposit insurance: it stabilizes the banking system, and it protects small, less-sophisticated depositors. The first justification, however, is based on a false premise. As shown already, government insurance programs tend to increase rather than reduce risk in the banking system. But what about the protection of small depositors? As Bradley points out, one justification given for federal deposit insurance during the congressional debates over the Banking Act of 1933 was simply "to protect the small depositor."[96] The argument goes that less-sophisticated depositors do not have the ability to monitor the soundness of large, complex banks and will be exposed to losses if the bank fails. However, only a minimal amount of deposit insurance is needed to protect these depositors, and the cost of deposit insurance, however small, is particularly harmful to lower-income consumers in several ways. First, low earners may only marginally be able to afford a bank account at all, and their financial alternatives such as check-cashing services and credit cards may be more costly. Second, deposit insurance fees have a proportionally larger impact on incomes that are lower and less disposable. Third, small depositors benefit less than large depositors from the implicit taxpayer subsidy created by deposit insurance. The current coverage limit of $250,000 is far beyond the amount needed by the typical depositor. Why should consumers be penalized by being forced to purchase a service they neither desire nor can afford?

Cutting the level of deposit insurance would also please economists who worry about moral hazard since more sophisticated depositors will have a greater incentive to monitor banks' risk-taking activities. FDIC Chairman William Isaac, for example, worried in the early 1980s that "[w]ith a perception of minimal risk, there is little incentive for larger depositors to exert the degree of market discipline present in other industries."[97] If the level of deposit insurance is reduced, more sophisticated investors will withdraw their deposits from banks that take excessive risk, thereby imposing a higher degree of market discipline, and less-sophisticated investors will still have some minimal level of protection.

Reducing the level of mandated coverage does not mean consumers would have no insurance at all, but rather that they would have the option of acquiring insurance through private means. American consumers are already able to insure their excess deposits through a variety of private insurance providers. As described in a report from the FDIC, "Private excess insurance already exists. . . . A small number of private insurance companies have offered this type of insurance over the past decade."[98] Although the insurance of excess deposits is most common at the individual level, it also appears that some institutions take it upon themselves to make sure all customer deposits are insured, even those beyond the FDIC coverage limit. "Among the some 300 institutions represented at FDIC outreach meetings . . . approximately one in ten indicated that they had purchased excess coverage."[99]

Credit unions use a similar system for insuring excess deposits. Like the FDIC, the National Credit Union Administration (NCUA) operates the National Credit Union Share Insurance Fund (NCUSIF) to protect its member institutions' deposits. This fund, however, is supplemented by private insurers. One of the largest private insurers is American Share Insurance (ASI), which provides primary and excess deposit insurance exclusively to credit unions. Excess deposit insurance from ASI is often used to insure deposits of up to $250,000 beyond the NCUA coverage limit of $250,000 for a total coverage of $500,000.

To protect itself against losses, ASI monitors the soundness and risk taking of its member credit unions. As described in an FDIC report, "American Share Insurance Company, a private primary and excess deposit insurer to credit unions, requires monthly financial reports from its members, examines them regularly, and supervises them closely."[100] As a private organization, ASI has more resources and expertise than federal agencies such as the NCUA for monitoring its credit union clients. For example, "NCUA conducts on-site examinations at 15% of federally insured credit unions annually, while ASI is on-site at 65% of its credit unions each year."[101] ASI is sometimes able to provide its services at a discount relative to FDIC insurance. According to the *Chicago Tribune*, "Craig Bradley, president of Kane County Teachers Credit Union in Illinois, said his organization switched to American Share in the early 1980s because the federal credit union deposit insurance fund was charging higher premiums."[102] The firm's website advertises that "ASI is owned by our insured credit unions . . . the corporation insures over 1.2 million credit union members, and no member has ever lost money in an ASI-insured account!"[103]

State-level cooperatives provide another example of private insurance. Massachusetts, for example, has a set of state-level deposit insurance funds that operate like the FDIC but are privately administered. "Massachusetts state law requires excess deposit insurance for the customers of state cooperative banks, savings banks, and state-chartered credit unions."[104] There are three main providers in the state: the Co-operative Central Bank, which insures cooperative banks; the Deposit Insurance Fund, which insures savings banks; and the Massachusetts Share Insurance Corporation, which insures credit unions. Although insurance for excess deposits is not required in most states, reducing the level of FDIC coverage would allow consumers to choose the level of insurance that is best for them through state-level providers, as is done in Massachusetts, or through private firms such as ASI.

Some opponents of private deposit insurance argue that the failure of the Ohio Deposit Guarantee Fund (ODGF) in 1985 proves state-level private deposit insurance is unreliable, but there is much confusion over whether the ODGF was, in practice, a private system. Alexander, for example, notes that although the ODGF was not intended to be an agency of the government, it was established by legislation to promote the public interest, and its structure, functions, and guarantees are specified in statute.[105] Although private in name, the ODGF was operated as a public agency, like the FDIC and FSLIC, that lacked the proper incentive structure of a truly private deposit insurance system. As Gattuso notes, "the 'private' Ohio insurance fund, far from being an example of unregulated private enterprise, was severely weakened by state regulation—indeed, it was modeled closely on the federal insurance corporations rather than normal private insurance systems."[106] Like the FSLIC, the ODGF was bankrupted by the bank failures of the 1980s S&L crisis. The state government chose to guarantee its losses which were ultimately borne by Ohio taxpayers. A similar state-level bailout took place for a state-level deposit insurance fund in Maryland. As the FDIC describes, "Ohio and Maryland S&L failures helped kill state deposit insurance funds."[107]

To some degree, depositors are able to circumvent the limits of deposit insurance coverage through programs like the Certificate of Deposit Account Registry Service (CDARS). CDARS allows each individual depositor to insure millions of dollars in deposits by splitting her total deposits among accounts at multiple banks, each of which is insured by the FDIC up to its $250,000 limit.[108] If the coverage limit on FDIC insurance is substantially lowered, some depositors would likely turn to services such as CDARS, while others would move to private insurance or other programs. Large depositors would have the option of earning a higher return on their uninsured accounts or earning a lower return by paying a fee to protect against potential losses.

Private Insurance without Mandated Coverage

A final recommendation for improving the deposit insurance system in the United States would combine the extreme cases of the previous two recommendations by lifting the mandate on deposit insurance completely and privatizing deposit insurance entirely. Although it is impossible to predict the response from private firms in the market or what institutional features would emerge, we can identify at least a few possibilities by looking to examples from the past.

As previously discussed, prior to the FDIC, several US states instituted their own state-level deposit insurance systems. Some states had schemes resembling the FDIC, whereas others relied more heavily on banks to self-regulate with a mutual guarantee system. During the antebellum period, for example, Indiana, Ohio, and Iowa had bank-liability schemes that largely resembled clearinghouses, run by a board of directors, whose members were appointed by individual banks.[109] According to Weber, "[T]he board had the power to close a branch, limit a branch's dividend payments, and restrict the ratio of its loans and discounts to capital."[110] Each member was mutually responsible for some of the bank's liabilities. As Calomiris notes, Indiana's system established strong supervisory authority that placed responsibility on the banks themselves, which gave them an incentive to implement it properly.[111] Some state-level examples exist today such as the programs in Massachusetts. As discussed previously, public state-level deposit insurance programs were historically less effective than their private counterparts.

In many states, clearinghouses emerged to facilitate transactions among banks and reduce the cost of clearing checks.[112] Clearinghouses in the nineteenth century resembled the clublike model of banking associations that provide deposit insurance in private systems, such as Germany's current system. Members had to satisfy certain rules of the clearinghouse, and failure to do so resulted in disciplinary actions such as fines or expulsion.[113] When runs occurred, the clearinghouse transformed into a quasi-deposit insurance scheme, "uniting the member banks in a hierarchical structure topped by the Clearinghouse Committee."[114] As Gorton and Mullineaux note, "individual banks had an incentive to lower the probability of other members' failures because of the information externalities."[115]

The most famous example of an effective clearinghouse is the Suffolk Bank of New England. Rather than forming from a banking organization, the Suffolk Bank was a private bank that evolved into a bankers' bank. It provided note-clearing services but also acted as a lender of last resort. Members were required to keep an interest-free deposit of 2 percent of capital at the Suffolk Bank, and if they ran a negative clearing position, they could borrow in the form of an overdraft. Instead of returning the bank's notes, the Suffolk Bank would hold on to them and return them as the member bank paid off the loan.[116] Rolnick, Smith, and Weber show that New England banks fared better during the banking Panic of 1837 and claim this outcome was due to the note-clearing and lender-of-last-resort services provided by the Suffolk Bank.[117] In the years leading up to the Civil War, the Suffolk Bank faced increasing competition from other clearinghouses and bankers' banks, most notably the Bank of Mutual Redemption. These regional clearing systems ultimately met a political end from "the suspension of specie payments in December 1861 and the passage of the National Banking System Act in 1863 with the resulting elimination of the bank-note issue of state banks."[118]

In addition to the benefits created through bank clearinghouses, other institutional mechanisms often developed to protect depositors and deter bank risk. One such mechanism described by White was the requirement that bank managers post performance bonds, often in the amount of multiple years' salary, which would be forfeited in the case that the bank became insolvent.[119] Many banks have recently adopted a similar tool, "clawback" clauses, that, in certain instances, allow the bank to reclaim salaries or bonuses paid to bank executives, but these mechanisms are not generally used to cover creditors' losses. "Such clauses are generally triggered by ethics violations rather than [by] performance alone."[120] Another pre-FDIC institutional feature adopted in several states was double or unlimited liability for bank stockholders.[121] According to Calomiris, "[S]tockholders were liable for bank losses up to twice their capital contribution and officers and directors of failed banks were presumed guilty of fraud until they proved otherwise. If they failed to prove their innocence, their liability was unlimited."[122] Double liability resulted in actual losses to creditors being extremely small.[123]

Although it may be hard to imagine gaining the political will to disband the FDIC in the United States, it is not hard to imagine how a developed economy could operate without a government deposit insurance system. Many countries have evolved sophisticated financial markets without the need for government deposit insurance. In 1970, only five countries had explicit deposit insurance systems, and in 1985 there were still only nineteen countries with deposit insurance systems, compared to the 112 countries that have such systems today.[124] Australia, Hong Kong, and Singapore all adopted deposit insurance as recently as 2004 and appear to have done so mostly in the face of political pressure rather than for any perceived benefit to the financial system. The Australian government, for example, worried that "[i]f we do not [insure deposits], Australian financial institutions could, over time, find it more difficult to borrow in international financial markets. They would become uncompetitive in attracting funds."[125] As discussed earlier, New Zealand adopted but then abolished its system of deposit insurance. Although its financial system is small relative to the US system, New Zealand provides a current example of both a financial system in a developed economy without the need for a deposit insurance program and, perhaps more important, a government that was able to recognize the harms created by deposit insurance and summon the political will to abandon its existing deposit insurance system.

Evidence from other developed nations and historical experiences in the United States suggests ending compulsory federal deposit insurance is both reasonable and practical. In the past, a variety of private mechanisms emerged to protect depositors and maintain stability in the banking system. The fact that financial systems in other developed nations functioned efficiently without deposit insurance in the recent past and even today indicates that eliminating deposit insurance is a realistic possibility for the United States as well.

Political Impact

The prospects of privatizing the administration of deposit insurance, lowering the level of coverage, or ending the FDIC entirely would require tremendous shifts in the political and regulatory environments. There would surely be serious political ramifications that might advance or impede competition and stability in the banking system. Even in the case that private firms are able to provide insurance for those who demand it, banks will lose the implicit subsidy they currently receive in terms of lower costs of borrowing. They may look to replace this advantage with other forms of rent-seeking and political protections. One could imagine that in the absence of FDIC insurance, Congress might offer even broader protections for banks and financial firms in times of economic turmoil. For example, Dodd-Frank enshrined the Federal Reserve's too big to fail policy by specifying the conditions under which banks can receive last-resort loans and specifying the process by which nonbank financial firms are designated as systemically important. Ending FDIC deposit insurance might create another opportunity for banks to expand their implicit and explicit subsidies.

Even with the threat of adverse political reactions, however, there are reasons that ending the FDIC might still be worthwhile. First, there is always a threat that Congress will grant banks new privileges. Banks will continue to lobby for subsidies and protections regardless of the existence of government deposit insurance, as they did before, during, and after the financial crisis. Second, if private firms are able to provide insurance to depositors, then these insurers might be harmed by additional bank subsidies. In this case, they might provide a counterbalance to the lobbyists of the banking industry and prevent further subsidies. Third, it is possible that future financial crises would be less severe in the absence of government deposit insurance, as demonstrated by the empirical evidence discussed in the previous sections. If so, banks may have less justification to call for government assistance. It is far from clear that any of these forces would, in fact, emerge or what the magnitude of their effects would be, but it is clear that ending the FDIC would provide a marginal step in the direction of greater financial stability and less government interference in the banking industry.

There are several examples of other industries that have been successfully deregulated in the past that provide hope for prospective changes to the deposit insurance system. Many industry deregulations have proven resounding successes, such as the Airline Deregulation Act of 1978, the reforms to the Interstate Commerce Commission and the Motor Carrier Act of 1980 that deregulated the trucking industry, and the breakup of AT&T's long-distance monopoly followed by the Telecommunications Act of 1996. Even the deregulation of the banking industry from the late 1970s through the 1990s was successful. For example, the Depository Institutions Deregulation and Monetary Control Act (DIDMCA), passed in 1980, was a landmark piece of legislation "to change some of the rules under which U.S. financial institutions [had] operated for nearly half a century."[126] This legislation deregulated the interest rate ceilings established by the Federal Reserve in 1933 through Regulation Q.[127] As the Federal Reserve Bank of Chicago notes, "in many cases these rules had been made obsolete by changes in the economy, the functioning of credit markets, technology, consumer demands for financial services, and the competitive environment." Similarly, the Garn–St. Germain Depository Institutions Act of 1982 took steps to deregulate S&Ls, such as allowing for new types of interest-paying accounts, allowing for overdraft loans, and expanding S&L investment powers.[128] The Gramm-Leach-Bliley Act of 1999 "repealed sections 20 and 32 of the Glass-Steagall Act, which had prevented commercial banks from being affiliated with investment banks."[129] Despite the flood of rules, restrictions, and regulations created pursuant to Dodd-Frank, the major provisions repealed by those Acts have not been reenacted.[130]

Critics of deregulation might object that although the historical evidence does show that increasing government deposit insurance (in terms of the amount covered or the level of government involvement) has tended to decrease stability in the banking system (in terms of more bank failures and financial crises), there is limited historical evidence that reducing government deposit insurance will increase stability. In some sense, this point is correct. Despite the fact that several countries such as Germany, Australia, Hong Kong, and Singapore adopted deposit insurance for political rather than economic reasons, New Zealand may be the only case in which government deposit insurance was actually repealed. Although the historical evidence strongly indicates that more government deposit insurance decreases stability in the banking system, it may be possible that some other factor could prevent such an increase in stability from occurring. For example, private companies might be slow to expand their offerings of deposit insurance, leaving many savers exposed to bank risk. Legislation or simple market failure might prevent banks from creating the types of mutual insurance systems that successfully minimized systemic risk prior to the creation of the Federal Reserve. It could even be the case that if government deposit insurance were repealed, banks might lobby for even greater subsidies and bailout guarantees than they have today. However, it is far from obvious that any of these objections will come to pass or that they would hinder the net benefits of reducing government deposit insurance.

There are several reasons based on economic theory and real-world evidence to think that reducing deposit insurance will help stabilize the banking system. First, one can always object that some new legislation or policy will prevent this deregulation from being effective, but how likely are such concerns? It would be no small task for supporters of deregulation to summon the political will to roll back FDIC insurance. If such monumental political change were to occur, then the threat of reactionary policies such as bailouts and bank protections seems much less likely. Similar "What if?" objections were surely made to every deregulation, and in each case, those worries were proven incorrect. It is possible, at least in theory, that breaking up the AT&T monopoly could have led to a consolidated industry with little competition and strong barriers to entry, but instead a vibrant communications industry has emerged today.[131] It is possible that deregulating the trucking industry might have caused transportation prices to increase, but instead they have greatly fallen. It is possible that deregulation might have given airlines the ability to price as oligopolies, especially given the small number of firms at the time, but instead, competition expanded and prices fell to the point that now air travel is affordable to more Americans than ever.[132] Critics of deregulation always argue that the final outcomes are unknown and that there could be unintended consequences. But these objections are often based on intuitions or gut feelings rather than any evidence that such negative events should be expected in the future. The evidence from previous deregulations does not support such fears.

Second, because we know that increasing government deposit insurance decreases banking stability, it is logical to assume that decreasing government deposit insurance will lead to increased stability. This simple theory of an inverse relationship between government insurance and stability does not account for many outside factors that might interfere with banking stability, but it is consistent with the notion of Occam's razor that, as Simon describes, a good theory should "make no more assumptions than necessary to account for the phenomena."[133] Unless strong evidence is found that outside factors will, in fact, prevent a decrease in government deposit insurance from creating an increase in stability, then these factors should not be included in our analysis.

The simple theory that higher government insurance reduces stability and lower government insurance increases stability is consistent with the historical evidence. Any theory indicating that reducing deposit insurance will *not* lead to greater stability must be based on special assumptions beyond the evidence discussed in this chapter.

It is also important to remember that ending *government* deposit insurance does not mean ending *all* deposit insurance. Private deposit insurance is widely available today and would surely become more common in the absence of government alternatives. As previously discussed, firms such as ASI already insure billions of dollars in deposits, often at rates that are comparable to or even lower than government insurance. An FDIC study found that roughly 10 percent of banks surveyed already provide private insurance on any deposits in excess of the FDIC limit.[134] In addition, the widespread availability of private deposit insurance is likely to quiet any cries for government intervention from the depositor side. Thus, calls from the big banks for bailouts or subsidies will hopefully be recognized as corporate welfare rather than a public benefit. Banks always have and always will seek special protections from the government, but ending FDIC insurance would be an important step in reducing cronyism in the United States.

CONCLUSION

Partly or fully privatizing the FDIC system of deposit insurance would increase efficiency and stability in the US banking system. Most laymen and economists alike believe FDIC deposit insurance increases stability by preventing bank runs. However, the widespread consensus in empirical studies is that the benefit of fewer bank runs is far outweighed by the cost of moral hazard, which increases individual bank failures and financial crises. Considering this evidence, the United States should attempt to improve banking stability by moving to a partly or fully privatized deposit insurance system.

This chapter offers three potential paths for improving the current system of FDIC deposit insurance. First, because international evidence indicates privately administered deposit insurance systems are more stable than government-administered systems, deposit insurance could be run by a private entity or an organization of private banks rather than by the FDIC. Second, empirical studies find that stability can be improved by reducing the level of mandatory deposit insurance coverage, allowing supplemental insurance to be provided through private means. Third, combining these recommendations, the United States could move to a fully privatized deposit insurance system with no required coverage. History suggests that alternative mechanisms would emerge to insure depositors and minimize bank risk. These changes could be instituted partly or in full, alone or in conjunction. Prior successful deregulations in banking and other industries indicate that such changes are possible and practical. Any changes that encourage banks to bear a greater burden of their own risk exposures will discourage excessive risk-taking activities and lessen the need for future bailouts. We hope future studies will explore these options in further detail to judge which will be the most efficient and politically feasible to be implemented in the United States.

NOTES

Acknowledgments: The authors thank Anthony J. Evans, Jack Tatom, Andy Young, two anonymous reviewers, and session participants at the Association for Private Enterprise Education annual conference, for their helpful comments and suggestions. We thank the Mercatus Center at George Mason University for generously supporting this research.

1. Crotty, "Structural Causes of the Global Financial Crisis"; Bhidé, "Accident Waiting to Happen."

2. Calomiris, "Financial Innovation, Regulation, and Reform"; Friedman, "Capitalism and the Crisis."

3. Diamond and Dybvig, "Bank Runs, Deposit Insurance, and Liquidity," has more than 1,000 citations and is among the top 25 most influential papers in economics, according to the Social Sciences Citation Index.

4. As Thomas Sargent describes the model, "People don't initiate bank runs because they trust that their deposits are safely insured. And a great thing is that it ends up not costing the government anything to offer the deposit insurance!" (Rolnick, "Interview with Thomas Sargent," 31). Hogan and Luther argue the Diamond and Dybvig ("Bank Runs, Deposit Insurance, and Liquidity") and other actuarially fair models of insurance are not appropriate for analyzing the FDIC. See Hogan and Luther, "Implicit Costs of Government Deposit Insurance."

5. We do not discuss the extended impact that changes to the deposit insurance system would have on other types of financial regulation. Historically, bank capital regulation was created to counteract the negative effects of deposit insurance by limiting the risk of moral hazard. Improving deposit insurance would therefore eliminate one of the primary justifications for most banking regulation, making such regulations superfluous. In the present day, however, regulators have expanded the scope and goals of financial regulation. Privatizing deposit insurance would surely involve additional regulations for this new section of the financial industry. It is therefore unclear whether reforming the deposit insurance system would lead to a net gain or reduction in the overall level and costs of financial regulation.

6. See FDIC, *Brief History of Deposit Insurance*, 20–27; Bradley, "Historical Perspective on Deposit Insurance," 1–4.

7. See Calomiris and Haber, *Fragile by Design*. They argue that, contrary to this common perception, the introduction of FDIC insurance did not play a causal role in ending bank runs in the Great Depression since "the banking crisis of 1932–33 ended months before the establishment of FDIC insurance" (190).

8. Although the bank failures of this period are often blamed on the supposedly unstable nature of banking, instability in the banking system was actually caused by ill-conceived banking regulations such as restrictions on branch banking. See Champ, Smith, and Williamson, "Currency Elasticity and Banking Panics"; Calomiris and White, "Origins of Federal Deposit Insurance."

9. See Friedman and Schwartz, *Monetary History of the United States*, 676; FDIC, *Brief History of Deposit Insurance*, 21; Bernanke, "Money, Gold, and the Great Depression."

10. FDIC, *Brief History of Deposit Insurance*, 22.

11. Ibid., 27.

12. Ibid., 30.

13. Even before government deposit insurance was introduced at the federal level, economists and politicians alike predicted its negative consequences. As Christine Bradley describes the Banking Act of 1933, "President Roosevelt was against a government guarantee of bank deposits. He was not alone: bankers, including the American Bankers Association, opposed an insurance program, maintaining that such a program rewarded inept banking operations" (Bradley, "Historical Perspective on Deposit Insurance," 5).

14. FDIC, *Brief History of Deposit Insurance*, 31.

15. Bradley, "Historical Perspective on Deposit Insurance," 9.

16. Hogan and Luther, "Explicit Costs of Government Deposit Insurance," 153–54.

17. Calomiris and Haber, *Fragile by Design*, 190.

18. Golembe, "Deposit Insurance Legislation of 1933"; Calomiris and White, "Origins of Federal Deposit Insurance"; White, "Legacy of Deposit Insurance"; Bradley, "Historical Perspective on Deposit Insurance"; Dehejia and Lleras-Muney, "Financial Development and Pathways of Growth," 239–72; Kroszner and Melick, "Lessons from the U.S. Experience."

19. Calomiris and White, "Origins of Federal Deposit Insurance," 158.

20. Cebula and Belton, "Empirical Note on the Impact of Federal Deposit Insurance," 281.

21. Shiers, "Deposit Insurance and Banking System Risk," 359.

22. Saltz, "FDIC Coverage on Bank Failures," 71.

23. Saltz, "Federal Deposit Insurance Coverage and Bank Failures," 3.

24. Kane, *S&L Insurance Mess*, 36.

25. Curry and Shibut, "Cost of the Savings and Loan Crisis," 33.

26. Barth, *Great Savings and Loan Debacle*, 1.

27. Curry and Shibut, "Cost of the Savings and Loan Crisis," 28.

28. Ibid., 33.

29. Kane, *S&L Insurance Mess*; Barth, *Great Savings and Loan Debacle*; Cebula, "Impact of Federal Deposit Insurance."

30. Dotsey and Kuprianov, "Reforming Deposit Insurance," 3.

31. Benston and Kaufman, "FDICIA after Five Years."

32. Ibid., 144.

33. Ibid., 147–48.

34. Balla, Prescott, and Walter, "Did the Financial Reforms of the Early 1990s Fail?," 2.

35. Ibid., 4.

36. Ibid.

37. Kaufman, "FDIC Losses in Bank Failures."

38. Admati and Hellwig, *Bankers' New Clothes*, 129, 136–39, 176–88.

39. Ibid., 136.

40. Ibid. Admati and Hellwig primarily focus on capital rules. Their argument is that because deposit insurance creates an incentive for moral hazard, capital regulations must be used to prevent banks from taking excessive risks, and these capital requirements should be much higher than the current levels. Our proposals to reform deposit insurance to reduce moral hazard would presumably have similar effects.

41. Hogan and Luther, "Implicit Costs of Government Deposit Insurance," 9.

42. Demirgüç-Kunt and Detragiache, "Does Deposit Insurance Increase?," 1386.

43. Barth, Caprio, and Levine, "Bank Regulation and Supervision," 237.

44. Demirgüç-Kunt and Huizinga, "Market Discipline and Deposit Insurance," 397, 393.

45. Demirgüç-Kunt and Detragiache, "Does Deposit Insurance Increase?," 1373.

46. Demirgüç-Kunt and Kane, "Deposit Insurance around the Globe," 193.

47. Demirgüç-Kunt and Huizinga, "Market Discipline and Deposit Insurance," 399.

48. Demirgüç-Kunt and Detragiache, "Determinants of Banking Crises," 81.

49. Demirgüç-Kunt and Detragiache, "Does Deposit Insurance Increase?," 1373.

50. Demirgüç-Kunt and Kane, "Deposit Insurance around the Globe," 184–85.

51. Barth, Caprio, and Levine "Bank Regulation and Supervision," 237.

52. Hohohan and Klingebiel, "Controlling the Fiscal Costs of Banking Crises," 1.

53. Demirgüç-Kunt and Kane, "Deposit Insurance around the Globe," 187.

54. Cecchetti and Krause, "Deposit Insurance and External Finance," 531.

55. Cull, Senbet, and Sorge, "Deposit Insurance and Financial Development," 73.

56. Demirgüç-Kunt and Kane, "Deposit Insurance around the Globe," 192.

57. Carr, Mathewson, and Quigley, "Stability in the Absence of Deposit Insurance," 1156.

58. Mondschean and Opiela, "Bank Time Deposit Rates," 179.

59. Chernykh and Cole, "Does Deposit Insurance Improve?," 388.

60. Beck, "Deposit Insurance as Private Club," 711.

61. Calomiris, "Is Deposit Insurance Necessary?," 283.

62. Thies and Gerlowski, "Deposit Insurance," 677.

63. Weber, "Bank Liability Insurance Schemes before 1865," 1.

64. White, "Deposit Insurance," 5.

65. Calomiris, "Is Deposit Insurance Necessary?," 286.

66. Calomiris, "Deposit Insurance."

67. Calomiris, "Is Deposit Insurance Necessary?," 288.

68. Dehejia and Lleras-Muney, "Financial Development and Pathways of Growth," 265.

69. Hooks and Robinson, "Deposit Insurance and Moral Hazard," 833.

70. Wheelock, "Deposit Insurance and Bank Failures"; Wheelock and Kumbhakar, "Which Banks Choose Deposit Insurance?"; Wheelock and Wilson, "Explaining Bank Failures."

71. Wheelock, "Deposit Insurance and Bank Failures," 530.

72. Spong and Regher, "Kansas Banking in the 1930s," 108.

73. Gorton, "Clearinghouses and the Origin of Central Banking," 277.

74. Macey and Miller, "Double Liability of Bank Shareholders," 34.

75. Dowd, "Deposit Insurance."

76. Demirgüç-Kunt, Kane, and Laeven, "Deposit Insurance Database," 37–38.

77. Demirgüç-Kunt, Karacaovali, and Laeven, "Deposit Insurance around the World," 60–64.

78. Esisuisse, *Articles of Association*, 1.

79. See Federal Assembly of the Swiss Confederation, "Federal Act on Banks and Savings Banks," art. 37a and art. 37h.

80. Ibid.

81. See ibid., and art. 37i.

82. Esisuisse, "2013 Annual Report," 78.

83. Ibid., 91.

84. Fondo Interbancario di Tutela dei Depositi (Interbank Deposit Protection Fund) Institution. Retrieved August 2016. https://www.fitd.it/Chi_Siamo/Istituzione.

85. Banca D'Italia, "Banking Act, Legislative Decree n.385" (translated from Italian), September 1, 1993, art. 96.

86. Fondo Interbancario.

87. Il Presidente Della Repubblica Italiana, "Legislative Decree n49 of 24th March 2011" (translated from Italian), March 24, 2011.

88. Fondo Interbancario, art. 11, art. 14.

89. Beck, "Deposit Insurance as Private Club," 712–13.

90. Bankenverband, "By-laws of the Deposit Protection Fund."

91. Demirgüç-Kunt, Kane, and Laeven, "Deposit Insurance Database," 34.

92. Beck, "Deposit Insurance as Private Club," 714.

93. Reserve Bank of New Zealand, "Release of the Reserve Bank."

94. Hoskin and Woolford, "Primer on Open Bank Resolution," 10.

95. Fiennes, "Handling Bank Failures."

96. Bradley, "Historical Perspective on Deposit Insurance," 5n47.

97. Isaac, "Prologue to Federal Deposit Insurance Corporation"; FDIC, *Brief History of Deposit Insurance*, iv.

98. FDIC, "Options Paper," 48.

99. Ibid.

100. Bradley and Valentine, "Privatizing Deposit Insurance," 26.

101. Cooke, "ASI Firing Back."

102. Allison, "Private Deposit Insurance Lives On."

103. ASI, Program Details.

104. NCUA, "Report to the Congress," 9.

105. Alexander, "Ohio Deposit Guarantee Fund," 431–32.

106. Gattuso, "Ohio Banking Crisis."

107. FDIC, "S&L Crisis."

108. CDARS, "How CDARS Works."

109. Calomiris, "Deposit Insurance," 10–30.

110. Weber, "Bank Liability Insurance Schemes before 1865," 5.

111. Calomiris, "Deposit Insurance," 16.

112. Gorton and Mullineaux, "Joint Production of Confidence," 460.

113. Ibid., 461.

114. Gorton, "Clearinghouses and the Origin of Central Banking," 280.

115. Gorton and Mullineaux, "Joint Production of Confidence," 464.

116. Weber, "Bank Liability Insurance Schemes before 1865."

117. Rolnick, Smith, and Weber, "Suffolk Bank and the Panic of 1837." In addition to the regulatory function of monitoring member banks, the Suffolk Bank also promoted economic stability by acting as a check on overexpansive monetary policy. Young and Dove examined state-level data on circulations and reserves from the Suffolk Banking System (1825–1858) and find a cointegrating relationship between state-level circulation and reserves, indicating that the Suffolk system was able to prevent in-concert overexpansions of banknotes. See Young and Dove, "Policing the Chain Gang."

118. Lake, "End of the Suffolk System," 205.

119. White, "Rethinking the Regulation of Banking," 6.

120. Hogan and Luther, "Explicit Costs of Government Deposit Insurance," 166.

121. Weber, "Bank Liability Insurance Schemes before 1865," 5.

122. Calomiris, "Deposit Insurance," 16.

123. Macey and Miller, "Double Liability of Bank Shareholders," 58.

124. Demirgüç-Kunt, Kane, and Laeven, "Deposit Insurance Database," table A.1.2.

125. Prime Minister of Australia, "Global Financial Crisis."

126. Federal Reserve Bank of Chicago, *Leveling the Playing Field*, 7.

127. Ibid.

128. Ibid.

129. White, "The Gramm-Leach-Bliley Act of 1999," 942.

130. Some economists, including a group of free-market economists known as the Shadow Financial Regulatory Committee, argue that section 619 of Dodd-Frank, known as the "Volcker Rule," has effectively reinstated the separation of commercial and investment banking, a primary component of the Glass-Steagall Act; see Acharya and Richardson, "Implications of the Dodd-Frank Act"; SFRC, "Glass-Steagall and the Volcker Rule." Others, however, argue that a stronger, modernized version of Glass-Steagall should be reenacted today; see Merkley and Levin, "Dodd-Frank Act Restrictions."

131. Jerry Hausman, for example, estimates that regulations delayed the introduction of new telecommunications services, which reduced consumer welfare by billions of dollars per year; see Hausman, "Valuing the Effect of Regulation." Hausman and Gregory Sidak argue that further welfare gains will be possible by moving toward "the end of regulation" in telecommunications; see Hausman and Sidak, "Telecommunications Regulation."

132. See Winston, "Economic Deregulation"; Crandall and Ellig, *Economic Deregulation and Customer Choice*; Winston, "U.S. Industry Adjustment to Economic Deregulation"; and Crandall, *Extending Deregulation.*

133. Herbert A. Simon, "Rational Decision Making in Business Organizations," *American Economic Review* 69, no. 4 (1979): 495.

134. FDIC, "2000 Options Paper," 48.

REFERENCES

Acharya, Viral V., and Matthew Richardson. "Implications of the Dodd-Frank Act." *Annual Review of Financial Economics* 4, no. 1 (2012): 1–38.

Admati, Anat, and Martin Hellwig. *The Bankers' New Clothes*. Princeton, NJ: Princeton University Press, 2013.

Alexander, Ronald E. "The Ohio Deposit Guarantee Fund: The Ohio Alternative to FSLIC." *Akron Law Review* 15, no. 3 (1983): 431–39.

Allison, Melissa. "Private Deposit Insurance Lives On." *Chicago Tribune,* January 30, 2002. http://articles.chicagotribune.com/2002-01-30/business/0201300227_1_deposit-insurance-federal-deposit-credit-unions.

American Share Insurance (ASI). Program Details. Retrieved January 2015. http://www.americanshare.com/ primaryshareinsurance/program-details.

Balla, Eliana, Edward S. Prescott, and John R. Walter. "Did the Financial Reforms of the Early 1990s Fail? A Comparison of Bank Failures and FDIC Losses in the 1986–92 and 2007–13 Periods." Working Paper 15-05, Federal Reserve Bank of Richmond, May 15, 2015.

Bankenverband. "By-laws of the Deposit Protection Fund of the Association of German Banks." August 2014.

Barth, James R. *The Great Savings and Loan Debacle*. Washington, DC: AEI Press, 1991.

Barth, James R., Gerard Caprio, and Ross Levine. "Bank Regulation and Supervision: What Works Best?" *Journal of Financial Intermediation* 13, no. 2 (2004): 205–48.

Beck, Thorsten. "Deposit Insurance as Private Club: Is Germany a Model?" *Quarterly Review of Economics and Finance* 42, no. 4 (2002): 701–19.

Benston, George J., and George G. Kaufman. "FDICIA after Five Years." *Journal of Economic Perspectives* 11, no. 3 (1997): 139–58.

Bernanke, Ben S. "Money, Gold, and the Great Depression." Remarks at the H. Parker Willis Lecture in Economic Policy, Washington and Lee University, Lexington, VA, March 2, 2004.

Bhidé, Amar. "An Accident Waiting to Happen: Securities Regulation and Financial Deregulation." In *What Caused the Financial Crisis*, edited by Jeffrey Friedman, 69–106. Philadelphia: University of Pennsylvania Press, 2011.

Bradley, Christine M. "A Historical Perspective on Deposit Insurance Coverage." *FDIC Banking Review* 13, no. 2 (2000): 1–25.

Bradley, Christine M., and Craig V. Valentine. "Privatizing Deposit Insurance: Results of the 2006 FDIC Study." *FDIC Quarterly* 1, no. 2 (2007): 23–32.

Calomiris, Charles W. "Deposit Insurance: Lessons from the Record." *Economic Perspectives* 13, no. 3 (1989): 10–30.

———. "Is Deposit Insurance Necessary? A Historical Perspective." *Journal of Economic History* 50, no. 2 (1990): 283–95.

———. "Financial Innovation, Regulation, and Reform." *Cato Journal* 29, no. 1 (2009): 65–91.

Calomiris, Charles W., and Stephen H. Haber. *Fragile by Design: The Political Origins of Banking Crises and Scarce Credit*. Princeton, NJ: Princeton University Press, 2014.

Calomiris, Charles W., and Eugene N. White. "The Origins of Federal Deposit Insurance." In *The Regulated Economy: A Historical Approach to Political Economy*, edited by Claudia Goldin and Gary D. Libecap, 145–88. Chicago: University of Chicago Press, 1994.

Carr, Jack L., Frank G. Mathewson, and Neil C. Quigley. "Stability in the Absence of Deposit Insurance: The Canadian Banking System, 1890–1966." *Journal of Money, Credit and Banking* 27, no. 4 (1995): 1137–58.

Cebula, Richard J. "The Impact of Federal Deposit Insurance on Savings and Loan Failures." *Southern Economic Journal* 59, no. 4 (1993): 620–28.

Cebula, Richard J., and Willie J. Belton. "An Empirical Note on the Impact of Federal Deposit Insurance on Bank Failures in the U.S." *International Advances in Economic Research* 3, no. 3 (1997): 281–87.

Cecchetti, Stephen G., and Stefan Krause. "Deposit Insurance and External Finance." *Economic Inquiry* 43, no. 3 (2005): 531–41.

Certificate of Deposit Account Registry Service (CDARS). "How CDARS Works." http://www.cdars.com/home/how-cdars-works/.

Champ, Bruce, Bruce D. Smith, and Stephen D. Williamson. "Currency Elasticity and Banking Panics: Theory and Evidence." *Canadian Journal of Economics* 29, no. 4 (1989): 828–64.

Chernykh, Lucy, and Rebel A. Cole. "Does Deposit Insurance Improve Financial Intermediation? Evidence from the Russian Experiment." *Journal of Banking and Finance* 35 (2011): 388–402.

Cooke, Sarah Snell. "ASI Firing Back at Private Insurance Nay Sayers." *Credit Union Times*, March 05, 2003. http://www.cutimes.com/2003/03/05/asi-firing-back-at-private-insurance-nay-sayers.

Crandall, Robert. *Extending Deregulation: Make the US Economy More Efficient*. Washington, DC: Brookings Institution, 2007.

Crandall, Robert, and Jerry Ellig. *Economic Deregulation and Customer Choice: Lessons for the Electric Industry*. Fairfax, VA: George Mason University, Center for Market Processes, 1997.

Crotty, James. "Structural Causes of the Global Financial Crisis: A Critical Assessment of the 'New Financial Architecture.'" *Cambridge Journal of Economics* 33, no. 4 (2009): 563–80.

Cull, Robert, Lemma W. Senbet, and Marco Sorge. "Deposit Insurance and Financial Development." *Journal of Money, Credit and Banking* 37, no. 1 (2005): 43–82.

Curry, Timothy, and Lynn Shibut. "The Cost of the Savings and Loan Crisis: Truth and Consequences." *FDIC Banking Review* 13 (2000): 26–35.

Dehejia, Rajeev, and Adriana Lleras-Muney. "Financial Development and Pathways of Growth: State Branching and Deposit Insurance Laws in the United States, 1900–1940." *Journal of Law and Economics* 50, no. 2 (2007): 239–272.

Demirgüç-Kunt, Asli, and Enrica Detragiache. "The Determinants of Banking Crises in Developing and Developed Countries." *IMF Staff Papers* 45, no. 1 (1998): 81–109.

———. "Does Deposit Insurance Increase Banking System Stability? An Empirical Investigation." *Journal of Monetary Economics* 49, no. 7 (2002): 1373–406.

Demirgüç-Kunt, Asli, and Harry Huizinga. "Market Discipline and Deposit Insurance." *Journal of Monetary Economics* 51, no. 2 (2004): 375–99.

Demirgüç-Kunt, Asli, and Edward J. Kane. "Deposit Insurance around the Globe: Where Does It Work?" *Journal of Economic Perspectives* 16, no. 2 (2002): 175–95.

Demirgüç-Kunt, Asli, Edward Kane, and Luc Laeven. "Deposit Insurance Database." IMF Working Paper 14-118, International Monetary Fund, Washington, DC, 2014.

Demirgüç-Kunt, Asli, Baybars Karacaovali, and Luc Laeven. "Deposit Insurance around the World: A Comprehensive Database." World Bank Policy Research Working Paper 3628, World Bank, Washington, DC, 2005.

Diamond, Douglas W., and Philip H. Dybvig. "Bank Runs, Deposit Insurance, and Liquidity." *Journal of Political Economy* 91 (1983): 401–19.

Dotsey, Michael, and Anatoli Kuprianov. "Reforming Deposit Insurance: Lessons from the Savings and Loan Crisis." *Federal Reserve Bank of Richmond Economic Review* 76, no. 2 (1990): 3–28.

Dowd, Kevin. "Deposit Insurance: A Skeptical View." *Federal Reserve Bank of St. Louis Review* 75 (1993): 14–17.

Esisuisse. "2013 Annual Report."

———. "Articles of Association." Version 14. November 2014.

Federal Assembly of the Swiss Confederation. "Federal Act on Banks and Savings Banks." SR 952.0. Translated from German, November 8, 1934.

Federal Deposit Insurance Corporation (FDIC). *A Brief History of Deposit Insurance in the United States*. Washington, DC: FDIC, 1998.

———. "2000 Options Paper." Washington, DC: FDIC, August 2000.

———. "The S&L Crisis: A Chrono-Bibliography." December 20, 2002. https://www.fdic.gov/bank/historical/sandl/.

Federal Reserve Bank of Chicago. *Leveling the Playing Field: A Review of the DIDMCA of 1980 and the Garn-St Germain Act of 1982*. Readings in Economics and Finance. Chicago: Federal Reserve Bank of Chicago, 1983.

Fiennes, Toby. "Handling Bank Failures." Speech delivered to the Institute of Directors in Wellington, New Zealand, April 11, 2013.

Friedman, Jeffrey. "Capitalism and the Crisis: Bankers, Bonuses, Ideology, and Ignorance." In *What Caused the Financial Crisis*, 1–68. Philadelphia: University of Pennsylvania Press, 2011.

Friedman, Milton, and Anna J. Schwartz. *A Monetary History of the United States, 1867–1960*. Princeton, NJ: Princeton University Press, 1963.

Gattuso, James L. "The Ohio Banking Crisis: Who's to Blame?" Heritage Foundation Executive Memorandum No. 77. Heritage Foundation, Washington, DC, March 22, 1985.

Golembe, Carter H. "The Deposit Insurance Legislation of 1933: An Examination of Its Antecedents and Its Purposes." *Political Science Quarterly* 75, no. 2 (1960): 181–200.

Gorton, Gary. "Clearinghouses and the Origin of Central Banking in the United States." *Journal of Economic History* 45, no. 2 (1985): 277–83.

Gorton, Gary, and Donald J. Mullineaux. "The Joint Production of Confidence: Endogenous Regulation and Nineteenth Century Commercial-Bank Clearinghouses." *Journal of Money, Credit and Banking* 19, no. 4 (1987): 457–68.

Hausman, Jerry A. "Valuing the Effect of Regulation on New Telecommunication Services." *Brookings Papers: Microeconomics* 28 (1997): 1–54.

Hausman, Jerry, and J. Gregory Sidak. "Telecommunications Regulation: Current Approaches with the End in Sight." In *Economic Regulation and Its Reform: What Have We Learned?*, edited by Nancy L. Rose, 345–406. Chicago: University of Chicago Press, 2014.

Hogan, Thomas L., and William J. Luther. "The Explicit Costs of Government Deposit Insurance." *Cato Journal* 34, no. 1 (2014): 145–70.

———. "The Implicit Costs of Government Deposit Insurance." *Journal of Private Enterprise* 31, no. 2 (Summer 2016): 1–13.

Hohohan, Patrick, and Daniela Klingebiel. "Controlling the Fiscal Costs of Banking Crises." World Bank Policy Research Working Paper 2241, World Bank, Washington, DC, 2000.

Hooks, Linda M., and Kenneth J. Robinson. "Deposit Insurance and Moral Hazard: Evidence from Texas Banking in the 1920s." *Journal of Economic History* 62, no. 3 (2002): 833–53.

Hoskin, Kevin, and Ian Woolford. "A Primer on Open Bank Resolution." *Reserve Bank of New Zealand Bulletin* 74, no. 3 (2011): 5–10.

Isaac, William M. "Prologue to Federal Deposit Insurance Corporation." In *The First Fifty Years: A History of the FDIC, 1933–1983*, iii–v. Washington, DC: FDIC, 1984.

Kane, Edward J. *The S&L Insurance Mess: How Did It Happen?* Washington, DC: Urban Institute Press, 1989.

Kaufman, George G. "FDIC Losses in Bank Failures: Has FDICIA Made a Difference?" *Federal Reserve Bank of Chicago Economic Perspectives* 28, no. 3 (2004): 13–25.

Kroszner, Randall S., and William R. Melick. "Lessons from the U.S. Experience with Deposit Insurance." In *Deposit Insurance around the World: Issues of Design and Implementation*, edited by A. Demirgüç-Kunt, E. Kane, and L. Leaven, 188–217. Cambridge, MA: MIT Press, 2008.

Lake, Wilfred S. "The End of the Suffolk System." *Journal of Economic History* 7, no. 2 (1947): 183–207.

Macey, Jonathan R., and Geoffrey P. Miller. "Double Liability of Bank Shareholders: History and Implications." *Wake Forest Law Review* 27, no. 1 (1992): 31–62.

Merkley, Jeff, and Carl Levin. "The Dodd-Frank Act Restrictions on Proprietary Trading and Conflicts of Interest: New Tools to Address Evolving Threats." *Harvard Journal on Legislation* 48 (2010): 515–53.

Mondschean, Thomas S., and Timothy P. Opiela. "Bank Time Deposit Rates and Market Discipline in Poland: The Impact of State Ownership and Deposit Insurance Reform." *Journal of Financial Services Research* 15, no. 3 (1999): 179–96.

National Credit Union Administration (NCUA). "Report to the Congress: Study of Further Possible Changes to the Deposit Insurance System." February 2007.

Prime Minister of Australia. "Global Financial Crisis." Press Release. October 12, 2008. http://pandora.nla.gov.au/pan/79983/20081112-0133/www.pm.gov.au/media/Release/2008/media_release_0534.html.

Reserve Bank of New Zealand. "Release of the Reserve Bank and Treasury's Advice on the Open Bank Resolution and Deposit Insurance." Press Release. April 19, 2013. http://www.rbnz.govt.nz/regulation_and_supervision/banks/oia-obr/.

Rolnick, Arthur J. "Interview with Thomas Sargent." *Federal Reserve Bank of Minneapolis: The Region* (September 2010): 26–39.

Rolnick, Arthur J., Bruce D. Smith, and Warren E. Weber. "The Suffolk Bank and the Panic of 1837." *Federal Reserve Bank of Minneapolis Quarterly Review* 24, no. 2 (2000): 3–13.

Saltz, Ira. "FDIC Coverage on Bank Failures: Cointegration Analysis Using Annual Data, 1942–91." *International Advances in Economic Research* 3, no. 1 (1997): 71–80.

———. "Federal Deposit Insurance Coverage and Bank Failures: A Cointegration Analysis with Semi-annual Data, 1965–91." *Journal of Economics and Finance* 21, no. 3 (1997): 3–9.

Shadow Financial Regulatory Committee. "Glass-Steagall and the Volcker Rule." Statement No. 334, December 10, 2012.

Shiers, Alden F. "Deposit Insurance and Banking System Risk: Some Empirical Evidence." *Quarterly Review of Economics and Finance* 34, no. 4 (1994): 347–61.

Simon, Herbert A. "Rational Decision Making in Business Organizations." *American Economic Review* 69, no. 4 (1979): 493–513.

Spong, Kenneth, and Kristen Regher. "Kansas Banking in the 1930s: The Deposit Insurance Choice and Implications for Public Policy." *Federal Reserve Bank of Kansas City Economic Review* (3rd Quarter 2012): 107–27.

Thies, Clifford F., and Daniel A. Gerlowski. "Deposit Insurance: A History of Failure." *Cato Journal* 8 (1989): 677–93.

Weber, Warren. "Bank Liability Insurance Schemes before 1865." Research Department Working Paper 679, Federal Reserve Bank of Minneapolis, 2010.

Wheelock, David C. "Deposit Insurance and Bank Failures: New Evidence from the 1920s." *Economic Inquiry* 30, no. 3 (1992): 530–43.

Wheelock, David C., and Subal C. Kumbhakar. "Which Banks Choose Deposit Insurance? Evidence of Adverse Selection and Moral Hazard in a Voluntary Insurance System." *Journal of Money, Credit and Banking* 27, no. 1 (1995): 186–201.

Wheelock, David C., and Paul W. Wilson. "Explaining Bank Failures: Deposit Insurance, Regulation, and Efficiency." *Review of Economics and Statistics* 77, no. 4 (1995): 689–700.

White, Eugene N. "Deposit Insurance." Policy Research Working Paper Series 1541, World Bank, Washington, DC, 1995.

———. "The Legacy of Deposit Insurance: The Growth, Spread, and Cost of Insuring Financial Intermediaries." In *The Defining Moment: The Great Depression and the American Economy in the Twentieth Century*, edited by Michael D. Bordo, Claudia Goldin, and Eugene N. White, 87–122. Chicago: University of Chicago Press, 1998.

———. "Rethinking the Regulation of Banking: Choices or Incentives?" Conference paper prepared for the Witherspoon Institute, December 5–6, 2011.

White, Lawrence J. "The Gramm-Leach-Bliley Act of 1999: A Bridge Too Far? or Not Far Enough?" *Suffolk University Law Review* 43, no. 4 (2010): 937–56.

Winston, Clifford. "Economic Deregulation: Days of Reckoning for Microeconomists." *Journal of Economic Literature* 31, no. 3 (1993): 1263–89.

———. "U.S. Industry Adjustment to Economic Deregulation." *Journal of Economic Perspectives* 12, no. 3 (1998): 89–110.

Young, Andrew T., and John A. Dove. "Policing the Chain Gang: Panel Cointegration Analysis of the Stability of the Suffolk System, 1825–1858." *Journal of Macroeconomics* 37 (2013): 182–96.

PART 2

ADDRESSING FAILURE

CHAPTER 4
Title II of Dodd-Frank

PETER J. WALLISON
American Enterprise Institute

Title II of the Dodd-Frank Wall Street Reform and Consumer Protection Act (Dodd-Frank), entitled the Orderly Liquidation Authority (OLA), was enacted as a reaction to the chaos that occurred after the bankruptcy of Lehman Brothers in September 2008. The sponsors of the Act, and many others at the time, believed that it was the Lehman bankruptcy filing that caused the enormous panic known as the financial crisis. In a sense, then, the OLA is really the heart of Dodd-Frank because it was designed to avoid another financial crisis by preventing the disruptive and disorderly failure of large financial firms.[1] That feature also allowed the act's sponsors to claim that it had solved the problem of financial firms that were too big to fail (TBTF) because the government—in fear of allowing them to fail—would inevitably bail them out.[2] With the OLA, said the act's proponents, the government had a way to liquidate or resolve these firms without disrupting the financial system.

Later analysis, however, has shown that it was incorrect to believe that the bankruptcies of large nonbank financial firms, such as Lehman, were inherently disorderly. The chaos that followed Lehman's bankruptcy did not occur because bankruptcy is an inherently disorderly process, but because of the government's unexplained and illogical reversal of a policy that it seemed to have established with the rescue of Bear Stearns, a much smaller investment bank, six months earlier. That rescue created significant moral hazard, persuading the managers of large financial firms that they would be rescued by the government if they encountered financial difficulties and thus did not have to raise much additional equity capital in order to reassure their creditors. This left the whole financial market vulnerable to a shock when the government—faced with the impending failure of Lehman—inexplicably reversed its policy and allowed Lehman to fail. It was this reversal that caused the ensuing panic, not Lehman's bankruptcy itself.

Far more important, however, is the fact that, while the Lehman failure caused losses throughout the financial system, no other large financial institution failed as a result of Lehman's sudden and unexpected bankruptcy filing.[3] What this shows is that Lehman, despite its size and its involvement in such sensitive activities as credit default swaps, was not so interconnected with other large firms that its bankruptcy caused those other firms to fail. American International Group (AIG), Wachovia, and Washington Mutual (WaMu) all had to be rescued after Lehman, but not because of their exposure to Lehman. They were brought down by the same factor that brought down Lehman—exposure to subprime and other risky mortgages when a massive housing bubble was collapsing. To be sure, one money market firm broke the buck, but in the end its investors received 99 cents on the dollar.[4] That no other large financial firm failed because of Lehman demonstrates something important: even when the market is in a weakened and fragile condition, the failure of a large nonbank financial firm will not drag down others.

In other words, nonbank financial firms are not so "interconnected" that the failure of one will cause a systemic event—or, in the words of Dodd-Frank's Title I, create "instability in the US financial system." This is probably because these large firms are highly diversified and are simply not exposed to one another to any significant extent. The government should have no interest in the failure of a company if that failure will not cause a systemic event. Accordingly, the OLA, which would permit the replacement of the private bankruptcy system with a government-run resolution system for large nonbank financial institutions, is unnecessary.

THE ORDERLY LIQUIDATION AUTHORITY

The OLA contemplates that when a large financial firm is in "material distress" the secretary of the Department of the Treasury can decide, with the approval of the Financial Stability Oversight Council (FSOC), to turn it over to the Federal Deposit Insurance Corporation (FDIC) for resolution.[5] The FDIC then has roughly the same powers it has under the Federal Deposit Insurance (FDI) Act to liquidate the failing firm.

The very existence of the secretary's power to direct a different form of resolution for large financial firms than for others has serious consequences, even if it is never exercised. It means that creditors of these firms cannot be sure of the outcome when firms that are eligible for this treatment are in material distress. Will the firm go through bankruptcy, which is a known process with disclosed rules that are followed by courts, or will it go through the FDIC's process, in which the agency has wide discretion and could prefer some classes of creditors over others?

This in itself will raise the costs of financing for the firms that are potentially within this charmed circle, and will be especially harmful when a weakening firm actually needs new financial support from the market. In that case, creditors will be reluctant to provide that support because there is no way of knowing what law will be applied if the firm ultimately fails. So, many more firms are likely to fail because of the uncertainty created by the OLA than would otherwise be the case.

Thus, in order to avoid unnecessary uncertainty and risk to the financial markets, the bankruptcy system should be the only method for resolving non-bank financial firms. There have been a number of reforms to the bankruptcy laws proposed by experts in the field that would tailor these bankruptcy procedures more effectively for financial firms.[6] These reforms are beyond the scope of this chapter but should be analyzed for their applicability to the bankruptcy of a large nonbank financial firm.

In Title I of Dodd-Frank, the FSOC was given the authority to designate certain nonbank financial firms as systemically important financial institutions (SIFIs). Firms so designated are then turned over to the Federal Reserve for what is called "stringent" regulation. This idea is founded on the assumption that more regulation will reduce their chance of failure and hence the possibility that these large firms will create systemic disruption through their alleged "interconnections" with one another.[7] The lesson of Lehman, however, is that interconnections, which certainly exist to some degree, are not so substantial as to create a danger of a systemic collapse.

What will cause a systemic collapse, however, as demonstrated in the 2008 turmoil, is the deterioration in the value of a widely held asset class; in 2008, this class was residential mortgages. When home and mortgage values deteriorated, beginning in 2007, all financial firms that held mortgages were weakened, and some of them—like Bear Stearns, Lehman, Wachovia, and WaMu—to the point of failure. So it is not the interconnections between financial firms that are important, but the *common shock* to which *all* similarly situated financial firms are subject when an asset class as large and significant as residential mortgages suddenly deteriorates in value. Other commentators, such as Professor Hal S. Scott of Harvard Law School, refer to the same concept as "contagion," but the point is that many firms are adversely affected by an external event and not by exposure to one another as they would be if they were significantly "interconnected."

Thus, to prevent another financial crisis like 2008, it makes no sense to designate one or more large financial firms as SIFIs; the additional regulation that SIFI designation invokes will not prevent the consequences of a collapse in value of a widely held asset class. If there is any useful prophylactic role for government, it is to recognize that an asset class is so large and widely held that it should be brought to the attention of regulators and the public. In the case of the financial crisis, it was government policy itself that created the widely held asset class—subprime and other low quality mortgages—that brought about the crisis.[8]

Indeed, the danger of a 2008-like systemic collapse may be made worse by subjecting more firms to greater regulation. Regulation tends to reduce diversification because regulators push firms into the activities or assets the regulators approve, increasing their vulnerability to unexpected economic changes. Two recent examples of this phenomenon are the collapse of the savings and loan (S&L) industry in the late 1980s and the failure of a large number of banks in the 2008 financial crisis. S&Ls were restricted to investing in housing and were severely weakened by the high interest rates in the late 1970s, leading to their eventual collapse in the late 1980s; risk-based capital incentives herded banks into private mortgage-backed securities based on risky subprime loans in the 2000s. Accordingly, the designation of large nonbank financial firms as SIFIs is unnecessary, and possibly harmful, as is the special FDIC resolution process for these large firms in the OLA.

THE SINGLE-POINT-OF-ENTRY (SPOE) STRATEGY

While the OLA adopted an unnecessary and counterproductive rule for non-bank financial firms, it failed to address the serious problem that very large insured banks may in fact be too big to fail. Large nonbank firms, as shown by Lehman's case, are not so interconnected with the rest of the financial system that their failure will produce a systemic event, but this is not true of the largest banks. Firms of all sizes keep their payrolls and other short-term ready cash resources and working capital in banks, and banks are the central nodes of the US and international payments system. Trillions of dollars flow daily through this system, and if any one of the largest banks should suddenly fail the entire US and international economic system would likely grind to a halt, with many firms of all sizes unable to meet their obligations. Dodd-Frank specifically exempted the insured banking system from the OLA, leaving the resolution of banks to the FDIC.

This is problematic because the FDIC has in the past simply merged failing banks with healthy ones, something that is no longer possible when there is already great concern that the largest banks are TBTF. Where mergers were not possible, the FDIC has resolved small banks by taking control of them, paying off depositors, and selling off their assets. This strategy can work for small banks, but not for the giant banks that created the TBTF problem. The FDIC simply does not have the financial resources to resolve the largest banks in this way.

The FDIC apparently recognizes this deficiency and has tried to adapt the OLA so that it could be used to recapitalize failing banks. This introduces some legal uncertainties, because two sections of Title II—201(a)(8)(B) and 201(a)(9)(A)—specifically forbid its use for banks. In addition, it is apparent that the OLA, which after all is named the Orderly *Liquidation* Authority, was not intended to be used to recapitalize *any* subsidiary, whether a bank or a nonbank. It was intended simply to provide for the liquidation of large nonbank financial firms, if necessary, outside of bankruptcy.[9]

Nevertheless, in December 2013, the FDIC announced what it called its single-point-of-entry strategy, which had an interesting and imaginative twist. It attempted to use the new OLA powers the FDIC had received for nonbank financial firms to take over the bank holding company (BHC) that controls a failing *bank* and to use the BHC's assets to recapitalize the bank and keep it operating. This would be good policy because, as noted previously, the failure of a large bank could be very disruptive for the US and global economy.

Thus, in its December 2013 public release on the SPOE strategy, the FDIC stated:

> The SPOE strategy is intended to minimize market disruption by isolating the failure and associated losses in a SIFI to the top-tier holding company while maintaining operations at the subsidiary level. In this manner, the resolution would be confined to one legal entity, the holding company, and would not trigger the need for resolution or bankruptcy across the operating subsidiaries, multiple business lines, or various sovereign jurisdictions.[10]

The FDIC has never explained how it would shoehorn the recapitalization of failing banks into the language of a law that was intended to provide for the liquidation of nonbanks, but its SPOE proposal nevertheless received a lot of praise from lawyers, academics, and lawmakers as a way to overcome the problem of TBTF banks. However, as I will discuss, even if the provisions of the OLA that exclude its use for banks are ignored, the SPOE strategy cannot work for the largest banks—the very institutions that pose the greatest danger to the financial system.

On the surface, if one ignores the obvious purpose of the OLA's language (to *liquidate* a nonbank financial firm), it is possible to use some of the OLA's language to support the SPOE strategy. For example, Section 203 of Dodd-Frank authorizes the secretary of the Treasury, with the approval of two-thirds of the voting members of the Board of Governors of the Federal Reserve System and two-thirds of the board of the FDIC, to begin the "orderly liquidation" of a covered financial company if, in the secretary's judgment, "the financial company is in default or in danger of default" and the failure of the company and its resolution under any other federal or state law "would have serious adverse effects on the financial stability of the United States."

When this test has been met, the Treasury secretary is authorized to take control of the financial company and appoint the FDIC as receiver with powers and duties enumerated under Section 204 of the Act. The secretary's authority to invoke the OLA is available for any covered financial company (the term "covered" refers to a firm that the secretary has designated under Section 203) and is not limited to BHCs with $50 billion in assets or more, or to firms that have been designated as SIFIs, so Section 203 can be invoked for any financial firm that the secretary believes would have serious adverse effects on financial stability if it were to default. If a BHC is treated as the covered failing company referred to in Section 203, the secretary can take over the BHC and appoint the FDIC as receiver.

Once appointed as receiver, the FDIC has considerable authority. Using the SPOE strategy, it can create a bridge company (Section 210 (h)) and transfer to it all the assets of the former BHC, subject only to the rights of secured creditors. The bridge company then becomes the new BHC for the bank. Left behind in the old BHC are all the unsecured liabilities and the old BHC's shareholders. Because the new BHC has assets (including the failing bank) and many fewer liabilities, it is then in theory able to raise debt and equity financing with which it will recapitalize its subsidiary bank and keep it operating. The idea is that this will be done so quickly and smoothly that there will be no market disruption and certainly no financial instability as a result.

However, there are a large number of legal and practical problems with this approach:

Threshold legal issues. As mentioned already, the language of the OLA says that it is not intended to be used to resolve banks, and the purpose of the OLA is to *liquidate* failing BHCs and other nonbank financial firms—not to use them as a source of recapitalization for their subsidiaries. OLA Section 204(a), for example, states clearly: "It is the purpose of this title to provide the necessary authority to *liquidate* failing financial companies that pose a significant risk to the financial stability of the United States in a manner that mitigates such risk and minimizes moral hazard" (emphasis added). If the OLA is ever invoked, the FDIC will argue that recapitalizing a subsidiary bank is within the powers of the FDIC after it becomes the receiver of the old BHC, and it is simply using the assets of the liquidated old BHC for a legitimate purpose under the law. This argument would appear to go well beyond anything the Supreme Court has yet treated with deference, but it is always possible that a court will be swayed by the argument that Dodd-Frank was emergency legislation and should be interpreted broadly in light of its purpose.

Meeting the statutory requirements. In order to take over the old BHC, the OLA provides that the Treasury secretary must find that it is "in default or in danger of default." This turns out to be an insurmountable obstacle for exactly the BHCs and banks that the SPOE strategy must cover. Most US banks are subsidiaries of BHCs, and in most cases the banks are by far a BHC's largest subsidiary. Accordingly, for most of the BHCs in the United States, if the largest bank controlled by a BHC is in danger of default the BHC itself is highly likely also to be in default or in danger of default. In that case, the secretary can easily point to the condition of the bank and say that the BHC is in danger of default, allowing the secretary to appoint the FDIC as the BHC's receiver. The SPOE strategy would work in that case, assuming it can pass the other legal tests outlined previously.

However, for the largest BHCs and banks—those in the high hundred billion or even the trillion-dollar category—it is not likely to be true that the failure of the BHC's largest subsidiary bank will also put the BHC in default or in danger of default. These BHCs have other bank and nonbank subsidiaries that are large enough so that the BHC will remain solvent even if it suffers the total loss of the investment in its largest subsidiary bank. In that case, then, the secretary would not have the legal authority to take over the BHC and appoint the FDIC as receiver. Table 1 lists the assets of the fifteen largest BHCs in relation to their investment in their largest subsidiary bank. It shows that for fourteen of the fifteen, the total loss of this investment would not leave the BHC insolvent or even close to insolvency. And this is particularly true for the largest four BHCs.

This has enormous implications for the usefulness of Title II in preventing any financial crisis in the future. While the SPOE strategy may work for nonbank financial firms and for small BHCs, neither of those entities is likely to cause a financial crisis if it fails. But for the largest BHCs—the firms that control the largest banks in the United States—the SPOE strategy cannot work because these BHCs will not be in default or in danger of default if their largest subsidiary bank should fail. Some may argue that the failure of a subsidiary bank will cause a run on the parent BHC or some other liquidity event at the parent that allows the secretary of the Treasury to declare the parent BHC in default or danger of default, but this is simply speculation. There is no way to know what financial resources a parent BHC may have in addition to its largest subsidiary bank. But as table 1 shows, with respect to the largest four banks, simply removing the parent BHC's investment in its subsidiary bank from the parent's balance sheet still leaves a firm with at least $40 billion in equity. Unless there is some reason to suspect enormously large losses at the parent BHC as a result of the subsidiary's failure, this concern is unfounded.

In other words, in the one area where it is most important—protecting the taxpayers and the economy against the failure of the largest banks—Dodd-Frank has failed. Despite the claims of its sponsors, there is still no way for the taxpayers to be sure that if one of the largest banks fails the government will not feel compelled to step in and rescue it with taxpayer funds.

The "source of strength" doctrine. Some proponents of the SPOE strategy may argue that BHCs have an obligation under the Fed's source-of-strength doctrine to recapitalize a failing subsidiary bank, and in some cases the recapitalization required could cause the parent BHC to become insolvent. That, in turn, would give the Treasury secretary some support for taking the position that the BHC is in default or in danger of default. Indeed, Section 616 of Dodd-Frank states:

> The appropriate Federal banking agency for a bank holding company or savings and loan holding company shall require the bank holding company or savings and loan holding company to serve as a source of financial strength for any subsidiary of the bank holding company or savings and loan holding company that is a depository institution.

Some commentators have described this as a "codification" of the source-of-strength doctrine,[11] and it may well be a codification of the idea, but that does not tell us what the source-of-strength doctrine actually requires, and hence what Congress actually codified. The doctrine as originally articulated by the Federal Reserve is that BHCs have an obligation to serve as sources of managerial and financial strength to their bank subsidiaries. This is a fairly general requirement, and its full meaning is not clear. In the most important case in which the scope of

Table 1. Parent BHC Capital after the Loss of Its Equity Investment in Its Largest Bank

Rank by Consolidated Asset Size	Holding Company	Consolidated BHC Assets	Parent Assets	Parent Equity	Equity in Bank Subsidiaries	Total Equity in Subsidiary Banks and Holding Companies	Book Equity of Largest Subsidiary Bank	Parent Equity Less Equity of Largest Bank Subsidiary
1	JPMorgan Chase	$2,476,986,000	$474,646,000	$227,314,000	$179,630,000	$209,059,000	$173,854,000	$53,460,000
2	Bank of America	$2,152,533,000	$466,366,000	$237,411,000	$0	$269,335,000	$180,119,000	$57,292,000
3	Citi Group	$1,894,736,000	$407,893,000	$211,362,000	$0	$150,325,000	$148,373,000	$62,989,000
4	Wells Fargo	$1,546,707,000	$302,139,000	$180,859,000	$0	$161,535,000	$139,286,000	$41,573,000
5	Goldman Sachs Group Inc	$915,705,000	$280,651,000	$81,629,000	$20,685,000	$20,685,000	$20,426,000	$61,203,000
6	Morgan Stanley	$831,381,000	$256,801,902	$70,755,318	$0	$24,948,264	$10,809,000	$59,946,318
7	American International Group	$547,111,000	$143,344,000	$103,833,000	$0	$0	$0	$103,833,000

8	General Electric	$516,971,228	$570,279,066	$85,809,299	$0	$14,033,659	$6,076,598	$79,732,701
9	US Bancorp	$371,289,000	$56,302,362	$42,700,000	$39,470,686	$39,470,686	$40,948,948	$1,751,052
10	Bank of New York Mellon	$368,241,000	$63,275,000	$38,326,000	$26,061,000	$26,337,000	$20,587,000	$17,739,000
11	PNC Financial	$323,586,973	$47,352,194	$44,204,590	$550,000	$41,548,462	$39,051,066	$5,153,524
12	HSBC North American Holding	$308,847,926	$37,043,283	$31,344,044	$0	$27,851,471	$18,458,031	$12,886,013
13	Capital One Financial	$290,886,180	$56,264,022	$43,814,768	$42,913,895	$42,913,895	$34,128,786	$9,685,982
14	State Street Corporation	$256,672,720	$30,806,288	$21,699,811	$21,102,481	$21,102,481	$20,254,266	$1,445,545
15	TD Bank US Holding Company	$237,493,754	$34,425,136	$25,153,278	$30,256,097	$30,256,097	$28,672,839	($3,519,561)

Source: Bank holding company data based on March 2014 regulatory reports publically available from the Federal Reserve National Information Center. Data on equity of the holding companies' banks subsidiaries is from the March 2014 FDIC Statistics on Depository Institutions.

the doctrine was tested, M Corp *v.* Board of Governors, 9 F.2d 852 (5th Cir. 1991), the court held that a BHC had no obligation to recapitalize a subsidiary bank, but the Supreme Court reversed the decision on other grounds and the issue was not litigated further. Thus, it is not at all clear what Congress actually codified.

Those who contend that the doctrine and its codification would require a BHC to become insolvent in order to recapitalize a subsidiary bank would have a difficult time convincing a court of this proposition, in the face of long-standing principles of corporate law that place no obligations on shareholders to pay the creditors of a corporation they control, or the similar principles of corporate separateness and a BHC's obligations to its own shareholders. Accordingly, the source-of-strength doctrine is unlikely to provide a basis for the Treasury secretary to argue that a BHC's obligations under the doctrine or its codification in Dodd-Frank would place it in default or danger of default.

So it is highly likely that the only government resources that will be available to address the failure of a very large bank will be the FDIC's powers under the FDI Act. As noted earlier, however, those powers may have reached the end of their useful life for the largest and most systemically important banks because policymakers have come to realize that the merger of large banks has created such large financial institutions that many observers consider them TBTF. There is no clear solution to the TBTF problem at the moment—breaking up these banks could create more problems than it will solve—and allowing the FDIC to follow its usual practice of merging weak or failing banks with strong ones will only make the TBTF problem worse.

The only alternative to merger is what is known as "open bank assistance," in which the FDIC provides financing to a bank while looking for a buyer, but this frequently allows the uninsured depositors to run, increasing the bank's losses, and the FDIC itself does not have sufficient funds to sustain the continuing losses that will occur as a trillion-dollar bank spirals down. It is also possible for the FDIC to take control of a failing bank, close it down to stanch its losses, and sell it off in pieces but, as discussed previously, for the largest banks this would be highly disruptive to the financial system and possibly bring about the kind of financial crisis that Dodd-Frank sought to avoid.

THE PERSISTENCE OF THE TBTF PROBLEM

Thus, the OLA in Title II of Dodd-Frank has not cured the TBTF problem for the largest systemic banks. There is still no way at this point to ensure that if such a bank fails it will not cause instability in the US financial system, requiring the government to step in with taxpayer funds. If it is still the objective of Congress to address the TBTF problem, it will be necessary to open up the Act for amendment and replace Title II with a resolution system that is adequate for resolving the largest banks.

How would this resolution system be structured? The FDIC's SPOE strategy is based on one important insight—if an operating bank can be kept operating through recapitalization, there would be no danger of a financial crisis. The FDIC attempted to implement this strategy in a way that did not fit within the language of the OLA, but making sure that the largest banks are always adequately capitalized may be the key to solving the TBTF problem.

This strategy would require the largest banks to have considerably more capital than they hold today, and it would require an adjustment in the prompt corrective action rules[12] so that these banks would never fall below this high level of capitalization. Prompt corrective action, which was instituted in the Federal Deposit Insurance Corporation Improvement Act (FDICIA) of 1991, has not been effective, probably because the capital positions of thousands of small banks could deteriorate too quickly for examiners to stop the risky practices that are causing the losses. In addition, the moral hazard implicit in insured deposits, and the FDIC's history of saving all depositors and creditors when banks are sold or merged, has eroded the usual effectiveness of market discipline. This has allowed banks that are losing money to "gamble for resurrection," suffering losses from risky loans that impair their capital positions before that information comes to the attention of their regulators.

But if large systemic banks were required to maintain, say, 16 or 20 percent capital, and prompt corrective actions were to take effect when their capital had declined to, say, 8 or 10 percent, taxpayers could have greater confidence that these banks are highly unlikely to fail. For the small number of banks to which these requirements would apply, it would be possible for regulators to keep accurate and current tabs on their capital positions.

In other words, rather than rely on parent holding companies to serve as sources of strength for their bank subsidiaries, the capital positions of the largest banks should be strengthened directly with infusions of capital from their holding companies before they become weak or insolvent. The BHC would borrow the necessary sums. The funds invested in the equity of subsidiary banks would still appear as equity on the consolidated balance sheets of the BHCs. This would also provide a basis for eliminating the Fed's capital and other regulation of BHCs, which is another source of the widely held view— supplementing TBTF—that the Fed is willing to assist the BHCs it regulates in order to prevent them and their subsidiaries from failing.

But the strengthening of capital requirements for subsidiary banks should not be extended to nonbank firms such as insurance companies, broker-dealers, and finance companies, let alone mutual funds, hedge funds, and other members of the capital markets. As Lehman's failure showed, these firms will not cause a financial crisis if they fail, and subjecting them to government capital requirements will inevitably lead to government prudential regulation that will stifle the competitiveness in the capital markets.

Requiring higher capital will undoubtedly be unpopular with the banks that will have to adopt this burden, and they will argue that higher capital will mean more costly loans and will reduce economic growth. Others may argue that higher capital requirements will only encourage banks to take more risks in order to attain the same return on equity. In February 2013, Douglas J. Elliott, then of the Brookings Institution, published a paper that argued that the effect on bank lending would not be costless. He pointed out that although in the ideal conditions posited by Modigliani and Miller, the greater the amount of a bank's capital the lower its borrowing rates, there are many elements in the real world that might interfere with this conclusion, including tax effects, the presence of government guarantees, the cost of raising capital, market perceptions of a bank's safety, and transitional effects. All these items make the ultimate result uncertain. Elliott's conclusion is that while the costs are unknown, there will still be costs.[13]

The alternatives, however, are not many. If it is true that the collapse of a large bank would have major disruptive effects on the US economy, which certainly seems plausible, and if it is also true that—as outlined in this chapter—Dodd-Frank does not provide a realistic basis for resolving the largest banks, then what remains are some unattractive choices. Breaking up these large banks would also have enormous disruptive consequences, and no one really knows what size would solve the TBTF problem anyway, or what would happen if a ceiling were placed on the growth of banks after they were broken up. There could be many more bank failures.[14]

Figure 1. US Commercial Banks, 1869–2015

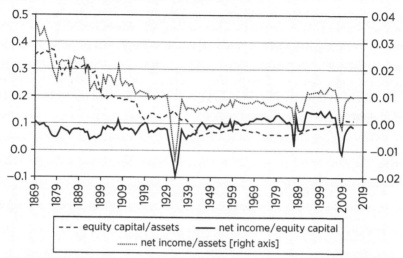

Source: Greenspan Associates LLC, using Federal Deposit Insurance Corporation and US Comptroller of the Currency data.

Alan Greenspan, for one, has long argued that raising bank capital is the answer, and his research has cut through a lot of debate about the issue by showing the consistency of bank returns on equity over an extended period during which capital requirements have declined precipitously. Figure 1 shows that despite aberrations during particularly disrupted times—and despite changes in capital requirements, taxes, regulatory policies, interest rates, the introduction of deposit insurance, altered perceptions of the government's role, and the rise of competition from the securities markets—bank managements have been able to adjust to all these challenges without substantial changes in banks' overall return on equity. This gives some hope that a gradual increase in capital requirements, allowing banks to adjust over time, will not cause an abrupt change in the financing costs.

CONCLUSION

If Congress is really interested in eliminating TBTF, there appears to be only one way to do it for the largest banks—ensure that their capital positions never erode to a point where they are in default or in danger of default. The simplest and most effective way to do this is to require a level of capitalization that can be watched continuously by regulators, with the regulators having authority to apply prompt corrective action when the banks' losses or potential losses reach a point where they have lost, say, half their required capital. This would not put a large bank in danger of default, but it would allow regulators and bank managements to take corrective steps that would eventually restore the bank to its required capitalization level. In this way, the taxpayers could be assured that they will never be called upon to rescue the largest banks.

NOTES

1. According to S. Rep. 111-176, 11th Cong. 2d Sess. (April 30, 2010), "[w]hen Lehman Brothers declared bankruptcy, the markets panicked and the crisis escalated. With no other means to resolve large, complex and interconnected financial firms, the government was left with few options other than to provide massive assistance to prop up failing companies in an effort to prevent the crisis from spiraling into a great depression. Despite initial efforts of the government, credit markets froze and the [US] problem spread across the globe. The crisis on Wall Street soon spilled over onto Main Street, touching the lives of most Americans and devastating many" (43–44).

2. Ibid., 4–6.

3. Scott, "Interconnectedness and Contagion," 2: "Evidence suggests the direct impact of Lehman's collapse on these counterparties was not as problematic or destabilizing as many feared it would be. In fact, no major financial institution failed as a result of its direct exposure to Lehman Brothers. Analyzing the potential impact of the AIG insolvency is also informative, as a similar conclusion follows: had AIG not been bailed out, direct losses imposed upon its counterparties would not have been a major problem either. The conclusion of each of these analyses is that given the relatively modest levels of losses involved, asset interconnectedness on its own was not a primary cause of the global financial crisis."

4. "Running from the Shadows."

5. See Federal Deposit Insurance Act §§ 203 and 204(b).

6. See, for example, Scott, Jackson, and Taylor, *Making Failure Feasible.*

7. Title I prescribes a number of elements that the FSOC should consider in designating a nonbank financial firm as a SIFI, including size, assets, liabilities, leverage, and interconnectedness, but none of these factors is important for determining the effect of a company's failure—that is, its likelihood to result in instability in the financial system—other than its interconnectedness with other firms.

8. See Wallison, *Hidden in Plain Sight.*

9. S. Rep. 111-176, 11th Cong. 2d Sess. at 4 (2010): "Once a failing financial company is placed under this authority, liquidation is the only option; the failing financial company may not be kept open or rehabilitated. The financial company's business operations and assets will be sold off or liquidated, the culpable management of the company will be discharged, shareholders will have their investments wiped out, and unsecured creditors and counterparties will bear losses."

10. 78 Fed. Reg. (December 18, 2013): 76623.

11. Lee, "Source-of-Strength Doctrine," 867, 868.

12. These rules were issued by the FDIC, under authority conferred by the Federal Deposit Insurance Corporation Improvement Act of 1991, and require that the FDIC impose increasingly strict limits on banks as their capital level declines.

13. Elliott, "Higher Bank Capital Requirements."

14. See, for example, Wallison, "Warren's Wall Street Reforms."

REFERENCES

Elliott, Douglas J. "Higher Bank Capital Requirements Would Come at a Price." Brookings Institution Paper, Washington, DC, February 20, 2013.

Lee, Paul L. "The Source-of-Strength Doctrine: Revered and Revisited—Part II." *Banking Law Journal* 129, no. 10 (November/December 2012): 867–68.

"Running from the Shadows." *The Economist*, November 24, 2012. http://www.economist.com /news/finance-and-economics/21567078-regulators-seek-shore-up-money-market-funds -against-runs-running.

Scott, Hal S. "Interconnectedness and Contagion." Committee on Capital Markets Regulation Paper, Cambridge, MA, November 20, 2012.

Scott, Kenneth E., Thomas H. Jackson, and John B. Taylor, eds. *Making Failure Feasible: How Bankruptcy Reform Can End "Too Big to Fail.* Stanford, CA: Hoover Institution Press, 2015.

Wallison, Peter J. *Hidden in Plain Sight: What Caused the World's Worst Financial Crisis and Why It Could Happen Again.* New York: Encounter Books, 2015.

———. "Warren's Wall Street Reforms Would Just Make Banks Riskier." *American Banker*, April 27, 2015. http://www.americanbanker.com/bankthink/warrens-wall-street-reforms-would-just -make-banks-riskier-1074013-1.html.

Wallison, Peter J., and Paul H. Kupiec. "Can the 'Single Point of Entry' Strategy Be Used to Recapitalize a Systemically Important Failing Bank?" *Journal of Financial Stability* 20 (October 2015): 184–97.

CHAPTER 5
The Rise of Bail-Ins and the Quest for Credible Laissez-Faire Banking

GARETT JONES

George Mason University

I n 2008 and the early weeks of 2009, I and others said that there was a practical alternative to bailouts.[1] There was an alternative to having the US Treasury buy shares in the big banks, an alternative to having the Federal Deposit Insurance Corporation (FDIC) guarantee bank bonds. That alternative was debt-to-equity conversions, a quick, efficient version of bankruptcy. Rather than have the government itself buy new bank shares as in a bailout, the troubled bank's own bondholders would instead be told, as Harvard's Greg Mankiw wrote in February 2009, "Congratulations, you are the new equity holders." By rapidly cutting away at unrealistic promises to bondholders while simultaneously increasing the amount of equity holdings, troubled banks would beef up their equity layer faster with no need for government cash.

The federal bailouts of 2008 seem inevitable in retrospect, but that is partly a case of hindsight bias. Economists including Harvard's Mankiw, Stanford's Robert Hall, Nobelist Joseph Stiglitz, and Chicago's Luigi Zingales explicitly offered some debt-to-equity conversion proposals in some form or another before, during, or in the months after the crisis—some as a plausible hypothetical, some as a more concrete, do-it-now plan.[2] In the years since, this approach has gone by various informal names: I offered "speed bankruptcy," but the less dangerous-sounding expressions such as "bondholder bail-in," "haircut," or "shared sacrifice" have caught on since then. In any case, it probably could have been done.

But it did not happen, and it is worthwhile to ask why. My claim is that the political temptation to act boldly and decisively in a crisis, the temptation to come to the market's rescue, creates a nearly insurmountable temptation for politicians to bail out big financial institutions. When a financial crisis hits, regardless of the rules on the books, politicians will almost always rescue the biggest financial institutions if there is any substantial threat of contagion. One can blame well-connected financial industry insiders for the pro-bailout bias, which surely is a problem, but the bigger issue is a deeply fearful voting public that wants to avoid a risky-sounding bankruptcy plan for the nation's biggest banks.

Therefore, a key goal for policymakers who want to avoid future bailouts should be to either reduce the likelihood of banking crises (partly by increasing the capital ratios for the biggest banks) or to make it politically feasible to take a leap into the dark by enacting a bondholder bail-in—a leap at least as large as the one Federal Reserve Chairman Ben Bernanke and Treasury Secretary Henry Paulson took when Lehman Brothers failed.

No democratically elected politician "wants another Lehman," so activists and policy advisers pushing for an alternative to bailouts need to demonstrate that their path is not going to lead to another Lehman. Politicians should plan today to create a world tomorrow where they themselves would be willing to press the button on financial discipline. It has been said that there are no atheists in foxholes, and no true believers in laissez-faire amid a financial crisis. At least in the halls of power, the latter statement is largely true, so individuals who want market-disciplined banking policy need to plan today if they want a more market-disciplined future. And as I argue, a loud and clear government promise of "no bailouts" might, alas, turn out to be an excellent way to create future bailouts.

Indeed, some form of bailout for financial institutions might be unavoidable—there might be heavily politically connected firms or some firms that genuinely are too big to fail, or politicians might understandably be afraid of taking that step into the dark. I suspect there is always going to be some set of financial institutions that politicians, openly or quietly, deem in need of a government guarantee. At the very least, the biggest banks are likely to receive massive government liquidity injections during a crisis. But when a potential financial crisis looms again in the rich countries, there should be real alternatives to 100 percent bailouts. There should be a continuum of options, not just pure laissez-faire versus blanket guarantees as far as the eye can see. Russ Roberts of the Hoover Institution has said this quite a few times since the crisis: If a policy of "no bailouts" was not feasible for some political or economic reasons, how did 100 percent bailouts for the big banks become the only alternative?[3]

Here I will set out why the market discipline approach is in fact safer than it seems, but since that story has been told well before, I will discuss it only briefly before reviewing how policymakers across the rich countries have enacted more pro-bail-in rules and regulations since 2008. That will demonstrate that the academic musings of 2008 and 2009 have become at least a partial political reality. Then I will turn to why bondholder bail-ins are important for the economy's long-run health, and why good economic policy should focus on nonutopian alternatives to 100 percent bailouts. Janos Kornai's work on the soft budget constraint, a feature of the economics of socialism, will be a focus of the penultimate section of the chapter. Future researchers will be able to judge to what extent the economics of socialism apply to the politics of banking policy.

BONDHOLDER BAIL-INS: A REVIEW

Consider a bank with one trillion dollars in assets, as in the top panel of table 1. One-third of the assets are conventional loans to customers, one-third are asset-backed securities (ABS)—essentially bonds backed by credit card repayments—and one-third are bonds and other readily tradable investments. In the United States, banks this large are not going to be funded solely by deposits and equity alone; it is a safe bet that at least a quarter of their funding will have come from the bond markets.

To keep it simple, consider a bank with a 10 percent capital ratio, so the other side of the balance sheet has $100 billion in publicly traded shares. Another $300 billion will be long-term bonds, so quite a few investors have placed long-term bets that this bank is reasonably safe. The remaining $600

Table 1. A Bail-In or Bondholder Haircut (in billions $)

		Precrisis: 10% Capital Ratio (100/1000)	
	Assets		Liabilities + Equity
Loans:	334	Deposits:	600
ABS:	333	Bonds:	300
Bonds:	333	Equity:	100
Total	1,000		1,000
		Crisis: A Plunge in Asset Values Causes a 0% Capital Ratio, Weaker Bond Prices	
	Assets		Liabilities + Equity
Loans:	334	Deposits:	600
ABS:	**133**	Bonds:	**200**
Bonds:	333	Equity:	**0**
Total	800	=	800
		Post-Bail-In: 25% Capital Ratio (200/800)	
	Assets		Liabilities + Equity
Loans:	334	Deposits:	600
ABS:	133	Bonds (wiped out, became new equity)	0
Bonds:	333	Equity:	**200**
Total	800	=	800

billion comes from depositors. One trillion in assets equals one trillion in liabilities and equity, so the balance sheet balances.

On a day-to-day basis, as financial markets react to good and bad news about the health of the bank's assets, it is the equity holders not the bondholders whose investment values fluctuate the most. The price of the stock rises on good news and sinks on bad news. Bonds react a little, but not too much, since bondholders have a contractual guarantee of repayment. Shareholders only get whatever is left over after everyone else is paid out—that is the peril of being the residual claimant.

But consider a case where devastating news hits the market for asset-backed securities. This time it is the credit card market, and investors are in grave doubt about whether Americans are going to repay their credit cards. And if credit cards do not get paid off, securities backed by credit card repayments will not get paid in full—they will head into some sort of default. So awful news about credit card–backed securities will surely cause the bank's share price to plummet. The bank's investors will start to wonder whether there is enough money around to pay the bondholder's regular coupon payments, whether the bank will be able to roll over its bonds that are coming due, even whether the bank can raise enough short-term cash in the money market to meet fluctuating day-to-day needs. Who wants to lend to a bank that might be bankrupt in a month? Consider an extreme case: If the asset-backed securities fall in value by \$200 billion, the bank is not worth enough to fully, credibly repay both its depositors and its bondholders: It now only has \$800 billion in assets but \$900 billion in contractual (bond + deposit) liabilities. The share price would drop to essentially zero, and the bank's bond prices would plummet by a third to reflect the impending doom.

In the corporate world, if you are able to meet eight-ninths of your legal financial obligations, you are just as bankrupt as if you are able to meet just one-ninth. Bankruptcy is (at least in principle, and often in practice) driven by balance sheets, not cash flows.

As a practical matter, the kind of megabank that is the focus here can only become critically illiquid if investors fear the bank might be gone in a week. A megabank can find willing short-term lenders if the market is convinced the megabank has a sound balance sheet. Indeed, as Taylor and Williams showed, during the financial crisis in the United States, a variety of forms of evidence suggested that the rise in interest rates looked more like solvency risk (in the form of counterparty risk) than a narrow liquidity problem.[4] Of course, central banks are there to provide emergency liquidity, but even before the Federal Reserve arrives with aid, other bank and nonbank firms with liquid wealth would be glad to earn big yields by lending to sound but illiquid megabanks. Solvency is the best line of credit.

So if the bank appears to be insolvent, what is the best solution? In the 2008 world, the answer was to have the government buy shares in the bank and to guarantee any new bond issues the bank made. The share purchases gave ready cash to the bank plus a de facto promise to keep the bank afloat. The bond guarantee meant investors would gladly lend to the bank, helping the bank to roll over old bonds. In the worlds of 2009 and 2010, the price of asset-backed securities recovered, so the government was able to sell its shares at a profit and the federal bond guarantees never had to be tested. So far, it sounds like it was a free lunch—but this was partly a classic case of the seen versus the unseen.

If instead the government had run the bank through a rapid bankruptcy-like process, it could have told the bondholders on Friday that on Monday they would be shareholders. In the simplest and most extreme case, the old shareholders would be wiped out, told that their shares were worthless and that the old bondholders would be handed new shares in proportion to their previous bondholdings. So an investor who owned 1 percent of the entire precrash face value of the bank's bonds would now own 1 percent of the shares in the firm. Now the bank's liabilities would be simple: $600 billion in deposits plus $200 billion in shares, just equal to the $800 billion in postcrisis asset value.

As I discussed in detail in my 2010 article on "Speed Bankruptcy,"[5] there are good reasons for being less generous to bondholders and for instead diluting the old shareholders rather than wiping them out. In our example, 1,000 shares could be divided up with 100 going to old shareholders and 900 going to the old bondholders. That would give the old shareholders a more-than-token $20 billion in value of the reborn firm ($20 billion = 10 percent of 25 percent of the $800 billion), and so the older, possibly better-informed investors would have a voice at the table. Also it would assuage legal concerns that shareholders had been unfairly treated; such concerns are not baseless, since after all there was always *some* chance the firm could have gambled for resurrection and won.

In addition, there are good reasons for cutting the promised face value of the bonds rather than wiping them out. That would work in our example: Cutting the value of the bonds by one-half or two-thirds and then also giving bondholders some shares in the new firm would be a practical option, since the remaining $800 billion in assets is still enough to guarantee *some* repayment to bondholders, even if it is not enough to guarantee dollar-for-dollar repayment. The depositors are owed a mere $600 billion, after all. Thirty-three or fifty cents on the dollar would then be the new face value of the bonds (leaving aside for now important details of maturity dates, present values, and coupons). In addition, the old bondholders would also receive shares in the new postcrisis bank.

Given a bankruptcy judge or an FDIC regulator with a strong mandate to quickly resolve the legal situation, this could be done in a matter of days. Bailing in the bondholders makes the bank sound: fewer debt promises and a restored layer of equity, all without a dollar of government aid. The bondholders took a risk when they invested in the bank; now they are experiencing the downside of risk.

Of course, in the 2008-type scenario, if the asset prices later recover, then the bondholders (and the diluted shareholders) can recover much or even all of their lost value. The loss on the downside is paired with potential benefit on the upside. This might be small comfort to the bondholder who thought she held a $10,000 bond but now holds a $3,000 bond and some paper shares, but if she had wanted government guaranteed repayment she could always have bought US Treasuries. The net result of speed bankruptcy is a highly solvent bank with no extra legal or regulatory entanglements. And since solvency is the best credit line, other self-interested financial institutions will have a strong incentive to line up to end any liquidity problems.

BONDHOLDER BAIL-IN REFORM: A VICTORY LAP FOR SPEED BANKRUPTCY

These examples are not just hypotheticals. Since the financial crisis, European governments as well as governments in Canada, Mexico, and Brazil have moved to make bondholder bail-ins more likely. How can one tell that it is not just smoke and mirrors, a vague promise that will be quickly forgotten in a crisis? The political battles over bail-ins, the blunt talk from credit rating agencies, and the sizable bondholder bail-ins during the Cyprus banking crisis all suggest that next time really will be different.

First, the political debate: European Union states are currently under mandates to reform their bankruptcy and finance laws to ensure that bail-ins would be practical and legal, particularly for senior debtholders. As Bloomberg put it, reporting on the debate over a German bill:

> After the European debt crisis turned German taxpayers
> into bailout masters, the country is trying to make sure more
> parties are on the hook for losses.[6]

And the bill that Germans debated is no piece of credibility-free, pie-in-the-sky legislation promising no bailouts ever. Instead, it builds on the EU's own law. Continuing with Bloomberg:

> The German bill is intended to facilitate the EU resolution
> law, which requires creditors to bear losses equivalent to

8 percent of a bank's liabilities, including senior debt if necessary, before recourse can be made to rescue funds.[7]

The EU's proposal—if actually deployed in a crisis—effectively raises the private capital ratio for the firm before the government comes in. Since 8 percent of liabilities is only slightly less than 8 percent of assets in today's heavily leveraged banks, this amounts to a massive increase in purely private, risk-bearing capital in the firm. For example, in the 2016 US bank stress tests, the biggest banks had to prove that in a deep financial crisis they would still maintain a Tier 1 leverage ratio of 4 percent of total assets. In that ratio, the numerator is overwhelmingly common stock and retained earnings, while the denominator is total bank assets, without any form of risk weighting. A layer of credible bail-in bonds worth 8 percent of assets effectively triples the private capital layer in the bank, providing perhaps as hard a budget constraint as one can imagine in the real world.

Germany is not the only country to move down the road to legal bail-ins. Ireland has substantially burned junior bondholders recently. Anglo Irish Bank posted Ireland's biggest corporate losses ever and had 50 billion euros in deposits, massive for a country of 5 million. And while the bank was nationalized and received government funds, it also forced losses on junior bondholders.[8] Likewise, the Cyprus banking crisis was resolved by burning bondholders and even some depositors. The response to the Cypriot banking crisis—which observers at the time said might set off global contagion—combined bail-ins and bailouts, something that may be the most market-oriented practical path forward.[9] Those considering investing in European bank bonds have good reason to think that next time actually will be different.

Do financial markets believe this? At the least the credit rating agencies appear to. Consider these two quotes from a 2015 Fitch Ratings report:

> EU [has made] progress in finding ways to resolve failed banks without disruption to financial stability and without requiring state resources . . .
> [and in] identifying senior debt as a distinct category of liability that can be "bailed in" ahead of counterparties and "uninsured" depositors.[10]

Another piece of evidence: Irish Finance Minister Michael Noonan's now-famous 2013 statement: "Bail-in is now the rule."[11] It has been repeated often enough that at the least, market participants are concerned about the risk of market discipline. And it has worked in practice: In 2013, the Dutch government wiped out over a billion dollars in subordinated debt in a bank as part of a government takeover. And as of 2015, a Moody's report finds that some Latin American governments are making progress, naming Brazil and Mexico for their relatively credible plans, although Moody's has doubts about the credibility of the bail-in proposals in other Latin American countries.

It appears that junior bondholders are already in the crosshairs of bank regulators. And while the categories of "junior" and "senior" investors are surely legally murky and a topic largely for attorneys rather than economists, senior bondholders are next in line, and Europe's bailout-weary voting public may be willing to accept some risk of financial contagion rather than bail out yet another banking system. Indeed, that the Cypriot banking crises failed to set off contagion and that weeks of bargaining with Greece's Syriza in 2015 set off little sustained contagion throughout European financial markets are signs that investors both believe and have good reasons to believe that contagion is harder to spread than was once feared.

Of course, doubts quite reasonably still exist, especially with senior debtholders, according to a 2014 *Wall Street Journal* "Heard on the Street" column:

> Despite political statements that bank creditors should bear
> the costs of poor lending decisions, senior bondholders have
> been protected in many cases.[12]

Among the likely reasons: When regulators consider holding bondholders accountable for their investments, concerns of "panic" are never far off. From the same *Wall Street Journal* column:

> The failure to protect bondholders of Washington Mutual in
> September 2008 when the bank was acquired by JPMorgan
> Chase probably contributed to greater panic in the US financial system.

Then again, the column continues, senior debtholders may in fact be on the hook:

> But the clock is ticking for senior debt's unofficial protected status. From 2016, Europe has ruled that it won't be excluded from being bailed-in, and could take losses in a restructuring if equity and subordinated debt proves insufficient.

The bondholder bail-in has become a standard talking point in financial circles since the global financial crisis, and when bail-ins have happened, long-lasting contagion did not. So major bail-ins are economically feasible.

And markets believe that bail-ins are relatively likely. A crucial example that itself is a tool for making bail-ins more likely: cocos. Cocos are "contingent convertible" bonds that become equity in time of need, such as when the bank's equity layer drops below 5 percent or when government regulators declare a financial crisis. Cocos are preplanned speed bankruptcy, and their issuance has exploded recently, partly because of favorable Basel rules.

At the time of my 2010 paper when I discussed cocos, they were little more than a theorist's dream, but in 2014 and again in 2015, over \$100 billion in cocos were issued globally. Cocos are now so widely traded that at least one market index for them exists, the Bank of America Merrill Contingent Capital Index (ticker symbol COCO). And indeed, the yield on the COCO index is about 2 percent higher than the yield on even high-yield European bonds.[13] That yield premium means markets believe cocos face a substantial likelihood of actually converting to equity at some point in the future. Another piece of evidence: During a wave of bad news about European banks early in 2016, European bank coco price movements started closely tracking the price movements of European banks. That is just what a finance theorist would expect if cocos were actually likely to convert into equity if the conversion trigger requirements were met.[14]

While the evidence suggests that markets believe bail-ins or haircuts of some sort are more likely in the next crisis—at least outside the United States—two important questions follow: What are the long-run costs of bailouts, and what precrisis policy actions can reduce the odds—and the size—of bailouts in the next crisis?

THE SOFT BUDGET CONSTRAINT: EASY CHOICES NOW, BIG COSTS LATER

Governments have a good reason for promising not to bail out firms: They do not want to subsidize bad behavior. It is a classic case of moral hazard. If banks know that any time they make a bad investment they can get bailed out, and in particular if the bank's top managers know they can accept a bailout and still keep their well-paying jobs, the bank has little incentive to behave prudently. It is tails I win, heads I win double. A world of bailouts offers all the thrills of the private sector—competition against worthy rivals, a chance to make it big—along with the vast safety net of the public sector—where if you make a big mistake it just might mean a slower promotion rather than a pink slip.

So in principle, a prudent government wants some degree of market discipline, but in the midst of a crisis it is tempted to say, in the spirit of the youthful Saint Augustine, "Lord, grant me market discipline, but not yet."

Here, the work of Hungarian economist Janos Kornai comes to the fore. He was the foremost economist of socialism, and his best-known work was on what he called the problem of the *soft budget constraint.* He noted that within socialism, there was little incentive for government enterprises to enforce any kind of budget discipline. If a government firm ran up debts because it produced too little output to cover its costs, it was easy for the government to cancel the debt. After all, the debt was just an accounting fiction, some amount of money that one government entity owed to another government entity. Why not forgive and forget? Of course, this created awful incentives, and as Kornai found, all of the solutions for the problem of the soft budget constraint contained their own problems. In an essay in the *Financial Times* in 2009, Kornai noted that the soft budget constraints were becoming a problem after the financial crisis:

> One strong concern expressed more than once in discussions on the present financial crisis has been this: the interventions by the state are smuggling a bit of socialism into the capitalist economy.[15]

The soft budget constraint is a form of the moral hazard. But soft budget constraints refer to a narrower class of problems: Soft budget constraints involve cases where one party is de facto or de jure spending someone else's money, while moral hazard can involve the decision to wear seat belts or to behave badly at work, or any of the thousands of situations where moral hazard has been studied. In addition, soft budget constraints by default involve work situations, just the kind of situations where one would expect instrumental rationality rather that emotion and caprice to rule. When a soft budget constraint exists, there are reasonably informed, reasonably rational parties, one of which is spending the other party's money.

When a government agency overspends for the year, knowing that it will be reimbursed by the legislature early next year, that is a case of the soft budget constraint; when a teenager runs up his credit card, knowing that his parents will bail him out, that is also a case of a soft budget constraint. And when a highly leveraged entrepreneur takes big risks with his company knowing that if the company fails, he can hand the firm over to the bank, that too is a soft budget constraint. A soft budget constraint deters the spender from shepherding his resources wisely. A soft budget constraint weakens prudence and causes misallocation. Whenever a person can count on outside help from a third party to pay the bills, it is a case of a soft budget constraint. Employees routinely face soft budget constraints at work; office supplies are an obvious example for desk jobs, and Johnny Cash's Cadillac built a piece at a time is an example from the assembly line. Business owners try to harden the budget constraint by making sure that employees do not steal or use business inputs for private use or waste time on smart phones when they should be working. And of course private business owners have reasonably strong incentives to harden budget constraints in a way that government managers (and indeed corporate managers) rarely do.

How might modern megabanks and systemically important financial institutions (SIFIs) shape their behavior in response to a soft budget constraint, an expectation of likely bailouts in the event of a crisis? How might bond buyers shape their behavior in response to an expectation that they will get blanket bailout coverage? How will these responses shape the overall economy?

The simple microeconomic story is the right place to start: If managers face less market discipline, they will tend to take bigger risks with the bank's money and they will be less cautious about cost control, or perhaps both. And potential bond buyers will put less effort into scrutinizing the bank's health if they believe it has a degree of de facto government insurance. The net effect is likely more financial resources poured into weaker, less efficient, less productive banks. The soft budget constraint makes both bond investors and managers less cautious, to society's loss.

And the soft budget constraint is not the only downside of government bailouts and bond guarantees. Government bailouts mean government ownership of banks, at least for a period of time. And here one can turn to an international empirical literature that looks into what happens to the financial sector and the overall economy when the government owns part of the banking sector. The comparison is not a perfect one, since international studies focus on long-term government ownership and bailout situations are typically short term. But even during the US Treasury's brief stint as a partial owner of major banks, government officials were faced with political pressures to urge the banks to pursue political rather than financial-value-maximizing goals. Since controlled experiments are so rare in economics, it is certainly worth a look at the international literature on government-owned banks to give us an idea of the possible downsides of government-owned banks.

In an influential paper, La Porta, Lopez-De-Silanes, and Shleifer looked at whether the economy grows faster or slower when the government owns part of the banking system and found that "higher government ownership of banks in 1970 [was] associated with slower subsequent financial development and lower growth of per capita income and productivity."[16] Notably, their study includes both banks that were partially owned by a nation's government and banks that were wholly government-owned. Even partial government ownership seems to predict weaker economic growth. In addition, a similarly influential paper by Demirgüç-Kunt and Detragiache looked at the effects of deposit insurance on the likelihood of bank collapses.[17] The FDIC's guarantees of bank bonds after the financial crisis were similar enough to deposit insurance that one should ask whether deposit insurance is likely to help rather than hurt financial stability. And both pieces of evidence should give bailout advocates pause: Even partial government ownership of banks appears to have bad effects on economic growth, and deposit insurance appears to predict more, not fewer, bank collapses. The advocate of laissez-faire who thinks that government intervention in the banking system is bound to lead to bad results can find a lot of support in this international literature.

Of course, cross-country comparisons might miss important differences: Perhaps one cannot compare permanently-partially-government-owned banks in middle-income countries to temporarily-partially-government-owned banks in the United States. That debate will not be settled here, but the international evidence should make us more interested in finding an alternative to bailouts and blanket bond guarantees. The international evidence should spur us to find a practical way to make greater market discipline a reality.

MAKING THE PERFECT THE ENEMY OF THE MARKET

Every politician and every government official involved in bank regulation should ask two questions when deciding whether a megabank's overall business strategy is prudent:

1. Would you let Fannie Mae and Freddie Mac follow this strategy?

2. If not, why would you allow complex, trillion-dollar banks to do it?

The megabanks have explicit protections from deposit insurance and implicit protections from the well-founded belief that governments will not allow big banks to wholly fail. They are all, to a substantial degree, Fannie and Freddie. One plausible response to the second question would be "because we credibly believe that these banks really will face market discipline in a crisis." But that "plausible" response only becomes a "good" response if that credibility is well-founded.

A 2014 GAO report found that markets do seem to believe that Dodd-Frank's new Orderly Liquidation Authority regime is at least somewhat credible. The best evidence for the new regime's credibility is that megabank bonds are no longer trading at substantially lower yields when compared to other somewhat smaller banks:

> GAO's analysis . . . suggests that large bank holding companies had lower funding costs than smaller ones during the financial crisis but provides mixed evidence of such advantages in recent years. [M]ost models suggest that such advantages [to megabanks] may have declined or reversed.[18]

But any such gains depend heavily on the government's willingness to enforce reasonably hard budget constraints. Plenty of politicians are happy to denounce bailouts, but if a politician's actions during normal times make bailouts more likely during a crisis, then that politician is pro-bailout in practice. What types of actions raise the probability of future bailouts? Here is a partial list:

1. Opposing higher capital requirements for the largest banks.

2. Insisting on a full-blown bankruptcy process for megabanks that fail, with strong rights of appeal that tie up megabanks and their assets in courts for years.

3. More speculatively, opposing medium-sized de facto bailout funds such as the borrowing powers included in Dodd-Frank's Orderly Liquidation Authority. Without such a fund, future politicians will be more likely to face a stark choice between a zero-bailout leap into the void versus another 2008-style crisis-enacted bailout fund. A medium-sized bailout fund may the best way to prevent a massive bailout.

In 2008, a divided House of Representatives voted against the Troubled Asset Relief Program (TARP) bailout fund only to vote for it a few days later: fear changed the vote. And if a legislature is against bailouts for 999 days in a row but votes for a bailout when a financial panic happens on the one-thousandth day, that legislature is objectively pro-bailout. Market participants try to figure out whether the government is bluffing when it says it is anti-bailout, and market participants often successfully call the government's bluff.

Legislatures and regulators who want to create an objectively lower-bailout future have to give politicians some non-bailout buttons they can reasonably press in a crisis. One of those is the debt-to-equity conversions discussed here. But even that would likely require serious advance planning, including well-rehearsed "funeral plans" and thick capital layers for the biggest banks: The Treasury and Fed might be willing to have a bondholder bail-in for one particularly troubled megabank, but it is hard to imagine them doing it for three or four separate trillion-dollar banks within a week. A combination of thick capital layers, cocos, or other explicitly subordinated debt and a range of emergency liquidity programs are the kind of *ex ante* plans that raises the odds that politicians will let the technocrats have *ex post* control during a crisis.

In the typical country, when the government owns bank shares and insures bank deposits, the economy grows more slowly and the banking system is less stable. Taking a few policy steps to make dollar-for-dollar bailouts less likely and to ensure that bank bonds are not as government-backed as bank deposits will help create a stronger economy and a more stable financial system. If the two options on the table are zero bailouts versus 100 percent bailouts, a politician in a crisis, regardless of party, will always choose 100 percent bailouts. But if the alternative to 100 percent bailouts is instead a well-rehearsed crisis contingency plan—not laissez-faire but a mix of cocos, capital planning, and a liquidity line—it is a lot easier to imagine a politician choosing greater market discipline. If policymakers remember what happened last time, then perhaps with some credible planning, next time really will be different.

NOTES

1. Among the others were Jones, "Imitate FDR's Treasury Secretary"; Zingales, "Cramdown," 8; Zingales, "Why Paulson Is Wrong"; and Mankiw, "Nationalization or Pre-Privatization?"

2. Clement, "Interview with Robert E. Hall"; see also Stiglitz, "Reforming the Global Economic Architecture"; and Jones, "Speed Bankruptcy."

3. Roberts, "Gambling with Other People's Money"; and "Roberts on the Crisis."

4. Taylor and Williams, "Black Swan in the Money Market," 58.

5. Jones, "Speed Bankruptcy."

6. Groendahl, "Two Shades of German Seniors."

7. Ibid., emphasis added.

8. See Gergeley, "Anglo Irish Bank"; O'Dwyer, "IBRC Junior Bondholders"; and Declan Brennan, "Anglo Irish Accounts."

9. Atkins and Watkins, "Cypriot Contagion Risk Rattles Investors."

10. Fitch Ratings, "Fitch."

11. Der Spiegel, "Bail-Ins."

12. Barley, "Senior Bondholders Keep Dodging Bullets."

13. Thompson, "Coco Sell-off Unveils High-yield Bargains." For more detail on the growing Coco market, see Greene, "Understanding CoCos."

14. Hale, "Music Stops for Buyers of Coco Debt."

15. Janos Kornai's comments appear in Buiter, "Kornai on Soft Budget Constraints."

16. La Porta, Lopez-de-Silanes, and Shleifer, "Government Ownership of Banks."

17. Demirgüç-Kunt and Detragiache, "Does Deposit Insurance Increase?"

18. GAO, "Large Bank Holding Companies."

REFERENCES

Atkins, Ralph, and Mary Watkins. "Cypriot Contagion Risk Rattles Investors." *Financial Times*, March 18, 2013. http://www.ft.com/intl/cms/s/0/e36274d4-8fe3-11e2-ae9e-00144feabdc0 .html.

Barley, Richard. "Senior Bondholders Keep Dodging Bullets." *Wall Street Journal Heard on the Street*, August 4, 2014. http://www.wsj.com/articles/heard-on-the-street-senior-bondholders -keep-dodging-bullets-1407168870.

Brennan, Declan. "Anglo Irish Accounts Did Not Link Funding with €7.2bn ILP Transactions." *Irish Times*, March 11, 2015. http://www.irishtimes.com/business/financial-services/anglo -irish-accounts-did-not-link-funding-with-7-2bn-ilp-transactions-1.2569643.

Buiter, William. "Kornai on Soft Budget Constraints, Bail-Outs and the Financial Crisis." *Financial Times*, October 14, 2009. http://blogs.ft.com/maverecon/2009/10/kornai-on-soft-budget -constraints-bail-outs-and-the-financial-crisis/.

Clement, Douglas. "Interview with Robert E. Hall." *The Region* 24, no. 2 (June 2010): 26–37.

Demirgüç-Kunt, Asli, and Enrica Detragiache. "Does Deposit Insurance Increase Banking System Stability? An Empirical Investigation." *Journal of Monetary Economics* 49, no. 7 (2002): 1373–406.

Der Spiegel. "Bail-Ins: EU Deal Protects Taxpayers in Bank Bailouts." June 27, 2015. http://www .spiegel.de/international/business/eu-deal-would-require-bail-ins-in-future-bank-rescue -plans-a-908175.html.

Fitch Ratings. "Fitch: German Senior Debt Law Would Improve Bank Resolvability." Press Release, March 24, 2015. https://www.fitchratings.com/site/fitch-home/pressrelease?id =981792.

Gergeley, Andras. "Anglo Irish Bank Posts Ireland's Biggest Loss Ever." *Reuters*, March 31, 2010. http://www.reuters.com/article/us-angloirishbank-idUSTRE62U38C20100331.

Government Accountability Office (GAO). "Large Bank Holding Companies: Expectations of Government Support." GAO-14-621, July 31, 2014.

Greene, Robert W. "Understanding CoCos: What Operational Concerns & Global Trends Mean for U.S. Policymakers." M-RCBG Associate Working Paper Series, No. 62, Harvard Kennedy School, June 2016.

Groendahl, Boris. "Two Shades of German Seniors Show Bail-In Pecking Order." *Bloomberg.com*, April 1, 2015. http://www.bloomberg.com/news/articles/2015-04-01/germany-leads-senior -bank-debt-revamp-to-ease-bail-in.

Hale, Thomas. "Music Stops for Buyers of Coco Debt." *Financial Times*, February 11, 2016. http:// www.ft.com/intl/cms/s/0/f921e592-d0af-11e5-831d-09f7778e7377.html.

Jones, Garett. "Imitate FDR's Treasury Secretary: Bankruptcy Not Bailouts." *U.S. Exchequer* (Fall 2008): 45–46.

———. "Speed Bankruptcy: A Firewall to Future Crises." *Journal of Applied Corporate Finance* 22, no. 3 (2010): 73–84.

La Porta, Rafael, Florencio Lopez-de-Silanes, and Andrei Shleifer. "Government Ownership of Banks." *Journal of Finance* 57, no. 1 (2002): 265–301.

Mankiw, Gregory. "Nationalization or Pre-Privatization?" *Greg Mankiw's Blog*. February 16, 2009. http://gregmankiw.blogspot.kr/2009/02/nationalization-or-pre-privatization.html.

Moody's. "Final Functionality of Bail-in Regimes in LatAm and Canada Is Uncertain." Announcement. January 22, 2015. https://www.moodys.com/research/Moodys-Final -functionality-of-bail-in-regimes-in-LatAm-and--PR_316970.

O'Dwyer, Peter. "IBRC Junior Bondholders Submit Claims of €285m." *Irish Examiner*, October 7, 2015. http://www.irishexaminer.com/business/ibrc-junior-bondholders-submit-claims-of -285m-357956.html.

Roberts, Russ. "Gambling with Other People's Money." Mercatus Working Paper, Mercatus Center at George Mason University, Arlington, VA, 2010.

———. "Roberts on the Crisis," *Econtalk Podcast*, May 17, 2010. http://www.econtalk.org/archives /2010/05/roberts_on_the_2.html.

Seleanu, David. "Canadian Banking Outlook Downgraded over 'Bail-In' Move, Adding to Recent Financial Stability Concerns." *Reuters*, July 17, 2014. http://blogs.reuters.com/financial -regulatory-forum/2014/07/17/canadian-banking-outlook-downgraded-over-bail-in -move-adding-to-recent-financial-stability-concerns.

Stiglitz, Joseph E. "Reforming the Global Economic Architecture: Lessons from Recent Crises." *Journal of Finance* 54, no. 4 (August 1999): 1508–21.

Taylor, John B., and John C. Williams. "A Black Swan in the Money Market." *American Economic Journal: Macroeconomics* 1, no. 1 (2009): 58–83.

Thompson, Christopher. "Coco Sell-off Unveils High-yield Bargains." *Financial Times*, August 14, 2014. http://www.ft.com/intl/cms/s/0/e9d5ffca-2308-11e4-a424-00144feabdc0.html.

Zingales, Luigi. "Cramdown: How to Fix the Credit Mess without a Government Bailout: Quickie Bankruptcies." *Forbes*, October 27, 2008. http://www.forbes.com/forbes/2008/1027/030 .html.

———. "Why Paulson Is Wrong." *The Economists' Voice* 5, no. 5 (2008): art. 2.

PART 3

REGULATING SECURITIES AND DERIVATIVES MARKETS

CHAPTER 6
US Broker-Dealer Regulation

HON. DANIEL M. GALLAGHER
Patomak Global Partners, LLC
Former Commissioner, US Securities and Exchange Commission

US FEDERAL BROKER-DEALER REGULATION

The US capital markets are inhabited by various types of market participants, each performing different roles and subject to different oversight regimes. Broker-dealers play a key role in these markets—among other things, they underwrite securities offerings, prepare research, make markets, and hold and service customer accounts for retail and institutional customers.

The Securities Exchange Act of 1934 (Exchange Act) defines the term "broker" as "any person engaged in the business of effecting transactions in securities for the account of others,"[1] and it defines "dealer" as "any person engaged in the business of buying and selling securities for such person's own account through a broker or otherwise."[2] Most firms function as both brokers and dealers, and thus are called broker-dealers.

Broker-dealers are subject to regulatory oversight by the federal government, the states, and self-regulatory organizations (SROs). The rules and regulations governing broker-dealers and their activity are encyclopedic in volume and detail. As such, this chapter provides only a survey of the federal oversight regime governing the operations and conduct of broker-dealers. It is intended to provide basic background on the subject of federal broker-dealer regulation in the United States and to demonstrate the extent of the regulatory requirements that apply to broker-dealers. These requirements generally fall into three main categories: (1) registration, (2) financial responsibility and customer protection, and (3) conduct.

The first part of this chapter consists of a high-level factual summary of the rules applicable to broker-dealers, while the second part consists of a normative, market-based critique of the broker-dealer regulatory regime. As will be seen, the broker-dealer regime does incorporate significant market-oriented elements. It would benefit, however, from a return to true self-regulation by SROs as well as increased economic analysis on the part of both the US Securities and Exchange Commission (Commission or SEC) and the SROs— in particular, analysis that takes into account the existing regulatory burden on broker-dealers.

Registration as a Broker-Dealer

The cornerstone of the federal regulatory regime for broker-dealers is registration with the SEC. Registration is required when firms engage in certain activities identified in the federal securities laws. Failure to register when required is a stand-alone cause of action in the securities laws.

Broker-dealers are required to register with the SEC pursuant to Section 15(a) of the Exchange Act.[3] A broker-dealer registers with the SEC by filing an application on Form BD, which requires extensive information about the background of the applicant, including the type of business in which it proposes to engage; the identity of the applicant's direct and indirect owners and other control affiliates; and whether the applicant or any of its control affiliates have been subject to criminal prosecutions, regulatory actions, or civil actions in connection with any investment-related activity.[4]

An SEC order granting registration generally will not become effective until a broker-dealer has become a member of at least one SRO.[5] Membership in one or more SROs, which consist of the Financial Industry Regulatory Authority (FINRA) and the national securities exchanges registered with the SEC, entails additional regulatory requirements for broker-dealers.[6] SROs are statutorily required to promulgate and enforce rules that govern all aspects of their members' securities business, including their financial condition, operational capabilities, sales practices, and the qualifications of their members' employees.[7]

A broker-dealer that limits its transactions to the national securities exchanges of which it is a member and meets certain other conditions may be required only to be a member of those exchanges;[8] however, any broker-dealer with a public customer business that effects securities transactions other than on a national securities exchange of which it is a member (including any over-the-counter business), must become a member of a "national securities association" as well, which in practice means FINRA, the only currently registered national securities association.[9] Lastly, firms that engage in transactions in municipal securities must also register with and comply with the rules of the Municipal Securities Rulemaking Board (MSRB), an SRO that makes rules governing transactions in municipal securities. Broker-dealers must comply with the rules of each of the SROs of which they are members.

The Exchange Act generally prohibits registered broker-dealers from conducting a securities business unless their associated persons who effect or are involved in effecting securities transactions are licensed in accordance with the qualification standards of each SRO of which they are members.[10] Most SROs have established various qualification exams for associated persons of broker-dealers, with licenses based on an associated person's job functions.[11] Broker-dealers and their associated persons may also need to register with the securities authority of one or more states, in accordance with the applicable laws of each state in which they do business.[12] The broker-dealer registration process is coordinated through the Central Registration Depository (CRD) system operated by FINRA.[13]

Financial Responsibility Rules

Broker-dealers must meet certain financial responsibility requirements under the Exchange Act. These requirements are designed to protect customers from the consequences of the financial failure of a broker-dealer by requiring the safeguarding of customer securities and funds held by the broker-dealer and requiring the broker-dealer to maintain minimum capital levels. The SEC's financial responsibility rules require broker-dealers to maintain more than a dollar of highly liquid assets for each dollar of liabilities, prohibit broker-dealers from using customer securities and cash to finance their own business, and require broker-dealers to maintain accurate books and records. The financial responsibility rules for broker-dealers are particularly complex; as such, the following represents a broad overview of the subject.

Net Capital Rule. Since 1942, the Commission has prescribed capital requirements for broker-dealers based on a net liquid assets test pursuant to Section 15(c)(3) of the Exchange Act and Rule 15c3-1 thereunder (the "net capital rule").[14] The net capital rule is designed to ensure that a broker-dealer holds, at all times, more than one dollar of highly liquid assets for each dollar of liabilities (e.g., money owed to customers and counterparties), excluding liabilities that are subordinated to all other creditors by contractual agreement.[15] The premise underlying the net capital rule is that if a broker-dealer fails, it should be in a position to meet all unsubordinated obligations to customers and counterparties and generate resources sufficient to wind down its operations in an orderly manner without the need of a formal proceeding.

The rule requires a broker-dealer to perform two primary calculations: (1) a computation of required minimum net capital (that is, the amount of net capital a broker-dealer must maintain in order to legally operate a securities business); and (2) a computation of actual net capital. A broker-dealer must ensure that its actual net capital exceeds its required minimum net capital at all times.

For most broker-dealers, the required minimum amount is the greater of a fixed-dollar amount or an amount computed using one of two financial ratios.[16] The first ratio provides that a broker-dealer shall not permit its aggregate indebtedness to all other persons to exceed 1,500 percent of its net capital (i.e., a 15-to-1 aggregate indebtedness to net capital requirement).[17] The second financial ratio, used by broker-dealers that carry customer accounts, provides that a broker-dealer shall not permit its net capital to be less than 2 percent of aggregate customer debit items (i.e., customer obligations to the broker-dealer).[18] After performing the applicable financial ratio calculation, the broker-dealer compares that amount to its applicable fixed-dollar requirement (e.g., $250,000). The larger amount—fixed-dollar or ratio—is the broker-dealer's required minimum.

Once the required regulatory net capital is determined, broker-dealers must undertake the calculation of their actual net capital. A broker-dealer begins this process by calculating its net worth using generally accepted accounting principles (GAAP).[19] It then subtracts illiquid, or "non-allowable," assets such as real estate or goodwill[20] and adds back qualified subordinated loans.[21]

Finally, a broker-dealer is required to subtract an amount, determined by taking percentage deductions (referred to as "haircuts"), from the mark-to-market value (i.e., the current market value) of each allowable asset (e.g., equity or debt securities). The size of the haircut for each allowable asset is prescribed by rule and depends on the inherent market and liquidity risk of the asset. In addition, certain larger broker-dealers may, upon application to and approval by the Commission, compute their actual net capital using an "alternative net capital" method, which entails the use of value at risk, or VaR, models in lieu of the standardized haircuts prescribed by the net capital rule.[22]

Customer Protection Rule. Exchange Act Rule 15c3-3 (the customer protection rule) applies to all registered broker-dealers, with certain exemptions. The customer protection rule imposes two important obligations on "carrying" broker-dealers—that is, broker-dealers that carry customer accounts—as well as on "clearing" broker-dealers, those through which other broker-dealers or customers clear their trades. First, each broker-dealer subject to the customer protection rule must obtain physical possession or control over customers' fully paid and excess margin securities,[23] meaning that the broker-dealer must hold these securities free of lien in one of several categories of locations specified in the rule (e.g., a bank or clearing agency).[24] Under Rule 15c3-3, a broker-dealer must make a daily determination from its books and records (as of the preceding day) of the quantity of fully paid and excess margin securities in its possession. Second, a broker-dealer must maintain at a bank or banks cash or qualified securities on deposit in a Special Reserve Bank Account for the Exclusive Benefit of Customers equaling at least the net amount computed by adding customer credit items (e.g., cash in securities accounts) and subtracting from that amount customer debit items (e.g., margin loans).[25]

The customer protection rule is designed to protect customer funds and securities by generally segregating them from the carrying broker-dealer's proprietary business activities. As such, if the carrying broker-dealer fails, customer funds and securities should be readily available to be returned to customers. The rule requires carrying broker-dealers to compute the customer reserve requirement on a weekly basis, except where customer credit balances do not exceed $1 million (in which case the computation can be performed monthly, provided that the broker-dealer maintains 105 percent of the required deposit amount).

Broker-dealers that do not hold customer funds or securities can claim an exemption from the requirements set forth in Rule 15c3-3.[26] For example, an "introducing" broker-dealer that clears all transactions with and for customers on a fully disclosed basis with a clearing broker-dealer, and who promptly transmits all customer funds and securities to the clearing broker-dealer, is not required to comply with Rule 15c3-3.[27]

Some broker-dealers that do not carry customer accounts receive securities and cash from customers for the limited purpose of effecting securities transactions. These broker-dealers can also claim an exemption from Rule 15c3-3 provided they promptly transfer all securities to customers and effectuate all financial transactions with customers through a bank's "Special Account for the Exclusive Benefit of Customers of [the broker-dealer]."[28] The amount of money that must be deposited into the account is the total amount of money the broker-dealer has received from customers. If the broker-dealer fails, the cash in this account is used to meet any outstanding obligations to customers (ahead of any general creditors of the broker-dealer).

Recordkeeping Requirements. Exchange Act Rule 17a-3 sets forth the basic recordkeeping requirements applicable to brokers and dealers. Examples of records required to be made and kept current under Rule 17a-3 include trade blotters itemizing trades, receipts, or deliveries of securities, as well as disbursements of cash and other debits and credits; a stock record of positions held in various securities; trial balances; a record of the firm's computation of net capital and aggregate indebtedness; trade confirmations; complaints regarding associated persons; and compliance records. Exchange Act Rule 17a-4 governs the retention periods for these records, which vary by record type, as well as for other records, such as information supporting a firm's financial reports and communications sent or received by the firm that relate to the firm's business.

Exchange Act Rule 17a-5 contains important reporting requirements for broker-dealers. Under Rule 17a-5, a broker-dealer is required, among other things, to periodically file unaudited reports. These reports—known as Financial and Operational Combined Uniform Single (FOCUS) Reports—contain information about a broker-dealer's financial and operational condition. Also under Rule 17a-5, a broker-dealer must annually file its financial statements and other reports, including a report covering the financial statements and reports prepared by the broker-dealer's independent public accountant, which must be registered with the Public Company Accounting Oversight Board (PCAOB). Rule 17a-5 reporting supports compliance with Rules 15c-3-1 and 15c3-3 and facilitates examinations by the SEC, state regulators, and SROs.

More specifically, under Rule 17a-5, broker-dealers must prepare and file with the SEC annual reports consisting of a financial report and either a compliance report or an exemption report prepared by the broker-dealer, as well as certain reports that are prepared by an independent public accountant covering the financial report and the compliance report or the exemption report. A broker-dealer must prepare and file a compliance report if the firm did not claim it was exempt from Rule 15c3-3 throughout the most recent fiscal year. A broker-dealer must prepare and file an exemption report if the firm did claim that it was exempt from Rule 15c3-3 throughout the most recent fiscal year.

General Conduct Rules

Like all securities market participants, broker-dealers must comply with the antifraud provisions of the federal securities laws,[29] which prohibit misstatements or misleading omissions of material facts, as well as fraudulent or manipulative acts and practices, in connection with the purchase or sale of securities. In practice, these prohibitions entail several broad conduct requirements.

For example, broker-dealers owe their customers a duty of "fair dealing" that "is derived from the antifraud provisions of the federal securities laws."[30] The Commission's interpretive statements and enforcement actions and court cases have filled out the requirement of fair dealing by identifying specific actions required of broker-dealers to fulfill that broad duty. As the Commission staff has noted, "these include the duties to execute orders promptly, disclose certain material information (i.e., information the customer would consider important as an investor), charge prices reasonably related to the prevailing market, and fully disclose any conflict of interest."[31]

Broker-dealers also have a "suitability" duty—that is, an obligation to recommend only those specific investments or overall investment strategies that are suitable for their customers. In practice, this duty obligates a broker-dealer to have an "adequate and reasonable basis" for any recommendation that it makes on a customer-specific basis.[32]

The duty of "best execution" requires a broker-dealer to seek to obtain the most favorable terms available under the circumstances for its customer orders.[33] Some SRO rules also include a duty of best execution. For example, FINRA members must use "reasonable diligence" to determine the best market for a security and buy or sell the security in that market, so that the price to the customer is as favorable as possible under prevailing market conditions.[34]

Broker-dealers also must comply with a number of SEC rules pertaining to specific circumstances. For example, Regulation SHO addresses the requirements that must be met for a "short sale" (i.e., the sale of a security the seller does not own), including a "locate" requirement, which requires a broker-dealer to have reasonable grounds to believe the relevant unowned security can be borrowed prior to its delivery date, as well as an additional "close-out" requirement for securities in which there are a relatively substantial number of extended delivery failures at a registered clearing agency.[35]

Additionally, broker-dealers must comply with Regulation M,[36] which applies when securities are being offered in a distribution. Regulation M prohibits broker-dealers (as well as underwriters and other distribution participants) from bidding for, purchasing, or attempting to induce any person to bid for or purchase, any security that is the subject of a distribution until the applicable restricted period has ended.[37]

Finally, broker-dealers are required to supervise their personnel and ensure their compliance with all relevant rules and regulations. Failure to do so could lead to "failure to supervise" liability under Section 15(b) of the Exchange Act.

A MARKET PERSPECTIVE ON US FEDERAL BROKER-DEALER REGULATION

A market-based critique of the broker-dealer regulatory regime must begin with an acknowledgement that the regime does, in fact, include significant market-oriented elements, especially in comparison with other extant financial regulatory regimes. Over the past several years, however, prudential regulators overseeing the banking sector have made efforts to bring the SEC's comparatively market-oriented approach to broker-dealer regulation more in line with the "safety and soundness" approach of banking regulations. This effort has intensified with the passage of the Dodd-Frank Wall Street Reform

and Consumer Protection Act (Dodd-Frank)[38] and the establishment and operation of the bank regulator-dominated Financial Stability Oversight Council
(FSOC). Tellingly, the FSOC has invoked Section 120 of Dodd-Frank, which
grants it the authority to "provide for more stringent regulation of financial activity by issuing recommendations to the primary financial regulatory agencies to
apply new or heightened standards and safeguards,"[39] only once, in an effort
to pressure the Commission to tailor its regulations governing money market
mutual funds in a manner more suitable to the prudential regulators of FSOC.[40]

One key difference between the banking and the broker-dealer regulatory
regimes is their differing capital rules. Bank capital rules are inherently centralized on both a national and a supranational basis, focusing on the safety
and soundness not only of individual banks but of the banking sector as a
whole. There is no broker-dealer equivalent to the Basel framework underlying
bank capital requirements throughout the developed world (although the largest broker-dealers are generally subsidiaries of bank holding companies, which
are subject to the Basel-based capital regime for banks). Crucially, there is
no acknowledgment in the SEC's net capital rule—tacitly or otherwise—of
the concept of a too big to fail broker-dealer. The SEC's net capital regime for
broker-dealers focuses not on "systemic risk" but instead on the protection of
individual investors.

Whereas bank capital requirements are predicated on the reduction of
risk and the avoidance of failure, broker-dealer requirements are designed
to *manage* failure by providing enough of a "cushion" to ensure that a failed
broker-dealer can liquidate in an orderly manner, allowing for the orderly
transfer of customer assets to another broker-dealer. Capital requirements for
broker-dealers reflect the fact that the capital markets are based, in large part,
on risk. They form a system designed to *encourage* investors and institutions
to take risks—informed risks that they freely choose in pursuit of a return
on their investments.

While bank failure is anathema to bank regulators, for broker-dealer regulators failure is a fact of life—an unavoidable element of the creative destruction
that underpins capitalism. The broker-dealer net capital regime, with its different haircut requirements for different investment products, is heavily weighted
in favor of highly liquid assets precisely because broker-dealers can, and do,
fail.[41] The goal of the net capital rule is to ensure that in the event of failure, a
broker-dealer will have the necessary assets not only to cover its liabilities but

to facilitate a quick and orderly self-liquidation of the firm. Crucially, the net capital rule is designed to work in conjunction with the customer protection rule—the segregation of customer assets is meant to ensure an easy transfer of accounts from a failing broker-dealer to a healthy one.

The Securities Investor Protection Corporation (SIPC), a nonprofit membership corporation created pursuant to the Securities Investor Protection Act (SIPA),[42] exists for the purpose of facilitating the liquidation of troubled broker-dealers and the return of customer property in a market-oriented manner. In a SIPA liquidation, SIPC (and in most cases a court-appointed trustee) work to return customers' securities and cash as quickly as possible. Unlike the Federal Deposit Insurance Corporation (FDIC), which is an independent federal agency providing, in essence, federally mandated deposit insurance, SIPC is primarily concerned with overseeing the liquidation of failed or failing firms with the goal of returning customer assets. SIPC's board of directors determines its policies and governs operations. Of its seven directors, five are appointed by the president subject to Senate approval. Three of those five directors represent the securities industry, while two are from the general public. The president is also responsible for designating a chairman and vice chairman. The remaining two directors are appointed by the secretary of the Department of the Treasury and the Federal Reserve Board from among the officers and employees of those organizations.

Another market-oriented element of broker-dealer regulation is the concept of self-regulation as embodied in the SRO construct. The Exchange Act codified the self-regulatory role of exchanges, requiring all existing exchanges to register with the newly formed SEC and function as SROs. Four years later, the Maloney Act of 1938 (Maloney Act)[43] authorized, and required the registration of, national securities associations to oversee over-the-counter (OTC) market participants. The legislative history of the Maloney Act explained Congress's desire to maintain and indeed increase its reliance on SROs, noting that relying solely on government regulation "would involve a pronounced expansion of the organization of the [SEC]; the multiplication of branch offices; a large increase in the expenditure of public funds; an increase in the problem of avoiding the evils of bureaucracy; and a minute, detailed, and rigid regulation of business conduct by law."[44]

In 1975, the US Congress passed a number of amendments to the Exchange Act (the "1975 Amendments"),[45] which, among other things, endorsed the role of SROs in securities regulation while simultaneously curtailing their independence. The legislative history of the 1975 Amendments explains Congress's determination that it was "distinctly preferable" to rely on "cooperative regulation, in which the task will be largely performed by representative organizations of investment bankers, dealers, and brokers, with the Government exercising appropriate supervision in the public interest, and exercising supplementary powers of direct regulation," especially in light of the "sheer ineffectiveness of attempting to assure [regulation] directly through the government on a wide scale."[46] The 1975 Amendments, however, fundamentally altered the role of SROs by requiring, for the first time, that any new SRO rule or rule amendment be approved by the SEC. This laid the groundwork for criticism of the SROs' enhanced role based on the belief that they are essentially quasi-governmental entities serving as "deputies" to the SEC.

As explained in a 2005 SEC "Concept Release Concerning Self-Regulation" (SRO Concept Release),[47] the Exchange Act, the Maloney Act, and the 1975 Amendments "reflect Congress' determination to rely on self-regulation as a fundamental component of U.S. market and broker-dealer regulation[.]" The SRO Concept Release noted a number of reasons for this determination, including the view that directly regulating the intricacies of the securities industry would be cost-prohibitive and inefficient, the desirability of SRO regulatory staff to be "intimately involved" with the complexities of rulemaking and enforcement, and the ability of SROs to set standards that exceeded those imposed by the Commission (e.g., just and equitable principles of trade and detailed proscriptive business conduct standards).[48] As the SRO Concept Release explained, "In short, Congress determined that the securities industry self-regulatory system would provide a workable balance between federal and industry regulation."[49]

Self-regulation is, in theory, significantly more market-oriented than external regulation. Executed properly, self-regulation empowers the parties most familiar with the actual workings of securities transactions and with the greatest stake in ensuring public trust and confidence in the markets. It is more cost-effective and fluid than governmental regulation, allowing its members to react quickly and decisively to changes in the industry that they observe directly on a daily basis. Furthermore, the status of each exchange as an SRO introduces an element of competition that, ideally, negates the possibility of a "race to the bottom," allowing investors displeased with the self-policing methods and results of a given exchange to transfer their business to one more suited to their tastes. Ironically, given prudential regulators' distaste for the decentralization and unpredictability of securities regulation, self-regulation embodies the concept of "skin in the game" mandated for securitizers of asset-backed securities in the "risk retention" provisions of Section 941 of Dodd-Frank.[50]

Unfortunately, the present-day implementation of the self-regulatory concept falls short of its market-oriented potential. Beginning with the 1975 Amendments' requirement that the SEC approve new rules or rule amendments by SROs, a number of developments over the past several decades have resulted in a significant move away from the traditional SRO construct. A 1996 settlement between the SEC and the National Association of Securities Dealers (NASD), the predecessor of FINRA and the owner of the NASDAQ electronic stock market, over the failure of the NASD to enforce its rules against anti-competitive pricing policies by NASDAQ market makers required the NASD to agree to a number of undertakings that led to profound changes in its governance structure. These changes included the addition of public members to the NASD board and the increased prominence of professional staff in NASD regulatory matters, which substantially decreased the role of NASD members in self-regulation. As such, they marked a watershed event in what has been referred to as "the NASD's transformation into a professional regulator largely independent of its membership."[51] Since then, the NASD and later FINRA have prioritized corporate governance issues (e.g., independent board membership) over member self-regulation, fundamentally altering the SRO concept.

An additional key development in the move away from the traditional SRO construct has been the transformation of exchanges into demutualized, for-profit entities. Notably, the then chairman and chief executive officer of the NASD highlighted, in a 2005 congressional hearing, "the concern . . . that for-profit, publicly traded exchanges will be faced with the conflicting goal [sic] of having to maximize profits while not compromising regulation."[52]

In 2007, the NASD merged with the regulatory arm of the New York Stock Exchange to form FINRA. Since this event, exchanges have increasingly delegated their regulatory responsibilities to FINRA, calling into question the role of exchanges as SROs. In a 2013 letter to SEC Chair Mary Jo White, the Securities Industry and Financial Markets Association (SIFMA) explicitly seconded my call for a "comprehensive market and regulatory structure review, including a review of the self-regulatory paradigm as a whole."[53] SIFMA noted that the incorporation of the role of SROs into federal securities law "was intended to serve two primary purposes: . . . it relieved the government of some of the burden of regulating the securities markets by instead delegating to and leveraging its oversight of the SROs [and] it was thought that regulation was more effective when conducted by an organization, such as an exchange, more familiar with the nuances of the business." SIFMA concluded, however, that "with exchanges having outsourced and delegated a substantial majority of regulatory functions to [FINRA], neither reason justifies why exchanges should continue to act as SROs."[54]

This decrease in the "self" aspect of FINRA's self-regulatory function has been accompanied by an exponential increase in its regulatory output. As FINRA acts more and more like a "deputy" SEC, concerns about its accountability grow more pronounced. While FINRA is generally required to address whether a proposed new rule or rule amendment would impose a burden on competition, conflict with the securities laws, or otherwise be inconsistent with the public interest or the protection of investors,[55] it is not required by statute or rule to conduct a benefit-cost analysis. However, FINRA's September 2013 announcement of a "Framework Regarding FINRA's Approach to Economic Impact Assessment for Proposed Rulemaking,"[56] a voluntary undertaking on its part to "help ensure that its rules are better designed to protect the investing public and maintain market integrity while minimizing unnecessary burdens,"[57] marked a significant positive development in this space.

FINRA's voluntary undertaking draws attention to perhaps the most significant deficiency, from a market-oriented perspective, in broker-dealer regulation: the lack of a calculation and acknowledgment of the cumulative cost of compliance for broker-dealers. Although the SEC is not required by law to conduct an extensive economic analysis for every proposed new rule or rule amendment, it has been the Commission's policy since the early 1980s to consider potential costs and benefits whenever it adopts rules. A staff memorandum issued in 2012 states that "[h]igh-quality economic analysis is an essential part of SEC rulemaking" and sets forth guidance for performing such analysis.[58] Even the Commission's most fulsome reviews of potential costs and benefits, however, fail to take into account the existing regulatory burden. This burden, substantial even before the financial crisis of 2008, has arguably grown significantly, and will continue to grow, due to the extensive requirements of Dodd-Frank.

Despite the lack of information on the cumulative cost to broker-dealers of the regulatory regime, one metric does stand out. In September 2007, there were 5,799 broker-dealers registered with the Commission. As of August 2016, that number had dwindled to 4,115.[59] Obviously, not all of this decrease can be attributed to the increased compliance costs facing broker-dealers in a post–Dodd-Frank world, especially given the intervening financial crisis. Only the most fervent free-market opponents, however, would deny that the ever-increasing cost of compliance has played a role in the reduction of the number of broker-dealers by almost 30 percent in less than a decade.

CONCLUSION

Although the broker-dealer regulatory regime does incorporate significant market-oriented elements, improvements can be made on both the self-regulatory and economic analysis fronts. Specifically, broker-dealer regulation would benefit from a return to true self-regulation by SROs, as opposed to the arguably quasi-governmental "deputy SEC" role they play today. In addition, broker-dealers and their customers would benefit from enhanced economic analysis on the part of both the SEC and the SROs, in particular analysis of the potential costs of new rules or rule amendments that takes into account the existing regulatory burden on broker-dealers.

NOTES

1. 15 U.S.C. § 78c(a)(4).

2. 15 U.S.C. § 78c(a)(5).

3. Section 15(a) of the Exchange Act requires broker-dealers to register with the SEC if the broker-dealer makes "use of . . . any means . . . of interstate commerce to effect any transaction in, or to induce or attempt to induce the purchase or sale of, any security" other than exempted securities. Section 3(a)(17) of the Exchange Act defines the term "interstate commerce" to include "trade, commerce, transportation, or communication among the several States, or between any foreign country and any State." Virtually any transaction-related contact between an intermediary meeting the definition of "broker" or "dealer" and the US securities markets or an investor in the United States involves interstate commerce and provides the basis for requiring the intermediary to register as a broker-dealer.

4. See Exchange Act Rule 15b1-1. Form BD also elicits information regarding whether the applicant or any of its control affiliates has been subject to a bankruptcy petition, had a trustee appointed under the Securities Investor Protection Act, has been denied a bond, or has any unsatisfied judgments or liens. Form BD is a consolidated form that was established by the Commission, SROs, and state regulators to allow an applicant to initiate registration with all relevant regulators using one form.

5. Exchange Act Section 15(b)(8). The Exchange Act defines an SRO as "any national securities exchange, registered securities association, or registered clearing agency, or (solely for the purposes of sections 19(b), 19(c) and 23(b) of [the Exchange Act]) the Municipal Securities Rulemaking Board established by section 15B. . . ." See Exchange Act Section 3(a)(26), 15 U.S.C. § 78c(a)(26).

6. There are twenty national securities exchanges registered with the SEC: BATS BZX Exchange, BATS BYX Exchange, BOX Options Exchange, C2 Options Exchange, Chicago Board Options Exchange, Chicago Stock Exchange, EDGA Exchange, EDGX Exchange, International Securities Exchange, The Investors Exchange, ISE Gemini, ISE Mercury, Miami International Securities Exchange, The NASDAQ Stock Market, NASDAQ BX, NASDAQ PHLX, National Stock Exchange, New York Stock Exchange, NYSE MKT, and NYSE Arca. Fast Answers: Exchanges, https://www.sec.gov/divisions/marketreg/mrexchanges.shtml (last retrieved August 8, 2016).

7. See, for example, Exchange Act Sections 6(b) and 15A(b), 15 U.S.C. §§ 78f(b) and 78o-3(b).

8. See Exchange Act Sections 6(b)(2) and 6(c), 15 U.S.C. §§ 78f(b)(2) and (c).

9. Exchange Act Section 15(b)(8). Pursuant to Exchange Act Rule 15b9-1, certain broker-dealers that are members of a national securities exchange, carry no customer accounts, and have annual gross income of no more than $1,000 that is derived from securities transactions effected otherwise than on a national securities exchange of which they are a member (not including income derived from proprietary trading) may be exempt from registration with a national securities association. However, the SEC has proposed to, among other things, limit the scope of Rule 15b9-1 by eliminating the proprietary trading exemption. See "Exemption for Certain Exchange Members," Exchange Act Release No. 74581 (March 25, 2015.

10. 17 C.F.R. § 240.15b7-1.

11. See, for example, National Association of Securities Dealers Rules 1022 and 1032, and Chicago Board Options Exchange Rule 3.6A(a).

12. Section 3(a)(16) of the Exchange Act defines "State" to mean "any State of the United States, the District of Columbia, Puerto Rico, the Virgin Islands, or any other possession of the United States." 15 U.S.C. § 78c(a)(16).

13. Exchange Act Rule 15b1-1(b). The CRD was developed and is maintained jointly by the North American Securities Administrators Association and FINRA. The CRD is an online registration data bank and application processing facility used by FINRA, the other SROs, state regulators, and the SEC in connection with the registration and licensing of broker-dealers and their personnel. The CRD was created, in part, to centralize the registration process, allowing applicants to file in one place, rather than filing separately in multiple jurisdictions. "Broker-Dealer Registration and Reporting," Exchange Act Release No. 41594 (July 2, 1999), 64 Fed. Reg. (July 12, 1999): 37586.

14. 15 U.S.C. § 78o(c)(3); 17 C.F.R. § 240.15c3-1.

15. Typically, affiliates (e.g., the holding company) or owners of the broker-dealer make subordinated loans to the broker-dealer for capital purposes.

16. The fixed-dollar amounts are based on the type of securities business in which the broker-dealer engages. For example, a broker-dealer that carries customer accounts has a fixed-dollar requirement of $250,000; a broker-dealer that does not carry customer accounts but engages in proprietary securities trading (defined as more than ten trades a year) has a fixed-dollar amount of $100,000; and a broker-dealer that does not carry accounts for customers or otherwise receive or hold securities and cash for customers, and does not engage in proprietary trading activities, has a fixed-dollar amount of $5,000.

17. Put another way, the broker-dealer must maintain, at a minimum, an amount of net capital equal to one-fifteenth (or 6.67 percent) of its aggregate indebtedness. This financial ratio is used by smaller broker-dealers that do not carry customer accounts.

18. Customer debit items—computed pursuant to Rule 15c3-3—primarily consist of margin loans to customers and securities borrowed by the broker-dealer to effectuate deliveries of securities sold short by customers. See 17 C.F.R. § 240.15c3-3 and 17 C.F.R. § 240.15c3-3a. This ratio is used by larger broker-dealers that maintain custody of customer securities and cash.

19. Net worth is the amount by which the broker-dealer's assets exceed its liabilities.

20. Non-allowable assets also include unsecured receivables and illiquid securities (e.g., securities that have no ready market).

21. Because of the net capital rule's strict asset liquidity requirements, broker-dealers typically rely on qualifying subordinated loans to meet their minimum net capital requirements. Typically, a control person of the broker-dealer, such as its parent holding company, makes the subordinated loan. The net capital rule prescribes a number of requirements for a subordinated loan to qualify as an add-back to net worth. Most important, the loan agreement must provide that the broker-dealer cannot repay the loan at term if doing so would reduce its net capital to certain levels above the minimum requirement. This contractual prohibition, in effect, makes the subordinated loan similar to preferred stock in that the loan would take on the characteristics of permanent capital if the broker-dealer could not repay it. 17 C.F.R. § 240.15c3-1d(b).

22. For a fuller expert discussion of the net capital rule, see Sirri (Director, Division of Trading and Markets, US Securities and Exchange Commission), "Remarks at the National Economist's Club."

23. 17 C.F.R. § 240.15c3-3(b)(1).

24. 17 C.F.R. § 240.15c3-3(c).

25. 17 C.F.R. § 240.15c3-3(a).

26. 17 C.F.R. § 240.15c3-3(k).

27. 17 C.F.R. § 240.15c3-3(k)(2)(ii).

28. See 17 C.F.R. § 240.15c3-3(k)(2)(i).

29. Exchange Act Sections 9(a), 10(b) and 15(c)(1) and (2); 15 U.S.C. §§ 78i(a), 78j(b), and 78o(c)(1)-(2).

30. See "Study on Investment Advisers and Broker-Dealers," 51. This SEC Staff study cites the "Report of the Special Study of Securities Markets of the Securities and Exchange Commission," H.R. Doc. No. 88-95, at 238 (1st Sess. 1963); "In the Matters of Richard N. Cea et al.," Exchange Act Release No. 8662 at 18 (August 6, 1969), involving excessive trading and recommendations of speculative securities without a reasonable basis; "In the Matter of Mac Robbins & Co. Inc.," Exchange Act Release No. 6846 (July 11, 1962).

31. "Guide to Broker-Dealer Registration."

32. See FINRA Rule 2111.

33. See FINRA Rule 5310.

34. Ibid. A member firm, in any transaction for or with a customer or a customer of another broker-dealer, is required to use "reasonable diligence" to determine the best market for a security and to buy or sell in such market so that the resultant price to the customer is as favorable as possible under prevailing market conditions. See also FINRA Regulatory Notice

to Members 12-13, March 2012, citing five factors that are among those to be considered in determining whether a firm has used reasonable diligence: (1) the character of the market for the security; (2) the size and type of transaction; (3) the number of markets checked; (4) the accessibility of the quotation; and (5) the terms and conditions of the order as communicated to the firm).

35. See 17 C.F.R. § 242.200-204

36. See 17 C.F.R. § 242.100-105.

37. Section 913 of the Dodd-Frank Wall Street Reform and Consumer Protection Act required the SEC to conduct a study to evaluate, among other things, the effectiveness of existing legal or regulatory standards of care for broker-dealers as well as whether there are legal or regulatory gaps in the protection of retail customers relating to the standards of care for broker-dealers. See the January 2011 "Study on Investment Advisers and Broker-Dealers." Dodd-Frank also granted the SEC authority to impose a fiduciary standard on broker-dealers. As of this writing, the SEC has not conducted any additional rulemaking pursuant to this grant of authority. The Department of Labor, however, proposed in 2010, reproposed in 2015, and adopted in 2016 a fiduciary standard for broker-dealers advising employee benefit plans under the Employee Retirement Income Security Act of 1974.

38. Dodd-Frank, Pub. L. No. 111-203, 124 Stat. 1376 (2010).

39. Pub. L. No. 111-203, 124 Stat. 1376, Sec. 120 (2010).

40. See "Financial Stability Oversight Council: Proposed Recommendations Regarding Money Market Mutual Fund Reform," 77 Fed. Reg. (November 2012): 69455–483.

41. That being said, however, far more banks fail. For example, nearly 550 banks have failed since October 1, 2000. See the FDIC, "Failed Bank List." In contrast, as of December 2015, the SIPC had processed a total of 328 proceedings since its inception in 1973. See SIPC, "2015 Annual Report," 8.

42. 15 U.S.C. § 78aaa-*lll*, as amended through July 22, 2010.

43. Maloney Act of 1938, Pub. L. 75-719, 52 Stat. 1070 (1938) (codified as amended at 15 U.S.C. § 78o, authorizing the US Securities and Exchange Commission to register national securities associations).

44. S. Rep. No. 1455, 75th Cong., 3d Sess. I.B.4. (1938); H.R. Rep. No. 2307, 75th Cong., 3d Sess. I.B.4. (1938) (duplicate text quoted in both reports).

45. Securities Acts Amendments of 1975, Pub. L. 29, 89 Stat. 97 (1975).

46. S. Rep. No. 94-75, 94th Cong., 1st Sess. 7, II (1975).

47. See Exchange Act 50700 (November 18, 2004), "Concept Release on SRO Structure," 60 Fed. Reg. (December 8, 2004): 71256.

48. "Concept Release on SRO Structure." See generally S. Rep. No. 1455, 73d Cong., 2d Sess. (1934); H.R. Doc. No. 1383, 73d Cong., 2d Sess. (1934); S. Rep. No. 1455, 73d Cong., 2d Sess. (1934).

49. See "Concept Release on SRO Structure," 71256.

50. Dodd-Frank, Pub. L. No. 111-203, 124 Stat. 1376, Sec. 941 (2010).

51. Black, "Punishing Bad Brokers," 36. See generally Peirce, "Financial Industry Regulatory Authority."

52. *Self-Regulatory Organizations: Exploring the Need for Reform, Hearing before the Subcommittee on Capital Markets, Insurance, and Government Enterprises of the Committee*

on Financial Services of the US House of Representatives, 109th Cong., 1st Session (November 17, 2005) (statement of Robert R. Glauber, chairman and chief executive officer, NASD), 3.

53. Letter from Chair of the SEC Mary Jo White to SIFMA, July 31, 2013 (citing Gallagher, "Market 2012").

54. Ibid., 4.

55. See 17 C.F.R. 240.19b-4 and Form 19b-4.

56. FINRA, "Framework Regarding FINRA's Approach."

57. FINRA, "FINRA Issues Public Statement."

58. "Current Guidance on Economic Analysis."

59. This number was calculated from SEC, Current Broker-Dealer Information Report.

REFERENCES

Black, Barbara. "Punishing Bad Brokers: Self-Regulation and FINRA Sanctions." *Brooklyn Journal of Corporate, Financial, and Commercial Law* 8, no. 1 (2013): 24–55.

"Current Guidance on Economic Analysis in SEC Rulemakings." March 16, 2012. https://www.sec .gov/divisions/riskfin/rsfi_guidance_econ_analy_secrulemaking.pdf.

Federal Deposit Insurance Corporation (FDIC). "Failed Bank List." Retrieved August 8, 2016. https://www.fdic.gov/bank/individual/failed/banklist.html.

Financial Industry Regulatory Authority (FINRA). "FINRA Issues Public Statement, Framework Regarding FINRA's Economic Impact Assessment for Proposed Rulemaking." Press Release. September 19, 2013. https://www.finra.org/newsroom/2013/finra-issues-public-statement -framework-regarding-finras-approach-economic-impact.

———. "Framework Regarding FINRA's Approach to Economic Impact Assessment for Proposed Rulemaking." September 2013. https://www.finra.org/sites/default/files/Economic%20 Impact%20Assessment_0_0.pdf.

Gallagher, Daniel M. "Market 2012: Time for a Fresh Look at Equity Market Structure and Self-Regulation." Remarks to SIFMA's 15th Annual Market Structure Conference, October 4, 2012.

———. "The Philosophies of Capital Requirements." Remarks to the Exchequer Club, January 15, 2014.

Peirce, Hester. "The Financial Industry Regulatory Authority: Not Self-Regulation after All." Mercatus Working Paper, Mercatus Center at George Mason University, Arlington, VA, January 2015.

Securities Investor Protection Corporation (SIPC). "2015 Annual Report."

Sirri, Erik R. Remarks at the National Economist's Club: Securities Markets and Regulatory Reform. Washington, DC, April 9, 2009.

US Securities and Exchange Commission. Current Broker-Dealer Information Report. Retrieved August 8, 2016. https://www.sec.gov/foia/bdreports/bd080116.txt.

US Securities and Exchange Commission Staff. "Guide to Broker-Dealer Registration." April 2008. https://www.sec.gov/divisions/marketreg/bdguide.htm.

———. "Study on Investment Advisers and Broker-Dealers." US Securities and Exchange Commission, January 2011. https://www.sec.gov/news/studies/2011/913studyfinal.pdf.

CHAPTER 7
Reconsidering the Dodd-Frank Swaps Trading Regulatory Framework

HON. J. CHRISTOPHER GIANCARLO*
Commissioner, US Commodity Futures Trading Commission

T hough there were a number of factors said to have contributed to the financial crisis of 2008,[1] many contend that bilaterally executed over-the-counter (OTC) swaps amplified and spread the crisis.[2] In response, the US Congress enacted the Dodd-Frank Wall Street Reform and Consumer Protection Act (Dodd-Frank),[3] which imposed a new regulatory framework for the OTC swaps market. One of Dodd-Frank's major reforms is a requirement that counterparties execute most clearing-mandate swaps on regulated trading platforms—that is, swap execution facilities (SEFs)[4] or designated contract markets (DCMs).[5] In enacting this reform, Congress put forth a fairly simple and flexible swaps trading framework suited to the episodic nature of swaps liquidity.

This chapter analyzes the flaws in the implementation by the US Commodity Futures Trading Commission (CFTC) of the swaps trading regulatory frame-

---

*The views expressed in this chapter reflect the views of the author and do not necessarily reflect the views of the US Commodity Futures Trading Commission (CFTC), other CFTC commissioners, or CFTC staff. This chapter is drawn from the author's White Paper, dated January 29, 2015, entitled: "Pro-Reform Reconsideration of the CFTC Swaps Trading Rules: *Return to Dodd-Frank*."

work under Title VII of Dodd-Frank and proposes a more effective alternative.[6] It asserts that there is a fundamental mismatch between the CFTC's swaps trading regulatory framework and the distinct liquidity and trading dynamics of the global swaps market. It explains that the CFTC's framework is highly overengineered, disproportionately modeled on the US futures market, and biased against both human discretion and technological innovation. As such, the CFTC's framework does not accord with the letter or spirit of Title VII of Dodd-Frank.

The CFTC's flawed swaps trading rules are triggering numerous adverse consequences, foremost of which is driving global market participants away from transacting with entities subject to CFTC swaps regulation, resulting in fragmented global swaps markets. The rules have also carved swaps trading into numerous artificial market segments, fragmenting markets domestically. This fragmentation has exacerbated the already inherent challenge in swaps trading—adequate liquidity—and thus is increasing market fragility and the systemic risk that Dodd-Frank reforms were predicated on reducing.

The alternative regulatory framework outlined in this chapter is pro-reform. It is comprehensive in scope and more flexible in application. This alternative focuses on raising standards of professional conduct for swaps market personnel rather than dictating prescriptive and ill-suited trading rules. It provides flexibility so that market participants can choose the manner of trade execution best suited to their swaps trading and liquidity needs. It better aligns regulatory oversight with inherent swaps market dynamics. Crucially, the alternative framework fully aligns with Title VII of Dodd-Frank to promote swaps trading under CFTC regulation and attract, rather than repel, global capital to US trading markets. The alternative approach seeks to lessen the market fragility and fragmentation that have arisen as a consequence of the CFTC's flawed swaps trading regime.

THE DODD-FRANK SWAPS TRADING REGULATORY FRAMEWORK

Title VII of Dodd-Frank requires execution of most clearing-mandate swaps on DCMs or SEFs via a straightforward trade execution requirement.[7]

Congress expressly permitted SEFs to offer various flexible execution methods for swaps transactions using "any means of interstate commerce." The law defines a SEF as a "trading system or platform in which multiple participants have the ability to execute or trade swaps by accepting bids and offers made by multiple participants in the facility or system, through any means of interstate commerce, including any trading facility, that—(A) facilitates the execution of swaps between persons; and (B) is not a designated contract market."[8] Despite continuing assertions to the contrary from some observers, Congress did not require SEFs to provide electronic execution.

Additionally, Congress articulated goals, not requirements, for this SEF framework in order to maintain its flexibility. Congress set two goals for SEFs in Title VII of Dodd-Frank: to promote (1) the trading of swaps on SEFs and (2) pre-trade price transparency in the swaps market.[9] Congress did not prescribe that the global swaps market be carved into an isolated US domestic market and then further sliced and diced into smaller and smaller domestic markets for swaps trading.[10]

Congress mandated "impartial" access to swaps markets rather than "open" access. It did not require SEFs to merge dealer-to-client and dealer-to-dealer market segments.[11] Indeed, in providing that a SEF must establish rules to provide market participants with impartial access to the market, Dodd-Frank requires a SEF to set out any limitation on this access.[12] This requirement confirms that Dodd-Frank does not demand that all market participants receive access to every market. There is no mandate or impetus for an all-to-all swaps market structure in Dodd-Frank.

Congress further laid out a core principles-based framework for SEFs and provided them with reasonable discretion to comply with these principles.[13] In short, Congress left it up to individual SEFs, not regulators, to choose their own business model based on their customer needs.

In crafting Title VII of Dodd-Frank, Congress got much of it right.[14] Unfortunately, the CFTC's implementation of the swaps trading rules widely misses the congressional mark.

THE CFTC'S FLAWED SWAPS TRADING REGULATORY FRAMEWORK

In response to political pressure to hurry the implementation of Dodd-Frank and likely influenced by the naïve view that centralized order-driven markets are the best way to execute all derivatives transactions, the CFTC acted expediently and modeled its swaps trading rules on the well-known and readily available regulatory template of the US futures market. Unfortunately, that framework is mismatched to the natural commercial workings of the global swaps market. It is a square peg being forced into a round hole. In adopting this framework, the CFTC failed to properly respond to congressional intent and Dodd-Frank's express goal of promoting swaps trading on SEFs.[15]

Limits on Methods of Execution

The SEF rules create two categories of swaps transactions, Required Transactions (i.e., any transaction involving a swap that is subject to the trade execution requirement)[16] and Permitted Transactions (i.e., any transaction not involving a swap that is subject to the trade execution requirement),[17] and prescribe execution methods for each category.[18] Required Transactions must be executed in an order book (Order Book)[19] or a Request for Quote (RFQ) System in which a request for a quote is sent to three participants operating in conjunction with an Order Book (RFQ System).[20] Any method of execution is allowed for Permitted Transactions,[21] but SEFs must also offer an Order Book for such transactions.[22]

There is no firm statutory support for segmenting swaps into two categories or for limiting one of those categories to two methods of execution. A footnote to the preamble of the final SEF rules justifies this segmentation by stating that Commodity Exchange Act (CEA) section 2(h)(8) *"sets out specific trading requirements* for swaps that are subject to the trade execution mandate . . . [and] [t]o meet these statutory requirements, [the SEF rule] defines these swaps as Required Transactions and provides *specific methods of execution for such swaps."*[23] The only thing that CEA section 2(h)(8) expressly requires, however, is that swaps subject to the trade execution requirement must be executed on a SEF or DCM.[24] The statute nowhere references the concept of Required Transactions with limited execution methods and Permitted Transactions via any method of execution. These artificial categories unnecessarily complicate Congress's simple and flexible swaps trading framework.

Rather, Dodd-Frank's SEF definition contemplates a platform where multiple participants have the ability to execute swaps with multiple participants through any means of interstate commerce, including a trading facility.[25] Congress clearly drafted this broad and flexible definition to allow execution methods beyond an Order Book or RFQ System for all swaps, not just some swaps. Dodd-Frank also permits SEFs to offer swaps trading "through any means of interstate commerce." The phrase "interstate commerce" has a rich constitutional history, which US federal courts have interpreted to cover almost an unlimited range of commercial and technological enterprise.[26] The CFTC rule construct is not supported by the plain language of the statute and expresses a bias for two specific execution methods over all others: one drawn from the all-to-all US futures markets and one that is generally one-to-many, not multiple-to-multiple.

The CFTC's limited execution method approach also does not comport with the way swaps actually trade in global markets. Trillions of dollars of swaps trade globally each day through a variety of execution methods designed to better account for their episodic liquidity. A swap product's particular liquidity characteristics determine the execution technology and methodology, which can change over time. This liquidity continuum necessitates flexible execution methods as rightly authorized by Dodd-Frank.

CFTC swaps trading rules, however, thwart trade execution flexibility and limit needed human discretion.[27] By requiring SEFs to offer Order Books for all swaps, even very illiquid or bespoke swaps,[28] the rules embody the uninformed and parochial view that centralized order-driven markets, like those in the US futures markets, are the best way to execute transactions for swaps. That flawed view is not reflective of global swaps market reality. The unique nature of swaps trading liquidity should drive execution methods, not the other way around.

Block Transactions: "Occurs Away" from SEF

The CFTC block trade definition—specifically, the "occurs away" requirement—is another example of artificial segmentation like the contrived distinction between Required Transactions and Permitted Transactions. A "block trade" is generally a transaction between two institutional traders for a large amount of the same product. Most organized trading markets delay public reporting of block trades so that the counterparties can complete the transaction and any associated hedging without the market moving against them. A block trade is defined by the CFTC as "a publicly reportable swap transaction that: (1) Involves a swap that is listed on a registered [SEF] or [DCM]; (2) 'Occurs away' from the registered [SEF's] or [DCM's] trading system or platform and is executed pursuant to the registered [SEF's] or [DCM's] rules and procedures;

(3) Has a notional or principal amount at or above the appropriate minimum block size applicable to such swap; and (4) Is reported subject to the rules. . . ."[29]

It is unclear what is being achieved by the CFTC in requiring block trades to be executed away from the SEF's trading platform. The "occurs away" requirement creates an arbitrary and confusing segmentation between non-block trades "on-SEF" and block trades "off-SEF," especially given that a SEF may offer any method of execution for Permitted Transactions. The off-SEF requirement also undermines the legislative goal of encouraging swaps trading on SEFs.

The block trade definition is a holdover from the futures model.[30] In futures markets, block trades occur away from the DCM's trading facility as an exception to the centralized market requirement.[31] In today's global swaps market, however, there are no on-platform and off-platform execution distinctions for certain-sized swaps trades. OTC swaps generally trade in very large sizes. These swaps are not constrained to Central Limit Order Books (CLOBs), but trade through one of a variety of execution methods appropriate to the product's trading liquidity.

Congress recognized these differences by not imposing on SEFs an open and competitive centralized market requirement with corresponding exceptions for certain noncompetitive trades as contained in DCM Core Principle 9.[32] Congress knew that counterparties executed swaps on flexible trading platforms in very large sizes. Rather, Congress expressly authorized delayed reporting for block transactions.[33] Congress got it right. The CFTC got it wrong. Its swaps block trade definition is inappropriate and unwarranted.

Unsupported "Made Available to Trade" Process

Congress included a trade execution requirement in CEA section 2(h)(8) that requires SEF[34] execution for swaps subject to the clearing mandate.[35] In a simple exception to this requirement, Congress stated that this trade execution requirement does not apply if no SEF "makes the swap available to trade."[36]

Rather than follow Congress's simple direction, the CFTC created an unnecessary regulatory mandate, referred to as the "made available to trade" (MAT) process, in order to identify those swaps subject to SEF execution.[37] Under this platform-controlled MAT process, a SEF submits a MAT determination for swaps products to the Commission pursuant to part 40 of the

CFTC's regulations after considering, as appropriate, certain liquidity factors for such swaps.[38] The CFTC reviews the SEF's determination, but may only deny the submission if it is inconsistent with the CEA or CFTC regulations.[39] Once made available to trade, these swaps are Required Transactions and counterparties must execute them on a SEF pursuant to the limited execution methods permitted by CFTC rules.[40]

A plain reading of the trade execution requirement demonstrates that Congress did not intend to create an entire regulatory mandate around the phrase "made available to trade." Unlike the clearing mandate in CEA section 2(h)(1), Congress provided no process in CEA section 2(h)(8) for determining which swaps must be traded on-SEF.[41] Congress could have instituted a regulatory mandate for the trade execution requirement as it did for the clearing mandate, but chose not to.[42] Congressional drafters of Title VII were aware that, unlike futures, newly developed swaps products are initially traded bilaterally and only move to a platform once trading reaches a critical stage. The trade execution requirement expresses this logic by requiring that a clearing-mandated swap must be executed on a SEF unless no SEF makes that swap available to trade (i.e., offers the swap for trading). Unfortunately, however, congressional intent was not followed and an entire regulatory mandate was created based on nothing more than the phrase "makes the swap available to trade."

Beyond Impartial Access

Congress required SEFs to have rules to provide market participants with impartial access to the market and to establish rules regarding any limitation on access.[43] The Commission, through the preamble to the final SEF rules, and staff appear to view these provisions as requiring SEFs to serve every type of market participant in an all-to-all market structure.[44] Given Dodd-Frank's reference to *limitations* on access, however, efforts to require SEFs to serve every type of market participant or to operate all-to-all marketplaces are unsupported by law.

There is no mandate for an all-to-all swaps market structure in Dodd-Frank. Congress knew that there were dealer-to-customer and dealer-to-dealer swaps markets before Dodd-Frank, just as there are in many other mature financial markets.[45] This structure is driven by the unique liquidity characteristics of the underlying swaps products.[46] This dynamic has not changed post–Dodd-

Frank, and the law's impartial access provisions do not require or support the alteration of the present swaps market structure.[47]

Dodd-Frank does not prohibit SEFs from serving separate dealer-to-dealer and dealer-to-customer markets. Its impartial access requirement must not be confused with open access.[48] Impartial access, as the Commission noted in the preamble to the final SEF rules, means "fair, unbiased, and unprejudiced" access.[49] This means that SEFs should apply this important standard to their participants; it does not mean that SEFs are forced to serve every type of market participant in an all-to-all futures-style marketplace. Congress could have imposed this mandate, but it chose not to do so. Even the Commission acknowledged in the preamble to the final SEF rules that a SEF may operate different markets and may establish different access criteria for each of its markets.[50] This preamble language and the statutory language regarding "any limitation on access" are meaningless if CFTC staff act under the supposition that SEFs are required to operate business models with the capacity to serve every type of market participant.

Unwarranted Void *Ab Initio*

The staffs of the Division of Clearing and Risk and the Division of Market Oversight (the Divisions) issued guidance that states that "any [swap] trade that is executed on a SEF . . . and that is not accepted for clearing should be void *ab initio*" (i.e., invalid from the beginning).[51] The guidance also states that this result is consistent with CEA section 22(a)(4)(B), which prohibits participants in a swap from voiding a trade, but does not prohibit the Commission or a SEF from declaring a trade to be void.[52]

The statute does not support the Divisions' justification for this policy. Although CEA section 22(a)(4)(B) does not prohibit the Commission or a SEF from voiding a trade, it does not require this outcome if a trade is rejected from clearing.[53] This section also does not prevent a SEF from implementing rules that allow a participant to correct errors and resubmit a trade for clearing.[54]

The CFTC staff's void *ab initio* policy creates a competitive disadvantage for the US swaps market relative to the US futures market. There are legitimate reasons, such as operational or clerical errors, that cause swaps trades to be rejected from clearing. In the futures market, DCMs have implemented rules to address the situation where an executed futures transaction is rejected from clearing.[55] Furthermore, the void ab initio policy introduces additional risk into the system. For example, after a participant executes a swap, the participant enters into a series of other swaps to hedge its risk. If the first swap is declared void ab initio and there is no opportunity to resubmit the trade, then the participant will not be correctly hedged, which creates additional market and execution risk.

Expansive Scope for Uncleared Swaps Confirmations

Under CFTC rules, a SEF is required to provide "each counterparty to a transaction . . . with a written record of all of the terms of the transaction which shall legally supersede any previous agreement and serve as a confirmation of the transaction."[56] Additionally, responding to public comments about a SEF's confirmation for uncleared swaps, footnote 195 to the preamble of the final SEF rules states, in part, that "[t]here is no reason why a SEF's written confirmation terms cannot incorporate by reference the privately negotiated terms of a freestanding master agreement . . . provided that the master agreement is submitted to the SEF ahead of execution . . ."[57]

The CFTC's approach to SEF confirmations is taken from the futures model. DCMs own their futures contracts and control the products' standardized terms. SEFs, however, do not own swaps products. The products' terms are akin to an open-source design that sell-side dealers created with their buy-side customers. Additionally, swaps market participants have long relied on master agreements that govern the overall trading relationship between counterparties. These master agreements set out the nontransaction-specific credit and operational terms that apply to all transactions entered into under them. As a result, SEFs do not know or have access to all of a swap's terms and corresponding documentation. This paradigm has not changed post–Dodd-Frank for uncleared swaps transactions.

Importantly, a master agreement and a confirmation serve different purposes and should be thought of as different documents. The CFTC swap documentation rules recognize the importance and distinct purposes of these documents.[58] The rules define a master agreement as including "all terms governing the trading relationship between the [parties]"[59] and a swap confirmation as documentation that "memorializes the agreement of the counterparties to all of the terms of the *swap transaction*."[60] The two are as alike as apples and oranges.

The burden of requiring a SEF to confirm and report "all of the terms" of a trading relationship to which it is not a party is significant. Absent reconsideration, the SEF confirmation requirements will continue to be an obstacle for the trading of uncleared swaps on SEFs.

Embargo Rule and Name Give-Up

Under the embargo rule, a SEF may not disclose swap transaction and pricing data to its market participants until it transmits such data to a swap data repository (SDR) for public dissemination.[61] To effect such SDR transmission, a SEF must first enrich and convert such transaction data as required by the SDR. Alternatively, the SEF may choose to use a third-party provider to transmit data to an SDR. Only then can the SEF disclose swap transaction data to market participants on its trading platform.

The embargo rule causes delays in transaction and data disclosure that inhibit the long-established "workup" process, whereby counterparties buy or sell additional quantities of a swap immediately after its execution on the SEF at a price matching that of the original trade.[62] The workup process may increase wholesale trading liquidity in certain OTC swaps by as much as 50 percent.[63] This rule has hindered US markets from continuing a well-established and crucial global trading mechanism. The effect of the embargo rule appears to prioritize public transparency—in a market that is closed to the general public[64]—at the expense of transparency for actual participants in the marketplace. It is difficult to justify this unbalanced restraint on swaps liquidity.[65]

Similarly, name give-up is a long-standing market practice in many swaps markets. With name give-up, the identities of the counterparties are disclosed to each other after they have been anonymously matched by a platform.[66] The origins of the practice lie in wholesale markets for self-cleared swaps and other products. There, counterparties to large transactions use name give-up to confirm the creditworthiness of their counterparties.

In markets with central counterparty (CCP) clearing of swaps, however, the rationale for name give-up is less clear cut. That is because the CCP and not the trading counterparty bears the credit obligations. Counterparties to CCP-cleared swaps primarily need assurance of each other's relation to the CCP and not the opposing counterparty's individual credit standing.

As the swaps market increasingly becomes a cleared market, it is reasonable to ask whether name give-up continues to serve a valid purpose. There are a variety of different views on both sides of this issue depending on one's position in the market. Some parties have urged the CFTC to flat-out ban the practice of name give-up. Yet, the impact of such a step must be carefully considered before taking any action.[67] What impact would a blanket ban have on swaps market liquidity? Would such a ban cause sell-side dealers to remove liquidity from the market or charge higher prices? Would new liquidity makers fully and consistently act in the market to make up any shortfall in liquidity? Because market illiquidity is increasingly recognized as a potential systemic risk to the US financial system,[68] any regulatory action to curtail the use of name give-up must be thoroughly analyzed for its impact on market liquidity and systemic risk.[69]

Prescriptive Rules Disguised as Core Principles

Congress provided a core-principles-based framework for SEFs based on the CFTC's historical principles-based regulatory regime for DCMs.[70] Unfortunately, Dodd-Frank missed the mark with respect to the SEF core principles, most of which are based on the DCM core principles. The successful futures regulatory model is an inappropriate template for core principles in swaps execution.

This problem has been magnified by unwarranted amendments to CFTC rules making SEFs self-regulatory organizations (SROs)[71] and requiring them to comply with very prescriptive rules modeled after futures exchange practices that are unsuitable for the way swaps trade. Although the SEF core principles place certain regulatory obligations on SEFs, Dodd-Frank does not require the CFTC to make SEFs SROs.[72] Additionally, it does not instruct the Commission to take a prescriptive rules-based approach to SEFs.[73] In fact, the statute provides SEFs with reasonable discretion to comply with the core principles.[74]

ADVERSE CONSEQUENCES OF THE CFTC'S SWAPS TRADING REGULATORY FRAMEWORK

Given the mismatch between the CFTC's flawed swaps trading regulatory framework and the manner in which swaps trade in global markets, the CFTC's swaps trading rules are threatening to cause and, in several cases, have already caused numerous adverse consequences for US market participants.

Global Market Fragmentation and Systemic Risk

Foremost among the adverse consequences is the reluctance of global market participants to transact with entities subject to CFTC swaps regulation. Non-US persons are avoiding financial firms bearing the scarlet letters of "US person" in certain swaps products to steer clear of the CFTC's problematic regulations.[75] As a result, global swaps markets are fragmenting into US person and non-US person liquidity pools.[76] The fragmentation of the global swaps market has fractured trading liquidity, exacerbating the inherent challenge of swaps trading— adequate liquidity.[77] Fragmentation has led to smaller, disconnected liquidity pools and less efficient and more volatile pricing. Divided markets are more brittle, with shallower liquidity, posing a risk of failure in times of economic stress or crisis.

Domestic Market Fragmentation

The CFTC's unwarranted slicing and dicing of swaps trading into a series of novel regulatory categories, such as Required Transactions and Permitted Transactions and block transactions "off-SEF" and non-blocks "on-SEF," has fragmented the US swaps market into artificial market segments. Like global fragmentation, domestic fragmentation has led to an artificial series of smaller and smaller pools of trading liquidity and increased market inefficiency.

Market Liquidity Risk

Several government studies and industry observations have focused on the liquidity shortfall in corporate and US government debt markets.[78] CFTC regulations and staff actions may be hazarding a similar structural imbalance between liquidity provided and liquidity demanded in the US swaps markets.[79]

Threatens SEF Survival

The CFTC's swaps regime threatens the survival of many SEFs and has erected enormous barriers to entry for future registrants. The CFTC's prescriptive and burdensome rules have ensured that operating a SEF is an expensive, legally intensive activity.[80] And the mismatch between the CFTC's swaps trading framework and the natural commercial workings of the swaps market has caused participants to avoid the CFTC's SEF regime, sharply depressing revenues.[81] As a result, big platforms get bigger, small platforms get squeezed out, and operating a SEF is unprofitable.[82]

Hinders Technological Innovation

In 1899, US Patent Commissioner Charles H. Duell is said to have pronounced that "everything that can be invented has been invented."[83] Not to be outdone, the CFTC's swaps trading rules presuppose that order book and RFQ methodologies are today and will always remain the only suitable technological means for US swaps execution. These restrictive SEF rules would close US swaps markets to promising technological advances while the rest of the world proceeds ahead in financial market innovation.[84]

Wastes Taxpayer Dollars

Fitting the square peg of the CFTC's swaps trading rules into the round hole of the established global swaps markets requires the CFTC to devote enormous resources to continuously explain, clarify, adjust, exempt, and manipulate rules sufficient for rough swaps market operability. The CFTC's current swaps trading regulatory framework requires enormous bureaucratic "make work" to ensure industry compliance. Yet, it is mostly unnecessary and unsupported by Title VII of Dodd-Frank. It wastes taxpayer dollars at a time when the Commission is seeking additional resources from Congress.

Harms Relations with Foreign Regulators

Instead of working with its counterparts abroad as agreed to by the Group of Twenty (G20),[85] the CFTC forged ahead with overreaching swaps rules, which are partially responsible for harming relations with foreign regulators. It is clear that Organized Trading Facilities (OTFs) under European swaps trading rules will not be similarly hidebound by CFTC-like restrictions in methods of trade execution, nor will swaps platforms in Singapore or Hong Kong.[86] This mismatch between CFTC and European rules may well be the basis down the road for another "equivalency" standoff similar to the prolonged dispute over central counterparty recognition.[87]

Threatens Job Creation and Human Discretion

The application of certain CFTC rules threatens jobs in the US financial services industry. Many overseas trading firms are considering cutting off all activity with US-based trade support personnel to avoid subjecting themselves to the CFTC's flawed swaps trading rules.[88] Also, underlying many CFTC rules is an unstated bias against human discretion in swaps execution.[89] Yet there is no legal support in Title VII of Dodd-Frank for restricting human discretion in swaps execution.

Increases Market Fragility

Nassim Nicholas Taleb, the well-known options trader who coined the phrase "black swan," has written about the increased fragility of today's top-down-designed, overly complicated economic systems.[90] He warns that naïve over-intervention in complex systems such as financial markets makes them more vulnerable, not less, to cascading runaway chains of reactions and ultimately fragile in the face of outsized crisis events.[91] The CFTC swaps trading rules, with their prescriptive complexity, limits on human discretion, and transaction methodology bias, seem to support this type of systemic fragility. That fragility increases rather than decreases the systemic risk—the risk of failure of the swaps markets and the broader US financial system—that Dodd-Frank was ostensibly designed to reduce.

ALTERNATIVE SWAPS TRADING REGULATORY FRAMEWORK

This section proposes a pro-reform reconsideration of many of the CFTC's swaps trading rules to align with natural swaps market dynamics and the express statutory framework of Title VII of Dodd-Frank. This reconsideration is drawn from five key tenets: comprehensiveness, cohesiveness, flexibility, professionalism, and transparency.

Comprehensiveness

The first tenet of this alternative framework is to subject a comprehensive range of US swaps trading to CFTC oversight. In this respect, the CFTC implemented a broad SEF registration requirement that applies "to facilities that meet the SEF definition in CEA section 1a(50)."[92] This alternative framework supports that comprehensive approach. Congress generally intended to bring all facilities for swaps trading into a comprehensive regulatory structure through its broad SEF registration provision.[93] Leaving platforms that solely facilitate the execution of swaps not subject to the trade execution mandate outside of CFTC oversight, and those that facilitate swaps subject to the mandate within creates bifurcated regulated and unregulated markets and invites abuses and evasion.[94]

The alternative approach proposed hereby adopts the CFTC's registration approach, but in a clear and noncircuitous manner. The scope of SEF registration would be defined through rules and not buried footnotes in the preamble text.[95] Similarly, all key components of the CFTC's swaps rules would reside in clear and definitive rule text and not in footnotes, staff advisories, and ad hoc no-action letters.

Cohesiveness

The second tenet of this alternative framework is regulatory cohesiveness. All CFTC-regulated swaps trading should fall within the same, cohesive, and undivided regulatory framework. This approach would remove the artificial segmentation between Required Transactions and their limited execution methods and Permitted Transactions and their broad execution methods, and between block transactions "off-SEF" and non-blocks "on-SEF." There is no statutory support for these divisions. They carry no ostensible policy justification. They are at odds with accepted global practices of swaps trading and hinder liquidity formation. They add large and unjustifiable regulatory costs and burdens and absorb limited agency resources.

Flexibility

This straightforward, comprehensive, and cohesive approach will only work if the CFTC returns to Dodd-Frank's express prescription for flexibility in swaps trading. This alternative framework proposes congressionally authorized flexibility in five key areas:

1. *Permitting trade execution through "any means of interstate commerce."* Markets, not regulators, must determine the various means of interstate commerce utilized in the swaps market, as Congress intended.

2. *Allowing swaps products to evolve naturally.* Follow Dodd-Frank's trade execution requirement and do away with the CFTC-created MAT process.

3. *Letting market structure be determined by the market.* Let market participants determine the optimal market structure (i.e., all-to-all markets or separate dealer-to-dealer and dealer-to-client marketplaces) based on their swaps trading needs and objectives.

4. *Accommodating beneficial swaps market practices.* Allow SEFs to implement workable error trade policies; narrow the scope of confirmations for uncleared swaps; better accommodate the activities of third-party commercial service providers, such as swaps data vendors, trade term affirmation providers, and trade confirmation vendors and allow compression, risk reduction, risk recycling, dynamic hedging, and other similar services.

5. *Treating core principles as general principles.* Implement a flexible core principles–based approach for SEFs that aligns with the way swaps actually trade.

Professionalism

The fourth tenet of this alternative framework is to raise standards of professionalism in the swaps market by setting standards of conduct for swaps market personnel. Rather than implementing highly prescriptive swaps trading rules that seek to limit the discretion of intermediaries (e.g., interdealer brokers, futures commission merchants [FCMs], introducing brokers [IBs]) through ill-suited execution methods, this alternative framework proposes to establish standards that would enhance the knowledge, professionalism, and ethics of personnel in the US swaps markets who exercise discretion in facilitating swaps execution.

It is noteworthy that US individuals who wish to broker or sell equities or debt securities must register with the US Securities and Exchange Commission (SEC) and join an SRO.[96] They must also pass the Series 7 exam, which seeks to measure the knowledge, skills, and abilities needed to perform the functions of a registered securities representative.[97] Similarly, in US futures markets certain persons must register with the CFTC and National Futures Association (NFA), a futures industry self-regulatory organization. Generally, all applicants for NFA membership must pass the Series 3 exam that seeks to measure futures markets proficiency.[98] Yet there is currently no examination that one must pass in the United States to broker swaps. There is no standardized measurement of one's knowledge and qualification to act with discretion in the world's largest and, arguably, most systemically important financial market—swaps.[99]

Transparency

The last tenet of this alternative framework focuses on promoting swaps trading and market liquidity as a prerequisite to increased transparency. The right measure of pre- and post-trade transparency can benefit market liquidity, but absolute and immediate transparency can harm liquidity and trading.[100] The regulatory objective must be to strike the right balance. Markets as complex as the swaps markets, where adequate liquidity is already a challenge, require care in the imposition of transparency mandates to ensure that this liquidity is not harmed.

Congress understood the liquidity challenge in the swaps market and thus set two goals for SEFs to be balanced against each other: (a) promoting the trading of swaps on SEFs and (b) promoting pre-trade price transparency in the swaps market. To date, CFTC rules have put greater weight on the side of the scale of pre-trade price transparency to the detriment of healthy trading liquidity.

A better way to promote price transparency is through a balanced focus on promoting swaps trading and market liquidity as Congress intended. Instead of taking a prescriptive approach to swaps execution that drives away participants, this framework would allow the market to innovate and provide execution through "any means of interstate commerce." That way, participants could choose the execution method that meets their needs based on a swap's liquidity characteristics, which in turn, responds to Congress's direction to promote trading on SEFs and liquidity.

CONCLUSION

The pro-reform proposals that I have set forth are a package. They stand together as a comprehensive whole. It would serve little purpose to reassert the broad reach of SEF registration without easing the rigid inflexibility of the CFTC's swap transaction rules. It would make little sense to seek to improve standards of participant conduct without removing the unwarranted restraints on their professional discretion. It would be pointless to seek greater market transparency while continuing to thwart market liquidity. These proposals work together to achieve the aims of Title VII of Dodd-Frank to improve the safety and soundness of the US swaps market. They should not be adopted on a piecemeal basis.

A smarter and more flexible swaps regulatory framework would enable the United States to take the global lead in smart regulation of swaps trading. It would allow American businesses to more efficiently hedge commercial risks, promoting economic growth. Such a framework would also stimulate the American jobs market. A smarter swaps regulatory regime would return to the express letter and language of Title VII of Dodd-Frank. It would eschew the artificial slicing and dicing of US trading liquidity and unwarranted restrictions on means of execution that are unsupported by the law. For decades the CFTC has been a competent and effective regulator of US exchange-traded derivatives. The opportunity is at hand to continue that excellence in regulating swaps markets. It is time to seize that opportunity.

NOTES

1. Financial Crisis Inquiry Commission, *The Financial Crisis Inquiry Report.*

2. Ibid., 45–51, 308, 343, 352, and 386. For dissenting views, ibid., 414, 426–27, and 447; and Tuckman, "In Defense of Derivatives."

3. Dodd-Frank Wall Street Reform and Consumer Protection Act, Pub. L. No. 111-203, 124 Stat. 1376 (2010).

4. A SEF is defined as a trading platform where multiple participants have the ability to execute or trade swaps by accepting the bids and offers of multiple participants on the platform, "through any means of interstate commerce." CEA § 1a(50); 7 U.S.C. § 1a(50).

5. 17 C.F.R. § 1.3(a) and (h); CEA § 2(h)(8); 7 U.S.C. § 2(h)(8).

6. In this chapter I argue, among other points, that the CFTC failed to follow its legislative mandate under Dodd-Frank in promulgating its swaps trading rules. I do not, however, seek to express a view as to whether the CFTC exceeded its general regulatory authority or acted in an arbitrary and capricious manner contrary to law.

7. CEA § 2(h)(8); 7 U.S.C. § 2(h)(8).

8. CEA § 1a(50); 7 U.S.C. § 1a(50).

9. CEA § 5h(e); 7 U.S.C. § 7b-3(e).

10. See the subsequent section in this chapter on the CFTC's Flawed Swaps Trading Regulatory Framework.

11. Given the episodic liquidity in many of the swaps markets, they have generally evolved over the past several decades into two-tiered marketplaces for institutional market participants; that is, "dealer to customer" marketplaces and "dealer to dealer" marketplaces. Traditionally, liquidity "taking" counterparties turn to sell-side dealers with large balance sheets that are willing to take on the liquidity risk in the swaps markets for a fee. Sell-side dealers then turn to the dealer-to-dealer marketplaces to instantly hedge the market risk of their large swaps inventory by trading with other primary dealers and sophisticated market-making participants. Dealers price their customer trades based on the cost of hedging those trades in the dealer-to-dealer markets. Without access to dealer-to-dealer markets, the risk inherent in holding swaps inventory would arguably require dealers to charge their buy-side customers much higher prices for taking on their liquidity risk, assuming they remained willing to do so.

12. CEA § 5h(f)(2); 7 U.S.C. § 7b-3(f)(2).

13. CEA § 5h(f)(1)(B); 7 U.S.C. § 7b-3(f)(1)(B).

14. Dodd-Frank missed the mark with respect to the SEF core principles. Most of the SEF core principles are based on the DCM core principles. Compare 7 U.S.C. § 7(d) (enumerating DCM core principles, including enforcement of exchange rules, monitoring of trading, recordkeeping and reporting, establishing position limits, adopting rules for emergency authority, requirements for financial resources, etc.), with 7 U.S.C. § 7b-3(f) (setting forth extremely similar core principles applicable to SEFs). However, the futures regulatory model is inappropriate for swaps trading, given the different liquidity and market structure characteristics of swaps.

15. CEA § 5h(e); 7 U.S.C. § 7b-3(e).

16. 17 C.F.R. § 37.9(a)(1).

17. 17 C.F.R. § 37.9(c)(1).

18. 17 C.F.R. §§ 37.9(a)(2) and 37.9(c)(2).

19. 17 C.F.R. §§ 37.3(a)(2), 37.3(a)(3), and 37.9(a)(2).

20. 17. C.F.R. §§ 37.9(a)(2) and 37.9(a)(3).

21. 17 C.F.R. § 37.9(c)(2).

22. 17 C.F.R. § 37.3(a)(2); "Core Principles and Other Requirements for Swap Execution Facilities," 78 Fed. Reg. (June 4, 2013): 33476, 33504.

23. SEF Rule at 33493n216 (emphasis added). The Commission further stated that to "distinguish these swaps from other swaps that are not subject to the trade execution mandate, [the SEF rule] defines such swaps . . . as Permitted Transactions and allows these swaps to be voluntarily traded on a SEF by using any method of execution." Ibid.

24. CEA § 2(h)(8); 7 U.S.C. § 2(h)(8).

25. CEA § 1a(50); 7 U.S.C. § 1a(50). I assert the context in which it is used makes clear that the reference to "interstate commerce" is substantive rather than a statement of Constitutional jurisdiction. See also SEF Rule at 33501.

26. See, for example, Gonzales v. Raich, 545 U.S. 1, 17 (2005); Katzenbach v. McClung, 379 U.S. 294, 302 (1964); Wickard v. Filburn, 317 U.S. 111, 125 (1942).

27. 17 C.F.R. § 37.9(a)(2).

28. See SEF Rule at 33504 (clarifying that a SEF must offer an Order Book for Permitted Transactions).

29. 17 C.F.R. § 43.2.

30. See "Alternative Executive, or Block Trading, Procedures for the Futures Industry," 64 Fed. Reg. (June 10, 1999): 31195; "Chicago Board of Trade's Proposal to Adopt Block Trading Procedures," 65 Fed. Reg. (September 27, 2000): 58051.

31. 17 C.F.R. § 38.500.

32. Ibid.

33. CEA § 2(a)(13)(E); 7 U.S.C. § 2(a)(13)(E). Established marketplaces worldwide have long recognized that for less liquid products where a smaller number of primary dealers and market makers cross larger size transactions, the disclosure of the intention of a major institution to buy or sell could disrupt the market and lead to poor pricing. If a provider of liquidity to the market perceives greater danger in supplying liquidity, it will step away from providing tight spreads and leave those reliant on that liquidity with poorer hedging opportunities. Hence, large size or "block" trades are generally afforded a time delay before their details are reported to the marketplace.

34. The trade execution requirement and the Commission's made available to trade process pertain to DCMs as well. Given this chapter's focus on SEFs, the references to DCMs in this section have been omitted.

35. CEA § 2(h)(8); 7 U.S.C. § 2(h)(8).

36. Ibid.

37. Ibid.; 17 C.F.R. §§ 37.10, 37.12, 38.11 and 38.12; "Process for a Designated Contract Market or Swap Execution Facility to Make a Swap Available to Trade, Swap Transaction Compliance and Implementation Schedule, and Trade Execution Requirement under the Commodity Exchange Act," 78 Fed. Reg. (June 4, 2013): 33606.

38. 17 C.F.R. §§ 37.10(a), (b), 38.12(a) and (b).

39. MAT Rule at 33607 and 33610. It is doubtful that the Commission could find that a MAT submission is inconsistent with the CEA or Commission regulations because neither the CEA nor the regulations contain any objective requirements that a swap must meet for a MAT determination to be valid.

40. 17 C.F.R. §§ 37.9(a)(1), 37.9(a)(2), 37.10, 37.12, 38.11, and 38.12.

41. Compare CEA §§ 2(h)(1), 2(h)(2) and 2(h)(3); 7 U.S.C. §§ 2(h)(1), 2(h)(2) and 2(h)(3), *with* CEA § 2(h)(8); § 7 U.S.C. § 2(h)(8).

42. Ibid.

43. CEA § 5h(f)(2); 7 U.S.C. § 7b-3(f)(2).

44. SEF Rule at 33507–8.

45. See supra note 14. Many swaps markets have evolved into two-tiered marketplaces for institutional market participants given the episodic liquidity in these markets.

46. Ibid.

47. In a McKinsey report, an overwhelming majority of buy-side participants interviewed acknowledged the important role that dealers play in providing liquidity and were "not interested in disintermediating dealers. . . ." See "Brave New World of SEFs," 5–6.

48. Open access is generally understood to mean universal, unrestricted access to all market participants.

49. SEF Rule at 33508.

50. Ibid.

51. US Commodity Futures Trading Commission, "Staff Guidance on Swaps."

52. Ibid.

53. CEA § 22(a)(4)(B); 7 U.S.C. § 25(a)(4)(B).

54. Ibid.

55. See, for example, Chicago Mercantile Exchange (CME) Rule 527.C. Outtrades Resolution, http://www.cmegroup.com/rulebook/CME/I/5/5.pdf; CME Rule 809.D. Reconciliation of Outtrades, http://www.cmegroup.com/rulebook/CME/I/8/8.pdf.

56. 17 C.F.R. § 37.6(b).

57. SEF Rule at 33491n195.

58. Compare 17 C.F.R. § 23.501 Swap Confirmation, with 17 C.F.R. § 23.504 Swap Trading Relationship Documentation.

59. 17 C.F.R. § 23.504(b)(1).

60. 17 C.F.R. § 23.500(c) (emphasis added).

61. 17 C.F.R. § 43.3(b)(3).

62. See SEF Rule at 33500 (explaining the workup process).

63. Author's professional observation based on marketplace experience.

64. The swaps market is closed to participants that are not eligible contract participants. CEA § 1a(18); 7 U.S.C. § 1a(18).

65. The preamble to the final real-time reporting rule did not respond to a public comment about the embargo rule's impact on the workup process. "Real-Time Public Reporting of Swap Transaction Data," 77 Fed. Reg. (January 9, 2012): 1182, 1200–2.

66. For example, after counterparties execute a swap through an anonymous order book, the identities of the counterparties are disclosed to each other. See Madigan, "CFTC to Test Role of Anonymity," discussing the name give-up issue; Burne, "CFTC to Look into Disclosure."

67. A question remains whether the CFTC has such authority under Dodd-Frank.

68. US Treasury Department, Office of Financial Research, 2014 Annual Report.

69. See the subsequent section on Adverse Consequences of the CFTC's Swaps Trading Regulatory Framework.

70. CEA § 5h(f); 7 U.S.C. § 7b-3(f).

71. 17 C.F.R. § 1.3(ee). "Adaptation of Regulations to Incorporate Swaps," 77 Fed. Reg. (November 2, 2012): 66288, 66290.

72. Ibid.

73. CEA § 5h(f)(1)(B); 7 U.S.C. § 7b-3(f)(1)(B).

74. Ibid.

75. Blater, "Cross-Border Fragmentation," says "the fracturing of the global interest rate swaps market that emerged in the aftermath of US swap execution facility rules coming into force in October 2013 shows no signs of reversing"; Stafford, "CFTC Calls for International Help," indicates that because of recent CFTC regulations, "Sefs have become US-centric venues [which] has led to concern that the market is fragmenting, damaging both economic growth and contributing to potential systemic market risk"; Stafford, "US Swaps Trading Rules," notes that "European dealers [have become] unwilling to trade with US counterparts" due to CFTC regulations; Burne, "Big U.S. Banks Make Swaps," notes that some banks are "changing the terms of some swap agreements made by their offshore units so they don't get caught by U.S. regulations."

76. Ibid.

77. Referring to the manifest liquidity split between London and New York, Dexter Senft, Morgan Stanley's co-head of fixed income electronic markets, said, "I liken [SEF liquidity] to a canary in a coal mine. It's not dead yet, but it's lying on its side." Hunter, "Growing Pains," 31. See also Burne, "Companies Warn of Swaps," on fragmentation and liquidity concerns.

78. The IMF ("Global Financial Stability Report," 49–53) explains that "unconventional monetary policies involving protracted, large-scale asset purchases" have depleted market liquidity by "drastically reduc[ing] the net supply of certain securities available to investors." The Bank for International Settlements ("85th Annual Report," 36–40) cites the increasing "liquidity illusion" in which credit markets appear liquid and well-functioning in normal times, only to become highly illiquid upon market shock. See also Krouse, "Wall Street Bemoans Bond Market"; Jersey and Marshall, "Interest Rate Strategy Focus," 3–5.

79. Madigan, "US End-Users Are Losers."

80. Contiguglia, "Sef Boss Spends His Days."

81. Ibid.

82. See Market Concentration section of Guest Lecture of Commissioner J. Christopher Giancarlo, Harvard Law School, Fidelity Guest Lecture Series on International Finance, December 1, 2015.

83. *Wikipedia's* "Charles Holland Duell" entry also states that this statement has been debunked as apocryphal.

84. Because of the technological transformation of markets, it is no surprise that a global contest is afoot among world financial centers to attract a new generation of financial technology ("FinTech") and the jobs it will create. In fact, investment in the British FinTech sector already exceeds that of New York. One key reason is the relative simplicity, transparency and innovation-friendly approach of British regulators. In contrast, US regulatory frameworks are seen as complex, conservative and, in some respects, opaque with limited regulatory initiatives directed toward financial technology. See generally Ernst and Young, UK FinTech, "On the Cutting Edge." I proposed five practical steps for the CFTC to encourage financial technology innovation: employ FinTech savvy regulatory staff, give FinTech firms "breathing room" to develop, collaborate in commercial FinTech experiments, listen and learn where

rules need to be adapted for technical advances and collaborate with other regulators here and abroad. See Giancarlo, "Blockchain."

85. At the 2009 Pittsburgh G20 Summit, one year after the financial crisis, global leaders agreed to work together to support economic recovery through a "Framework for Strong, Sustainable and Balanced Growth." The Pittsburgh participants pledged to work together to "implement global standards" in financial markets while rejecting "protectionism." See "G20 Leaders' Statement," 7, 20, 22.

86. See Statement of Edwin Schooling Latter, Head of Markets Policy, UK Financial Conduct Authority: "We're not prescriptive in the EU about the execution methods that the venues have to employ. So, for example, taking MTFs [multilateral trading facilities] and OTFs, they can use central limit order books, they can have quote-driven systems, they can do RFQ, they can use undeveloped hybrids of all of those." Division of Market Oversight (DMO) Public Roundtable regarding the Made Available to Trade Process, archived webcast, July 15, 2015, http://www.cftc.gov/PressRoom/Events/opaevent_cftcstaff071515. See also Regulation 600/2014, 2014 O.J. (L173) 85-86 (EU).

87. Brunsden and Stafford, "EU and US Strike Derivatives Regulation Deal."

88. CFTC Staff Advisory No. 13-69, "Applicability of Transaction-Level Requirements to Activity in the United States," November 14, 2013; CFTC Letter No. 16-64, "Extension of No-Action Relief: Transaction-Level Requirements for Non-US Swap Dealers," August 4, 2016.

89. The bias is seen in a range of CFTC positions, including allowing only two specific types of execution methods for Required Transactions, requiring an RFQ System to operate in conjunction with an Order Book, requiring an RFQ to be sent to three market participants, and placing various conditions around basis risk mitigation services.

90. See generally Taleb, *Antifragile*.

91. Ibid.

92. 17 C.F.R. § 37.3(a)(I); SEF Rule at 33481, 33483.

93. The SEF registration requirement states that "no person may operate a facility for the trading or processing of swaps unless the facility is registered as a [SEF] or as a [DCM] under this section." CEA § 5h(a)(1); 7 U.S.C. § 7b-3(a)(1).

94. For example, a platform meeting the SEF definition could shift its offerings to eliminate swaps imminently subject to a trade execution mandate in order to stay outside of CFTC oversight.

95. See SEF Rule at 33481n88.

96. See SEC, "Guide to Broker-Dealer Registration," April 2008.

97. See Financial Industry Regulatory Authority, General Securities Representative Qualification Examination (Series 7) Content Outline (2015), retrieved August 12, 2016, http://www.finra.org/web/groups/industry/@ip/@comp/@regis/documents/industry/p124292.pdf.

98. See NFA, "Registration: Who Has to Register," retrieved August 12, 2016, http://www.nfa.futures.org/NFA-registration/index.HTML; NFA, "Proficiency Requirements," http://www.nfa.futures.org/NFA-registration/proficiency-requirements.HTML; NFA, "Examination Subject Areas National Commodity Futures Exam," http://www.nfa.futures.org/NFA-registration/study-outlines/SO-Series3.pdf.

99. Dodd-Frank requires registration of swap dealers (SDs) and major swap participants (MSPs) and directed the CFTC to promulgate specific business conduct requirements and "such

other standards and requirements as the Commission may determine are appropriate in the public interest, for the protection of investors, or otherwise in furtherance of the purposes of this Act." CEA §§ 4s(a), 4s(h) and 4s(h)(3)(D); 7 U.S.C. §§ 6s(a), 6s(h) and 6s(h)(3)(D). Pursuant to this direction the Commission issued business conduct standards for SDs and MSPs in Part 23 of its regulations. Those regulations do not require any sort of proficiency testing, however. Moreover, associated persons of SDs and MSPs are not required to register under Dodd-Frank or the Commission's regulations. See "Registration of Swap Dealers and Major Swap Participants," 77 Fed. Reg. (January 19, 2012): 2613.

100. There are historical examples of markets that have sought to achieve full market transparency without adequate exemptions. In 1986, the London Stock Exchange (LSE) enacted post-trade reporting rules designed for total transparency with no exceptions for block sizes. What ensued was a sharp drop in trading liquidity as market makers withdrew from the market due to increased trading risk. To bring back trading, the LSE thereafter engaged in a series of amendments to make its block trade rules more flexible and detailed over time. See, for example, ISDA and SIFMA, "Block Trade Reporting," 8–9.

REFERENCES

Bank for International Settlements. "85th Annual Report." Basel, June 28, 2015.

Blater, Audrey Costabile. "Cross-Border Fragmentation of Global Interest Rate Derivatives: Second Half 2015 Update." International Swaps and Derivatives Association Research Note, May 10, 2016, 1–6.

"The Brave New World of SEFs: How Broker-Dealers Can Protect Their Franchises." McKinsey and Company Working Paper No. 4 on Corporate and Investment Banking, June 2014.

Brunsden, Jim, and Philip Stafford. "EU and US Strike Derivatives Regulation Deal." *Financial Times*, February 10, 2016. http://www.ft.com/cms/s/0/b7f72eda-cfef-11e5-92a1-c5e23e f99c77.html#axzz4J2AgI4xV.

Burne, Katy. "Companies Warn of Swaps Rules' Impact on Hedging." *Wall Street Journal*, April 8, 2014. http://www.wsj.com/articles/SB10001424052702304819004579489493056041978 ?autologin=y.

———. "Big U.S. Banks Make Swaps a Foreign Affair." *Wall Street Journal*, April 27, 2014. http://www .wsj.com/articles/SB10001424052702304788404579520302570888332?autologin=y.

———. "CFTC to Look into Disclosure of Identities of Swap Counterparties." *Wall Street Journal*, November 12, 2014. http://www.wsj.com/articles/cftc-to-look-into-disclosure-of-identities -of-swap-counterparties-1415834947.

Contiguglia, Catherine. "Sef Boss Spends His Days 'Worrying about Costs.' " *Risk.net*. September 24, 2014. http://www.risk.net/risk-magazine/news/2371788/sef-boss-spends-his -days-worrying-about-costs.

Ernst and Young, UK FinTech. "On the Cutting Edge: An Evaluation of the International FinTech Sector." 2016. https://www.gov.uk/government/uploads/system/uploads/attachment_data /file/502995/UK_FinTech_-_On_the_cutting_edge_-_Full_Report.pdf.

Financial Crisis Inquiry Commission. *The Financial Crisis Inquiry Report: Final Report of the National Commission on the Causes of the Financial and Economic Crisis in the United States.* Washington, DC: US Government Printing Office, 2011.

Giancarlo, J. Christopher. "Pro-Reform Reconsideration of the CFTC Swaps Trading Rules: *Return to Dodd-Frank*." White Paper, US Commodity Futures Trading Commission,

January 29, 2015. http://www.cftc.gov/idc/groups/public/@newsroom/documents/file/sefwhitepaper012915.pdf.

———. "Blockchain: A Regulatory Use Case." Keynote Address before the Markit Group, 2016 Annual Customer Conference, New York, May 10, 2016.

The Group of Twenty (G20) Leaders' Statement at the Pittsburgh Summit. September 24–25, 2009. http://www.treasury.gov/resource-center/international/g7-g20/Documents/pittsburgh _summit_leaders_statement_250909.pdf.

Hunter, Kim. "Growing Pains." *Markit Magazine*, Winter 2014, 31–34.

International Monetary Fund (IMF). "Global Financial Stability Report." October 2015.

International Swaps and Derivatives Association (ISDA) and SIFMA, "Block Trade Reporting for Over-the-Counter Derivatives Markets." January 18, 2011. http://www.isda.org/speeches/pdf /Block-Trade-Reporting.pdf.

Jersey, Ira, and William Marshall. "Interest Rate Strategy Focus: Downside of Prudential Regulation: Lower Liquidity." Credit Suisse. May 8, 2014. https://plus.credit-suisse.com /researchplus/ravDocView?docid=tiK8uA.

Krouse, Sarah. "Wall Street Bemoans Bond Market Liquidity Squeeze." *Wall Street Journal*, June 2, 2015. http://blogs.wsj.com/moneybeat/2015/06/02/wall-street-bemoans-bond-market -liquidity-squeeze/.

Madigan, Peter. "US End-Users Are Losers in Swaps Liquidity Split." *Risk.net*. April 28, 2014. http://www.risk.net/risk-magazine/feature/2340854/us-end-users-are-the-losers-in-swaps -liquidity-split.

———. "CFTC to Test Role of Anonymity in Sef Order Book Flop." *Risk.net*. November 21, 2014. http://www.risk.net/risk-magazine/feature/2382497/cftc-to-test-role-of-anonymity-in-sef -order-book-flop.

Stafford, Philip. "US Swaps Trading Rules Have 'Split Market.'" *Financial Times*, January 21, 2014. http://www.ft.com/intl/cms/s/0/58251f84-82b8-11e3-8119-00144feab7de .html#axzz3CHQbMKxU.

———. "CFTC Calls for International Help on Derivatives Oversight." *Financial Times*, November 14, 2014. http://www.ft.com/intl/cms/s/0/3aeabbb0-6b63-11e4-9337 -00144feabdc0.html#axzz3OX6k3roi.

Taleb, Nassim Nicholas. *Antifragile: Things That Gain from Disorder.* New York: Random House 2012.

Tuckman, Bruce. "In Defense of Derivatives." Cato Institute Policy Analysis No. 781, Washington, DC, September 29, 2015.

US Commodity Futures Trading Commission Staff. "Staff Guidance on Swaps Straight-Through Processing." September 26, 2013. http://www.cftc.gov/ucm/groups/public/@newsroom /documents/file/stpguidance.pdf.

US Treasury Department, Office of Financial Research. "2014 Annual Report." December 2, 2014, 30–33.

CHAPTER 8
Rethinking the Swaps Clearing Mandate

HESTER PEIRCE AND VERA SOLIMAN*
Mercatus Center at George Mason University

T he remaking of the United States derivatives markets is among the most celebrated pieces of the Dodd-Frank Wall Street Reform and Consumer Protection Act of 2010 (Dodd-Frank).[1] These regulatory reforms have unnecessarily destabilized the financial markets through mandatory reliance on central counterparties (CCPs).[2] CCPs are financial institutions that collect derivatives transactions from many market participants and manage the associated risks. We outline a better approach that would not include a central clearing mandate or the associated trading mandate and instead would allow the derivatives markets to develop through voluntary—not regulatory—mechanisms. Combined with principles-based regulation for CCPs and robust regulatory reporting, an organically developed market structure would enable the derivatives markets to mitigate risk—including through the voluntary use of CCPs—without undermining financial stability.

*For the article on which this chapter is based, see Hester Peirce, "Derivatives Clearinghouses: Clearing the Way to Failure," *Cleveland State Law Review* 61 (June 2016): 589–660.

OTC DERIVATIVES, CLEARING, AND THE NEW REGULATORY FRAMEWORK

Derivatives are financial contracts that derive their value from the price of something else, such as a commodity, stock, bond, index, or currency. These contracts—which include futures, forwards, swaps, and options—enable companies and individuals to shift risks to parties willing to bear that risk. Derivative contracts can last for weeks, months, or even years. Financial and nonfinancial companies use derivatives to manage a wide array of risks, including foreign exchange risk, interest rate risk, and counterparty risk. Another important role derivatives play is price discovery and liquidity: derivatives provide information about the products or financial instruments on which they are based and can improve liquidity in the markets for those products or financial instruments.[3]

Many derivatives trade on exchanges and are cleared through CCPs, which are often affiliated with the exchange.[4] These derivatives adhere to a standard set of terms governing each aspect of the contract. Derivatives also can be executed off-exchange in a bilateral transaction between a dealer (usually a large bank)[5] and another dealer or customer. These bilateral transactions—also known as over-the-counter (OTC) derivatives—afford substantial flexibility in contract terms to accommodate the customer's unique needs.[6] Many OTC derivatives are interest rate derivatives,[7] which allow firms, for example, to exchange a floating interest rate for a fixed interest rate. OTC derivatives are sometimes called swaps "because many OTC deals involve cash flows, or obligations, that are swapped or exchanged between two parties at defined intervals."[8] Parties to these OTC derivatives generally have not cleared them through CCPs.

In the United States, voluntarily established clearinghouses have long served the equities, options, futures, and fixed income markets.[9] Clearinghouses match, confirm the terms of, net, and settle executed trades.[10] Of particular importance for this chapter, once a trade is executed, a clearinghouse that serves as a CCP steps in as buyer for every seller and as seller for every buyer. To protect itself and its members, the CCP collects contributions to a guaranty fund and collateral (also known as margin)[11] from each clearinghouse member.[12] If a party defaults and losses exceed the collateral provided by that party, remaining losses are allocated according to a preset default waterfall.[13]

Dodd-Frank proffers mandatory central clearing as necessary to bring order to the large OTC derivatives markets. By forcing OTC derivatives into central clearing, Dodd-Frank purportedly reduces systemic risk; big financial institutions' exposures to one another are limited and replaced with exposures to CCPs. Advocates also point to the value of central clearing in enhancing transparency, introducing margin uniformity and discipline, mutualizing losses, and limiting the need for market participants to monitor one another.[14] Importantly, CCPs also can help to contain the consequences of a failure by a large financial firm.[15]

In addition to implementing central clearing mandates, Dodd-Frank directs regulators—the US Commodity Futures Trading Commission (CFTC), US Securities and Exchange Commission (SEC), the Board of Governors of the Federal Reserve System (Federal Reserve), and other banking regulators— to impose margin, trading, reporting, registration, risk management, and business conduct requirements on swaps markets. Dodd-Frank changes are rooted in an international postcrisis effort to impose a new, more formal regulatory structure on the OTC derivatives markets, which had previously not been subject to the same degree of regulation as, for example, the futures markets.[16]

The Dodd-Frank swaps framework includes several key features. First, it identifies the major market participants (i.e., "swap dealers" and "major swap participants"),[17] requires them to register with the CFTC or SEC,[18] and subjects them to certain business conduct requirements.[19] Second, Dodd-Frank requires the CFTC and SEC to identify OTC derivatives or categories that are subject to a clearing mandate.[20] In making these determinations, the agencies must consider factors such as market size and liquidity, the availability of pricing data, swap infrastructure adequacy, systemic risk considerations, competitive considerations, and legal certainty.[21] Third, Dodd-Frank mandates that these swaps— except for those involving nonfinancial companies hedging their business risks—be cleared at clearinghouses registered with the SEC or CFTC.[22] Fourth, if a trading venue is available, cleared swaps must trade on an exchange or a swap execution facility (SEF)—a new type of trading venue created by Dodd-Frank for the swaps markets.[23] Fifth, Dodd-Frank rules prescribe how, when, and by whom cleared and uncleared swap transactions must be reported to a swap data repository, another new registered entity created under Dodd-Frank to house swap transaction data.[24] Sixth, Dodd-Frank requires public transparency about swap transactions.[25] Seventh, the Act requires regulators to set capital and margin requirements in connection with cleared and uncleared swaps.[26]

The final component of the regulatory framework is focused on safeguarding the CCPs that play such a central role in Dodd-Frank. Ben Bernanke, the former Federal Reserve chairman, put it this way: "As Mark Twain's character Pudd'nhead Wilson once opined, if you put all your eggs in one basket, you better watch that basket."[27] Titles VII and VIII of Dodd-Frank, which address numerous aspects of CCPs, facilitate efforts to "watch the basket." OTC derivatives clearinghouses must register with either the CFTC as a derivatives clearing organization (DCO)[28] or the SEC as a clearing agency.[29] The statute allows the CFTC and SEC to exempt from registration CCPs that are supervised by the other commission or a foreign regulator.[30] Dodd-Frank builds on the existing regulatory framework for the DCOs and clearing agencies that existed before Dodd-Frank to clear exchange-traded derivatives and securities. The Act modifies the regulatory structure for CCPs in a number of ways. First, Congress authorizes the CFTC and SEC to write tailored rules for swaps CCPs.[31] Second, the statute directs the commissions to write rules governing conflicts of interest at CCPs if "necessary or appropriate to improve the governance of, or to mitigate systemic risk, promote competition, or mitigate conflicts of interest."[32] Third, Title VII prescribes an "open access" model for swaps CCPs pursuant to which they must accept swaps for clearing, regardless of where the transactions are executed.[33] Fourth, Title VII includes a modified and expanded set of "core principles" for DCOs.[34]

The final component of Dodd-Frank's changes for CCPs is in Title VIII of the legislation, which posits a more stringent regulatory regime for CCPs designated to be currently or potentially systemically important by the Financial Stability Oversight Council (FSOC).[35] Title VIII charges the SEC and CFTC with writing and enforcing heightened risk management standards for designated CCPs and gives the Federal Reserve a backup regulatory role.[36] The Act requires cooperation among the CFTC, SEC, and the Federal Reserve in developing a joint risk management supervisory framework for designated CCPs.[37] CCP standards must cover a number of specific risk management areas, including margin and default procedures, but the statute allows the regulators wide latitude to write standards covering other areas.[38] A designated CCP must seek preapproval from its regulator for changes in rules, procedures, and operations that would "materially affect the nature or level of risks presented by" the CCP.[39]

US CCP regulation draws heavily from international standards. These global standards predate the financial crisis,[40] but—as Dodd-Frank notes—have been "evolving" since the crisis.[41] Most significant among the postcrisis efforts is the revised set of standards for financial market infrastructures, including CCPs, issued in 2012 by the Committee on Payment and Settlement Systems (CPSS)—subsequently renamed the Committee on Payments and Market Infrastructures (CPMI)—and the International Organization of Securities Commissions (IOSCO).[42] Drawing the appropriate balance between safety of and access to CCPs is a key theme of the CPSS/IOSCO standards. Covered areas include governance, credit and liquidity risk management, access, transparency, and default management.

As the length and breadth of the international standards illustrate, CCP risk management is a complex undertaking. Inserting regulators deeply into that exercise further complicates risk management. The next section discusses this and other problems with the existing regulatory framework.

PROBLEMS WITH THE CURRENT REGULATORY FRAMEWORK

Together, the clearing mandate, the regulatory influences on the design and operation of CCPs, and the implicit government backstop threaten to destabilize CCPs, individual firms' risk management, and the broader financial system. As Professor Craig Pirrong has warned, "a wholesale re-engineering of the structure of derivatives markets via legislative fiat is fraught with danger."[43] There are a number of concerns associated with the new framework.

Expanded CCPs Could Destabilize the Financial System

CCPs, expanded pursuant to the clearing mandate, could pose a risk to the broader financial system. By nature, CCPs are deeply interconnected with large financial companies and potentially with other CCPs. They have direct relationships with clearing members and settlement banks, which tend to be large firms. They have indirect relationships with clearing members' customers, which also may be large financial firms. These interconnections are channels through which problems could be transmitted across the financial system.

CCPs function by making and receiving payments according to a strict timeline. This feature normally protects the CCP and its members, but may cause problems during a crisis. In addition to the initial margin that a CCP collects in connection with a transaction to protect against future price movements, the CCP collects variation margin from, and credits it to, the accounts of its counterparties in response to price changes throughout the life of the derivatives contract. Paying on time is important to ensure that clearing members to whom payments are due are able to meet their obligations to other parties.[44] CCPs typically collect variation margin daily, but, to protect themselves during times of market stress, CCPs are likely to make multiple and perhaps large collateral calls in a single day.[45] Mark Roe points out that because "the collateral available to one creditor, namely the clearinghouse, is value denied to other creditors," the CCP may not serve to reduce systemic risk.[46] Knott and Mills note that a CCP's protective margin calls could cause members "to sell assets in a second market, driving down prices there."[47] They further explain that if margin payments are delayed, "the CCP may redistribute part of its risk to liquidity providers such as banks."[48] Pirrong cites the potential for CCPs to shift risk from derivatives counterparties to other creditors of failed firms, increase borrowing to meet margin requirements, create large demands for liquid assets during times of great stress, and impose losses on firms through the default fund at times when those firms can least bear them.[49]

Further complicating matters, clearing members are likely to be large financial institutions that play multiple roles and have multiple relationships with each CCP. Only a small number of firms are clearing members.[50] Clearing members may themselves be, or may be affiliated with, the settlement banks or the providers of lines of credit on which CCPs rely.[51] Prearranged lines of credit might not materialize during a crisis, particularly if the lending bank is a stressed clearing member.[52] Federal Reserve Governor Jerome Powell points out that "the failure of a large clearing member that is also a key service provider could disrupt the smooth and efficient operation of one or multiple CCPs, and vice versa."[53] The CCP has to consider the full scope of its relationship with clearing members when, for example, it forecasts the effects of a member default or a margin call or assessment on surviving members.[54]

The 1987 stock market crash illustrated how closely CCPs are tied to the banking system, how important payment timing is, how serious the ramifications of operational issues can be, and how CCPs interact with the financial system during a crisis.[55] Ben Bernanke, who studied the incident, concluded that the clearing and settlement system suffered from "malfunctions of communications and information processing systems" and "financial gridlock as banks and other creditors became cautious about transferring funds to individuals or institutions whose solvency might be in doubt."[56] These fears seemed to have helped to drive prices down.[57] Bernanke further notes that clearinghouses' margin calls "were widely criticized in postmortems for 'draining liquidity from the system.' "[58] Federal Reserve intervention kept the system functioning through the 1987 crisis.[59] Since 1987, systems have improved,[60] but real concerns remain about how expanded CCPs would function in the face of similar market stress. Because of new liquidity rules after the most recent crisis, liquid assets will be at even more of a premium than they were in 1987.[61]

Default management also might be difficult in the Dodd-Frank world of stricter capital standards and mandatory clearing. Capital requirements may prevent nondefaulting clearing members from taking on the defaulter's client's portfolios.[62] Particularly if the defaulter's portfolio contains unusual products, the CCP may have trouble borrowing trading personnel with the requisite knowledge of the products from nondefaulting members to manage the defaulter's portfolio.[63]

A further complication is that multiple CCPs may be competing for the same liquid assets, personnel, capacity of clearing members to take on additional positions from defaulters' portfolios, and perhaps even capacity of clearing members to replenish guaranty funds or meet unfunded assessments. If one CCP were affected, others would likely also be affected.[64]

If a CCP stopped meeting its obligations altogether, it could greatly impede markets. A CCP that cannot meet its payment obligations could stop the markets for which it clears from functioning.[65] Because CCPs tend to dominate particular markets, there might not be a substitute CCP, so the market for any OTC derivatives cleared at the failing CCP and subject to the clearing mandate would lock up.[66] Adding to the disruption, the status of existing contracts at a failing CCP would also be uncertain.[67]

During a crisis, CCPs operating in an environment of clearing mandates may aggravate, rather than mitigate, problems in the financial system. As the next section describes, even during normal times, a CCP may have unintended adverse effects on risk management in the financial system.

Clearing Mandate Could Undermine Risk Management *Outside* the CCP

Dodd-Frank's clearing mandate affects the way firms manage their business risks and exposures to other firms. Some of these changes may be positive, but others may disrupt existing bilateral relationships and may result in risks being borne by parties not well equipped to bear them.

Bilateral transactions are often part of a larger customer relationship between a company and a dealer bank. That relationship may include unique collateral arrangements (e.g., not having to post collateral below a certain threshold or being permitted to post illiquid assets as collateral). Forcing swaps into CCPs, which cannot replicate these accommodations, will disrupt these bilateral relationships. Both clearing members and their customers will have to post collateral in the liquid form demanded by CCPs.[68] Customers may enter into new relationships to borrow collateral. If banks meet the demand by lending liquid assets to their customers to post as collateral, "the tail risk may not leave their books," as central clearing proponents hoped it would.[69]

Nonstandardized, bilateral agreements enable companies to manage their risks with a greater precision than they can with standardized products. The clearing mandate and associated disincentives to use uncleared swaps—such as higher margin requirements for uncleared swaps, capital charges, and anti-evasion provisions—may discourage firms from dealing in and using uncleared swaps. Risks may go unhedged as firms forgo derivatives-based hedging altogether or use a less tailored cleared product to imperfectly hedge their risk.[70] Alternatively, Columbia University scholar Ilya Beylin argues that market participants seeking to avoid the clearing mandate could resort to more complicated, less transparent, and riskier transactions.[71]

Mandatory clearing undercuts the ability of firms to engage in bilateral netting—the process by which dealers are able to net their exposures to one another. Although CCPs facilitate multilateral netting, bilateral netting opportunities with a particular counterparty decrease if some transactions with that counterparty are moved to a CCP.[72]

Mandated Central Clearing Could Impair Counterparty Monitoring

One of the main functions of a CCP is to eliminate the need for a buyer of a derivatives contract to monitor the seller, and vice versa. Buyers and sellers planning to centrally clear can be indifferent about the identity of their counterparty.[73] Loss is mutualized and risk management is centralized by CCPs. As a consequence, less interdealer monitoring will take place than it did prior to the clearing mandate.[74] CCPs pool risks, which means that there is still an incentive for each member to conduct some monitoring to avoid having to cover a portion of the losses from a defaulting member.[75] The clearing mandate tempers those incentives by forcing participation in the CCP and limiting members in their ability to influence CCP access and risk management rules.

CCPs have certain risk management advantages. They offer centralized risk management by requiring clearing members to meet certain threshold requirements and contribute to a guaranty fund that can be tapped if a member defaults.[76] CCPs monitor their members and may impose risk-specific restrictions on them—including position limits—to prevent being overexposed to any particular firm.[77] CCPs may be able to monitor risk more thoroughly than a single dealer could since CCPs have broad access to information about clearing members and their positions.[78] Pirrong has argued, however, that CCPs have lower quality information than the hedge funds and banks that "specialize precisely in understanding risks and pricing . . . especially . . . for more complex and novel derivative instruments."[79] CCP staff may have a broader view of a member's portfolio, but they may not be able to fully understand the risks of the portfolio since they do not have the expertise of the individuals who trade particular products daily.

The clearing mandate could incentivize firms to enter into transactions that they otherwise would avoid, because they know the attendant risks will be the CCP's. Former British central banker Paul Tucker makes the point that "firms using a CCP have incentives to take more counterparty credit risk in their market transactions than otherwise, discriminating less when choosing with whom to trade because their credit exposure is not to their market counterparty but rather to the clearing house—unless the tail risk is credibly mutualized."[80] Efforts to increase the CCP's share of the losses in the event of a member default could exacerbate the problem of clearing members' offloading risk—intentionally or carelessly—to CCPs.[81]

CCPs are generally very reliable counterparties, but firms have to consider the possibility that something could go wrong. If a CCP member defaults, the other members may bear some of the losses, but how much a particular firm will bear is difficult to estimate in advance. To enable more precise modeling of their exposure to CCPs, clearing members are pushing for greater *ex ante* clarity about what will happen if a CCP runs into trouble.[82] Members also have an interest in strong risk management, but the clearing mandate undercuts clearing members' leverage by making it hard to eschew doing business with a poorly managed CCP that clears a product subject to the mandate. Incentives to monitor CCPs and choose carefully which ones to use may be further hampered by Dodd-Frank's practice of assigning the right to select a CCP to the nondealer party to a transaction—the party with the least incentive to monitor the CCP.[83] Assessing and managing exposure to CCPs may be particularly difficult because, as the next sections discuss, regulatory developments are changing CCPs.

Mandated Clearing Could Force Improper Risks into CCPs

The clearing mandate, when combined with other regulatory and economic pressures, encourages CCPs to open their doors to more products in higher volumes than they would have absent the mandate. Carefully choosing products for clearing is an important way that CCPs protect themselves.[84] Considerations include how a product's prices have moved over time, how the product might interact with other products cleared by the CCP, and how those interactions might change in response to market developments. As figure 1 shows, cleared volumes have risen markedly in recent years. Some of the newly cleared products have features that make risk management difficult. An international body focused on CCP risk management explained in modifying its recommendations for OTC derivative CCPs: "because of the complex risk characteristics and market design of OTC derivatives products, clearing them safely and efficiently through a CCP presents unique challenges that clearing listed or cash-market products may not."[85] Manmohan Singh similarly warns that "pushing CCPs to clear riskier and less-liquid financial instruments, as the regulators are now demanding, may increase systemic risk and the probability of a bailout."[86] Today's CCPs, therefore, must grapple with new risks.

The risks associated with certain types of swaps are particularly difficult to manage. Single-name credit default swap (CDS) contracts, for example, present a jump-to-default risk that makes them more difficult to properly margin than standard interest rate contracts.[87] A portfolio of swaps may behave unremarkably during normal market conditions, but may be prone to unanticipated, dramatic price moves.[88] Liquidity may fluctuate during a swap's lifetime.[89] Interproduct correlations are also not constant over time.[90] CCPs' margin models—developed for more standardized, highly liquid derivatives—may

Figure 1. US Central Clearing Market Share of Interest Rate Derivatives and CDS Index Swaps, 2013–2015

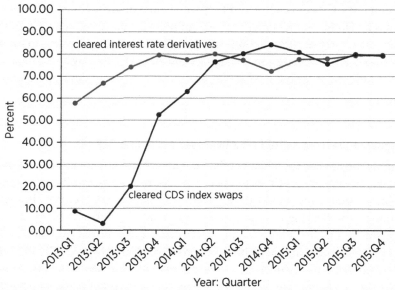

Year: Quarter

Source: Financial Stability Oversight Council, "FSOC 2016 Annual Report Data," June 21, 2016, https://www.treasury.gov/initiatives/fsoc/studies-reports/Pages/2016-Annual-Report.aspx.

Note: FSOC uses SwapInfo (ISDA) data.

not properly accommodate the unique features of these new products and their correlations with other products.[91]

In deciding which products to clear and how to margin them, CCPs also must be alert to changes in correlations among cleared products and clearing members:

> [R]isk may be amplified due to a correlation among risk factors. For example, a CCP clearing CDS could experience a "double default" where a reference entity defaults and a CCP's participant defaults simultaneously because the participant had a large short position (i.e., sold credit protections) in the reference entity or where the credit risk of a reference entity and that of a participant with a large

short position are highly correlated. In another scenario, a defaulting participant with a short position may turn out to be the reference entity (self-referencing CDS).[92]

Dodd-Frank acknowledges that the clearing mandate is not appropriate for all OTC derivatives. The statute directs regulators, in deciding whether to impose a clearing mandate on a swap or a group of swaps, to consider a number of factors including "the existence of significant outstanding notional exposures, trading liquidity, and adequate pricing data" and operational and legal frameworks.[93] However, other statutory factors—systemic risk mitigation and competitive implications[94]—give regulators a nudge to opt *for* a clearing mandate, even if there are concerns about inadequate liquidity or pricing data.[95]

Strong commercial, financial, and competitive incentives intensify pressure to extend clearing mandates to additional categories of swaps. CCPs seeking to expand their businesses[96] and market participants chafing under dealers' tight control of the bilateral markets might favor extended clearing mandates. Mandated central clearing brings with it new profit opportunities for firms that do not have large bank balance sheets and therefore may not have been attractive counterparties in the bilateral context. Users of CCPs may also encourage broader clearing mandates as expanded CCPs offer multilateral netting, which can reduce collateral demands.[97]

Regulatory advantages to clearing bolster the market impetus for broad central clearing mandates. Among these advantages are potential margin savings because margin requirements on uncleared swaps are intended to be more stringent than they would be in the cleared context.[98] Basel capital rules also offer favorable capital treatment for swaps cleared through a CCP that meets international standards—a qualifying CCP.[99] Uncleared OTC derivatives also carry legal and reputational risk as Dodd-Frank requires the SEC and CFTC to take steps to prevent "evasion of the mandatory clearing requirements."[100]

Regulatory Conflicts of Interest Could Impair CCP Risk Management

CCPs, as originally conceived, brought together a group of members that voluntarily pooled and cooperatively managed risks. The new model replaces voluntary cooperative efforts with regulatory mandates. That regulatory involvement not only brings new risks into CCPs, it complicates risk management.

Because of the important place CCPs have in the government-made OTC market structure and the implicit government backstop, it is not surprising that many policymakers and academics call for intense regulation of CCPs.[101] A counter-concern is that such regulation may be guided by objectives other than sound risk management.

First, regulators may be moved by factors other than risk management in setting guidelines for membership standards—a key risk management feature of CCPs. Membership rules have stability implications; a broad membership distributes "the costs of default across a greater number of members,"[102] but a homogeneous, robust membership may generate more stable CCPs.[103] Membership rules also have competitive implications because a firm that does not meet the minimum requirements must clear through a member (or through a member's client) or forgo trading in swaps subject to a clearing mandate.[104] The CFTC claims to allow DCOs "discretion to balance restrictions on participation with legitimate risk management concerns" because they are "in the best position in the first instance to determine the optimal balance."[105] Yet it specifically prohibits DCOs from setting "a limit on the number of market participants that may become clearing members,"[106] setting more than a $50 million minimum capital requirement for membership,[107] and requiring "members to post a minimum amount of liquid margin or default guarantee contributions, or to participate in a liquidity facility."[108] These decisions highlight what Professor Jo Braithwaite refers to as "the membership dilemma" created by "regulators having framed compulsory legislation around a private sector legal device designed to mutualise losses for selected participants."[109] As Professor Hal Scott explains, "A clearinghouse is just an association, so it's only as strong as the member firms. If you were hell-bent on fairness, and opened this thing to everybody, that would increase the risk to the clearinghouse."[110]

Second, the mandated use of CCPs has given them a quasi-public character in regulators' eyes, which introduces competing interests in CCP governance. Economist Norbert Michel points out that Dodd-Frank's classification of CCPs as financial market utilities "marks a dangerous shift in the relationship between government and private markets because it implies that private financial firms cannot—or should not—competitively provide financial services."[111] The CPSS/IOSCO principles, which heavily inform US regulation, emphasize the responsibility of financial market infrastructures to "support the stability of the broader financial system, other relevant public interest considerations, and the objectives of relevant stakeholders"[112] and call for governance to balance the interests of a CCP's owners, board of directors, managers, clearing members, regulators, and "other stakeholders."[113] Directing CCPs—in the nebulous name of public interest—to serve multiple constituencies with potentially conflicting objectives may have the perverse effect of destabilizing CCPs and the financial system. CCPs that are run with a member-focus are more likely to elevate risk management than CCPs required to consider a host of other constituencies (such as regulators and other nonmember "stakeholders") who do not face the prospect of absorbing CCP losses.

Third, regulators face pressure to view purported risk management measures as the product of competitive machinations by dealers. In a comment letter to the CFTC, the Department of Justice worried that anticompetitive behavior in connection with CCP access "could be explained away . . . by expressing risk management–related concerns" and urged the CFTC to adopt stricter conflict of interest standards for CCPs.[114] This view may cause regulators to disallow legitimate risk management measures. It also helps to drive calls for governance and ownership restrictions on CCPs intended to limit the influence of clearing members and other large financial firms on clearinghouse management. Many observers favor replacing or supplementing dealer influence in governance and risk management with public interest and regulatory representation.[115] Under Dodd-Frank's conflict of interest mandates, the SEC and CFTC have contemplated individual and aggregate ownership caps and independent director involvement in governance to temper clearing member influence.[116]

Fourth, regulators may be tempted to employ one-size-fits-all regulations that distract CCPs from conducting their own tailored risk management and may prevent them from responding effectively to problems as they arise. Stress tests are one area in which this concern exists. Although calling for "[m]ore standardized stress tests" across jurisdictions,[117] former CFTC Commissioner Mark Wetjen, warned that "[w]hile standardization and uniformity are appealing, they could inadvertently impede innovation and thoroughness. Would we start to teach to the test instead of evaluating and refining the stress test methodologies as appropriate?"[118]

Fifth, a prescriptive regulatory regime applicable to a small number of firms with a vital role in the financial system seems fertile ground for regulatory capture.[119] Economist George Stigler warned that "as a rule, regulation is acquired by industry and is designed and operated primarily for its benefit."[120]

There are a small number of CCPs, and Dodd-Frank legally mandates that they be used. There are also relatively few large firms that serve as clearing members. Although the new regulatory framework is burdensome for these firms, CCPs and clearing members could seek to use these burdens to their advantage in blocking entry by domestic and foreign rivals. Alternatively, the Shadow Financial Regulatory Committee suggested that CCPs could "exploit opportunities for regulatory arbitrage and regulatory capture to lessen the costs of government oversight."[121] Moreover, CCPs are likely to put pressure on regulators to dissuade the use of noncleared derivatives, which can serve as substitutes for cleared products. The authority of multiple regulators in this space might make regulatory capture more difficult, but divided regulatory authority brings its own challenges.

Sixth, conflicts among regulators could exacerbate risk by adding complexity to CCP management. The SEC and CFTC directly regulate CCPs, and the Federal Reserve plays a backup role under Title VIII of Dodd-Frank. The approaches taken by these agencies are not always consistent, in part because of historical differences in the way the agencies have overseen CCPs.[122] There have also been calls for the involvement of the FSOC in CCP regulation.[123] Moreover, despite the common G20 commitment to central clearing, global regulators have had difficulty working together in overseeing this international market, and the lack of coordination could worsen during a crisis as regulators strive to keep assets in CCPs within their jurisdiction.[124] As clearing mandates take hold around the world, the pressure for linkages among CCPs is likely to grow,[125] which will only further complicate regulatory oversight.

Finally, the desire to increase the proportion of swaps that is cleared is likely to affect regulators' oversight of key risk management decisions. As discussed earlier, a pro-clearing outlook may color determinations to impose a clearing mandate. More subtly, a desire to make clearing more attractive could affect decisions related to how much margin is collected, the form margin may take, and how it is invested. If margins are set improperly, the CCP may be at risk.[126] There is not a widely accepted formula for setting margin, and there is a lot of room for nonrisk considerations to affect regulators' views on margin methodologies.[127] Consequences of regulatory mistakes may not manifest themselves until a crisis. Similarly, on questions related to CCP default management, regulators may favor the approach that imposes the least additional immediate cost on clearing services, even if that approach misaligns market participants' incentives and lays the groundwork for problems should a member later default.

Mandated Clearing Risk Could Increase Bailout Risk

In an era of clearing mandates, a shuttered CCP could devastate markets as market participants must centrally clear transactions subject to the clearing mandate. If clearing members could not prop up a CCP, presumably the government that imposes the clearing mandate and supervises CCPs would go to great lengths to keep the troubled CCP in operation. If regulators have acquiesced in or encouraged CCP under-margining, inadequate guaranty funds, or some other risk management misstep, they are particularly likely to be pressured to bail out a failing CCP. If problems emanate from products under a clearing mandate, regulators will likewise face bailout pressure. If only one CCP clears a product, that pressure will be particularly intense.[128]

The likely availability of government support for a failing CCP is reflected in Dodd-Frank in two ways. First, the Orderly Liquidation Authority in Title II, Dodd-Frank's alternative to bankruptcy for large financial institutions, does not explicitly apply to CCPs; whether a CCP could be resolved under Title II is an open question.[129] The absence of a resolution mechanism could be interpreted as leaving open the door for a government bailout. Second, Title VIII gives the Federal Reserve authority to loan money through the discount window to systemically important CCPs in "unusual or exigent circumstances."[130] Dodd-Frank also allows the Federal Reserve to establish accounts for systemically important CCPs and provide services to them, such as currency and coin services, check clearing and collection services, wire transfer services, automated clearinghouse services, settlement services, securities safekeeping services, and Federal Reserve float.[131] The Federal Reserve could use these powers to conduct a bailout.[132] Despite messages to the contrary,[133] the availability of emergency lending could encourage carelessness by both CCPs and regulators.[134]

A possible rejoinder to the concern about bailouts is that CCPs rarely fail. There have been failures, however, and today's more complex CCPs—reshaped by clearing mandates and attendant regulation—are not immune from failure.

Past failures include the French Caisse de Liquidation in 1974, the Kuala Lumpur Commodity Clearing House in 1983, and the Hong Kong Futures Exchange Clearing Corp. in 1987.[135] In each case, the problem related to margin.[136] Brazil's BM&F CCP almost failed in 1999 when there was inadequate margin after a currency devaluation caused two clearing members to default.[137] In December 2013, a Korean CCP dipped into its guaranty fund after one of its members—a small broker-dealer—defaulted because of a trading error.[138] Problems at CCPs emerge quickly and come with a high price tag—precisely the conditions on which government bailouts are built.

A BETTER APPROACH TO MANAGING RISK

To achieve greater financial stability and serve financial markets and the broader economy effectively, the current top-down regulatory framework for OTC derivatives needs to be replaced with a regulatory approach that leaves clearing decisions and the consequences of those decisions in the private sector. The new structure would not include clearing mandates or associated trading mandates. Provisions designating CCPs systemically important and providing them access to Federal Reserve backstops would likewise not be part of the new structure. The replacement framework would instead allow market participants to choose central clearing and would substitute a principles-based regulatory approach for the current, increasingly prescriptive approach to CCP regulation. A comprehensive reporting regime for cleared and uncleared swaps would ensure that firms and their regulators have better insight into where derivatives exposures are than they did in the last crisis.

Elimination of the Clearing Mandate

The first step toward enhancing financial stability would be to eliminate the clearing mandate. Admittedly, doing so would be a stark departure from one of Dodd-Frank's core features. On the other hand, as noted earlier, the Act recognizes that clearing is not always appropriate. Dodd-Frank embraced the clearing mandate to shore up financial stability, but there is a growing realization that clearing is not unambiguously positive for stability. To effectively eliminate the mandate, capital and margin incentives to clear also would have to be eliminated. The clearing mandate and associated regulatory nudges impede market participants' ability to make choices that are both consistent with strong risk management and serve customer needs. As attorney Paul McBride points out, much can be done with "voluntary, rather than compulsory clearing, [which enables] market participants . . . to exercise discretion in order to strike the optimal balance between the costs and benefits of clearing."[139] Eliminating the mandate would also ease concerns that a failing CCP would lock up markets since market participants would be able to continue transacting in uncleared products without running afoul of the clearing mandate.

It is likely that CCPs would continue to clear many of the swaps that they currently clear and add new products to meet organic market demand for central clearing. Even before Dodd-Frank's clearing mandate was put in place, some OTC derivatives, in response to market demand, were centrally cleared.[140] Affording market participants the ability to choose whether to clear would allow them to avoid, or use their leverage to improve, poorly managed CCPs. In the current model, once a mandate is in place, CCPs have a government-granted privilege. A mandate-less model would give CCPs an incentive to earn customer business by managing risk well.[141]

The trading mandate, which was established by Dodd-Frank as a companion of the clearing mandate, is likewise unnecessary. Market participants will choose how and where to trade based on a wide variety of considerations that they are best positioned to balance. The swap execution facilities called into life by Dodd-Frank would continue to exist, if they meet organic market demand.

Principles-Based Regulation

Eliminating the clearing mandate would not obviate the need for regulatory oversight of CCPs. The regulatory regime, however, should be principles-based. Primary responsibility for designing and running CCPs should remain with the owners and members. A prescriptive regulatory regime inappropriately shifts this responsibility to regulators by placing the full array of risk management decisions in their hands. A principles-based regulatory regime would allow CCPs broad discretion to operate in the manner that best suits the products they clear and the market participants they serve. Within this framework, CCPs would have the room to make swift changes to operational, technical, or risk management procedures as weaknesses emerge, risks are better understood, or available technology improves. CCPs are self-regulatory organizations, which means that—subject to oversight by the CFTC or SEC—they are able to write and enforce rules applicable to their members. In line with the approach used by the CFTC, CCPs could be permitted to self-certify to their regulator that each new rule complies with the principles.

To allow CCPs sufficient discretion, core principles should be broad, not prescriptive. Increasingly prescriptive regulation can have the perverse effect of frustrating effective and adaptive CCP risk management, dulling clearing-member monitoring of CCPs, and homogenizing CCPs so that all are subject to similar vulnerabilities. As former Federal Reserve Governor Randall Kroszner explained, "More intense government regulation of CCPs may prove counterproductive if it creates moral hazard or impedes the ability of CCPs to develop new approaches to risk management."[142] The CPSS/IOSCO risk management principles and other relevant standards can inform the core principles and CCPs' compliance with those principles. To facilitate member monitoring, CCPs would need to disclose policies governing topics including member obligations, the complete default waterfall, risk management, governance, resolution and recovery procedures, and margin methodologies, as many CCPs already do in their rulebooks.

Regulators could continue to monitor CCPs for improper practices. Pirrong has called for regulators to be able to revise membership requirements if the regulators "can show that they were adopted for anti-competitive reasons, or place an undue burden on competition not justified by any prudential benefit."[143] This principle makes sense applied more broadly to other CCP risk management and operational measures.

To augment regulatory oversight of CCPs, CCPs could obtain private insurance[144] or issue convertible bonds. Although these options require further analysis, they could supplement the monitoring provided by regulators and members.

Properly Aligned CCP Ownership and Governance

CCPs are most likely to serve the public interest of promoting financial stability if their ownership and governance structures correspond to economic interests. Randall Kroszner has explained that "market forces can produce private regulations that address the concerns about safety, soundness, and broader financial stability."[145] As traditionally constructed, clearinghouses were a group of financial firms that pooled certain risks, managed them jointly, and shared any losses. Risk management is an essential ingredient of such an arrangement.[146] CCP control restrictions of the sort contemplated by Dodd-Frank that would prohibit such an arrangement may have the unintended consequence of undermining the proper functioning of incentives for risk management.[147] As a result of demutualization, today's CCPs tend not to be member-owned; most CCPs are affiliated with an exchange.[148] Clearing members, however, continue to be the primary loss-bearers when they fail. Consequently, as others have argued, clearing members must play a role in designing risk controls for, and managing, CCPs.[149] Regulations should accommodate and encourage active member involvement in CCP oversight.

Although the mutual ownership CCP model is attractive for financial stability reasons, the for-profit model that dominates the swaps landscape would more effectively contribute to stability if the clearing mandate were eliminated. CCPs would no longer have an essentially guaranteed stream of business, which would give market participants more leverage to influence CCP risk management practices. Members will be reluctant to use a CCP that exposes them to large or difficult-to-estimate risk. Now the only option for clearing members concerned about poor CCP risk management is to cease trading products subject to clearing mandates.

The suggestion that members with money on the line in the default fund must play a central role in risk management runs directly counter to the recommendations of others who worry about the undue control that dealers exercise in CCPs.[150] These commentators worry that, if permitted, large dealers will limit entry to CCPs and prevent them from accepting products for clearing to keep products in the more profitable (for dealers) bilateral market.[151] Some call for ownership and governance restrictions of the sort permitted by Dodd-Frank and proposed by the SEC and CFTC.[152] Some advocate replacing the voices of clearing members with those of public interest directors in risk management and other key committees or securing a place for regulatory representatives on CCP boards.[153] Concerns about dealer control of CCPs are understandable in light of their dominant role in these markets, but attempts to readjust the power dynamics at CCPs may unintentionally destabilize them. Regulatory principles should encourage the involvement of properly incentivized, knowledgeable experts in CCP management and oversight.

Prohibitions against anticompetitive activity modeled on existing statutory prohibitions should suffice to prevent CCPs from being used for improper competitive purposes. For example, DCOs are prohibited from making rules and taking actions that restrain trade or impede competition unless the DCO has a statutorily legitimate reason for doing so.[154] As noted earlier, regulators could have the authority to abrogate CCP rules or other actions upon demonstrating that the action was being undertaken for anticompetitive reasons rather than to bolster the soundness of the CCP.[155] The task of identifying inappropriate, anticompetitive behavior is best left to the functional regulators, rather than to the realm of antitrust law.[156]

No Implicit or Explicit Promises of Bailouts

Regulatory changes to end bailout expectations would support financial stability. As Kroszner explains, "a promise of government financial support in the event of a risk-management failure" can "eviscerate . . . private-market discipline, which has served private and public interests in the stability of CCP arrangements so well for so long."[157] Restoring private discipline requires eliminating explicit and implicit government guarantees on CCPs.

Central to eliminating government guarantees is ending the FSOC's power to designate systemically important financial market utilities under Title VIII of Dodd-Frank and related provisions. The designation carries with it an implicit message that the government will not let designated entities fail. Designated CCPs have access to Federal Reserve accounts and services, which could allow the Federal Reserve to prop up a failing CCP in a future crisis.

The elimination of the clearing mandate also would help to send the message that the government is not a CCP guarantor. As long as the government requires market participants to use CCPs, market participants will anticipate that the government will step in to keep a failing CCP operating to ensure that transactions subject to the mandate and cleared solely by that CCP would not cease.

A final way to build private discipline is to encourage private-sector efforts involving CCPs and their members to define CCPs' default waterfalls clearly, realistically explore tail risks, and plan for recapitalization and resolution in the event of failure due to defaults or nondefault problems (e.g., operational issues).[158] Although current conversations about these issues have been spurred by the increase in clearing brought about by the clearing mandate, they are valuable in the absence of a mandate. Credible plans by CCPs to deal with failures in risk management or operational systems are a critical part of eliminating implicit expectations of government bailouts.

Regulatory Reporting

One of the concerns during the last crisis was that neither regulators nor market participants had a good picture of the OTC derivatives market. CCPs provide a discipline that prevents the buildup of the backlogs that plagued pre-crisis markets,[159] but a reporting regime could do the same thing. A new regulatory regime would not only provide regulators the information they need to monitor the derivatives markets, but would ensure that market participants are aware of their exposures to CCPs and other counterparties.

Elements of Dodd-Frank's reporting regime achieve these objectives. Under the Act, market participants report swap transactions to a swap data repository (SDR) or to the SEC or CFTC.[160] The SDR collects and confirms trade details and stores trade data for regulators to access. SDRs could be retained for these purposes.[161] Requiring that transactions be reported as soon as reasonably possible would help to avoid the buildup of backlogs of unconfirmed transactions. Dodd-Frank specifies which entities possess the reporting obligation, but under a new framework, this determination could be part of contractual negotiations.

Even if regulators have timely and comprehensive access to information about the OTC derivatives markets, policymakers should not assume that regulators will identify and preemptively solve emerging problems in those markets.[162] As with other areas, markets are more agile at gathering, analyzing, and reacting to information than regulators are, particularly if market participants bear the consequences of their own decisions. The recognition of regulators' limits underlies a regulatory framework that leaves risk management decisions and consequences with market participants.

CONCLUSION

The combination of clearing mandates, government prescriptions regarding clearinghouse design, and government support for CCPs threatens financial stability. A preferable approach would eliminate government backstops and leave decisions about which products should be centrally cleared and how CCPs should operate to private decision makers. The current regulatory framework would be replaced by a principles-based regulatory approach and mandatory reporting of swaps transactions.

Despite good intentions, the Dodd-Frank framework has given rise to a new set of risks by compromising the effectiveness of clearinghouse risk management while simultaneously encouraging CCPs to embrace new risks. The drive for clearing colors regulatory oversight and impedes markets and regulators from thinking clearly about the associated risks. Prescriptive regulation displaces or distorts CCPs' own risk management initiatives. The risk management focus of CCPs is further dulled by calls to dampen the influence of clearing members and populate their boards with independent directors. The preference given to cleared instruments has a secondary effect of making it more difficult for parties to manage risk outside CCPs and less imperative for parties to monitor one another. Moreover, the growth and change of CCPs in response to government policy builds bailout expectations.

To foster financial stability, policymakers should eliminate clearing mandates, the attendant prescriptive regulatory regime for CCPs, systemic designations of CCPs, and special Federal Reserve privileges for CCPs. A replacement regulatory framework could consist of a broad set of principles for CCPs, a reporting framework for cleared and uncleared swaps, a governance framework for CCPs that includes market participants who bear the risks, and a clear delineation of default waterfalls and CCP recovery plans. A return to private ordering in the OTC derivatives space would diminish bailout expectations and allow market participants to benefit from central clearing where it makes sense, continue to use uncleared swaps where they best manage risk, and monitor and manage both CCP and non-CCP risk effectively.

Domestic political realities and the shared international commitment to mandatory clearing may stand in the way of the proposed return to private ordering. If clearing mandates remain in place, policymakers can benefit from considering the concerns raised here and elsewhere about the risks associated with mandatory clearing and the regulatory structure. Regulators need to be keenly aware of the deleterious effect poor regulatory requirements can have on CCPs' risk management. Supervisors should apply clearing mandates carefully and only after a full consideration of the risks informed by adequate data. Policymakers should afford CCPs and their participants the regulatory flexibility necessary to manage risk effectively and should monitor CCPs closely, but not micromanage them. Regulators and market participants should continue to work together to understand how CCPs would perform under stressed scenarios and how losses from the default of one or more clearing members would be allocated. Relationships among CCP supervisors have been tense in recent years, but cooperation is critical. Regardless of whether the clearing mandate remains in place, CCPs will continue to play an important role in the financial system. Accordingly, efforts by regulators, market participants, and academics to better understand, manage, and monitor CCP risks are well worth the commitment of resources, time, and attention.

NOTES

1. Pub. L. No. 111-203, 124 Stat. 1376 (2010).

2. Professor Craig Pirrong raised concerns about the clearing mandate early, eloquently, and often. See, for example, Pirrong, "Bill of Goods," 55, and "Clearinghouse Cure." Others also have raised concerns. See Levitin, "Response," 445, 453; Roe, "Clearinghouse Overconfidence," 1641; Wibaut and Wilford, "Markets for CCPs and Regulation," 102. While citing the risk-reducing aspects of CCPs, the Office of Financial Research and Financial Stability Oversight Council also identified CCPs as a potential source of systemic risk. Financial Stability Oversight Council, "2015 Annual Report," 11, identifies CCPs as a "potential emerging threat and vulnerability." Office of Financial Research, "2014 Annual Report," 66, notes that "[b]anks could face significant losses if a CCP experienced losses and transmitted them to clearing members" and highlights potential liquidity effects of margin requirements.

3. Acharya et al., "Derivatives," 234.

4. In the US futures markets, exchanges typically are vertically integrated with clearinghouses, whereas clearinghouses in the equities and options markets are independent of exchanges. For a historical and regulatory discussion of why these markets developed differently, see Wolkoff and Werner, "History of Regulation," 313.

5. The US derivatives market is concentrated; four commercial banks—JPMorgan Chase Bank, Bank of America, Citibank, and Goldman Sachs—have approximately 90 percent of the banking industry's derivatives. Office of the Comptroller of the Currency, OCC's Quarterly Report on Bank Derivatives Activities Third Quarter 2015, 1, graphs 4 and 5 (based on notional amounts).

6. In addition to carefully crafted risk management, there were historically other reasons, such as accounting reasons, for using these specially tailored derivatives. See Heckinger, Ruffini,

and Wells, "Over-the-Counter (OTC) Derivatives," 27, which discusses the reasons for using the OTC derivatives markets.

7. Office of the Comptroller of the Currency, OCC's Quarterly Report on Bank Trading and Derivatives Activities Third Quarter 2015, 10, observes that "interest rate contracts continue to represent the lion's share of the derivatives market at 76.9% of total derivatives. FX and credit derivatives are 16.7% and 4.3% of total notionals, respectively. Commodity and equity derivatives collectively are only 2.1% of total notional derivatives."

8. Heckinger, Ruffini, and Wells, "Over-the-Counter (OTC) Derivatives." This chapter uses the term "swaps" as a rough shorthand for OTC derivatives.

9. For a concise history of clearinghouses in the United States, see Bernanke, "Clearinghouses, Financial Stability, and Financial Reform," 9.

10. See, for example, Knott and Mills, "Modelling Risk," 162n2. These services need not be provided by a CCP. See, for example, Ledrut and Upper, "Clearing Post-Trading Arrangements for OTC Derivatives," 92: "Given that CCP services have been limited to a restricted set of contracts," they write, "market participants have explored other avenues to obtain some of the benefits of CCPs [including] centralization of information or multilateral netting. . . ."

11. Initial margin, which is collected at the outset of a transaction and adjusted periodically, "is designed to cover the worst-case close out costs (due to the need to find replacement transactions) in the event a member defaults." Gregory, Central Counterparties, § 3.2.4. Variation margin, which is adjusted at least daily, reflects net changes in the market value of clearing members' portfolios. Compare 17 C.F.R. § 1.3(ccc), which defines initial margin as "money, securities, or property posted by a party to a futures, option, or swap as performance bond to cover potential future exposures arising from changes in the market value of the position," with 17 C.F.R. § 1.3(fff), which defines variation margin as "a payment made by a party to a futures, option, or swap to cover the current exposure arising from changes in the market value of the position since the trade was executed or the previous time the position was marked to market." For further discussions of margin, see Duffie, Li, and Lubke, "Policy Perspectives on OTC Derivatives," 7–9 and app. C; Gregory, Central Counterparties, chap. 6 and § 8.3.3; McPartland, "Clearing and Settlement"; Turbeville, "Derivatives Clearinghouses," 9–12.

12. Because the burdens of CCP membership are high, most swap market participants prefer indirect access through a clearing member or—even more indirectly—through a clearing member's client. See, for example, Braithwaite, "Legal Perspectives on Client Clearing," 9: "The membership criteria for clearing services for OTC derivatives are onerous, even by the standards of other clearing services. This is because a CCP faces more risk clearing OTC derivatives, which have very high values and long maturities compared to other cleared contracts (e.g., for commodities), while the operational complexities involved in clearing OTC derivatives are also far greater." Gregory, Central Counterparties, § 8.3.2, explains that some market participants, "particularly buy side and smaller financial institutions," either may not be eligible for membership or "may find the indirect clearing route more efficient."

13. Under international guidelines, systemically important CCPs are supposed to be prepared to handle the simultaneous default of their two largest clearing members and their affiliates (the so-called Cover 2 standard). CPSS/IOSCO, "Principles for Financial Market Infrastructures," 36. According to principle 4, "a CCP that is involved in activities with a more-complex risk profile or that is systemically important in multiple jurisdictions should maintain additional financial resources sufficient to cover a wide range of potential stress scenarios that should include, but not be limited to, the default of the two participants and their affiliates that would potentially cause the largest aggregate credit exposure to the CCP in extreme but plausible market conditions."

14. See, for example, Yellen, "Interconnectedness and Systemic Risk," 15–16.

15. See, for example, Squire, "Clearinghouses as Liquidity Partitioning," 857.

16. The Group of Twenty (G20) nations, meeting after the crisis, made "[i]mproving over-the-counter derivatives markets" a key element of their postcrisis regulatory reform plans:

   "All standardized OTC derivative contracts should be traded on exchanges or electronic trading platforms, where appropriate, and cleared through central counterparties by end-2012 at the latest. OTC derivative contracts should be reported to trade repositories. Non-centrally cleared contracts should be subject to higher capital requirements."

   See G20 Leaders' Statement at the Pittsburgh Summit, 9.

17. Dodd-Frank § 721 (codified at 7 U.S.C. § 1a (2012)) defines "swap dealers" and "major swap participants." A parallel provision—Dodd-Frank § 761 (codified at 15 U.S.C. § 78c(a) (2012))—defines "security-based swap dealer" and "major security-based swap participant." Dodd-Frank directs the CFTC and SEC to further define all of those terms and "swap," "security-based swap," "eligible contract participant," and "security-based swap agreement"; see Dodd-Frank § 712(d)(1) (codified at 15 U.S.C. § 8302 (2012)). These definitions are important as they help to determine which transactions are subject to Dodd-Frank requirements.

18. Dodd-Frank § 731 (codified at 7 U.S.C. § 6s(a) (2012)) provides for registration of swap dealers and major swap participants; Dodd-Frank § 764 (codified at 15 U.S.C. § 78o-10 (2012)) provides for registration of security-based swap dealers and major security-based swap participants.

19. Dodd-Frank § 731 (adding 7 U.S.C. § 6s(h)) imposes business conduct requirements on swap dealers and major swap participants; Dodd-Frank § 764 (adding 15 U.S.C. § 78o-8(h) (3)) imposes business conduct requirements on security-based swap dealers and major security-based swap participants.

20. Dodd-Frank § 723(a) (codified at 7 U.S.C. § 2(h)(2) (2012)) directs the CFTC to determine "on an ongoing basis" which swaps must be cleared; Dodd-Frank § 763(a) (codified at 15 U.S.C. § 78c-3(b) (2012)) directs the SEC to determine "on an ongoing basis" which security-based swaps must be cleared.

21. Dodd-Frank § 723(a) (codified at 7 U.S.C. § 2(h)(2) (2012)) sets forth clearing determination factors for the CFTC; Dodd-Frank § 763(a) (codified at 15 U.S.C. § 78c-3(b) (2012)) sets forth clearing determination factors for the SEC.

22. Dodd-Frank § 723(a) (codified at 7 U.S.C. § 2(h) (2012)) establishes a swaps clearing requirement; Dodd-Frank § 763(a) (codified at 15 U.S.C. § 78c-3) (2012)) establishes a security-based swaps clearing requirement.

23. Dodd-Frank § 733 (codified at 7 U.S.C. § 7b-3 (2012)) establishes swap execution facilities; Dodd-Frank § 723(a) (codified at 7 U.S.C. § 2(h)(8) (2012)) requires trade execution for swaps; Dodd-Frank § 763(a) (codified at 15 U.S.C. § 78c-3(h) (2012)) requires trade execution for security-based swaps made available to trade; Dodd-Frank § 763(c) (codified at 15 U.S.C. § 78c-4) (2012)) establishes security-based swap execution facilities.

24. Dodd-Frank § 727 (codified at 15 U.S.C. § 2(a) (2012)) provides for swap data repository registration and requires that all swaps be reported to a registered repository; Dodd-Frank § 729 (codified at 7 U.S.C. § 6r (2012)) requires reporting for uncleared swaps; Dodd-Frank § 763(i) (codified at 15 U.S.C. § 78(m), (n) (2012)) provides for security-based swap data repository registration and requires that all security-based swaps be reported to a registered repository; Dodd-Frank § 766 (codified at 15 U.S.C. § 78m-1 (2012)) requires reporting for uncleared security-based swaps.

25. Dodd-Frank § 727 (codified at 7 U.S.C. § 2(a) (2012)) requires public reporting of swap transaction data; Dodd-Frank § 763(i) (codified at 15 U.S.C. § 78(m) (2012)) requires public reporting of security-based swap transaction data.

26. Dodd-Frank § 731 (codified at 7 U.S.C. § 6s(e) (2012)) provides for capital and margin requirements for swaps; Dodd-Frank § 764 (codified at 15 U.S.C. § 78o-8(e) (2012)) provides for capital and margin requirements for security-based swaps.

27. Bernanke, "Clearinghouses, Financial Stability, and Financial Reform," 9.

28. Dodd-Frank § 725(a) (codified at 7 U.S.C. § 7a-1 (2012)).

29. Dodd-Frank § 763(b) (codified at 15 U.S.C. § 78q-1(g) (2012)). Entities providing clearing services for securities must register with the SEC under, and meet the requirements set forth in, section 17A of the Securities Exchange Act of 1934 (codified at 15 U.S.C. § 78q-1(b)) and rule 17Ab2-1, 17 C.F.R. § 240.17Ab2-1 (2016)).

30. Dodd-Frank § 725(b) (codified at 7 U.S.C. § 7a-1(h) (2012)) authorizes the CFTC to exempt comparably supervised CCPs; Dodd-Frank § 763(b) (codified at 15 U.S.C. § 78q-1(k) (2012)) authorizes the SEC to exempt comparably supervised CCPs.

31. Dodd-Frank § 725(c) (codified at 7 U.S.C. § 7a-1(c)(2)(A)(i) (2012)) requires DCOs to adhere to rules imposed by the CFTC pursuant to 7 U.S.C. § 12a(5); Dodd-Frank § 763(b) (codified at 15 U.S.C. § 78q-1(i), (j) (2012)) authorizes the SEC to write security-based swap clearing agency standards.

32. Dodd-Frank § 726 (codified at 15 U.S.C. § 8323 (2012)) directs the CFTC to review the need for and adopt conflict-mitigating rules; Dodd-Frank § 765 (codified at 15 U.S.C. § 8343 (2012)) provides a parallel provision for the SEC. See also Dodd-Frank § 725(d) (2010) (codified at 7 U.S.C. § 7a-1 note (2012)), which directs the CFTC to "adopt rules mitigating conflicts of interest in connection with the conduct of business by a swap dealer or a major swap participant with a [swaps DCO] in which the swap dealer or major swap participant has a material debt or material equity investment." Congress considered more stringent limits on control and voting rights as a way to prevent large dealers from becoming too influential at CCPs. The Lynch Amendment—in the words of its sponsor, Representative Stephen Lynch—would have "prevent[ed] those big banks and major swap participants, like AIG, from taking over the police station—these new clearinghouses . . . by limiting to a 20 percent voting stake the ownership interest in those banks and the governance of the clearing and trading facilities." 155 Cong. Rec. H14, 713 (daily edition, December 10, 2009).

33. Dodd-Frank § 725(c) (codified at 7 U.S.C. § 7a-1(c)(2)(C)(iii)(III) (2012)) requires that DCOs provide "fair and open access"; Dodd-Frank § 763 (codified at 15 U.S.C. § 78c-3(a) (2)(B) (2012)) requires that clearing agencies "provide for non-discriminatory clearing of a security-based swap executed bilaterally or on or through the rules of an unaffiliated national securities exchange or security-based swap execution facility." Open access stands in contrast with the futures model in which DCOs clear the contracts traded on a particular exchange.

34. Dodd-Frank § 725(c) (codified at 7 U.S.C. § 7a-1(c)(2) (2012)).

35. Dodd-Frank § 804 (codified at 12 U.S.C. § 5463 (2012)). For a general overview of Title VIII, see Michel, "Financial Market Utilities." Among the designated financial market utilities (FMUs) are the Chicago Mercantile Exchange, Inc. and ICE Clear Credit LLC, both of which clear swaps. See FSOC Designations, last retrieved April 3, 2015, http://www.treasury .gov/initiatives/fsoc/designations/Pages/default.aspx#FMU.

36. Dodd-Frank § 805(a)(2) (codified at 12 U.S.C. § 5464(a)(2) (2012)) relates to setting standards; Dodd-Frank § 807 (codified at 12 U.S.C. § 5466 (2012)) is related to examination and enforcement.

37. Dodd-Frank § 813 (12 U.S.C. § 5472 (2012)); see also Board of Governors of the Federal Reserve System, SEC and CFTC, "Risk Management Supervision of Designated Clearing Entities," July 2011, a joint report required by section 813 of the Act.

38. Dodd-Frank § 805(c) (codified at 12 U.S.C. § 5464(c) (2012)).

39. Dodd-Frank § 806(e) (codified at 12 U.S.C. § 5465(e) (2012)).

40. See, for example, BIS, "Report of the Committee on Interbank Netting Schemes"; and its Committee on Payment and Settlement Systems and Technical Committee of the International Organization of Securities Commissions, "Recommendations for Central Counterparties."

41. See 15 U.S.C. §78q-1(i) (2012), suggesting that the SEC "conform [security-based swap clearing agency] standards or oversight to reflect evolving United States and international standards."

42. CPSS/IOSCO, "Principles."

43. Pirrong, "Inefficiency of the Clearing Mandate," 33.

44. See, for example, Parkinson, "CCP Liquidity Risk Management," 2–3, which notes that "the central concern with respect to CCP liquidity risk is that a failure of one or more clearing members to meet variation margin calls on time could cause the CCP itself to be unable to meet its own payment obligations as and when expected" and that "[s]uch a failure could jeopardize the ability of its nondefaulting clearing members to meet their payment obligations when expected and thus is a potential vector for financial contagion."

45. Gregory, *Central Counterparties*, § 9.1.4, states that "CCPs may make one or more intra-daily margin calls per day and typically only return margin once a day. Such effects would be most pronounced during volatile markets where large price moves may cause CCPs to ask for very large intraday margins from some participants covering their losses, whilst possibly not returning immediately the equivalent margin against gains of other clearing members."

46. Roe, "Clearinghouse Overconfidence," 1664, 1671–72. Others argue that CCPs are stability enhancing because they ensure that some creditors get paid quickly without slowing down payments to other creditors; see Squire, "Clearinghouses as Liquidity Partitioning," 857.

47. Knott and Mills, "Modelling Risk," 164. See also Domanski, Gambacorta, and Picillo, "Central Clearing," 72. They write that "extreme price movements in cleared financial instruments could result in large variations in the exposure of clearing members to the CCPs and therefore in the need for some of them to make correspondingly large variation margin payments. Such payments can be large, even if margin requirements remain unchanged. But they may be exacerbated if the CCP increases initial margins and/or tightens collateral standards in the face of unusually large price movements. The interaction of such sudden and large shifts in collateral flows with the wider financial system is untested. . . . The demands and dispositions of CCPs could lead to big shifts in collateralized markets, adding to risk aversion and increasing pressure to reduce leverage in a procyclical manner."

48. Knott and Mills, "Modelling Risk," 164.

49. Pirrong, "Bill of Goods," 62–74. See also Tarullo, "Advancing Macroprudential Policy Objectives," which raises concerns about, among other things, CCPs imposing losses on large firms during crises.

50. See Rahman, "Over-the-Counter (OTC) Derivatives," 290. The author writes that "there are a relatively small number of clearing members for these CCPs, and fewer still that

offer client clearing. Those clearing members that do offer client clearing become more important within the system because non-clearing member firms would otherwise be unable to access central clearing, hindering their ability to undertake OTC derivatives transactions (especially if these contracts become subject to the clearing obligation)" (footnote omitted).

51. Wendt, "Central Counterparties," 9. "Global systemically important banks (G-SIBs) and other commercial banks," Wendt writes, "may fulfill roles of general clearing member (clearing for clients), liquidity provider, depository bank, custodian and settlement bank."

52. See, for example, Parkinson, "CCP Liquidity Risk Management," 4; Steigerwald, "Central Counterparty Clearing," 21–22.

53. Powell, "Financial System Perspective," 4: "To carry out their critical functions, CCPs rely on a wide variety of financial services from other financial firms, such as custody, clearing, and settlement. Many of these services are provided by the same global financial institutions that are also the largest clearing members of the CCPs." See also Domanski, Gambacorta, and Picillo, "Central Clearing," 68: "The CCP's own liquid assets and backup liquidity lines made available by banks may provide effective insurance against liquidity shocks resulting from the difficulties of one or a few clearing members. But they can hardly provide protection in the event of a systemic shock, when a large number of clearing participants—potentially including the providers of liquidity lines—become liquidity-constrained, thereby triggering domino effects."

54. See, for example, Wendt, "Central Counterparties," 9, which explains that a CCP is "particularly vulnerable to the default of a service-providing clearing member . . . not only because it has to cover the default of the clearing member, but because it may also lose access to the collateral kept by that clearing member in its role as custodian[,] may lose access to the credit lines that were provided by the defaulting clearing member and it may face operational problems due to the loss of one of its settlement banks."

55. See generally *Report of the Presidential Task Force on Market Mechanisms*. Known as the Brady Commission Report, it describes the events of the 1987 crash. See also McPartland, "Clearing and Settlement," 3, which explains that "a CCP can only remove market risk from its clearing system when the national banking system is open," adding that "late settlement payments associated with derivatives markets were one of the root causes of near payments gridlock during the 1987 market crash."

56. Bernanke, "Clearing and Settlement during the Crash," 133, 146–47. The IMF points to the role that operational weaknesses played during the 1987 crash in the near failures of the Chicago Mercantile Exchange (CME) and the Options Clearing Corporation (OCC); see IMF, "Making Over-the-Counter Derivatives Safer," 18–19.

57. Bernanke, "Clearing and Settlement during the Crash," 133, 148.

58. Ibid., 133, 147.

59. Ibid., 149. Bernanke writes that "the Federal Reserve, in its lender-of-last-resort capacity . . . induce[d] the banks (by suasion and by the supply of liquidity) to make loans on customary terms, despite chaotic conditions and the possibility of severe adverse selection of borrowers."

60. Some operational concerns still remain. See Anderson and Jõeveer, "Economics of Collateral," which finds that "moving toward central clearing with product specialized CCPs can greatly increase the numbers of margin movements which will place greater demands on a participant's operational capacity and liquidity."

61. See, for example, "Liquidity Coverage Ratio: Liquidity Risk Measurement Standards," 79 Fed. Reg. (October 10, 2014): 61439.

62. See, for example, transcript of the CFTC Market Risk Advisory Committee Meeting, Washington, DC, April 2, 2015, 95 (statement of Emily Portney, JPMorgan).

63. See, for example, transcript of CFTC Market Risk Advisory Committee Meeting, 89 (statement of Scott Flood, Citi's Institutional Client Group).

64. See Domanski, Gambacorta, and Picillo, "Central Clearing," 68–69. The authors explain that "[i]n the extreme case, the default of common clearing members could threaten the resilience of several CCPs at the same time [which], in turn, would impose strains on the surviving clearing members, propagating systemic risk."

65. See, for example, Parkinson, "CCP Liquidity Risk Management," 3. "If confidence in a CCP is shattered and, as is often the case, no other CCP serves the market, the market would cease functioning."

66. The statutory framework does not explicitly allow for emergency termination or suspension of the clearing mandate. FIA Europe raised a permutation of this issue—a CCP would have to continue clearing a product subject to a clearing mandate and taking on the associated risk during a crisis. FIA Europe, "Review of the Cumulative Impact," 12: "[T]he clearing obligation cannot be terminated or suspended as a matter of urgency in extreme circumstances. This means that CCPs may find themselves clearing more risk in a contract or product than there would be market capacity to manage upon a member default. A CCP may therefore have no option but to encourage participants to reduce these clearing provisions by increasing margin requirements to levels at which it is uneconomic to hold the positions and thus force the risk to be closed out."

67. See, for example, Elliott, "Central Counterparty Loss-Allocation Rules," sec. 4, which discusses the potential adverse effects of a CCP failure.

68. For a discussion of the association between central clearing and high collateral demands, see Singh, "Making OTC Derivatives Safe," 5.

69. Ibid., 9.

70. For an excellent discussion of the potential for lost hedging opportunities and increased costs for swaps end-users as a result of the central clearing mandate, see McBride, "The Dodd-Frank Act and OTC Derivatives," 1111–19. Market observers have noted that futures products are emerging to take the place of certain types of swaps. See, for example, CFTC, Transcript of the Public Roundtable on Futurization of Swaps.

71. Beylin, "Reassessment of the Clearing Mandate," 15, 48.

72. See Singh, "Making OTC Derivatives Safe," 4: "Offloading only standard contracts will adversely impact the net exposure on their books as this will 'unbundle' netted positions. . . ." For a general discussion of this topic, see McBride, "The Dodd-Frank Act and OTC Derivatives," 1106–8.

73. See McPartland, "Clearing and Settlement," 2: "In an electronic trading environment, clearing provides valuable anonymity; buyer and seller (and buying clearing member and selling clearing member) rarely know (or need to know) each other's identity."

74. See Roe, "Clearinghouse Overconfidence," 1641, 1694–95.

75. Knott and Mills, "Modelling Risk," 172, explains, for example, that ". . . residual exposure to the uncovered losses of the CCP . . . creates an incentive for clearing members to take an active interest in the overall standard of a CCP's risk management."

76. Gregory, *Central Counterparties*, § 3.2.6, explains that a key to the CCP "loss mutualisation" model is the requirement that "all members pay into [a] default fund [and thus] all

contribute to absorbing an extreme default loss." See also IMF, "Making Over-the-Counter Derivatives Safer," 17, which notes that "guarantee fund contributions should be related to the [clearing member's] market position and the nature of its exposures and be reevaluated regularly."

77. See CME Rulebook, sec. 8F010, which explains that "if the Clearing House determines in good faith that, based on the exercise of prudent risk management standards, that an OTC Clearing Member poses undue risk to the Clearing House based on its OTC Derivatives portfolio, the Clearing House may take any or all of the following actions with respect to such OTC Clearing Member: 1) impose an additional performance bond requirement; 2) prohibit the addition of any new OTC Derivative positions, or 3) require the reduction or unwinding of OTC Derivatives positions." ICE Clear Credit Rulebook (2015), 16, explains that "for the protection of ICE Clear Credit and the Participants, ICE Clear Credit shall be authorized: (i) to impose such additional capital, Margin or other requirements on a Participant; (ii) to allow such Participant to submit Trades for liquidation only; (iii) to limit or restrict the type of Contracts that may be cleared by such Participant in any of its accounts with ICE Clear Credit; or (iv) to limit or restrict the aggregate notional or other reference amount of positions in Contracts that are permitted to be maintained by such Participant in any of its accounts with ICE Clear Credit."

78. See, for example, Parkinson, "CCP Liquidity Risk Management," 6, which suggests that "perhaps the most important reason a CCP can reduce risk is that a CCP has a more complete picture of the aggregate risks posed by participants than do counterparties to uncleared transactions."

79. Pirrong, "Economics of Central Clearing," 14 (footnote omitted).

80. Tucker, "Are Clearing Houses the New Central Banks?," 2. See also Chang, "Systemic Risk Paradox," 773. "Lulled by a false sense of security and goaded by improvements in hedging from DCOs," the author writes, "players might take on more derivatives at greater notional values. Counterparties might monitor each other less, trusting that DCOs are doing so— whereas counterparties trading bilaterally likely understand each other better than a DCO would" (footnotes omitted).

81. See, for example, Cœuré, "Ensuring an Adequate Loss-Absorbing Capacity": "In fact, a substantial increase of 'skin in the game' could provide clearing members with a false sense of security, by reducing their potential contribution to the loss-allocation process. This could lead them to be less vigilant in monitoring risks, which may have severe consequences for the safety of CCPs. . . . [I]t seems reasonable that an increase in prefunded resources, should it become necessary, should be mainly borne by clearing members" (footnote omitted).

82. See Rundle, "Helping Clearing Houses Avoid a Crash." The author writes, "Not surprisingly, clearing members are wanting more transparency on how clearing houses will operate in a crisis. Concerns are high that the stress-testing methodologies they use and the extent to which members might be required to prop up a clearer are ill-defined, to the point that it may increase risk in stressed markets." CCPs are not particularly sympathetic to this concern. See, for example, CME Group et al., letter to Jacob L. Lew, 3: "With full transparency into a CCP's financial safeguards and default management practices, clearing members and participants have sufficient information to evaluate the risk profile of the CCP and manage their own exposures."

83. See, for example, 17 C.F.R. § 23.432, which requires swap dealers and major swap participants to disclose "that the counterparty has the sole right to select the derivatives clearing organization at which the swap will be cleared." The nondealer's clearing member presumably will monitor the CCP, but requiring that the nondealer choose the CCP still removes the decision from the party with the most direct access to information about the CCP.

84. For the considerations that go into decisions whether to clear, see Gregory, *Central Counterparties*, § 12.1.3.

85. CPSS/IOSCO, "Guidance on the Application," iii. The document provides an extensive discussion of the unique complexities of an OTC derivatives CCP.

86. Singh, "Making OTC Derivatives Safe," 9. See also Cohn, "Clearing Houses Reduce Risk." The Goldman Sachs president and chief operating officer sets forth an argument that nonstandardized products in deeply liquid markets can safely be cleared, but "in other markets, clearing houses can themselves become centres of concentrated risk and sources of contagion, amplifying systemic problems instead of alleviating them." Cohn explains that forcing central clearing on "complex, illiquid products that are susceptible to sudden and severe price gaps . . . can have serious repercussions."

87. CPSS/IOSCO, "Guidance on the Application," 13, notes that "some products may have nonlinear risk characteristics (e.g., jump-to-default risk in a single-name CDS)."

88. See Knott and Mills, "Modelling Risk," 172, which notes that "it will be important for CCPs to develop and enhance scenario-based stress-testing procedures which assess the impact of low probability, but nonetheless plausible events, which may have no precedent in the current historical record."

89. Pirrong, "Economics of Central Clearing," 18, explains that "in many OTC products, liquidity tends to decline over time, and these positions are often retained for extended periods."

90. See Wibaut and Wilford, "Markets for CCPs and Regulation," 112. The authors explain that correlations "are unlikely to hold when it matters most—a systemic disruption with significant market contagion."

91. See Knott and Mills, "Modelling Risk," 170: "As CCPs expand into new markets, . . . there is a question about how effectively SPAN [a common margin methodology] can be adapted to deal with the more complex portfolios that result."

92. CPPS/IOSCO, "Guidance on the Application," 13.

93. Dodd-Frank §723(a)(2) (adding 7 U.S.C. § 2(h)(2)(D)(ii)).

94. Ibid.

95. As an illustration, in the following clearing determination, the CFTC repeats the standard arguments for clearing without applying them specifically to the CDS indices allegedly being analyzed:

> "Clearing the CDS indices subject to this determination will reduce systemic risk in the following ways: mitigating counterparty credit risk because the DCO would become the buyer to every seller of CDS indices subject to this determination and vice-versa; providing counterparties with daily mark-to-market valuations and exchange of variation margin pursuant to a risk management framework set by the DCO and reviewed by the Commission's Division of Clearing and Risk; posting initial margin with the DCO in order to cover potential future exposures in the event of a default; achieving multilateral netting, which substantially reduces the number and notional amount of outstanding bilateral positions; reducing swap counterparties' operational burden by consolidating collateral management and cash flows; and eliminating the need for novations or tear-ups because clearing members may offset opposing positions."

CFTC, "Clearing Requirement Determination under Section 2(h) of the CEA," 77 Fed. Reg. (December 13, 2012): 74283, 74297.

96. For example, Carr, "CCPs Mull Equity Swaps," reports that a number of CCPs are "exploring the possibility of clearing a broader range of equity swap products," which could ultimately lead to new clearing mandates; see also Domanski, Gambacorta, and Picillo, "Central Clearing," 72, which notes that "most CCPs are for-profit entities—typically vertically integrated with other financial market infrastructures, such as exchanges—that are strongly motivated to generate revenues by expanding their product offering and capturing market share. However, new products could bring incremental risk, which clearing members may end up bearing if the CCP does not increase its capital commensurately."

97. Professors Darrell Duffie and Haoxiang Zhu show that "[r]elative to the case of fully bilateral netting (no clearing), substantial [counterparty risk reduction] benefits can be obtained by the joint clearing of the four major classes of derivatives" and call for "the joint clearing of standard interest-rate swaps and credit default swaps in the same clearinghouse." Duffie and Zhu, "Does a Central Clearing Counterparty?," 88, 90. See also Squire, "Clearinghouses as Liquidity Partitioning," 919, which argues that, in order to increase netting opportunities, regulators should follow "the aphorism 'in for a dime, in for a dollar.'"

98. See CFTC, "Final Rule and Interim Final Rule: Margin Requirements for Uncleared Swaps for Swap Dealers and Major Swap Participants," 81 Fed. Reg. (January 6, 2016): 671: "The final rule implements the new statutory framework . . . which requires the Commission to adopt capital and initial and variation margin requirements for [covered swap entities] on all uncleared swaps in order to offset the greater risk to the swap entity and the financial system arising from the use of swaps and security-based swaps that are not cleared." See CFTC, "Proposed Rule: Margin Requirements for Uncleared Swaps for Swap Dealers and Major Swap Participants," 79 Fed. Reg. (October 3, 2014): 59901: "Given the Congressional reference to the 'greater risk' of uncleared swaps and the requirement that margin for such swaps 'be appropriate for the risk,' the Commission believes that establishing margin requirements for uncleared swaps that are at least as stringent as those for cleared swaps is necessary to fulfill the statutory mandate." See also Yellen, "Interconnectedness and Systemic Risk," 19–20, which explains that "a more robust and consistent margin regime for non-centrally cleared derivatives will not only reduce systemic risk, but will also diminish the incentive to tinker with contract language as a way to evade clearing requirements."

99. See generally Basel Committee on Banking Supervision, "Capital Requirements." For a discussion of how capital rules apply to uncleared and cleared transactions, see Office of the Comptroller of the Currency and Board of Governors of the Federal Reserve System, "Regulatory Capital Rules: Regulatory Capital, Implementation of Basel III, Capital Adequacy, Transition Provisions, Prompt Corrective Action, Standardized Approach for Risk-Weighted Assets, Market Discipline and Disclosure Requirements, Advanced Approaches Risk-Based Capital Rule, and Market Risk Capital Rule," 78 Fed. Reg. (October 11, 2013): 62094–103.

100. Dodd-Frank §§ 723(a) (adding 7 U.S.C. §2(h)(4)) directs the CFTC to prevent evasion of clearing mandate with respect to swaps; 763(a) (adding 15 U.S.C. § 78c-3(d)) directs the SEC to prevent evasion of clearing mandate with respect to security-based swaps. See also CFTC-SEC Conflicts Roundtable, 40 (comments of Heather Slavkin, AFL-CIO, which suggests that there would be "spurious customization" to avoid the clearing mandate); and Financial Stability Board, "Implementing OTC Derivatives," 21, which warns regulators to be wary of customization as a way to avoid clearing.

101. See Massad, Keynote Address, which underscores the importance of CCP regulation "because of the increased importance we have placed on central clearing." See also Allen, "Derivatives Clearinghouses and Systemic Risk," 1106, which calls for strict regulation and a prefunded guaranty fund with a government backstop; Bernanke, "Clearinghouses," 9, which explains that a robust prudential regulatory regime must accompany access to emergency credit facilities;

Powell, "Financial System Perspective," which explains that international CCP standards are "essential given that, in the interest of transparency and improved risk management, policymakers have encouraged the concentration of activities at these key nodes"; Tucker, "Are Clearing Houses the New Central Banks?," 12. A former UK central bank official, Tucker explains that "[l]ike central banks, clearing houses are part of the essential financial plumbing of modern economies." He argues that CCPs should be macroprudentially "regulated utilities." See also Levitin, "Response," 462, which identifies a potential role for regulation of CCP rules but argues principally for high capital standards to serve as a "financial sea wall" for CCPs.

102. See Greenberger, "Diversifying Clearinghouse Ownership," 245, 257. See also Nosal, "Clearing Over-the-Counter Derivatives," 143–44, which argues that broad membership fosters liquidity and competition, so any firm that "can cover the risk that it brings into the CCP, by providing appropriate levels of collateral and making contributions to the guarantee fund," should be allowed membership.

103. See Pirrong, "Economics of Central Clearing," 27, which explains that "CCPs with more diverse memberships are more prone to conflict, more cumbersome to manage, less effective at responding to changes in the marketplace and less effective at responding to crises that are likely to have disparate impacts on different types of firms," and they are more vulnerable to "moral hazard problems." Angela Armakola and Jean-Paul Laurent underscore the important relationship between CCP resilience in the face of stress scenarios and the strength of a CCP's member base. See Armakola and Laurent, "CCP Resilience and Clearing Membership," 26, which urges regulators to be "cautious about . . . subsidising of low quality [clearing members] that might overload a CCP at the expense of others, thus jeopardizing the efficiency of the new risk-sharing mechanisms."

104. See Braithwaite, "Legal Perspectives on Client Clearing," 16–17, which observes that the clearing mandate could effectively shut certain parties out of OTC markets subject to a mandate if they are neither eligible to be members nor desirable clients for a member. See also SEC, "Final Rule: Clearing Agency Standards," 77 Fed. Reg. (November 2, 2012): 66240, which explains that "the success of correspondent clearing arrangements depends on the willingness of participants to enter such arrangements with non-participant firms that may act as direct competitors to the participants in the participants' capacity as dealers or security-based swap dealers in the market for the relevant securities."

105. CFTC, "Final Rule: Derivatives Clearing Organization General Provisions and Core Principles," 76 Fed. Reg. (November 8, 2011): 69353.

106. Ibid.

107. Ibid., 69355. The CFTC argued that "the addition of smaller clearing members does not eliminate the role that larger clearing members can play in default management—it merely spreads the risk," and that "[s]ubject to appropriate safeguards, outsourcing of certain obligations can be an effective means of harmonizing these goals" (69356). It is questionable whether these outsourcing arrangements would be honored during a crisis when they would most likely be called upon.

108. Ibid., 69357.

109. Braithwaite, "Legal Perspectives on Client Clearing," 12.

110. "Q&A with Hal Scott of Harvard Law."

111. Michel, "Financial Market Utilities," 10.

112. CPSS/IOSCO, "Principles," 1.

113. Ibid., 26.

114. Varney et al., Letter to CFTC, 7. See also Chang, "Systemic Risk Paradox," 795, 810–12. The author writes that "because big banks, which tend to be the powerhouse derivatives dealers, control clearinghouses, there is a danger that big banks can leverage the dominance of clearinghouses to consolidate their share in the dealer market" and argues for the application of the "essential facilities doctrine" for the purpose of "clarifying when rivals of clearinghouse members might be able to pursue a private right of action" (footnote omitted). See also Johnson, "Commentary on the Abraham L. Pomerantz Lecture," 696–701, which argues that large dealer CCP members' "rent-seeking motives" could lead CCPs to make decisions that undermine the role of CCPs in risk mitigation.

115. See, for example, Greenberger, "Diversifying Clearinghouse Ownership," 265–66n, which calls for at least half of directors to be independent; Griffith, "Governing Systemic Risk," 1240, which argues for half of directors on CCP boards to be selected by regulators and thus attuned to systemic risk considerations; Johnson, "Governing Financial Markets," 221, 240, which points to the "conflict between regulators' expectations and . . . clearinghouse owners' priorities" and calls for a regulator-appointed monitor to serve as a board watchdog who "would report directly to and receive compensation from" regulators; Kelleher, letter to David A. Stawick, 16, which advocates that a CCP's risk management committee "be controlled in form and substance by independent decision-makers"; Varney et al., letter to CFTC, 7, which calls for the risk management committee to be populated with a majority of independent directors.

116. For a description and analysis of the different proposed approaches, see Griffith, "Governing Systemic Risk," 1212–26.

117. Wetjen, "Ensuring the Promise." See also Bailey, "Bank of England's Perspective." Bailey called for "[s]tandardised stress tests" to "complement more tailored and potentially much more rigorous internal stress testing, developed and implemented by individual CCPs." See also Powell, "Financial System Perspective." "Not all CCPs are alike," according to Powell, "[b]ut there may be approaches that could bring some of the benefits of standardization while allowing tailoring of some scenarios to the activities of particular CCPs or groups of CCPs."

118. Wetjen, "Ensuring the Promise."

119. An anonymous peer reviewer raised this concern. A full analysis of regulatory capture in the post-Dodd-Frank derivatives markets is beyond the scope of this chapter but would be a productive area for further research.

120. Stigler, "Theory of Economic Regulation," 3.

121. Shadow Financial Regulatory Committee, "Dangers of Substituting Foreign Compliance," 1.

122. See CFTC and SEC, "Joint Report," 88. "The CFTC does not have clear authority, for example, to set rules for risk management for exchanges and clearinghouses. The CFTC's authority contrasts with the authority of other regulators, such as the SEC or regulators in foreign jurisdictions."

123. Saltzman, letter to Jacob Lew, 2, requested "that the FSOC coordinate and work with its member agencies with authority over CCPs to strengthen the ability of CCPs to mitigate and manage systemic risks arising from CCP operations." Others have argued against the one-size-fits-all regulation that might be introduced by active FSOC involvement in CCP regulatory issues; see Duffy et al., letter to Jacob J. Lew.

124. See Wendt, "Central Counterparties," 12: "International coordination among authorities will be challenging, in case of a default impacting multiple jurisdictions, as interests may differ. The home authority may give priority to maintaining the CCP's operations, whereas the authorities of other countries may prioritize the stability of their financial system or local banks." See also Swinburne, Speech before the World Federation of Exchanges/IOMA

Conference. Swinburne commented that she did "not want to see a scenario where the banking regulator of a large clearing member refuses to allow that member to participate in refills of a CCPs default fund as it is concerned about that bank having enough capital to refill one of its own domestically supervised CCPs."

125. Linking can take different forms. See IMF, "Making Over-the-Counter Derivatives Safer," 24–25, box 3.7.

126. Ibid., 18, box 3.5. The IMF discusses CCP failures and highlights the role that failure to properly increase margin requirements played in the failures of the French Caisse de Liquidation, the Malaysian Kuala Lumpur Commodity Clearing House, and the Hong Kong Futures Exchange.

127. Wibaut and Wilford point out, for example, that regulators' role in setting the type of margin that CCPs can accept could be influenced by the same forces that drove regulators to treat German and Greek bonds as equivalent. Wibaut and Wilford, "Markets for CCPs and Regulation," 102n7.

128. To avoid the problem of a sole CCP failing, BlackRock has recommended that the clearing mandate only apply to products cleared by two or more CCPs. BlackRock, "Central Clearing Counterparties," 2. Alternatively, if there were a failure, the government could encourage another already operational and healthy CCP that clears other types of products to begin clearing the products formerly cleared by the failing CCP. Such an expansion, however, would likely take considerable time because it would require the expanding CCP to analyze the risk associated with the new product and any new clearing members and to gain regulatory approval to clear the product. Presumably a willing regulator could expedite such a process in an emergency, but doing so would raise new risk concerns.

129. See Lubben, "Failure of the Clearinghouse," which argues that CCPs likely are not encompassed in the list of companies that can proceed through resolution and that, had CCPs been intended to be covered, the CFTC would have been granted a role in deciding whether a CCP should be put into the Orderly Liquidation Authority; Duffie, "Financial Market Infrastructure," 3, which discusses questions about whether Title II, particularly as interpreted by the Federal Deposit Insurance Corporation, applies to CCPs. But see also Allen, "Derivatives Clearinghouses and Systemic Risk," 1103, which argues that, although Title II applies to CCPs, "the logistical complexities of applying the Orderly Liquidation Authority procedures to an insolvent clearinghouse make government intervention before initiation of the receivership process the most likely outcome."

130. Dodd-Frank § 806(b) provides: "The Board of Governors may authorize a Federal Reserve Bank . . . to provide a designated financial market utility discount and borrowing privileges only in unusual or exigent circumstances, upon the affirmative vote of a majority of the Board of Governors . . . after consultation with the Secretary, and upon a showing by the designated financial market utility that it is unable to secure adequate credit accommodations from other banking institutions." See also Baker, "Federal Reserve's Supporting Role," 180, which explains: "The failure of a systemically significant clearinghouse could be catastrophic. It would threaten widespread, domino-like disruptions of critical money flows that its members and other financial institutions count on to meet their own financial obligations all over the world. Intervention by a government backstop—a last resort clearinghouse—would likely be needed to avert the collapse of a systemically significant clearinghouse. Due to critical but little understood reforms in Title VIII, the Federal Reserve can now assume this role in certain situations."

131. Dodd-Frank § 806(a).

132. The likelihood that the provision will be used for a bailout may be increased by the fact that—as Colleen Baker points out—the phrase "unusual or exigent circumstances" is

broader than the "unusual and exigent circumstances" used in the Federal Reserve's emergency lending authority under Section 13(3) [12 U.S.C. § 343(3)(A) (2012)]. Baker, "Federal Reserve's Supporting Role," 180n38.

133. See Powell, "Financial System Perspective," which advises "CCPs and their members" that they "must plan to stand on their own and continue to provide critical services to the financial system, without support from the taxpayer."

134. See Baker, "Federal Reserve's Supporting Role," 184, which argues that "the very presence of a potential central bank backstop for systemically significant clearinghouses—essentially the possibility of catastrophic liquidity insurance—creates a significant moral hazard"; Singh, "Making OTC Derivatives Safe," 17, which points out that the availability of emergency liquidity support "may lead to moral hazard that may manifest itself, for example, in CCPs not requiring full collateral from their existing members/clients, quite possibly with the acquiescence of regulators."

135. See Hills et al., "Central Counterparty Clearing Houses," 129–30, which provides a helpful discussion of the causes of each CCP failure; Moody's Investors Service, "Proposed Clearing House Rating Methodology," exhibit 16. See also Gregory, *Central Counterparties*, §14.2, which discusses "historical CCP failures and near failures"; Tucker, "Counterparties in Evolving Capital Markets," 180, which describes the fallout from the Hong Kong failure.

136. See IMF, "Making Over-the-Counter Derivatives Safer," 18, box 3.5, which highlights the role that failure to properly increase margin requirements played in the CCP failures.

137. See Quarry et al., "OTC Derivatives Clearing," 6.

138. Kong, "Trading Error"; Vaghela, "Korea Clearing Structure"; Whan-woo, "HanMag Debacle Hits Brokerages."

139. McBride, "The Dodd-Frank Act and OTC Derivatives," 1121–22.

140. See, for example, Culp, "OTC-Cleared Derivatives," 1, which notes that CCPs started clearing OTC derivatives in the late 1990s; Kroszner, "Central Counterparty Clearing," 39.

141. The notion that clearing members do not care about CCP risk management is belied by the widespread industry concern about uncapped exposures to CCP risk. See, for example, Saltzman, letter to Jacob Lew, which notes that The Clearing House Association "continues to share the serious concerns raised by regulators regarding the need to address and mitigate systemic risks presented by all CCPs" and details concerns and recommendations for improved risk management.

142. Kroszner, "Central Counterparty Clearing," 37.

143. Pirrong, "Economics of Central Clearing," 28–29.

144. Some have proposed insurance to cover potential losses at the end of the default waterfall. See, for example, Leising, "Catastrophe Prevention Drives Pitch," which describes the formation of an insurance consortium to offer insurance to clearinghouses.

145. Kroszner, "Central Counterparty Clearing," 38.

146. IMF, "Making Over-the-Counter Derivatives Safer," 16, which explains that a race to the risk management bottom "will be counteracted provided that users, who bear the risk of each other's default, have a sufficient voice in governance and particularly if the CCP is user-owned"; Kroszner, "Central Counterparty Clearing," 38: "The mutualization of risk creates incentives for all of the exchange's members to support the imposition of risk controls that limit the extent to which the trading activities of any individual member expose all of [the] other members to losses from defaults. Moreover, because members own the clearinghouse, they have the capability to act on their incentives for effective CCP risk management."

147. See Dodd-Frank § 726, which allows the CFTC to "adopt rules which may include numerical limits on the control of, or the voting rights with respect to, any derivatives clearing organization that clears swaps . . . by a bank holding company . . . with total consolidated assets of $50,000,000,000 or more, a nonbank financial company . . . supervised by the Board, an affiliate of such a bank holding company or nonbank financial company, a swap dealer, major swap participant, or associated person of a swap dealer or major swap participant."

148. See Domanski, Gambacorta, and Picillo, "Central Clearing," 63, which notes that "in 83% of the cases, CCPs are directly owned or managed by the company operating the stock exchange"; Evanoff, Russo, and Steigerwald, "Policymakers, Researchers, and Practitioners," 12, which notes that, "[i]n the U.S., there has been a recent movement away from the traditional model of mutual ownership of exchanges and their clearing and settlement providers, toward a for-profit, stock ownership," which "could have a potential impact on the incentive structure and, possibly, the risk aversion of the organizations."

149. See Hills et al., "Central Counterparty Clearing Houses," 130, which notes that if risk monitoring incentives are to be effective, "providers of the central counterparty's guarantee fund or other capital should also be its owners, or at least . . . management should be accountable to them in some way"; Kroszner, "Central Counterparty Clearing," 39, which explains that "governance arrangements must provide those with 'skin in the game' with substantial influence over the CCP's risk controls"; Pirrong, "Economics of Central Clearing," 26, which argues that "those who bear the counterparty risks assumed by a CCP should have the power to make decisions that affect the riskiness of the CCP, and the distribution of that risk"; Scott, "Reduction of Systemic Risk," 701, which argues against ownership and control restrictions that "would limit the ability of swap dealers and major swap participants, who are the parties with the greatest expertise in risk management, to exercise influence over the policies and operations of a clearinghouse."

150. See Greenberger, "Diversifying Clearinghouse Ownership," 245, which argues for strong limits on the economic interests of swap dealers in CCPs.

151. See Johnson, "Governing Financial Markets," 222–25, which contends that large swap dealers have incentives to limit CCP membership and product eligibility.

152. See Greenberger, "Diversifying Clearinghouse Ownership," 245, which argues "that the CFTC should strengthen its proposed governance standards for DCOs in order to safeguard swap users' access to clearing against the possibility that the CFTC's participant eligibility requirements fail to increase DCO membership" (footnote omitted); Johnson, "Governing Financial Markets," 239–41, which argues for a board monitor or observer to provide a link between CCP boards and regulators.

153. See Griffith, "Governing Systemic Risk," 1212–26, which acknowledges that "dealers must exert a level of control over clearinghouse operations that is commensurate with their exposure to risk through the clearinghouse" but advocates that CCP boards include some directors elected by regulators to ensure systemic risk considerations are taken into account"; Turbeville, "Derivatives Clearinghouses," 13, which states: "At a minimum, the public's interest should be represented by membership on the risk committees of major clearinghouses. Regulatory representation, or representation by other public interest organization, would legitimize the process . . ."; Varney et al., letter to CFTC, 7, which calls for 100 percent independent directors on nominating committees and majority independent risk management and executive committees.

154. 7 U.S.C. § 7a-1(c)(2)(N)(2013). See also 15 U.S.C. § 78q-1(b)(3)(I)(2013): "The rules of the clearing agency do not impose any burden on competition not necessary or appropriate in furtherance of the purposes of this title."

155. As noted earlier, Craig Pirrong called for something similar with respect to risk management measures. Pirrong, "Economics of Central Clearing," 28–29, which calls for regulators to be able to revise membership requirements if the regulators "can show that they were adopted

for anti-competitive reasons, or place an undue burden on competition not justified by any prudential benefit."

156. The Supreme Court's reasoning for not allowing an antitrust suit to proceed in Credit Suisse v. Billing, which related to initial public offering underwriter syndicates, seems applicable here. 551 U.S. 264, 285 (2007). The court refused to apply antitrust law based on "the difficulty of drawing a complex, sinuous line separating securities-permitted from securities-forbidden conduct, the need for securities-related expertise to draw that line, the likelihood that litigating parties will depend upon the same evidence yet expect courts to draw different inferences from it, and the serious risk that antitrust courts will produce inconsistent results that, in turn, will overly deter syndicate practices important in the marketing of new issues."

157. Kroszner, "Central Counterparty Clearing," 40.

158. For thoughtful discussions of these issues, see Committee on Payments and Market Infrastructures and Board of the International Organization of Securities Commissions, Recovery of Financial Market Infrastructures (comments on the report are available at http://www.bis.org/cpmi/publ/comments/d109/overview.htm); Duffie, "Resolution of Failing Central Counterparties"; ISDA, "CCP Loss Allocation"; JPMorgan Chase, "What Is the Resolution Plan?"; LCH.Clearnet, "CCP Risk Management."

159. See Duffie, Li, and Lubke, "Policy Perspectives on OTC Derivatives," 2, which explains that "In 2005, the exponential growth of the credit derivatives market had outpaced the capabilities of dealers' processing systems, leading to large backlogs of unconfirmed trades. These unconfirmed trades had potentially uncertain legal statuses, often for lengthy periods of time, and limited the ability of dealers to accurately determine their counterparty exposures . . ."; Ledrut and Upper, "Clearing Post-Trading Arrangements," 92, which notes that "high access standards by CCPs can serve as a catalyst for improvements in back office processes."

160. See Dodd-Frank § 727 (adding 7 U.S.C. § 2a(13)(G)), which notes that "each swap (whether cleared or uncleared) shall be reported to a registered swap data repository," and § 729 (adding 7 U.S.C. § 6o-1(a)(1)), which allows uncleared swaps to be reported to the CFTC. (Parallel provisions exist for security-based swaps.)

161. Swap data repositories are defined in Dodd-Frank to mean "any person that collects and maintains information or records with respect to transactions or positions in, or the terms and conditions of, swaps entered into by third parties for the purpose of providing a centralized recordkeeping facility for swaps." Dodd-Frank § 721 (adding 7 U.S.C. § 1a(48)). Entities that meet this definition *must* register with the CFTC. Dodd-Frank § 728 (adding 7 U.S.C. § 24a(1)(A)). Allowing SDRs to choose whether to register would enable SDRs to choose to serve nonregulatory audiences without registering.

162. See Hayek, "Pretence of Knowledge": "The recognition of the insuperable limits to his knowledge ought indeed to teach the student of society a lesson of humility which should guard him against becoming an accomplice in men's fatal striving to control society—a striving which makes him not only a tyrant over his fellows, but which may well make him the destroyer of a civilization which no brain has designed but which has grown from the free efforts of millions of individuals."

REFERENCES

Acharya, Viral, Menachem Brenner, Robert Engle, Anthony Lynch, and Matthew Richardson. "Derivatives—the Ultimate Financial Innovation." In *Restoring Financial Stability: How to Repair a Failed Financial System,* edited by Viral Acharya and Matthew Richardson, 233–50. Hoboken, NJ: Wiley, 2009.

Allen, Julia Lees. "Derivatives Clearinghouses and Systemic Risk: A Bankruptcy and Dodd-Frank Analysis." *Stanford Law Review* 64 (2012): 1079–108.

Anderson, Ronald W., and Karin Jõeveer. "The Economics of Collateral." Discussion Paper No. 732, Financial Markets Group, May 2014.

Armakola, Angela, and Jean-Paul Laurent. "CCP Resilience and Clearing Membership." November 20, 2015. http://papers.ssrn.com/sol3/Delivery.cfm/SSRN_ID2693427 _code1859873.pdf?abstractid=2625579&mirid=1.

Bailey, David. "The Bank of England's Perspective on CCP Risk Management, Recovery, and Resolution Arrangements." Speech at the Deutsche Boerse Group and Eurex Exchange of Ideas Conference, London, November 24, 2014.

Baker, Colleen M. "The Federal Reserve's Supporting Role behind Dodd-Frank's Clearinghouse Reforms." *Harvard Business Law Review Online* 3 (2013): 177–86.

Bank for International Settlements. "Report of the Committee on Interbank Netting Schemes of the Central Banks of the Group of Ten Countries" (Lamfalussy Report). November 1990. http://www.bis.org/cpmi/publ/d04.pdf.

Bank for International Settlements, Committee on Payment and Settlement Systems and Technical Committee of the International Organization of Securities Commissions. "Recommendations for Central Counterparties." November 2004. http://www.bis.org/cpmi/publ/d64.htm.

Basel Committee on Banking Supervision. "Capital Requirements for Bank Exposures to Central Counterparties." April 2014. http://www.bis.org/publ/bcbs282.pdf.

Bernanke, Ben S. "Clearing and Settlement during the Crash." *Review of Financial Studies* 3 (1990): 133–51.

———. "Clearinghouses, Financial Stability, and Financial Reform." Speech at the 2011 Financial Markets Conference, Stone Mountain, GA, April 4, 2011.

Beylin, Ilya. "A Reassessment of the Clearing Mandate: How the Clearing Mandate Affects Swap Trading Behavior and the Consequences for Systemic Risk." Unpublished draft, May 18, 2015.

BlackRock. "Central Clearing Counterparties and Too Big to Fail." April 2014. https://www .blackrock.com/investing/literature/whitepaper/viewpoint-ccp-tbtf-april-2014.pdf.

Board of Governors of the Federal Reserve System, US Commodity Futures Trading Commission, and US Securities and Exchange Commission. "Risk Management and Supervision of Designated Clearing Entities." July 2011.

Braithwaite, Jo. "Legal Perspectives on Client Clearing." Law, Society, and Economy Working Paper 14, London School of Economics, 2015.

Carr, Gillian. "CCPs Mull Equity Swaps Clearing Solutions," *Risk.net*, March 20, 2015. http:// www.risk.net/structured-products/news/2399385/ccps-mull-equity-swaps-clearing -solutions.

Chang, Felix B. "The Systemic Risk Paradox: Banks and Clearinghouses under Regulation." *Columbia Business Law Review* (April 2014): 747–816.

CME Group, DTCC, ICE, and OCC. Letter to Jacob L. Lew, Chairman, Financial Stability Oversight Council, March 9, 2015. https://www.theice.com/publicdocs/CME_DTCC_ICE _OCC_Letter.pdf.

Cœuré, Benoît. "Ensuring an Adequate Loss-Absorbing Capacity of Central Counterparties." Speech at the Federal Reserve Bank of Chicago 2015 Symposium on Central Clearing, April 10, 2015.

Cohn, Gary. "Clearing Houses Reduce Risk, They Do Not Eliminate It." *Financial Times*, June 22, 2015. http://www.ft.com/intl/cms/s/0/974c2c48-16a5-11e5-b07f-00144feabdc0.html ?siteedition=intl#axzz3e1ggkHg4.

Committee on Payment and Settlement Systems and Technical Committee of the International Organization of Securities Commissions (CPSS/IOSCO). "Guidance on the Application of the 2004 CPSS-IOSCO Recommendations to OTC Derivatives CCPs." May 2010. http://www .iosco.org/library/pubdocs/pdf/IOSCOPD320.pdf.

———. "Principles for Financial Market Infrastructures." April 2012. http://www.bis.org/cpmi /publ/d101a.pdf.

Committee on Payments and Market Infrastructures and Board of the International Organization of Securities Commissions. Recovery of Financial Market Infrastructures. October 2014. http://www.bis.org/cpmi/publ/d121.pdf.

Culp, Christopher L. "OTC-Cleared Derivatives: Benefits, Costs, and Implications of the 'Dodd-Frank Wall Street Reform and Consumer Protection Act.'" *Journal of Applied Finance* 20 (2010): 1–27.

Domanski, Dietrich, Leonardo Gambacorta, and Cristina Picillo. "Central Clearing: Trends and Current Issues." *BIS Quarterly Review* (December 2015): 59–76.

Duffie, Darrell. "Financial Market Infrastructure: Too Important to Fail." Economics Working Paper 14101, Hoover Institution, January 2014.

———. "Resolution of Failing Central Counterparties." Stanford Graduate School of Business Working Paper 3256, December 17, 2014.

Duffie, Darrell, Ada Li, and Theo Lubke. "Policy Perspectives on OTC Derivatives Market Infrastructure." Federal Reserve Bank of New York Staff Report No. 424, revised March 2010.

Duffie, Darrell, and Haoxiang Zhu. "Does a Central Clearing Counterparty Reduce Counterparty Risk?" *Review of Asset Pricing Studies* 1 (2011): 74–95.

Duffy, Terrence A., Robert Druskin, Scott A. Hill, and Craig S. Donohue. Letter to Jacob J. Lew, Chairman, Financial Stability Oversight Council, March 9, 2015. http://www.optionsclearing .com/components/docs/about/press/comment-letters/20150309-FSOC.pdf.

Elliott, David. "Central Counterparty Loss-Allocation Rules." Financial Stability Paper No. 20, Bank of England, April 2013.

Evanoff, Douglas D., Daniela Russo, and Robert S. Steigerwald. "Policymakers, Researchers, and Practitioners Discuss the Role of Central Counterparties." In *The Role of Central Counterparties*, 6–25. European Central Bank and Federal Reserve Bank of Chicago Conference, July 2007.

FIA Europe. "A Review of the Cumulative Impact of European Derivatives Law Reform." June 2015. https://europe.fia.org/sites/default/files/content_attachments/FIA%20Europe_%20 A%20review%20of%20the%20cumulative%20effect%20of%20European%20derivatives%20 reform_Position%20Paper.pdf.

Financial Stability Board. "Implementing OTC Derivatives Market Reforms." October 25, 2010. http://www.fsb.org/2010/10/fsb-report-on-implementing-otc-derivatives-market-reforms/.

Financial Stability Oversight Council. "2016 Annual Report." Washington, DC.

Greenberger, Michael. "Diversifying Clearinghouse Ownership in Order to Safeguard Free and Open Access to the Derivatives Clearing Market." *Fordham Journal of Corporate and Financial Law* 18 (2013): 245–68.

Gregory, Jon. *Central Counterparties: Mandatory Clearing and Bilateral Margin Requirements for OTC Derivatives.* West Sussex: Wiley, 2014.

Griffith, Sean J. "Governing Systemic Risk: Towards a Governance Structure for Derivatives Clearinghouses." *Emory Law Journal* 61 (2012): 1153–240.

The Group of Twenty Leaders' Statement at the Pittsburgh Summit. September 24–25, 2009. http://www.treasury.gov/resource-center/international/g7-g20/Documents/pittsburgh_summit _leaders_statement_250909.pdf.

Hayek, Friedrich A. "The Pretence of Knowledge." Prize Lecture to the Memory of Alfred Nobel, December 11, 1974.

Heckinger, Richard, Ivana Ruffini, and Kirstin Wells. "Over-the-Counter (OTC) Derivatives." In *Understanding Derivatives: Markets and Infrastructure*, 27–38. Chicago: Federal Reserve Bank of Chicago, 2014.

Hills, Bob, David Rule, Sarah Parkinson, and Chris Young. "Central Counterparty Clearing Houses and Financial Stability." *Financial Stability Review* (June 1999): 122–34.

International Monetary Fund. "Making Over-the-Counter Derivatives Safer: The Role of Central Counterparties." In *Global Financial Stability Report: Meeting New Challenges to Stability and Building a Safer System*, 91–118. Washington, DC, 2010.

International Swaps and Derivatives Association. "CCP Loss Allocation at the End of the Waterfall." August 2013. https://www2.isda.org/attachment/NTc5Nw==/CCP_loss _allocation_waterfall_0807.pdf.

Johnson, Kristin N. "Commentary on the Abraham L. Pomerantz Lecture: Clearinghouse Governance: Moving beyond Cosmetic Reform." *Brooklyn Law Review* 77 (2012): 681–708.

———. "Governing Financial Markets: Regulating Conflicts." *Washington Law Review* 88 (2013): 185–244.

JPMorgan Chase. "What Is the Resolution Plan for CCPs?" *Perspectives*, September 2014. https://www.jpmorganchase.com/corporate/About-JPMC/document/resolution-plan-ccps.pdf.

Kelleher, Dennis M. Letter from President and CEO, Better Markets, to David A. Stawick, Secretary, CFTC, November 17, 2010. http://bettermarkets.com/sites/default/files/documents/CFTC -%20CL-%20Conflicts%20of%20Interest%20SEFs%2C%20DCOs%2011-17-10.pdf.

Knott, Raymond, and Alastair Mills. "Modelling Risk in Central Counterparty Clearing Houses: A Review." *Financial Stability Review* (December 2002): 162–74.

Kong, Kanga. "Trading Error Leaves Korean Broker Scrambling." *Wall Street Journal*, December 18, 2013. http://blogs.wsj.com/korearealtime/2013/12/18/trading-error-leaves -korean-broker-scrambling/.

Kroszner, Randall S. "Central Counterparty Clearing: History, Innovation, and Regulation." *Federal Reserve Bank of Chicago Economic Perspectives* (4th Quarter 2006): 37–41.

LCH.Clearnet. "CCP Risk Management, Recovery, and Resolution." November 7, 2014.

Ledrut, Elisabeth, and Christian Upper. "Clearing Post-Trading Arrangements for OTC Derivatives." *BIS Quarterly Review* (December 2007): 83–95.

Leising, Matthew. "Catastrophe Prevention Drives Pitch to Congress." *Bloomberg*, March 11, 2014. http://www.bloomberg.com/news/articles/2014-03-11/catastrophe-prevention-drives -insurance-pitch-to-clearinghouses.

Levitin, Adam J. "Response: The Tenuous Case for Derivatives Clearinghouses." *Georgetown Law Journal* 101 (2013): 445–66.

Lubben, Stephen J. "Failure of the Clearinghouse: Dodd-Frank's Fatal Flaw?" *Virginia Law and Business Review* 10 (2015): 150–51.

Massad, Timothy G. Keynote Address before the District of Columbia Bar, Washington, DC, July 23, 2015.

McBride, Paul M. "The Dodd-Frank Act and OTC Derivatives: The Impact of Mandatory Central Clearing on the Global OTC Derivatives Market." *International Lawyer* 44 (2010): 1077–22.

McPartland, John W. "Clearing and Settlement of Exchange Traded Derivatives." *Chicago Fed Letter* 267 (October 2009): 2.

Michel, Norbert J. "Financial Market Utilities: One More Dangerous Concept in Dodd-Frank." Heritage Foundation Backgrounder 3005, Washington, DC, March 20, 2015.

Moody's Investors Service. "Proposed Clearing House Rating Methodology." June 22, 2015. https://www.moodys.com/research/Proposed-Clearing-House-Rating-Methodology --PBC_181095.

Nosal, Ed. "Clearing Over-the-Counter Derivatives." *Federal Reserve Bank of Chicago Economic Perspectives* (4th Quarter 2011): 137–46.

Office of Financial Research. "2014 Annual Report."

Office of the Comptroller of the Currency. OCC's Quarterly Report on Bank Derivatives Activities Third Quarter 2015.

Parkinson, Patrick M. "CCP Liquidity Risk Management and Related Failure Management Issues." Speech to Federal Reserve Bank of Chicago Annual Over-the-Counter Derivatives Symposium, April 11, 2014.

Pirrong, Craig. "The Clearinghouse Cure." *Regulation* 44 (Winter 2008–2009): 44–51.

———. "The Inefficiency of the Clearing Mandate." Cato Policy Analysis, Washington, DC, July 21, 2010.

———. "The Economics of Central Clearing: Theory and Practice." ISDA Discussion Papers Series No. 1, International Swaps and Derivatives Association, May 2011.

———. "A Bill of Goods: Central Counterparties and Systemic Risk." *Journal of Financial Market Infrastructures* 2 (2014): 55–85.

Powell, Jerome H. "A Financial System Perspective on Central Clearing of Derivatives." Speech at the 17th International Banking Conference, Chicago, November 6, 2014.

"Q&A with Hal Scott of Harvard Law: Clearinghouse Ownership and Risk." *DerivAlert.* October 20, 2010. http://www.tradeweb.com/Blog/Q-A-With-Hal-Scott-of-Harvard-Law --Clearinghouse-Ownership-and-Risk/.

Quarry, Jason, Barrie Wilkinson, Toby Pittaway, and Jay Cheah. "OTC Derivatives Clearing: Perspectives on the Regulatory Landscape and Considerations for Policymakers." Oliver Wyman Report, May 31, 2012.

Rahman, Arshadur. "Over-the-Counter (OTC) Derivatives, Central Clearing and Financial Stability." *Bank of England Q3 Quarterly Bulletin* (2015): 283–95.

Report of the Presidential Task Force on Market Mechanisms. Washington, DC: Treasury Department, 1988.

Roe, Mark J. "Clearinghouse Overconfidence." *California Law Review* 101 (2013): 1641–704.

Rundle, James. "Helping Clearing Houses Avoid a Crash." *Financial News*, May 20, 2015. http://www .efinancialnews.com/story/2015-05-20/helping-rescuers-avoid-turbulence-clearing-houses.

Saltzman, Paul. Letter from President, The Clearing House Association LLC, to Jacob Lew, Chairman, Financial Stability Oversight Council (FSOC), January 9, 2015.

Scott, Hal. "The Reduction of Systemic Risk in the United States Financial System." *Harvard Journal of Law and Public Policy* 33 (2010): 671–734.

Shadow Financial Regulatory Committee. "The Dangers of Substituting Foreign Compliance for US Supervision of Financial Derivatives Activity." Statement No. 340, May 13, 2013.

Singh, Manmohan. "Making OTC Derivatives Safe—A Fresh Look." IMF Working Paper 11/66, International Monetary Fund, Washington, DC, 2011.

Squire, Richard. "Clearinghouses as Liquidity Partitioning." *Cornell Law Review* 99 (2014): 857–924.

Steigerwald, Robert S. "Central Counterparty Clearing." In *Understanding Derivatives—Markets and Infrastructure*. Chicago: Federal Reserve Bank of Chicago, 2013.

Stigler, George J. "The Theory of Economic Regulation." *Bell Journal of Economics and Management Science* 2 (1971): 3–21.

Swinburne, Kay. Speech before the World Federation of Exchanges/IOMA Conference, Sao Paulo, May 5, 2015.

Tarullo, Daniel K. "Advancing Macroprudential Policy Objectives." Speech at the Office of Financial Research and Financial Stability Oversight Council's Fourth Annual Conference on Evaluating Macroprudential Tools: Complementarities and Conflicts, Arlington, VA, January 30, 2015.

Tucker, Paul. "Counterparties in Evolving Capital Markets: Safety, Recovery and Resolution." *Banque de France Financial Stability Review* 17 (2013): 179–84.

———. "Are Clearing Houses the New Central Banks?" Speech at the Over-the-Counter Derivatives Symposium, Chicago, April 11, 2014.

Turbeville, Wallace C. "Derivatives Clearinghouses in the Era of Financial Reform." Conference Paper, Roosevelt Institute, New York, 2010.

US Commodity Futures Trading Commission. Transcript of the Public Roundtable on Futurization of Swaps, Washington, DC, January 31, 2013. http://www.cftc.gov/idc/groups /public/@swaps/documents/dfsubmission/dfsubmission13_013113-trans.pdf.

US Commodity Futures Trading Commission and US Securities Exchange Commission. "A Joint Report of the SEC and the CFTC on Harmonization of Regulation." October 16, 2009.

———. Transcript of the Public Roundtable on Governance and Conflicts of Interest in the Clearing and Listing of Swaps, Washington, DC, August 20, 2010. http://www.cftc.gov/idc /groups/public/@swaps/documents/dfsubmission/dfsubmission9_082010.pdf.

Vaghela, Viren. "Korea Clearing Structure in Question after HanMag Trading Error." *Risk.net*. March 5, 2014. http://www.risk.net/asia-risk/feature/2331225/korea-clearing-structure-in -question-after-hanmag-trading-error.

Varney, Christine A., Carl Shapiro, Gene I. Kimmelman, James J Tierney, Scott A. Scheele, Ihan Kim, Robert A. Potter, Samuel N Weinstein, Jeffrey M. Wilder, Charles S. Taragin, and Fan Zhang. Letter from Department of Justice, Assistant Attorney General to US Commodity Futures Trading Commission, December 28, 2010. http://comments.cftc.gov /PublicComments/ViewComment.aspx?id=26809&SearchText.

Wendt, Froukelien. "Central Counterparties: Addressing Their Too Important to Fail Nature." IMF Working Paper 15/21, International Monetary Fund, Washington, DC, January 2015.

Wetjen, Mark P. "Ensuring the Promise of a Centrally Cleared, Global Swaps Market: Next Steps." Remarks before the Futures Industry Association Asia Derivatives Conference, Singapore, December 4, 2014.

Wibaut, Serge, and D. Sykes Wilford. "Markets for CCPs and Regulation: Considering Unintended Consequences." *The Capco Institute Journal of Financial Transformation* 34 (2012): 103–17.

Wolkoff, Neal L., and Jason B. Werner. "The History of Regulation of Clearing in the Securities and Futures Markets and Its impact on Competition." *Review of Banking and Financial Law* 30 (2010–2011): 313–81.

Yellen, Janet L. "Interconnectedness and Systemic Risk: Lessons from the Financial Crisis and Policy Implications." Remarks at the American Economic Association/American Finance Association Joint Luncheon, San Diego, CA, January 4, 2013.

Yi, Whan-woo. "HanMag Debacle Hits Brokerages." *Korea Times*, December 17, 2013. http://koreatimes.co.kr/www/news/biz/2013/12/602_148108.html.

CHAPTER 9
The Past and Future of
Exchanges as Regulators

EDWARD STRINGHAM
Trinity College

If the Exchange had been nothing more than a meeting-
place for buyers and sellers of securities, and the borrowers
and lenders of funds based on securities—a huge automatic
dial to register vibrating values, and a legalized centre of
speculation—it would even then have been worthy of an
important place in the national annals. But though created
only for these functions, it has come to discharge another
and more striking one. In so doing it has formed that connection with the country's development which may be reck-
oned the most valuable feature in its history.
                    —Edmund Stedman and Alexander Easton[1]

Well-functioning stock markets benefit investors, publicly traded companies, and the financial intermediaries who bring them together. They help individual investors become involved with large-scale commerce without requiring them to be involved in any details of the company, and they vastly expand firms' access to capital. Stock markets, however, have the potential to expose investors to financial mismanagement or outright fraud from the company selling shares or from any number of financial intermediaries. Fraud not only harms the investors who lose, but it scares away future investors and reduces the pool of capital and business opportunities for legitimate enterprises and financial intermediaries that serve them. How can the good aspects of markets be encouraged and the fraudulent schemes or lesser forms of self-dealing be reduced? Most people assume that the only or best way to deal with fraud is with government rules or regulations. University of Chicago professors Rajan and Zingales[2] maintain that "market transactions require a central authority to enforce them promptly and at low cost" and "politics—for better or worse—lays the foundations for markets, and thus for prosperity."[3] Such thinking is also behind those who have advocated more government regulation of markets with the 2002 Sarbanes-Oxley Act (also known as the Public Company Accounting Reform and Investor Protection Act) and the Dodd-Frank Wall Street Reform and Consumer Protection Act of 2010 (Dodd-Frank).

Yet if one looks at the history of all the world's first successful stock markets one can see that they were regulated in a very different way—privately. In seventeenth-century Amsterdam, eighteenth-century London, and nineteenth-century New York, government officials commonly viewed stock markets with suspicion and passed various laws that made most of the sophisticated transactions in stock markets unenforceable. Despite government not enforcing entire classes of contracts, trading in stock markets continued and actually thrived. Rather than relying on government, market participants relied on various private enforcement mechanisms, or private governance, to mitigate fraud and facilitate exchange. Stockbrokers adopted private rules and regulations, not because they were required to, but because they wanted to make the markets more attractive for themselves, companies, and investors. The regulatory environment can best be viewed as open and competitive with different broker groups experimenting with different types of rules in order to attract business to their market.

Relying on the market to regulate the market was not a short-lived historical anomaly. Instead private rules and regulations underpinned all of the world's first stock markets for hundreds of years.[4] Studying the history of private rules and regulations helps us see how markets can operate without government oversight and how market incentives have led markets to find ways to reduce fraud and facilitate trade. Rules ranged from rules about trading, which help ensure contractual compliance among brokers, to rules about listing requirements for publicly traded firms. A system of competitive and private regulation offers an attractive alternative to one-size-fits-all and often heavy-handed government regulation advanced in recent years. Economists[5] describe exchange-created rules as the microstructure of markets; Mahoney refers to the role of the exchange as regulator; and Romano outlines how such competition encourages exchanges to create rules that investors trust.[6]

A 2007 McKinsey and Company report sponsored by former New York City Mayor Michael R. Bloomberg and Senator Charles Schumer interviewed fifty financial services CEOs and surveyed hundreds of others and found that burdensome government regulations are making American financial markets much less competitive than they could be. Five percent of Americans work in financial services, and the sector represents 8 percent of GDP,[7] not to mention *all* of the private enterprise made possible because of financial intermediation and other financial services. Yet many suggest that government rules and regulations have gone overboard and are bogging down markets. Bloomberg and Schumer state:

> The findings are quite clear: First, our regulatory framework is a thicket of complicated rules, rather than a streamlined set of commonly understood principles, as is the case in the United Kingdom and elsewhere. The flawed implementation of the 2002 Sarbanes-Oxley Act (SOX), which produced far heavier costs than expected, has only aggravated the situation, as has the continued requirement that foreign companies conform to U.S. accounting standards rather than the widely accepted—many would say superior—international standards.[8]

Respondents told McKinsey that compared to London, New York is lacking on the following issues: "government and regulators are responsive to business needs," "fair and predictable legal environment," and "attractive regulatory environment."[9] Policymakers appear to have gotten us into this problematic situation by overestimating the efficacy of government rules and regulations and ignoring many costs. Unfortunately, legislators and regulators who write statutes and regulations that end up costing investors and provide negligible benefits receive little market feedback and are not penalized for any harm they impose on investors, companies, or financial intermediaries.

An alternative to the heavy-handed approach of government is to move back to the system that enabled all the world's first successful stock markets to thrive: allow investors and their agents to opt into or out of competitively provided regulatory regimes that cater to investor wants. A system of private regulations encourages market participants to search for rules and regulations that help investors. Those that fail to offer basic assurances to investors or have rules and regulations that are onerous and provide few benefits will lose market share, and those that offer better protections gain. Instead of subjecting everyone to government mandates regardless of their efficacy or costs, there is the option of moving back to a system of freely adopted private rules and regulations that made all the world's successful stock markets possible.

LESSONS FROM THE HISTORY OF STOCK EXCHANGES AS PRIVATELY GOVERNED CLUBS[10]

Private Rules and Regulations in Seventeenth-Century Amsterdam

Although most people believe that commandments like "Thou shalt not steal" are just and ought to be followed, exactly how a market deals with problems like underperformance or nonperformance of a contract are open questions. What should the repercussion against nonperformance be? Should a market have retribution, restitution, or simple expulsion for underperformance, default, or fraud? Should an unintentional defaulter be treated the same as an intentional defaulter? If fines exist, should they be flat or graduated, and who should determine them? What should happen when a defaulter has no funds to pay? If market participants rely on expulsion, should expelled members ever be let back in, and if so under what circumstances? These are all tough questions that could long be debated in legislative chambers, regulatory hearings, courts of law, and academic journals, but instead the private governance in stock markets left the judgment to the market. The broker who reported to customers, "I didn't think about our counterparty default risk, and I don't actually have the shares that you paid for," would be at a severe disadvantage to brokers who traded in venues that minimized such problems. As such, market participants had incentive to search for rules that would make their market more orderly and more attractive.

Companies with transferable shares may date back to ancient Rome,[11] but the first stock market with a considerable secondary market was in seventeenth-century Amsterdam. The Dutch East India Company, created in 1602, was originally intended as short-lived endeavor, but by 1609 the company directors made it an ongoing venture. The modern notion of having shares in a company evolved gradually, starting as " 'paerten,' 'partieen,' or 'partijen,' the word being taken over from the practice of 'participation' in the shipping business," and was eventually referred to as an "actie" or share by 1606.[12] Investors wishing to sell their shares had to go with a buyer to the company's offices and pay a fee to have the shares transferred. There is nothing inherently wrong with going to headquarters to transfer shares, but imagine having to go to Redmond, Washington, anytime you wanted to buy or sell your Microsoft shares. The East India Company charged transfer fees and did not have a streamlined process. Neal describes the process:

> The transfer books were available 4 or 5 days a week and recorded the ledger entries for both the seller and the buyer, the amount of stock transferred, and the names of two witnesses and the clerk. A very small transfer fee was charged per share. Delays did occur due to the sloppiness of the clerks in recording entries and the necessity of checking to make sure the seller had at least the number of shares being sold to his or her credit in the main ledger.[13]

Over time, however, an independent secondary market for shares emerged.

Brokers who had specialized in trading in commodities or other financial instruments began specializing in trading shares and would keep track of their transactions and settle at *rescontre* dates established every three months.[14] At settlement time, brokers would net out the shares they owe and could either hand over shares for cash or settle using payment of differences. For example, suppose you make a contract to buy a share from me for 3,000 guilders in three months, but at settlement the current price turns out to be 3,300. I (with a short position) could procure the share for 3,300 and give the share to you (with a long position) in exchange for 3,000 guilders. An easier way of settling such a trade would be to have a payment-of-differences contract, where I would simply pay you 300 guilders and we would call it even. Contracts with future

229

settlement dates, whether with delivery of shares or payment of differences, eliminated the need to go to the company's office after each trade and pay fees. But moving away from the equivalent of a spot market with immediate settlement introduced the possibility for unintentional default or intentional fraud come settlement date. If I owed you 300 guilders but at settlement date I simply did not show up, what would you do?

A modern reader may assume that you need to take the defaulter to court to get your money back. But as Petram points out, "lawsuits that were ultimately brought before the Court of Holland could take anywhere between three-and-a-half and twelve years."[15] More important, however, a three- to twelve-year trial was not even an option for the majority of transactions. In 1608 shares in the East India Company fell by 35 percent and officials believed that outlawing short selling would prevent further price drops.[16] Officials passed ordinances against short sales, prohibiting selling "in blanco" (selling something you do not own) as well as "windhandel" (trading in wind). The new ordinances required that only owners of shares could make sales and that sellers had to actually transfer their shares within a month.[17] In the following decades official prohibitions continued; additional ordinances were passed in 1621, 1623, 1624, 1630, 1636, and 1677[18] that outlawed all but the simplest transactions. Many contracts had uncertain legal status while others such as short sales were outright prohibited.

Despite the unenforceability of most contracts, trading in such transactions continued and actually thrived. In addition to forward contracts with long and short sales, brokers developed many other sophisticated transactions including options, hypothecation (where people can pledge stocks as collateral for a loan), and other derivatives that enabled people who could not purchase a full share to trade. How is that possible? One seventeenth-century stockbroker, de la Vega (1688),[19] wrote a book describing the market and throughout he highlights the unenforceable status of most of these contracts. But he also describes informal private mechanisms that brokers used for encouraging contractual performance. Consider Adam Smith's commentary on why people would follow through on an unenforceable contract:

> Of all the nations in Europe, the Dutch, the most commercial, are the most faithful to their word. . . . This is not at all to be imputed to national character, as some pretend. . . . It

is far more reduceable to self interest, that general principle which regulates the actions of every man, and which leads men to act in a certain manner from views of advantage, and is as deeply implanted in an Englishman as a Dutchman. A dealer is afraid of losing his character, and is scrupulous in observing every engagement. When a person makes 20 contracts in a day, he cannot gain so much by endeavouring to impose on his neighbours, as the very appearance of a cheat would make him lose.[20]

Trading never takes place in a vacuum, and those who want to conduct business must persuade others to deal with them. Parties can cheat, but when they do so, they not only sour the relationship with their victims, but they sour their relationship with everyone else who finds out.

Greif[21] refers to this as a multilateral reputation mechanism, and in many circumstances it takes the place of formal enforcement. Even if two parties have never interacted before and have no intention of interacting again, both will think twice about damaging their reputation for a short-run gain. Many passages in de la Vega illustrate the importance of reputation and the need to follow through with one's word to remain in business.[22] As de la Vega explains,

He states, "[To be sure, there is widespread honesty and expedition on the Exchange. For example,] the business in stocks and the bustle of the sales which are made when unforeseen news arrives is wonderful to behold. Nobody changes the decisions which he makes in his momentary passion, and his words are held sacred even in the case of a price difference of 50 per cent; and, although tremendous business is done by the merchants without the mediation of brokers who could serve as witnesses, no confusion occurs and no quarrels take place. . . . Such honesty, co-operation, and accuracy are admirable and surprising."[23]

How successful was this market? De la Vega describes how people talked about the market for shares all over the city. By the end of the seventeenth century the Dutch East India Company had 20,000 employees, over 300 ships traveling between the East Indies and Europe,[24] and some estimate that it had the equivalent market capitalization of $7 trillion in modern US dollars, making it the most valuable company in history. The East India Company helped make the Golden Age possible, and it financed Henry Hudson's voyage where he charted Manhattan in 1607. The Dutch West India Company also founded New Amsterdam (New York) in 1624, so the influences of the Dutch stock market are long lasting. None of this would have been possible without a market for secondary shares, and that market was only made possible because of the informal rules and regulations on these markets.

Private Rules and Regulations in Eighteenth-Century London

The world's second major stock market developed in London starting at the end of the seventeenth century, and, as in Amsterdam, government officials were hardly supportive of it. England's first major joint stock company was the "Mystery and Company of Merchant Adventurers for the discovery of regions, dominions, islands, and places unknown," founded in 1551 (and later known as the Muscovy Company, chartered in 1555), and other major English companies included the Levant Company, the English East India Company, and the Virginia Company, chartered in 1581, 1600, and 1606, respectively.[25] By the end of the seventeenth century the number of joint stock companies increased and people began specializing in trading stocks.[26]

In 1696, however, the government passed an act "To Restrain the Number and the Practice of Brokers and Stockjobbers." Stockbrokers were prohibited from trading at the Royal Exchange, so instead congregated by "Change Alley around Cornhill and Lombard streets."[27] Especially after London prohibited them from congregating on the street in 1700, their main trading venues became Jonathan's and Garraway's coffeehouses. One broker had put out the following advertisement in 1695 in *Collection for Improvement of Husbandry and Trade*: "John Castaing at Jonathan's Coffee House on Exchange, buys and sells all Blank and Benefit Tickets; and all other Stocks and Shares."[28] Another successful stockbroker was described by his peers as "the leader and oracle of Jonathan's Coffee House."[29]

Government officials always looked down on this trade, as Sir Robert Walpole made clear in 1716: "Every one is aware how the administration in this country has been distressed by stock-jobbers."[30] In addition to passing rules restricting stockbrokers, the government all but outlawed the formation of new joint stock companies in 1720 with the passing of the Bubble Act. This 1734 bill, "[t]o prevent the infamous Practice of Stock-jobbing," also banned options, forward contracts, and margin trading, and government animosity toward stock traders persisted for well over a century.[31]

The government considered most contracts with future settlement dates as illegitimate. In his 1766 *Lectures on Jurisprudence*, Adam Smith wrote:

> This practice of buying stocks by time is prohibited by government, and accordingly, tho' they should not deliver up the stocks they have engaged for, the law gives no redress. There is no natural reason why 1000£ in the stocks should not be delivered or the delivery of it enforced, as well as 1000£ worth of goods. But after the South Sea scheme this was thought upon as an expedient to prevent such practice.[32]

Palgrave describes that time bargains referred to any contract that did not involve immediate settlement, and that includes long and short forward contracts and options contracts:

> Time bargains are contracts entered into between two parties for the transfer at a fixed price of a certain quantity of a commodity, security, or right from one to the other on a specified future date or within a specified time from the date of the contract. In colloquial language they fall under two heads, viz. (1) sale or purchases for "future" or "forward" delivery; (2) options.[33]

These advanced contracts were pervasive, as Palgrave explains: "on the stock market all contracts are for future delivery unless otherwise specified."

Another interesting distinction that government officials made, most likely due to a poor understanding of economics and finance, was between trades with settlement involving (1) actual delivery of the stock in return for money versus (2) cash settlement or payment of differences between the previously agreed on price and the market price on settlement date. Leaving aside the major transaction costs of handing over the shares or other contracted item, contracts with physical or cash settlement have near identical economic effects on each party and the market as a whole. Many British officials, however, considered a contract with physical settlement to be a "bona fide contract," whereas a "time bargain for payment of differences" was a form of "gaming or wagering."[34] The same was true in America, and Freedman[35] describes how in the latter half of the nineteenth century the Chicago Board of Trade helped promulgate the argument, likely with hopes of having government restrict the activities of its "bucketshop" competitors.

Although British officials made most contracts that occurred on the exchange illegal, Smith wrote that the law "proved ineffectual." Contracts were unenforceable but not punishable, so stockbrokers engaged in them anyway:

> In the same manner all laws against gaming never hinder it, and tho' there is no redress for a sum above 5£, yet all the great sums that are lost are punctually paid. Persons who game must keep their credit, else no body will deal with them. It is quite the same for stockjobbing. They who do not keep their credit will be turned out, and in the language of Change Alley be called lame duck.[36]

Stockbrokers initially relied on the discipline of repeat dealings and reputation mechanisms similar to brokers in Amsterdam. Calling someone a lame duck sounds pretty damaging!

Over time brokers began to create more formal private rules and regulations to deal with unintentional default or intentional fraud. To do this brokers decided to transform coffeehouses into private clubs. In 1761 Thomas Mortimer wrote, "The gentlemen at this very period of time . . . have taken it into their heads that some of the fraternity are not so good as themselves . . . and have entered into an association to exclude them from J——'s coffee-house."[37] In 1762, one hundred and fifty brokers formed a club and contracted with Jonathan's Coffeehouse to use it exclusively. Creating this exclusive club, or privatizing the commons, was not without controversy. A 1772 letter in *Town and Country Magazine* writes critically that "the brokers at Jonathan's admit none but their own fraternity into their coffee-house, which to prevent strangers intruding amongst them."[38] One excluded broker ended up going to government and suing to break up this newly formed club. Government intervened and declared that Jonathan's Coffeehouse did not have the right to exclude outsiders. In 1773, as an alternative strategy, brokers organized and purchased a building for their own use. This new building was known as New Jonathan's and was open to anyone who paid the daily admission fee, which covered expenses such as rent.[39] In 1773 the *Gentlemen's Magazine* reported, "New Jonathan's came to the resolution that instead of its being called New Jonathan's, it should be called The Stock Exchange, which is to be wrote over the door."[40]

Brokers experimented with different rules and regulations, and documented many of them in their first rulebook in 1812. The stated resolutions were "but an attempt (the first indeed that has ever yet been made in this House) to reduce into a regular method the rules and regulations, by which so very important a class of society is to be governed."[41] Although the Committee said some disputes can be settled within the exchange using "the known Laws of the Land," they added that "many others (which, form their nature and extent, preclude the possibility of forming any general laws on the subject, so as to meet every contingency) may also be adjusted by the known custom and practice of the market."[42]

To give an idea of how their rules worked, consider a few of the Committee's 1812 resolutions passed for "the safety and protection of the property and interests of the members of the Stock-Exchange." The Exchange had rules in the following categories:

Admissions	(14 resolutions)
Bargains	(10 resolutions)
Clerks	(8 resolutions)
Committee	(18 resolutions)
Failures	(12 resolutions)
Partnerships	(1 resolution)
Puts and calls	(1 resolution)
Passing of tickets	(3 resolutions)
Quotation of prices	(5 resolutions)
Settling days	(3 resolutions)

Without writing in a legalistic way, they stated they wanted to make the resolutions "as clear and comprehensive as possible."[43] The need to attract business made the Exchange act in a judicious manner.[44]

How did the London Stock Exchange enforce its rules? Its main rule-enforcing body was the Committee for General Purposes, which had thirty members, a chairman, and a deputy-chairman elected by the members each year. The Committee would deal with "management, regulation, and direction" of the Stock Exchange. The secretary of the Committee would keep records of applications and report "the name of every defaulter that may have been declared in the Stock-Exchange, and insert the same into the minute book."[45] The Committee had "the right to expel any of their members from the Committee who may have been guilty of dishonourable or disgraceful conduct; or who may be otherwise highly objectionable to them" provided they created a sub-committee to vote on the matter and two-thirds agreed.[46]

The Committee also dealt with membership applications, which had to be renewed each year. All new applicants had to be recommended by two members who "have knowledge of the party and his circumstances"[47] and could explain them to the admission committee. Anyone who objected to a new member could express that to the Committee for consideration. People whose membership was not accepted could reapply after thirty days, and if rejected again they would have to wait until the next year. At any point in time, "Every defaulter ceases to be a member" and "Every subscriber, who shall become bankrupt ceases to be a member." Losing membership was not necessarily permanent if a defaulter rectified certain wrongs. The rules and regulations stated, however, certain actions could lead to expulsion: "Every member, who may be guilty of dishonourable or disgraceful conduct, or who may violate any of the fundamental laws of the Stock-Exchange, shall be liable to expulsion."[48] The expulsion process required a hearing before a committee where at least three-fourths of the members voting decided on expulsion.

Members could also request to have clerks admitted, and members were required to assume responsibility for their clerks. A list of approved clerks and their employers "shall be put up and remain in a conspicuous part of the House." To get permission the member "must send the name of such a clerk to the Committee for General Purposes for their approbation; without whose consent no such clerk shall be admitted."[49] Clerks were not permitted to trade on their own account and would be expelled if they did. Clerks were generally forbidden to engage in time bargains (i.e., forward contracts or options) unless approved by the Committee. They stated "a list of such clerks shall be put up and remain in a conspicuous part of the Stock-Exchange, together with the names of their employers." Given that time bargains involve considerably more risk, one can understand such a rule.

The Exchange had rules about settlement[50] and what would go wrong in the event of a dispute. The rulebook stated that "[a]ll disputes between individuals (not affecting the general interests of the Stock-Exchange) shall be referred to arbitration" and added "the Committee [for General Purposes] will not interfere in such disputes, unless that resource may have proved ineffectual, or unless arbitrators cannot be found ready and willing to determine the case." Here brokers appear to have two levels of adjudication within the Exchange.

The Exchange also had various rules about what would happen to default-ers. All creditors whose counterparty defaulted were required to report the default to the Committee for General Purposes. Any creditor who violated the rule would have his name "affixed in a conscious part of the Stock-Exchange."[51] Other rules specified the equivalent of rules for bankruptcy proceedings. If someone in default was scheduled to be paid money from another set of trades, the proceeds would go the creditors of the defaulter and split equally among them. This prevented a strategic defaulter from reneging on some contracts but collecting on others. A defaulter would lose his membership but could reapply for membership if he furnished "his books of accounts and a state-ment of the sums owing to him and owed by him in the Stock-Exchange" and met a few other conditions. A defaulter applying for readmission "shall have his name fixed in a conspicuous part of the Stock-Exchange, at least eight days previous to the application being considered during this Committee." If any members reported "that the conduct of such defaulter has been dishonour-able, or marked with any circumstances of impropriety," readmission would be denied and the name of the person would be written on "the *Black Board* in the Stock-Exchange."[52]

The Committee stated that "order and decorum" were "so essentially neces-sary to be observed in all places in this business" and that they needed to inhibit "rude and trifling practices" that would be "injurious to the best interests of the House."[53] The Exchange had fairly strict rules, but none of them seem dra-conian. As long as defaulters repaid their debts (indicating they had not acted with bad intentions when they defaulted) they could be let back in. The rules seem to be adopted to inhibit bad behavior and encourage good behavior. The rules have continued to evolve over time, and to this day the London Stock Exchange is experimenting with different levels of strictness between its

Main Market and its more flexible Alternative Investment Market (AIM). As the London Stock Exchange did a couple hundred years ago, it has rules of conduct to retain membership and has procedures against those who violate them.

London was the financial capital of the world, at least until World War I, and the London Stock Exchange, with its system of private regulation, played a crucial role. In 1877 one government report stated that the Stock Exchange's rules "had been salutary to the interests of the public" and that the Exchange acted "uprightly, honestly, and with a desire to do justice." It concluded saying that the Exchange's private rules were "capable of affording relief and exercising restraint far more prompt and often satisfactory than any within the read of the courts of law."[54]

Private Rules and Regulation in Nineteenth-Century New York

Similar to its European counterparts, the New York Stock Exchange (so named since 1863) evolved over time and also was privately governed. The earliest available written agreements between brokers date to 1791, when signatories agreed to fourteen rules about trade, and 1792, when twenty-four brokers signed the Buttonwood Tree Agreement, where they agreed to "solemnly promise and pledge ourselves to each other."[55] An association of merchants created the New York Tontine Coffee House Company between 1791 and 1792, and opened the Tontine Tavern and Coffee House in 1793 "for the purpose of a Merchants Exchange with 203 subscribers at $200 each."[56] In 1794 one commentator wrote,

> The Tontine Tavern and Coffee House is a handsome, large
> brick building; you ascend six or eight steps under a portico,
> into a large public room, which is the Stock Exchange of
> New York, where all bargains are made. Here are two books
> kept, as at Lloyd's, of every ship's arrival and clearing out.
> This house was built for the accommodation of the mer-
> chants, by Tontine shares of two hundred pounds each. It is
> kept by Mr. Hyde, formerly a woolen draper in London. You
> can lodge and board there at a common table, and you pay
> ten shillings currency a day, whether you dine out or not.[57]

Brokers adopted a "Constitution And Nominations of the Subscribers To The Tontine Coffee-House" as early as 1796, and by 1817 brokers created a more formal membership club and trading venue, the New York Stock and Exchange Board.[58] The 1817 "Rules to be adopted and observed by the 'New York Stock and Exchange Board'" were quite simple and included "fines for non-attendance at the calling of the Stocks" and guidance on how "any member refusing to comply with the foregoing rules may have a hearing before the Board, and if he shall still persist in refusing, two-thirds of the Board may declare him no longer a member."[59] Members added different resolutions over the years, and by the 1860s, in addition to blacklisting those who did not follow through with their contracts, they had rules prohibiting "indecorous language" (suspension for a week), fines for "smoking in the Board-room, or in the ante-rooms" (five dollars), and fines for "standing on tables or chairs" (one dollar), as such rules made sure everyone was proper.[60] By 1865 the initiation fee was $3,000 and by 1868 one's membership seat became a valuable property right that could be sold to potential members.[61]

In 1899, accounting author David Keister[62] reported, "The rules of the Stock Exchange are very strict; a high standard of integrity is maintained, and all disputes are settled by a committee of arbitration." In 1922 an economist for the New York Stock Exchange stated,

> The regulations of the Stock Exchange relating to the business conduct of its members go beyond the common law in the earnest attempt to maintain "just and equitable principles of trade," and that these regulations are immediately and thoroughly enforced. From the inherent nature of the transactions which take place in an organized securities market, such a high and ethical spirit of legislation is necessary. The general recognition of this necessity by Exchange members, in fact, is responsible for the severe and instant punishment to which they have voted to make themselves liable.[63]

In addition to having rules of membership, the New York Stock Exchange started having rules about the securities that could be listed. Letting any "enterprise," including likely fraudulent ones, approach investors had the potential to create a tragedy of the commons situation where the fraudulent ventures crowded out the good. To deal with this problem, the Exchange adopted listing and disclosure requirements to make the market more transparent.

By 1865 the New York Stock Exchange had two lists of securities, the regular list and the secondary list, and the first list would be called at the "First Board." Similar to over-the-counter or pink sheet stocks in modern times, the secondary list did not have strict listing requirements. The stocks traded on the regular list had more liquidity, and members had to attend the morning session for their trading. To be on the first list, companies had to give their "applications for placing of Stocks on the regular list, [which] shall be made directly to the Board, with a full statement of capital, number of shares, resources, &c."[64] The financial journal *Bradstreet's* reported, "The New York Stock Exchange has, to a certain extent, taken upon itself an important public duty in requiring companies, whose securities are to be placed on its lists, to make much fuller statements of their organization and affairs."[65]

The New York Stock Exchange later adopted stricter listing requirements and required companies to maintain a transfer agency and registrar that is approved by the Exchange[66] to obtain permission from the Committee on Stock before issuing initial or subsequent shares;[67] and to comply with various rules of the New York Stock Exchange Governing Committee, which had the authority to suspend dealings or remove a company's shares from the exchange.[68] By the 1920s, the New York Stock Exchange[69] (1925) required various reports and disclosures from companies. Before the passage of the Securities Act of 1933 and the Securities Exchange Act of 1934, all firms listed on the New York Stock Exchange provided information about assets and liabilities and were audited by certified public accountants.[70] Firms that no longer met the requirements would be suspended or delisted or, as they referred to at the time, "stricken from the list."

Although each listing and disclosure requirement involves costs to listing firms, requirements can bestow certain benefits to investors and listing firms alike.[71] One can think of the New York Stock Exchange as solving a collective-action problem between individual investors and firms. A listing firm nominally bears the costs of compliance, but it willingly does so because the rules increase the value of its stock. If investors value transparency through listing or disclosure requirements, the New York Stock Exchange can require them. That means individual investors need not visit a company's offices if investors know that a stock exchange and auditors have reviewed the company's books.[72]

Adopting stricter rules had the potential to attract more market participants or it had the potential to push them away to less strict competitors. The New York Stock Exchange always had to compete for business and throughout the years faced competition from the Open Board of Brokers, which merged with the New York Stock Exchange in 1869;[73] the Curb Market and its more formal outgrowth, the New York Curb Exchange (founded in 1921 and renamed the American Stock Exchange in 1953); the Consolidated Stock Exchange of New York (founded in the 1880s, it included many mining companies); and regional exchanges including the Boston Exchange and Philadelphia Stock Exchange (founded in 1834 and 1754, respectively, the latter in London Coffee House). Investors also could have focused on "the Coal and Iron Exchange, the Coffee Exchange, the Cotton Exchange, the Maritime Exchange, the Metal Exchange, the New York Insurance Exchange, and the Leaf Tobacco Board of Trade,"[74] to name a few.

Those running the New York Stock Exchange made a lot of good choices, and by World War I, the New York Stock Exchange surpassed the London Stock Exchange as the most important exchange in the world. The New York Stock Exchange with its system of private rules and regulations helped finance American industry to become the economic powerhouse that it is today.

LESSONS FROM HISTORY FOR TODAY: LETTING PEOPLE OPT INTO OR OPT OUT OF DIFFERENT REGULATORY REGIMES

Private governance of stock exchanges underpinned the world's three most successful stock markets for centuries when government officials were unknowledgeable about or uninterested in supporting stock markets. Although many people assume that rules and regulations to underpin markets must come from government, the history of stock markets shows rules and regulations coming from markets themselves. When rules and regulations enhance market transparency and the value of markets, market participants have incentives to search for them.

What are some potential policy implications? In modern times, a system of private regulation would allow stock exchanges to compete on various margins to help improve the microstructure of their markets. Private rules and regulations could govern everything from different ways of matching and filling orders to what firms can become listed. Historically, exchanges bundled various sets of rules, although there is no reason that listing requirements and market design need to be decided by the same entity. A New York Stock Exchange or London Stock Exchange could compete to offer various listing and disclosure requirements and either require all of its listed firms to be traded on that exchange or allow some or all of its listed firms to be traded in various exchanges such as Bats Global Markets, an electronic communication network founded as Better Alternative Trading System in 2005, or newer exchanges like IEX Group. Yale Law School professor Jonathan Macey, for example, has discussed how exchanges can offer a bundle of off-the-rack rules of corporate governance and serve as reputational intermediaries for listed firms, and more recently he has proposed having an increased number of stock exchanges be exclusive forums for listed stocks.[75] Think of a stock exchange as acting like the Underwriters' Laboratories to help set standards for, certify, and put a stamp of approval on member firms.

In each case a private regulator must offer a set of rules that is ultimately attractive to investors and the publicly traded firms that want to cater to them. For example, the London Stock Exchange's AIM provides a much more flexible approach for firms that want to go public and gives firms a "comply or explain" option for many rules that allows listed firms to give reasons why complying with a certain guideline does not make sense for them.[76] Rather than having to pass a litany of bureaucratic rules, firms simply must have the seal of approval of a Nominated Adviser, a third-party financial company approved by the London Stock Exchange, to go public and remain publicly traded.[77] For any potential rule for publicly traded firms, such as recent proposals to require firms to rotate auditors, stock exchanges would be allowed to experiment with having or not having the rule. Those that adopt rules that benefit investors would see an increased demand for their market, and those that adopt onerous rules would see a decrease in demand. The process of competition would thus encourage stock exchanges to offer the set of rules and regulations that investors want. Recently proposed rules like auditor rotation need not be mandated for all firms.

For those who believe that the current set of government regulations is always, or at least sometimes, beneficial, it would be quite easy to keep most regulations in existence but at the same time let investors opt out of them if they desire. Just as international investors are allowed to invest in (and have been investing in) foreign markets over American ones, and just as institutionally qualified investors are able to invest in companies that do not follow all of the rules for publicly traded companies, ordinary Americans need not be deprived of those same liberties and investment options. For example, the US Securities and Exchange Commission's 500-page Regulation NMS (National Market System) includes a set of provisions that mandate that all investors get the "best price" for orders of publicly traded securities, but it neglects the wishes of investors who want to opt into venues that optimize on other margins. "Best price" regulations both undermine the time-tested specialist system of the New York Stock Exchange and act as a hurdle for newer exchanges like IEX attempting to devise systems to match orders in a potentially more orderly way. My modest proposal would allow some exchanges to advertise that they are compliant with Regulation NMS and others to say they are not and offer the choice to investors. Such a setup would require stock exchanges to get approval from their customers (i.e., their rules would need to pass the market test), not the SEC, for offering a set of rules and regulations that differs from their competitors'.

The New York Stock Exchange, now publicly traded as part of the Intercontinental Exchange Inc., is still tremendously important and can be even more important in the future, but since 2000, prosecutors and regulators have stripped the New York Stock Exchange of much of its power to regulate its market. For example, before Regulation NMS mandated immediacy and "best price" of order execution over all other factors, the New York Stock Exchange, NASDAQ, and other trading venues competed to offer attractive ways of executing orders (e.g., the individual specialists in the New York Stock Exchange versus the plethora of market makers in NASDAQ), and the market decided what venue was best. One-size-fits-all regulations like Regulation NMS, however, both undermine the specialist system of the New York Stock Exchange[78] and preclude many other types of innovation and experimentation from competing electronic communication networks.[79]

Another way to move away from monopoly mandates would be to allow private regulatory organizations like the Financial Industry Regulatory Authority (FINRA) to continue to do most of what they do, but not mandate their authority on all securities firms.[80] To the extent that consumers want to deal with firms that comply with and are monitored by FINRA or another competitor, firms will opt into the system. A voluntary and competitive system would contrast with the current system that relies on society-wide mandates of previously untested but subsequently difficult-to-repeal government rules, no matter how bad they turn out to be. Those who believe the existing set of regulations are beneficial to investors can willingly comply with the Securities Act of 1933 and the Securities Exchange Act of 1934 or the thousands of pages of government regulations added since. If government regulations were anything close to as good as public officials say, then safety and returns in these markets would be superior and investors would flock to them. The fact that investors are not given this choice is, however, prima facie evidence that these rules and regulations would be unable to pass any market test.[81] A major advantage of private over government regulation is the former's flexibility and ability to more fluidly evolve over time. Like generals preparing for previous wars, government regulators often devise plans to deal with old problems and do a poor job at predicting future ones. Regulators are also often slow to eliminate antiquated and unnecessary regulations. Instead of having a set of rules and regulations to solve problems at hand, markets are often left with layers of legalistic mandates that offer few benefits for companies or investors.

Moving to a system of regulatory competition would allow investors to opt into sets of rules and regulations that they consider best, and competing stock exchanges to provide that option. In much the same way that car buyers do not need to evaluate each of the 30,000 parts in their car, investors need not evaluate every single rule or regulation in the market they are opting into. Competing stock exchanges help provide an off-the-shelf package of rules for corporate governance, and the costs and benefits of that package become internalized within each exchange. And in much the same way that a competitive market for automobiles gives us far superior cars than if all cars were produced by the government, the same was and can again be true with rules and regulations provided through the market.

NOTES

1. Stedman and Easton, "History of the New York Stock Exchange," 18.

2. Rajan and Zingales, *Saving Capitalism from the Capitalists*.

3. Likewise Mancur Olson writes that without "institutions that enforce contracts impartially," a society loses "most of the gains from those transactions (like those in the capital market) that require impartial third-party enforcement." See Olson, "Big Bills Left on the Sidewalk," 22. Israel M. Kirzner writes, "Without these institutional prerequisites—primarily, private property rights and freedom and enforceability of contract—the market cannot operate. It follows that those institutions cannot be created by the market itself." See Kirzner, *Driving Force of the Market*, 83.

4. This chapter focuses on the world's three most successful stock markets and identifies many similarities between them. Another set of useful research could look for patterns in the economies that did not end up developing successful stock markets. For example, a century and a half before the stock market in Amsterdam, Antwerp had what many consider the first successful bourse, albeit not one with a major market for equities. Having the Antwerp bourse grow into one with a flourishing secondary market for equities could have been a natural extension. But the government eventually passed a series of economically illiberal policies, which included expelling the Jewish population (Bloom, *Economic Activities of the Jews*, 181) and banning ships traveling directly to the city (Israel, *Dutch Primacy in World Trade*, 30). Around that time many of those people and commercial enterprises moved up to Amsterdam. Elsewhere, the Hanseatic Stock Exchange (referring here to a bourse that did not trade equities at its formation) at Hamburg was founded in 1558, the Frankfurt Stock Exchange was founded in 1585, and the Berlin Stock Exchange was founded in 1686, but they only began listing equities in the early nineteenth century; see Baker, *German Stock Market*, 35–36. Neal, *Concise History of International Finance*, discusses how in seventeenth-century France, the financial "innovation" was simply government efforts to increase taxation rather than to create opportunities for people to invest in private enterprise. They had "no Stock Exchange or bank" (67) and did not develop a capitalism for the people, a term used by Luigi Zingales.

    The legal origins literature—see Glaeser and Shleifer, "Legal Origins"—hypothesizes that successful stock markets can be attributed to more legal protections for shareholders in common law countries and fewer in civil law countries. Although a large degree of correlation between common law and present stock market development may exist, the story glosses over the fact that stock markets were invented in a country without a common law tradition and that legal mandates that allegedly protect shareholders are a relatively recent invention. Four centuries ago, Amsterdam was home to an eighty-year Dutch revolt against Spain, but not home to an advanced legal system designed to protect stock market participants. Another major point of weakness for the legal origins hypothesis is the fact that up until a hundred years ago, many of the world's most developed stock markets were in civil law countries; see Musacchio, "Can Civil Law Countries Get Good Institutions?" Ultimately I believe McCloskey (*Bourgeois Virtues*) makes a compelling case that the Netherlands and England became the centers of early modern capitalism because their people embraced individualism and markets. I will add that a tremendously important factor that enabled these markets to grow was the existence of stock markets.

5. O'Hara, *Market Microstructure Theory*; Carlos and Neal, "Micro-Foundations of the Early London Capital Market"; Neal and Davis, "Evolution of the Rules and Regulations"; Neal and Davis, "Evolution of the Structure and Performance."

6. Mahoney, "Exchange as Regulator"; Romano, "Empowering Investors."

7. McKinsey and Company, *Sustaining New York's and the US' Global Financial Services*, 7.

8. Ibid., ii.

9. Ibid., 65.

10. Much of this section draws from my book *Private Governance*. Readers looking for more details are invited to read that work, too.

11. Malmendier, "Law and Finance at the Origin"; Romano, "Empowering Investors."

12. See Kellenbenz, "Introduction to Confusion De Confusiones," 134. The other main publicly traded company was the Dutch West India Company, founded in 1621; see Israel, *Dutch Republic*, 326–27. The Dutch West India Company attracted a similar amount of initial capital, but it was never as successful as the Dutch East India Company.

13. Neal, *Rise of Financial Capitalism*, 195.

14. Neal, "On the Historical Development of Stock Markets," 62.

15. Petram, "World's First Stock Exchange," 92.

16. Kellenbenz, "Introduction to Confusion De Confusiones," 134.

17. Wilson, *Anglo-Dutch Commerce in the Eighteenth Century*, 14; Kellenbenz, "Introduction to Confusion De Confusiones," 134–35.

18. Dehing and Hart, "Linking the Fortunes," 55; Garber, "Tulipmania," 78; De Vries and Van Der Woude, *First Modern Economy*, 151.

19. de la Vega, *Confusion De Confusiones*.

20. Smith, *Lectures on Jurisprudence*, 538.

21. Greif, "Contract Enforceability and Economic Institutions."

22. For example, de la Vega writes, "The Exchange business is comparable to a game. Some of the players behave like princes and combine strength with tenderness and amiability with intelligence, but there are some participants who lose their reputation and others who lack devotion to their business even before play begins" (*Confusion De Confusiones*, 172). Who wants to deal with an untrustworthy broker? De la Vega writes, "Since the status, the insignificant capital, the low reputation, and the limited trustworthiness of such people are well known, they do not dare attempt to carry on any considerable business" (201).

23. Ibid., 172.

24. Israel, *Dutch Primacy in World Trade*, 258; and *Dutch Republic*, 942.

25. Many of these companies were given privileges by government, but those protections were not unlimited. For example, the English East India Company faced competition from the Dutch East India Company, the Danish East India Company, the French East India Company, the Portuguese East India Company, and the Swedish East India Company. If one goes by the dictionary definition of monopoly as "exclusive supply," then no monopoly existed.

26. Kindleberger, *Financial History of Western Europe*, 96.

27. Reed, *History of James Capel & Co.*, 5.

28. Reprinted in Mirowski, "Rise (and Retreat) of a Market," 564.

29. Morgan and Thomas, *London Stock Exchange*, 46.

30. Francis, *Chronicles and Characters of the Stock Exchange*, 23.

31. Harris, *Industrializing English Law*, 225.

32. Smith, *Lectures on Jurisprudence*, 538.

33. Palgrave, *Dictionary of Political Economy*, 542.

34. *Law Times Reports of Cases*, 612.

35. Freedman, *Introduction to Financial Technology*, 164.

36. Smith, *Lectures on Jurisprudence*, 538.

37. Reprinted in Smith, "Early History of the London Stock Exchange," 215.

38. Anti-Lounger, "Letter to the Printer," 525.

39. Wincott, *Stock Exchange*.

40. Reprinted in Jenkins, *Stock Exchange Story*, 45.

41. Committee for General Purposes of the Stock-Exchange, *Rules and Regulations*, 10.

42. Ibid.

43. Ibid., 6.

44. Boot, Greenbaum, and Thakor, "Reputation and Discretion in Financial Contracting."

45. Committee for General Purposes of the Stock-Exchange, *Rules and Regulations*, 33.

46. Ibid., 31.

47. Ibid., 17.

48. Ibid., 18–19.

49. Ibid., 23.

50. Ibid., 20.

51. Ibid., 34–35.

52. Ibid., 36–37.

53. Ibid., 46.

54. Reprinted in Wincott, *Stock Exchange*, 27.

55. Banner, *Anglo-American Securities Regulation*, 250–51, argues against the somewhat popular belief that these agreements cartelized markets.

56. Werner and Smith, *Wall Street*, 216.

57. Quoted in Bayles, *Old Taverns of New York*, 360–61.

58. Tontine Coffee House, *Constitution and Nominations of the Subscribers*; Stedman and Easton, *History of the New York Stock Exchange*, 62.

59. Stedman and Easton, *History of the New York Stock Exchange*, 64.

60. Hamon, *New York Stock Exchange Manual*, 26–29; New York Stock Exchange, *Constitution and By-Laws*, 31–33.

61. Hamon, *New York Stock Exchange Manual*, 12; New York Stock Exchange, *About Us/History/Timeline*.

62. Keister, *Keister's Corporation Accounting*, 260.

63. Meeker, *Work of the New York Stock Exchange*, 352.

64. New York Stock Exchange, *Constitution and By-Laws*, 16–17.

65. "Restrictions for Company Promoters."

66. New York Stock Exchange, *Constitution of the New York Stock Exchange*, art. XXXIII, sec. 1.

67. Ibid., sec. 2, sec. 5.

68. Ibid, sec. 4.

69. New York Stock Exchange, *Constitution of the New York Stock Exchange (as Revised in 1925)*.

70. Benston, "Required Disclosure and the Stock Market," 133.

71. Manne, "Hydraulic Theory of Disclosure Regulation."

72. Macey, *Death of Corporate Reputation*.

73. Stedman and Easton, "History of the New York Stock Exchange," 214.

74. Markham, *Financial History of the United States*, 6.

75. Macey and Kanda, "Stock Exchange as a Firm"; Macey and Swensen, "Cure for Stock-Market Fragmentation."

76. Stringham and Chen, "Alternative of Private Regulation."

77. The London Stock Exchange, *Guide to AIM*, 6, reports that firms listed on the AIM face "no minimum market capitalization, no trading record requirement, no prescribed level of shares to be in public hands, no prior shareholder approval for most transactions, [and] admission documents [are] not pre-vetted by the Exchange nor by the UKLA [United Kingdom Listing Authority] in most circumstances."

78. Arnuk and Saluzzi, *Broken Markets*, 14.

79. White, "ECNs RIP."

80. Because private regulatory groups like FINRA are state sanctioned and must comply with government rules, many people infer that private regulation is only possible because government ultimately enforces it. Historically, however, many private regulatory groups had rules that were at odds with the laws of the land. As Neal points out, "the formal self-regulation of the London Stock Exchange evolved circumspectly to avoid state-regulation." Because government considered most of the trading on the exchange as a form of illegal gambling it is clear that these private regulatory groups were not made possible because of government. See Neal, "Evolution of Self- and State Regulation," 300.

    Evidence from countries with more obviously less developed legal systems is also revealing. For example, after the fall of communism, the law often offered little protection for most market participants; see Frye, *Brokers and Bureaucrats*. Although the outcomes were far from perfect, stock markets in these countries emerged and helped encourage the privatization process. See Stringham, Boettke, and Clark, "Are Regulations the Answer?" But the amount of support from government is questionable at best. Consider the fate of Yukos Oil, which had its CEO jailed and $50 billion assets expropriated, or the holding company Sistema, which also had its CEO arrested and billions of dollars' worth of oil assets expropriated (see Davies, Stubbs, and Escritt, "Court Orders Russia to Pay $50 Billion"; Bashneft, "Bashneft Is Notified of a Change"). Cases like these cast doubt on the claim that successful publicly traded companies are only possible because of government rules and regulations.

81. A more explicitly paternalistic argument posits that typical investors are not smart enough to understand what stock exchange is likely to offer them attractive sets of rules. But if one wants to push this line of thinking, how will these same people be smart enough to select politicians with even a basic understanding of economics? While each investor has to bear the cost of his good or bad decisions, and thus has incentives to become more informed and make good decisions, individual voters do not bear the full cost of voting for economically ignorant politicians; see Caplan, *Myth of the Rational Voter*; Caplan and Stringham, "Privatizing the Adjudication of Disputes." If one assumes, as paternalists do, that the average person is ill-informed or even stupid, that is one of the best arguments for taking important financial and regulatory decisions out of the hands of the masses. Personally, I believe I am much more qualified to decide where to invest my money rather than being forced to have 12 percent of my lifetime income "invested" in an unfunded and actuarially unsound Social Security system.

REFERENCES

Anti-Lounger. "Letter to the Printer of Town and Country Magazine." *Town and Country Magazine*, October 23, 1772, 524–25.

Arnuk, Sal, and Joseph Saluzzi. *Broken Markets: How High Frequency Trading and Other Predatory Practices on Wall Street Are Destroying Investor Confidence and Your Portfolio*. Saddle River, NJ: FT Press, 2012.

Baker, James C. *The German Stock Market*. New York: Praeger Publishers, 1970.

Banner, Stuart. *Anglo-American Securities Regulation: Cultural and Political Roots, 1680–1860.* Cambridge: Cambridge University Press, 1998.

Bashneft. "Bashneft Is Notified of a Change of a Majority Shareholder." Press Release, Moscow, December 10, 2014. http://www.rustocks.com/index.phtml/Pressreleases/0/5/38226?filter =2014.

Bayles, W. Harrison. *Old Taverns of New York.* New York: Frank Allaben Genealogical Company, 1915.

Benston, George J. "Required Disclosure and the Stock Market: An Evaluation of the Securities Exchange Act of 1934." *American Economic Review* 63, no. 1 (1973): 132–55.

Bloom, Herbert Ivan. *The Economic Activities of the Jews of Amsterdam in the Seventeenth and Eighteenth Centuries.* Williamsport, PA: Bayard Press, 1937.

Boot, Arnoud, Stuart Greenbaum, and Anjan Thakor. "Reputation and Discretion in Financial Contracting." *American Economic Review* 83 (1993): 1165–83.

Caplan, Bryan. *The Myth of the Rational Voter: Why Democracies Choose Bad Policies.* Princeton, NJ: Princeton University Press, 2007.

Caplan, Bryan, and Edward Peter Stringham. "Privatizing the Adjudication of Disputes." *Theoretical Inquiries in Law* 9, no. 2 (2008): 503–28.

Carlos, Ann, and Larry Neal. "The Micro-Foundations of the Early London Capital Market: Bank of England Shareholders during and after the South Sea Bubble, 1720–1725." *Economic History Review* 59, no. 3 (August 2006): 498–538.

Committee for General Purposes of the Stock-Exchange. *Rules and Regulations Adopted by the Committee for General Purposes of the Stock-Exchange.* London: Stephen Couchman Printers, 1812.

Davies, Megan, Jack Stubbs, and Thomas Escritt. "Court Orders Russia to Pay $50 Billion for Seizing Yukos Assets." *Reuters,* July 28, 2014. http://www.reuters.com/article/us-russia-yukos -idUSKBN0FW0TP20140728.

Dehing, Pit, and Marjolein 't Hart. "Linking the Fortunes: Currency and Banking, 1550–1800." In *A Financial History of the Netherlands,* edited by Marjolein 't Hart, Joost Jonker, van Zanden, and Jan Luiten, 37–63. New York: Cambridge University Press, 1997.

de la Vega, Josef Penso. *Confusion De Confusiones.* New York: John Wiley & Sons, 1688 [1996].

De Vries, Jan, and Ad Van Der Woude. *The First Modern Economy: Success, Failure, and Perseverance of the Dutch Economy, 1500–1815.* New York: Cambridge University Press, 1997.

Francis, John. *Chronicles and Characters of the Stock Exchange.* Boston: Wm. Crosby and H. P. Nichols, 1850.

Freedman, Roy S. *Introduction to Financial Technology.* Burlington, MA: Academic Press, 2006.

Frye, Timothy. *Brokers and Bureaucrats: Building Market Institutions in Russia.* Ann Arbor: University of Michigan Press, 2000.

Garber, Peter. "Tulipmania." In *Speculative Bubbles, Speculative Attacks, and Policy Switching,* edited by Robert Flood and Peter Garber, 55–82. Cambridge: MIT Press, 1994.

Glaeser, Edward, and Andrei Shleifer. "Legal Origins." *Quarterly Journal of Economics* 117, no. 4 (2002): 1193–229.

Greif, Avner. "Contract Enforceability and Economic Institutions in Early Trade: The Maghribi Traders' Coalition." *American Economic Review* 83 (1993): 525–48.

Hamon, Henry. *New York Stock Exchange Manual: Containing Its Different Modes of Speculation: Also, a Review of the Stocks Dealt in on 'Change*. New York: John F. Trow, 1865.

Harris, Ron. *Industrializing English Law: Entrepreneurship and Business Organization, 1720–1844*. New York: Cambridge University Press, 2000.

Israel, Jonathan. *Dutch Primacy in World Trade, 1585–1740*. New York: Oxford University Press, 1989 [1991].

———. *The Dutch Republic: Its Rise, Greatness, and Fall 1477–1806*. New York: Oxford University Press, 1995.

Jenkins, Alan. *The Stock Exchange Story*. London: Heinemann, 1973.

Keister, David. *Keister's Corporation Accounting and Auditing*. Cleveland: Burrows Brothers Company, 1889.

Kellenbenz, Hermann. "Introduction to Confusion De Confusiones." In *Extraordinary Popular Delusions and the Madness of Crowds by Charles MacKay and Confusion De Confusiones by Joseph de la Vega*, edited by Martin Fridson, 125–46. New York: John Wiley & Sons, 1957 [1996].

Kindleberger, Charles P. *A Financial History of Western Europe*. London: George Allen and Unwin, 1984.

Kirzner, Israel M. *The Driving Force of the Market: Essays in Austrian Economics*. New York: Routledge, 2000.

The Law Times Reports of Cases Decided in the House of Lords, the Privy Council, the Court of Appeal, etc. London: Horace Cox, Windsor Hourse, Bream's Buildings, E. C., 1892.

Leeson, Peter T. "Escaping Poverty: Foreign Aid, Private Property, and Economic Development." *Journal of Private Enterprise* 23 (2008): 39–64.

———. *Anarchy Unbound: Why Self-Governance Works Better than You Think*. Cambridge: Cambridge University Press, 2014.

The London Stock Exchange. *A Guide to AIM*. London: London Stock Exchange, 2010.

Macey, Jonathan. *The Death of Corporate Reputation: How Integrity Has Been Destroyed on Wall Street*. Upper Saddle River, NJ: Pearson Education, 2013.

Macey, Jonathan, and Hideki Kanda. "The Stock Exchange as a Firm: The Emergence of Close Substitutes for the New York and Tokyo Stock Exchanges." *Cornell Law Review* 75 (1990): 1007–52.

Macey, Jonathan, and David Swensen. "The Cure for Stock-Market Fragmentation: More Exchanges." *Wall Street Journal*, May 31, 2015.

Mahoney, Paul. "The Exchange as Regulator." *Virginia Law Review* 83 (1997): 1453–500.

Malmendier, Ulrike M. "Law and Finance at the Origin." *Journal of Economic Literature* 47, no. 4 (2009): 1076–108.

Manne, Geoffrey A. "The Hydraulic Theory of Disclosure Regulation and Other Costs of Disclosure." *Alabama Law Review* 58 (2007): 473–511.

Markham, Jerry. *A Financial History of the United States. Vol. 2. From J. P. Morgan to the Institutional Investor*. New York: M. E. Sharpe, 2002.

McCloskey, Deirdre N. *The Bourgeois Virtues*. Chicago: University of Chicago, 2006.

McKinsey and Company. *Sustaining New York's and the U.S.' Global Financial Services Leadership*. New York: McKinsey and Company, 2007.

Meeker, James Edward. *The Work of the New York Stock Exhange*. New York: Ronald Press Company, 1922.

Mirowski, Philip. "The Rise (and Retreat) of a Market: English Joint Stock Shares in the Eighteenth Century." *Journal of Economic History* 41, no. 3 (1981): 559–77.

Morgan, E. Victor, and W. A. Thomas. *The London Stock Exchange*. New York: St. Martin's Press, 1969.

Musacchio, Aldo. "Can Civil Law Countries Get Good Institutions? Lessons from the History of Creditor Rights and Bond Markets in Brazil." *Journal of Economic History* 68, no. 1 (2008): 80–108.

Neal, Larry. *The Rise of Financial Capitalism: International Capital Markets in the Age of Reason*, New York: Cambridge University Press, 1990

———. "On the Historical Development of Stock Markets." In *The Emergence and Evolution of Stock Markets*, edited by Horst Brezinski and Michael Fritsch, 59–79. Cheltenham: Edward Elgar Publishing, 1997.

———. "The Evolution of Self- and State Regulation of the London Stock Exchange, 1688–1878." In *Law and Long-Term Economic Change: A Eurasian Perspective*, edited by Debin Ma and Jan Luiten van Zanden, 300–322. Palo Alto, CA: Stanford University Press, 2011.

———. *A Concise History of International Finance*. Cambridge: Cambridge University Press, 2015.

Neal, Larry, and Lance Davis. "The Evolution of the Rules and Regulations of the First Emerging Markets: The London, New York and Paris Stock Exchanges, 1792–1914." *Quarterly Review of Economics and Finance* 45 (2005): 296–311.

———. "The Evolution of the Structure and Performance of the London Stock Exchange in the First Global Financial Market, 1812–1914." *European Review of Economic History* 10, no. 3 (2006): 279–300.

New York Stock Exchange. *Constitution and By-Laws of the New York Stock Exchange*. New York: Martin England, 1869.

———. *Constitution of the New York Stock Exchange and Resolutions Adopted by the Governing Committee: With Amendments to February 1914*. New York: Searing & Moore Company, 1914.

———. *The Constitution of the New York Stock Exchange (as Revised in 1925)*. New York: New York Stock Exchange, 1925.

———. *About Us/History/Timeline*. New York: New York Stock Exchange, 2013.

O'Hara, Maureen. *Market Microstructure Theory*. Oxford: Blackwell, 1995.

Olson, Mancur. "Big Bills Left on the Sidewalk: Why Some Nations Are Rich, and Others Poor." *Journal of Economic Perspectives* 10, no. 2 (1996): 3–24.

Palgrave, Robert Harry Inglis. *Dictionary of Political Economy, Volume III*. London: Macmillan and Co., 1910.

Petram, Lodewijk Otto. "The World's First Stock Exchange: How the Amsterdam Market for Dutch East India Company Shares became a Modern Securities Market, 1602–1700." Dissertation, University of Amsterdam, 2011.

Rajan, Raghuram, and Luigi Zingales. *Saving Capitalism from the Capitalists: Unleashing the Power of Financial Markets to Create Wealth and Spread Opportunity*. Princeton, NJ: Princeton University Press, 2004.

Reed, M. C. *A History of James Capel & Co*. London: James Capel & Co, 1975.

"Restrictions for Company Promoters." *Bradstreet's*, June 24, 1899, 388.

Romano, Roberta. "Empowering Investors: A Market Approach to Securities Regulation." *Yale Law Journal* 107 (1998): 2365–99.

Smith, Adam. *Lectures on Jurisprudence*. Indianapolis, IN: Liberty Classics, 1766 [1982].

Smith, C. F. "The Early History of the London Stock Exchange." *The American Economic Review* 19, no. 2 (1929): 206–16.

Stedman, Edmund C., and Alexander N. Easton. "History of the New York Stock Exchange." In *The New York Stock Exchange: Its History, Its Contribution to National Prosperity, and Its Relation to American Finance at the Outset of the Twentieth Century*, edited by E. C. Stedman, 15–410. New York: Stock Exchange Historical Company, 1905.

Stringham, Edward. *Private Governance: Creating Order in Economic and Social Life*. New York and Oxford: Oxford University Press, 2015.

Stringham, Edward Peter, Peter J. Boettke, and J. R. Clark. "Are Regulations the Answer for Emerging Stock Markets? Evidence from the Czech Republic and Poland." *Quarterly Review of Economics and Finance* 48, no. 3 (August 2008): 541–66.

Stringham, Edward Peter, and Ivan Chen. "The Alternative of Private Regulation: The London Stock Exchange's Alternative Investment Market as a Model." *Economic Affairs* 32, no. 3 (2012): 37–43.

Tontine Coffee House. *The Constitution and Nominations of the Subscribers to the Tontine Coffee-House*. New York: Tontine Coffee House, 1796.

Werner, Walter and Steven T. Smith. *Wall Street*. New York: Columbia University Press, 1991.

White, Derek N. "ECNs RIP: How Regulation NMS Destroyed Electronic Communication Networks and All Their Market Improvements." Working Paper, University of Colorado Law School, 2008.

Wilson, Charles. *Anglo-Dutch Commerce in the Eighteenth Century*. New York: Cambridge University Press, 1941.

Wincott, Harold. *The Stock Exchange*. London: Sampson Low, Marston and Company, 1946.

CHAPTER 10
Using the Market to Manage Proprietary Algorithmic Trading

HOLLY A. BELL

University of Alaska Anchorage

E ven before Michael Lewis[1] published his popular and controversial[2] book on high-frequency trading (HFT), traditional traders and regulators were asking what they should do about this new evolution in financial market trading technology in which traders use algorithms—computerized trading programs—to automatically trade securities in financial markets. But what exactly about high-frequency trading do traders and regulators wish to see controlled, and can these issues be regulated away? Or are there better, more market-based solutions to address the issues associated with evolving market technology?

The intent of this chapter is to broadly discuss categories of concerns about algorithmic and, more specifically, proprietary algorithmic trading based on issues regulators and legislators themselves have given as rationale for market intervention, but not to explore in detail every possible issue that might be raised. The chapter defines algorithmic and proprietary trading and describes how the technology and regulatory environments have gotten us to today's financial market structure. I present some of the broad concerns algorithmic trading technologies have created for regulators, legislators, the public, and other stakeholders, then explore one proposed legislative solution, financial transaction taxes (FTTs), and the outcomes of five cases in which an FTT has been implemented. The chapter concludes with market-based solutions that work toward cooperative rather than regulatory resolutions to concerns about market integrity and fairness, including how competition and a self-reporting system for human and technology errors may help manage the concerns some have with computerized trading and proprietary algorithmic trading (PAT) in particular.

TYPES OF ALGORITHMIC TRADING

Algorithmic trading uses computer programs with complex mathematical formulas to analyze internal and external market data to determine trading strategies and place trades. Hasbrouck and Saar divide algorithmic trading into two broad categories: (1) agency algorithms (AA) and (2) proprietary algorithms (PA). The properties of each are unique. AA are "used by buy-side institutions as well as the brokers who serve them to buy and sell shares"[3] with the goal of minimizing the cost of executing trades. These types of algorithms break up large orders into smaller ones to be distributed across multiple trading venues and are generally used by portfolio managers with longer-term investment horizons than those utilizing PA.

Those using PA are attempting to profit from the trading environment itself rather than from investments in securities. PA can be subdivided into two broad categories of users: (1) electronic market making and (2) statistical arbitrage trading. Electronic market makers "buy and sell their own account in a list of securities,"[4] carry low inventories, and profit from small differences between bid and ask prices and liquidity rebates.

Statistical arbitrage trading "is carried out by the proprietary trading desks of large financial firms, hedge funds, and independent specialty firms."[5] They analyze the historical data of stocks and asset groups for trading patterns and compare them with current patterns to identify deviations that can be turned into short-run profit opportunities. PA also look for changes in market behavior that indicate a large order is being executed that creates temporary price imbalances that can be capitalized on. It is important to note that market making and arbitrage trading are not new; they existed in nonautomated markets and were historically executed by specialists. The difference today is the speed with which these strategies can be executed due to automation.

The term "high-frequency trading" is generally associated with proprietary algorithms that operate in the millisecond environment and post and cancel orders frequently as they look for market-making and arbitrage opportunities. I use the term proprietary algorithmic trading in this chapter whenever possible and high-frequency trading when necessary due to context, such as when I am discussing what someone else has said. The two terms should be considered synonymous within this chapter.

CONCERNS ABOUT PROPRIETARY ALGORITHMIC TRADING

Analyzing the goals regulators themselves state as reasons why they seek to regulate PAT finds they generally fall into two broad categories: market integrity and "fairness."[6]

Market Integrity

When it comes to market integrity, most stakeholders are in agreement that markets should be secure, reliable, and orderly to enable effective price discovery and limit market manipulation and abuses. No one ultimately has anything to gain in a chaotic and unstable financial market, and no market participant wishes to compete in such an environment.

While every day 5 billion to 6 billion equity shares are efficiently and effectively traded with an extremely low failure rate,[7] concerns that a major market-disrupting event is inevitable continues to drive calls for increased regulation of both PAT and computerized trading more broadly. Since the 1970s regulators have looked for regulatory solutions to solve the same perceived market failures they believe threaten market integrity today. Among them are market fragmentation and price synchronization across venues, information dissemination problems (including market technology problems), and previous policy failures. Yet these issues persist with only the regulatory targets changing over time. The current target is PAT.[8]

To understand how PAT became the current market integrity concern, it is important to understand some of the history of market structure, regulation, and the concerns of critics. In the early 1970s the US Securities and Exchange Commission (SEC), concerned about increased market fragmentation and the resulting challenges with price synchronization across exchanges, began pursuing a national market system. The purpose was to develop a consolidated communication and data processing network to synchronize price quotations.[9] It was implemented in 1975.

Regulators were happy with this system until Black Monday of October 19, 1987. Several factors caused stress in the markets in the days leading up to Black Monday, including a higher-than-expected federal budget deficit and new proposed legislation to eliminate the tax benefits associated with corporate mergers. This news led to dollar value declines. Actions taken by the Federal Reserve in the months leading up to the crash had also led to rapidly rising interest rates. These factors together were creating downward pressure on equity prices and generating higher trading volumes. The high volumes were greater than the system technology could handle and technical pricing problems developed. On the day of the crash there was so much sell pressure that some market makers postponed trading for an hour after opening. They simply refused to answer their phones. Doing so meant market indexes had become stale, which led to difficulties pricing securities accurately. The chaotic market environment with impaired and disorderly trading ultimately led to the crash.[10]

Black Monday of 1987 was viewed as a failure of the market structure established by the national market system. To modernize and strengthen it, the Regulation National Market System (NMS) was implemented to correct the previous policy's failures.[11] The goals of Regulation NMS were to improve the dissemination of market information, reduce computerized technical problems, and better synchronize prices across exchanges. Prior to Regulation NMS, most trading was taking place on the New York Stock Exchange (NYSE) and the NASDAQ because the scale of their operations meant there was significant liquidity available and little incentive to trade elsewhere. With the implementation of Regulation NMS and its Order Protection (Trade Through) Rule—which requires trading centers to make price quotations immediately and automatically accessible to ensure orders are executed at the best price, regardless of which exchange it resides on—price competition and liquidity increased across trading venues, creating incentives for other venues to enter the marketplace. It was this competition that led to the improved liquidity, reduced spreads, and lowered transaction costs seen in markets today.

However, there were a couple of new problems created under this market structure. It was assumed, but not required, that all prices would be synchronized within the Securities Information Processor (SIP), however the technology driving it quickly became too old and too slow to keep up with the speed of trading. Prices from the SIP generally lag well behind the actual price present in the market, creating problems for traders who could trade faster than the quotes could update. The benefit of Regulation NMS to resolve technological price synchronization and information dissemination problems was short-lived as trading technology quickly outpaced centralized quoting. So traders adapted by purchasing direct feeds to market data that was closer to real-time. Instead of having access to SIP-processed output quotes, these firms had access to the data at the same time it was input into the SIP, eliminating significant delays. However, it is worth noting that prices change so rapidly in markets that displayed prices, even through direct feeds, are never a complete and accurate reflection of the prices securities are actually trading at in the market. There is always some delay.

Critics like Arnuk and Saluzzi[12] have blamed the increased market fragmentation created by Regulation NMS as leading to the proliferation of PAT. Yet there is little empirical evidence to support a link between Regulation NMS and the emergence of PAT specifically. In a speech before the Economic Club of New York in June 2014,[13] SEC Chair Mary Jo White points out that multiple countries have seen the same levels (or higher) of HFT growth in their markets even though they are not subject to Regulation NMS or similar types of regulation. Even highly centralized markets that like the Chicago Mercantile Exchange have similar levels of HFT activity in their E-mini trading as more fragmented markets that are subject to Regulation NMS. Another example is Japan, where 90 percent of all stock trading is centralized on the Tokyo Stock Exchange and there are no maker/taker fees and rebate payments for order flow, yet in 2014 HFT accounted for as much as 72 percent of trades.[14] The cause of HFT is more likely simply the evolution of market technology.

A criticism of technology advances and the increased use of algorithms within markets is that PAT has caused average order sizes on the NYSE to plunge 67 percent between 2005 and 2010.[15] In 2009, the average order size on the NYSE was about 400 shares;[16] by October 2014 the average trade size was 187 shares, which represented a 22.3 percent decrease on a year-over-year basis.[17] But the question to consider is whether this is a PAT-related issue or a regulatory-initiated problem. By requiring trade price to be the primary measure of execution quality, Regulation NMS ignores other execution factors that might be important to institutional or individual traders. In the central-ized pricing requirements created under Regulation NMS, it becomes nearly impossible to execute a large order without moving the overall market price. It is this centralization and the removal of the ability to display block orders exclusively to other institutional buy-side firms under the SEC's Regulation of Exchanges and Alternative Trading Systems (Regulation ATS)[18] that has led to the proliferation of dark pools—and a lack of order transparency even among large block traders within them—as well as smaller order sizes on lit markets.[19]

With Regulation NMS and Regulation ATS as root causes, PAT has become a tool that helps the market absorb large numbers of small orders to ensure they do not become a significant problem for markets. An opinion written by investment management company BlackRock states there is little reason to be concerned about reductions in order sizes because "investors should be generally indifferent to receiving 10 fills of 300 shares vs. 1 fill of 3,000 shares provided that execution quality and aggregate liquidity are equivalent."[20] PAT and its market-making function help keep liquidity high.

Another market integrity concern is the opportunity for technical problems with trading algorithms and their related systems. In an attempt to resolve these concerns, the SEC developed Regulation Systems Compliance and Integrity (SCI), which became effective February 3, 2015, and was fully implemented in November 2015. The two primary purposes of the regulation are to ensure market participants:

> (1) have comprehensive policies and procedures in place to help ensure the robustness and resiliency of their techno-logical systems, and also that their technological systems operate in compliance with the federal securities laws and with their own rules; and (2) provide certain notices and reports to the Commission to improve Commission over-sight of securities market infrastructure.[21]

For the previous twenty-six years, the SEC relied on a cooperative set of principles outlined in the Commission's Automated Review Policy (first imple-mented in 1989[22] and revised in 1991[23]) and its associated inspection program to oversee the technology of the US securities markets. These policy statements were not "rules" in the formal regulatory sense, but suggestions and guidelines for how participants could design their systems, including capacity, contingencies, and security, as well as testing policies and procedures and independent system audits. It also established guidelines for reporting significant system changes, problems, and outages to the Commission. Participants could also request an inspection from regulators to evaluate their key systems and make recommendations for improvement.

Under increased pressure by lawmakers and the public to improve Commission oversight after the Flash Crash of May 6, 2010, the SEC took what participants were already doing voluntarily and turned it into formal regulation with Regulation SCI. There is at least one downside here. Regulation SCI moves the relationship between market participants and regulators away from cooperation and toward a more punitive, adversarial relationship. Imposing formal regulation implies the desire to impose sanctions when there is a technological failure or other problem with trading systems. A punitive rather than cooperative environment may discourage innovation and expeditious self-reporting of system events to the public and regulators in order to avoid fines.

There are strong, shared market integrity goals between traders, exchanges, and regulators that make a cooperative solution preferable. As mentioned earlier, no market participant benefits from a chaotic market or technology failures, and there are significant market incentives to maintain practices that promote secure, reliable, and orderly financial markets and market systems that enable effective price discovery. The financial loss experienced by Knight Capital due to its algorithmic trading errors demonstrates one such market incentive.

Fairness

The compatible interests of stakeholders diverge once regulators begin to discuss the imposition of "fairness" on markets. These policies are usually based on normative value judgments about what market outcomes *should* be, based on the subjective ideals of individuals or regulators about social optimality. For example, the ability of proprietary algorithms to rapidly analyze internal and external market data, allowing them to quickly identify profitable trades, has been criticized. Economist Joseph Stiglitz believes the use of HFT should be discouraged through financial transaction taxes because, in part, there is no social value and only personal reward in obtaining information before someone else does, and personal rewards fail to provide the greatest value to society as a whole.[24]

Others, like British professor John Kay, believe the strategy employed by PAT of holding stocks only in the short term should be discouraged, while owning stocks over the long term should be encouraged. His rationale is that trading decisions that maximize a trader's utility in the short run cannot possibly reflect the trader's long-term financial interests or the interests of society.[25]

While these arguments may seem somewhat extreme, they are resonant with concerns that many others, including more moderate commentators, have about the challenges associated with competition within financial markets. As markets become faster and more competitive, can everyone compete? Or, as Lewis suggests, have markets become "rigged"?

When discussing issues of market fairness related to PAT, I think it is prudent to mention some relevant philosophical and factual points that counter the arguments made by Stiglitz and Kay. First, attempts to control "fairness" of market outcomes in the pursuit of "social optimality" is challenging at best. There is no all-knowing, neutral third party in society who has all information, past, present, and future, and who can decide what the moment-by-moment or long-run socially optimal outcome should be. It is this ignorance that requires us to rely on markets to determine that outcome. In this way markets are indifferent to whether participants are behaving as fully rational "social" optimizers or as "individual" utility maximizers, provided they are making the best choice possible in response to the decision-making of others. The individual profit maximizers can reach an outcome in which no other market participant will be better off by unilaterally changing his or her strategy, implying the socially optimum outcome is being moved toward.[26] Even if individuals are not making the best choice possible, the market is indifferent; it simply reflects their suboptimal choice.

Regarding concerns about the ability of all to compete in the marketplace, it is important to note significant competitive forces have always been present in financial markets. Professional institutional investors have always had more time, information, and resources at their disposal than individual investors or even smaller firms. One market solution to this problem was the creation of mutual funds so that all investors could benefit from the advantages of institutional investors.[27] Mutual fund ownership has risen from 5.7 percent of US households in 1980 to 46.3 percent of households including 96.2 million individuals in 2013, with 93 percent held in retirement funds, primarily in employer pension programs.[28] These trends indicate that an increasing number of investors are receiving the benefits of institutional investor knowledge and trading.

On an institutional investor level, while increased market fragmentation created by Regulation NMS has added additional competitive forces to markets, markets remain procedurally fair in the sense that the same rules apply to PAT as to other traders. One example is that all traders are permitted to buy a computer, colocate it in an exchange data center, and develop or purchase computer programs to execute trades.[29]

While individuals like Stiglitz and Kay believe there are no social benefits associated with the improvements in information dissemination, competition, and shorter hold times associated with PAT, there have been empirically demonstrated benefits to investors. HFT has improved liquidity by lowering spreads; has reduced trading costs, making markets accessible to a greater number of people; has improved price synchronization of related securities; performs a stabilizing function during extreme market price movements; has increased direct price improvements for retail investors; and in some cases has made pricing more efficient. Market makers make a fraction of what they used to make per trade, and the savings have been passed on to investors. While markets and market competition are not perfect, they remain the best ways to maximize efficiency.[30]

HFT is also not taking over the markets as some have claimed.[31] While PAT had some advantages early on, as others have figured out their trading strategies, they have been better able to compete with PAT in the marketplace, reducing both the market share and profits of PAT. At its peak in 2009, HFT represented 61 percent of US equity volume,[32] but its market impact was reduced dramatically to 49 percent of volume by June 2016, as reported by the Tabb Group.[33] In 2009 profits from HFT were $7.2 billion; by 2014 profits had declined to an estimated $1.3 billion.[34]

One of the great challenges in imposing regulation is that often by the time a new market structure regulation is proposed or implemented, the market has already evolved beyond the identified problem. The perceived problem of the proliferation of PAT within the market making it difficult for others to compete is one example. While for a brief period around 2009 HFTs held a technological and competitive position in equity markets that made competing with them challenging—primarily because others lacked an understanding of their methods—market forces have reduced their competitive position as non-PAT firms improved their knowledge of PAT and executed new competitive and technological strategies. One of the first competitive strategies was the software program called Thor, developed by Brad Katsuyama when he was at the Royal Bank of Canada, which competed directly with the order routing speed of PAT.[35]

Even though market share and profit potential for PAT has diminished over time, it remains a predominant topic for politicians and regulators particularly as it relates to issues of fairness. As Maureen O'Hara in a Cambridge University interview stated, HFT has become politicized because fast trading sounds bad to the average person and the media promotes this fear.[36]

PROPOSED FINANCIAL TRANSACTION TAXES

While basic rules and regulations associated with organized financial markets are necessary, it is difficult for regulators and legislators to stay ahead of technology, foresee all possible market disruptions, or determine what a socially optimal market outcome might look like. Regulators and legislators also generally lag behind market forces in correcting market inequities and either end up creating ineffective policies or disrupt a functional market-based solution. Even with these challenges, globally a plethora of existing and proposed regulations are designed to disrupt market modernization through computerized algorithmic trading and PAT. Among them are policies that require market makers to provide liquidity regardless of market conditions, controls on direct market access, minimum hold times, maximum order-to-trade ratios, circuit breakers, algorithm approval processes, standardized system testing, reduction in order types, batch auctions, and eliminating maker/taker fees.[37] While the limited space of this chapter does not allow me to address each of these proposals in depth, these resolutions do have second and third order consequences that may have negative consequences on markets overall; therefore the costs and benefits of these market interventions must be carefully considered.

A FTT has been proposed recently in the United States. The current "high-roller fee" proposed by Chris Van Hollen—a top Democrat on the House Budget Committee—and similar actions supported by presidential candidates Hillary Clinton[38] and Bernie Sanders[39] are being proposed as a way to "raise tens of billions of dollars each year" to give back to "workers" in the form of tax relief and to eliminate computerized high-speed trading. The congressman claims there will be no adverse consequences from the tax because the European Union (EU) and others already have or are imposing trading fees and these fees will be "imperceptible" to high-rolling investors.[40] Others like Nobel Prize–winning economists Joseph Stiglitz and James Tobin, and former Treasury Secretary Lawrence Summers, have long supported a FTT as a means of reducing speculation and market "noise," thereby reducing market volatility and the risk of a market-disrupting event.[41] Yet there is empirical evidence to indicate that financial transaction taxes are harmful to markets.

The state of New York imposed a Securities Transaction Tax on all equity transactions from 1905 until its repeal in 1981. In 1932 during the Great Depression, New York doubled the transaction tax in order to increase state revenue. In 1968, the New York Stock Exchange threatened to leave the state because the tax was putting it at a competitive disadvantage compared to out-of-state exchanges; the taxes were gradually reduced until they were completely abandoned in 1981.

A study of the impacts of the transaction tax between 1932 and 1981 found that NYSE volume declined, average stock volatility and transaction costs for investors increased, volume was reduced, there were higher price impacts, and bid-ask spreads increased, thereby reducing liquidity.[42]

In 2012, Canada implemented a transaction tax based on the total number of market messages including trades and order submissions, cancellations, and modifications. A study on the impacts of the transaction tax found that while trades, quotes, and order cancellations—the "noise" some consider harmful— dropped 30 percent, bid-ask spreads increased by 9 percent. The researchers also found that as "message-intensive" (noisy) algorithmic traders reduced their activity, retail traders' intraday returns were negatively impacted—with limit order returns having the greatest decrease—while large institutional traders' returns from market orders increased.[43]

In a related issue, Canadian brokers who wish to avoid fees and take advantage of maker/taker payment for order flow are routing about 40 percent of Canadian retail trade orders to the United States—about half of all Canadian interlisted trading.[44] Regulators who wish to remove the maker/taker model because they believe it will discourage HFT need to consider that it also attracts capital.

Sweden's experiment with a financial transaction tax actually caused the government to lose tax revenue rather than create new revenue sources that could be redistributed to working Swedes. Sweden introduced a 1 percent tax on equity transactions in 1984 that was later raised to 2 percent in 1986. A study found that when the tax was raised in 1986 volatility failed to decline, but average equity prices did decrease. The most damaging outcome from the tax was that 60 percent of the trading volume of the eleven most actively traded Swedish trade classes migrated to London to avoid paying the tax.

Assuming US markets will not be impacted similarly because EU markets are also implementing FTTs is shortsighted. Unless all world markets have the identical tax, there remains incentive for other countries to compete globally for capital by lowering or eliminating taxes.

In the United States, one of the goals of proposed FTTs is to reduce the high frequency of trades; however, the Swedish experience provides an additional warning against reducing turnover rates. In Sweden, significant turnover rate reductions caused revenues from capital gains taxes to decline to a level offsetting any gains from taxes raised from the financial transaction tax in 1988.[45]

Shortly after financial transaction taxes were implemented in Italy and France, their shares of European equity turnover plummeted. Within six months after Italy introduced its tax, equity turnover dropped from €101 billion in 2012 to €50 billion for the same time period in 2013. This drop happened even as overall European volumes increased 7 percent.

In 2012, France implemented a package of financial transaction taxes. The first tax, designed to eliminate HFT by making it unprofitable, was a 0.01 percent "nontransaction" tax on modified or canceled stock orders exceeding 80 percent of all orders transmitted in a month. HFTs are subject to the tax if they transmit, modify, or cancel their orders within a half second. Additionally, a 0.20 percent transaction tax on purchased shares of French companies with market capitalizations of at least €1 billion was included in the package.[46]

The consequences for France have been significant decreases in market liquidity. France's share of European equity turnover was reduced from 23 percent in 2011 to an estimated 12.85 percent in 2013.[47]

Based on theorists' and regulators' own policy proposals, the goals of financial transaction taxes worldwide appear to be to generate revenue for the government, redistribute wealth, reduce trading and its perceived market integrity risk, eliminate HFT, or engineer an unknown "socially optimal" market outcome.[48] Yet it is important to consider second and third order consequences of such actions including reduced liquidity, higher transactions costs, volatility and spread increases, and market flight.

The International Monetary Fund (IMF) warns that because FTTs are not well targeted but "levied on every transaction, the cumulative, 'cascading' effects of an FTT . . . can be significant and non-transparent"[49] with costs falling primarily on final consumers rather than financial institutions. These costs include, but are not limited to, reduced returns on savings, higher costs of borrowing, or increases in final commodity prices. A study has concluded that a 0.5 percent financial transaction tax leads to a 1.33 percent increase in the cost of capital.[50] A higher cost of capital initiated by a financial transaction tax could "reduce the flow of profitable projects, shrinking levels of real production, expansion, capital investment and even employment," according to the study.[51]

A speech by former SEC Commissioner Daniel M. Gallagher speaks to the long-term consequences of regulation on US capital markets:

> Legislators and regulators are layering on law after law, regulation after regulation—strangling entrepreneurs, their enterprises, and of course their employees and customers. We are not even resting on our laurels—we are actively throwing those laurels on a bonfire.[52]

Commissioner Gallagher goes on to describe how since 2007 the United States has been steadily losing market share to other international financial centers due, in part, to an "increasingly costly regulatory environment and the burdensome level of civil litigation," loss of economic freedom, and failure to respond to global competition. He cites multiple studies that indicate the United States is losing its position in the world as a leader in capital markets as other countries find ways to modernize and enhance their markets. Places like Dubai, Qatar, Singapore, Turkey, Tokyo, China, Brazil, Mexico, and even Moscow are all trying to reduce their impediments to capital formation in their markets through modifications in regulation, taxes, or fees.[53]

TOWARD MARKET-BASED SOLUTIONS

More than forty years of regulatory efforts to deal with issues of market fragmentation and price synchronization, information dissemination and market technology problems, and previous policies have failed to eliminate these issues. In the current market environment PAT is the focus. However, it is important to understand that issues like information dissemination and price synchronization will never be perfect and there will always be market technology problems that crop up; they are inherent in markets. The key is to find cooperative market-based solutions that minimize competition between regulators and market participants on the development of market structure and the monitoring of market integrity. While markets are already managing the proliferation of HFT in financial markets, there are a couple of other market-based solutions to managing PAT.

The first is competition. While market fragmentation has been a criticism associated with Regulation NMS, US stock market ownership is not highly fragmented. Of the eleven exchanges, four are owned by BATS, three each by Intercontinental Exchange and NASDAQ, and one by the Chicago Stock Exchange.[54] Off-exchange dark pools do compete with the "lit" markets and add fragmentation, but there is competition there as well.

As public concerns about HFT emerged, so did several competitive solutions. The one most people are familiar with is the Investors' Exchange (IEX), the dark pool featured in Michael Lewis's book *Flash Boys*. The intention of IEX is to equalize the speed of transactions to eliminate any speed advantage experienced by HFTs.[55] In June 2016, IEX's application to become a national stock exchange was approved and a target date of September 2, 2016, was set for implementation.[56] IEX adds a fifth competitor within the US marketplace.

Responding to the challenges of executing large block trades and concerns that HFT activity is not always being disclosed in dark pools has motivated fund managers at nine large firms—including majority holder Fidelity in cooperation with BlackRock, T. Rowe Price, and JPMorgan, and others—to develop a new dark pool called Luminex that specializes in large stock trades.[57] Luminex Trading & Analytics began trading on November 3, 2015, with eighty-four investment management firms subscribed to the platform.[58] As of June 2016, Luminex was reporting a subscriber base of 132 clients trading an average block size of 32,000 shares and volume in excess of 155 million shares.[59]

A similar effort is under way by Europe-based Plato Partnership Ltd.—a consortium of asset managers and broker dealers—designed to increase transparency, simplify markets, and trade large blocks of stock without detection by HFTs.[60] The consortium would be organized as a not-for-profit trading utility.[61] No launch date has been set as of this writing.

Aequitas Neo Exchange (ANE), a new stock exchange in Canada, intends to equalize the speed of transactions much like IEX does, but also plans to waive market data fees for some investors. Retail investors will not be charged for "real-time displayed market data for securities listed on the primary and venture TSX [Toronto Stock Exchange] exchanges." Professional investors will have fees waived on the ANE until their volumes reach 5 percent of market share.[62]

ANE launched in March of 2015 and as of April 2016 was averaging over 6 percent of Canadian securities market share by volume traded in 2016. For the month of April 2016 ANE's average trade size exceeded that of all other Canadian marketplaces in the most actively traded securities.[63]

Whether these competitors are arising due to real concerns about HFT or investor sentiment, as long as there is demand for competing trading venues the market will provide them. If the competitors offer a superior service for the majority of investors, HFT will be eliminated through market forces as it falls out of fashion.

Additional competition is available in the form of self-learning, predictive algorithms[64] and software that detects HFT strategies[65] that will allow retail investors to be more competitive with HFT. For regulatory intervention to be necessary, a market failure must exist, such as HFT holding a monopoly position within the market, not just being highly competitive. The rapidly rising direct competitors indicate an HFT monopoly does not exist and that market forces are keeping HFT in check.

As concerns have increased that technology problems may lead to major market events like a Flash Crash, regulators have responded by formalizing testing and system integrity protocols under Regulation SCI. However, there are no rules that can eliminate human/technology interface errors. The best alternative is to look for patterns of errors that might indicate a need for preventive measures. For example, on May 6, 2010, markets were stressed due to negative political and economic news, including the European debt crisis, and significantly reduced buy-side liquidity. Contributing to the market stress was a UK trader named Navinder Singh Sarao who was, according to the US Department of Justice, engaging in aggressive "spoofing" activity in an effort to move market prices in a direction favorable to his trading strategy[66]—the potential for which is another criticism of PAT and a practice already illegal under US and European law. However, the tipping point of the Flash Crash of 2010 was reached during a human/technology interface error[67] when a large firm chose to execute an algorithm that was inappropriate for the current market conditions.

One solution is to develop a database for confidentially self-reporting human and technology errors for research. The purpose is to gather data on human and technology errors in order to analyze the data for patterns and prevent major market events, through awareness, training, and if all else fails, specific regulatory intervention.[68] The goal is to move toward a cooperative approach between traders and regulators to solve issues related to human errors and technology glitches by encouraging self-reporting without punishing recovered errors.

Human errors would include issues like selecting the wrong or inappropriate algorithm for market conditions, accidentally deleting computer code, entering the wrong quantity, or entering a sell order when it was supposed to be a buy. An example of a technology failure is when the algorithm does not work as intended and/or is stopped during its operation due to a problem.

The airline industry uses a similar self-reporting system that is administered by NASA as a neutral third party. NASA removes any identifying information from the reports and the data is compiled, analyzed, and reported on.[69] Human error is a significant factor in aviation incidents, but like errors in finance, they rarely lead to a major event like a crash. However, between June 2009 and July 31, 2015, there were 31,045 human factor errors reported to NASA.[70] The vast majority of these airline incidents were not required to be reported to a regulating body, yet analyzing this data for patterns of errors has led to measures designed to minimize potential major aircraft incidents. The database is also made public, so companies, academics, and agencies can also analyze the data and propose solutions.

A suitable neutral third party would need to be established for the financial sector to encourage reporting.[71] Advisory committees could also be formed to work with trading firms and venues to establish action plans, develop performance improvement reporting, and when cooperative solutions are inadequate or unsuccessful, propose regulatory solutions to improve the human-automation interface.

CONCLUSION

US financial markets have a long history of cooperation and self-regulation,[72] and the SEC has repeatedly maintained "that competition and innovation in the provision of trading services should be encouraged." This includes using competition as a means of technological advances. The statement by the SEC upon release of the Market 2000 Report in 1994 also asserts that "competition would drive the evolution of the markets," that "the Commission [should] cultivate an atmosphere in which innovation is welcome, without dictating a particular structure," and that it should allow "competitive forces to shape market structure within a fair regulatory field."[73]

Even though there is evidence that competition is containing PAT in financial markets, we are moving away from allowing markets to move through their evolution. This has created a market environment that pits market participants against regulators in a contentious battle to shape market structure, technological advancement, and oversight. This is an outcome that calls into question the social optimality of introducing additional regulatory intervention in financial markets rather than approaching the evolution of markets from a cooperative perspective through competition and the reporting and analysis of human and technology errors to form cooperative solutions.

NOTES

1. Lewis, *Flash Boys*.

2. For one comprehensive criticism, see Kovac, *Flash Boys*.

3. Hasbrouck and Saar (2010), "Low-Latency Trading," 12.

4. Ibid., 13.

5. Ibid.

6. Bell and Searles, "Analysis of Global HFT Regulation."

7. Berman, "Trading Stocks in America."

8. Jarrow and Protter, "Dysfunctional Role of High Frequency Trading"; Zhang, "High-Frequency Trading"; Boehmer, Fong, and Wu, "International Evidence on Algorithmic Trading."

9. Seligman, "Rethinking Securities Markets."

10. Carlson, "Brief History of the 1987 Stock Market Crash."

11. US Securities and Exchange Commission, Regulation NMS, 17 C.F.R. Parts 200, 201, 230, 240, 242, 249, and 270 (August 2005).

12. See chapter 1 in Arnuk and Saluzzi, *Broken Markets*, 7–21.

13. White, "Intermediation in the Modern Securities Markets."

14. Nakamura and Hasegawa, "Humans Lose Out."

15. Grant, "Average Trading Order Size Falls by Half."

16. Skeete, *Future of the Financial Exchanges*, 6.

17. Mondo Visione, "October 2014 FIF."

18. US Securities and Exchange Commission, "Regulation of Exchanges and Alternative Trading Systems," 17 C.F.R. Parts 202, 240, 242 and 249 (1998).

19. Blume, "Competition and Fragmentation in Equity Markets"; Bunge, "Suspect Emerges in Stock-Trade Hiccups"; Foley, "How Reg ATS Destroyed Buy-Side Price."

20. Blackrock, "US Equity Market Structure," 3.

21. US Securities and Exchange Commission, "Regulation Systems Compliance and Integrity," 17 C.F.R. Parts 240, 242, and 249 (2013), 6.

22. Policy Statement: Automated Systems of Self-Regulatory Organizations, Release No. 34-27445, File No. S7-29-89 (1989).

23. Policy Statement: Automated Systems of Self-Regulatory Organizations (II), Release No. 34-29185, File No. S7-12-91 (1991).

24. Stiglitz, "Tapping the Brakes."

25. Kay, "Kay Review of UK Equity Markets."

26. For more see Bell and Searles, "Analysis of Global HFT Regulation."

27. Fox, *Myth of the Rational Market*; Bell, "High Frequency Trading."

28. Investment Company Institute, "Characteristics of Mutual Fund Owners," 101–20.

29. Angel and McCabe, "Fairness in Financial Markets."

30. Hendershott, Jones, and Menkveld, "Does Algorithmic Trading Improve Liquidity?"; Gerig, "High-Frequency Trading"; Malinova, Park, and Riordan, "Taxing High Frequency Market Making"; Hasbrouck and Saar (2013), "Low-Latency Trading"; Hendershott and Riordan, "Algorithmic Trading and Information"; Benos et al., "Interactions among High-Frequency Traders"; Brogaard et al., "High-Frequency Trading and Extreme Price Movements"; Weisberger, "Dear Michael Lewis."

31. Taggart, "Eric Hunsader."

32. Meyer, Massoudi, and Stafford, "Casualties Mount."

33. Cheng, "Stocks Close Well Off Lows."

34. Russolillo, "Larry Tabb."

35. Lewis, *Flash Boys*.

36. "High Frequency Trading and Finance."

37. Bell and Searles, "Analysis of Global HFT Regulation."

38. Epstein, "Hillary Clinton to Propose High-Frequency Trading Tax."

39. Lieber, "Tax to Curb Excessive Trading."

40. Hollen, "Action Plan to Grow the Paychecks of All."

41. Stiglitz, "Using Tax Policy"; Summers and Summers, "When Financial Markets Work Too Well"; Tobin, "Proposal for International Monetary Reform."

42. Pomeranets and Weaver, "Securities Transaction Taxes and Market Quality."

43. Malinova, Park, and Riordan, "Taxing High Frequency Market Making."

44. Nicoaou, "Toronto Stock Exchange."

45. Umlauf, "Transaction Taxes."

46. KattenMuchinRosenman LLP, "France Releases Details"; Rosenthal, "In France"; Nouel, "France-FTT and High-Frequency Trading."

47. "Liquidity Dries Up in FTT Countries-Report."

48. Bell and Searles, "Analysis of Global HFT Regulation."

49. IMF, "Fair and Substantial Contribution."

50. Amihud and Mendelson, "Transaction Taxes and Stock Values," cited in Pomeranets, "Financial Transaction Taxes."

51. Pomeranets, "Financial Transaction Taxes," 9n37.

52. Gallagher, "Can the U.S. Be an International Financial Center?"

53. Ibid. See also Bell and Searles, "Analysis of Global HFT Regulation."

54. Mostowfi, "TABB Equity Market Structure Survey."

55. McCrank, "Exclusive."

56. SEC, "SEC Approves IEX Proposal"; Katsuyama, "Letter from Brad Katsuyama."

57. Foley, "Big Fund Managers Form New Dark Pool."

58. Luminex, "Luminex Successfully Commences Operations."

59. Luminex, "Luminex Delivers Significant Subscriber Savings."

60. Hadfield, "Banks Turn to Plato."

61. Plato Partnership, "Our Mission."

62. Shart and Rocha, "Canada's Neo Stock."

63. Aequitas NEO Exchange, "NEO Exchange Canadian Market Share."

64. Anan, " 'I Know First.' "

65. Albinus, "Trade Informatics' Anti-Gaming Solution."

66. United States of America v. Navinder Singh Sarao, Docket Number 1: 15 CR, 75 (February 11, 2015).

67. US Commodity Futures Trading Commission and SEC, "Findings Regarding the Market Events."

68. Bell, "Beyond Regulation."

69. For more information, see the website of the Aviation Safety Reporting System, https://asrs.arc.nasa.gov/.

70. NASA, "Aviation Safety Reporting System Database."

71. For more detailed information, see Bell, "Beyond Regulation."

72. Gallagher, "Market 2012."

73. SEC, "Statement by the Securities and Exchange Commission," 4–6.

REFERENCES

Aequitas NEO Exchange. "NEO Exchange Canadian Market Share in Excess of 6% as ETF Trading Surges." Press Release, Toronto, May 2, 2016. https://aequitasneoexchange.com/en/notices/may-2-16-neo-exchange-canadian-market-share-in-excess-of-6-as-etf-trading-surges/.

Albinus, Phil. "Trade Informatics' Anti-Gaming Solution Hunts HFT Predators." *Traders Magazine*, February 27, 2015. http://www.tradersmagazine.com/news/buyside/trade-informatics-anti-gaming-solution-hunts-hft-predators-113524-1.html.

Amihud, Yakov, and Haim Mendelson. "Transaction Taxes and Stock Values." In *Modernizing U.S. Securities Regulation: Economic and Legal Perspective*, edited by Kenneth Lehn and Robert W. Kamphuis, 477–500. New York: Irwin Professional Publishing, 1992.

Anan, Ritesh. " 'I Know First': An Advanced Self-Learning, Predictive Algorithm for Everyone." *Benzinga*, January 14, 2015. http://www.benzinga.com/small-business/15/01/5136357/i-know-first-an-advanced-self-learning-predictive-algorithm-for-everyone.

Angel, James J., and Douglas McCabe. "Fairness in Financial Markets: The Case of High Frequency Trading." December 21, 2010. http://www.sec.gov/comments/s7-02-10/s70210-316.pdf.

Arnuk, Sal, and Joseph Saluzzi. *Broken Markets: How High Frequency and Predatory Practices on Wall Street Are Destroying Investor Confidence and Your Portfolio*. Upper Saddle River, NJ: FT Press, 2012.

Bell, Holly A. "High Frequency Trading: Do Regulators Need to Control This Tool of Informationally Efficient Markets?" Cato Institute Policy Analysis 731, Washington, DC, July 22, 2013.

———. "CFTC Proposal for High-Speed Trading May Drive Business Offshore." *American Banker*, December 18, 2013.

———. "Beyond Regulation: A Cooperative Approach to High-Frequency Trading and Financial Market Monitoring." Cato Institute Policy Analysis 771, Washington, DC, April 8, 2015.

Bell, Holly A., and Harrison Searles. "An Analysis of Global HFT Regulation: Motivations, Market Failures, and Alternative Outcomes." Mercatus Working Paper, Mercatus Center at George Mason University, Arlington, VA, April 2014.

Benos, Evangelos, James Brugler, Eric Hjalmarsson, and Filip Zikes. "Interactions among High-Frequency Traders." Working Paper 523, Bank of England, February 2015.

Berman, Gregg E. "Trading Stocks in America: Key Policy Issues." Panel discussion transcript, Brookings Institution, Washington, DC, January 30, 2014.

Blackrock. "US Equity Market Structure: An Investor Perspective." April 2014. https://www.blackrock.com/corporate/en-us/literature/whitepaper/viewpoint-us-equity-market-structure-april-2014.pdf.

Blume, Marshall E. "Competition and Fragmentation in Equity Markets: The Effects of Regulation NMS." The Wharton School, Rodney L. White Center for Financial Research, 2007.

Boehmer, Ekkehart, Kingsley Y. L. Fong, and Juan Wu. "International Evidence on Algorithmic Trading." AFA 2013 San Diego Meetings Paper, September 17, 2015.

Brogaard, Jonathan, Ryan Riordan, Andriy Shkilko, and Konstantin Sokolov. "High-Frequency Trading and Extreme Price Movements." 2014. http://dx.doi.org/10.2139/ssrn.2531122.

Bunge, Jacob. "A Suspect Emerges in Stock-Trade Hiccups: Regulation NMS." Wall Street Journal, January 27, 2014. http://www.wsj.com/articles/SB10001424052702303281504579219962494432336.

Carlson, Mark. "A Brief History of the 1987 Stock Market Crash with a Discussion of the Federal Reserve Response." Finance and Economics Discussion Series. Washington, DC: Divisions of Research and Statistics and Monetary Affairs Federal Reserve Board, 2006.

Cheng, Evelyn. "Stocks Close Well off Lows; Energy, Financials Weigh." CNBC. June 10, 2016. http://www.msn.com/en-us/money/markets/stocks-close-flat-as-dow-recovers-from-triple-digit-loss/ar-AA9gluo.

Epstein, Jennifer. "Hillary Clinton to Propose High-Frequency Trading Tax, Volcker Rule Changes." Bloomberg, October 7, 2015. http://www.bloomberg.com/politics/articles/2015-10-08/hillary-clinton-to-propose-high-frequency-trading-tax-volcker-rule-changes.

Foley, Kevin. "How Reg ATS Destroyed Buy-Side Price Discovery and Block Liquidity." Tabb Forum, March 11, 2015. http://tabbforum.com/opinions/how-reg-ats-destroyed-buy-side-price-discovery-and-block-liquidity?page=2.

Foley, Stephen. "Big Fund Managers Form New Dark Pool Equity Trading Venue." Financial Times, January 19, 2015. http://www.ft.com/intl/cms/s/0/372de622-a034-11e4-aa89-00144feab7de.html#axzz3U7Gj3D62.

Fox, Justin. The Myth of the Rational Market: A History of Risk, Reward, and Delusion on Wall Street. New York: Harper Business, 2009.

Gallagher, Daniel M. "Market 2012: Time for a Fresh Look at Equity Market Structure and Self-Regulation." Speech presented at SIFMA's 15th Annual Market Structure Conference, October 4, 2012.

———. "Can the U.S. Be an International Financial Center?" Speech presented at the Women in Housing and Finance Public Policy Luncheon, Washington, DC, January 13, 2015.

Gerig, Austin. "High-Frequency Trading Synchronizes Prices in Financial Markets." 2012. https://arxiv.org/abs/1211.1919.

Grant, Jeremy. "Average Trading Order Size Falls by Half." Financial Times, February 22, 2010. http://www.ft.com/intl/cms/s/0/22556abc-1f52-11df-9584-00144feab49a.html.

Hadfield, Will. "Banks Turn to Plato for New European Equity Platform." Bloomberg Business, December 17, 2014. http://www.bloomberg.com/news/articles/2014-12-17/banks-turn-to-plato-for-new-european-equity-platform.

Hasbrouck, Joel, and Gideon Saar. "Low-Latency Trading." Working Paper, New York, October 2010.

———. "Low-Latency Trading." Journal of Financial Markets 16 (2013): 646–79.

Hendershott, Terrence, Charles M. Jones, and Albert J. Menkveld. "Does Algorithmic Trading Improve Liquidity?" Journal of Finance 66, no. 1 (2011): 1–33.

Hendershott, Terrence, and Ryan Riordan. "Algorithmic Trading and Information." Working Paper, CA, 2011.

"High Frequency Trading and Finance." *Cambridge-INET: Conversations in Economics*. YouTube video, June 9, 2014.

Hollen, Chris Van. "An Action Plan to Grow the Paychecks of All, Not Just the Wealthy Few." January 12, 2015. http://democrats.budget.house.gov/action-plan.

International Monetary Fund (IMF). "A Fair and Substantial Contribution by the Financial Sector-Final Report for the G20." June 2010.

Investment Company Institute. "Characteristics of Mutual Fund Owners." In *2014 Investment Company Fact Book: A Review of Trends and Activities in the U.S. Investment Company Industry*, 54th ed., 101–20. Washington, DC: ICI, 2014.

Jarrow, Robert A., and Philip A. Protter. "A Dysfunctional Role of High Frequency Trading in Electronic Markets." *International Journal of Theoretical and Applied Finance* 15, no. 3 (2012).

Katsuyama, Brad. "Letter from Brad Katsuyama, CEO." *IEX*, June 17, 2016.

KattenMuchinRosenman LLP. "France Releases Details of Financial Transaction Tax." *HFT Review*, February 16, 2012. http://www.hftreview.com/pg/blog/kattenlaw/read/38536/france -releases -details-of-financial-transaction-tax.

Kay, John. "The Kay Review of UK Equity Markets and Long-Term Decision Making." July 2012. https://www.gov.uk/government/uploads/system/uploads/attachment_data/file/253454/bis -12-917-kay-review-of-equity-markets-final-report.pdf.

Kovac, Peter. *Flash Boys: Not So Fast*. Directissima Press, 2014.

Lewis, Michael. *Flash Boys: A Wall Street Revolt*. New York: W. W. Norton, 2014.

Lieber, Ron. "A Tax to Curb Excessive Trading Could Be a Boon to Returns." *New York Times*, October 2, 2015. http://www.nytimes.com/2015/10/03/your-money/a-tax-to-curb-excessive -trading-could-be-a-boon-to-returns.html?_r=0.

"Liquidity Dries Up in FTT Countries-Report." *The Trade*, September 3, 2013. http://www.thetradenews .com/news/Asset_Classes/Equities/Liquidity_dries_up_in_FTT_countries_-_report.aspx.

Luminex. "Luminex Successfully Commences Operations of Equity Trading Venue." Press Release, Boston, November 3, 2015. http://luminextrading.com/wp-content/uploads/2016/01 /Luminex-Launch-Day-Press-Release-vF-20151102.pdf.

———. "Luminex Delivers Significant Subscriber Savings and Strong Subscriber Growth in First Six Months of Operations." Press Release, Boston, June 2, 2016. http://luminextrading.com /wp-content/uploads/Luminex-6-Month-Anniversary-Press-Release_20160602.pdf.

Malinova, Katya, Andreas Park, and Ryan Riordan. "Taxing High Frequency Market Making: Who Pays the Bill?" 2016. http://papers.ssrn.com/sol3/papers.cfm?abstract_id=2183806.

McCrank, John. "Exclusive: IEX Eyes Stock Exchange Status." *Reuters*, April 5, 2014. http://www .reuters.com/article/2014/04/05/us-iex-exchange-idUSBREA3400620140405.

Meyer, Gregory, Arash Massoudi, and Philip Stafford. "Casualties Mount in High-Speed Trading Arms Race." *Financial Times*, January 22, 2015. http://www.ft.com/intl/cms/s/0/38a1437e -a1eb-11e4-bd03-00144feab7de.html.

Mondo Visione. "October 2014 FIF [Financial Information Forum] Market Dynamics Report-Executive Summary." m.mondovisione.com/_assets/files/FIF_October_2014_Executive _Summary_Market_Dynamics.pdf.

Mostowfi, Sayena. "TABB Equity Market Structure Survey." *Tabb Forum*, January 13, 2015. http:// tabbforum.com/opinions/market-structure-survey.

Nakamura, Yuji, and Toshiro Hasegawa. "Humans Lose Out as Robots Take Tokyo Stock Exchange." *Bloomberg Business*, March 4, 2015. http://www.bloomberg.com/news/articles /2015-03-05/robots-take-tokyo-as-high-frequency-equity-infiltration-hits-70-.

National Aeronautics and Space Administration (NASA). "Aviation Safety Reporting System Database." July 31, 2015. http://asrs.arc.nasa.gov/search/database.html.

Nicoaou, Anna. "Toronto Stock Exchange Warns on Trade Flow to US Markets." *Financial Times*, February 16, 2015. http://www.ft.com/intl/cms/s/0/d8ae480c-b39e-11e4-a6c1-00144feab7de .html#axzz3U7Gj3D62.

Nouel, Gide Loyrette. "France-FTT and High-Frequency Trading." 2012. http://www.aima.org /objects_store/gide_note_re_french_ftt_-_august_2012.pdf.

Plato Partnership. "Our Mission." http://www.platopartnership.com.

Pomeranets, Anna. "Financial Transaction Taxes: International Experiences, Issues, and Feasibility." *Bank of Canada Review* (Autumn 2012): 3–13.

Pomeranets, Anna, and Daniel G. Weaver. "Securities Transaction Taxes and Market Quality." Working Paper 2011-26, Bank of Canada, February 8, 2013.

Rosenthal, Steven. "In France, High-Frequency Traders Now Get Taxed for Fictitious Orders." *Christian Science Monitor*, August 9, 2012. http://www .csmonitor.com/Business/Tax-VOX /2012/0809/In-France-high-frequency-traders-now -get-taxed-for-fictitious-orders.

Russolillo, Steven. "Larry Tabb: 'No, Mr. Lewis. The Markets Are Not Rigged.'" *Wall Street Journal*, April 1, 2014. http://blogs.wsj.com/moneybeat/2014/04/01/larry-tabb-no-mr-lewis-the -markets-are-not-rigged/.

Seligman, Joel. "Rethinking Securities Markets: The SEC Advisory Committee on Market Information and the Future of the National Market System." *Business Lawyer* 57, no. 2 (2002): 637–80.

Shart, Alastair, and Euan Rocha. "Canada's Neo Stock Exchange to Waive Market Data Fees for Some." *Reuters*, March 11, 2015. http://www.reuters.com/article/2015/03/11/markets-canada-neoexchange-idUSL1N0WD28C20150311.

Skeete, Herbie. *The Future of the Financial Exchanges: Insights and Analysis from The Mondo Visione Exchange Forum*. Burlington, MA: Elsevier, 2009.

Stiglitz, Joseph E. "Using Tax Policy to Curb Speculative Short-Term Trading." *Journal of Financial Services Research* 3 (1989): 101–15.

———. "Tapping the Brakes: Are Less Active Markets Safer and Better for the Economy?" Presenta- tion at the Federal Reserve Bank of Atlanta Financial Markets Conference: Tuning Financial Regulation for Stability and Efficiency, Atlanta, GA, April 15, 2014.

Summers, Lawrence H., and Victoria P. Summers. "When Financial Markets Work Too Well: A Cautious Case for a Securities Transactions Tax." *Journal of Financial Services Research* 3 (1989): 261–86.

Taggart, Adam. "Eric Hunsader: Investors Need to Realize the Machines Have Taken Over." *Peak Prosperity*, October 6, 2012. http://www.peakprosperity.com/podcast/79804/nanex-investors -realize-machines-taken-over.

Tobin, James. "A Proposal for International Monetary Reform." Presented at Eastern Economic Association, Washington, DC, 1978.

Umlauf, Steven R. "Transaction Taxes and the Behavior of the Swedish Stock Market." *Journal of Financial Economics* 33, no 2 (1993): 227–40.

US Commodity Futures Trading Commission and US Securities and Exchange Commission. "Findings Regarding the Market Events of May 6, 2010." September 30, 2013. http://www.sec.gov/news/studies/2010/marketevents-report.pdf.

US Securities and Exchange Commission. "Statement by the Securities and Exchange Commission upon the Market 2000 Report." In *Market 2000: An Examination of Current Equity Market Developments*. Washington, DC: Division of Market Regulation, SEC, 1994.

———."SEC Approves IEX Proposal to Launch National Exchange, Issues Interpretation on Automated Securities Prices." Press Release, Washington, DC, June 17, 2016.

Weisberger, David. "Dear Michael Lewis: If You Don't Understand Something, Please Ask for Assistance." *Tabb Forum*, March 23, 2015. http://tabbforum.com/channels/equities/opinions/dear-michael-lewis-if-you-don%27t-understand-something-please-ask-for-assistance.

White, Mary Jo. "Intermediation in the Modern Securities Markets: Putting Technology and Competition to Work for Investors." Speech presented at the Economic Club of New York. New York, July 20, 2014.

Zhang, Frank. "High-Frequency Trading, Stock Volatility, and Price Discovery." Working Paper, New Haven, CT, December 2010.

CHAPTER 11
Offering and Disclosure Reform

DAVID R. BURTON
The Heritage Foundation

B oth the US Congress and the US Securities and Exchange Commission
(SEC) are seriously considering reform to mandatory disclosure
requirements.[1] This chapter examines the law and economics of securities offerings and disclosure requirements. It explains the current disclosure
system and analyzes the principles that should govern policymakers as they
craft a reformed disclosure regime. It offers a program of interim reforms to
improve the existing disclosure system to the benefit of both investors and
issuers. It also offers a much simpler, more coherent fundamental reform proposal that would replace the existing fourteen disclosure regimes with three—
public, quasi-public, and private, the first two of which would be scaled.

THE BASIC FRAMEWORK OF US DISCLOSURE REQUIREMENTS

The Securities Act of 1933[2] makes it generally illegal to sell securities unless
the offering is registered with the SEC.[3] Making a registered offering (often
called "going public") is a very expensive proposition and well beyond the
means of most small and startup companies. The SEC has estimated that "the
average cost of achieving initial regulatory compliance for an initial public
offering is $2.5 million, followed by an ongoing compliance cost, once public,

of $1.5 million per year."[4] The Act, however, exempts various securities and transactions from this requirement.[5]

The most important exemption is the exemption for private offerings (often called a private placement).[6] This is the means chosen by most businesses, large and small, to raise capital. This is also the reason local business people can start a restaurant or store without registering the securities with the SEC.

Regulation D,[7] adopted in 1982 during the Reagan administration,[8] is the primary means of implementing this exemption, particularly for companies offering stock to investors who are not issuer officers, directors, or other insiders, friends, or family.[9] According to the SEC, Regulation D accounted for $1.3 trillion (62 percent) of private offerings in 2014.[10] Although private offerings do not necessarily have to be in compliance with Regulation D, it provides a regulatory safe harbor such that if an issuer meets the requirements of Regulation D, the issuer will be treated as having made a private offering. Regulation D investments are generally restricted to accredited investors. Generally, accredited investors are financial institutions or affluent individuals with a residence-exclusive net worth of more than $1 million or an income of $200,000 or more ($300,000 joint).[11] Thus, approximately 90 percent of Americans are effectively prevented from investing in Regulation D securities.[12]

The "small issues exemption" was meant to provide an exemption for small firms.[13] This exemption is implemented by Regulation A.[14] Although this exemption is important in principle, it has been, in practice, of virtually no value to small firms due to overregulation (primarily by state regulators). Until 2015, it was almost never used.[15] The 2012 Jumpstart Our Business Startups (JOBS) Act provisions, often called "Regulation A plus," may change this. On April 20, 2015, the SEC adopted final rules,[16] which were effective June 19, 2015, to implement Title IV of the JOBS Act.[17] The SEC's revisions to Regulation A, while a marked improvement over the current rule, nevertheless are cause for serious concern.[18] It is very doubtful that the problems with Regulation A have been solved. In the first year, approximately forty-four Regulation A offerings have been qualified.[19] In contrast, in 2014, there were 2,752 public offerings and 33,429 Regulation D offerings.[20]

Registered companies must file periodic reports. The Form 10-K is an annual report and the Form 10-Q is a quarterly report.[21] In addition, a

Form 8-K must be filed when major events of importance to investors must be reported.[22] Nonfinancial disclosure requirements for public or registered companies (also called reporting or public companies) are provided by SEC Regulation S-K.[23] Regulation S-K imposes approximately 150 different requirements. A PDF of Regulation S-K in small type is 136 pages long. Financial or accounting disclosure requirements are set forth in SEC Regulation S-X.[24] A PDF of Regulation S-X in small type is ninety-six pages long. Regulation S-X, however, incorporates many other requirements by reference.[25]

Registered companies do not all have the same obligations. Companies with a public float of less than $75 million are deemed "smaller reporting companies" and have less onerous disclosure obligations and do not need to comply with the Sarbanes-Oxley Act Section 404(b) internal control reporting requirements.[26] In general, an issuer with an aggregate worldwide common equity market value of $75 million or more (but less than $700 million) that is not a smaller reporting company is an accelerated filer.[27] An accelerated filer must file its 10-Qs within forty days of the close of the quarter and its 10-Ks within seventy-five days of the close of the year. A "large accelerated filer" is, in general, an issuer with an aggregate worldwide common equity market value of $700 million or more.[28] A large accelerated filer must file its 10-Qs within forty days of the close of the quarter and its 10-Ks within sixty days of the close of the year.

Title I of the JOBS Act created a new concept of "emerging growth companies" (EGCs).[29] Generally, a company qualifies as an emerging growth company if it has total annual gross revenues of less than $1 billion during its most recently completed fiscal year and, as of December 8, 2011, had not sold common equity securities under a registration statement. For five years, EGCs are excused from complying with a number of onerous disclosure requirements and from Sarbanes-Oxley Act Section 404(b) internal control reporting requirements. Moreover, they may submit confidential draft registration statements to the SEC for review.[30]

FRAUD

The primary purpose of securities law is to deter and punish fraud.[31] Fraud is the misrepresentation of material facts or the misleading omission of material facts for the purpose of inducing another to act, or to refrain from action, in reliance upon the misrepresentation or omission.[32] Federal law prohibits fraudulent securities transactions.[33] So do state securities laws.[34] State laws governing securities are known as blue sky laws.[35]

Requiring certain written affirmative representations in public disclosure documents deters fraud because proving fraud becomes easier if the public, written representations are later found by a trier of fact to be inconsistent with the facts. Such an approach is analogous to the Statute of Frauds (1677)[36] and Uniform Commercial Code § 2-201,[37] which require certain contracts to be in writing in order to be enforceable. Modern US securities laws go further, requiring the disclosure documents of public companies to not only be in writing but to be publicly available and provided to government regulators.

DISCLOSURE

The second important purpose of securities laws is to foster disclosure by firms that sell securities to investors of material facts about the company needed to make informed investment decisions.[38] Appropriate mandatory disclosure requirements can promote capital formation, the efficient allocation of capital, and the maintenance of a robust, public, and liquid secondary market for securities.[39] Among the reasons disclosure mandates can be effective are: (1) the issuer is in the best position to accurately and cost-effectively produce information about the issuer;[40] (2) information disclosure promotes better allocation of scarce capital resources or has other positive externalities;[41] (3) the cost of capital may decline because investors will demand a lower risk premium;[42] (4) disclosure makes it easier for shareholders to monitor management;[43] and (5) disclosure makes fraud enforcement easier because evidentiary hurdles are more easily overcome.

The baseline for measuring the benefits of mandatory disclosure is not zero disclosure. Firms would disclose considerable information even in the absence of legally mandated disclosure. It is generally in their interest to do so.[44] Even before the New Deal securities laws mandating disclosure were enacted, firms made substantial disclosures and stock exchanges required disclosure by listed firms.[45] Firms conducting private placements today make substantial disclosures notwithstanding the general absence of a legal mandate to do so.[46] The reason is fairly straightforward. In the absence of meaningful disclosure about the business and a commitment, contractual or otherwise, to provide continuing disclosure, few would invest in the business and those that did would demand substantial compensation for the risk they were undertaking by investing in a business with inadequate disclosure.[47] Voluntary disclosure allows firms to reduce their cost of capital; therefore they undertake to disclose information even in the absence of a legal mandate to do so.

As I will discuss in detail, mandatory disclosure laws impose costs, often very substantial costs. These costs do not increase linearly with company size. Offering costs are larger as a percentage of the amount raised for small offerings. They therefore have a disproportionate adverse impact on small firms. Moreover, the benefits of mandated disclosure are also less for small firms because the number of investors and amount of capital at risk is less. Since the costs are disproportionately high and the benefits lower for smaller firms, disclosure should be scaled so that smaller firms incur lower costs.[48]

Disclosure also has a dark side in countries with inadequate property rights protection. In a study examining data from 70,000 firms, the World Bank has found that in developing countries mandatory disclosure is associated with significant exposure to expropriation, corruption, and reduced sales growth.[49]

Nor should it be forgotten that many large businesses and large broker-dealers are quite comfortable with high levels of regulation because regulatory compliance costs constitute a barrier to entry and limit competition from smaller, potentially disruptive competitors; high compliance costs have a disproportionately negative impact on their smaller competitors.[50] Some have been quite forthright about this. Goldman Sachs CEO Lloyd Blankfein, for example, recently said:

> More intense regulatory and technology requirements have raised the barriers to entry higher than at any other time in modern history. This is an expensive business to be in, if you don't have the market share in scale. Consider the numerous business exits that have been announced by our peers as they reassessed their competitive positioning and relative returns.[51]

The securities bar, accounting firms doing compliance work, and regulators all also have a strong pecuniary interest in maintaining complex rules.[52]

The benefits, and to a lesser extent the costs, of mandatory disclosure are notoriously difficult to measure, although the benefits are probably substantially less than commonly thought.[53] This is no doubt partially a function of the fact that the SEC does a very poor job of collecting and publishing relevant data, a deficiency that should be remedied.[54] There is no small degree of truth in the observation of Georgetown law professors Donald Langevoort and Robert Thompson that "[m]ost all of securities regulation is educated guesswork rather than rigorous cost-benefit analysis because we lack the ability to capture the full range of possible costs or benefits with anything remotely resembling precision."[55] The limited empirical literature examining the issue tends to find little, and often no, net benefit.[56] As Yale Law School Professor Roberta Romano has written, "The near total absence of measurable benefits from the federal regulatory apparatus surely undermines blind adherence to the status quo."[57]

On the other hand, the United States securities markets are the largest, deepest capital markets in the world. At over $18 trillion, the 2012 US stock market capitalization was five times the size of China's ($3.7 trillion) and Japan's ($3.7 trillion) and six times that of the United Kingdom ($3 trillion).[58] The US stock market dwarfs the securities markets of most countries.[59] US market capitalization as a percentage of GDP is greater than all major developed countries except for the United Kingdom and Switzerland.[60] US private capital markets are broad and deep compared to other countries.[61] This implies that the US securities regulatory regime is broadly reasonable compared to those in most other countries, although other factors such as property rights protection, taxation (of both domestic and foreign investors), the legal ability or willingness of banks to undertake equity investment, and the degree of corruption should also be considered. An alternative explanation would be that US capital markets are so strong that they can readily absorb the adverse impact of poor regulation.

The core problem with the current US securities regulation system is its negative impact on small startup and emerging growth companies and, therefore, the adverse impact it has on entrepreneurship and the growth potential of the economy.[62] It is quite clear that existing regulations, usually imposed in the name of investor protection,[63] go beyond those necessary to deter fraud and achieve reasonable, limited, scaled disclosure for small firms.[64] Existing rules seriously impede the ability of entrepreneurial firms to raise the capital they need to start, to grow, to innovate, and to create new products and jobs.[65]

INVESTOR PROTECTION EXAMINED

Investor protection is a central part of the SEC's mission.[66] But the term "investor protection" is a very ambiguous term that can cover, at least, four basic ideas. The first is protecting investors from fraud or misrepresentation. This is a fundamental function of government. The second is providing investors with adequate information to make informed investment decisions. Although a legitimate function of the securities laws, this requires policymakers to carefully balance the costs (which are typically underestimated by regulators and policymakers) and the benefits (which are typically overestimated by regulators and policymakers) of mandatory disclosure.[67] The third is protecting investors from investments or business risks that regulators deem imprudent or ill-advised. This is not an appropriate function of government and can be highly counterproductive. The fourth is protecting investor freedom of choice or investor liberty and thereby allowing investors to achieve higher returns and greater liquidity. This primarily requires regulators to exercise restraint or eliminate existing regulatory barriers, both in the regulation of primary offerings by issuers and of secondary market sales by investors to other investors. In practice, this aspect of investor protection is almost entirely ignored by state and federal regulators.

Disclosure requirements have become so voluminous that they obfuscate rather than inform, making it more difficult for investors to find relevant information.[68] Over the past twenty years, the average number of pages in annual reports devoted to footnotes and "Management's Discussion and Analysis" has quadrupled.[69] The number of words in corporate annual 10-Ks has increased from 29,996 in 1997 to 41,911 in 2014.[70] This means that the *average* 10-K is now nearly as lengthy as some famous novels.[71]

Very few investors, whether professional or retail, are willing to wade through lengthy disclosure documents, often running hundreds of pages of dense legalese, available on the SEC EDGAR database[72] or multitudinous state blue sky filings in the forlorn hope that they will find something material to their investment decision that is not available elsewhere in shorter, more focused, more accessible materials. Many of these more accessible materials are, of course, synopses of both the mandated disclosure documents[73] and other voluntarily disclosed information such as shareholder annual reports or materials provided to securities analysts by companies. But the fact that the vast majority of investors rely on these summary materials strongly implies that the legal requirements exceed what investors find material to their investment decisions.

The law should not, even in principle, adopt a regulatory regime that is designed to protect all investors from every conceivable ill. Even in the case of fraud, there needs to be a balancing of costs and benefits. Securities law should deter and punish fraud but, given human nature, it will never entirely eliminate fraud. The only way to be certain that there would be no fraud would be to make business impossible. In other words, the socially optimal level of fraud is not zero.[74] While fraud imposes significant costs on the person who is defrauded, preventing fraud also has significant costs (both to government and to law-abiding firms or investors) and at some point the costs of fraud prevention exceed the benefits, however defined, of preventing fraud.[75] It is up to policymakers to assess this balance and make appropriate judgments in light of the evidence.

About three-fifths of the states conduct what is called "merit review."[76] Under merit review, state regulators decide whether a securities offering is too risky or unfair to be offered within their state, effectively substituting their investment judgment for that of investors. Merit review is wrong in principle. Moreover, it is very unlikely that regulators make better investment decisions than investors. Lastly, merit review is expensive and it delays offerings considerably.[77]

In a free society, it is inappropriate paternalism for the government to prevent people from choosing to invest in companies that they judge to be good investment opportunities or may choose to invest in for reasons other than pecuniary gain (personal relationship or affinity for the mission of the enterprise).[78] Individuals, not government, should be the judge of what is in their own interest. This idea, however, is under sustained assault both by progressives and by those who called themselves "libertarian paternalists."[79] Both progressives and libertarian paternalists rely on the commonsense findings of behavioral economics that people are not always rational, sometimes make poor decisions, and respond to sales pressure or disclosure documents differently.[80] Securities regulators are increasingly looking to this body of literature to inform or justify their actions.[81]

There are at least eight reasons to doubt that government regulators have better investment judgment than private investors investing their own money. First, there is an inability for a central regulatory authority to collect and act on information as quickly and accurately as dispersed private actors.[82] Government has a reputation for being ponderous and slow to act for a reason.[83] In the context of securities regulation, it is highly doubtful that government regulators have a better understanding of business and the markets than those participating in those markets. Second, private investors have strong incentives to be good stewards of their own money, both in the sense of not taking unwarranted risk and in the sense of seeking high returns. In addition, investors may seek to invest for reasons that do not involve pecuniary gain, including support of the persons launching an enterprise or support for a social enterprise that has a dual mission. Government regulators have an entirely different set of incentives. Third, individuals, not government officials, know their own risk tolerance and their own portfolios. Investing in a riskier security[84] can reduce the overall risk of a portfolio if the security in question is negatively correlated or even not highly covariant with price movements of the overall portfolio.[85] Fourth, government officials are people too, and they exhibit the same irrationality and tendency to sometimes make poor decisions as anyone else. There is absolutely no reason to believe that regulators are less subject to the concerns identified by behavioral economics and the "libertarian paternalists" than are others.[86] Moreover, since most securities regulators are lawyers and a legal education provides no training to make investment decisions, there is no particular reason to believe they have any relevant "expertise" that will make their investment decisions objectively better than those investing their own money. Fifth, as public choice economics has demonstrated, government officials are not angels but act in their own self-interest.[87] This too is in keeping with basic common sense. Government officials have an interest in enlarging their agencies, increasing their power, and improving their employment prospects.[88] They are no more benevolent than any other group of people, including issuers and investors, and there is no particular reason to believe that government regulators will act in the interest of investors when those interests conflict with their own interest. The analysis of politics, and the politicians and regulators that conduct politics, should be stripped of its "romance."[89] Sixth, government officials trying to make investments have a notoriously bad track record.[90] Perhaps the most famous example of poor regulator entrepreneurial investment judgment is when securities regulators in Massachusetts barred Massachusetts citizens from investing in Apple Computer during its initial public offering.[91] It was deemed too risky of an investment. Seventh, in their capacity as regulators assessing risk, regulators have an increasingly obvious bad track record. Government regulators in the most recent financial crisis did no better than private actors in understanding risk.[92] Eighth, it is a reasonable hypothesis that government regulators are unduly risk-averse for at least two reasons: Government tends to attract people who are risk averse. They have a lower risk tolerance than those making entrepreneurial investments.[93] Moreover, the incentives for government regulators tend to make them unduly risk-averse. An investment that goes bad may make the headlines and their regulatory judgment may be criticized. An investment that never happens because it does not receive regulatory approval will not make the headlines and the regulators' judgment will not be second-guessed.

The approximately two-fifths of states that do not undertake merit review[94] rely on antifraud laws and the disclosure of the material facts by issuers but allow investors to make their own decisions, just as federal securities laws rely primarily on disclosure and antifraud enforcement.[95]

While doing little to actually protect investors, the current array of state and federal regulatory excesses imposes costly requirements and restrictions that have a disproportionate negative impact on small and startup firms. Furthermore, although the JOBS Act mitigated the problem, existing rules often, in practice, force these firms to use broker-dealers or venture capital firms to raise capital.[96] Having to hire outside firms raises issuer costs. Being reliant on broker-dealers or venture capital firms to raise capital also increases the likelihood that entrepreneurs will lose control of the company they founded because these firms so often require large fees, a large share of the ownership of the company, or effective control of the firm when raising capital for new, unseasoned issuers. The law should allow entrepreneurs to cost-effectively seek investors without reliance on broker-dealers or venture capital firms.

UNMOORING DISCLOSURE FROM INVESTMENT VALUATION

Title XV of the Dodd–Frank Wall Street Reform and Consumer Protection Act[97] contains three provisions requiring public companies to report in their disclosure documents with respect to conflict minerals, mine safety, and resource extraction. In addition, Title IX Section 953(b) requires disclosure of the ratio between a company's CEO pay and the median pay of all other employees. The primary purpose of these requirements is to further political objectives. They are unrelated to the purpose of the securities laws and the mission of the SEC.

The politically motivated requirements in Title XV distract—or in the case of the proposals for new disclosure requirements, would distract—the SEC from its mission. Moreover, the requirements do nothing to further the securities laws' purpose of protecting shareholders or providing them with information that is material to their investment decisions. Shareholders, when presented with an opportunity to vote on whether to require such disclosure, have almost always voted not to do so.[98]

These Dodd-Frank provisions are part of a continuing trend of using the securities laws to mandate disclosures that are not material to assessing the expected return from investing in a company (that is, its valuation) to further political objectives. For example, there is a major effort under way to pressure the SEC into issuing a rule requiring disclosure of corporate "political spending."[99] The campaign promoting this rulemaking has generated over one million comments to the SEC.[100] The information disclosed in compliance with this rule would not be used by investors to assess the value of their investments, but by activists to pressure corporation management with respect to political issues. Issuance of such a rule has been temporarily barred by Congress.[101]

Legislation has also been introduced in Congress to require both disclosure and a shareholder vote before public corporations can make political expenditures, including independent expenditures, or give money to a trade association for certain purposes. Spending made in contravention of the rules set forth in the legislation would give rise to joint and several liability by a corporation's officers and directors equal to treble the amount spent.[102] The requirements would not apply to private corporations, labor unions, or tax-exempt organizations. There is also a recent petition that asks the SEC to require public companies to disclosure "gender pay ratios."[103]

These requirements impose unwarranted costs on issuers that reduce the return on shareholder investments.[104] The SEC estimates that the conflict minerals, mine safety, resource extraction, and CEO pay ratio requirements combined will have initial compliance costs of approximately $5 billion and ongoing costs of $1.5 billion annually.[105] Furthermore, by adding to already voluminous disclosure requirements, they tend to make it more difficult for investors to find material information in disclosure documents.

THE PRIVATE-PUBLIC DISTINCTION

The securities laws draw a distinction between public and private companies, imposing a wide variety of obligations on public companies that are not imposed on private companies. Originally, this distinction was generally a distinction between firms whose securities were trading on stock exchanges and those whose securities were not. The Securities Acts Amendments of 1964[106] broadened the requirements to register and make periodic disclosures to any company with 500 or more shareholders of record.[107] Thus, the distinction between public and private firms is probably best thought of as between a firm with widely held ownership (public) as opposed to closely held ownership (private).[108] Given the breadth of ownership, the aggregate value of investments made, the fact that management is a more effective producer of information than multiple outside investigators with limited access to the relevant facts absent mandatory disclosure, the agent-principal or collective action problem and various other factors, imposing greater disclosure obligations on larger, widely held firms is appropriate. It is, however, important that even the disclosure and other obligations of public companies be scaled. Compliance costs have a disproportionate adverse impact on small firms, and the benefits are correspondingly less because small firms have fewer investors with less capital at risk.

It is far from clear that the current "holder of record" method of drawing the distinction between public and private firms is the best. The number of beneficial owners, public float, or market capitalization—all metrics used in connection with other securities law provisions—are probably better than the traditional shareholder of record measure.[109] The number of holders of record bears little relationship to any meaningful criteria of when disclosure should be mandated or when disclosure or other requirements should be increased. Its primary virtue is ease of administration.

A SUMMARY OF PRESENT LAW REQUIREMENTS

Post–JOBS Act, there are at least fourteen categories of firms issuing securities. They are

1. private companies using section 4(a)(2);

2–6. private companies using Regulation D Rule 504, Rule 505 (with and without nonaccredited investors), and primarily Rule 506 (with and without nonaccredited investors);[110]

7–8. small issuer Regulation A companies (two tiers);

9–11. crowdfunding companies (three tiers);

12. smaller reporting companies;

13. emerging growth companies; and

14. fully reporting public companies.

Each of these categories has different initial and continuing disclosure obligations, different classes of investors that can invest in the offering, and a host of other differences. The existing disclosure regime is not coherent in that in many cases smaller firms have greater disclosure requirements and the degree and type of disclosure differs significantly by the type of offering, even for firms that are otherwise comparable in all meaningful respects.

INTERIM SECURITIES REGULATION REFORM

Fundamental securities regulation reform is necessary, as I will discuss. In the interim, there are steps that should be taken to improve the regulatory environment for small firms seeking access to the capital markets. The major components of an interim reform program are outlined here.

Recommendations Reducing Barriers to Raising Private and Quasi-Public Capital

Regulation A. The original 1933 Securities Act contained the small issue exemption that is the basis for Regulation A. Congress has increased the dollar amount of the exemption over the years.[111] Overly burdensome regulation by state regulators (and, to a lesser extent, by the SEC), combined with the opportunity for issuers to avoid burdensome blue sky laws since 1996[112] via Rule 506 of Regulation D, have rendered Regulation A ineffective—a dead letter that is virtually never used.[113] In 2011, only one Regulation A offering was completed.[114] SEC data show that Regulation A between 2009 and 2012 was used to raise only $73 million. This compares to comparably sized Regulation D offerings of $25 billion and comparably sized public offerings of $840 million.[115] Thus, in the aggregate, over that three-year period, Regulation A accounted for less than three-tenths of 1 percent of the capital raised in offerings of $5 million or less.[116]

Title IV of the JOBS Act demonstrates a clear bipartisan consensus that this is unacceptable and that the section 3(b) small issues exemption needs to be rethought to promote small business capital formation. Title IV has come to be known as Regulation A-plus. It would allow Regulation A offerings of up to $50 million. The SEC promulgated a rule implementing Title IV that was effective June 19, 2015.[117] This regulation would create two tiers, but only the more heavily regulated second tier would be blue sky exempt and even "Tier 2" secondary offerings are not exempt. Smaller "Tier 1" companies remain subject to the expense and delay of blue sky laws. For small businesses to efficiently use Regulation A, legislative changes are needed:

1. Congress should preempt state registration and qualification laws governing all Regulation A company securities. These companies have substantial initial and continuing disclosure obligations. Congress should either define "covered securities" under the National Securities Markets Improvement Act (NSMIA) to include securities sold in transactions exempt pursuant to Regulation A or define qualified purchasers to include all purchasers of securities in transactions exempt under Regulation A, or both. The recent Regulation A-plus rule would do this for "Tier 2" companies' primary offerings.[118]

2. Congress should simplify the statutory small issue exemption. Specifically, amend Securities Act section 3(b)(1) so that "Tier 1" Regulation A offerings have reasonable requirements for offering statements and periodic disclosure and provide that the provisions are self-effectuating without having to wait for the promulgation of SEC regulations. The current rules are nearly as complex as those governing smaller reporting companies.

3. Congress should eliminate application of the section 12(g)(1) holder of record thresholds for Regulation A securities. Regulation A securities are much less likely to be held in street name through a broker-dealer. Thus, the number of "holders of record" may approach the number of beneficial owners. The current limit of 500 shareholders is too low.[119]

Regulation D. The Securities Act provides an exemption for offerings "not involving any public offering." Regulation D, adopted in 1982, provides a safe harbor such that offerings that are compliant with the requirements of Regulation D are deemed not to involve a public offering.[120]

Regulation D has three parts. Rule 504[121] and Rule 505[122] were meant for use by small firms. Rule 504 allows firms to raise up to $1 million annually.[123] Rule 505 allows firms to raise up to $5 million annually.[124] In practice, 99 percent of capital raised using Regulation D is raised using Rule 506.[125] This is because Rule 506 offerings, in contrast to Rule 504 or Rule 505 offerings, are exempt from state blue sky registration and qualification requirements.[126] Issuers using Rule 506, therefore, do not have to bear the expense and endure the delay of dealing with as many as fifty-two regulators, about three-fifths of whom engage in "merit review" where regulators purport to decide whether an investment is fair or a good investment.[127] Regulation D has become the dominant means of raising capital in the United States, particularly for entrepreneurs. In 2013, approximately $1.3 trillion annually was raised using Regulation D.[128]

Most Regulation D offerings are sold entirely to accredited investors because selling to nonaccredited investors triggers additional disclosure requirements under Regulation D and creates other regulatory risks.[129] In general, an accredited investor is either a financial institution or a natural person who has either income greater than $200,000 ($300,000 joint) or a residence exclusive net worth of $1 million or more.[130] There is a major push by progressive, pro-regulatory organizations and state regulators to increase these thresholds dramatically.[131]

Rule 506 also permits up to thirty-five "sophisticated investors" to purchase Rule 506 offerings. The problem is that the regulatory definition of what constitutes a sophisticated investor is very amorphous. It turns on whether the investor has such "knowledge and experience in financial and business matters" that the investor "is capable of evaluating the merits and risks of the prospective investment."[132] For Regulation D to be an effective avenue for small businesses to raise money:

4. Congress should establish a statutory definition of accredited investor for purposes of Regulation D offerings that (a) sets the income and net worth requirements for natural persons at current levels and (b) establishes specific bright line tests for sophistication.[133]

5. Congress should prevent the promulgation of the Regulation D amendments proposed in July 2013.[134] These rules would substantially increase the regulatory burden for smaller companies seeking to use Regulation D and have no appreciable positive impact.[135] They would require filing three forms instead of one and impose a variety of other burdensome requirements.[136]

Crowdfunding. The story of the investment crowdfunding exemption is an object lesson in how a simple, constructive idea can be twisted by the Washington legislative process into a complex morass. Representative Patrick McHenry introduced his Entrepreneur Access to Capital Act on September 14, 2011.[137] It was three pages long, less than one page if the actual legislative language were pasted into a Word document. It would have allowed issuers to raise up to $5 million and limited investors to make investments equal to the lesser of $10,000 or 10 percent of their annual income.[138] The exemption would have been self-effectuating, requiring no action by the SEC in order to be legally operative. The bill reported out of committee and ultimately passed by the House was fourteen pages long.[139] By the time the Senate was done with it, it had expanded to twenty-six pages.[140] Many of the additions were authorizations for the SEC to promulgate rules or requirements that it do so. The bill was incorporated into the JOBS Act as Title III. Firms may raise no more than $1 million annually using Title III crowdfunding.[141] So it is only an option for the smallest of firms. The PDF of the October 23, 2013, proposed crowdfunding rule was 585 pages long (although double spaced) and sought public comments on well over 300 issues raised by the proposed rule.[142] The PDF of the final rule was 685 pages (229 pages as published in the *Federal Register*).[143]

If Congress decides to work with the current crowdfunding statute rather than start over, there are at least eight changes that should be made if crowdfunding is to achieve its promise as a viable way for small companies to obtain financing. Only two of them relate to disclosure:[144]

6. Congress should eliminate the audit requirements in crowdfunding offerings over $500,000 required by Securities Act section 4A(b)(1)(D)(iii).

7. Congress should reduce the mandatory disclosure requirements on crowdfunding issuers. They are much too burdensome for the very small firms that are permitted to use Title III crowdfunding.

Congress would probably do better by simply starting over and replacing the existing Title III with a simpler statute more appropriately crafted for very small firms.

Other Improvements. In order to allow extremely small firms to raise capital without complying with complex securities:

8. Congress should amend the Securities Act to create a statutory "micro-offering" safe harbor so that any offering is deemed not to involve a public offering for purposes of section 4(a)(2) if the offering (1) is made only to people with whom an issuer's officers, directors, or 10 percent or more shareholders have a substantial preexisting relationship; (2) involves thirty-five or fewer purchasers; or (3) has an aggregate offering price of less than $500,000 (within a twelve-month period).[145]

Recommendations Reducing Regulatory Burdens on Small Public Companies

Regulation S-K[146] is the key regulation governing nonfinancial statement disclosures of registered (i.e., public) companies. Regulation S-X[147] generally governs public company financial statements in registration statements or periodic reports. These two rules, including the various rules and accounting policies that they incorporate by reference—including those of the SEC, the Public Company Accounting Oversight Board (PCAOB) and the Financial

Accounting Standards Board (FASB)—impose the vast majority of the costs incurred by public companies.

The SEC has estimated that "the average cost of achieving initial regulatory compliance for an initial public offering is $2.5 million, followed by an ongoing compliance cost, once public, of $1.5 million per year."[148] This is probably a significant underestimate for many firms.

Costs of this magnitude make going public uneconomic for most smaller firms. Table 1 shows the composition and magnitude of the costs, according to the SEC. It also shows that the costs are disproportionately higher for firms conducting offerings of $50 million or less.

Although there have been some efforts to scale disclosure requirements, notably the emerging growth company provisions contained in Title I of the JOBS Act and the smaller reporting company rules, public company compliance costs have grown sufficiently high that many smaller firms are "going private."[149] Sarbanes-Oxley (2002),[150] Dodd-Frank (2010),[151] other legislation, and regulatory actions have contributed to these costs. Moreover, US initial public offering (IPO) costs are considerably higher than those abroad.[152] To address the disproportionate costs that small companies face under the securities laws:

Table 1. Initial Public Offering–Related Fees as a Percentage of Offering Size, 1996–2012

	All Offerings (n = 4,868) %	Offerings $5–$50 Million (n = 2,017) %	Offerings > $50 Million (n = 2,851) %
Total fees	9.55	11.15	8.44
Compliance fees	1.39	1.91	1.03
Registration fees	0.03	0.04	0.02
Blue Sky fees	0.03	0.07	0.01
Accounting fees	0.53	0.72	0.40
Legal fees	0.80	1.08	0.60
Underwriter fees	6.45	6.87	6.17
Printing fees	0.32	0.47	0.22

Source: US Securities and Exchange Commission, Division of Economic and Risk Analysis; "Proposed Rule Amendments for Small and Additional Issues Exemptions Under Section 3(b) of the Securities Act," 79 Fed. Reg. (January 23, 2014): 3978.

Note: Analysis excludes IPOs from non-Canadian foreign issuers and blank-check companies.

9. Congress should preempt blue sky registration and qualification requirements with respect to public companies not listed on national exchanges.

10. Congress should increase the smaller reporting company threshold to $300 million and conform the accelerated filer definition.

11. Congress should make all emerging growth company advantages permanent for smaller reporting companies.

12. Congress should improve the disclosure requirements under Regulation S-K for smaller reporting companies.[153]

FUNDAMENTALS

There is a need to fundamentally rethink the regulation of small company capital formation. A coherent, scaled disclosure regime should be developed and implemented by Congress, with respect to both initial and continuing disclosure, that is integrated across the various exemptions and categories of reporting company such that larger firms with more investors and more capital at risk have greater disclosure obligations. Congress should consider the cost of compliance; the investor protection benefits of the added disclosure; the cost to investors of being denied investment opportunities by investment restrictions; and the cost to the public of lost economic growth, capital formation, innovation, and job creation caused by the regulation of issuers.

It is worth considering a simplified set of exemptions. One possibility is to establish three categories, as shown in table 2.

In such a regime, private companies would have no legally mandated disclosure requirements. Disclosure requirements would be negotiated by the private parties involved, much as they usually are now. A company would be deemed private if it did not engage in general solicitation, was below some specified number of beneficial owners[154] or, perhaps, some measure of non-insider share value (analogous to public float)—call this threshold A—and its shares were not traded on a venture exchange or a national securities exchange.

Public companies could engage in general solicitation and would (1) be above a specified measure of size (threshold B) or (2) have shares traded on a national securities exchange. Disclosure obligations would be scaled based on some measure of size (probably public float). This is the category into which

Table 2. A Proposal for a Reformed Disclosure Regime

Type of Issuer	Type of Solicitation		Size (Public Float/ Number of Beneficial Owners)		Secondary Market Status
Private	Private	and	Below specified threshold A	and	Not national securities exchange and not venture exchange traded
Quasi-public	General	or	Above specified threshold A	and	Not national securities exchange traded (venture exchange trading permitted)
Public (registered)	General	and	Above specified threshold B	or	National securities exchange traded

most companies that are full reporting companies, smaller reporting companies, emerging growth companies, and perhaps some Regulation A-plus companies would fall.

Companies that are neither "public" nor "private" would be intermediate "quasi-public" companies. They could engage in general solicitation and sell to the public. Disclosure obligations would be scaled based on some measure of size (perhaps public float if traded on a venture exchange or the number of beneficial owners otherwise). These are the kind of companies that are meant to use the crowdfunding, Rule 505, and Regulation A exemptions and would include some companies that are smaller reporting companies today.

Blue sky laws regarding registration and qualification would be preempted in all cases. State antifraud laws would remain operative.

Companies would report based on their category (private, quasi-public, or public). Disclosure obligations would be scaled within the quasi-public and public category. Registration statements would be dramatically simplified, describing the security being offered but the quarterly (10-Q), annual (10-K), and major event (8-K) reporting would become the core of the disclosure system rather than registration statements (except in the case of initial quasi-public offerings transitioning from private company status, or initial public offerings transitioning from private or quasi-public status).

Although it is far from clear that the accredited investor distinction should be retained, some accredited investor limitations measuring wealth, income, or sophistication could be applied to private offerings should policymakers wish to limit those who may invest in private companies. In that case, however, something similar to the current section 4(a)(2) exemption or a statutory exemption for micro issuers should remain. Otherwise, two guys starting a bar would run afoul of the securities laws when they tried to raise money from their family and friends.

Such a regime would constitute a major improvement over the current one. It would be simpler, result in fewer regulatory difficulties and costs, protect investors, and promote capital formation.

CONCLUSION

Because the benefits of mandatory disclosure are so much smaller than usually assumed, policymakers need to adopt a more skeptical posture toward the existing disclosure regime. The costs are significant and have dramatically increased in recent years. The adverse impact on small and startup entrepreneurial firms, innovation, job creation, and economic growth is substantial. Moreover, disclosure requirements have become so voluminous that they defeat their alleged purpose. They obfuscate rather than inform. Finally, disclosure requirements that are not material to security valuation should be repealed.

Because the costs are disproportionately high and the benefits lower for smaller firms, disclosure should be scaled so that smaller firms incur lower costs. The current system—a set of fourteen different disclosure regimes—is incoherent. In many cases, under current law smaller firms have greater disclosure requirements than large firms, and the degree and type of disclosure differs significantly by the type of offering even for firms that are otherwise comparable in all meaningful respects.

Blue sky laws raise costs and create delays. States that engage in merit review are particularly problematic. There is ample evidence that blue sky laws are one of the central impediments to both primary offerings by small companies and secondary market trading in small company securities by investors. There is little evidence that the registration and qualification provisions of state blue sky laws protect investors. In fact, there is evidence that they hurt investors. State blue sky registration and qualification provisions should be preempted by Congress with respect to companies that have continuing reporting obligations, including public companies and those issuing securities under Regulation A or under Regulation Crowdfunding.

In this chapter I have outlined a program of interim reforms to improve the existing disclosure regime and recommended specific changes to Regulation A, crowdfunding, Regulation D, and the regulation of small public companies and of secondary markets that, taken as a whole, would dramatically improve the current regulatory environment. A program of fundamental reform, which I have also outlined, would dramatically simplify the existing disclosure regime to the benefit of both investors and issuers. This proposal would create three disclosure regimes—public, quasi-public, and private—and disclosure under the first two categories would be scaled based on either public float or the number of beneficial shareholders.

NOTES

1. See Disclosure Modernization and Simplification, Title LXXII of the Fixing America's Surface Transportation (FAST) Act, Pub. L. No. 114–94 (December 4, 2015); "Business and Financial Disclosure Required by Regulation S–K Concept Release," 81 Fed. Reg. (April 22, 2016): 23915.

2. Securities Act of 1933, Pub. L. No. 73-22, 48 Stat. 74 (1933), 15 U.S.C. § 77a et seq. (as amended through Pub. L. No. 112-106 [2012]).

3. See § 5 of the Securities Act of 1933.

4. Proposed Rules, "Crowdfunding," 78 Fed. Reg. (November 5, 2013): 66509.

5. See generally Securities Act §§ 3-4.

6. Section 4(a)(2) of the Securities Act exempts "transactions by an issuer not involving any public offering," 15 U.S.C. § 77d(a)(2). Prior to the Jumpstart our Business Startups Act of 2012 (JOBS Act), Pub. L. No. 112-106, 126 Stat. 306 (2012), the exemption was in §4(2).

7. 17 C.F.R. § 230.500 et seq.; see also US Securities and Exchange Commission, "Regulation D—Rules 504, 505 and 506."

8. See "Revision of Certain Exemptions from Registration for Transactions Involving Limited Offers and Sales" (Release No. 33-6389), 47 Fed. Reg. (March 16, 1982): 11251. Regulation D is found at 17 C.F.R. § 230.500 through §230.508. See "Revision of Certain Exemptions from the Registration Provisions of the Securities Act of 1993 for Transactions Involving Limited Offers and Sales" (Release No. 33-6339), 46 Fed. Reg. (August 18, 1981): 41791, for the original proposed rule.

9. Insiders, friends, and family will often rely on the private offering exemption (Section 4(a)(2)) without using Regulation D.

10. Bauguess, Gullapalli, and Ivanov, "Capital Raising in the US."

11. See SEC Rule 501(a).

12. Gullapalli, "Accredited Investor Pool."

13. See § 3(b) of the Securities Act of 1933.

14. 17 C.F.R. § 230.251 et seq.; see also US Securities and Exchange Commission, "Regulation A."

15. "Factors That May Affect Trends"; Campbell, "Regulation A."

16. Final Rule, "Amendments for Small and Additional Issues Exemptions under the Securities Act (Regulation A)," 80 Fed. Reg. (April 20, 2015): 21806–925.

17. Title IV, the Jumpstart Our Business Startups (JOBS) Act of 2012, Pub. L. No. 112-106 (2012).

18. Burton, "Regulation A+ Proposed Rule"; and Comments on "Proposed Rule Amendments"; Campbell, "Regulation A and the JOBS Act."

19. Wan, "Progress Report."

20. See Bauguess, Gullapalli, and Ivanov, "Capital Raising in the US," 7.

21. Pursuant to § 13 or 15(d) of the Securities Exchange Act of 1934.

22. Ibid.

23. 17 C.F.R. Part 229.

24. 17 C.F.R. Part 210.

25. Notably the voluminous requirements of the Public Company Accounting Oversight Board (PCAOB) and the Financial Accounting Standards Board (FASB).

26. 17 C.F.R. § 240.12b-2; 17 C.F.R. § 229.10 (Item 10(f)(1)).

27. 17 C.F.R. § 240.12b-2(1).

28. 17 C.F.R. § 240.12b-2(2).

29. Section 2(a)(19) of the Securities Act of 1933 (15 U.S.C. § 77b(a)(19)).

30. Section 6(e) of the Securities Act of 1933 (15 U.S.C. § 77f(e)).

31. A transaction induced by fraud (misrepresentation) is not voluntary or welfare enhancing in that it would not be entered into in the absence of the fraud (or would be entered into at a different price). This principle has been recognized at common law since time immemorial—see, for example, Blackstone, *Commentaries on the Laws of England*, book III, chap. 9—and is recognized by virtually all political theorists. Securities fraud was illegal long before New Deal securities laws or even blue sky laws were enacted (Banner, *Anglo-American Securities Regulation*). See also Easterbrook and Fischel, "Mandatory Disclosure," 669; Walker, "Securities Regulation"; Mahoney, *Wasting a Crisis*.

32. See *Restatement of the Law, Second, Torts, Volume 3* (Philadelphia: American Law Institute, 1977) at § 525 Liability for Fraudulent Misrepresentation; § 526 Conditions under which Misrepresentation Is Fraudulent (Scienter); § 529 Representation Misleading because Incomplete; and §551 Liability for Nondisclosure.

33. See Securities Exchange Act of 1934 § 10(b) [15 U.S.C. § 78j(b)], Regulation of the Use of Manipulative and Deceptive Devices. See also 17 C.F.R. § 240.10b-5, Employment of manipulative and deceptive devices.

34. See, for example, § 501 of the Uniform Securities Act (2002), which reads:

> "General Fraud. It is unlawful for a person, in connection with the offer, sale, or purchase of a security, directly or indirectly:

(1) to employ a device, scheme, or artifice to defraud;

(2) to make an untrue statement of a material fact or to omit to state a material fact necessary in order to make the statement made, in the light of the circumstances under which it is made, not misleading; or

(3) to engage in an act, practice, or course of business that operates or would operate as a fraud or deceit upon another person."

35. For a discussion of the history of blue sky laws, see Macey and Miller, "Origin of the Blue Sky Laws"; and Mahoney, "Origins of the Blue Sky Laws."

36. Charles II, "Act for Prevention of Frauds and Perjuryes."

37. Uniform Commercial Code § 2-201. Formal Requirements; Statute of Frauds.

38. For a general introduction, see Posner, "Financial Markets."

39. Prentice, "Economic Value of Securities Regulation"; Black, "Legal and Institutional Preconditions"; Enriques and Gilotta, "Disclosure and Financial Market Regulation."

40. Kahan, "Securities Laws"; Coffee, "Market Failure"; Seligman, "Historical Need," 1.

41. Wurgler, "Financial Markets"; Mclean, Zhang, and Zhao, "Why Does the Law Matter?"; Dye, "Mandatory versus Voluntary Disclosures"; Bushee and Leuz, "Economic Consequences"; Franco, "Why Antifraud Provisions Are Not Enough"; Healy and Palepu, "Information Asymmetry"; Admati and Pfleiderer, "Forcing Firms to Talk."

42. Botosan, "Evidence That Greater Disclosure Lowers the Cost"; Himmelberg, Hubbard, and Love, "Investor Protection."

43. The interests of shareholders and management are often not coincident and may considerably conflict. Corporate managers often will operate firms as much for their own benefit as that of shareholders, and shareholders may have difficulty cost-effectively preventing this. The incongruity of interest is often described as the agent-principal problem or collective action problem and is significant in larger firms where ownership and management of the firm are separate and ownership is widely held. See Jensen and Meckling, "Theory of the Firm"; Mahoney, "Mandatory Disclosure"; Fox, "Retaining Mandatory Securities Disclosure."

44. Romano, *Advantage of Competitive Federalism*; Healy and Palepu, "Information Asymmetry.

45. Easterbrook and Fishel, *Economic Structure of Corporate Law*; Fishman and Hagerty, "Disclosure Decisions"; Stigler, "Public Regulation"; Benson, "Required Disclosure."

46. The Regulation D safe harbor imposes certain additional requirements if the issuer sells securities under Rule 505 or 506(b) to any purchaser that is not an accredited investor. See 17 C.F.R. § 230.502(b).

47. See, for example, O'Hara and Easley, "Information and the Cost of Capital."

48. Lewis, "Future of Capital Formation"; Schwartz, "Law and Economics," 347; Bradford, "Transaction Exemptions." There is also a strong argument that scaling should be a function of the age of the firm so that relatively young firms with limited compliance experience and, typically, limited cash flow and resources should have lesser disclosure requirements than more mature firms. See table 3.3 in Phillips and Zecher, *SEC and the Public Interest*. See also US Securities and Exchange Commission, "Economic Analysis," "Proposed Rule Amendments for Small and Additional Issues Exemptions under Section 3(b) of the Securities Act," 79 Fed. Reg. (January 23, 2014): 3972–93.

49. Liu et al., "Dark Side of Disclosure."

50. Eklund and Desai, "Entry Regulation," 25; Woodward, "Regulatory Capture"; Stigler, "Theory of Economic Regulation."

51. "Regulation Is Good for Goldman."

52. See, for example, Karmel, *Regulation by Prosecution*, 18, where she states:

> "The other Commissioners seemed to feel that the staff was their constituency and that by supporting staff they were necessarily acting in the public interest. . . .
> Most of my close business and personal friends are securities lawyers, and many of them are SEC alumni. I belong to a tight-knit community of interesting and decent people, whose livelihoods depend on the continued existence and vitality of the SEC."

Karmel was an SEC Commissioner from 1977–1980. For a general discussion of these issues, see Rubin and Bailey, "Role of Lawyers"; White, "Legal Complexity."

53. See Enriques and Gilotta, "Disclosure and Financial Market Regulation"; Ben-Shahar and Schneider, "Failure of Mandated Discourse."

54. The lack of data available to policymakers regarding the private capital markets, compliance costs, SEC and other regulator enforcement actions, and the types of securities laws violations that occur in practice is startling. Steps need to be taken to rectify this lack of data so that policymakers can make policy in something other than a largely data-free environment. Specifically, the SEC should collect and publish times series data with respect to the initial offering and continuing regulatory costs incurred by small public and Regulation A companies (including both those whose offerings are declared effective or qualified and those whose offerings are not) and in connection with private placements (primary Regulation D offerings), the amount of capital raised, and the nature of the investors. The SEC should also collect and publish data regarding enforcement actions taken in connection with private, Regulation A, and small public company offerings, disclosure obligations, and secondary market activity. Specifically, the SEC should collect and publish information showing what types of disclosures, misrepresentations, or omissions are the source of enforcement actions; what types of issuers and exemptions give rise to enforcement actions; the frequency and severity of different types of violations (including the amount lost by investors); and whether the primary or the secondary market is the source of most problems.

55. Langevoort and Thompson, " 'Publicness.' "

56. de Fontenay, "Do the Securities Laws Matter?"; Daines and Jones, "Truth or Consequences"; Leuz and Wysocki, "Economic Consequences"; Healy and Palepu, "Information Asymmetry"; Zecher, "Economic Perspective"; Easterbrook and Fischel, "Mandatory Disclosure"; Phillips and Zecher, *SEC and the Public Interest*, chap. 3; Kripke, *SEC and Corporate Disclosure*; Benson, *Corporate Financial Disclosure*, and "Corporate Financial Disclosure." For two pioneering economic studies finding no measurable benefit from the Securities Act of 1933, see Stigler, "Public Regulation," and Benson, "Required Disclosure."

57. Romano, "Empowering Investors."

58. See Quandl, 2012 World Bank Market Capitalization Data.

59. Ibid.

60. World Bank, "Market Capitalization of Listed Companies."

61. Broad in the sense that a high number of firms participate in equity markets and deep in the sense that markets are liquid with large numbers of investors investing large amounts of capital.

62. Once the discussion is broadened to financial regulation generally speaking, other major problems also must be considered, including "too big to fail," bank regulation, federal loan guarantees, monetary policy, and the like.

63. There are exceptions. The disclosure requirements with respect to conflict minerals, mine safety, resource extraction, and the ratio between a company's CEO pay and the median pay of all other employees are examples. See Burton, "How Dodd-Frank Mandated Disclosures Harm."

64. See, for example, Romano, "Regulating in the Dark," esp. 89–90, which explains that the Sarbanes-Oxley Act has been particularly costly for small firms; Campbell, "Wreck of Regulation D," which discusses how Regulation D does not work the way it is supposed to for small companies because of state blue sky laws; Campbell, "Regulation A," 77–122, esp. 121–22, which explains that "[f]ederal and state securities laws exacerbate" the already difficult task of small firms trying to raise capital; Campbell, "Regulation A and the JOBS Act"; SEC Commissioner Gallagher, "Whatever Happened to Promoting Small Business?"; Cohn and Yadley, "Capital Offense"; Burton, "Reducing the Burden."

65. For a more complete discussion of the economic importance of entrepreneurship and existing impediments to entrepreneurship, see Burton, "Building an Opportunity Economy."

66. "The mission of the US Securities and Exchange Commission is to protect investors, maintain fair, orderly, and efficient markets, and facilitate capital formation." US Securities and Exchange Commission, "What We Do," retrieved October 31, 2016, https://www.sec.gov /about/whatwedo.shtml#intro. The SEC's statutory charge is: "Whenever pursuant to this title the Commission is engaged in rulemaking and is required to consider or determine whether an action is necessary or appropriate in the public interest, the Commission shall also consider, in addition to the protection of investors, whether the action will promote efficiency, competition, and capital formation." See § 3(f) of the Securities Exchange Act of 1934 and § 2(b) of the Securities Act of 1933.

67. See, for example, sec. III, "Some Limits and Drawbacks of MD," in Enriques and Gilotta, "Disclosure and Financial Market Regulation."

68. Paredes, "Blinded by the Light"; and, as commissioner, "Remarks at The SEC Speaks." See also, Higgins (Director, Division of Corporation Finance), "Disclosure Effectiveness."

69. Ernst & Young, "Now Is the Time."

70. Monga and Chasan, "109,894-Word Annual Report."

71. For example, Ray Bradbury's *Fahrenheit 451* (46,118 words), F. Scott Fitzgerald's *The Great Gatsby* (47,094), and Stephen Crane's *The Red Badge of Courage* (47,180).

72. The Electronic Data Gathering, Analysis, and Retrieval (EDGAR) system is a free search tool at http://www.sec.gov/edgar/searchedgar/webusers.htm#.U_ZaTmOC2So.

73. Usually, these documents are the federal Forms 10-K, 10-Q, or 8-K.

74. Becker, "Crime and Punishment"; Posner, "Economic Theory."

75. This short discussion abstracts away from many subsidiary issues, including the relative efficacy of civil and criminal penalties, the degree of deterrence that is socially optimal, measurement issues, and the like. For a recent review of some of the issues, see Hylton, "Theory of Penalties."

76. For a dated but detailed look at blue sky laws, see "Report on the Uniformity." For a critique of blue sky laws, see Campbell, "Federalism Gone Amuck," 578: "In retrospect, there can be little doubt that the failure of Congress to preempt state authority over the registration of securities was a significant blunder." See also Karmel, "Blue-Sky Merit Regulation." The North American Securities Administrators Association, "Application for Coordinated Review," delineates between merit review and disclosure jurisdictions. There are forty-nine participating jurisdictions, including Puerto Rico, the US Virgin Islands, and the District of Columbia. Of the states, twenty-eight are merit review states, sixteen are disclosure states,

and two (New Jersey and West Virginia) are "disclosure" states that "reserve the right" to make "substantive comments." Four states do not, at this time, participate.

77. Campbell, "Insidious Remnants"; Manne and Mofsky, "What Price Blue Sky"; Maynard, "Future of California's Blue Sky Law"; Sargent, "Future for Blue Sky"; Mofsky and Tollison, "Demerit in Merit Regulation"; Mofsky, *Blue Sky Restrictions*; Bell and Arky, "Blue Sky Restrictions."

78. A discussion of the role of benefit corporations (or benefit LLCs) and social enterprises is beyond the scope of this chapter. However, it is my strong contention that if there is full disclosure and investors understand the dual mission of the enterprise, investors should be free to invest in such enterprises and the founders of such enterprises should be free to sell securities in such enterprises.

79. Jolls, Sunstein, and Thaler, "Behavioral Approach to Law"; Thaler and Sunstein, "Libertarian Paternalism"; Sunstein and Thaler, "Libertarian Paternalism Is Not an Oxymoron"; O'Donoghue and Rabin, "Studying Optimal Paternalism." See also Whitman, "Against the New Paternalism."

80. Jolls, Sunstein, and Thaler, "Behavioral Approach to Law"; Korobkin and Ulen, "Law and Behavioral Science."

81. See, for example, Stein, "Remarks before the Consumer Federation"; Elan, "Annotated Bibliography"; US Securities and Exchange Commission Investor Advisory Committee, minutes of May 17, 2010 meeting.

82. Hayek, "Pretence of Knowledge"; *Individualism and Economic Order*; "Use of Knowledge in Society"; and "Economics and Knowledge."

83. Schuck, *Why Government Fails So Often*; Winston, *Government Failure*; Peirce, *Bureaucratic Failure*.

84. A "riskier security" is here defined as a security with a high degree of unique risk (as opposed to market or systemic risk).

85. This is often called a negative beta or low beta investment. For a discussion of these issues, see, for example, Brealey, Meyers, and Allen, "Introduction to Risk" or most introductory finance textbooks.

86. Choi and Pritchard, "Behavioral Economics and the SEC."

87. Tullock, Seldon, and Brady, *Government Failure*.

88. For a specific discussion of this issue with respect to securities regulation, see Enriques and Gilotta, "Disclosure and Financial Market Regulation."

89. Shughart, "Public Choice"; Buchanan, *Collected Works of James M. Buchanan*, 46, from a lecture originally given at the Institute for Advanced Studies in Vienna, Austria in 1979. Buchanan stated: "My primary title for this lecture, 'Politics without Romance,' was chosen for its descriptive accuracy. Public choice theory has been the avenue through which a romantic and illusory set of notions about the workings of governments and the behavior of persons who govern has been replaced by a set of notions that embody more skepticism about what governments can do and what governors will do, notions that are surely more consistent with the political reality that we may all observe about us. I have often said that public choice offers a 'theory of governmental failure' that is fully comparable to the 'theory of market failure' that emerged from the theoretical welfare economics of the 1930s and 1940s."

90. Folsom and Folsom, *Uncle Sam Can't*; Pack and Saggi, in "Case for Industrial Policy," 1, write: "Overall, there appears to be little empirical support for an activist government policy even though market failures exist that can, in principle, justify the use of industrial policy."

91. Rustin and Lynch, "Apple Computer Set."

92. For example, in February 2008, then Federal Reserve Board Chairman Ben Bernanke said, "Among the largest banks, the capital ratios remain good and I don't anticipate any serious problems of that sort among the large, internationally active banks that make up a very substantial part of our banking system." See "Fed Chairman." Only seven months later, the Emergency Economic Stabilization Act of 2008 established the Troubled Asset Relief Program (TARP), with Bernanke's support, to bail out the big banks.

93. Roszkowski and Grable, "Evidence of Lower Risk Tolerance."

94. See the discussion at note 77 and North American Securities Administrators Association, "Application for Coordinated Review of Regulation A Offering."

95. There is, however, a creeping introduction of a type of merit review into federal securities laws. Notably, Title III of the JOBS Act limits investments to a specified percentage of income or net worth and the new Regulation A-plus rules do the same. It does not take too much imagination to envision a federal regulatory regime that has specified diversification or other requirements for most investors that would seriously limit investors' options and that most entrepreneurs starting a business with their own funds would fail. Indeed, the Financial Industry Regulatory Authority (FINRA) Rule 2111 relating to suitability requirements already imposes the broad outlines of such a system for transactions recommended by a broker-dealer. The Department of Labor's fiduciary standards under the Employee Retirement Income Security Act (ERISA) raise similar issues.

96. Examples would include the SEC's continued limitations on paying finders (or private placement brokers) who bring capital to a small business, limits on peer-to-peer lending, the unduly restrictive rules governing Regulation D general solicitation, and the crowdfunding rules that quite probably make non-broker-dealer funding portals uneconomic. Moreover, the sheer complexity of SEC and FINRA regulation of broker-dealers acts to limit competition and to create a cartel, resulting in higher broker-dealer fees than would obtain in a genuinely competitive market. The Financial Crimes Enforcement Network (FinCEN) proposed rules applying the Anti-Money Laundering/Know Your Customer (AML/KYC) rules to funding portals, even though they are prohibited from holding customer funds and the financial institutions holding the funds must do AML due diligence, are a further example. See "Amendments to the Definition of Broker or Dealer in Securities," 81 Fed. Reg. (April 4, 2016): 19086–94.

97. Dodd-Frank, Pub. L. No. 111-203, 124 Stat. 1376 (2010).

98. The Conference Board, "Corporate Political Spending"; and Welsh and Passoff, "Proxy Preview 2016," 64–65.

99. Michaels, "Democrats Pressure SEC"; and "SEC Action on Corporate Political Spending Disclosure," letter signed by ninety-four senators and representatives.

100. "Petition for Rulemaking on Disclosure by Public Companies of Corporate Resources Used for Political Activities," File No. 4-637-2, April 15, 2014; and "Comments on Rulemaking Petition: Petition to Require Public Companies to Disclose to Shareholders the Use of Corporate Resources for Political Activities," File No. 4-637, https://www.sec.gov/comments/4-637/4-637 .shtml.

101. Consolidated Appropriations Act, 2016, Pub. L. No. 114-113, H.R. 2029, 114th Cong. (December 18, 2015), Section 707, Title VII, Division O: "None of the funds made available by any division of this Act shall be used by the Securities and Exchange Commission to finalize, issue, or implement any rule, regulation, or order regarding the disclosure of political contributions, contributions to tax exempt organizations, or dues paid to trade associations." This act governs spending through FY 2016, which ended September 30, 2016.

102. The Shareholder Protection Act of 2015, S. 214, H. R. 446, 114th Cong.

103. "Request for rulemaking to require public companies to disclose gender pay ratios on an annual basis, or in the alternative, to provide guidance to companies regarding voluntary reporting on pay equity to their investors," submitted by PAX Ellevate Management LLC, File No.4-696, February 1, 2016.

104. For example, the US Chamber of Commerce estimates, based on survey data, that the CEO pay-disclosure-rule compliance costs $711 million annually, substantially more than the SEC estimate. See Brannon, "Egregious Costs of the SEC's Pay-Ratio." The SEC estimated that the initial cost of compliance with the conflict minerals rule "is between approximately $3 billion to $4 billion, while the annual cost of ongoing compliance will be between $207 million and $609 million." See "Conflict Minerals," Final Rule, 77 Fed. Reg. (September 12, 2012): 56351.

105. Burton, "How Dodd-Frank Mandated Disclosures Harm."

106. The Securities Acts Amendments of 1964, Pub. L. No. 467, 78 Stat. 565 (August 20, 1964). See also Phillips and Shipman, "Analysis of the Securities Acts Amendments."

107. See section 12(g) of the Securities Exchange Act. The 2012 JOBS Act liberalized this rule by allowing a firm to have up to 2,000 accredited investors before having to register. In addition, under the JOBS Act, investors who bought securities pursuant to the Title III crowdfunding exemption are not counted toward the section 12(g) limit. It is also important to note that "holder of record" is not the same as beneficial owner. Most investors hold their stock under "street name" so that all of the stock held by various customers of a particular broker-dealer is held on the records of the company as one holder of record—the broker-dealer. In addition, many investors may combine to form and invest in a special-purpose vehicle that in turn actually invests in the company. The special-purpose vehicle counts as only one shareholder of record. The regulations do not require the issuer to "look-through" the special-purpose vehicle investor. In addition, mutual funds, closed-end funds, or private equity funds are, in effect, entities that represent the investment of many individual investors, yet they too would constitute just one holder of record.

108. Regulation A and crowdfunding securities are public in the sense they may be sold to all investors and the securities are not restricted securities (in the case of crowdfunding, after one year). They are not public in the sense that the issuer is not subject to the requirements of a reporting company. The term quasi-public is meant to encompass these types of companies and companies that would be in a similar situation under alternative regulatory regimes.

109. For a discussion of these issues, see Langevoort and Thompson, " 'Publicness.' "

110. Rule 502(b) imposes significantly greater disclosure requirement on issuers that sell to non-accredited investors in both Rule 505 and Rule 506(b) offerings.

111. Securities Act of 1933 section 3(b); 15 U.S.C. § 77c(b). It was originally $100,000 and was increased to $300,000 in 1945, to $500,000 in 1970, to $2 million in 1978, and to $5 million in 1980. The JOBS Act in 2012 created section 3(b)(2), which allows certain Regulation A offerings to raise as much as $50 million. This is so-called Regulation A-plus.

112. See section 102 of the National Securities Markets Improvement Act of 1996 (Pub. L. No. 1040-290, October 11, 1996) incorporating the Capital Markets Efficiency Act of 1996 as section 18(b)(4)(E) of the Securities Act (15 U.S.C. § 77r(b)(4)(E)), which treats as covered securities those securities not involving a public offering under Securities Act section 4(a)(2). Rules 504 and 505 were promulgated under Securities Act section 3(b) and therefore transactions using these rules are not blue sky exempt.

113. See, for example, Campbell, "Regulation A"; Cohn and Yadley, "Capital Offense"; "Factors That May Affect Trends."

114. See "Factors That May Affect Trends," 9.

115. "Proposed Rule Amendments for Small and Additional Issues Exemptions under Section 3(b) of the Securities Act," 3928.

116. Roughly $73 million out of $25,840 million. If section 4(a)(2) private offerings made without use of the Regulation D safe harbor were considered, the percentage would be substantially lower still.

117. "Amendments for Small and Additional Issues Exemptions under the Securities Act."

118. Massachusetts and Montana challenged the authority of the SEC to preempt state law. Lynch, "Two States Sue U.S. SEC." On June 14, 2016, the US Court of Appeals for the District of Columbia Circuit ruled against the states and for the SEC. To the author's knowledge, the state regulators have not indicated whether they will file a Petition for a Writ of Certiorari with the US Supreme Court.

119. Securities Exchange Act section 12(g)(1). For a more detailed discussion, see Burton, Comments on "Proposed Rule Amendments."

120. See "Revision of Certain Exemptions from Registration for Transactions Involving Limited Offers of Sales" (Release No. 33-6389), 11251. Regulation D is found at 17 C.F.R. § 230.500 through §230.508.

121. 17 C.F.R. § 230.504. See also US Securities and Exchange Commission, "Rule 504 of Regulation D," retrieved October 31, 2016, https://www.sec.gov/answers/rule504.htm.

122. 17 C.F.R. § 230.505. See also US Securities and Exchange Commission, "Rule 505 of Regulation D," retrieved October 31, 2016, https://www.sec.gov/answers/rule505.htm.

123. Rule 504 offerings are exempt from the additional disclosure requirements for sales to non-accredited investors. See Rule 504(b)(1). General solicitation is permitted only in certain specified circumstances.

124. Rule 505 allows up to thirty-five nonaccredited investors but investments by nonaccredited investors trigger additional disclosure requirements under Rule 502(b).

125. See Bauguess, Gullapalli, and Ivanov, "Capital Raising in the US," 12.

126. This has been true since the passage of the National Securities Markets Improvement Act (NSMIA) of 1996, which amended section 18 of the Securities Act (15 U.S.C. § 77r) to exempt from state securities regulation any "covered security." 15 U.S.C. § 77r(b)(4)(E) provides that "[a] security is a covered security with respect to a transaction that is exempt from registration under this subchapter pursuant to . . . commission rules or regulations issued under section 77d(2) of this title, except that this subparagraph does not prohibit a State from imposing notice filing requirements that are substantially similar to those required by rule or regulation under section 77d(2) of this title that are in effect on September 1, 1996." Section 77d(2) is a reference to section 4(2) of the Securities Act (now section 4(a)(2)), to wit, transactions by an issuer not involving any public offering. Only Rule 506 of Regulation D relied on this provision. See US Securities and Exchange Commission, "Revision of Certain Exemptions from Registration for Transactions Involving Limited Offers and Sales," 11251. Rule 505 and Rule 504 rely instead on section 3(b) of the Securities Act. See 17 C.F.R. § 230.504(a) and 17 C.F.R. § 230.505(a). Accordingly, Rule 504 and Rule 505 offerings are not treated as covered securities by the SEC or the state regulators.

127. The fifty-two regulators are the fifty states, the District of Columbia, and the SEC.

128. Bauguess, Gullapalli, and Ivanov, "Capital Raising in the US"; Burton, "Don't Crush the Ability."

129. See Rule 502(b).

130. 17 C.F.R. § 230.501(a) (SEC Rule 501).

131. For details, see Burton, "Don't Crush the Ability."

132. Rule 501(e) excludes all accredited investors from the calculation of the number of purchasers. Rule 506(b)(2)(ii) requires that "each purchaser who is not an accredited investor either alone or with his purchaser representative(s) has such knowledge and experience in financial and business matters that he is capable of evaluating the merits and risks of the prospective investment, or the issuer reasonably believes immediately prior to making any sale that such purchaser comes within this description." The shorthand for this requirement is that he must be a "sophisticated investor."

133. The Fair Investment Opportunities for Professional Experts Act (H.R. 2187, 114th Cong.), which passed the House by a vote of 347–48 on February 1, 2016, would take steps in this direction by statutorily setting the thresholds at current level and indexing them prospectively, by treating certain financial professionals as sophisticated, and by allowing the SEC with FINRA to broaden the definition.

134. The Private Placement Improvement Act of 2016 (H.R. 4852, 114th Cong.) would prevent promulgation of these rules. This bill was reported out of the House Financial Services Committee on June 16, 2016. For proposed rules, see Release No. 33-9416; Release No. 34-69960; Release No. IC-30595; File No. S7-06-13; RIN 3235-AL46, "Amendments to Regulation D, Form D and Rule 156," 78 Fed. Reg. (July 24, 2013): 44806–55 and Release No. 33-9458; Release No. 34-70538; Release No. IC-30737; File No. S7-06-13; RIN 3235-AL46; "Amendments to Regulation D, Form D and Rule 156; Re-Opening of Comment Period," 78 Fed. Reg. (October 3, 2013): 61222.

135. See Burton, Comments to the SEC on "Amendments to Regulation D."

136. However, filing a simple closing Form D indicating the amount actually raised is justified by the need to have improved information about this critical market.

137. Entrepreneur Access to Capital Act, H.R. 2930, 112th Cong. (2011–2012).

138. It also excluded crowdfunding investors from the holders of record count, preempted blue sky laws, and entitled issuers to rely on investor self-certification as to income level.

139. H.R. 2930, 112th Cong. (November 3, 2011).

140. Senate Amendment to Title III of H.R. 3606 (March 22, 2012).

141. Securities Act section 4(a)(6).

142. There were 284 actual requests for comment, but many of them are multipart requests. US Securities and Exchange Commission Proposed Rules, "Crowdfunding," October 23, 2013. For the Federal Register version of these proposed rules, see 78 Fed. Reg. (November 5, 2013): 66428–601; citations to the Crowdfunding proposed rules discussed in the text are to this version.

143. Crowdfunding, Final Rule, 80 Fed. Reg. (November 16, 2015): 71388.

144. The other proposed changes are: (1) permit funding portals to be compensated based on the amount raised by the issuer; (2) make it clear that funding portals are not issuers and not subject to the issuer liability provisions; (3) repeal the restriction on providing investment advice entirely or, alternatively, explicitly permit "impersonal investment advice," making it clear that a portal may bar an issuer from its platform if the portal deems an offering to be of inadequate quality without fear of liability to issuers or investors and that this would not constitute providing prohibited investment advice; (4) reduce the administrative and compliance burden on funding portals; (5) allow intermediaries to rely on good faith efforts by third-party certifiers for purposes of complying with the investment limitation in section

(4)(a)(6)(B); and (6) amend the Bank Secrecy Act to make it clear that federal AML/KYC rules do not apply to finders, business brokers, or crowdfunding web portals since they are prohibited by law from holding customer funds. FinCEN has proposed rules to make funding portals subject to the AML/KYC rules. See "Amendments to the Definition of Broker or Dealer in Securities."

145. The Micro Offering Safe Harbor Act, H.R. 4850, 114th Cong. (2015–2016) is designed to address this issue. The version as originally introduced would do so. The amended version reported out of the House Financial Services on June 16, 2016, is very narrow and will have only a limited impact. Burton, "Starting a Small Business."

146. 17 C.F.R. Part 229.

147. 17 C.F.R. Part 210.

148. Proposed Rules, "Crowdfunding," 78 Fed. Reg. (November 5, 2013): 66509.

149. See, for example, Committee on Capital Market Regulation, "Interim Report"; Kamar, Karaca-Mandic, and Talley, "Going-Private Decisions"; Bartlett, "Going Private but Staying Public."

150. The Sarbanes-Oxley Act of 2002, Pub. L. No. 107-204, 116 Stat. 745 (2002).

151. Dodd-Frank, Pub. L. No. 111-203, 124 Stat. 1376 (2010).

152. See, for example, Meoli et al., "Cost of Going Public."

153. See Burton, "Reducing the Burden."

154. There would be a need to have reasonable, administrable look-through rules if beneficial ownership were to replace the holder of record threshold. However, in the contemplated regulatory regime, the impact of the step-up from private to quasi-public status would not be so discontinuous as the step-up from private to public today, therefore this break point would be of less importance.

REFERENCES

Admati, Anat R., and Paul C. Pfleiderer. "Forcing Firms to Talk: Financial Disclosure Regulation and Externalities." *Review of Financial Studies* 13, no. 3 (Fall 2000): 479–519.

Banner, Stuart. *Anglo-American Securities Regulation: Cultural and Political Roots, 1690–1860.* Cambridge: Cambridge University Press, 2002.

Bartlett, Robert P., III. "Going Private but Staying Public: Reexamining the Effect of Sarbanes-Oxley on Firms' Going-Private Decisions." *University of Chicago Law Review* 76, no. 1 (2009): 7–44.

Bauguess, Scott, Rachita Gullapalli, and Vladimir Ivanov. "Capital Raising in the US: An Analysis of the Market for Unregistered Securities Offerings, 2009–2014." US Securities and Exchange Commission, October 2015.

Becker, Gary S. "Crime and Punishment: An Economic Approach." In *Essays in the Economics of Crime and Punishment,* edited by Gary S. Becker and William M. Landes, 1–54. New York: Columbia University Press, 1974.

Bell, John P. A., and Stephen W. Arky. "Blue Sky Restrictions on New Business Promotions." *Business Lawyer* 27, no. 1 (November 1971): 361–65.

Ben-Shahar, Omri, and Carl E. Schneider. "The Failure of Mandated Discourse." *University of Pennsylvania Law Review* 159 (2011): 647–749.

Benson, George J. "Required Disclosure and the Stock Market: An Evaluation of the Securities Exchange Act of 1934." *American Economic Review* 63, no. 1 (March 1973): 132–55.

——. *Corporate Financial Disclosure in the U.K. and the U.S.A.* London: Institute of Chartered Accountants, 1976.

——. "Corporate Financial Disclosure in the UK and the USA." *The Accounting Review* 53, no. 4 (October 1978): 1019–21.

Black, Bernard S. "The Legal and Institutional Preconditions for Strong Securities Markets." *UCLA Law Review* 48 (2001): 781–855.

Blackstone, William. *Commentaries on the Laws of England, Book III: Private Wrongs.* Oxford: Clarendon Press, 1765.

Botosan, Christine A. "Evidence That Greater Disclosure Lowers the Cost of Equity Capital." *Journal of Applied Corporate Finance* 12, no. 4 (2000): 60–69. Reprinted in *Corporate Governance at the Crossroads: A Book of Readings*, edited by Donald H. Chew Jr. and Stuart L. Gillan. New York: McGraw-Hill/Irwin, 2005.

Bradford, C. Steven. "Transaction Exemptions in the Securities Act of 1933: An Economic Analysis." *Emory Law Journal* 45 (1996): 591–671.

Brannon, Ike. "The Egregious Costs of the SEC's Pay-Ratio Disclosure Rule." Center for Capital Markets. May 2014. http://www.centerforcapitalmarkets.com/wp-content/uploads/2013/08/Egregious-Cost-of-Pay-Ratio-5.14.pdf.

Brealey, Richard A., Stewart C. Meyers, and Franklin Allen. "Introduction to Risk, Return and the Opportunity Cost of Capital." In *Principles of Corporate Finance*, 8th ed. New York: McGraw-Hill, 2006.

Buchanan, James M. *The Collected Works of James M. Buchanan, The Logical Foundations of Constitutional Liberty*, vol. 1. Indianapolis, IN: Liberty Fund, 1999.

Burton, David. Comments to the SEC on "Amendments to Regulation D, Form D and Rule 156." November 4, 2013. http://www.sec.gov/comments/s7-06-13/s70613-462.pdf.

——. "Don't Crush the Ability of Entrepreneurs and Small Businesses to Raise Capital." Heritage Foundation Backgrounder 2874, February 5, 2014.

——. Comments on "Proposed Rule Amendments for Small and Additional Issues Exemptions under Section 3(b) of the Securities Act." March 21, 2014. http://www.sec.gov/comments/s7-11-13/s71113-52.pdf.

——. "Regulation A+ Proposed Rule Needs Work." *The Daily Signal*, April 8, 2014. http://dailysignal.com/2014/04/08/regulation-plus-proposed-rule-needs-work/.

——. "Reducing the Burden on Small Public Companies Would Promote Innovation, Job Creation, and Economic Growth." Heritage Foundation Backgrounder 2924, June 20, 2014.

——. "Building an Opportunity Economy: The State of Small Business and Entrepreneurship." Testimony before the Committee on Small Business, US House of Representatives, Heritage Foundation, March 4, 2015.

——. "How Dodd-Frank Mandated Disclosures Harm, Rather than Protect, Investors." Heritage Foundation Issue Brief 4526, March 10, 2016.

——. "Starting a Small Business Could Break This Federal Law." *Daily Signal*, March 24, 2016. http://dailysignal.com/2016/03/24/how-starting-a-small-company-could-break-this-federal-law/.

Bushee, Brian J., and Christian Leuz. "Economic Consequences of SEC Disclosure Regulation: Evidence from the OTC Bulletin Board." *Journal of Accounting and Economics* 39, no. 2 (2005): 233–64.

Campbell, Rutherford B., Jr. "The Insidious Remnants of State Rules Respecting Capital Formation." *Washington University Law Quarterly* 78 (2000): 407–34.

———. "Regulation A: Small Businesses' Search for a Moderate Capital." *Delaware Journal of Corporate Law* 31, no. 1 (2006): 77–123.

———. "Federalism Gone Amuck: The Case for Reallocating Governmental Authority over the Capital Formation Activities of Businesses." *Washburn Law Journal* 50, no. 3 (Spring 2011): 573–82.

———. "The Wreck of Regulation D: The Unintended (and Bad) Outcomes for the SEC's Crown Jewel Exemptions." *Business Lawyer* 66 (2011): 919–42.

———. "Regulation A and the JOBS Act: A Failure to Resuscitate." *Ohio State Entrepreneurial Business Law Journal* 7, no. 2 (2012): 317–33.

Charles II. "An Act for Prevention of Frauds and Perjuryes." In *Statutes of the Realm: Volume 5, 1628–80*, edited by John Raithby, 839–42. 1819. http://www.british-history.ac.uk/statutes-realm/vol5/pp839-842.

Choi, Stephen J., and A. C. Pritchard. "Behavioral Economics and the SEC." *Stanford Law Review* 56, no. 1 (October 2003): 1–73.

Coffee, John C., Jr. "Market Failure and the Economic Case for a Mandatory Disclosure System." *Virginia Law Review* 70 (1984): 717–53.

Cohn, Stuart R., and Gregory C. Yadley. "Capital Offense: The SEC's Continuing Failure to Address Small Business Financing Concerns." *New York University Journal of Law and Business* 4, no. 1 (2007): 1–87.

Committee on Capital Market Regulation. "Interim Report of the Committee on Capital Markets Regulation." November 30, 2006.

The Conference Board. "Corporate Political Spending: Shareholder Activity." Updated October 30, 2014. https://www.conference-board.org/politicalspending/index.cfm?id=6256.

Daines, Robert, and Charles M. Jones. "Truth or Consequences: Mandatory Disclosure and the Impact of the 1934 Act." Working Paper, Stanford Law School, May 2012.

de Fontenay, Elisabeth. "Do the Securities Laws Matter? The Rise of the Leveraged Loan Market." *Journal of Corporation Law* 39 (2014): 725–68.

Dye, Ronald A. "Mandatory versus Voluntary Disclosures: The Cases of Financial and Real Externalities." *Accounting Review* 65, no. 1 (1990): 1–24.

Easterbrook, Frank H., and Daniel R. Fischel. "Mandatory Disclosure and the Protection of Investors." *Virginia Law Review* 70 (1984): 669–715.

———. *The Economic Structure of Corporate Law*. Cambridge, MA: Harvard University Press, 1991.

Eklund, Johan E., and Sameeksha Desai. "Entry Regulation and Persistence of Profits in Incumbent Firms." Swedish Entrepreneurship Forum Working Paper, Stockholm, December 15, 2013.

Elan, Seth L. "Annotated Bibliography on the Behavioral Characteristics of U.S. Investors." Report Prepared by the Federal Research Division, Library of Congress under an Interagency Agreement with the US Securities and Exchange Commission, August 2010.

Enriques, Luca, and Sergio Gilotta. "Disclosure and Financial Market Regulation." In *The Oxford Handbook on Financial Regulation*, edited by Eilís Ferran, Niamh Moloney, and Jennifer Payne, 511–36. Oxford: Oxford University Press, 2015.

Ernst & Young. "Now Is the Time to Address Disclosure Overload." To the Point 2012-18, June 21, 2012.

"Fed Chairman: Some Small US Banks May Go Under." CNBC with Reuters and AP. February 28, 2008. http://www.cnbc.com/id/23390252.

Fishman, Michael J., and Kathleen M. Hagerty. "Disclosure Decisions by Firms and the Competition for Price Efficiency." *Journal of Finance* 44, no. 3 (1989): 633–46.

Folsom, Burton W., Jr., and Anita Folsom. *Uncle Sam Can't Count: A History of Failed Government Investments, from Beaver Pelts to Green Energy*. New York: HarperCollins, 2014.

Fox, Merritt B. "Retaining Mandatory Securities Disclosure: Why Issuer Choice Is Not Investor Empowerment." *Virginia Law Review* 85, no. 7 (1999): 1335–419.

Franco, Joseph A. "Why Antifraud Provisions Are Not Enough: The Significance of Opportunism, Candor and Signaling in the Economic Case for Mandatory Securities Disclosure." *Columbia Business Law Review*, no. 2 (2002): 223–362.

Gallagher, Daniel M. "Whatever Happened to Promoting Small Business Capital Formation?" September 17, 2014. http://www.heritage.org/events/2014/09/commissioner-gallagher.

Gullapalli, Rachita. "Accredited Investor Pool." Presentation to the Forum on Small Business Capital Formation, Division of Economic and Risk Analysis, US Securities and Exchange Commission, November 20, 2014.

Hayek, Friedrich A. "Economics and Knowledge." *Economica* (February 1937): 33–54.

———. "The Use of Knowledge in Society." *American Economic Review* 34, no. 4 (September 1945): 519–30

———. *Individualism and Economic Order*. Chicago: University of Chicago Press, 1948.

———. "The Pretence of Knowledge." Lecture to the Memory of Alfred Nobel, December 11, 1974.

Healy, Paul M., and Krishna G. Palepu. "Information Asymmetry, Corporate Disclosure, and the Capital Markets: A Review of the Empirical Disclosure Literature." *Journal of Accounting and Economics* 31 (2001): 405–40.

Higgins, Keith F. "Disclosure Effectiveness." Remarks before the American Bar Association Business Law Section Spring Meeting, April 11, 2014.

Himmelberg, Charles P., R. Glenn Hubbard, and Inessa Love. "Investor Protection, Ownership, and the Cost of Capital." World Bank Policy Research Working Paper 2834, World Bank, Washington, DC, 2002.

Hylton, Keith N. "The Theory of Penalties and the Economics of Criminal Law." *Review of Law and Economics* 1, no. 2 (2005): 175–201.

Jensen, Michael C., and William H. Meckling. "Theory of the Firm: Managerial Behavior, Agency Costs and Ownership Structure." *Journal of Financial Economics* 3, no. 4 (1976): 305–60. Reprinted in *Economics of Corporation Law and Securities Regulation*, edited by Kenneth E. Scott and Richard A. Posner. New York: Aspen Publishers, 1980.

Jolls, Christine, Cass R. Sunstein, and Richard Thaler. "A Behavioral Approach to Law and Economics." Faculty Scholarship Series Paper 1765, Yale Law School, 1998.

Kahan, Marcel. "Securities Laws and the Social Cost of 'Inaccurate' Stock Prices." *Duke Law Journal* 41, no. 5 (1992): 977–1044.

Kamar, Ehud, Pinar Karaca-Mandic, and Eric Talley. "Going-Private Decisions and the Sarbanes-Oxley Act of 2002: A Cross-Country Analysis." Working Paper, Kauffman–RAND Institute for Entrepreneurship Public Policy, February 2008.

Karmel, Roberta S. *Regulation by Prosecution: The Securities and Exchange Commission vs. Corporate America*. New York: Simon & Schuster, 1982.

———. "Blue-Sky Merit Regulation: Benefit to Investors or Burden on Commerce?" *Brooklyn Law Review* 53 (1987): 105–25.

Korobkin, Russell B., and Thomas S. Ulen. "Law and Behavioral Science: Removing the Rationality Assumption from Law and Economics." *California Law Review* 88, no. 4 (2000): 1051–144.

Kripke, Homer. *The SEC and Corporate Disclosure: Regulation in Search of a Purpose*. New York: Harcourt Brace Jovanovich, 1979.

Langevoort, Donald C., and Robert B. Thompson. "'Publicness' in Contemporary Securities Regulation after the JOBS Act." *Georgetown Law Journal* 101 (2013): 337–86.

Leuz, Christian, and Peter D. Wysocki. "Economic Consequences of Financial Reporting and Disclosure Regulation: A Review and Suggestions for Future Research." Working Paper, Social Science Research Network, March 2008.

Lewis, Craig M. "The Future of Capital Formation." Chief Economist and Director of the Division of Economic and Risk Analysis, MIT Sloan School of Management's Center for Finance and Policy's Distinguished Speaker Series, April 15, 2014.

Liu, Tingting, Barkat Ullah, Zuobao Wei, and Lixin Colin Xu. "The Dark Side of Disclosure: Evidence of Government Expropriation from Worldwide Firms." World Bank Policy Research Working Paper 7254, World Bank, Washington, DC, May 2015.

Lynch, Sarah N. "Two States Sue U.S. SEC over JOBS Act Public Offer Rules." *Reuters*, May 26, 2015. http://www.reuters.com/article/2015/05/27/sec-states-lawsuit-idUSL1N0YH0VR20150527.

Macey, Jonathan R., and Geoffrey P. Miller. "Origin of the Blue Sky Laws." *Texas Law Review* 70, no. 2 (1991): 347–97.

Mahoney, Paul G. "Mandatory Disclosure as a Solution to Agency Problems." *University of Chicago Law Review* 62, no. 3 (1995): 1047–112.

———. "The Origins of the Blue Sky Laws: A Test of Competing Hypotheses." UVA Law and Economics Research Paper 01-11, University of Virginia, December 2001.

———. *Wasting a Crisis: Why Securities Regulation Fails*. Chicago: University of Chicago Press, 2015.

Manne, Henry G., and James S. Mofsky. "What Price Blue Sky: State Securities Laws Work against Private and Public Interest Alike." In *The Collected Works of Henry G. Manne*, vol. 3, edited by Fred S. McChesney, 84–93. Indianapolis, IN: Liberty Fund, 1996.

Maynard, Therese H. "The Future of California's Blue Sky Law." *Loyola of Los Angeles Law Review* 30 (1997): 1531–56.

Mclean, R. David, Tianyu Zhang, and Mengxin Zhao. "Why Does the Law Matter? Investor Protection and Its Effects on Investment, Finance, and Growth." *Journal of Finance* 67, no. 1 (2012): 313–50.

Meoli, Michele, Katrin Migliorati, Stefano Paleari, and Silvio Vismara. "The Cost of Going Public: A European Perspective." *International Journal of Economics and Management Engineering* 2, no. 2 (May 2012): 1–10.

Michaels, Dave. "Democrats Pressure SEC to Force Disclosure of Political Spending." *Bloomberg*, August 31, 2015. http://www.bloomberg.com/politics/articles/2015-08-31/democrats-pressure-sec-to-force-disclosure-of-political-spending.

Mofsky, James S. *Blue Sky Restrictions on New Business Promotions*. New York: Matthew Bender & Company, 1971.

Mofsky, James S., and Robert D. Tollison. "Demerit in Merit Regulation." *Marquette Law Review* 60 (1977): 367–78.

Monga, Vipal, and Emily Chasan. "The 109,894-Word Annual Report: As Regulators Require More Disclosures, 10-Ks Reach Epic Lengths; How Much Is Too Much?" *Wall Street Journal*, June 1, 2015. http://blogs.wsj.com/cfo/2015/06/02/the-109894-word-annual-report/.

North American Securities Administrators Association. "Application for Coordinated Review of Regulation A Offering." http://www.nasaa.org/industry-resources/corporation-finance/coordinated-review/regulation-a-offerings/.

O'Donoghue, Ted, and Matthew Rabin. "Studying Optimal Paternalism, Illustrated by a Model of Sin Taxes." *American Economic Association Papers & Proceedings* (May 2003): 186–91.

O'Hara, Maureen, and David Easley. "Information and the Cost of Capital." *Journal of Finance* 59, no. 4 (August, 2004): 1555–83.

Pack, Howard, and Kamal Saggi. "The Case for Industrial Policy: A Critical Survey." World Bank Policy Research Working Paper 3839, World Bank, Washington, DC, February 2006.

Paredes, Troy A. "Blinded by the Light: Information Overload and Its Consequences for Securities Regulation." *Washington University Law Quarterly* 81 (2003): 417–85.

———. "Remarks at The SEC Speaks in 2013." Washington, DC, February 22, 2013.

PAX Ellevate Management LLC, Request for Rulemaking, File No.4-696, February 1, 2016. https://www.sec.gov/rules/petitions/2016/petn4-696.pdf.

Peirce, William S. *Bureaucratic Failure and Public Expenditure*. New York: Academic Press, 1981.

Phillips, Richard M., and Morgan Shipman. "An Analysis of the Securities Acts Amendments of 1964." *Duke Law Journal* (1964): 706–845.

Phillips, Susan M., and J. Richard Zecher. *The SEC and the Public Interest*. Cambridge, MA: MIT Press, 1981.

Posner, Richard A. "An Economic Theory of the Criminal Law." *Columbia Law Review* 85 (1985): 1193–231.

———. "Financial Markets." In *Economic Analysis of the Law*, 9th ed. New York: Wolters Kluwer Law & Business, 2014.

Prentice, Robert A. "The Economic Value of Securities Regulation." *Cardozo Law Review* 28, no. 1 (2006): 333–89.

Quandl. 2012 World Bank Market Capitalization Data. https://www.quandl.com/c/economics/stock-market-capitalization-by-country.

"Regulation Is Good for Goldman." *Wall Street Journal*, February 11, 2015. http://www.wsj.com/articles/regulation-is-good-for-goldman-1423700859.

Romano, Roberta. "Empowering Investors: A Market Approach to Securities Regulation." *Yale Law Journal* 107 (1998): 2359–430.

———. *The Advantage of Competitive Federalism for Securities Regulation.* Washington, DC: AEI Press, 2002.

———. "Regulating in the Dark and a Postscript Assessment of the Iron Law of Financial Regulation." *Hofstra Law Review* 43 (2014): 25–93.

Roszkowski, Michael J., and John E. Grable. "Evidence of Lower Risk Tolerance among Public Sector Employees in their Personal Financial Matters." *Journal of Occupational and Organizational Psychology* 82, no. 2 (June 2009): 453–63.

Rubin, Paul H., and Martin J. Bailey. "The Role of Lawyers in Changing the Law." *Journal of Legal Studies* 23, no. 2 (1994): 807–31.

Rustin, Richard E., and Mitchell C. Lynch. "Apple Computer Set to Go Public Today: Massachusetts Bars Sale of Stock as Risky." *Wall Street Journal,* December 12, 1980, 5.

Sargent, Mark A. "A Future for Blue Sky." *University of Cincinnati Law Review* 62 (1993): 471–512.

Schuck, Peter. *Why Government Fails So Often and How It Can Do Better.* Princeton, NJ: Princeton University Press, 2014.

Schwartz, Jeff. "The Law and Economics of Scaled Equity Market Disclosure." *Journal of Corporation Law* 39 (2014): 347–94.

"SEC Action on Corporate Political Spending Disclosure." Letter to SEC Chair Mary Jo White, December 22, 2015. http://www.menendez.senate.gov/imo/media/doc/Letter%20to%20 SEC%20on%20omnibus%20provision%202015-12-22%20FINAL1.pdf.

Seligman, Joel. "The Historical Need for a Mandatory Corporate Disclosure System." *Journal of Corporation Law* 9, no. 1 (1983): 1–61. Reprinted in *Selected Articles on Federal Securities Law,* edited by F. E. Gill. Chicago: American Bar Association Section of Business Law, 1991.

Shughart, William F. "Public Choice." In *Concise Encyclopedia of Economics,* edited by David R. Henderson, 427–30. Indianapolis, IN: Liberty Fund, 2007.

Stein, Kara M. "Remarks before the Consumer Federation of America's 27th Annual Financial Services Conference." Washington, DC, December 4, 2014.

Stigler, George J. "Public Regulation of the Securities Markets." *Business Lawyer* 19, no. 3 (April 1964): 721–53.

———. "The Theory of Economic Regulation." *Bell Journal of Economics and Management Science* 2, no. 1 (1971): 3–21.

Sunstein, Cass R., and Richard H. Thaler. "Libertarian Paternalism Is Not an Oxymoron." *University of Chicago Law Review* 70 (2003): 1166–87.

Thaler, Richard H., and Cass R. Sunstein. "Libertarian Paternalism." *American Economic Association Papers & Proceedings* (May 2003): 175–79.

Tullock, Gordon, Authur Seldon, and Gordon L. Brady. *Government Failure: A Primer in Public Choice.* Washington, DC: Cato Institute, 2002.

US Government Accountability Office. "Factors That May Affect Trends in Regulation A Offerings." GAO-12-839. Washington, DC, July 2012.

US Securities and Exchange Commission. "Revision of Certain Exemptions from Registration for Transactions Involving Limited Offers and Sales" (Release No. 33-6389), 47 Fed. Reg. (March 16, 1982): 11251.

———. "Report on the Uniformity of State Regulatory Requirements for Offerings of Securities That Are Not 'Covered Securities.'" October 11, 1997.

———. "Rule 504 of Regulation D." Retrieved October 31, 2016. https://www.sec.gov/answers /rule504.htm.

———. "Rule 505 of Regulation D." Retrieved October 31, 2016, https://www.sec.gov/answers /rule505.htm.

US Securities and Exchange Commission Investor Advisory Committee. Minutes of May 17, 2010 meeting.

Walker, Gordon. "Securities Regulation, Efficient Markets and Behavioural Finance: Reclaiming the Legal Genealogy." *Hong Kong Law Journal* 36, no. 3 (2006): 481–517.

Wan, Amy. "Progress Report: Looking at Regulation A+ One Year Later." *Crowdfund Insider*, July 11, 2016. http://www.crowdfundinsider.com/2016/07/87745-looking-regulation-one -year-later/.

Welsh, Heidi, and Michael Passoff. "Proxy Preview 2016." http://www.proxypreview.org/proxy -preview-2016/.

White, Michelle J. "Legal Complexity and Lawyers' Benefit from Litigation." *International Review of Law and Economics* 12, no. 3 (1992): 381–95.

Whitman, Glen. "Against the New Paternalism: Internalities and the Economics of Self-Control." Cato Institute Policy Analysis 563, Washington, DC, February 22, 2006.

Winston, Clifford. *Government Failure versus Market Failure: Microeconomics Policy Research and Government Performance.* Washington, DC: American Enterprise Institute and the Brookings Institution, 2006.

Woodward, Susan E. "Regulatory Capture and the U.S. Securities and Exchange Commission." In *Restructuring Regulation and Financial Institutions*, edited by James R. Barth, R. Dan Brumbaugh, and Glenn Yago, 99–117. New York: Springer, 2001.

World Bank. "Market Capitalization of Listed Companies (% of GDP)." 2012 data. http://data .worldbank.org/indicator/CM.MKT.LCAP.GD.ZS.

Wurgler, Jeffrey. "Financial Markets and the Allocation of Capital." *Journal of Financial Economics* 58, no. 187 (2000): 187–214.

Zecher, J. Richard. "An Economic Perspective of SEC Corporate Disclosure." *Journal of Comparative Business and Capital Market Law* 7, no. 3 (1985): 307–15.

PART 4

REGULATING CONSUMER FINANCE

CHAPTER 12
Market-Reinforcing versus Market-Replacing Consumer Finance Regulation

TODD J. ZYWICKI

Antonin Scalia Law School, George Mason University

The run-up to and aftermath of the financial crisis that began around 2008 produced a wave of new consumer financial protection regulations and institutions unique in recent American history in terms of their combined impact on consumers and the economy. From credit cards and mortgages to payday loans and debt collectors, the regulatory regime that came into being in the wake of the financial crisis has directly impacted every corner of consumer financial services and indirectly impacted millions of small businesses that rely on their founders' personal credit for financing.

But while the details of the current wave of regulatory institutions and initiatives created in the postcrisis era are new, the ideas that underlie them are not. Indeed, the most recent wave of regulation is just the latest in the cycle of history of the regulation of consumer credit in the United States. Command-and-control regulation of consumer finance from prior eras was abandoned when economists and policymakers came to realize that those regulations tended to harm those they were purportedly intended to benefit. In the short

319

time since the financial crisis, the new regulatory regime is already having the same effect. Regulation has dried up access to financial services for millions of low-income Americans, driving them out of the mainstream financial system and into less-preferred alternatives. While the particular initiatives and institutions have changed, the underlying economics of consumer credit and its regulation have not. Thus, there is no reason to believe that the end results of this episode of regulation will be any different from those in the past—higher prices, less innovation, less competition, and worse outcomes for consumers.

The lessons of history suggest that the command-and-control regulatory approach of the postcrisis era is likely doomed to failure as its negative consequences for consumers and the economy come to be better understood. But this collapse of old-style regulation also presents an opportunity for a new, modern approach to consumer financial protection to take its place. Developments in technology have transformed consumer finance, from credit cards to payday loans to debt collection practices, making consumer products safer, more secure, more convenient, and more innovative than ever before. In recent decades, consumer finance has exploded as a national market and consumers have come to expect twenty-four-hour, instantaneous, secure access to bank accounts and credit anywhere in the world (even the most remote areas), on demand. Yet today's regulators persist in trying to impose an early-twentieth-century regulatory mindset on this flourishing Internet-age consumer finance system.

This chapter offers a new way forward. The premise is that the basic mindset that has characterized the postcrisis era is little more than new wine in old wineskins—the basic ideas have been tried, and failed, before. And from those failures it is possible to anticipate why they are unlikely to be more successful this time than in the past. At the same time, developments in technology and market competition provide a greater opportunity than ever to construct a regulatory regime that will serve consumers and the economy, promoting choice, competition, and innovation.

I will distinguish between two basic regulatory approaches to consumer credit: "market-replacing" regulation, on one hand, versus "market-reinforcing" regulation, on the other. Market-replacing regulatory strategies seek to limit choice and competition through prohibitions or restrictions on particular products and terms, such as price controls on interest rates (known as usury regulations) or de facto or de jure bans on particular products such as payday loans or bank deposit advance products. Market-replacing regulations are characterized by a decision by regulators or legislatures to replace the terms to which the parties would voluntarily bargain with terms dictated by the regulator, and to prohibit consumers from entering into certain contracts even if those consumers believe that purchasing that product furthers their own goals. A market-reinforcing regulatory strategy, by contrast, seeks to promote competition and choice so that consumers can find those products that they think are best for themselves and their families. Whereas market-replacing regulation limits the range of choices available to consumers or favors some options over others, market-reinforcing regulation generally assumes that individual choice is a given and consumers generally know their personal needs better than regulators, so it seeks to promote innovation and consumer choice in order to facilitate discovery of those products that best suit consumers' needs.[1]

WHAT IS THE CURRENT REGULATORY APPROACH?

The history of the regulation of consumer credit has been dominated by the market-replacing approach. While the use of credit is ancient (it appears that credit was used extensively in early agricultural settlements, for example, to deal with the seasonal nature of farming), regulation of credit is ancient as well. Laws (both political and religious) date back to at least the Code of Hammurabi (1750 BC), which limited interest charges to 33.3 percent on loans of grain repayable in-kind and 20 percent on loans of silver.[2] While the Code of Hammurabi appears to be the first recorded evidence of interest rate price controls it certainly was not the last—since that time, market-replacing regulation, usually in the form of interest rate ceilings, has been ubiquitous, including for most of the history of the United States.

The Long History of Substantive Regulation

Several arguments have been advanced over time to support interest rate ceilings and prohibitions or limits on other terms.[3] In general, however, they boil down to two basic arguments. First, consumer credit contracts are "contracts of adhesion" in which a lender is posited to have monopoly power and the consumer, with unequal bargaining power, is "forced" into the terms of the contract on a "take it or leave it" basis. This is especially the case for avowedly unsophisticated or desperate parties who are thought to be particularly prone to exploitation. For example, in earlier eras, supporters of regulation argued that retailers preyed on "math-impaired females," who supposedly were unable to understand the full cost of the credit that they were using. Second, consumers are thought to lack self-control and be able to be "goaded" into purchasing products that they cannot afford and thus use credit to try to live beyond their means. For example, the theory of "conspicuous consumption" developed by economist Thorsten Veblen in the nineteenth century pointed to consumer credit as one of the drivers of the conspicuous consumption race. Today, the modern theories of behavioral economics have been used to update this argument, drawing on purported biases such as the problem of "hyperbolic discounting" or other cognitive biases that lead consumers to spend excessively today and to therefore save insufficient amounts of money for the future.

Although frequently used interchangeably as rationales for regulation, these two theories generate different predictions about the patterns of the supply and demand of consumer credit. Under the first rationale, regulation is seen as a mechanism for constraining purported monopoly power by lenders that can enable lenders to extract monopoly rents from consumers. In that case, regulation is seen as a way of reducing prices to consumers, but it is thought that there would be little or no restriction in the supply of credit made available to consumers. Under the second theory, however, it is anticipated that usury restrictions will in fact have the effect of reducing the availability of certain high-cost credit products. In some instances this is seen as a desired effect, as restricting access to high-cost credit is a way of protecting poor consumers from exploitation by so-called predatory lenders offering high-cost credit products.

Economic analysis has rejected the first hypothesis that consumer lenders exercise monopoly power over borrowers and thus can dictate the terms of consumer credit, including interest rates.[4] The real interest rates on consumer credit are set by market forces of supply and demand, not by regulation. Thus, contrary to that theory, unregulated interest rates do *not* tend to rise to the maximum rate permitted by law (unless the maximum rate is set very low), but instead are readily explicable by standard economic forces such as default risk, cost of funds, and other costs of operations.[5] Where usury ceilings are binding, by contrast, higher-risk borrowers are typically rationed out of the market, which suggests that there are real economic effects from imposing a price ceiling at a rate below the equilibrium price.[6] There is also no evidence that lenders earn permanent monopoly returns on consumer credit operations where entry is allowed, although certain types of regulation can artificially segment markets and dampen competition among providers.[7]

Interest rate ceilings are binding, however, when the market price of credit as established by the forces of supply and demand exceeds the statutorily permitted interest rate ceiling. A detailed discussion of interest rate ceilings and their impact is presented in chapter 13. For current purposes, however, usury laws provide a prototypical example of market-replacing regulation that can be applied to any regulation of specific terms of consumer loan contracts. Thus, economic studies of usury regulations are relied on here to illustrate the nature of market-replacing regulation and why this long-standing approach to regulation fell into intellectual disrepute until reinvigorated by the postcrisis regulatory environment.

Market-replacing substantive regulations of terms and products will have their intended effect but will also have several unintended consequences. The intended effects are usually easy to predict: if interest rates are capped at a certain rate—say, 10 percent—then lenders subject to the law cannot legally lend at a rate above 10 percent.

On the other hand, for lenders to be willing to make a loan, they must be able to do two things—to accurately set the price and other terms to reflect the predicted riskiness of the loan, and if they cannot, to reduce their risk exposure by either making loans to fewer people (especially excluding higher-risk borrowers) or by lending less to the same people (such as by reducing credit lines). Unintended consequences of the regulation of consumer credit can have three basic effects and frequently a fourth effect: (1) term repricing, (2) product substitution, (3) rationing, and in many cases (4) dynamic competitive effects. Consider each in turn.

First, term repricing (sometimes called "circumvention") describes the process by which borrowers and lenders agree to adjust some terms of the contract to offset the regulations on other terms of the contract in order to make the loan feasible. Because the price of a consumer loan is set by supply and demand, politicians cannot change the total price of a loan, just the combination of price and nonprice terms. For example, in the high-interest rate periods of the 1970s, when usury ceilings on credit cards were binding constraints, card issuers imposed annual fees on credit cards to make up for the inability to charge a market rate of interest on credit card loans. Thus, unsurprisingly, when credit card interest rates were effectively deregulated by the Supreme Court's decision in Marquette National Bank v. First of Omaha Service Corporation,[8] interest rates were permitted to be set at market rates and annual fees for standard credit cards quickly disappeared.[9] For loans other than credit cards, where interest rates are subject to binding interest rate caps, other terms of the contract may also be adjusted, such as requiring a higher down payment, artificially extending the maturity of the loan, requiring the borrower to post collateral, or requiring the borrower to borrow a greater sum of money so as to reduce the measured interest rate on the loan. Thus, while a borrower who receives a loan does so at a lower interest rate than would otherwise be the case, she will likely confront other less-desirable terms on other elements of the loan, such as being forced to borrow more money than she desires, thereby increasing her risk of default. Moreover, the effect is not limited just to interest rates—for example, when useful debt-collection remedies are restricted, which will increase the risk of lending and the expected loss rate on loans, lenders will offset that heightened risk by increasing interest rates, down payments, and other terms to compensate for the increased risk of loss. The effect of term repricing, therefore, will be to limit the stated price of the loan to the borrower but it will not affect the total cost of the loan to the borrower, as other terms of the loan will be adjusted to offset the parties' inability to contract for their preferred terms with respect to interest rates, down payments, loan size, and so on.

Second, if the borrower and lender are unable to effectively reprice the terms of the loan to offset the inability to contract at their preferred terms, some borrowers will be unable to obtain their preferred types of credit and will be forced to use alternatives, an adjustment known as "product substitution." Thus, for example, when strict regulation of credit card interest rates made it impossible for many consumers to acquire general-purpose bank-type cards and other unsecured credit, borrowers and lenders substituted and made greater use of other types of products instead, such as pawn shops and retail store credit. In many states, pawn shops traditionally have been regulated under a different set of rules than unsecured credit that often permit pawnbrokers to charge higher rates of interest. Thus, consumers who could not be approved for credit cards or could not gain a sufficient line of credit to meet their needs instead turned to pawnbrokers to fill the gap. Moreover, whereas credit card issuers could impose annual fees on credit cards to make up for their losses, pawnbrokers could reduce the amount they agreed to pay for pawned goods, thereby providing a more effective means of circumventing usury limits (where applicable). Department stores were also barred by usury ceilings from charging high prices on their credit programs, thus they typically ran their credit operations at a loss to subsidize their retail operations. But they were able to recoup those losses by raising the price of the goods that they sold, especially items such as appliances, which were typically sold on credit, thereby giving them a comparative advantage in circumventing usury limits.[10] For example, according to a 1979 study by economists William Dunkelberg and Robin De Magistris, in states with very low usury ceilings (Arkansas in their case) retailers originated a much larger percentage of consumer credit transactions (as opposed to banks and finance companies) than in states with less-restrictive usury ceilings.[11] Thus, because some providers of credit (such as pawnbrokers and retailers) either were not bound by the same usury ceiling or were able to evade usury restrictions more easily than others (such as credit card issuers) consumers would substitute those alternative types of credit for their preferred types of credit.

Third, even after these other adjustments, some consumers would find themselves unable to obtain legal credit on any terms. This led to the problem of credit-rationing—not being able to obtain legal credit at all. Reducing the supply of credit, however, did not eliminate the demand, especially for higher-risk borrowers. Thus, where consumer credit regulations were most severe, illegal loan sharks arose to meet that demand.[12] Even if consumers do not turn to loan sharks, however, they will still face the hardship associated with lack of access to financial services—bounced checks, late bill payments, lack of wealth-building potential, and the inability to acquire goods and services that can improve their lives.

Fourth, by prompting all of these adjustments in response to the distorting effects of substantive restrictions on lending terms, the total effect of usury restrictions was to make the terms of consumer credit products more complicated and less transparent. As a result, it became more difficult for consumers to compare across products and balkanized markets by erecting a series of ad hoc regulations designed to address particular evasions that arose with respect to particular products. Consider, for example, the practice of charging an annual fee on a credit card as a response to the inability to charge a market rate of interest. Not only does that substitution make both the borrower and lender worse off by forcing them to depart from their preferred set of lending terms, the presence of an annual fee functions as a sort of "tax" on holding a credit card. Thus, rather than a consumer holding several credit cards at any given time that are all competing for his business, if he is required to pay an annual fee he is likely to only carry one credit card and consider switching each year only at the time the annual fee is to be paid.

Similarly, by reducing the comparative advantage of retailers in engaging in term repricing behavior through raising the price of the goods that they sell, deregulation of consumer credit terms also eliminated the competitive advantage that large department stores held over smaller retailers because of their superior ability to bear the cost and risk of maintaining an in-house credit operation.[13] Deregulation of interest rates, therefore, not only prompted greater competition in consumer credit markets but in retail markets as well, enabling smaller (and eventually online) retailers to compete directly with large department stores without having to maintain costly credit operations.

Finally, although these regulations usually were supposedly intended to benefit low-income people, they invariably had a regressive distributional effect. For example, to the extent that interest rate ceilings rationed some people out of the market for legal credit, it was the higher-risk borrowers— who are disproportionately younger and have lower incomes—who were excluded. Indeed, by drying up the supply of lending capital to higher-risk borrowers, usury restrictions might have actually diverted capital to lower-risk markets, resulting in a higher supply and lower prices for middle- and high-income borrowers at the expense of low-income borrowers.[14]

The Rise of Disclosure Regulation

Over time, therefore, a consensus emerged that the costs of substantive, market-replacing regulation—especially the recurrent dangers of loan-sharking— exceeded the benefits to consumers and the market.[15] Thus, beginning in the 1960s, economists and regulators began to consider a different approach to consumer credit regulation—disclosure-based regulation. As first embodied in the Truth in Lending Act (TILA), disclosure-based regulation was an effort to implement a market-reinforcing approach to consumer credit regulation.[16] Rather than fixing prices or other terms of consumer credit contracts, the architects of TILA sought to harness the beneficial effects of market competition for the benefit of consumers. Rather than paternalistically seeking to protect consumers from themselves, TILA largely rested on the idea that individuals were the best judge of their own needs, preferences, and circumstances and that the most effective use of regulation would be to facilitate the provision of information from competing lenders in standardized and simplified formats that will enable consumers to compare competing credit offers.

More recently, however, this view of TILA has been eroded through excessive disclosure as the result of litigation and regulations that have piled more and more disclosures on consumers.[17] Consumers today are overwhelmed by pages and pages of disclosures mandated by regulation or provided defensively out of fear of litigation for failure to disclose a salient term. In addition, disclosures suffer from the creep of substantive regulation into disclosure regulation—a sort of "normative disclosure" whereby politicians and regulators require disclosure of terms that they believe consumers *should* care about, even if they do not.[18] "Normative disclosure" reflects a temptation to try to mold consumer decision-making through the use of disclosures, rather than heavy-handed substantive regulation. In so doing, however, regulators have stripped away the focus of the original market-reinforcing goal of TILA, producing a jumble of disclosure and substantive regulation.

Consider, for example, the requirement that each credit card statement prominently include a calculation of how long it would take consumers to pay off their credit card balance if they make only the minimum monthly payment. Providing this information to consumers in the form of a mandatory disclosure in every monthly statement is expensive for both card issuers and consumers—given the limited space and attention span available for consumers, there are myriad different pieces of information that an issuer could provide in that prominent location on the consumer's statement each month that instead is occupied with a particular disclosure. Yet based on research by former Federal Reserve economist Thomas Durkin, it appears that no more than 4 percent of consumers would find that information to actually be useful to their behavior, as that represents the percentage of consumers who would consider paying off their credit cards by making only the minimum monthly payment and, importantly, would also be willing to stop using the credit card while paying off the balance (because any new charges would, of course, change the payoff time).[19] Given the low percentage of consumers who actually care about this piece of information, the requirement that it be disclosed each month on every cardholder's statement more likely reflects the political sense of what consumers *should* care about and an effort to try to shape consumer behavior, rather than simply trying to provide consumers with the terms and information that they need in order to make their decisions.

WHAT IS WRONG WITH THE CURRENT APPROACH?

The period since the financial crisis has witnessed a resurgence of a belief in substantive, market-replacing regulation, as regulators have begun to again dictate terms and to prohibit certain terms and products. And, unfortunately, as they resuscitate discredited regulatory strategies, they are again reaping the predictable sorrows that invariably follow in their wake.

Consider the effect of recent restrictions on credit card pricing. In May 2008, the Federal Reserve Board proposed new rules that regulated credit card contract terms; the rules became final in December 2008, although those new rules were not scheduled to go into effect until July 1, 2010. In 2009, however, the US Congress passed the Credit Card Accountability, Responsibility, and Disclosure Act of 2009 (the CARD Act),[20] which legislated many of the terms of the Fed's regulation, thereby superseding the Fed's action. In August 2010 the Federal Reserve issued its rules implementing the CARD Act. Thus, even though the final regulations were not implemented until August 2010, banks were aware by May 2008 at the latest (and presumably by 2007 or early 2008) of pending regulation governing credit card terms.

Both the Federal Reserve's regulations and the CARD Act significantly limit the flexibility of credit card issuers to adjust the terms of the agreement when a consumer's risk changes. For example, except for introductory rates and variable rate cards, issuers are required to provide forty-five days' notice before increasing interest rates and fees and are prohibited from increasing interest rates on existing balances unless the account falls deeply in arrears. Moreover, such rate increases must be reevaluated every six months. The rules also limit the size of the fees that can be assessed relative to the issuer's cost. These provisions limit the ability to adjust card pricing based on a consumer's observed risk.

As expected, the Federal Reserve's regulations and the CARD Act did in fact have the intended effect of limiting the size of the fees that were subjected to new regulation under the law.[21] But analysis has also generally found that interest rates, annual fees, and other fees (such as cash-advance fees) increased after the Federal Reserve regulations and CARD Act went into effect. In addition, the introduction of new rules that limited the ability to engage in risk-based pricing had the expected effect of reducing access to credit card credit, both by reducing total credit lines outstanding but, even more, reducing access to credit cards for lower-income (and generally higher-risk) borrowers. In turn, those who lost access to credit cards presumably had to turn to alternative types of credit that are more expensive, such as payday loans, personal installment loans, or other types of credit. Thus while some consumers benefited as a result of the CARD Act—namely, those who otherwise would have paid fees for exceeding their credit limits or incurring other fees—other consumers were harmed by paying higher interest rates or higher annual fees or by losing access to credit cards altogether and being forced to turn to alternative, more expensive credit.

A second example of the negative unintended consequences of the current regulatory approach is the effects of the so-called Durbin Amendment to Dodd-Frank Wall Street Reform and Consumer Protection Act, which imposed price controls on the interchange fees that could be charged on debit cards issued by larger banks (with more than $10 billion in assets).[22] Interchange fees are part of the "merchant discount" fee that is paid by merchants when they accept a payment card to complete a transaction to compensate the bank issuing the card to the consumer. Prior to Dodd-Frank, interchange fees on debit cards were set by market forces. The result was that debit cards rapidly became one of the most popular and quickly adopted consumer banking innovations in American history.

Debit card usage soared during the decade of the 2000s, rapidly displacing checks in terms of consumer (and merchant) popularity and passing credit cards as well by mid-decade.[23] Perhaps more important, as a result of the growing popularity of debit cards and the interchange fee revenues they generated, banks were able to extend to consumers greater access to free checking accounts, to reduce other bank fees and the minimum balances necessary to gain access to free checking, and to make major quality investments in retail banking services such as the development of online and mobile banking products. Between 2001 and 2009, for example, access to free checking rose dramatically, from less than 10 percent of all bank accounts to 76 percent of all bank accounts. In turn, this expansion of access to free checking expanded financial inclusion, bringing into the mainstream financial system millions of consumers who historically had been unable to afford a bank account.

The imposition of the Durbin Amendment, however, reversed these trends, with particularly harsh consequences for low-income consumers. The Durbin Amendment provided that any interchange fee for a debit card issued by a covered bank is required to be "reasonable and proportional to the cost incurred by the issuer with respect to the transaction" plus a small addition for fraud losses. The primary effect of the rule, therefore, is to permit issuers to recover interchange fees tied to consumer transactions but not to enable recovery of fixed and other operating costs, such as the cost of acquiring consumers, bank branches, customer service, or card issuance. As implemented by the subsequent Federal Reserve rulemaking, the end effect of the Durbin Amendment was to cut the interchange fee per transaction approximately in half with an estimated total loss of $8.5 billion in annual interchange fee revenue.[24]

The Durbin Amendment had its intended effect of reducing the interchange fees paid by merchants who choose to accept payment cards by billions of dollars annually, but the bulk of the savings flowed to very large merchants, such as big-box retailers, department stores, and Amazon.com. In fact, there is no evidence that small and medium-sized merchants experienced any savings in the period following the Durbin Amendment, and many merchants who process many small-dollar transactions actually experienced an increase in the size of the fees that they paid. But while the Durbin Amendment reduced the amount paid by merchants to support the payment card network, those costs did not disappear. Instead, they were simply shifted in the first instance over to card issuers and then, as would be predicted in a highly competitive market such as retail banking, on to consumers.

A study by Zywicki, Manne, and Morris on the effects of the Durbin Amendment found that while the per-transaction and total interchange fees paid by merchants declined following the Durbin Amendment's enactment, those revenue losses were simply shifted on to consumers in the form of higher bank fees and loss of access to free checking.[25] Access to free checking fell from 76 percent of bank accounts in the immediate pre-Durbin period (2009) to only 38 percent by 2013. Moreover, this decline in free checking was experienced *only* at larger banks subjected to the Durbin Amendment—smaller banks did not reduce access to free checking and may have actually increased it (by some measures). In addition, monthly maintenance fees for non-free checking accounts increased dramatically, and did so in the period immediately following the enactment of the Durbin Amendment. Other bank fees and the mandatory minimum balance necessary to gain access to free checking rose dramatically as well.

Most tragic, the higher bank fees and reduced access to free checking caused by the Durbin Amendment reversed many of the gains in access to bank accounts experienced by low-income consumers in the preceding decade. According to the Federal Deposit Insurance Corporation, between 2009 and 2011 the number of unbanked consumers increased by one million.[26] While a number of factors might have contributed to this increase in the number of unbanked households, the increase in bank fees and loss of free checking caused by the Durbin Amendment presumably contributed. Moreover, because of the increase in the minimum balances necessary to maintain free checking, many low-income consumers who maintained bank accounts were now forced to pay monthly maintenance fees or saw the size of those and other fees increase. In addition, banks terminated rewards programs and other perks offered on debit cards, thereby reducing their quality and attractiveness to consumers.

At the same time, while large merchants saved billions of dollars as a result of the Durbin Amendment, there is no evidence that any of these cost savings were passed through to consumers in the form of lower prices or higher quality. As a result, Zywicki, Manne, and Morris estimate that the overall effect of the Durbin Amendment is a wealth transfer of approximately $1 billion to $3 billion per year to large retailers and their shareholders. Moreover, these costs were almost entirely regressive—higher-income consumers were either able to avoid the impact of higher bank fees by increasing the size of their minimum balances or using other bank services or simply shifted their purchase volume from debit cards to credit cards, for which interchange fees remained unregulated and for which rewards remained in effect.[27]

As these examples illustrate, the trend in recent years back toward market-replacing regulation in the form of the substantive regulation of the terms and conditions of consumer credit products is having effects identical to past efforts. Regulation of some terms, such as the ability to adjust interest rates or fees on credit cards in response to changing consumer risk, simply led to the repricing of other fees, such as higher interest rates for all consumers. In addition, interfering with the ability to price risk efficiently has led to a reduction in access to credit cards, especially for low-income consumers, forcing them to substitute and to rely more heavily on alternative products such as payday lending that are typically more expensive and less preferred by consumers. Finally, to the extent that regulators are increasingly taking away access to those products, such as by restricting access to payday loans, this in turn is pushing consumers further down the pecking order to still less-desirable alternatives and further out of the mainstream financial system. It is difficult to see how this process of systematically restricting choices for those who already have limited choices is a strategy that is likely to benefit low-income consumers.

These detailed examples are only illustrative. The return of market-replacing regulation that mandates, prohibits, or limits certain substantive terms of consumer credit contracts is becoming more aggressive. For example, in 2015 alone the Bureau of Consumer Financial Protection (CFPB) announced a proposal that would impose new underwriting requirements on all short-term credit products (such as payday and auto title loans), a proposal that is predicted to reduce the revenues of payday lenders by 82 percent, driving most small lenders out of the market and thereby reducing competition and consumer choice.[28] The CFPB's Qualified Mortgage and Ability-to-Repay rules governing residential mortgages, which dictate the terms of purportedly safe mortgages, are driving many community banks out of the mortgage market, thereby reducing competition and consumer choice.[29] And finally, in October 2015 the CFPB announced a preliminary proposal that would prohibit enforcement of provisions in consumer credit contracts that require arbitration and limit consumer access to class actions.[30] In each situation, the CFPB has intervened to impose substantive limits on contract terms and products without any tangible showing of consumer harm or lack of capacity to understand the relevant terms.

TOWARD A MARKET-REINFORCING APPROACH TO CONSUMER CREDIT

Given the centuries of evidence that market-replacing regulation of consumer credit products does not work and actually tends to harm those it is supposedly intended to help, it is time for a new approach to the regulation of consumer credit. Such an approach can be referred to as a market-reinforcing approach to consumer credit regulation.

But it must be stressed that a true market-reinforcing approach to consumer credit regulation is not simply a return to disclosure-based regulation. The criticisms of disclosure-based regulation are well taken—in particular that disclosures are not well tailored to meet the particular needs of consumers. Instead, disclosure-based regulation inevitably tended toward the production of long, prolix, complicated disclosures written primarily to placate regulators and to avoid class-action litigation. Risk-averse regulators and financial institutions have felt it safer to "err on the side of disclosure," disclosing all terms and conditions in excruciating detail, rather than risking a failure to disclose some term in sufficient detail that might later give rise to the claim by a class-action lawyer that a salient term was not disclosed properly or fully. Thus, while disclosure regulation was generally preferable to substantive regulation of terms and products, it was still not truly consumer- and competition-centered, as it failed to take into account how consumers actually make decisions and how markets actually work.

Disclosure regulation also suffers from a second problem. As with any other bureaucratic system, once particular disclosures are mandated by legislation or regulation they are frozen in place and are difficult to update or modify as market conditions change. Consider, for example, the so-called Schumer Box, which imposes a requirement that all credit card offers highlight certain terms and conditions that regulators considered (at the time) to be especially important for consumers to know. While some of the terms that must be prominently disclosed may (or may not) have been important at the time Schumer Box disclosures were mandated, many of them are largely irrelevant today or relevant only to very few consumers. For example, virtually every credit card charges a "minimum interest charge" of $0.50. In addition, only a small number of consumers take cash advances on their credit cards, yet the Schumer Box requires disclosure of the cash-advance fee at the time of applying for a card. By mandating disclosure of terms that are irrelevant for most consumers, mandated disclosure requirements tend to overload consumers and make it more difficult for them to actually find and focus on the terms that are most relevant and important to them.

The failure of disclosure regulation to accomplish its intended purposes has led some analysts to draw a different—and, in many cases, opposite—conclusion, but one that is equally flawed. Some scholars, mostly working under the flag of "behavioral law and economics," have argued that certain financial products are excessively complicated for consumers to understand and that consumer financial products should be forcibly simplified so that their salient terms can be disclosed to consumers. For example, professors Michael Barr, Sendhil Mullainathan, and Eldar Shafir have argued for the primacy of "plain vanilla" consumer financial products, which financial institutions would be required to offer consumers and consumers would be required to affirmatively reject before those financial institutions would be permitted to offer alternative and more complicated products.[31] For example, before a lender could offer to a consumer an adjustable-rate mortgage, a lender would be required to offer consumers the option of a thirty-year fixed-rate mortgage and to explain to the borrower the advantages of the plain vanilla product, which the consumer would be required to affirmatively reject. Indeed, this novel idea proved so influential that it was included in the Obama administration's original legislative proposal that eventually became Dodd-Frank.[32]

But the flaws of the plain-vanilla approach to consumer financial protection are in many ways the opposite of the flaws in the disclosure regime. The criticism of a disclosure regime is that some products are so complicated that it is difficult to disclose all of the potentially relevant terms up-front without creating information overload problems for consumers. The criticism of a plain-vanilla regime, by contrast, is that the complexity of product offerings would be bounded by the limits of what a consumer can understand at the time of entering into a credit contract. Thus, the logic of a plain-vanilla regulatory regime is to work backward from what can be reasonably disclosed and understood by a consumer at the time of entering into a contract and then limit the number of terms in that fashion.

The flaws in such a regime, however, are obvious. While one can require the offer of plain-vanilla products, advocates of the plain-vanilla regulatory regime have yet to identify any plain-vanilla consumers for whom these one-size-fits-all products are appropriate. Consumer credit products are complicated because consumers are complicated and the products that they use are complicated. About half of consumers never or rarely revolve balances on their credit card—those consumers pay little attention to the annual percentage rate (APR) or related credit features of a credit card, but pay substantial attention to terms like the annual fee or rewards. Consumers also differ with respect to what kinds of rewards they value. Other consumers do revolve balances at different frequencies, or use their credit cards abroad, or use their personal credit cards for business purposes or even as a source of financing for a small business. It becomes apparent very quickly that in the face of consumer heterogeneity, a plain-vanilla regulatory strategy will soon turn one-size-fits-all into one-size-fits-none. Moreover, as exemplified by the CARD Act, when certain risk-based pricing terms are limited, such as over-the-limit fees or the ability to adjust interest rates in the face of changes in risk, it favors those advantaged consumers but does so at the expense of other consumers who have to pay higher interest rates and annual fees, or lose access to credit cards entirely.

A market-based approach to consumer financial protection, therefore, will be one that does not drown consumers in excessive disclosures of irrelevant terms but also does not force consumers and financial institutions into oversimplifying their product offerings just to shoehorn them into standardized formats. Instead, a true market-reinforcing consumer financial protection regime will start with a foundation that consumers are the best judge of the terms and products that are best for themselves and their families and that the purpose of regulation should be to help consumers to identify their preferred products most efficiently.

A market-based consumer financial protection regime would begin by specifying the market failure that purportedly is to be addressed by the regulation.[33] Thus, if the problem to be addressed is one of information (i.e., that consumer preferences are taken as given and it is a matter of enabling them to find their preferred products efficiently), then the remedy should be informational. But if the problem is substantive (i.e., that regulators do not want consumers to make certain choices), then one should not invoke informational remedies. Thus, for example, if politicians believe that consumers take on too much credit card debt and do not pay it off fast enough, trying to change consumer behavior through disclosure-based regulation (such as requiring conspicuous disclosure of how long it will take to pay off the balance if one makes only the minimum payment) will be an ineffective way to achieve that end.

Indeed, using disclosure to try to accomplish substantive goals of changing consumer behavior can actually be counterproductive. For example, evidence indicates that the new required disclosure on credit card statements actually may have caused the number of consumers who only made the minimum monthly payment to *increase*.[34] In a similar vein, when the Department of Housing and Urban Development proposed a rule that would have required separate disclosure of fees charged by mortgage brokers (which were irrelevant

335

to the price of the loan to the consumer), a study by economists at the Federal Trade Commission found that the proposed disclosure actually *increased* consumer confusion and led them to make mistakes about the overall cost of the loan.[35] In both instances, the proposed disclosure remedy was not well tailored to the problem it was supposed to address.

But markets actually already offer a better way. Consider a website such as cardhub.com, which is operated by a former credit card industry executive.[36] The website reads through the dense pages of credit card terms and disclosures and interprets the card terms for consumers. Moreover, rather than throwing a bunch of generic disclosures at consumers—disclosures that are both overinclusive and underinclusive for virtually every consumer—cardhub.com enables consumers to search for cards with the specific attributes that particular consumers value, whether a low APR, zero foreign transaction fee, gasoline rewards, or frequent flyer miles. In effect, cardhub.com and other similar websites allow consumers to tailor disclosures to the terms that they consider most relevant at the time that they make their decision and then to find other terms as needed. In addition, terms that have become obsolete with respect to a consumer's decision (such as the minimum finance charge) can be ignored unless a consumer specifically wants to know that term. In contrast to the cumbersome one-size-fits-all strategy of government-mandated disclosure, cardhub.com provides a model that lets consumers wade through the inherently complex nature of modern credit cards without forcing financial institutions to artificially simplify their products to shoehorn them into a preexisting model of disclosure.

In this sense, shopping for a credit card has become no different from shopping for any other multifeature product, such as a car, refrigerator, or computer. In such markets consumers rely on their own experiences, information from advertising, and independent third-party rating institutions such as Consumer Reports, Angie's List, or Carfax. Credible third-party rating agencies can provide information to help consumer decision-making.

Moreover, simplicity itself is a product attribute consumers value in competitive markets. For example, the global popularity of Apple's iPhone is attributable in substantial part to its simplicity of use in comparison to Android-based phones, even though Androids are less expensive. There is good reason to believe that financial institutions will respond to consumer demand for simplicity as well. For example, consider general-purpose reloadable (GPR) prepaid cards, which serve as a payment alternative to debit and credit cards.[37] When GPR cards were first introduced and started to become mainstream, they were laden with multiple fees—activation fees, cash-withdrawal fees, transaction fees, and so on. As the GPR prepaid market has expanded and competition has grown, however, both the number and dollar amount of the fees charged on the cards have fallen dramatically. Today, cards issued by American Express (through Walmart), JPMorgan Chase, US Bank, and others, all offer high functionality with a very simplified fee structure. Indeed, by the time that financial regulators actually started considering regulating the number and size of fees on prepaid cards, market competition was already delivering to consumers quality cards with fewer and smaller fees. Indeed, today the largest obstacle to competition and consumer choice in the prepaid card market is the Durbin Amendment, which requires that to avoid its punitive price controls, large-bank issuers subject to its terms (over $10 billion in assets) must offer cards with reduced functionality that effectively cannot serve as a mobile banking substitute for a traditional bank account.

Finally, the Durbin Amendment itself is one of the more glaring examples of how not to create a market-reinforcing regulatory regime. The growth of free checking and improved quality of bank accounts during the 2000s, combined with the great popularity of debit cards as a payment instrument, is a remarkable story of pro-consumer competition and innovation. The growth of debit cards enabled banks to expand free checking to many groups that traditionally did not have access to bank accounts—for instance, low-income and young consumers. More important, the growth of debit cards and the interchange fees that they generated turned these low-income Americans into valued bank customers—banks had an incentive to open new branches, including branches in untraditional locations such as grocery stores, in order to attract a new class of customers. Banks had an incentive to expand their mobile banking platforms and online banking systems to attract tech-savvy younger consumers (many of whom had limited access to credit cards, in part because of regulations limiting access to credit cards by college students), among whom uptake of debit cards was especially popular. In short, the growth of debit card interchange fee revenues created a whole new class of consumers who were actually profitable and thus valued customers.

The Durbin Amendment, however, changed that calculus. Because the Durbin Amendment prohibits the recovery of the full cost of debit card issuance and servicing, it has effectively turned what had been a profit center into a loss. Banks now offer debit cards at a loss and must recoup their losses by selling other services to their customers or requiring larger minimum deposit balances to support their operation. Indeed, according to one report, as a result of the Durbin Amendment, JPMorgan Chase now estimates that approximately 70 percent of its customers with less than $100,000 in assets are unprofitable for the bank.[38]

The Durbin Amendment has effectively eliminated low-income and young consumers as profitable customers of the bank, and the consequences have been predictable—these consumers are exiting the banking system or never entering it. One fears that confronted with a growing class of unbanked consumers, regulators will essentially force banks to offer bank accounts at a loss to consumers.[39] Wouldn't it be better for all—and especially the consumers themselves—to provide economic incentives to treat low-income consumers as valued customers, rather than forcing them to serve those customers as a charity case?

A modern approach to consumer credit regulation should recognize and embrace the dynamic and innovative nature of consumer credit and payments. Mobile phone technology offers the potential to empower consumers to gain access to new information and make better decisions about the products that they choose. The reimposition of old-style command-and-control regulation, by contrast, threatens to stifle this innovation, competition, and flexibility.

NOTES

1. These conceptual categories are not intended to provide a taxonomic categorization of all regulations but to illustrate different approaches to regulation.

2. Durkin et al., *Consumer Credit and the American Economy*, 483.

3. These arguments are reviewed in ibid., chap. 11.

4. See ibid.

5. See ibid., 504; see also Zywicki, "Economics of Credit Cards" (credit cards), and "Case against New Restrictions."

6. See Durkin et al., *Consumer Credit and the American Economy*, chap. 5.

7. Regulation can dampen competition among providers, such as by imposing different usury ceilings for different products or providers or by erecting regulatory barriers to entry such as licensing of entrants. In such situations it is more plausible that certain firms could have monopoly power. See ibid., 506–9.

8. Marquette National Bank v. First of Omaha Service Corporation, 439 U.S. 299 (1978).

9.   Today, most cards that carry annual fees also provide some sort of reward program (such as frequent flyer miles) for which the annual fee is used to defray some of the costs of the program operation. The frequency and size of annual fees has risen since the enactment of the Credit Card Accountability Responsibility and Disclosure (CARD) Act of 2009, especially for higher-risk borrowers. See Durkin, Elliehausen, and Zywicki, "Assessment of Behavioral Law."

10. See Zywicki, "Case against New Restrictions."

11. Dunkelberg and De Magistris, "Measuring the Impact of Credit Regulation."

12. See Zywicki, "Consumer Financial Protection Bureau," 856.

13. Some smaller retailers outsourced their credit operations to consumer finance companies to try to keep costs down.

14. See Boyes, "In Defense of the Downtrodden."

15. See, for example, Samuelson, "Statement before the Committee of the Judiciary"; see also Friedman, "Defense of Usury," which says, "I know of no economist of any standing from [Bentham's] time to this who has favored a legal limit on the rate of interest that borrowers could pay or lenders receive—though there must have been some."

16. See Durkin and Elliehausen, *Truth in Lending*.

17. See Durkin et al., *Consumer Credit and the American Economy*; see also Ben-Shahar and Schneider, *More than You Wanted to Know*.

18. See Zywicki, "Market for Information," 13.

19. Durkin, "Requirements and Prospects," 26.

20. Credit Card Accountability Responsibility and Disclosure Act of 2009, Pub. L. No. 111–24, 123 Stat 1734 (2009) codified at 15 U.S.C. § 1601.

21. For a summary of the evidence on the effects of the CARD Act, see Durkin et al., "Assessment of Behavioral Law," which this discussion summarizes.

22. 15 U.S.C. §16930-2(a)(2).

23. Zywicki, Manne, and Morris, "Price Controls on Payment Card Interchange Fees."

24. See Wang, "Debit Card Interchange Fee Regulation."

25. Zywicki, Manne, and Morris, "Price Controls on Payment Card Interchange Fees."

26. FDIC, "2011 FDIC National Survey," 10.

27. In the period immediately following the enactment of the Durbin Amendment, usage of debit cards flatlined while usage of credit cards increased substantially, which reversed a multiyear trend of declining credit card purchase volume. Moreover, virtually all of the growth in credit card usage was for transactional users who pay their debts in full at the end of each month, suggesting that the increase in credit cards was for transactions for which debit cards otherwise would have been used.

28. See Baines, Courchane, and Stoianovici, "Economic Impact on Small Lenders."

29. See Zywicki "Dodd-Frank Act Five Years Later."

30. CFPB, "Small Business Advisory Review Panel." For a criticism of the study on which the proposal is based, see Johnston and Zywicki, "Consumer Financial Protection Bureau's Arbitration Study."

31. Barr, Mullainathan, and Shafir, "Behaviorally Informed Financial Services Regulation."

32. Department of the Treasury, "Financial Regulatory Reform."

33. See Zywicki, "Market for Information," 13.
34. Navarro-Martinez et al., "Minimum Required Payment."
35. Lacko and Pappalardo, "Improving Consumer Mortgage Disclosures."
36. This observation is not intended to endorse this particular website over myriad similar competitors; it is provided for illustrative purposes.
37. See Zywicki, "Economics and Regulation."
38. Marcinek, "JP Morgan Sees Clients."
39. See Cordray, Letter to CEO of Unnamed Financial Institution.

REFERENCES

Baines, Arthur, Marsha Courchane, and Steli Stoianovici. "Economic Impact on Small Lenders of the Payday Lending Rules under Consideration by the CFPB." Prepared by Charles River Associates for Community Financial Services Association of America, May 12, 2015.

Barr, Michael S., Sendhil Mullainathan, and Eldar Shafir. "Behaviorally Informed Financial Services Regulation." Policy Paper, New America Foundation, Washington, DC, October 2008.

Ben-Shahar, Omri, and Carl E. Schneider. *More than You Wanted to Know: The Failure of Mandated Disclosure*. Princeton, NJ: Princeton University Press, 2014.

Boyes, William J. "In Defense of the Downtrodden: Usury Laws?" *Public Choice* 39, no. 2 (1982): 269–76.

Consumer Financial Protection Bureau (CFPB). "Small Business Advisory Review Panel for Potential Rulemaking on Arbitration Agreements: Outline of Proposals under Consideration and Alternatives Considered." October 7, 2015.

Cordray, Richard (Director, Bureau of Consumer Financial Protection). Letter to CEO of Unnamed Financial Institution, February 3, 2016. http://files.consumerfinance.gov/f/201602_cfpb_letter-to-banks-on-lower-risk-accounts.pdf.

Department of the Treasury. "Financial Regulatory Reform, a New Foundation: Rebuilding Financial Supervision and Regulation." June 17, 2009.

Dunkelberg, William C., and Robin De Magistris. "Measuring the Impact of Credit Regulation on Consumers." In *The Regulation of Financial Institutions, Conference Series No. 21*, 44–62. Boston: Federal Reserve Bank of Boston, 1979.

Durkin, Thomas A. "Requirements and Prospects for a New Time to Payoff Disclosure for Open End Credit under Truth in Lending." Finance and Economics Discussion Series Working Paper 2006-34, Divisions of Research & Statistics and Monetary Affairs Federal Reserve Board, Washington, DC, October 2006.

Durkin, Thomas A., and Gregory Elliehausen. *Truth in Lending: Theory, History, and a Way Forward*. New York: Oxford University Press, 2011.

Durkin, Thomas A., Gregory Elliehausen, Michael E. Staten, and Todd J. Zywicki. *Consumer Credit and the American Economy*. New York: Oxford University Press, 2014.

Durkin, Thomas A., Gregory Elliehausen, and Todd J. Zywicki. "An Assessment of Behavioral Law and Economics Contentions and What We Know Empirically about Credit Card Use by Consumers." *Supreme Court Economic Review* 22 (2014): 1.

Federal Deposit Insurance Corporation (FDIC). "2011 FDIC National Survey of Unbanked and Underbanked Households." September 2012.

Friedman, Milton. "Defense of Usury." *Newsweek*, April 6, 1970, 79.

Johnston, Jason Scott, and Todd J. Zywicki. "The Consumer Financial Protection Bureau's Arbitration Study: A Summary and Critique." Mercatus Working Paper, Mercatus Center at George Mason University, Arlington, VA, August 2015.

Lacko, James M., and Janis K. Pappalardo. "Improving Consumer Mortgage Disclosures: An Empirical Assessment of Current and Prototype Disclosure Forms." Federal Trade Commission Staff Report, June 2007.

Marcinek, Laura. "JP Morgan Sees Clients with Less than $100,000 Unprofitable." *Bloomberg Business*, February 28, 2012. http://www.bloomberg.com/news/articles/2012-02-28/jpmorgan-views-clients-with-less-than-100-000-to-invest-as-unprofitable.

Navarro-Martinez, Daniel, Linda Court Salisbury, Katherine N. Lemon, Neil Stewart, William J. Matthews, and Adam J. L. Harris. "Minimum Required Payment and Supplemental Information Disclosure Effects on Consumer Debt Repayment Decisions." *Journal of Marketing Research* 48 (special issue 2011): S60–S77.

Samuelson, Paul A. "Statement before the Committee of the Judiciary of the General Court of Massachusetts in Support of the Uniform Consumer Credit Code (January 29, 1969)." In *Statements of Former Senator Paul Douglas and Professor Paul Samuelson on the Uniform Credit Code 7*. Boston: National Conference of Commissioners on Uniform State Laws, 1969.

Wang, Zhu. "Debit Card Interchange Fee Regulation: Some Assessments and Considerations." *Federal Reserve Bank of Richmond Economic Quarterly* 98, no. 3 (3rd Quarter 2012): 159–83.

Zywicki, Todd J. "The Economics of Credit Cards." *Chapman Law Review* 3 (2000): 79.

———. "The Case against New Restrictions on Payday Lending." Mercatus Working Paper 09-28, Mercatus Center at George Mason University, Arlington, VA, July 2009.

———. "The Market for Information and Credit Card Regulation." *Banking and Financial Services Policy Report* 28, no. 1 (2009): 13–16.

———. "The Consumer Financial Protection Bureau: Savior or Menace?" *George Washington Law Review* 81 (2013): 856–928.

———. "The Economics and Regulation of Network Branded Prepaid Cards." *Florida Law Review* 65 (2013): 1477.

———. "The Dodd-Frank Act Five Years Later: Are We More Stable?" Testimony before the House of Representatives Financial Services Committee, July 9, 2015.

Zywicki, Todd J., Geoffrey Manne, and Julian Morris. "Price Controls on Payment Card Interchange Fees: The U.S. Experience." ICLE Financial Regulatory Research Program White Paper 2014-2, 2014.

CHAPTER 13
Examining Arguments Made by Interest Rate Cap Advocates

THOMAS W. MILLER JR.
Mississippi State University

HAROLD A. BLACK
University of Tennessee, Knoxville (Emeritus)

The lending of money is one of the world's oldest professions, which probably accounts for the recurring skepticism about its value.

—*Irving Michelman*[1]

Personal credit use, and its price, has been a controversial societal topic—likely since the dawn of recorded history. Theologians, historians, politicians, economists, and others have offered disparate views. At the center of this topic are the questions of whether individuals should use personal credit and—if they do—what the "appropriate" price, or interest rate, is. The focus of this chapter is on the second question as applied to two widely used small-dollar loan products today.

Every day, consumers make choices based on the price of money—just as they respond to prices of other goods and services. Despite teeth-gnashing and hand-wringing by philosophers, advocates, reformers, legislators, and others, the market for credit is not "special" or "different." Simply stated, the market for credit obeys the laws of supply and demand.

Through the ages, monarchs, governments, and organized religions have made many attempts to influence this market, often through usury laws that set a maximum rate of interest. Homer and Sylla, however, detail how difficult it is for lawmakers to eliminate the concept of interest.[2] Systems will arise to create promises to pay more in the future than the money received today. Some market participants could find that the maximum interest rate is too low, so they create a loan contract at their preferred rate. In such a case, these market participants will either ignore the law or add clever elements to the deal to stay within the letter of the law.

As does any binding price ceiling, an interest rate cap interferes with the gains from trade flowing to both borrowers and lenders. This chapter discusses the effects of interest rate caps on borrowers and lenders. We begin the chapter with a brief discussion of the history of interest rate caps, which is followed by a description of the economics of price ceilings, particularly interest rate caps.

We then present a discussion of research addressing the arguments advocates of interest rate caps make to justify these caps. In that section, we show that rigorous academic research does not support any of these common arguments. We then discuss how consumer advocates and capitalists in the early twentieth century created the installment loan business designed to outcompete illegal loan sharks.

Following that section, we briefly discuss how the interest rate regulatory environment evolved in the traditional installment loan business, and we present discussions on the current state-based regulatory environment for two popular small-dollar credit products: traditional installment loans and payday loans. We then outline a path going forward that will benefit borrowers and lenders in the small-dollar loan market.

A BRIEF HISTORY OF INTEREST RATE CAPS

Interest rate caps, in the form of usury laws, likely represent the longest, and most repeated, government intervention in financial markets.[3] The earliest advocates of usury laws favored an interest rate of zero. Aristotle asserted that money was sterile and should earn no interest. Governments dating from ancient Egypt through the modern day have imposed interest rate ceilings for a variety of reasons.[4]

Glaeser and Scheinkman state that usury laws play many roles throughout history and seek to explain why interest rate caps have had a pervasive historical presence.[5] In their formal model, assuming money is available to borrow at the cap rate, interest rate caps are welfare-enhancing because they provide a means for individuals to insure themselves cheaply against income shocks. In their model, consumers cannot self-insure with savings so they must borrow from other consumers.

Because usury laws play many roles, no single theory can explain all the roles. One theory to explain interest rate caps is rent-seeking by those who set them. Ekelund, Herbert, and Tollison, for example, argue that interest rate caps continued to exist in the Middle Ages because low rates benefited the Catholic Church, which was a heavy borrower.[6]

In the eighteenth century, usury laws in Britain mandated a 5 percent interest rate ceiling. The British laws formed the basis for usury laws in America. Against this historical backdrop, Benmelech and Moskowitz examined usury laws in America.

Benmelech and Moskowitz show that the maximum legal interest rate by state from 1641 to 1891 ranged from 5.73 percent (Virginia) to unbounded (California).[7] The maximum legal rate had a median of 8 percent. The higher rate caps enacted in America likely helped to attract investment capital. Durkin, Elliehausen, and Zywicki state that legal limits were not always binding in the colonial period because they sometimes exceeded prevailing market interest rates.[8] Benmelech and Moskowitz find that usury laws, when binding, reduce credit and economic activity.

To test why usury rates existed, Benmelech and Moskowitz use two competing theories: private interests with political power capture rents from others, versus public interests protect the underserved. They also suggest an interpretation of their results: that "regulation designed to serve the politically and financially weak has the unintended consequence of exacerbating their plight."[9]

In 1836, William Cullen Bryant, the editor of the *New York Evening Post*, argued against interest rate caps. Bryant, in his passionate editorial, forcefully declared:

> Such attempts [at restricting interest rates] have always been, and always will be, worse than fruitless. They not only do not answer the ostensible object, but they accomplish the reverse. They operate, like all restrictions on trade, to the injury of the very class they are framed to protect; they oppress the borrower for the advantage of the lender; they take from the poor to give to the rich.[10]

In a later section of this chapter, we present evidence from rigorous research that corroborates Bryant's viewpoint. The evidence shows that interest rate caps harm the exact people who they are designed to protect. In addition, restrictions of interest rates result in a shift of resources from the credit impaired to those that are not credit impaired.

THE ECONOMICS OF INTEREST RATE CAPS

> Economists may not know much. But we know one thing very well: how to produce shortages and surpluses. Do you want a shortage? Have the government legislate a maximum price that is below the price that would otherwise prevail. If you want to create a shortage of tomatoes, for example, just pass a law that retailers can't sell tomatoes for more than two cents per pound. Instantly you'll have a tomato shortage.[11]

Although his eloquent example features tomatoes, Milton Friedman's argument above applies to all markets—including credit markets. If the rate cap is set above the market-clearing interest rate, then the interest rate cap does not restrain trade: competition and interactions between borrowers and lenders will set the rate when the market interest rate is below the rate cap. If the rate cap imposed is lower than the market-clearing interest rate, an excess demand by consumers for credit will exist because the quantity of loanable funds demanded at that rate will be greater than the amount that lenders are willing to lend.

As shown in tables 1 and 2, some states have capped interest rates on small-dollar loans at a level that makes these loan products unprofitable for lenders. The demand, however, for small-dollar loans in these states is not zero. Borrowers will continue to seek credit through legal and illegal sources.

Table 1. State Regulations Concerning Traditional Installment Lending

Current and Historic Interest Rate Caps

State	2014 Maximum Annual Percentage Rate (APR) on a $1,000 Loan (Source: AFSA)	2014 Dollar Interest Paid on a 12-Month, $1,000 Loan at State's Maximum APR (Source: Author Calculations)	1935 Maximum Annual Percentage Rate (APR) on a $100 Loan ($1,728 in 2014 Dollars) (Source: Foster (1941))
Panel A. Low rate cap states			
1 *Arkansas*	17	94	10
2 *Connecticut*	17	94	36
3 *Massachusetts*	23	129	36
4 Pennsylvania	*24(a)*	135	36
5 *District of Columbia*	24	135	12
6 *Nebraska*	24	135	10
7 *Rhode Island*	24	135	36
8 *Vermont*	24	135	30
9 Hawaii	25	141	42
10 *Michigan*	25	141	36
11 *New York*	25	141	36
12 *Washington*	25	141	—
13 Alabama	*26(a)*	146	8
14 *California*	30	170	30
15 Florida	30	170	42
16 Maine	30	170	36
17 New Jersey	30	170	30
18 *North Carolina*	30	170	—
19 Oklahoma	30	170	—
20 Maryland	33	188	42
21 Minnesota	33	188	36
22 West Virginia	33	188	42
23 *Ohio*	*28(a)*	158	36
24 Tennessee	*34(a)*	194	6
Panel B. States with rate cap of about 36%			
1 Alaska	36	206	—
2 *Arizona*	36	206	42

Table 1. (continued)

State	2014 Maximum Annual Percentage Rate (APR) on a $1,000 Loan (Source: AFSA)	2014 Dollar Interest Paid on a 12-Month, $1,000 Loan at State's Maximum APR (Source: Author Calculations)	1935 Maximum Annual Percentage Rate (APR) on a $100 Loan ($1,728 in 2014 Dollars) (Source: Foster (1941))
3 Colorado	36(a)	206	10
4 *Indiana*	36	206	36
5 Iowa	36	206	36
6 *Kansas*	36	206	—
7 Kentucky	36	206	42
8 Louisiana	36	206	42
9 Mississippi	36	206	10
10 Montana	36	206	—
11 New Hampshire	36	206	24
12 *Oregon*	36	206	36
13 *Virginia*	36	206	42
14 Wyoming	36	206	—
Panel C. States with higher rate caps			
1 Georgia	40(b)	230	18
2 Nevada	40	230	—
3 Texas	80	484	10
4 Illinois	99	613	36
Panel D. States with no rate cap			
1 Delaware	No Cap	----(c)	8
2 Idaho	No Cap		—
3 Missouri	No Cap		36
4 New Mexico	No Cap		10
5 North Dakota	No Cap		—
6 South Carolina	No Cap, over $640		—
7 South Dakota	No Cap		—
8 Utah	No Cap		36
9 Wisconsin	No Cap		30

Sources: (a) National Consumer Law Center, "Installment Loans" (b) "The Cost of Personal Borrowing in the United States"; American Financial Services Association (AFSA), "State Small Loan Lending Law Categories," 2014, www.afsaonline.org. Historic APRs are from Foster, "Personal Finance Business under Regulation," 154–72, table 1. States in bold italic are states that AFSA identifies as states without traditional installment lending, www.afsaonline.org. (c) With no cap, the amount paid is competitively determined.

Note: For a one-year $1,000 loan, the allowable APR is 28%. However, the state of Ohio allows credit services organizations to charge an additional—uncapped—fee for arranging a loan.

Table 2. State Regulations Concerning Payday Lending

Legality, Interest Rate Caps, Maximum Loan Amounts, and Fees

State	Maximum Annual Percentage Rate (APR) on $100 2-Week Payday Loan (Source: Consumer Federation of America)	Maximum Annual Percentage Rate (APR) on $100 2-Week Payday Loan (Source: Community Financial Services Association of America)	Dollar Fee Paid on a $100 2-Week Payday Loan at State's Maximum APR (Source: Community Financial Services Association of America)	Maximum Dollar Amount Permitted to Be Borrowed (Source: Consumer Federation of America)	Maximum Dollar Amount Permitted to Be Borrowed (Source: Community Financial Services Association of America)
Panel A. Prohibited per CFED website					
1 Arizona	—	—	—	—	—
2 Arkansas	—	—	—	—	—
3 Connecticut	—	—	—	—	—
4 District of Columbia	—	—	—	—	—
5 Georgia	—	—	—	—	—
6 Maine	—	—	—	—	—
7 Maryland	—	—	—	—	—
8 Massachusetts	—	—	—	—	—
9 New Jersey	—	—	—	—	—
10 New York	—	—	—	—	—
11 North Carolina	—	—	—	—	—
12 Pennsylvania	—	—	—	—	—
13 Vermont	—	—	—	—	—
14 West Virginia	—	—	—	—	—
Panel B. Legal per CFED website, but de facto prohibited					
1 Montana	36	—	—	300	Not specified
2 New Hampshire	36	—	—	500	Not specified
3 Oregon	36	—	—	Not specified	Not specified
4 Maine(a)	43(a)	—	—	None	Not specified
5 Colorado	—	—	(b)	500	500
Panel C. Legal per CFED website, rate capped					
1 Alabama	456	455	$17.50	500	500
2 Alaska	443	520	$20.00	500	500

Table 2. (continued)

State	Maximum Annual Percentage Rate (APR) on $100 2-Week Payday Loan (Source: Consumer Federation of America)	Maximum Annual Percentage Rate (APR) on $100 2-Week Payday Loan (Source: Community Financial Services Association of America)	Dollar Fee Paid on a $100 2-Week Payday Loan at State's Maximum APR (Source: Community Financial Services Association of America)	Maximum Dollar Amount Permitted to Be Borrowed (Source: Consumer Federation of America)	Maximum Dollar Amount Permitted to Be Borrowed (Source: Community Financial Services Association of America)
3 California	460	459	$17.65	300	300
4 Florida	342	390	$15.00	500	500
5 Hawaii	460	459	$17.65	600	600
6 Illinois	404	429	$16.50	1,000	1,000
7 Indiana	391	390	$15.00	550	605 or 20% of gross inc.
8 Iowa	358	433	$16.67	500	500
9 Kansas	391	390	$15.00	500	500
10 Kentucky	471	485	$18.65	500	500
11 Louisiana	574	783	$30.12	350	350
12 Michigan	375	402	$15.45	600	600
13 Minnesota	235	390	$15.00	350	350
14 Mississippi	572	520	$20.00	400	500
15 Missouri	1,955	—	—	500	500
16 Nebraska	460	459	$17.65	500	500
17 New Mexico	409	416	$16.00	2,500	25% of gross inc.
18 North Dakota	520	538	$20.68	500	600
19 Ohio(c)	390(c)	—	$15.00(c)	500	800
20 Oklahoma	396	405	$15.46	500	500
21 Rhode Island	261	260	$10.00	500	500
22 South Carolina	391	400	$15.40	550	550
23 Tennessee	313	459	$17.65	425	500
24 Texas	309	—	$11.87	Not specified	Not specified
25 Virginia	610	686	$26.38	500	500
26 Washington	390	390	$15.00	700	700 or 30% of gross inc.
27 Wyoming	313	780	$30.00	Not specified	No limit

(continued)

Table 2. (continued)

State	Maximum Annual Percentage Rate (APR) on $100 2-Week Payday Loan (Source: Consumer Federation of America)	Maximum Annual Percentage Rate (APR) on $100 2-Week Payday Loan (Source: Community Financial Services Association of America)	Dollar Fee Paid on a $100 2-Week Payday Loan at State's Maximum APR (Source: Community Financial Services Association of America)	Maximum Dollar Amount Permitted to Be Borrowed (Source: Consumer Federation of America)	Maximum Dollar Amount Permitted to Be Borrowed (Source: Community Financial Services Association of America)
Panel D. Legal per CFED website, rate not capped by state					
1 Delaware	—	—	—	500	1,000
2 Idaho	—	—	—	1,000	1,000 or 25% of gross inc.
3 Nevada	—	—	—	25% of Gross Inc.	25% of gross inc.
4 South Dakota	—	—	—	500	500
5 Utah	—	—	—	No limit	No limit
6 Wisconsin	—	—	—	1,500	1,500 or 35% of gross inc.

Sources: (a) Barth et al., "Do State Regulations Affect Payday Lender Concentration?" The Consumer Federation of America website (www.paydayloaninfo.org) says payday lending in Maine is prohibited. The Community Financial Services Association of America (www.cfsaa.com) has no data for Maine. (b) Colorado law provides a six-month minimum loan term with multiple payments. (c) Barth et al., "Do State Regulations Affect Payday Lender Concentration?"

Note: Community Financial Services Association (CFSA) information is as of July 1, 2014. Consumer Federation of America (CFED) information is as of October 20, 2015.

Blitz and Long state, "Legal rate ceilings may reduce the price of personal loan credit to some borrowers, but when ceilings are sufficiently low to affect the observed market rate in a significant way, there is a substantial reduction on the number of borrowers included in the legal market. Relatively low risk borrowers who remain in the legal lending market appear to benefit from the lower cost loans made when higher risk potential borrowers are excluded."[12]

Durkin, Elliehausen, Staten, and Zywicki present a detailed discussion of the theoretical and empirical evidence on this issue.[13] For example, Daniel Villegas studies the effect of interest rate caps on the quantity of credit provided to different risk classes of borrowers. He finds that rate ceilings negatively affect the quantity of credit available to low- and middle-income households living in states with rate caps.[14] Economists would predict, however, that if the credit market cannot eliminate the excess demand for credit by high-risk borrowers simply by raising the price (i.e., the interest rate) of the loans, then lenders will allocate their loanable funds through other means.

Consider the following example. Suppose an effective interest rate cap exists in a credit market. Lenders will supply some, but not all, of the loan funds demanded at the interest rate cap. This point is an important one: when lenders cannot use price to allocate loans, they must use some other criteria to allocate loanable funds. The result is almost surely that the credit demand of higher-risk borrowers will go unfulfilled.

Despite the many ways in which lending discrimination is illegal in the United States, an effective interest rate cap actually provides an incentive for lenders to discriminate when choosing borrowers. Research indicates, as one might expect, that lenders, when faced with binding interest rate caps, favor less risky and generally wealthier borrowers over those who are more risky.

Considerable research evidence exists that laws imposing interest rate caps harm the very people the proponents of the law are seeking to protect. For example, Bowsher states that the effects of interest rate caps are "arbitrary and weigh heaviest on those credit seekers generally considered most risky."[15] He also points out that a low interest rate cap prevents higher-risk individuals from competing for loanable funds. As a result, a greater share of the available loan funds flows to lower risk applicants—thereby increasing the volume of credit flowing to relatively wealthier borrowers. Relatively poorer borrowers, therefore, have a reduced access to credit.

Zinman shows that imposing a binding interest rate cap harms those with high debt burdens, because decreasing access to credit increases foreclosures, defaults, and bankruptcies.[16] He, and Peterson and Falls,[17] find that these borrowers are forced to shift into more expensive substitutes for installment loans. A shift into products such as check overdrafts and pawn shops worsens the financial conditions of borrowers.[18] Zywicki contends that imposing more regulations on payday lenders will "make consumers worse off, stifle competition, and do little to protect consumers from concerns of over-indebtedness and high-cost lending."[19] He argues that unintended consequences, such as shifting borrowers into more expensive credit products, can occur because of heavy restrictions on payday lenders.

RESEARCH ON ARGUMENTS MADE FOR IMPOSING INTEREST RATE CAPS

Advocates of interest rate caps offer many arguments for the "need" for interest rate caps in small-dollar loan markets. One can collectively view these arguments simply as "being in the best interest of consumers." From our synthesis of the literature, popular arguments for interest rate caps include:

    a. Borrowers are naïve and simply do not understand the loan terms.

    b. Groups thought, by advocates, to be most vulnerable to exploitation by lenders—namely minorities, women, and the poor—need protection from "predatory" lenders.

    c. Even if consumers are willing to borrow at high interest rates, society should protect these consumers from themselves because they are making themselves worse off.

    d. Lenders, especially small-dollar lenders, make abnormally high profits from lending at high interest rates because they have considerable market power.

Borrowers Are Naïve and Do Not Understand Loan Terms

The literature on awareness of loan terms, especially annual percentage rates (APRs), is extensive, as summarized by Durkin and Elliehausen. They distill survey evidence that shows that consumers believe that it is not difficult to obtain information on credit costs.[20] Although consumer awareness of APRs extends to many credit products, this section mostly summarizes evidence regarding payday loans.

Elliehausen and Lawrence directly examine the question of whether borrowers who demand short-term credit are naïve and do not understand the terms of the loan. Presenting the results of a 2001 national survey of borrowers in the payday lending market, they find little, if any, support for the "naïve borrower" hypothesis.[21] The survey results show that consumers understand the dollar cost (i.e., the finance charge) of payday loans. The survey results also show, however, that consumers generally do not recall the APR of these loans—even though the lender discloses the APR to the consumer. Elliehausen and Lawrence postulate that the result concerning recollection of the APR possibly stems from the desire of borrowers to know the dollar charges they face—such as check overdraft charges and late payment fees. Then, borrowers can compare these charges when making the financial decision to use a payday loan.

If so, this conjecture implies that APR is not likely to have as much influence on borrower behavior as does dollar cost. Rather than being uninformed and naïve, high interest rate customers appear to be making rational decisions based on the dollar cost of short-term credit. Zinman posits that perhaps the closest substitute for a payday loan is bank overdraft protection—a considerably more expensive option.[22] If one views these bank overdraft fees as interest charges, they could be much greater than the average APR calculation for a payday loan because the overdraft fee applies to even small check amounts relative to a typical payday loan.

Empirical studies also suggest that most consumers choose credit contracts that suit their needs. Recently, Miller presents the results of a survey for the state of Mississippi. Two questions in this survey are whether consumers know where to go to get a loan that suits their needs and whether they understand the terms of these loan products. Concerning the first question, Miller reports that whether the respondent has a bank account or not matters, and so does whether the person's education level stops at high school. Concerning the second question, he reports that what matters is whether the educational level of the respondent stops at high school.[23] If consumers make significant mistakes concerning credit, Durkin, Elliehausen, Staten, and Zywicki discuss how consumers tend to correct them.[24]

The Most Vulnerable Need Protection from Predatory Lenders

Advocates of interest rate caps perceive consumers of high APR products as being the most "vulnerable" members of society—namely, women, minorities, and the poor. Advocates of rate caps call other potentially vulnerable members of society "unbanked" or "underbanked."

Empirical Evidence Concerning Income of Borrowers. Barr presents evidence that low-income consumers in Detroit use high-rate borrowing.[25] He surveys these consumers and finds that their expenditures on these loans were quite low. His results suggest that these consumers are quite good at finding ways to avoid fees. That is, his results suggest that low-income consumers have some sophistication in using financial services that are appropriate to their circumstances and that users of high-rate credit products might not be as vulnerable to predatory lenders as critics suggest—despite their modest incomes and lower levels of formal education.

The empirical evidence drawn from payday borrowers shows that the typical payday loan customer is a young family that is credit-constrained. Moreover, these payday borrowers do not fit the typical profile of "the unbanked" because borrowers must have a steady job and a checking account to qualify for a payday loan. Thus, one would expect that payday loan customers would not typically have the lowest incomes of small-dollar borrowers. Indeed, the 2001 national survey by Elliehausen and Lawrence[26] reported that, on average, only 23 percent of payday borrowers have family incomes below $25,000 ($31,759 in 2011 dollars), while 25 percent have incomes greater than $50,000 ($63,518).

In 2003, Stegman and Faris looked at the incomes of payday customers by certain states and noted the average incomes of payday borrowers were between $25,000 to $30,000 ($38,111 in 2011 dollars) in Indiana, $24,000 ($30,489) in Illinois, and $19,000 ($24,137) in Wisconsin. DeYoung and Phillips reported an average income of $41,500 ($43,512 in 2011 dollars) in Colorado.[27]

Despite the differences in income levels, there are some common characteristics reported in these studies. Payday customers are more likely to be younger families, employed, and credit constrained. Elliehausen and Lawrence report that these consumers are more likely than the population at large to have more debt and to have filed for bankruptcy. In addition, they report that payday borrowers are more likely to have poor credit and more likely to have been denied credit. About 94 percent of payday borrowers have attained a formal education level of at least a high school diploma.[28]

Economics of the Physical Location of the Lenders. It is reasonable to assume that suppliers of a product prefer to locate near their customers. Locational studies have shown that convenience is a major determinant in consumer decisions regarding where to buy. Convenience is one method whereby firms compete with each other. Increasing convenience lowers search costs to the customer. Thus, greater convenience is a benefit to the borrowers.

As Stegman states, payday lenders compete with other lenders through both location and service.[29] One would predict that payday lending operations are more likely to be located in minority census tracts or near military bases. This prediction is based on the expectation that payday lenders would likely locate in census tracts with a high demand for their products—that is, in census tracts with lower incomes.

Locating in Minority Neighborhoods and Near Military Bases. To our knowledge, there are no nationwide studies on the location of payday lenders, although existing studies reveal the distribution of payday loans by the race of the borrower. Stegman and Faris report that African-American families in North Carolina and Texas were found to be "about twice as likely to borrow from a payday lender as whites."[30] Stegman's results suggest that neighborhoods with high minority populations would be more likely to have payday lending stores than areas with smaller percentages of minorities.[31]

Graves and Peterson's study of military bases in twenty states showed that there is a higher concentration of payday lenders around military bases than elsewhere in these states.[32] Morgan notes this concentration simply signals a higher demand for loans by the residents of this area; Stegman buttresses this signaling notion by concluding that active-duty military personnel have a greater demand for payday loans than do civilians.[33] In addition, Morgan's empirical analysis shows a beneficial impact on borrowers when the number of payday stores increases, finding that interest rates fall as the number of payday lending stores per capita increases. Competition among lenders benefits borrowers.

The Department of Defense issued a 2006 report on the demand for payday loans by military personnel. This report likely led to the Talent-Nelson Amendment that became law in October 2007.[34] Among other restrictions, the Talent-Nelson Amendment imposes a nationwide 36 percent interest rate cap on loans to members of the military.

Carrell and Zinman estimate the effects of payday loan access on military readiness and performance using Air Force personnel data. They find that payday borrowing is negatively correlated to military readiness—an assertion they attribute to the Department of Defense. Their findings are strongest among relatively inexperienced and financially unsophisticated airmen.[35]

One would predict that the Talent-Nelson Amendment would likely curtail payday lending to members of the military—to their detriment. Brown and Cushman argue that income characteristics of military enlisted personnel are essentially similar to civilians of similar age.[36] Although military compensation is stable, cash expenditures are not because of features of the military lifestyle. Brown and Cushman find that all kinds of consumer credit, including credit cards and other short-term loans, can be appropriate for military personnel under circumstances that they, as rational consumers, determine for themselves. They find no evidence that the economic welfare of military enlisted personnel will be enhanced by restricting the types of credit available to them.

Society Should Protect Consumers from Themselves

Those who advance the hypothesis that consumers make themselves worse off by borrowing at high rates make an argument as follows: high rate borrowers cannot see how high interest rate products could harm them; therefore, others must protect these consumers from themselves. Two basic assertions these advocates make are that (1) lenders lure these consumers into borrowing at high interest rates and that, consequently, (2) many of them will spiral into an inextricable cycle of debt—commonly referred to as the "debt trap." Ernst et al. states that the Center for Responsible Lending estimates the annual cost of the debt trap is $3.4 billion.[37] Many advocates favor a ban on high interest rate loans to protect consumers from making decisions that will trap them in debt.[38] By extension, advocates of a ban on payday lending believe that consumers will have fewer financial problems if access to a legal, high interest rate loan product is eliminated.[39]

The "Debt Trap." Although anecdotal evidence regarding debt traps exists, rigorous research, not anecdotes, must provide the basis for sound policy concerning consumer credit markets. In a 2008 study to empirically test the "debt trap" hypothesis, Morgan and Strain examined the impact on consumers when legislation in Georgia (2004) and North Carolina (2005) closed payday lending operations in these two states.[40] In general, their findings do not support the predictions of the "debt trap" hypothesis. Instead, after the ban, Georgia households bounced more checks, had more complaints about debt collectors, and were more likely to file for bankruptcy under Chapter 7.[41] Rather than finding that Georgia and North Carolina households had fewer financial difficulties after banning payday lending, Morgan and Strain find that residents of these states had more financial difficulties. That is, despite the intention to enhance consumer welfare, banning payday lending reduces consumer welfare.

In a separate study, Morgan also finds evidence contrary to the debt trap hypothesis.[42] Households in states without usury ceilings on payday loans are less likely to be turned down for credit and do not report higher levels of debt. These households are also less likely to have missed a debt payment during the previous year. Morgan finds that this result is consistent with the notion that payday borrowing is used to avoid missing payments on other debt.

In a clever paper, Morse studies whether payday lending is wealth reducing or wealth enhancing by examining whether payday lenders "help distressed individuals bridge financial shortfalls without incurring the greater expense of delinquency or default on obligations."[43] Morse examines the response to natural disasters as an experiment. Looking at California for the period 1996–2005, she finds that while natural disasters induce an increase in foreclosures, payday loans significantly offset this increase. She further examines whether banks are substitutes for payday lenders and finds that they are substitutes in only two of sixteen specifications. Morse concludes that payday lending is welfare enhancing and that "a move to ban payday lending is ill advised."

Evidence from Arkansas and Oregon. Peterson, and Peterson and Falls, study the effects on Arkansas borrowers after a constitutional amendment made a 10 percent interest rate cap binding on all consumer loans.[44] Both studies find that after the 10 percent cap was imposed (1) small loan credit was not readily available, (2) many consumer finance companies ceased operations, and (3) depository lenders often stopped making small consumer loans. They also find that pawnbrokers in the state proliferated.

Peterson and Falls also note that when the Arkansas interest rate cap became binding, commercial banks and credit unions rationed credit by increasing the minimum size of a personal loan to more than two and one-half times the average minimum size of loans in other states. This action denies credit to consumers with a loan demand for a small-dollar amount. They also find that a higher proportion of Arkansas customers were rejected for credit than in other states, and find shorter loan maturities in Arkansas.[45] These results are consistent with the rationing of credit at the lower rates.

Arkansas consumers who were unable to find credit at the 10 percent cap substituted credit from pawn shops and point-of-sale credit.[46] As a result, point-of-sale credit purchase prices rose to levels that were higher in Arkansas than in the other states studied. The implication is that the state-imposed interest rate cap ceiling was welfare reducing. Higher-risk consumers had to patronize pawnbrokers and incur higher prices on point-of-sale credit purchases than consumers in other states.[47]

As Collins and Sonstegaard note, the most serious effect of Arkansas' legal restrictions on interest rates is that while affluent consumers can borrow out of state—the less affluent could find it difficult to borrow the funds needed during an emergency.[48] Thus, if the constitutionally imposed interest rate cap in Arkansas was designed to protect the poor, it failed to do so.

Zinman[49] studied the impact of the imposition of binding interest rate caps on consumer lending in Oregon. In 2007, Oregon instituted an APR interest rate cap of 150 percent. Because the bordering state of Washington did not impose such restrictions, Zinman constructed a careful study comparing the impact of interest rate caps on the access to credit in both states. He shows that the production costs of making these loans results in a breakeven APR rate of 390 percent for these payday lenders. After Oregon imposed the interest rate cap, the number of payday lenders in Oregon dropped from 346 to 82 by September 2008.

Zinman finds that the Oregon interest rate cap reduced the supply of credit for payday borrowers and that their financial condition worsened. After the cap was imposed, Oregon payday borrowers were more likely to "experience an adverse change in financial condition."[50] In addition, borrowers in Oregon who would have been customers at payday lenders, shifted into what Zinman refers to as "incomplete and plausibly inferior substitutes" such as pawnbrokers and Internet lenders.[51] Thus, the results presented by Zinman buttress the findings of the earlier study by Peterson.

Lenders Make Abnormally High Profits Because They Have the Market Power to Charge High Interest Rates

In this argument, market power enables lenders to set interest rates higher than those that would exist in a competitive market. Consequently, the argument continues, imposing an interest rate cap lowers the interest rate toward a competitive market interest rate. This argument, however, provides no answer to the following question. If one wants an interest rate closer to the competitive market rate, it is reasonable to ask; "Why not simply allow competitive interactions between borrowers and lenders and set market-clearing interest rates for various loan products?"

The economic argument for interest rate caps is that lenders likely have sufficient market power that they use to command "artificially" high interest rates. Economists, however, would find it quite curious that anyone could view an industry growing as fast as the payday lending industry as having concentrated market power and influence over interest rates.

Basic economics predicts that if an industry is earning abnormal profits, these profits will be competed away—either by price competition or by entry of new firms. As of 2014, the CFPB estimates that there are 15,766 payday store locations in the United States—hardly a concentration of market power.[52] In addition, there are many other competitors such as check cashing shops, pawnbrokers, consumer finance companies, banks, savings and loans, mutual savings banks, and credit unions. Consequently, this competition almost surely results in loan rates being lower than they would be without competition.

Morgan illustrates the effect of competition when he finds that the number of pawnshops in the United States stopped growing after the advent of the payday lending industry. He also points out that the payday lending industry is heavily regulated—therefore the costs of compliance are actually high.[53] High compliance costs limit entry, drive some existing firms out of business, and drive up costs to the remaining firms. Industry-wide, higher costs result in higher rates, and fewer dollars lent.

DeYoung and Phillips study payday loan interest rates in Colorado between 2000 and 2006,[54] and report results similar to those of Flannery and Samolyk. In the early years of their sample, DeYoung and Phillips found price competition among payday lenders. In the latter years of their sample, however, they found that payday lending rates moved toward the statutory limit and that noninterest rate competition emerged. They postulate that the lenders appear to be competing with convenience of the stores and the provision of customer service. DeYoung and Phillip also found that the firms practiced price differentiation, charging lower prices to first-time borrowers and higher prices to repeat customers. Multiple-location payday lenders charged higher prices than single store lenders.

At least two studies specifically investigate the payday lender profits. Flannery and Samolyk study payday store costs and profitability using proprietary store-level data from two large payday lenders. They do not find evidence of abnormally large profits and note: "To a great extent, the high APRs implied by payday loan fees can be justified by the fixed costs of keeping stores open and the relatively high default losses suffered on these loans."[55]

Huckstep compares the profitability of seven publicly traded payday lenders versus six mainstream commercial lenders and finds that "when compared to many other well-known lending institutions, payday lenders may fall far short in terms of profitability."[56] Payday lenders averaged a 3.6 percent profit margin while mainstream commercial lenders had a profit margin of 13.0 percent. Because the payday lending profit margin is roughly one-fourth the size of the profit margin of mainstream commercial lenders, Huckstep concludes that abnormally high profits for payday lenders are more myth than reality.

Although the payday lenders charge high fees, they incur high costs. Stegman and Faris state that banks have moved away from the brick and mortar model and have reduced branches by substituting electronic transactions; as a result, "fringe banks" have filled this void by offering more locations and extended business hours.[57] Huckstep adds that the cost of providing convenience to borrowers results in high rent costs, high wage costs, and high fixed costs associated with writing small loans.[58] Additional costs arise from high loan default rates and loan-monitoring activities to reduce the incidence of default.

The empirical evidence concerning the effects of competition in the installment lending business is also compelling. The National Commission on Consumer Finance (NCCF) devoted an entire chapter of its report to the issue of "Rates and Availability of Credit." The Commission forcefully states: "The implications of these findings for public policy seem obvious: the only truly effective way of gaining ample supplies of personal loan credit for consumers *and* reasonable rates too, is to increase competition while simultaneously relaxing inordinately restrictive rate ceilings."[59]

LEGISLATION FOCUSED ON SMALL-DOLLAR LOANS

In the early twentieth century, lenders generally could not legally profit from making small-dollar loans at the state-imposed interest rates.[60] As a result, illegal lenders, eventually known as "loan sharks," filled the demand for small-dollar loans.

During this period, many social reform causes, collectively known as the Progressive Movement, were under way in the United States.[61] In 1907, the philanthropist Margaret Olivia Sage established the Russell Sage Foundation for "the improvement of social and living conditions in the United States." In 1909, the Russell Sage Foundation turned its attention to consumer credit reform. Spearheaded by Arthur Ham, the Foundation sought ways to spread access to credit to workers. The credit reformers during this Progressive era did not seek to alter or regulate the behavior of those they wanted to protect. Instead, they sought ways, through research, to attract "legitimate" capital into the business of small-dollar installment lending. Importantly, reformers at the time recognized that the needs of both lenders and borrowers had to be satisfied to create a sustainable alternative to the "loan shark."[62]

An Innovative Approach to Interest Rate Regulation and the Creation of an Industry

As detailed by Carruthers, Guinnane, and Lee,[63] the intent of the reformers was to pass laws that would allow specially licensed lenders to make small installment loans to consumers at interest rates above state-imposed caps. Through a series of rigorous studies, reformers decided that the costs and risks of providing small-dollar lending merited an interest rate of 3 percent to 3.5 percent per month—at least six times higher than the prevailing legal rates of about 6 percent per year.[64]

In partnership with businesses willing to risk capital in lending small-dollar amounts to consumers, reformers, led by Arthur Ham, framed a pioneering model state law called the Uniform Small Loan Law of 1916. Members of the Russell Sage Foundation, academics, and legislatures deliberated, debated, and studied this model legislation as variants were enacted by states. By the early 1940s, as discussed in Hubachek, thirty states plus Hawaii, which was not a state at that time, had comprehensive small loan laws, nine had ineffective small loan laws, and nine had no small loan laws.[65]

The Shift to More Federal Regulation in Consumer Credit Markets

Since the 1900s, state legislatures were heavily involved in regulating the small loan market. Michelman states that from 1904 to 1933, there were 1,078 bills relating to small loans introduced in state legislatures.[66] Many of these bills concerned the allowable rate of interest on these loans. Foster summarizes the state-mandated interest rate caps in effect in 1935.[67]

In the ensuing three-quarters of a century, there have been many modifications to small loan laws in the various states. Table 1 (which is discussed in detail in a later section) summarizes the net result of state legislation from the mid-1930s to the present. Seventeen states (and the District of Columbia) currently have lower rate caps than they did in 1935. Sixteen states currently have higher rate caps than they did in 1935, and five currently have the same rate cap as they did in 1935. Foster did not report data for the remaining twelve (by current count) states.

The history of interest rate cap legislation in the various states between 1935 and 2015 remains a fertile area for research. State legislatures in particular would be interested in such a review and history.[68] From the mid-1930s until the late 1960s, states regulated the pricing terms in consumer credit markets. Starting in the mid-1960s, the federal government became more active in regulating the consumer credit market. In May 1968, the US Congress passed the Consumer Credit Protection Act. Title I of that Act was the Truth in Lending Act (TILA), commonly referred to as Regulation Z. Other federal legislation, like the Equal Credit Opportunity Act, followed in the 1970s.

Durkin, Elliehausen, Staten, and Zywicki detail many changes in the consumer credit market since the end of World War II.[69] A seminal Supreme Court ruling in 1978 concerned maximum interest rates on credit cards. In the landmark case, Marquette National Bank of Minneapolis v. First of Omaha Service Corp., the Supreme Court ruling allowed credit card issuers to "export" nationally whatever interest rate was allowed in the state in which they were headquartered. To induce the companies to relocate, some states simply dropped their usury laws. Several large issuers relocated to these states. As a result of removing rate caps, market competition and the risk level of borrowers helped determine interest rates on credit cards.

As shown in Durkin, Elliehausen, Staten, and Zywicki, credit card borrowing increased dramatically after the ruling.[70] The impact on the installment loan business was that their "low risk" borrowers likely had more access to credit cards than their "high risk" borrowers did. If they did, this shift pressured profit margins for small-dollar lenders through an increase in bad debt expense. It is likely that installment lenders would have responded by improving underwriting techniques.

In addition, installment lenders could restore profit margins by making larger loans. As loan production costs increased, it is likely that, at some point, installment lenders could not make money by making loans below a certain size—likely less than $1,000. If so, the unprofitability of these loans likely created a "credit desert" for a time in this loan space.[71] Markets, like nature, abhor a vacuum.

Growth of the Payday Loan Industry

The payday loan industry emerged in the early 1990s and grew because of strong consumer demand and changing conditions in the financial services marketplace. One important change was "the exiting of traditional financial institutions from the small-denomination, short-term credit market—a change largely due to its high cost structure."[72]

Today, consumer demand for the payday loan product is considerable and the market supply response to provide the payday loan product has been impressive. Bair states that payday lenders were virtually unheard of "15 years ago" (i.e., around 1990).[73] Caskey writes, "At the beginning of the 1990s, there were probably fewer than 200 payday loan offices nationally."[74] Stegman reports that payday lenders lent about $8 billion in 1999; Bair cites a study from a research firm that estimates that there were more than 22,000 payday store locations in 2004 and these stores extended about $40 billion in short term loans.[75] In 2000, the industry consisted of 7,000 to 10,000 payday loan offices, rising to a peak of about 24,000 storefronts in 2006.[76]

Hecht reports that, in 2013, there were about 17,800 payday loan storefront locations that provided $30 billion in loans. He also reports that another $15 billion was supplied by Internet payday lenders.[77] The continued existence of payday lenders is consistent with the notion that these lenders are fulfilling a demand for loans by borrowers that other lenders will not, or cannot, meet.

Dodd-Frank and the Creation of the Bureau of Consumer Financial Protection

In response to the financial crisis that peaked in the fall of 2008, the 848-page Dodd-Frank Wall Street Reform and Consumer Protection Act (Dodd-Frank) became law only eighteen months later.[78] There was scant time for any rigorous research on the effects of Dodd-Frank regulations on many aspects of financial markets. An important part of Dodd-Frank is Title X. In its 108 sections and 158 pages, Title X established, and detailed the authority of, the Bureau of Consumer Financial Protection (CFPB). One of the general powers of the CFPB is to ensure that, "with respect to consumer financial products and services . . . consumers are protected from unfair, deceptive, or abusive acts and practices. . . ." Although the CFPB has broad authority to regulate financial markets, Title X does not grant the CFPB authority to impose interest rate caps on any loan or other extension of credit. Nonetheless, the existence of the CFPB and its organizational structure pose considerable "regulatory risk" for small-dollar lenders and their customers.[79]

CURRENT STATE OF SMALL-DOLLAR LOAN LEGISLATION

Strictly speaking, there are two bona fide forms of non–credit card, small-dollar loans available to consumers today.[80] One—the payday loan—is a lump-sum loan paid back with interest at the end of the loan period. These loans typically have a two-week term. The other is a traditional installment loan. In an installment loan agreement, the borrower receives the proceeds today and pays back the loan in equal payments over the life of the loan. In an install-ment loan, the amount owed to the lender declines over the length of the loan. When the borrower makes the last payment, the borrower has paid back all interest and the principal. The appendix of this chapter contains a description and examples of the workings of these two loan products. States heavily and thoroughly regulate these loan products.

Existing Legislation in the Traditional Installment Loan Market

Table 1 contains a summary of existing small-dollar traditional installment loan laws, by state. The main data source in the table is the industry trade group for traditional installment lenders, the American Financial Services Association (AFSA). One can trace AFSA's roots back to the days when it, consumer advo-cates, and businesses sought to create alternatives to the "loan shark." AFSA publishes a report on "State Small Loan Lending Law Categories." Two addi-tional raw data sources used to augment the AFSA publication are the appendix to a 2015 report from the National Consumer Law Center and a report called "The Cost of Personal Borrowing in the United States," by Carleton Inc.

It is important to note that rate ceilings are not always a single APR for all loans. In fact, many states have ceilings, graduated by size of loan, that are higher for smaller loans than for larger loans. In Mississippi, for example, as of 2015 the Small Loan Regulatory Law allowed 36 percent on the first $1,000; 33 percent on an amount over $1,000 but not exceeding $2,500; 24 percent on an amount over $2,500 but not exceeding $5,000, and 14 percent on the remainder. Comparing graduated rate ceilings is difficult. The data from the AFSA in table 1 represents an attempt to convert these ceilings to APRs. This conversion helps make comparisons among states easier.

The rates provided by the AFSA report are interest rate ceilings only. That is, these APRs are the estimated interest charges on a $1,000 loan. These APRs do not reflect other fees or costs of ancillary products (like credit insurance).

Foster[81] contains data for the maximum APR allowed on a $100 loan in 1935 (about $1,728 in 2014 dollars). These maximum rates appear in column three of table 1.[82]

No state bans traditional installment lending. Per AFSA, however, traditional installment lenders operate in only thirty-three states. In the remaining seventeen states and the District of Columbia, state-imposed interest rate caps are such that lenders cannot profitably make installment loans. In these states, the APR of the state-imposed interest rate cap ranges from 17 percent (Arkansas) to 36 percent (Indiana and Virginia). It is interesting to note, however, that in seventeen of the states where traditional installment lenders operate, the state-imposed maximum interest rate is 36 percent or less.[83]

The data in table 1 are presented in four groups. Panel A contains a list of states with "Low" rate caps, most 33 percent and below; of the twenty-three states for which Foster presents data, fourteen have a current rate cap lower than the cap in 1935 and four states (and the District of Columbia) have a current rate cap higher than the cap in 1935. Panel B contains a list of fourteen states with a current interest rate cap of 36 percent; of these states, Foster presents data for ten of them. Four have a current cap rate lower than the cap in 1935, three have a higher rate, and three states have rate caps today equal to the rate cap in 1935.

Panel C lists four states with a current rate cap greater than 36 percent. As shown in panel D of table 1, only nine states—Delaware, Idaho, Missouri, New Mexico, North Dakota, South Carolina (on loans over $640), South Dakota, Utah, and Wisconsin—have no rate cap. Instead, these states allow borrowers and lenders to agree on a rate appropriate for the loan size, likely resulting in a wide range of possible loan sizes in these states. Two others, Texas and Illinois, offer rates that likely result in a wide range of possible loan sizes. As shown in table 1, Foster presents data for eight of the thirteen states listed in panels C and D. All eight have a current rate cap that exceeds the rate cap in 1935.

Consequences of a 36 Percent Interest Rate Cap on Installment Loans

Twenty-three states and the District of Columbia have current rate caps less than 36 percent, fourteen states have an interest rate cap of 36 percent, and two more have caps slightly higher. The consequences of this rate cap level combined with inflation has likely led to a widespread "loan desert" for installment loans for amounts less than $1,000. The reason is simple. The interest income on a $1,000 loan with a 36 percent APR is the same amount, $206, regardless of what year the loan is made, but costs increase over time with inflation.[84]

In making an installment loan, there are significant production costs that increase over time with inflation. In the period 1971–1972, the NCCF, a federal government study commission authorized by the federal Consumer Credit Protection Act, studied the breakeven APR by loan size. These breakeven APRs were calculated using careful cost estimates from Smith.[85] The NCCF estimates a fixed cost of $50 to produce and collect the loan. In addition, the NCCF adds an 11 percent variable cost markup. This 11 percent variable cost allowance includes, presumably, a "normal" economic pretax profit.

Under these assumptions, the NCCF estimates that a $300 loan in 1972 has a 39.6 percent breakeven APR. For other loan sizes, the breakeven APRs (in parentheses) were estimated as $400 (32.7 percent), $500 (28.3 percent), $700 (23.5 percent), $1,000 (19.8 percent), $2,100 (15.2 percent), and $2,600 (14.4 percent) breakeven APR.

Durkin, Elliehausen, and Hwang update the NCCF estimates by restating the costs of making these loans into 2013 dollars.[86] They find that a $700 loan has a breakeven APR of 91.4 percent and a $1,000 loan has a breakeven APR of 77.9 percent, a $2,100 loan has a breakeven APR of 42.0 percent, and a loan of $2,600 has a breakeven APR of 36 percent.

Traditional installment lenders are competitive enterprises that must make a profit to remain in business. In states with a 36 percent rate cap, the implication of these higher breakeven rates is that traditional installment lenders will be making larger dollar loans in 2013 than they were in 1972 (or in any year with an inflation index lower than the level in 2013). The consequence of these higher breakeven rates, coupled with a 36 percent rate cap, is that there is likely an installment "loan desert" below some loan size, perhaps $2,600.

Figure 1 shows this loan desert graphically; in the figure a breakeven loan size of $2,500 is assumed. A one-year installment loan of $2,500 at 36 percent APR paid monthly generates $514 of interest. Suppose $514 represents the total fixed costs, variable costs, and normal profit for making an installment loan. Figure 1 compares a rate cap of 36 percent to the APR required in order

Figure 1. Approximate APR Required to Generate $514 Interest Income, by Loan Size (Assuming One-Year Loan with Monthly Payments)

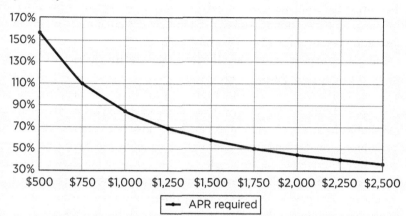

Note: *Original loan production cost and risk data are from Smith,* "Recent Trends in the Financial Position of Nine Major Consumer Finance Companies." *Smith's data appears in the report of the National Commission on Consumer Finance,* Consumer Credit in the United States, *exhibit 7-16, under rates that would "allow for enlargement of the market through a higher degree of risk acceptance." Durkin, Elliehausen, and Hwang, in* "Rate Ceilings and the Distribution of Small Dollar Installment Loans," *discuss the Commission's procedure in detail and they update the Commission's exhibit in their figure 1 by restating the costs per loan in 2013 dollars, so that a loan size somewhere between $2,200 and $2,700 has a breakeven rate of 36 percent (2013 dollars). In figure 1 as shown here, a break-even loan size of $2,500 is assumed. A one-year installment loan of $2,500 at 36 percent APR paid monthly generates $514 of interest; as shown here the APR must increase as the loan size decreases in order to generate $514 of interest.*

to generate $514 of interest as the loan size decreases. One can see that the APR required increases as the loan size decreases.

In states with a higher rate cap, however, there will be a wider range in the dollar amount lent by traditional installment lenders. Durkin, Elliehausen, and Hwang show that nearly half the installment loans in their study occur in five states with rate caps ranging from 40 percent to uncapped.[87] The median loan size ranged from $701 (Texas) to $1,102 (Illinois).

Existing Payday Loan Legislation

Payday loans are a popular type of lump-sum loan. In a payday loan transaction, a borrower writes a check to a lender in exchange for a short-term cash loan, generally for about two weeks. The lender agrees to cash the check on, or after, the date specified in the loan. Table 2 contains a summary of existing payday loan laws, by state. Data for this table is primarily from two sources: (1) the Community Financial Services Association of America (CFSA), which provided information privately, and (2) a web resource provided by the Consumer Federation of America (CFED), which attempts to maintain an information resource for advocates and consumers.[88]

As displayed in panel A of table 2, thirteen states and the District of Columbia prohibit the lump-sum payday lending product. As shown in panel B of table 2, the laws in three other states do not expressly prohibit payday lending, but the state-imposed interest rate cap in those states likely makes payday lending unprofitable. Maine appears in both panels because one database classifies it as prohibiting payday lending, while another classifies it as having an APR of 43 percent.[89] The new payday lending law in Colorado does not allow lump-sum payday lending. Instead, the law requires multiple payments on a payday loan.

States regulate payday lenders in many different ways. One common way is to set a maximum fee allowed on a payday loan transaction. Sources often annualize and report this fee, which, as reported in table 2, ranges from $10.00 to $30.12 on a two-week $100 payday loan. A second common way that states regulate payday loan transactions is by the amount of money that a payday lender can loan to a borrower in a payday loan. Panel C contains a list of states with caps on fees (and their annualized rates) and with a cap on the state-allowed amount borrowed. Two columns in panel C show the annualized rates at the time the raw data was gathered. Two other columns show the state-allowed maximum amount borrowed. This maximum amount is either a stated amount or a percentage of the borrower's gross income. The last two columns in panel C show these maximum amounts.

At the time the raw data was gathered, all states but three, Texas, Wyoming, and Utah, set a maximum borrowing amount for payday loans.[90] The maximum allowable amount ranges from $300 (California and Montana) to $2,500 (New Mexico). The most common maximum amount is $500 (fifteen states per CFSA and seventeen states per CFED), with one (or two per the CFED) at $550, three (or two) at $600, and one (per the CFED) at $700. Only four states allow a maximum loan amount of $1,000 or more: Idaho and Illinois at $1,000; Wisconsin at $1,500; and New Mexico at $2,500.

Panel D of table 2 contains a list of the six states where payday lending is legal and without one (or both) of the state-imposed restrictions. Only one, Utah, has neither restriction.

CONCRETE ACTIONS FOR ADVOCATES, ACADEMICS, AND LEGISLATURES IN MOVING FORWARD IN SMALL-DOLLAR LOAN LEGISLATION

Consider Adding Other Measures of the Cost of Small-Dollar Loans

It is easy for consumer advocates and others to catch "APR fever." After all, most consumer advocates have had personal experience with traditional credit products, such as home mortgages, wherein APRs and changes in APR matter. For example, all else equal, an interest rate increase of 1 percent (i.e., 100 basis points) on a $200,000 fixed-rate, thirty-year mortgage increases the interest cost to the consumer by $40,000 over the life of the loan.[91]

The APR is a useful disclosure for a wide range of consumer credit products. Consumers can readily compare the costs of many consumer credit products offered by different types of lenders using the APR, even if they do not understand the mathematics. However, the APR is not useful and is potentially misleading in some circumstances. Durkin and Elliehausen argue that these circumstances include joint purchases of credit and other products, such as credit insurance.[92] Durkin and Elliehausen also argue that APRs are not useful and are perhaps misleading for short-term (less than a year) loans.[93]

Some credit decisions are inherently difficult and a single number should likely not be used to make these decisions. Mors provides a good discussion on assessing the cost of credit and argues that depending on circumstances, several types of information may be useful, including an effective interest rate (APR), finance charge, monthly payment and term to maturity, and simple interest rate.[94]

In the small-dollar loan market, using only an APR as a loan cost indicator presents a skewed view of the cost of borrowing. Research results show that consumers are more concerned about the dollar costs of borrowing than the APR. Consumers can easily compare the dollar costs of loans and can easily understand them. Elliehausen and Lawrence show that borrowers only recall dollar costs, even though lenders disclose APR as well as dollar costs;[95] one study of the small-dollar loan market posits that dollar costs are a better loan cost indicator than APR for consumers.[96] DeYoung and Phillips show that APR is a poor predictor of the behavior of payday borrowers with respect to payday loan pricing.[97]

Consumers who do not have enough money to pay their current bills know that they could face charges for nonsufficient funds, penalties and late fees, as well as reconnection fees for their utilities. For example, the Center for

Responsible Lending reports that consumers were assessed $10 billion in over-draft charges in 2005 alone.

If one converts these charges to an implied APR, the costs of paying these charges exceed the interest rates from lump-sum payday lenders. Suppose a consumer writes a $100 check, but does not have sufficient funds in the account. Furthermore, suppose the overdraft fee is $40. If the consumer pays the $40 overdraft fee in two weeks, the computed APR is $1,040.[98] By contrast, a $100 two-week payday loan with an APR of 520 percent, costs the consumer only $20—half as much as the potential overdraft fee.

Tescher advocates the "TIP" calculation as a standard "by which to judge comparably the cost of short-term, small-dollar loans, regardless of what they are called."[99] The TIP ratio is calculated by dividing the total interest by the principal of the loan. A two-week $500 lump sum payday loan with a 20 percent fee (an APR of 520 percent) has a TIP ratio of 20 percent. A twelve-month $1,000 traditional installment loan with an APR of 36 percent has a TIP ratio of 21 percent.[100]

The TIP ratio is much lower for the lump-sum payday loans and traditional installment loans than it is for a traditional fixed rate mortgage. A $200,000 thirty-year mortgage at a 4 percent APR has a TIP ratio of 72 percent. A $1,000 traditional installment loan with an APR of 96 percent has a TIP ratio of 59 percent.[101] Mortgages are neither short term in nature nor do they involve small amounts of money. However, these loans are expensive for consumers via the TIP calculation when compared to any of the lump-sum payday loans or traditional installment loans given. The lesson from a TIP calculation is that focusing only on the APR conceals the dollar costs paid by the consumer.

Allow Different Interest Rates for Different Amounts Borrowed

Recall that rate ceilings are not always a single APR. In fact, many states have ceilings graduated by size of loan that are higher for smaller loans than for larger loans. The Uniform Small Loan Law of 1916 provides a classic example of a graduated rate. From Section 13:

> Every licensee hereunder may lend any sum of money not
> to exceed three hundred dollars ($300) in amount and may

> contract for and receive thereon charges at a rate not exceeding
> three and one-half per centum (3½ percent) per month on
> that part of the unpaid principal balance of any loan not in
> excess of one hundred dollars ($100) and two and one-half
> per centum (2½ percent) per month on any remainder of
> such unpaid principal balance.

Today, some states allow much higher rates for very small loan sizes. Durkin, Elliehausen, and Hwang[102] illustrate the effect of these higher rate ceilings on the distribution of loan sizes and APRs. In general, one observes small loan sizes when the law allows higher rates for small loan sizes.

Installment loans, like other goods, have production costs.[103] The biggest production cost facing installment lenders is underwriting the loan, which involves employees spending time assessing the ability of the borrower to repay the loan and filling out paperwork required by regulation. After making the loan, the lender faces another significant cost—the time spent monitoring the loan to ensure timely repayment. Lenders must pay for the money that they acquire to lend to their borrowers and, like any brick-and-mortar business, the lender has rent, utilities, salaries, and benefits costs.

Because production costs for small-dollar loans are roughly the same as production costs of larger-dollar loans, loans with low principal amounts are not as likely to be made under binding interest rate caps. To make small-dollar loans, lenders must earn a dollar profit that supports offering these loans. Under a binding interest rate cap, these small-dollar loans do not provide sufficient income to cover costs. Breakeven interest rates, therefore, increase as the loan size falls. Durkin, Elliehausen, and Hwang summarize the compelling evidence from the National Commission on Consumer Finance that a rate cap precludes the offering of a wide range of small-dollar loans.[104]

Study the Effects of Interest Rate Caps Thoroughly before Imposing Them

Michelman states that social reformers of the early 1900s placed great emphasis on thoroughly and carefully studying an issue first, and only then passing laws based on the results of these studies.[105] In 1909, the Russell Sage Foundation took this approach when it charged Arthur H. Ham to "study the Remedial Loan Associations of the country, to give advice to societies already established as to methods of work, and to give advice to those who wish to know about the formation of new societies."[106]

Anderson reports that in November 1911, Arthur Ham addressed the fifth annual convention of the Maine Conference of Charities and Corrections.[107] At a time when rate ceilings made profitable small-loan lending impossible, Ham outlined the need for small-dollar loan reform by saying:

> We should not lose sight of the fact that the average annual earnings of the workingman in American cities is hardly more than $500 and . . . that the average family . . . cannot maintain a normal standard of living on this amount of income. Consequently, it becomes immediately apparent that in time of sickness or similar crisis almost every wage-earner is forced to borrow money. . . . It is a regrettable fact that . . . the small loan business in this country has been almost entirely, and even now, is very largely in the hands of discredited and disreputable people [i.e., "loan sharks"], who . . . fatten upon the misfortunes and the necessities of the deserving.

Arthur Ham's plea for freeing citizens from "discredited and disreputable" lenders (i.e., "loan sharks") is consistent with access to credit being an important aspect of the fundamental freedom to enter wealth-enhancing contracts.

The problems American consumers face concerning income disruptions and expense shocks have not materially changed in the past 100 years. What has changed in the interest rate legislation arena is the abandonment of a deliberate legislative process following careful study. Let us return to that culture of studying interest costs through rigorous and unbiased study. The best example of this approach is the 1972 report of the National Commission on Consumer Finance. Perhaps it is time for another large-scale study of the current state of consumer credit in the United States.

Revise or Eliminate Interest Rate Caps

A comment in Hubachek's 1941 article is still relevant. It begins:

> The maximum rate of charge of 3½ per cent a month on
> that part of any loan balance not exceeding $100 and 2½ per
> cent a month on that part exceeding $100 is recommended
> as an initial rate in all states. This combination of rates per-
> mits a maximum charge ranging from 3½ per cent a month
> on outstanding balances of $100 or less to 2.83 per cent a
> month on outstanding balances of $300. The rate is designed
> to attract aggressive competition by licensed lenders follow-
> ing the enactment of the law in order to drive unlicensed
> lenders out of business. *This rate should be reconsidered after
> a reasonable period of experience with it.* (emphasis added)[108]

Clearly, 100-plus years certainly exceeds "a reasonable period." There is a
need for exhaustive, and extensive, research that examines any small-dollar loan
market where buyers and sellers contractually agree to loan terms, particularly
the interest rate. As shown in table 1, many states have kept interest rate caps on
traditional installment loans at the maximum APR of 36 percent or below.

In the lump-sum payday loan space, there is only one state, Utah, with no
limit on the dollar amount of a payday loan or an interest rate cap. Five other
states, Delaware, Idaho, Nevada, South Dakota, and Wisconsin, impose no rate
cap on lump-sum payday loans, but limit the dollar amount. Missouri imposes
a 1,955 percent APR on payday loans.

In the traditional installment loan space, there are a few more states available for researchers to study a loan market where borrowers and lenders can
freely enter into loan agreements (i.e., no rate cap). As shown in table 1, states
that allow borrowers and lenders to enter into loans by contract are Delaware,
Idaho, Missouri, New Mexico, North Dakota, South Carolina (for amounts
over $640), South Dakota, Utah, and Wisconsin. Additionally, Texas and
Illinois allow for rates higher than the bulk of the other states.

Legislatures can learn from the range of loan sizes in these "by contract"
states and the frequency of these loans. If a wide range of loan sizes exists, this
fact is consistent with the notion that the borrower has access to a loan that

is "right" for her. Then, one can compare the range and frequency of loan sizes across interest rate cap categories. By doing so, one can estimate the costs of interest rate caps to consumers.

The National Commission on Consumer Finance makes a strong statement on this issue. It states,

> The Commission recommends that each state evaluate the competitiveness of its markets before considering raising or lowering rate ceilings from present levels. Policies designed to promote competition should be given the first priority, with adjustment of rate ceilings used as a complement to expand the availability of credit. As the development of workably competitive markets decreases the need for rate ceilings to combat market power in concentrated markets, such ceilings may be raised or removed.[109]

CONCLUSION

For a variety of reasons, since the beginning of recorded history, lawmakers have looked on the ownership of money, and the charges for its use, differently from the ownership of other assets and the charges for their use. Consequently, setting interest rap caps on loans has long been a focus of religious leaders and a wide variety of governments and their agents. A belief in the effectiveness of interest rate caps endures despite many empirical studies showing that not only are interest rate caps ineffective, they harm their intended beneficiaries.

Fundamentally, because interest rate caps are a market-distorting action, imposing an interest rate cap or banning loan products reduces the well-being of parties who would have otherwise engaged in trade. Nonetheless, advocates continue to argue for interest rate caps. Their arguments fall into four general categories:

1. Borrowers are naïve and simply do not understand the loan terms.

2. Groups thought to be most vulnerable to exploitation by lenders—namely minorities, women, and the poor—need protection from predatory lenders.

3. Even if consumers are willing to borrow at high interest rates, society should protect these consumers from themselves because they are making themselves worse off.

4. Lenders, especially small-dollar lenders, make abnormally high profits from lending at high interest rates because they have considerable market power.

This chapter summarizes a large body of rigorous research that examines these arguments. Little, if any, empirical evidence supports any of these four arguments.

Many consumer advocates have had personal experience with traditional credit products such as high-limit credit cards, home mortgages, and personal lines of credit. Few, however, share the daily budgetary concerns facing many hourly workers. These workers generally have lower income levels and lower levels of wealth. As a result, income disruptions and/or expense shocks have a profound impact on their ability to pay bills.

Today, there are two dominant forms of small-dollar loan products available to consumers who seek nonbank-provided credit: a lump-sum payday loan, paid back with interest at the end of the loan period, and a traditional installment loan, in which the borrower makes equally spaced, equal payments over the life of the loan.

Existing payday and traditional installment lending legislation severely restricts access to these credit products. Twelve (or thirteen, depending on Maine's classification) states and the District of Columbia place outright bans on the payday lending product. The laws in four other states do not expressly prohibit payday lending, but the state-imposed interest rate cap in those states likely precludes the lump-sum payday lending product. In addition, Colorado law imposes an installment payment plan instead of allowing the lump-sum loan product.

All states but one, Utah, set a maximum borrowing amount for payday loans. The maximum allowable amount ranges from $300 (California and Montana) to $2,500 (New Mexico), while the most common maximum amount is $500 (seventeen states).

Where legal, the maximum APR of payday lending interest rates range from 36 percent (Montana, New Hampshire, and Oregon) to 1,955 percent (Missouri). Only six states allow the parties to the loan to set the interest rate by contract.

Advocates and legislators often ignore the actual dollar cost of a payday loan. For a $100, fourteen-day payday loan with an APR of 790 percent, the interest expense to the consumer is only $30. Clearly, it is easier to foster and bolster passion to oppose an APR of 790 percent than the corresponding $30 interest expense.

No state bans traditional installment lending. The AFSA trade association reports, however, that traditional installment lenders do not operate in seventeen states (or the District of Columbia). The names of these states appear in bold italics in table 1. The APR in these seventeen states and the District of Columbia ranges from 17 percent (Arkansas and Connecticut) to 36 percent (Arizona, Indiana, Kansas, Oregon, and Virginia).

Moving forward, we propose four concrete actions for researchers to study and provide results to consumer advocates and legislators. These actions are:

1. Include other ways to measure the cost of small-dollar loans.

2. Allow different interest rates for different amounts borrowed.

3. Return to studying interest rates thoroughly before regulating them.

4. Revise, or eliminate, interest rate caps.

Each of these actions allows or enhances voluntary exchange that benefits both borrowers and lenders. Both parties in a voluntary trade are better off after the trade than they were before the trade. If they were not, they would not trade. In lending, there would be no loan agreement unless both parties were better off by making the loan.

Every day, consumers make choices based on the price of money—just as they respond to prices of other goods and services. The market for credit is not "special" or "different"; it also obeys the laws of supply and demand. Consequently, as in any market that obeys the laws of supply and demand, letting the market determine prices and quantities will greatly benefit the participants in the small-dollar loan market.

APPENDIX

Suppose a consumer desires to obtain a bona fide small-dollar loan from an in-the-flesh lender. This consumer essentially has two choices: a traditional installment loan from a finance company or a payday loan.[110]

Traditional Installment Loans

In the early 1900s, a battle raged against illegal "loan sharks" and an alternate new loan source emerged through the collaboration of lenders who wanted to offer this new product and consumer advocates, notably Arthur H. Ham of the Russell Sage Foundation. What emerged was the Uniform Small Loan Law written in 1916. By the 1960s, almost all states had adopted some version of this model law.[111]

The striking feature of this law was that it allowed for interest rates higher than allowed under existing usury laws. Of course, both illegal "loan sharks" and those who favored low interest rate ceilings lobbied long and hard against this legislation. When collaborating on the Uniform Small Loan Law, the parties agreed on the following: (1) Legal installment lenders must be able to earn a reasonable profit. Therefore, the interest rate was initially set at 3 to 3.5 percent per month; (2) small loans were defined as "up to $300" (in today's dollars, about $7,137), and (3) the interest rate would be reexamined periodically to sustain the industry.

As an example of an installment loan, suppose a consumer wants to borrow $1,000 to pay for vehicle repairs. The terms of the loan are twelve months, an annual interest rate of 36 percent (3 percent per month), and no closing fee (for ease of calculation). To calculate the loan payment, we use the following two equations:

$$\$P = \$C \left[\frac{1 - Present\ Value\ Factor}{r} \right]$$

where:

$$Present\ Value\ Factor = \frac{1}{(1+r)^T}.$$

In this example, the Present Value Factor is $= \frac{1}{(1+.03)^{12}} = 0.70138$. The resulting monthly payment is

$$\$1{,}000 = \$C\left[\frac{1-0.70138}{.03}\right] = \$C\,[9.9540],$$

and we can calculate $\$C = \$100.46$. The total of interest and principal payments equals the payment times the number of payments, or $\$100.46$ times 12, or $\$1{,}205.55$. The consumer borrowed $\$1{,}000$, so the consumer pays $\$205.55$ in interest over the life of the loan. Notice that the consumer does NOT pay $\$1{,}000$ times 0.36, or $\$360$, in interest. The difference between $\$360$ and $\$205.55$ occurs because the amount owed each month declines, or amortizes, over the length of the loan. Therefore, even though the interest rate of 36 percent determines the size of the installment payment, the interest income received by the lender is $\$205.55$, or 20.56 percent of $\$1{,}000$.

Payday Loans

A payday loan is a short-term, lump-sum loan. Most of the loans are for a term of thirty days or less. (Payday loans are also known as cash advance loans, delayed deposit loans, and deferred presentment loans.) In a traditional payday loan, a borrower writes a check to a lender in exchange for a short-term cash loan. The lender agrees not to cash the check until a date specified in the loan agreement.

To obtain a payday loan, lenders generally require borrowers to have an active checking account, provide proof of income, show valid identification, and be at least eighteen years old. Payday lenders generally do not require a traditional credit report.

As of September 6, 2016, according to the website for the National Conference of State Legislatures: "Thirty-eight states have specific statutes that allow for payday lending. Eleven jurisdictions do not have specific payday lending statutory provisions and/or require lenders to comply with interest rate caps on consumer loans . . . [while] . . . Arizona and North Carolina allowed pre-existing payday lending statutes to sunset. Arkansas repealed its pre-existing statute in 2011."[112]

Mississippi law, for example, allows a payday lender to charge a fee of up to $\$20$ per $\$100$ advanced to the borrower. For example, if a borrower writes a check for $\$240$, the lender advances $\$200$ to the borrower and keeps the check, which includes $\$40$ in fees. Assuming this loan is for two weeks, the annual percentage rate is $\$40/\$200$ times $26 = 520$ percent.

NOTES

Acknowledgments: The authors thank Carolyn Moore Miller, Ted Bolema, Tom Durkin, Greg Elliehausen, and two anonymous reviewers for editorial comments and helpful suggestions. We thank Wenqing Gao for research assistance. An early version called "An Overview of Usury Ceilings and Their Impact on Borrowers" contains some of the content herein. The National Installment Lenders Association (NILA) supported that March 2009 document. NILA had no editorial control over the content in the earlier write-up or over this version.

1. Michelman, *Consumer Finance*, 87–88.

2. Homer and Sylla, *History of Interest Rates*.

3. For the interested reader, many authors document the history of interest rates and lending. An incomplete list includes Michelman, *Consumer Finance*; Homer and Sylla, *History of Interest Rates*; Smith, "Rethinking Usury Laws"; Horack, "Survey of the General Usury Laws," 36–53; Glaeser and Scheinkman, "Neither a Borrower nor a Lender Be," 1–6; Calder, *Financing the American Dream*; Botticini, "Tale of 'Benevolent' Governments," 164–89; Anderson, "Experts, Ideas, and Policy Changes," 271–310; Graeber, *Debt*; Durkin, Elliehausen, and Hwang, "Rate Ceilings"; Durkin, Elliehausen, and Zywicki, "Consumer Credit and the American Economy"; Durkin et al., *Consumer Credit and the American Economy*.

4. See Homer and Sylla, *History of Interest Rates*.

5. Glaeser and Scheinkman, "Neither a Borrower nor a Lender Be."

6. Ekelund, Herbert, and Tollison, "Economic Model of the Medieval Church," 307–31. They do not claim that the Church invented the doctrine of interest rate restrictions merely for economic gain. Rather, they state that the doctrine was imposed (and modified through time) for other religious reasons. The Church likely did recognize, however, the benefit of low rates when it borrowed.

7. Benmelech and Moskowitz, "Political Economy of Financial Regulation," 1029–73.

8. Durkin, Elliehausen, and Zywicki, "Consumer Credit and the American Economy."

9. Benmelech and Moskowitz, "Political Economy of Financial Regulation," 1030.

10. Bryant, "On Usury Laws."

11. Milton Friedman cited in Friedman and Friedman, *Free to Choose*, 219.

12. Blitz and Long, "Economics of Usury Regulation," 608–19.

13. Durkin et al., *Consumer Credit and the American Economy*.

14. Villegas, "Impact of Usury Ceilings on Consumer Credit," 126–41.

15. Bowsher, "Usury Laws," 18.

16. Zinman, "Restricting Consumer Credit Access," 546–56.

17. Ibid.; Peterson and Falls, "Impact of a Ten Percent Usury Ceiling."

18. Ernst, Farris, and King, "Quantifying the Economic Costs." They contend that banning high interest rate loans benefits consumers with high debt burdens and argue that because consumers spend $3.4 billion (in their study) in interest charges, consumers will instead save most of this amount. Morgan and Strain in "Payday Holiday" point out that Ernst et al. ignore the interest costs resulting from customers resorting to higher cost loans and the costs of increased financial stress.

19. Zywicki, "Case against New Restrictions," 1.

20. Durkin and Elliehausen, *Truth in Lending.*

21. Elliehausen and Lawrence, "Payday Advance Credit in America."

22. Zinman, "Restricting Consumer Credit Access," 548n18: "Bouncing checks is quite costly due to insufficient funds and returned-check fees . . . the bank often charges the account holder [a] fee of $20 or more; hence in many cases getting a payday loan is cheaper than over-drawing the checking account (particularly if the account holder runs the risk of overdraw-ing multiple checks)."

23. Miller, "Differences in Consumer Credit Choices."

24. Durkin et al., *Consumer Credit and the American Economy.*

25. Barr, *No Slack.*

26. Elliehausen and Lawrence, "Payday Advance Credit in America."

27. See Stegman and Faris, "Payday Lending"; DeYoung and Phillips, "Payday Loan Pricing." Dollar values are adjusted by the Consumer Price Index from the St. Louis Federal Reserve Bank.

28. Elliehausen and Lawrence, "Payday Advance Credit in America," Table 5-6.

29. Stegman, "Payday Lending."

30. Stegman and Faris, "Payday Lending." This finding is consistent with African-American households typically having worse credit, and less income, than white households do.

31. Stegman, "Payday Lending." Interestingly, Flannery and Samolyk ("Payday Lending") note that while mature stores are located in zip codes with higher proportions of African-Americans, the lenders in their study typically locate their newer stores in zip codes with lower proportions of African-Americans and Hispanics.

32. Graves and Peterson, "Predatory Lending and the Military."

33. Morgan, "Defining and Detecting Predatory Lending"; Stegman, "Payday Lending."

34. In 2006, Congress enacted the Talent-Nelson Amendment to the John Warner National Defense Authorization Act of 2007. The amendment, also known as Section 670, is meant to regulate the terms of certain credit extensions, including payday loans, vehicle title loans, and refund anticipation loans, to active-duty service members and their dependents. See Department of Defense, "Report on Predatory Lending Practices," 50580, 50584.

35. Carrell and Zinman, "In Harm's Way?," 2805–40.

36. Brown and Cushman, "Compensation and Short-Term Credit Needs."

37. See Ernst, Farris, and King, "Quantifying the Economic Costs." Ernst et al. notes that this estimate is conservative because it includes only the direct costs of payday lending. The esti-mate does not include the costs associated with what they term "payday lending induced bankruptcies."

38. To our knowledge, proponents are silent on the actions by other consumers who pay the minimum monthly payment on their credit cards. Credit cards have a lower APR than payday loans or traditional installment loans, but paying the minimum monthly payment drastically extends the amount of time to pay off a credit card. See, for example, the calcula-tor available at www.greenpath.com.

39. Proponents once advocated for a ban on the production, transportation, and sale of alco-holic beverages, which resulted in the Eighteenth Amendment to the US Constitution. These proponents mistakenly believed that these bans would then result in nearly zero levels of alcohol consumption.

40. Morgan and Strain, "Payday Holiday."

41. Ibid. Morgan and Strain reported similar results for North Carolina.

42. Morgan, "Defining and Detecting Predatory Lending."

43. Morse, "Payday Lenders," 28–44.

44. Peterson, "Usury Laws and Consumer Credit"; Peterson and Falls, "Impact of a Ten Percent Usury Ceiling."

45. Peterson and Falls, "Impact of a Ten Percent Usury Ceiling."

46. Peterson, "Usury Laws and Consumer Credit." Although credit card rates were subject to the interest rate cap, merchants accepting credit cards could mark up prices so that they could lend at the state-imposed interest rate.

47. Pawnbrokers typically charge a fee of 10 to 20 percent per month.

48. Collins and Sonstegaard, "Hey Buddy Can Ya' Spare a Dime?"

49. Zinman, "Restricting Consumer Credit Access."

50. Ibid. Adverse condition is defined as being unemployed or having a negative subjective assessment about one's overall or future financial condition. Although Zinman's results are consistent with the notion that payday lending is welfare enhancing rather than welfare destructive, he cautions that more research is needed in this area.

51. Ibid., 547.

52. Bureau of Consumer Financial Protection, Payday Loans and Deposit Advance Products, 81 Fed. Reg. (July 22, 2016): 47863, 47871.

53. Morgan, "Defining and Detecting Predatory Lending."

54. DeYoung and Phillips, "Payday Loan Pricing."

55. After controlling for loan volume, Flannery and Samolyk also find that the economic and demographic conditions in the neighborhoods where the stores are located do not have much of an effect on profitability. Flannery and Samolyk, "Payday Lending."

56. Huckstep, "Payday Lending," 204.

57. Stegman and Faris, "Payday Lending."

58. Huckstep, "Payday Lending."

59. National Commission on Consumer Finance, Consumer Credit in the United States.

60. Smith ("Rethinking Usury Laws") reports that state laws codified usury as charging interest over the legal maximum. In the early twentieth century, legal lending rates were typically 6 percent. Under the laws at the time, a lender was equally guilty of usury for charging 7 percent per year or charging 7 percent per month.

61. These movements included women's suffrage, temperance, child worker laws, pensions for workers, and pure food and drug laws.

62. See Calder, Financing the American Dream, and Anderson, "Experts, Ideas, and Policy Changes," for detailed descriptions of the Progressive era, the Russell Sage Foundation, and credit reform.

63. Carruthers, Guinnane, and Lee, "Bringing 'Honest Capital,'" 393–418.

64. The Russell Sage foundation, as well as the Progressive Movement of the early twentieth century, placed considerable weight on the value of rigorous research to underpin social

legislation. This emphasis extended to the setting of interest rates. The emphasis on the value of rigorous research has faded, but the rates from a hundred years earlier remain. For example, lacking the support of rigorous research, the Talent-Nelson Amendment and the national usury ceiling proposed by Senator Dick Durbin both propose keeping annual interest rate caps of 36 percent (i.e., 3 percent per month).

65. Hubachek, "Development of Regulatory Small Loan Laws," 108–45. Appendix C in ibid., "Sixth Draft: General Form of Uniform Small Loan Law," distills all the work and thought on this topic into a model law. The language of the sixth draft grew to fill eight pages in twenty-five years: six pages that outline the model law and two pages that contain nineteen notes on various aspects of it.

66. Michelson, *Consumer Finance.*

67. Foster, "Personal Finance Business," 154–72.

68. For this chapter, this history is not germane. The origin of the Uniform Small Loan Law, the origin of the 36 percent rate cap, and current state-mandated interest rate caps are much more important.

69. Durkin et al., *Consumer Credit and the American Economy.*

70. Ibid.

71. One of the authors is currently researching the costs of installment loan production over time versus the income from installment loans of various sizes. The purpose of the project is to identify when installment lenders migrated away from loans less than a particular size (say, $1,000).

72. Community Financial Services Association of America, "About the Payday Advance Industry," retrieved October 27, 2016, http://cfsaa.com/about-the-payday-advance-industry.aspx.

73. Bair, "Low-Cost Payday Loans."

74. Caskey, "Payday Lending," 1–14.

75. Stegman, "Payday Lending"; Bair, "Low-Cost Payday Loans," citing Stephens Inc., "Industry Report."

76. The CFPB estimated that the number of payday lending stores operating in 2014 was 15,766. Bureau of Consumer Financial Protection, "Payday, Vehicle Title, and Certain High-Cost Installment Loans; Proposed Rule," 81 Fed. Reg. (July 22, 2016): 47864, 47871.

77. Hecht, "Alternative Financial Services."

78. Within a week in July 2009, the US House of Representatives held a hearing on "The Proposed Consumer Finance Protection Agency: Implications for Consumers and the FTC," and the US Senate held a hearing titled "Creating a Consumer Financial Protection Agency: A Cornerstone of America's New Economic Foundation." On July 21, 2010, the 848 pages of H.R. 4173 became Pub. L. 111-203, commonly called Dodd-Frank. See Law Librarians' Society of Washington, DC, "Dodd-Frank Wall Street Reform and Consumer Financial Protection Act: A Brief Legislative History with Links, Reports and Summaries."

79. See Zywicki, "Consumer Financial Protection Bureau," 856–928, for a carefully detailed presentation of the implications of the "rush to regulate" approach manifested in this massive agency.

80. One might be inclined to include online payday loans, but the focus in this chapter is on "brick-and-mortar lenders." One might also be inclined to include pawn loans or title loans. These transactions, however, are not loans in the traditional sense because the borrower has the right simply to exchange the good (or vehicle) for cash and walk away. Although the borrower has the option to redeem the proceeds for the pawned item, there is no recourse for the

lender. In addition, credit cards might not be available to some consumers. Other consumers might have access to credit cards, but have no available credit remaining on their cards.

81. Foster, "Personal Finance Business."

82. Rate ceilings were also graduated in many states in the 1930s.

83. The careful reader will wonder why installment lenders operate in these states. Our conjecture is that dollar loan levels in these states are, on average, significantly higher than in states with higher interest rate caps.

84. Because the principal is paid down each month, it is important to note that at a 36 percent APR, the dollar amount of interest paid on a $1,000 twelve-month installment loan is $206. That is, it is *not* the simple interest amount of $1,000 times 0.36, or $360. An APR of 61 percent results in an interest cost of $360.

85. The estimates come from Smith, "Recent Trends." Exhibit 7-16 of the NCCF report incorporates the cost data from 1964.

86. Durkin, Elliehausen, and Hwang, "Rate Ceilings."

87. Ibid., table 9. These states are Texas, South Carolina, Illinois, Missouri, and Georgia.

88. For the CFSA, see www.cfsaa.com and, for the CFED website, www.paydayloaninfo.org. Two other useful resources are at www.ncsl.org, which is provided by the National Conference of State Legislatures, and "Resource Guide: Protections from Predatory Short-Term Loans," from the CFED, cfed.org/assets/scorecard/2013/rg_PredatoryLending_2013.pdf. Data for Maine and Ohio are from Barth et al., "Do State Regulations Affect Payday Lender Concentration?" Data was gathered directly from each state's regulatory authorities.

89. Compare CFED with Barth et al., "Do State Regulations Affect Payday Lender Concentration?"

90. However, the website, paydayloaninfo.org, does not specify a limit for two states where it is unlikely that payday lending operates, Maine and Oregon, and does not specify a limit for two other states, Texas and Wyoming, where payday lending likely operates.

91. A careful reader would notice that, to be useful in a mortgage, an APR would have to reflect when the borrower expects to repay the mortgage—something that the borrower cannot always predict. To make an intelligent mortgage loan decision, the borrower might need more than the APR or any other single number.

92. Durkin and Elliehausen, *Truth in Lending*.

93. Durkin and Elliehausen, "Assessing the Price of Short Term Credit."

94. See Mors, *Consumer Credit Finance Charges*. We thank an anonymous reviewer for providing this discussion.

95. Elliehausen and Lawrence, "Payday Advance Credit in America."

96. Buch, Rhoda, and Talaga, "Usefulness of the APR." Buch et al. note similar difficulties in mortgage borrowers making comparisons in selecting mortgages based on APR.

97. DeYoung and Phillips, "Payday Loan Pricing."

98. To see how to calculate APR, go to www.moneyandhappiness.com/blog/?p=26.

99. Tescher, "Letter to Mr. Robert E. Feldman."

100. The monthly payment on a $1,000 one-year installment loan with an APR of 36 percent is $100.46, which means the total interest paid is $205.55.

101. The monthly payment on a $200,000 thirty-year mortgage with an APR of 4 percent is $954.83, which means the total interest paid is $143,739. The monthly payment on a $1,000

one-year installment loan with an APR of 96 percent is $132.70, which means the total interest paid is $592.34.

102. Durkin, Elliehausen, and Hwang, "Rate Ceilings."

103. As detailed in Michelman, *Consumer Finance*; National Commission on Consumer Finance, *Consumer Credit in the United States*; Durkin, Elliehausen, Staten, and Zywicki, *Consumer Credit and the American Economy*; and Durkin, Elliehausen, and Hwang, "Rate Ceilings."

104. Durkin, Elliehausen, and Hwang, "Rate Ceilings"; National Commission on Consumer Finance, *Consumer Credit in the United States*.

105. Michelman, *Consumer Finance*.

106. Quote from Glenn, Brandt, and Andrews, *Russell Sage Foundation 1907–1946*. Remedial Loan Societies in the early 1900s exemplified the principle of "philanthropy and 6 percent" by lending small amounts of money at rates high enough to cover their operating costs and yield a "fair" return on capital invested. Given the number of illegal lenders operating at the time, the Remedial Loan Societies obviously could not supply all demand for small loans.

107. Anderson, "Experts, Ideas, and Policy Changes."

108. Hubachek, "Development of Regulatory Small Loan Laws," app. C, n14.

109. National Commission on Consumer Finance, *Consumer Credit in the United States*.

110. One might be inclined to include online payday loans, but the borrower here prefers to deal with a lender in the flesh. One might also be inclined to include pawn loans or title loans. These transactions, however, are not traditional loans because they are nonrecourse—that is, the borrower has the right simply to exchange the good (or vehicle) for cash and walk away.

111. Durkin et al., *Consumer Credit and the American Economy*, 491.

112. See National Conference of State Legislatures, Payday Lending State Statutes. For more information, see Consumer Federation of America, "Legal Status of Payday Loans by State."

REFERENCES

American Financial Services Association. "State Small Loan Lending Law Categories." Washington, DC, 2014.

Anderson, Elisabeth. "Experts, Ideas, and Policy Changes: The Russell Sage Foundation and Small Loan Reform, 1909–1941." *Theory and Society* 37, no. 3 (June 2008): 271–310.

Bair, Sheila. "Low-Cost Payday Loans: Opportunities and Obstacles." Annie E. Casey Foundation, University of Massachusetts at Amherst, 2005.

Barr, Michael S. *No Slack: The Financial Lives of Low-Income Americans*. Washington, DC: Brookings Institution, 2012.

Barth, James R., Jitka Hilliard, John S. Jahera, and Yanfei Sun. "Do State Regulations Affect Payday Lender Concentration?" *Journal of Economics and Business* 84 (March–April 2016): 14–29, app. 2.

Benmelech, Efraim, and Tobias J. Moskowitz. "The Political Economy of Financial Regulation: Evidence from U.S. Usury Laws in the 19th Century." *Journal of Finance* 65 (2010): 1029–73.

Blitz, Rudolph C., and Millard F. Long. "The Economics of Usury Regulation." *Journal of Political Economy* 73, no. 6 (1965): 608–19.

Botticini, Maristella. "A Tale of 'Benevolent' Governments: Private Credit Markets, Public Finance, and the Role of Jewish Lenders in Medieval and Renaissance Italy." *Journal of Economic History* 60 (2000): 164–89.

Bowsher, Norman N. "Usury Laws: Harmful When Effective." *Federal Reserve Bank of St. Louis Review*, August 1974, 16–23.

Brown, William O., Jr., and Charles B. Cushman Jr. "Compensation and Short-Term Credit Needs of U.S. Military Enlisted Personnel." Consumer Credit Research Foundation, 2006.

Bryant, William Cullen. "On Usury Laws." *New York Evening Post*, September 26, 1836.

Buch, Joshua, Kenneth L. Rhoda, and James Talaga. "The Usefulness of the APR for Mortgage Marketing in the USA and the UK." *International Journal of Bank Marketing* 20, no. 2 (2002): 76–85.

Calder, Lendol. *Financing the American Dream: A Cultural History of Consumer Credit.* Princeton, NJ: Princeton University Press, 1999.

Carrell, Scott, and Jonathan Zinman. "In Harm's Way? Payday Loan Access and Military Personnel Performance." *Review of Financial Studies* 27 (2014): 2805–40.

Carruthers, Bruce G., Timothy W. Guinnane, and Yoonseok Lee. "Bringing 'Honest Capital' to Poor Borrowers: The Passage of the Uniform Small Loan Law, 1907–1930." *Journal of Interdisciplinary History* 42 (2012): 393–418.

Caskey, John P. "Payday Lending." *Journal of Financial Counseling and Planning* 12 (2001): 1–14.

Collins, Jeffrey T., and Miles H. Sonstegaard. "Hey Buddy Can Ya' Spare a Dime?: Arkansas Usury Laws Revisited." *Arkansas Business and Economic Review* 32, no. 3 (Fall 1999): 7–10.

Community Financial Services Association of America. Data on file with the authors.

Consumer Federation of America. "Legal Status of Payday Loans by State." December 2014. http://www.paydayloaninfo.org/state-information.

"The Cost of Personal Borrowing in the United States." Publication No. 830. South Bend, IN: Financial Publishing Co., 1998 (updated through subscription).

Department of Defense. "Report on Predatory Lending Practices Directed at Members of the Armed Forces and Their Dependents." August 9, 2006.

DeYoung, Robert, and Ronnie J. Phillips. "Payday Loan Pricing." The Federal Reserve Bank of Kansas City, February 2009.

Durkin, Thomas A., and Gregory Elliehausen, 2013. "Assessing the Price of Short Term Credit." Working Paper, Board of Governors of the Federal Reserve System, Division of Research and Statistics.

Durkin, Thomas A., Gregory Elliehausen, and Min Hwang. "Rate Ceilings and the Distribution of Small Dollar Installment Loans from Consumer Finance Companies: Results of a New Survey of Small Dollar Cash Lenders." Working Paper, George Washington University, Washington, DC, 2015.

Durkin, Thomas A., Gregory Elliehausen, Michael Staten, and Todd Zywicki. *Consumer Credit and the American Economy.* New York: Oxford University Press, 2014.

Durkin, Thomas A., Gregory Elliehausen, and Todd Zywicki. "Consumer Credit and the American Economy." *Journal of Law, Economics, and Policy* 11, no. 3 (2015): 279–302.

Ekelund, Robert, Robert Hébert, and Robert Tollison. "An Economic Model of the Medieval Church: Usury as a Form of Rent Seeking." *Journal of Law, Economics and Organization* 5 (1989): 307–31.

Elliehausen, Greg, and Edward C. Lawrence. "Payday Advance Credit in America: An Analysis of Customer Demand." Credit Research Center, Georgetown University, 2001.

Ernst, Keith, John Farris, and Uriah King. "Quantifying the Economic Costs of Predatory Payday Lending." Center for Responsible Lending, Durham, NC, February 24, 2004.

Flannery, Mark, and Katherine Samolyk. "Payday Lending: Do the Costs Justify the Price?" Federal Deposit Insurance Corporation. Working Paper 2005-09, Federal Deposit Insurance Corporation Center for Financial Research, Arlington, VA, 2005.

Foster, William Trufant. "The Personal Finance Business under Regulation." *Law and Contemporary Problems* 8, no. 1 (Winter 1941): 154–72.

Friedman, Milton, and Rose Friedman. *Free to Choose*. New York: Harcourt Brace Jovanovich, 1979.

Glaeser, Edward L., and Jose Scheinkman. "Neither a Borrower nor a Lender Be: An Economic Analysis of Interest Restrictions and Usury Laws." *Journal of Law and Economics* 41 (1998): 1–36.

Glenn, John M., Lilian Brandt, and F. Emerson Andrews. *Russell Sage Foundation 1907–1946*. Vol. 1. New York: Russell Sage Foundation, 1947.

Graeber, David. *Debt: The First 5,000 Years*. Brooklyn, NY: Melville House, 2014.

Graves, Steven M., and Christopher L. Peterson. "Predatory Lending and the Military: The Law and Geography of 'Payday' Loans in Military Towns." *Ohio State Law Journal* 66, no. 4 (2005): 653–832.

Hecht, John. "Alternative Financial Services: Innovating to Meet Consumer Needs in an Evolving Regulatory Framework." 14th Annual Meeting and Conference, Community Financial Services Association (CFSA) Solutions, 2014.

Homer, Sidney, and Richard Sylla. *A History of Interest Rates*, 4th ed. Hoboken, NJ: Wiley Finance, 2005.

Horack, Benjamin S. "A Survey of the General Usury Laws." In "Combating the Loan Shark," special issue, *Law and Contemporary Problems* 8, no. 1 (Winter 1941): 36–53.

Hubachek, F. B. "The Development of Regulatory Small Loan Laws." In "Combating the Loan Shark," special issue, *Law and Contemporary Problems* 8, no. 1 (Winter 1941): 108–45.

Huckstep, Aaron. "Payday Lending: Do Outrageous Prices Necessarily Mean Outrageous Profits?," *Fordham Journal of Corporate and Financial Law* 12, no. 1 (2007): 203–31.

Michelman, Irving S. *Consumer Finance: A Case History in American Business*. New York: Frederick Fell, 1966.

Miller, Thomas W., Jr. "Differences in Consumer Credit Choices by Banked and Unbanked Mississippians." *Journal of Law, Economics, and Policy* 11, no. 3 (2015): 367–412.

Morgan, Donald P. "Defining and Detecting Predatory Lending." Staff Report 273, Federal Reserve Bank of New York, 2007.

Morgan, Donald P., and Michael R. Strain. "Payday Holiday: How Households Fare after Payday Credit Bans." Staff Reports, Federal Reserve Bank of New York, 2008.

Mors, Wallace. *Consumer Credit Finance Charges*. New York: National Bureau of Economic Research, 1965.

Morse, Adair. "Payday Lenders: Heroes or Villains?" *Journal of Financial Economics* 102 (2011): 28–44.

National Commission on Consumer Finance. *Consumer Credit in the United States: The Report of the National Commission on Consumer Finance.* Washington, DC: Government Printing Office, 1972.

National Conference of State Legislatures. Payday Lending State Statutes. September 29, 2016.

National Consumer Law Center. "Installment Loans: Will States Protect Borrowers from a New Wave of Predatory Lending?" Boston, 2015.

Peterson, Richard L. "Usury Laws and Consumer Credit: A Note." *Journal of Finance* 38, no. 4 (September 1983): 1299–304.

Peterson, Richard L., and Gregory A. Falls. "Impact of a Ten Percent Usury Ceiling: Empirical Evidence." Working Paper 40, Credit Research Center, Purdue University, 1981.

Smith, Paul F. "Recent Trends in the Financial Position of Nine Major Consumer Finance Companies." In *The Consumer Finance Industry: Its Costs and Regulation*, edited by John M. Chapman and Robert P. Shay, 29–53. New York: Columbia University Press, 1967.

Smith, Reginald H. "Rethinking Usury Laws." *Annals of the American Academy of Political and Social Science* 196 (March 1938): 189–92.

Stegman, Michael A. "Payday Lending." *Journal of Economic Perspectives* 21, no. 1 (Winter 2007): 169–90.

Stegman, Michael A., and Robert Faris. "Payday Lending: A Business Model That Encourages Chronic Borrowing." *Economic Development Quarterly* 17, no. 1 (February 2003): 8–32.

Stephens Inc. "Industry Report: Payday Loan Industry." May 24, 2004.

Tescher, Jennifer. "Letter to Mr. Robert E. Feldman, FDIC." On behalf of The Center for Financial Services Innovation, 2007.

Villegas, Daniel J. "The Impact of Usury Ceilings on Consumer Credit." *Southern Economic Journal* 56 (1989): 126–41.

Zinman, Jonathan. "Restricting Consumer Credit Access: Household Survey Evidence on Effects around the Oregon Rate Cap." *Journal of Banking and Finance* 34 (2010): 546–56.

Zywicki, Todd. "The Case against New Restrictions on Payday Lending." Working Paper 09-28, Mercatus Center at George Mason University, Arlington, VA, 2009.

———. "The Consumer Financial Protection Bureau: Savior or Menace?" *George Washington Law Review* 81 (2013): 856–928.

PART 5

FACILITATING INNOVATION

PART 2

FACILITATING INNOVATION

CHAPTER 14
Regulating Bitcoin—On What Grounds?

WILLIAM J. LUTHER

Kenyon College

B itcoin is a relatively new technology with much promise. As the world's first successful cryptocurrency, it functions as an alternative means of making electronic payments. Its cryptography keeps transactions secure and protects merchants from chargeback fraud. Its use of a blockchain, or public ledger, and distributed peer-to-peer network to process these transactions seems likely to lower the costs of transacting. The Bitcoin protocol, which simultaneously rewards those on the network known as miners for processing blocks of transactions and ensures that the bitcoin supply grows at a steady, known rate, prevents users from spending balances they do not have while removing the prospect of unexpected and undesirable monetary expansions. Seeing these benefits, some customers and businesses, large and small, have already turned to bitcoin. And bitcoin proponents believe many others will make use of it as the benefits become more apparent.

Despite these benefits, many regulators seem concerned. In the New Jersey legislature, the Financial Institutions and Insurance Assembly Committee held a hearing on February 5, 2015, to consider how best to regulate bitcoin.[1] In the same week, the New York Department of Financial Services released a revised draft version of its BitLicense proposal that would require some entities in the bitcoin community to be licensed by the state.[2] At the federal level, the Financial Crimes Enforcement Network (FinCEN) has offered guidance on how bitcoin will be treated within its existing regulatory framework.[3] The US Commodity Futures Trading Commission (CFTC) took action against an unregistered bitcoin options trading platform in September 2015.[4] In December 2015, the US Securities and Exchange Commission (SEC) charged two bitcoin mining companies and their founder with fraud.[5] In all of the efforts to regulate or apply existing regulations to bitcoin to date, there is a strong presumption that something must be done.

There are three principal justifications for regulating bitcoin: to protect consumers, to prevent illegal transactions and transfers, and to promote broader macroeconomic policy goals. Such justifications imply that there are potential benefits to regulating bitcoin. Of course, regulations also impose costs. In addition to compliance costs, excessive regulation could dissuade some or all users from transacting in bitcoin and, hence, from realizing the benefits thereof. Efficient regulation requires that the rules adopted, and the extent to which those rules are enforced, are limited to cases in which the benefits exceed the costs.

In this chapter, I consider the three principal justifications for regulating bitcoin. Since efficient regulation is the goal, I consider the merits of each justification by assessing the extent of the problem regulation might address, the likely effectiveness of regulation in addressing that problem, and the likely costs of regulation on the regulated actors and the system as a whole. I conclude by offering some simple guidelines for regulators. Ideally, such guidelines would bring about a superior regulatory framework. If nothing else, though, one can hope that some regulatory clarity will emerge soon.

CONSUMER PROTECTION

Justifications for consumer protection regulation generally come in naïve and more sophisticated forms. Both views suggest that some consumers will be exploited, defrauded, misled, or otherwise taken advantage of in the absence of regulation.[6] The naïve view assumes, at least implicitly, that (1) consumers are never willing to acquire the requisite information to prevent being mistreated, (2) that competition or the threat of competition is never sufficient to prevent mistreatment, and/or (3) that the optimal amount of mistreatment is equal to zero. A more sophisticated view recognizes that consumers are generally interested in protecting themselves and will incur costs to do so; that firms are generally interested in maintaining relationships with consumers over a long period of time and regularly incur costs to keep consumers satisfied; and that, at some point, the cost of providing additional protection to consumers exceeds the benefits. Regulation is desirable, in this more sophisticated view, when it lowers the information costs to consumers or more properly aligns the incentives of firms. Even then, regulation is unlikely to prevent all instances of abuse.

When considering regulation on the basis of consumer protection, it is important to understand who is being protected and from whom they are being protected. In the case of bitcoin, the relevant agents include individual users, small business users, large business users, e-wallet services, exchanges, miners, and mining pool administrators. The term "user" refers to one making, accepting, or receiving payments in bitcoin. E-wallet services refer to counterparties that enable users to send, accept, receive, or store bitcoin more conveniently. Exchanges refer to services that allow one to exchange bitcoin for traditional or other virtual currencies. Miners are those processing bitcoin transactions via the Bitcoin protocol in exchange for new bitcoin or transaction fees. Mining pool administrators refer to those organizing a collection of miners and/or distributing payments to miners in the pool.

The National Association of Attorneys General (NAAG) lists three risks to consumers using bitcoin: exchange rate volatility, lack of security, and the inability to execute chargebacks.[7] Let me consider each in turn.

Exchange Rate Volatility

One concern with bitcoin is that, to date, it has been characterized by a highly volatile exchange rate. Over a twelve-month period, the dollar per bitcoin closing price on the BitStamp exchange has ranged from a low of $209.72 in August 2015 to a high of $467.42 in April 2016.[8] The average closing price was $340.32. The Bitcoin Volatility Index shows that the exchange rate is less volatile today than it has been in the past.[9] Still, with a thirty-day estimated volatility around 1.52 percent, it is more volatile than gold (1.2 percent) and other major currencies (0.5 to 1.0 percent).

The supply of bitcoin is exogenously determined and known in advance. The observed fluctuations in the exchange rate, then, reflect changes in demand. Demand is volatile for many reasons. Since the network of bitcoin users is relatively small at present, a user's decision to buy or sell relatively small amounts of bitcoin can have a significant effect on the price.[10] Of course, such fluctuation becomes less prevalent as the network grows. Uncertainty surrounding the future network size of bitcoin also contributes to this volatility. If everyone knew that everyone else would use bitcoin in the future, it would be very valuable today. On the other hand, if no one will use bitcoin in the future, it would not be very valuable today. Unfortunately, the future is, to some extent, unknown and unknowable. As our best guess of the future network size of bitcoin changes, so too does the current trading price. Finally, the future network size depends, in part, on the regulatory environment. The regulatory environment is unclear at the moment and expectations about the future regulatory environment might change as new evidence becomes available.[11] Hence, if nothing else, clarifying the regulatory approach to bitcoin could reduce exchange rate volatility.

A volatile exchange rate makes bitcoin risky to hold. One might suffer huge losses or realize huge gains over short periods of time. Fortunately, most agents are already aware of the volatility and have taken steps to mitigate the downsides. Others are being compensated for (knowingly) bearing this risk. As such, regulations intended to mitigate the risks of exchange rate fluctuations are limited to (1) reducing uncertainty by clarifying the regulatory environment and (2) providing general information to users about the volatility of bitcoin.

At present, most bitcoin users—be they individuals, small businesses, or large businesses—do not hold much wealth in bitcoin. They merely use bitcoin as a convenient means of payment. Intermediaries, like Coinbase, function as an exchange and e-wallet service. They permit users to convert traditional currencies into bitcoin at the time of making a payment and permit the conversion of bitcoin into traditional currencies.[12] Hence, a typical transaction involves a dollar to bitcoin exchange, a bitcoin transfer from payer to payee, and a bitcoin to dollar exchange. The payer can spend bitcoin without having held wealth in bitcoin. The payee can accept bitcoin without having to hold bitcoin. Both incur a small fee to convert into and out of bitcoin on the spot to make a transaction.[13] If neither payer nor payee holds bitcoin for an extended period of time, they need not be concerned with—and will not suffer losses from—the fluctuating exchange rate.[14] As such, there is not much scope for protecting these users with regulation.

Of course, someone must be holding bitcoin and, hence, bearing the risk of a fluctuating exchange rate. Intermediaries accept this risk by (1) agreeing to convert dollars to bitcoin and bitcoin to dollars at the current market rate when a transaction is made and (2) holding bitcoin between transactions. Given that they knowingly accept this risk and are compensated with a fee paid by the payer and/or payee for intermediating the transaction, there is little reason to think they are in need of regulatory protection. Moreover, the risk is arguably quite low for these entities to the extent that they deal in a large number of transactions. Sometimes they will incur losses. Other times they will experience gains. While the losses and gains from a fluctuating exchange rate will generally cancel out, the gains from fees and a general tendency for the value of bitcoin to increase over time with the size of the network makes intermediating transactions a profitable venture.

Although not specifically addressed by the NAAG, one might also consider protecting miners and mining pools from a volatile exchange rate. Miners incur costs to process transactions. Since only the first miner to successfully process a batch of transactions is rewarded with new bitcoin, miners frequently join pools to share the rewards in proportion to the computing power each miner employs.[15] Some miners might incur costs on the expectation that bitcoin will have a given value at the time a reward is issued, only to be disappointed when bitcoin has a lower value than expected. Still, there are at least three reasons to believe miners would not benefit greatly from regulation. First, miners (like the intermediaries discussed) tend to be sophisticated participants. They already know about the volatility of bitcoin and have chosen to participate anyway. Second, rewards are paid out roughly every ten minutes and miners have the option to exchange rewards for traditional currencies on the spot. As with users, they need not hold their wealth—even that obtained through mining—in bitcoin for an extended period of time. Third, miners have the option to join mining pools and, if they do, receive a steady stream of payments from mining. As with intermediaries, the gains and losses from a volatile exchange rate will largely cancel out for miners receiving rewards (or a fraction thereof) regularly.

There is no denying that the exchange value of bitcoin is much more volatile than that of many other assets. However, there is not much scope for improving matters in this regard with regulation. The fluctuation stems from changes in demand. It is widely known. And those in the bitcoin system have already taken steps to allocate risk efficiently and compensate those individuals bearing the risk. As such, regulatory improvements in this regard are limited to (1) reducing uncertainty concerning the future network size by clarifying the regulatory environment and (2) providing general information to users about the volatility of bitcoin. The latter is desirable insofar as the regulatory authority can provide this information at a lower cost than each individual user would incur collecting it.

Security Concerns

Another concern with bitcoin is the degree to which one's electronic balance is secure. Regulators naturally worry that the bitcoin system might be hacked;[16] that a large mining pool might compromise the system;[17] and that digital balances might be lost or stolen.[18] Some of these concerns are unfounded or might be alleviated with some simple precautionary actions, as I will discuss. Others are genuine, providing some scope for regulatory action on the grounds of consumer protection.

Concerns about the core Bitcoin protocol are largely unfounded. Dan Kaminsky, renowned security expert and Chief Scientist of White Ops, famously tried—and failed—to hack the Bitcoin protocol in 2011.[19] Based on this experience, Kaminsky concluded that "the core technology actually works, and has continued to work, to a degree not everyone predicted." By relying on algorithmic and open source governance, the bitcoin system is able to process transactions securely and ensure that only those users with the appropriate credentials can transfer and receive a given balance of bitcoin.[20]

Recognizing that concerns regarding the core Bitcoin protocol are largely unfounded is not to accept that the system is immune from attack. It is widely recognized, for example, that the system could be compromised if a miner or mining pool controlled more than 50 percent of the computing power on the network.[21] Since the Bitcoin protocol recognizes the longest blockchain on the peer-to-peer network as legitimate, and since computing power is the limiting factor for adding new blocks to a blockchain, a miner or group of miners with more than 50 percent of the computing power could outcompete other miners to produce the longest blockchain. And, with such power, a miner or mining pool could prevent other users from making transactions or undo past transactions, enabling users to double-spend balances.

While possible, such an attack seems less likely in practice. For one, it would require gaining and *maintaining* more than 50 percent of the computing power. When legitimate miners recognize a threat, they have an incentive to increase the computing power they contribute to the system. If legitimate miners can regain control, they can undo what has been done. Moreover, it is not clear that such an attack is in the interest of the attacker.[22] In weakening the system, an attack would discourage users from participating. The value of bitcoin would fall as existing users exit the system and potential new users refuse to join. Recall that miners are rewarded with bitcoin after successfully processing a block of transactions. It is therefore in their interest to promote the integrity of the system, since that would bolster the value of the newly created coins they earn.

Recent experience confirms the idea that those in a position to make a 51 percent attack are unlikely to do so. On June 12, 2014, the mining pool GHash.io maintained majority power for twelve hours.[23] It did not attempt to undermine the system by double-spending or preventing transactions.[24] A statement issued by the mining pool noted that "the threat of a 51% attack . . . is damaging not only to us, but to the growth and acceptance of Bitcoin long term, which is something we are all striving for."[25] Still, the price of bitcoin fell as some users feared such an attack, thereby discouraging even benevolent mining pools from gaining majority computing power.[26]

A law limiting the processing power of individual miners or mining pools to something less than 50 percent might mitigate the threat of attack. However, for reasons discussed previously, that threat is probably overstated in popular accounts. Moreover, to the extent that miners can coordinate activities in private, it would be difficult to enforce such a law. Finally, if such a law were applied broadly to other cryptocurrencies, it might rule out permissioned blockchain protocols where a smaller fraction of known users verify transactions.

Another security concern exists in the relationship between miners and mining pool administrators. Recall that miners contribute computing power to a mining pool in exchange for a share of the reward earned by any member of the pool. Hence, miners must trust that the mining pool administrator will deliver on the promise to distribute the reward. In practice, this is not much of a concern. Most pools pay their miners several times a day.[27] As such, exploits along these lines are significantly limited. Still, the relationship between miners and pool administrators could be governed by standard contract law. It would not require additional regulation.

For reasons discussed, the benefits from regulations aimed at protecting the system from malicious miners and mining pools or miners from malicious mining pool administrators are probably quite small. Moreover, the costs of such regulations—to the extent that they discourage mining or the development and implementation of alternative protocols—could be large. Recall that the bitcoin system depends crucially on a large, diverse base of miners to ensure that only legitimate transactions are executed. Discouraging mining would therefore undermine the system's ability to fend off attacks. Likewise, alternative protocols—like permissioned blockchains—might provide many of the benefits of bitcoin at an even lower cost. The regulatory framework should not discourage such innovations except in cases where there is a clear and significant risk of abuse.

Other, more plausible security problems exist. Consider the prospect that an inexperienced user loses bitcoin. Bitcoin can be lost when one loses a private key, the hardware where one secures a private key fails, or the private key is not transferred in the event of one's death. In an oft-cited case, one UK man lost 7,500 bitcoin—worth approximately $1.90 million today—when he threw out an old hard drive in 2013.[28] Although most instances of lost bitcoin have involved early adopters who left the network before bitcoin was very valuable, the potential for losing bitcoin remains a problem for users.

The problem of lost bitcoin has some rather straightforward solutions. Users could keep a backup of their private key; they could keep a paper wallet—that is, a physical copy of their private key—and they could make arrangements for private keys to be passed on in the event of death. Other solutions involve trusting a third party (usually an e-wallet provider) with your primary key or employing a multisignature wallet, which requires two of three digital signatures to make a transaction, with the e-wallet provider maintaining one of the three signatures. In the first case, access is recoverable by providing sufficient identifying information to the third party. In the second case, access is recoverable in the event that one but not both keys held by the user is lost or irretrievable.

There are two problems with these solutions to lost bitcoin. First, the users most likely to lose their bitcoin are probably least likely to obtain information on how to prevent such a loss in advance. Their relative inexperience drives both results. The bitcoin community has certainly taken steps to make this information widely available. And, as noted, some e-wallet providers go beyond the mere provision of information by requiring multiple signatures and/or maintaining a copy of the private key. Nonetheless, regulators could potentially improve the flow of information and, in doing so, might help those in the community discover and establish appropriate security and insurance standards. Second, while reducing the likelihood of losing bitcoin, the solutions outlined increase the risk that one's bitcoin will be stolen. Storing multiple copies of your private key increases the number of places where your private key might be discovered. Trusting a third party with a private key provides the opportunity for that trust to be broken. Moreover, inexperienced users—those most likely to lose bitcoin—are probably also less likely to secure private keys appropriately and less able to assess the trustworthiness of a given third party. As such, the possible remedies to the lost bitcoin problem might be worse than the disease.

What is the likelihood that a bitcoin is stolen? Perhaps it is greater than one might think. According to one 2014 estimate, some 918,142.965 bitcoin worth roughly $415.99 million had been stolen.[29] Considering that, at the time of this writing, there are roughly 15,558,175 bitcoin in circulation, a little more than 5.9 percent, or 1 in 17, have been stolen.[30] Bitcoin can be stolen when one does not take the necessary precautions to protect a private key.[31] The biggest heists, however, involve third parties holding access to the accounts of multiple users. For example, the Japan-based bitcoin exchange Mt. Gox tops the list, losing an estimated 850,000 of its users' bitcoin in what the company described as a "transaction malleability" attack that had taken place— unbeknownst to users—over several years.[32] A Tokyo Metropolitan Police investigation concluded that cyberattacks were responsible for only 1 percent of the missing balances at Mt. Gox.[33] Whether such losses result from outside attacks, embezzlement, or the mere mismanagement of funds, they illuminate the difficulties of keeping bitcoin secure.

The blockchain technology presents an interesting problem for thieves. Although users are pseudonymous—that is, their physical identities can be kept private—all transactions taking place on the blockchain are publicly observable. Any user can follow a stolen balance of bitcoin as it is transferred from one address to the next.[34] Indeed, a small team of computer scientists, using only publicly available data, was able to trace bitcoin stolen in well-known thefts to popular exchanges. As they note, "following stolen bitcoins to the point at which they are deposited into an exchange does not in itself identify the thief; however, it does enable further de-anonymization in the case in which certain agencies can determine (through, for example, subpoena power) the real-world owner of the account into which the stolen bitcoins were deposited."[35] Others point out that "a well-equipped law enforcement agency could de-anonymise the network even further."[36]

The prospect of theft presents, perhaps, the strongest case for regulating bitcoin on consumer protection grounds. On one hand, bitcoin is vulnerable like other electronic payment mechanisms and should be regulated as such. On the other hand, bitcoin has unique features that might be leveraged by regulators to create an even more robust system. If thieves can be prevented from cashing out large sums at exchanges, for example, they are reduced to cumbersome alternatives to convert digital balances into usable wealth. Knowing they will be unable to liquidate large balances easily, some thieves will be deterred from stealing balances altogether. However, the costs of preventing or delaying large-scale liquidations—the legitimacy of which might be difficult to assess over short periods of time—might be overly burdensome, discouraging some users from participating in the network altogether. And, to the extent that exchanges or e-wallet service providers are participating in the theft or mismanagement of funds, such regulations would have little effect. A better option, then, would be to require e-wallet and exchange services to (1) register with the proper authorities and (2) collect identifying information on users before exchanging large amounts of bitcoin. In the event of a theft, the victim would then have recourse to go after the appropriate exchange for assisting—knowingly or otherwise—in the transfer of stolen funds and the authorities could subpoena the information held by the exchange or e-wallet service provider. Such regulations would be imperfectly designed and imperfectly enforced. Still, they could have a significant effect on reducing the extent of bitcoin theft.

Chargebacks

Some regulators might be concerned by the inability to execute chargebacks under the Bitcoin protocol without the current owner of a balance agreeing to return the funds in question. This stands in sharp contrast to traditional, centralized payment processing mechanisms that can reverse a transaction when a dispute is made. Indeed, the inability to reverse transactions contributes to the problem of theft: it is impossible to return funds to their rightful owner without consent of the thief. But more mundane instances—like receiving a product of inferior quality or not receiving a product at all—come to mind.

In being unable to execute chargebacks, the Bitcoin protocol is no different than cash.[37] And there are good reasons to permit such a payment mechanism. For one, it prevents the sort of chargeback fraud that plagues small businesses.[38] Indeed, some shopkeepers save so much from the elimination of chargeback fraud that they give their customers steep discounts for paying with bitcoin.[39] It promotes international business as well.[40] High rates of fraud have led traditional payment processors to forgo business in over fifty countries, preventing individuals in those countries from making convenient payments to American businesses. In eliminating a large class of fraud, bitcoin makes transacting with individuals in those countries possible—and profitable.[41] Hence, bitcoin has the potential to increase commerce for small and large businesses alike.

For better or worse, the inability to execute chargebacks under the Bitcoin protocol is part of what it means to transact with bitcoin. Some users will no doubt prefer a payment mechanism that gives them recourse when dealing with potentially unscrupulous sellers. Provided that they are willing to pay the higher fees that come with the ability to execute chargebacks, such users should eschew bitcoin for traditional payment mechanisms. Others can enjoy the lower fees and unique transaction networks made possible with bitcoin. Provided that consumers are aware of the inability to execute chargebacks when making payments with bitcoin, there is no compelling reason to reduce consumer choice in payment mechanisms.

ILLICIT TRANSACTIONS AND TRANSFERS

Bitcoin has attracted a lot of attention from regulators on the grounds that it might facilitate illegal transactions and transfers.[42] Senator Charles Schumer (D-NY) was among the first to take note, describing bitcoin as "an online form of money laundering used to disguise the source of money, and to disguise who's both selling and buying the drug."[43] Senator Joe Manchin (D-WV) also recommended regulation, given the "clear ends of Bitcoin for either transacting in illegal goods and services or speculative gambling."[44] Indeed, many seem to believe "bitcoin is basically for criminals."[45] Others have warned that bitcoin might be used to fund terrorism.[46] So, I will discuss the merits of regulating bitcoin on these grounds.

To date, the sort of black market transactions of concern to Schumer, Manchin, and others seems to comprise a small fraction of the total bitcoin economy. The US Treasury Department found no evidence of bitcoin's widespread use in funding terrorism.[47] Similarly, while media reports have directed much attention at mail-order drug sites conducting business in bitcoin, the volume of transactions actually made through these sites is quite small. Consider the Silk Road, which operated from February 2011 to October 2013 and was described by one media outlet as the Amazon of drugs.[48] The best available evidence, collected over eight months from late 2011 to early 2012, suggests that roughly $1.2 million worth of transactions were made on the Silk Road each month.[49] More recent estimates put the figure at roughly $4.7 million per month for the life of the site.[50] By either estimate, the volume of trading is quite small for a global marketplace.[51] Moreover, the monthly transaction volume for the entire bitcoin system averaged roughly $206.34 million from February 2011 to October 2013.[52] In other words, Silk Road transactions comprised less than 2.28 percent of all transactions. Hence, even if regulations could eliminate all illegal sales conducted in bitcoin, the benefits would be small. And the costs would be borne, at least in part, by the much larger class of users employing bitcoin for legitimate ends.

As I have argued elsewhere, the "US government should find it awkward to regulate bitcoin on the grounds that it facilitates illegal transactions. Its own currency—and the $100 bill in particular—has done so for years."[53] A recent study maintains that 48 percent of the US currency stock is employed in the domestic underground economy.[54] When this analysis is extended to the world, one finds that roughly 76 percent of the US currency stock, or $960 billion, is used to facilitate exchange beyond the reach of tax and law enforcement authorities.[55] To the extent that bitcoin is like cash, the regulatory authority should treat it as such.

Of course, bitcoin is not exactly like cash. It enables electronic transfers. As such, it creates a trail for law enforcement authorities not possible with cash. Although transactions are pseudonymous—that is, virtual addresses are not necessarily tied to physical identities—all transactions are recorded in the public ledger, or blockchain. So, once a criminal is identified in the physical world and linked to a digital address, law enforcement agencies could potentially uncover a string of past criminal transactions. Had they been conducted in cash, these past transactions would be nearly impossible to trace. Moreover, to the extent that exchanges and e-wallet services cooperate—or can be compelled to cooperate—the authorities could uncover and investigate a criminal's past trading partners, who might also be involved in criminal activity.[56] Hence, law enforcement agencies would perhaps be better served by working with the bitcoin network rather than against it.

Furthermore, legal uses of bitcoin are likely to be more sensitive to regulation than illegal uses.[57] Legal users often conduct business with a physical presence; even those conducting business exclusively online often make their physical identities known. Illegal users, in contrast, typically employ anonymizing technology like Tor, preferring to conduct business on the so-called dark web. Hence, the illicit transactions justifying regulatory action are exceptionally difficult to stamp out. To the extent that regulatory efforts make transacting with bitcoin more costly or cumbersome, one should expect legitimate users to exit the network while illegitimate users merely avoid the channels through which such laws are enforced.

There is no denying that bitcoin can be used to make illegal transactions and transfers. The relevant question is whether the benefits of regulating bitcoin on these grounds exceed the costs. Given that the fraction of bitcoin users engaged in illicit transactions or transferring funds to terrorist groups is probably quite small and regulatory efforts to stamp out such transactions are unlikely to succeed, it seems unlikely that regulating on these grounds would produce many benefits. On the other hand, the costs imposed on a system comprised primarily of legitimate users in search of a few bad apples could be substantial. As such, the prudent course of action would seem to require investing in the requisite technology to de-anonymize users in the event that they are suspected of criminal activity.

MACROECONOMIC POLICY

Regulators might also worry that bitcoin could impede the government in promoting broader macroeconomic policy goals. As one commentator put it, bitcoin "looks like it was designed as a weapon intended to damage central banking and money issuing banks, with a Libertarian political agenda in mind—to damage [states'] ability to collect tax and monitor their [citizens'] financial transactions."[58] Having addressed issues of financial monitoring and oversight previously, I now turn to the extent to which the government would lose revenues or be unable to conduct monetary policy effectively if individuals used bitcoin instead of dollars.

Budgetary Policy

When discussing illicit transactions and transfers, I have limited the analysis to black market transactions. However, governments might also be concerned with gray market transactions—that is, buying and selling legal goods or services illegally in order to avoid sales or income tax. Whereas governments want to prevent black market transactions altogether, they do not want to discourage the underlying transactions taking place on the gray market. Rather, they want to force these transactions out of the gray market so that they can collect taxes on the sales and incomes supported by these transactions.

Tax evasion is already a significant problem in the United States. It has been estimated that between 18 to 19 percent of total reportable income goes unreported, reducing tax revenues by $400 billion to $500 billion per year.[59] To the extent that bitcoin obscures one's identity, it could replace cash in such transactions. It is unclear, however, whether bitcoin would promote *additional* tax evasion. On the one hand, it is easier to hold and transact with large balances of bitcoin than cash, which occupies physical space. As such, bitcoin might increase the scope of tax evasion. But, as noted already, bitcoin offers law enforcement authorities a trail of transactions to follow that they would not have if those transactions were made with cash. Hence, bitcoin might fail to replace cash entirely in this domain. In any event, it seems unlikely that the effect of bitcoin on tax evasion would be large, if only because tax evasion is so pervasive already.[60]

In addition to revenues raised through taxing income and sales, governments earn seigniorage revenue from issuing base money. Seigniorage revenue results from holding interest-bearing assets purchased with base money. In the United States, the Treasury's Bureau of Engraving and Printing produces currency and sells it to the Federal Reserve System at cost. The Federal Reserve uses this currency and the balances it creates on its books as reserves held at the

Federal Reserve to purchase interest-bearing assets. Then, after covering its operating costs, the Federal Reserve remits the net income to the Treasury. If demand for base money—that is, currency and reserves held at the Federal Reserve— were to fall as individuals switch to bitcoin, the Federal Reserve would earn less income and therefore remit less to the Treasury. As such, some have warned that the federal government would lose seigniorage revenues if bitcoin were adopted.[61]

In practice, the loss of revenues would be small. In 2013, Fed remittances to the Treasury totaled $79.6 billion—just 0.53 percent of current expenditures by the federal government.[62] Moreover, the extent of revenues lost would be proportional to the number of users switching from dollars to bitcoin. If bitcoin were to function as a niche currency, adopted by a subset of potential users or used in conjunction with dollars, the decline in revenues would be far less than the total amount of remittances.[63] Hence, the benefits of regulating bitcoin on these grounds are quite small. Moreover, sustaining seigniorage revenues in the face of competition from bitcoin would require dissuading some or all users from transacting with bitcoin when, by their own assessments, bitcoin is the preferred alternative. Hence, the costs of regulating bitcoin on these grounds—roughly equal to the losses that users experience from employing an inferior base money—could be quite large. As such, regulating bitcoin on the grounds that it would reduce revenues would almost certainly be inconsistent with the principle of efficient regulation.

Monetary Policy

Others are concerned that bitcoin will prevent the Federal Reserve from conducting monetary policy effectively.[64] Indeed, this is in part why Nobel Prize– winning economist Paul Krugman advanced the claim that "bitcoin is evil."[65] The view is relatively straightforward: if individuals use bitcoin instead of dollars as money, the Federal Reserve will not be able to control the supply of money in circulation. There is some truth to this view. The supply of bitcoin is built into the Bitcoin protocol. A central monetary authority cannot control it. Moreover, the protocol cannot be modified without the consent of a majority of users on the system. And, at least for bitcoin, changes to the money supply rule are widely considered to be off the table.[66]

Many users like the money supply constraint embedded in the Bitcoin protocol. The protocol ensures that a predetermined amount of bitcoin enters the system every ten minutes. The precise amount of bitcoin created, which serves as a reward for those processing transaction blocks, is cut in half roughly every four years. Prior to November 2012, the reward totaled 50 bitcoin. Later it was halved to 25 and again to 12.5. Roughly every two weeks, the system confirms that a block of transactions was processed every ten minutes on average. It then adjusts the difficulty of the cryptographic problem required to process transactions to ensure that the ten-minute processing time is achieved. Since new bitcoin are only created when a block is processed, the supply grows steadily at a declining rate over time.

There are at least two problems with the view that bitcoin undermines the Federal Reserve's ability to conduct monetary policy, thereby generating macroeconomic instability. First, bitcoin will have little effect on macroeconomic fluctuation if the dollar continues to function as the actual or effective unit of account.[67] Textbook models of macroeconomic fluctuation depend on so-called sticky prices that do not adjust instantaneously. If prices are denominated in dollars, the Federal Reserve will not lose control of monetary policy.

It seems likely that the dollar will continue to serve as the unit of account. Most bitcoin transactions at present involve goods or services actually priced in dollars, with the transaction being made at the current market rate. One entrepreneur has even developed digital price tags that update the bitcoin-price of products at current market rates, given the dollar prices chosen by merchants.[68] Hence, even when bitcoin prices are employed, the dollar often continues to function as the effective unit of account. If such a state persists, one need not be concerned that bitcoin will generate undesirable macroeconomic fluctuation.

Second, the Fed only loses control of monetary policy to the extent that individuals choose to switch from dollars to bitcoin. Considering that network effects favor the incumbent money, such a switch would indicate that the net gains from switching to bitcoin are perceived to be large.[69] Such gains would be large, for example, if the Federal Reserve were not very good at managing the money supply. But, in this case, the Federal Reserve could discourage the switch by committing to offer better monetary policy. In this view, bitcoin would function as a desirable check on monetary mischief.

The potential effect of bitcoin on monetary policy ranges from inconsequential to serving as a desirable check on the monetary authority. In the former case, there are no gains from regulating bitcoin on these grounds. In the latter case, regulation would almost certainly reduce the attractiveness of monetary policy. Hence, bitcoin should be welcomed on the grounds of promoting monetary stability.

CONCLUSION

Bitcoin—and the blockchain technology at its core—offers users many benefits over existing alternatives. When considering regulation, then, one should think carefully about the likely costs and benefits. I have reviewed the three principal justifications for regulating bitcoin. The scope for efficient regulation is limited in two ways. First, private governance structures and fee-based services have already begun addressing many of the known problems, such as protecting consumers from volatile exchange rates and preventing them from losing access to their accounts. As such, the benefits from regulation are typically low. Second, since most regulations would have the (intended or unintended) consequence of discouraging use, the costs—in terms of technological gains forgone—are potentially high. Nonetheless, there seems to be some scope for regulation in the provision of information and requirement of registration, thereby ensuring one has recourse in the event of theft.

Regulators interested in efficient regulation would do well to follow certain guidelines.

1. **Clarify the regulatory framework.** Provided that the gains from bitcoin are as large as many proponents believe, entrepreneurs can find ways to work within a wide range of regulatory frameworks. However, they cannot move forward confidently until the regulatory framework is settled.[70] Much clarity is needed, at the moment, over (1) who the appropriate regulators are, (2) what existing rules apply to bitcoin, and (3) what future rules are likely to be adopted. Clarity along these lines will enable entrepreneurs to take the requisite actions today. It will also allow users to make a more informed decision regarding whether the currency will be useful for their desired ends.

2. **Regulate transactions—not the transactions medium.** To the extent that some transactions and transfers are deemed undesirable, the

government should attempt to prevent them, at least insofar as the benefits of preventing them exceed the costs. However, the government should attempt to prevent these transactions without criminalizing the transactions medium. In the case of drug transactions, for example, that means buy-busts and monitoring similar to that currently employed for such transactions traditionally made in cash. Attempting to prevent such transactions by regulating the transactions medium imposes costs on legitimate users while having little effect on criminal users.

3. **Regulate exchanges—not users, miners, mining pool administrators, or software developers.** Many of the benefits of regulation can be realized by merely requiring large exchanges to register and collect identifying information on users exchanging bitcoin. Moreover, since such enterprises are large nodes in the bitcoin system, the costs of regulating them are probably low. Regulations that discourage users from adopting bitcoin, miners from processing blocks of transactions, or software developers from offering new programs to track, store, or transfer bitcoin, by contrast, are likely to impose large costs. As such, the latter should be avoided.

4. **Err on the side of technological progress.** Technological change is the primary driver of economic growth. New technologies are often disruptive, but entrepreneurs often react to these growing pains by making improvements to the underlying technology or developing ancillary products and services to ease the transition. Regulators should encourage technological progress by committing to an environment of *permissionless innovation*.[71] Reaffirm that those who venture out in search of better ways of doing things will be rewarded when they succeed. And, to the extent possible, reduce the barriers to such ventures.

Bitcoin is still in its infancy. Over the last seven years, users have joined the network; exchanges have made it easier to enter and exit; e-wallet services have made it more convenient to store and transact with bitcoin; miners have found ways to lower costs of processing transactions; and entrepreneurs more generally have developed a host of products in the bitcoin system. There are still problems with the bitcoin system—it is far from perfect. Some of these problems can and will be addressed with additional innovation. Others will, no doubt, require regulation. However, in pursuing the latter, one would do well to keep an eye to the future. Regulators should not let the minor problems of today justify preventing major gains in the future. Instead, regulators should aim to adopt only those regulations that deliver large benefits at a low cost.

NOTES

1. Higgins, "Bitcoin Panel Seeks New Take."

2. Rizzo, "Breaking Down New York's Latest BitLicense Revision."

3. FinCEN, "Application of FinCEN's Regulations."

4. CFTC, "CFTC Orders Bitcoin Options Trading Platform Operator."

5. SEC, "SEC Charges Bitcoin Mining Companies."

6. This need not imply that all consumers will be treated poorly; nor that all firms will engage in unscrupulous practices. It merely states that, in the absence of regulation, some firms will take advantage of some consumers. Of course, some firms might continue to take advantage of some consumers in the presence of regulation—though those employing the naïve justification often overlook this prospect.

7. The NAAG separates security issues into "hacking of virtual wallets or Bitcoin platforms" and "fraudulent transactions." Both are considered in this chapter under the general heading Security Concerns. NAAG, "An Explanation of Bitcoin."

8. All exchange rate data used herein comes from BitcoinCharts.com.

9. The Bitcoin Volatility Index measures volatility as the standard deviation of daily returns for the preceding thirty- and sixty-day windows. Dourado, "Bitcoin Volatility Index."

10. On the network effects problem as it pertains to bitcoin, see Luther, "Cryptocurrencies."

11. See Brito and Dourado, "Comments to the New York Department of Financial Services." Under New York's proposal, for example, it was "unclear whether individual cryptocurrency miners would be required to obtain a BitLicense" (4); whether software wallets and multi-signature wallets are engaged in Virtual Currency Business Activity (VCBA) and, hence, are subject to regulation as such (5–6); whether introducing an AltCoin constitutes VCBA (10); what criteria will be employed by the superintendent to offer exemptions to chartered banks (13); whether exempted banks are subject to custodial limitations (14); and so on.

12. Luther and White, "Can Bitcoin Become a Major Currency?"

13. At the moment, fees are in the neighborhood of 1 percent of the transaction value—much less than traditional merchant accounts. Some, like BitPay, have forgone fees based on transaction value in favor of a flat annual or monthly fee.

14. Brito, "Benefits and Risk of Bitcoin," 3.

15. This distribution scheme prevails because computing power determines the likelihood of success.

16. "Virtual currencies are targets for highly sophisticated hackers, who have been able to breach advanced security systems." CFPB, "Risks to Consumers."

17. The CFPB warns that the blockchain "is maintained by vast unidentified private computer networks spread all over the world. It is possible that elements of these networks could abuse

the power that comes with maintaining the ledger, for example by undoing transactions that you thought were finalized." See ibid.

18. In its 2014 consumer advisory, the CFPB states, "If you store your virtual currency yourself" and "you lose your private keys, you have lost all access to your funds." Moreover, "virtual currency wallet companies may disclaim responsibility for replacing your virtual currency if it is stolen on their watch." See ibid.

19. Kaminsky, "I Tried Hacking Bitcoin."

20. Algorithmic governance refers to the actual code, which limits what users in the bitcoin network can do. Open source governance refers to the formal rules and informal norms that have emerged between Bitcoin Core developers, other developers, miners, and users. For a full discussion of these issues, see Dourado and Brito, "Cryptocurrency."

21. Berkman, "What Is a 51 Percent Attack?"

22. Indeed, Dourado and Brito ("Cryptocurrency," 5–6) "observe some self-regulation by the mining pools, which are heavily invested in the success of Bitcoin. Whenever the top pool starts to approach 40% or so of computing power of the network, some participants exit the pool and join another one."

23. Goodin, "Bitcoin Security Guarantee."

24. Farivar, "After Reaching 51% Network Power."

25. Smith, "GHashi.io Is Open for Discussion."

26. Hornyak, "One Group Controls 51 Percent."

27. Dourado and Brito, "Cryptocurrency," 4.

28. Sparkes, "The £625m Lost Forever."

29. "List of Major Bitcoin Heists."

30. While considering the role governments might play in *preventing* bitcoin thefts, it is also worth noting that government officials have *perpetrated* bitcoin thefts. In August 2015, former Secret Service agent Shaun Bridges plead guilty to money laundering and obstruction charges in connection with the theft of more than $800,000 in bitcoin. He is suspected of additional thefts as well. Higgins, "US Prosecutors Believe Ex–Secret Service Agent."

31. Victims of theft are not limited to relatively inexperienced or unsophisticated users. See, for example, Brandom, "Anatomy of a Hack."

32. Rizzo and Southurst, "Mt. Gox Allegedly Loses $350 Million."

33. Stucky and Adelstein, "Japanese Bitcoin Heist."

34. Edwards, "Thief Is Attempting to Hide $100 Million."

35. Meiklejohn et al., "Fistful of Bitcoins."

36. Dourado and Brito, "Cryptocurrency," 7.

37. As with cash, transactions with bitcoin can be charged back when an escrow service is employed; see Dourado, "Stop Saying Bitcoin Transactions Aren't Reversible." Indeed, the company Bitrated offers such a service; see Perez, "How Bitrated Wants to Put the Trust."

38. Maltby, "Chargebacks Create Business Headaches."

39. Wile, "Brooklyn Bodega Owner."

40. Brito, "Benefits and Risk of Bitcoin," 2.

41. Love, "Guy Who Owns a Bitcoin-Only Electronics Store."

42. Brito, "Beyond Silk Road."

43. Wolf, "Bitcoin Exchanges."

44. Greenberg, "Senator Calls for Bitcoin Ban."

45. Edwards, "CLAIM."

46. Brantly, "Financing Terror Bit by Bit."

47. Dougherty and Farrell, "Treasury's Cohen Sees."

48. Chen, "Underground Website."

49. Christin, "Traveling the Silk Road," 213–24.

50. These estimates, reported by Brito, "Beyond Silk Road," 2n2, are based on a forthcoming study by Nicolas Christin that is not publicly available at present. Brito also explains why estimates put forward by the FBI in the criminal complaint against Ross William Ulbricht overstate the volume of transactions.

51. For comparison, annual revenues at Amazon totaled $74.45 billion in 2013. At roughly $6.2 billion per month, that is more than 370 times the highest monthly transaction volume estimated for the Silk Road.

52. Figures calculated by author using data from "Estimated USD Transaction Value," Blockchain .info, last modified October 26, 2016, https://blockchain.info/charts/estimated-transaction -volume-usd?timespan=all.

53. Luther, "Dark Dollar Dealings."

54. Feige, "New Estimates of U.S. Currency Abroad."

55. Luther, "Dark Dollar Dealings."

56. Indeed, some exchanges already seem to be cooperating. See Sparshott, "Bitcoin Exchange Makes Apparent Move."

57. Brito and Castillo, *Bitcoin*, 26–27.

58. Stross, "Why I Want Bitcoin to Die."

59. Feige and Cebula, "America's Underground Economy."

60. Bitcoin might make it easier to hide more of one's wealth in financial assets. But that wealth is only valuable insofar as it can be exchanged for other goods and services. Suggesting that bitcoin will have a significant effect on tax evasion amounts to claiming individuals are able to hide a significantly larger portion of their purchases. Given that just a little less than one-fifth of income is going unreported already, that seems unlikely.

61. Davies, "Bitcoin."

62. Hendrickson, Hogan, and Luther, "Political Economy of Bitcoin."

63. Luther, "Cryptocurrencies," 30–34, discusses bitcoin's prospects as a niche currency.

64. Note that such a view implicitly accepts that the Fed is able to conduct monetary policy effectively in the absence of bitcoin. The historical record raises doubts on this point. See Selgin, Lastrapes, and White, "Has the Fed Been a Failure?"

65. Krugman, "Bitcoin Is Evil." A vice president of the Federal Reserve Bank of St. Louis has acknowledged that "the threat of Bitcoin (and of currency substitutes in general) places constraints on monetary policy"; see Andolfatto, "Bitcoin and Central Banking." Similarly, a

representative of the Bank of Canada has warned that, if bitcoin were widely adopted, "central banks would struggle to implement monetary policy"; see Higgins, "Bank of Canada."

66. Dourado and Brito, "Cryptocurrency," 5.

67. Ibid., 6.

68. Luther and White, "Can Bitcoin Become a Major Currency?"

69. Luther, "Cryptocurrencies."

70. Some banks have refused to work with bitcoin companies, citing regulatory uncertainty; see Rizzo, "Bank Stops Working with Bitcoin Exchange." Bitcoin ATMs have also been halted; Rizzo, "Bitcoin ATM Shutdown."

71. Thierer, *Permissionless Innovation.*

REFERENCES

Andolfatto, David. "Bitcoin and Central Banking." *MacroMania*, November 12, 2015. http://andolfatto.blogspot.com/2015/11/bitcoin-and-central-banking.html.

Berkman, Fran. "What Is a 51 Percent Attack, and Why are Bitcoin Users Freaking Out about It Now?" *The Daily Dot*, June 13, 2014. http://www.dailydot.com/business/bitcoin-51-percent-attack/.

Brandom, Russell. "Anatomy of a Hack: A Step-by-Step Account of an Overnight Digital Heist." *The Verge*, March 4, 2015. http://www.theverge.com/a/anatomy-of-a-hack.

Brantly, Aaron. "Financing Terror Bit by Bit." *CTC Sentinel*, October 31, 2014. https://www.ctc.usma.edu/posts/financing-terror-bit-by-bit.

Brito, Jerry. "Beyond Silk Road: Potential Risks, Threats, and Promises of Virtual Currencies." Testimony before the Senate Committee on Homeland Security and Governmental Affairs, Mercatus Center at George Mason University, Arlington, VA, November 18, 2013.

———. "Benefits and Risk of Bitcoin for Small Businesses." Testimony before the House Committee on Small Business, Mercatus Center at George Mason University, Arlington, VA, April 2, 2014.

Brito, Jerry, and Andrea Castillo. *Bitcoin: A Primer for Policymakers.* Arlington, VA: Mercatus Center at George Mason University, 2013.

Brito, Jerry, and Eli Dourado. "Comments to the New York Department of Financial Services on the Proposed Virtual Currency Regulatory Framework." Public Interest Comment, Mercatus Center at George Mason University, Arlington, VA, August 14, 2014.

Bureau of Consumer Financial Protection (CFPB). "Risks to Consumers Posed by Virtual Currencies." *Consumer Advisory*, August 11, 2014. http://files.consumerfinance.gov/f/201408_cfpb_consumer-advisory_virtual-currencies.pdf.

Chen, Adrien. "The Underground Website Where You Can Buy Any Drug Imaginable." *Gawker*, June 1, 2011. http://gawker.com/the-underground-website-where-you-can-buy-any-drug-imag-30818160.

Christin, Nicolas. "Traveling the Silk Road: A Measurement Analysis of a Large Anonymous Online Marketplace." Proceedings of the 22nd International World Wide Web Conference, May 2013.

Davies, Gavyn. "Bitcoin: Miracle or Madness?" *Financial Times*, January 19, 2014. http://blogs.ft.com/gavyndavies/2014/01/19/bitcoin-miracle-or-madness/.

Dougherty, Carter, and Greg Farrell. "Treasury's Cohen Sees No Widespread Criminal Bitcoin Use." *Bloomberg*, March 18, 2014. http://www.bloomberg.com/news/articles/2014-03-18 /treasury-s-cohen-says-regulation-helps-virtual-currencies.

Dourado, Eli. "Stop Saying Bitcoin Transactions Aren't Reversible." *Eli Dourado*, December 4, 2013. https://elidourado.com/blog/bitcoin-arbitration/.

———. "The Bitcoin Volatility Index." Retrieved March 26, 2015. https://btcvol.info/.

Dourado, Eli, and Jerry Brito. "Cryptocurrency." In *The New Palgrave Dictionary of Economics Online Edition*, edited by Steven N. Durlauf and Lawrence E. Blume. New York: Palgrave Macmillan, 2014.

Edwards, Jim. "CLAIM: Bitcoin Is Basically for Criminals." *Business Insider*, November 27, 2013. http://www.businessinsider.com/claim-bitcoin-is-basically-for-criminals-2013-11.

———. "A Thief Is Attempting to Hide $100 Million in Stolen Bitcoins—and You Can Watch It Live Right Now." *Business Insider*, December 3, 2013. http://www.businessinsider.com/a-thief -is-attempting-to-hide-100-million-in-stolen-bitcoins-and-you-can-watch-it-live-right -now-2013-12.

Farivar, Cyrus. "After Reaching 51% Network Power, Bitcoin Mining Pool Says 'Trust Us.'" *Ars Technica*, June 16, 2014.

Feige, Edgar L. "New Estimates of U.S. Currency Abroad, the Domestic Money Supply and the Unreported Economy." MPRA Paper No. 34778, Munich Personal RePEc Archive, September 2011.

Feige, Edgar L., and Richard Cebula. "America's Underground Economy: Measuring the Size, Growth and Determinants of Income Tax Evasion in the US." MPRA Paper No. 29672, Munich Personal RePEc Archive, January 2011.

Financial Crimes Enforcement Network (FinCEN). "Application of FinCEN's Regulations to Persons Administering, Exchanging, or Using Virtual Currencies." Guidance FIN-2013-G001, March 18, 2013. http://www.fincen.gov/statutes_regs/guidance/html/FIN -2013-G001.html.

Goodin, Dan. "Bitcoin Security Guarantee Shattered by Anonymous Miner with 51% Network Power." *Ars Technica*, June 15, 2014. http://arstechnica.com/security/2014/06/bitcoin -security-guarantee-shattered-by-anonymous-miner-with-51-network-power/.

Greenberg, Andy. "Senator Calls for Bitcoin Ban in Letter to Financial Regulators." *Forbes*, February 26, 2014. http://www.forbes.com/sites/andygreenberg/2014/02/26/senator-calls -for-bitcoin-ban-in-letter-to-financial-regulators/.

Hendrickson, Joshua R., Thomas L. Hogan, and William J. Luther. "The Political Economy of Bitcoin." *Economic Inquiry* 54, no. 2 (2016): 925–39.

Higgins, Stan. "Bitcoin Panel Seeks New Take on Regulation at New Jersey Hearing." *CoinDesk*, February 6, 2015. http://www.coindesk.com/bitcoin-panel-regulation-redo-new-jersey/.

———. "Bank of Canada: Bitcoin Could Create 'New Monetary Order.'" *CoinDesk*, November 16, 2015. http://www.coindesk.com/bank-of-canada-chief-bitcoin-monetary-policy/.

———. "US Prosecutors Believe Ex–Secret Service Agent Stole More Bitcoin from Silk Road." *CoinDesk*, February 24, 2016. http://www.coindesk.com/us-government-secret-service-agent-stole-silk-road-bitcoins/.

Hornyak, Tim. "One Group Controls 51 Percent of Bitcoin Mining, Threatening Security Sanctity." *PCWorld*, June 16, 2014. http://www.pcworld.com/article/2364000/bitcoin-price-dips-as-backers-fear-mining-monopoly.html.

Kaminsky, Dan. "I Tried Hacking Bitcoin and I Failed." *Business Insider*, April 12, 2013. http://www.businessinsider.com/dan-kaminsky-highlights-flaws-bitcoin-2013-4.

Krugman, Paul. "Bitcoin Is Evil." *New York Times*, December 28, 2013. http://krugman.blogs.nytimes.com/2013/12/28/bitcoin-is-evil/?_r=0.

"List of Major Bitcoin Heists, Thefts, Hacks, Scams, and Losses." *Bitcoin Forum*, April 19, 2014, posted by "dree12." https://bitcointalk.org/index.php?topic=576337#post_toc_71.

Love, Dylan. "A Guy Who Owns a Bitcoin-Only Electronics Store Is Revealing Everything on Reddit." *Business Insider*, March 18, 2014. http://www.businessinsider.com/e-commerce-with-bitcoin-2014-3.

Luther, William J. "Dark Dollar Dealings." *U.S. News & World Report*, February 23, 2015. http://www.usnews.com/opinion/economic-intelligence/2015/02/23/us-has-no-business-regulating-bitcoin-because-of-illegal-dealings.

———. "Cryptocurrencies, Network Effects, and Switching Costs." *Contemporary Economic Policy* 34, no. 3 (2016): 553–71.

Luther, William J., and Lawrence H. White. "Can Bitcoin Become a Major Currency?" *Cayman Financial Review*, August 8, 2014. http://www.compasscayman.com/cfr/2014/08/08/Can-bitcoin-become-a-major-currency-/.

Maltby, Emily. "Chargebacks Create Business Headaches." *Wall Street Journal*, February 10, 2011. http://www.wsj.com/articles/SB10001424052748704698004576104554234202010.

Meiklejohn, Sarah, Marjori Pomarole, Grant Jordan, Kirill Levchenko, Damon McCoy, Geoffrey M. Voelker, and Stefan Savage. "A Fistful of Bitcoins: Characterizing Payments among Men with No Names." *;login:* 38, no. 6 (December 2013): 10–14.

National Association of Attorneys General (NAAG). "An Explanation of Bitcoin and Its Implications for Consumer Protection." *NAAGazette* 8, no. 6–7 (July 24, 2014). http://www.naag.org/publications/naagazette/volume-8-number-6/an-explanation-of-bitcoin-and-its-implications-for-consumer-protection.php.

Perez, Yessi Bello. "How Bitrated Wants to Put the Trust Back in Bitcoin." *CoinDesk*, April 12, 2015. http://www.coindesk.com/how-bitrated-is-aiming-to-put-trust-back-in-bitcoin/.

Rizzo, Pete. "Bank Stops Working with Bitcoin Exchange CampBX Due to 'Regulatory Uncertainty.'" *CoinDesk*, February 1, 2015. http://www.coindesk.com/bank-stops-working-bitcoin-exchange-campbx-regulatory-uncertainty/.

———. "Breaking down New York's Latest BitLicense Revision." *CoinDesk*, February 5, 2015. http://www.coindesk.com/breaking-down-new-york-bitlicense-revision/.

———. "Bitcoin ATM Shutdown Spotlights Regulatory Uncertainty in Vermont." *CoinDesk*, February 17, 2015. http://www.coindesk.com/bitcoin-atm-shutdown-regulation-vermont/.

Rizzo, Pete, and Jon Southurst. "Mt. Gox Allegedly Loses $350 Million in Bitcoin (744,400 BTC), Rumoured to Be Insolvent." *CoinDesk*, February 25, 2014. http://www.coindesk.com/mt-gox-loses-340-million-bitcoin-rumoured-insolvent/.

Selgin, George, William D. Lastrapes, and Lawrence H. White. "Has the Fed Been a Failure?" *Journal of Macroeconomics* 34, no. 3 (2012): 569–96.

Smith, Jeffrey. "GHashi.io Is Open for Discussion." GHashi.io Press Release, June 16, 2014. http://www.scribd.com/doc/229951141/GHash-Press-Release-June-16-2014.

Sparkes, Matthew. "The £625m Lost Forever—The Phenomenon of Disappearing Bitcoins." *Telegraph*, January 23, 2015. http://www.telegraph.co.uk/technology/news/11362827/The -625m-lost-forever-the-phenomenon-of-disappearing-Bitcoins.

Sparshott, Jeffrey. "Bitcoin Exchange Makes Apparent Move to Play by U.S. Money-Laundering Rules." *Wall Street Journal*, June 28, 2013. http://online.wsj.com/article/SB100014241278873 23873904578574000957464468.html.

Stross, Charlie. "Why I Want Bitcoin to Die in a Fire." *Charlie's Diary*, December 18, 2013. http:// www.antipope.org/charlie/blog-static/2013/12/why-i-want-bitcoin-to-die-in-a.html.

Stucky, Nathalie-Kyoko, and Jake Adelstein. "Japanese Bitcoin Heist 'an Inside Job,' Not Hackers Alone." *The Daily Beast*, December 31, 2014. http://www.thedailybeast.com /articles/2014/12/31/japanese-bitcoin-heist-an-inside-job-not-hackers-alone.html.

Thierer, Adam. *Permissionless Innovation: The Continuing Case for Comprehensive Technological Freedom, Revised and Expanded Edition*. Arlington, VA: Mercatus Center at George Mason University, 2016.

US Commodity Futures Trading Commission. "CFTC Orders Bitcoin Options Trading Platform Operator and Its CEO to Cease Illegally Offering Bitcoin Options and to Cease Operating a Facility for Trading or Processing of Swaps without Registering." Press Release, September 17, 2015. http://www.cftc.gov/PressRoom/PressReleases/pr7231-15.

US Securities and Exchange Commission. "SEC Charges Bitcoin Mining Companies." Press Release 2015-271, December 1, 2015.

Wile, Rob. "A Brooklyn Bodega Owner Told Us Why All Merchants Should Start Accepting Bitcoin." *Business Insider*, November 11, 2013. http://www.businessinsider.com/brooklyn -bitcoin-bodega-2013-11.

Wolf, Brett. "Bitcoin Exchanges Offer Anti-Money-Laundering Aid." *Reuters*, June 15, 2011. http:// www.reuters.com/article/2011/06/15/financial-bitcoin-idUSN1510930920110615.

CHAPTER 15
Financial Technology

HOUMAN B. SHADAB

Center for Business and Financial Law
New York Law School

T his chapter analyzes important developments in financial technology (fintech) and their implications for US regulation in three areas: personal finance, consumer payments, and access to capital. It establishes principles that regulators should follow to foster innovation while protecting consumers and pursuing other policy goals. Overall, fintech innovation benefits market participants by reducing fees and other costs and by improving access to capital and other financial services. While the US financial regulatory framework has enabled fintech to develop, in certain areas regulation can be improved to allow fintech to develop even further.

Technology is causing innovation, competition, and even disruption across a range of industries, including financial services. The growing use of technology has resulted in financial services that are cheaper, faster, safer, and more accessible. These benefits may be relatively mundane improvements, such as more efficient automatic teller machines and data-driven bank relationships with customers. But they also include more radical innovations that potentially remove the need for traditional financial intermediaries to invest, make electronic payments, and raise capital. A major benefit of fintech is making financial services more competitive. According to a March 2015 Goldman

Sachs report, competition from fintech startups has the potential to disrupt $4 trillion in revenues and $470 billion of profits at existing financial institutions.[1]

Since 2010, global fintech investment has been rapidly increasing, and 2015 was a record year with $19.1 billion invested globally.[2] The large amount of capital backing fintech firms indicates that the nature of financial services is fundamentally changing and accordingly warrants attention from regulators.

The growth of fintech has many causes. They include more powerful computing, the need to reduce costs and risk and comply with regulation in the wake of the financial crisis, and dissatisfaction among consumers with existing institutions and services. Another cause is the already large amount of spending done by financial institutions on information technology, which was estimated by Gartner to be $485 billion in 2014.[3]

Fintech applies to nearly all aspects of the broad and diverse world of finance and financial markets. However, there are certain features and drivers that have come to typify the fintech industry, most importantly:

- **Peer-to-peer (disintermediation).** Parties transacting (more) directly by removing intermediaries that charge fees and commissions, act as gatekeepers, and are focal points for regulation.

- **Data-driven and automated.** Replacing paper-based information and manual decision-making with those that are digital, automated, and involve data analysis, including using algorithms to make lending decisions and detect fraudulent payments.

- **Open source software and widely accessible data.** Moving away from proprietary technology and closed systems to software code that can be used and modified by anyone and data made accessible to third-party software developers.

- **Mobile.** Payments, trading, borrowing, and other financial services are increasingly being offered on smart phones, wearables, and other mobile devices.

- **Social.** Users and producers of financial services are communicating through social media platforms, including to discuss stock trades and make electronic payments.

- **Accessibility and inclusion.** Expanding the reach of financial services, such as banking and electronic payments, to traditionally underserved individuals and companies, including those without bank accounts and assets traditionally accepted as collateral by lending institutions.

- **Blockchains (distributed ledgers).** Undertaking and recording transactions without a centralized intermediary by using a blockchain network software protocol that creates a shared ledger among multiple institutions. The potential benefits are widely applicable to financial services and include increased transaction security, speed, and transparency.

- **Cryptocurrencies.** Peer-to-peer payment networks that operate using public-key cryptography to create digital tokens that are not backed by any government and do not require any financial institution or other centralized intermediary to be transferred. The most prominent cryptocurrency is bitcoin.

FINTECH REGULATION: A PRO-INNOVATION APPROACH

Fintech innovation seems to have benefited consumers and companies by reducing costs and delays, increasing transparency about fees, improving accessibility to financial services, and making it easier to diversify investment portfolios. As technology becomes increasingly ubiquitous in all aspects of financial services, regulators should expect that innovation and change—from the introduction of new products and services to the disruption of entire companies and sectors—will become the norm.

Depending on the circumstances, a single fintech innovation may implicate a wide range of regulations and agencies. For example, a mobile phone application that permits users to borrow funds, transfer money, and make investments could potentially implicate state and federal lending laws, anti–money laundering regulation, and securities regulations that relate to consumer protection, recordkeeping and disclosure, and prevention of criminal finance. Accordingly, this chapter establishes principles that foster innovation across a range of financial sectors and regulatory regimes while maintaining policy goals.

The widely recognized observation that successful innovation requires entrepreneurs to develop a tolerance for failure also applies to lawmakers. An overly precautionary approach that seeks to prevent all instances of fraud or other harms that may accompany innovation should not be the basis for policy decisions. A pro-innovation approach should create room for innovation by permitting new financial products to come to market without being subject to all of the regulations applicable to established firms. This can be accomplished by using legal and policy devices such as:

- Safe harbors or no-action letters that provide exemptive relief from regulation for firms that produce significant benefits or offer their products only to sophisticated persons, or that operate on a small scale.

- Scaled-down or flexible requirements for startups and other small or young firms.

- Government initiatives such as "sandboxes" that permit firms to experiment and develop new products in a cooperative arrangement with regulators.[4]

A potentially promising regulatory sandbox was enacted on February 18, 2016, when the Bureau of Consumer Financial Protection (CFPB) finalized rules relating to its Project Catalyst sandbox initiative.[5] Project Catalyst seeks to create legal certainty for entrepreneurs by empowering the CFPB to provide no-action regulatory relief from certain legal requirements if entrepreneurs are developing new products with potentially significant benefits to consumers in an area where application of existing law is unclear.[6] However, the CFPB sandbox is not likely to be widely used because the application process is costly, the CFPB retains power to revoke any regulatory relief granted, and its determinations are not binding on courts or other agencies. Indeed, the CFPB itself notes that its no-action relief will be granted only in exceptional circumstances. A lesson from the limited scope of Project Catalyst is that relief for innovators must be broad and not costly to obtain to have a significant impact. The United Kingdom's Financial Conduct Authority, by contrast, seems to have a more promising approach for a fintech sandbox due to it being run more like a competitive startup incubator than a narrowly tailored administrative program.[7]

To properly promote innovation, policymakers should also avoid subjecting firms to redundant or conflicting rules and obligations. Fintech products are typically offered nationally or internationally and may cut across several regulatory boundary lines. However, being required to comply with numerous federal and state licensing, registration, or regulatory requirements may hinder innovation without advancing policy goals. Avoiding such problems may be accomplished by

- coordination among federal regulatory authorities;
- establishing uniform laws among states;
- creating a single federal regime that preempts duplicative and differing state requirements; or
- state regulators recognizing that registration or licensure in another state, or with the federal government, is sufficient for operating within their state.

A pro-innovation approach requires regulators to introduce new rules as a last resort, and only after becoming informed about the use of new technology and making a determination that applying existing rules is insufficient to cure a recognized market failure. Private contract law, technological developments, industry initiatives, and competitive pressures have a successful history and should in part be relied on to protect consumers and companies. The payments industry's protection of consumer data and control of fraud is a good example. First, the Payment Card Industry Data Security Standard established by the major credit card networks provides a robust security framework applicable to merchants, financial institutions, and vendors. Second, the contractual liabilities imposed on merchants and banks provide incentives to protect customer data and reduce fraud. Third, fintech payments and technology providers more generally have gone beyond minimum requirements to incorporate stronger data protection technologies (such as tokenization, which is discussed later) and biometric authentication. As a result, in 2014, gross loss from fraud in credit and debit card transactions was only 0.057 percent (or 5.7 cents per $100).[8]

When new regulations are necessary, regulators should seek to foster innovation with flexible rules. This approach generally requires preferring government registration over robust licensure requirements, and regulation over prohibition.[9] Regulators should also avoid targeting specific technologies. Instead, regulators should target problematic activities and harms that may be enabled by new technologies. Regulating specific technologies may be underinclusive because it may not capture problems that are caused by technologies that fall outside the scope of the regulation. Technology-specific regulation may also be overinclusive by capturing activities undertaken by a particular technology that are unrelated to the actual harms that concern regulators. For example, data security rules applicable only to mobile phone payments software may fail to capture problems that may arise from other types of mobile payment devices such as smart clothing. Likewise, rules targeting mobile phones may not be necessary for certain mobile phones with their own built-in hardware security features. Regulating a specific technology could be particularly onerous in financial services where multiple regulators may have jurisdiction over the same technology, potentially exacerbating the under/overinclusive problems.

Instead of adopting new rules on a technology-by-technology basis, regulators should adapt existing rules and frameworks to new technology. This can be accomplished by clarifying whether existing rules and policies apply to new technological implementations and amending existing rules if required. In adapting rules to new technology, regulators should focus on actual risks and harms and avoid using metaphors and analogical reasoning that often fail to accurately reflect the real benefits and risks of new technology. Regulators should be cautious even when mandating disclosure. Although some level of disclosure certainly benefits consumers and investors, disclosure mandates suffer from well-known problems due to the inability of individuals to process large amounts of information and behavioral biases such as limited attention spans and confirmation bias.[10] For example, requiring startups to disclose audited financial statements may confuse investors due to the constantly changing nature of a young company's business.

Financial regulators should not directly regulate intermediaries and third parties that do not interact with consumers and only provide a technology-driven service to regulated firms or firms that are sophisticated. Examples include software providers and service vendors that enable financial services, but are not financial firms themselves. Financial regulation is often predicated on regulating intermediaries such as exchanges, brokers, and lending institutions. Fintech, however, often poses a challenge to this regulatory paradigm by enabling companies and individuals to exchange value directly (on a peer-to-peer basis) through online platforms or decentralized networks. When technology enables financial markets to become decentralized and function without intermediaries, regulators should reconsider subjecting investors, traders, and other users to rules that would apply if they were interacting with

421

a regulated firm. Decentralized markets may not pose standard concerns due to a lack of unequal bargaining power and asymmetric information in such markets. Decentralized markets generally serve as platforms that enable parties to interact directly and have a strong incentive to establish their own rules that protect consumers and meet other regulatory goals as a way to attract users. In addition, limitations on enforceability may also require regulators to permit bilateral exchange. There are significant challenges in implementing an oversight regime potentially applicable to millions of individuals transacting bilaterally around the globe.

Overall, given the speed of fintech innovation and the expertise required to understand its operations and benefits and risks for the public, regulators should adopt an approach that emphasizes flexibility, focuses on outcomes, and incorporates industry feedback and validation. This approach broadly fits under what is often referred to as "principles-based regulation" and similar approaches that favor regulation that is adaptable to diverse and rapidly changing industries.[11] The Office of the Comptroller of the Currency's stated intent to host forums and workshops with innovators is a promising example of incorporating industry perspectives in commercial banking.[12] Regulators may also be able to play an important role by providing education and informational resources to the public and potentially vulnerable market participants about any new risks or costs from fintech innovation.

PERSONAL FINANCE

In the United States, savings are typically held in banks and some mixture of real estate and investment funds that hold stocks and bonds. Many of these holdings are in tax-preferred accounts, such as qualified pensions and Individual Retirement Accounts (IRAs). Before the rise of fintech, individuals seeking to purchase public company stocks often did so by using full-service investment advisers and brokers charging significant commissions and fees, including household names such as Charles Schwab and Salomon Smith Barney. These practices were challenged with the development of widely available discount online brokers in the early 1990s such as E-Trade. Around the same time, a wide variety of financial products gave ordinary investors new and cheaper ways to access a broader range of investments. These usually came in the form of stock and bond mutual funds and exchange-traded funds.

Against this backdrop arose fintech firms targeting all aspects of a person's personal financial management. One basic service is to consolidate an individual's accounts and present in a single platform a complete picture of one's finances. This includes one's assets, spending patterns, and investment gains or losses. A leading firm in this area is Mint, founded in 2006, which provides users with a complete financial snapshot and also the ability to pay bills, file taxes, and establish a budget that is monitored and reported back to the user.

Other services provided by personal investment advisers and wealth managers are also being targeted by fintech. A fundamental fintech innovation is providing low-cost, automated financial advice that is tailored to an individual's goals and preferences, with low to no minimum account sizes and with transparent fee structures. So-called robo-advisers provide services in the form of online and mobile platforms that offer services that determine how savers should allocate and diversify their savings among stocks, bonds, and less traditional investments. The platforms automatically adjust a customer's portfolio between different asset classes in accordance with their goals.

Automation allows these firms to reduce costs for investors. Betterment, for example, offers an all-inclusive management fee as low as 0.15 percent of assets, and Wealthfront charges an annual advisory fee of 0.25 percent for accounts with over $10,000 in assets. Robinhood provides zero-commission stock brokerage for its clients. Acorns circumvents minimum investment requirements often imposed by asset managers by using technology to allow investors to literally invest their spare change. As of 2015, automated services controlled a small portion of assets relative to traditional investment advisers, but they are estimated to grow to $2.2 trillion by 2020.[13]

Fintech also gives investors greater autonomy over their investments by offering a wider range of choices. Since 2007, discount online brokers have offered customers the ability to invest in foreign stocks directly using local currencies.[14] Motif offers investors over 150 investment themes ranging from recent initial public offerings (IPOs) to drugs that battle cancer to wearable technology.

Fintech advisers and investment platforms are also helping to increase financial literacy. This includes giving customers access to their credit scores and advice on how to improve them, and making available a range of savings and investment options, from stocks and bonds to mortgages and life insurance. Fintech investment platforms are also integrating social media into

423

investing, such as by integrating social features into investment platforms that enable investors to learn from differing points of view. Most fintech investment platforms target the largest possible range of investors and, at low cost, make advisory services more affordable.

Automated investment advisers are subject to standard registration and regulatory requirements by the US Securities and Exchange Commission (SEC) under the Investment Advisers Act of 1940. The Act prohibits fraud and misleading statements by advisers, imposes fiduciary duties of care and loyalty, and requires disclosures on Form ADV as well as the establishment of a compliance program.[15] Automated investment advisers typically operate an affiliated broker-dealer subject to SEC regulation under the Securities Exchange Act of 1934.

Regulation of fintech investment advisers has generally permitted innovation. The SEC has not singled out firms just because they are online, automated, or offer investors a wider range of investments and investment strategies than previously available. On May 8, 2015, the SEC played an educational role by issuing an alert about the nature and potential pitfalls of automated investment advisers.[16]

CONSUMER PAYMENTS

Fintech is bringing a wide variety of changes, both large and small, to global and local payment systems that offer greater accessibility and convenience. By the turn of the century, the ability to make noncash payments was widely available through credit and debit card networks such as Visa, MasterCard, and American Express. Plastic credit and debit cards require a simple swipe of a magnetic stripe to initiate a transaction and may require a personal identification number (PIN) code to process. For each transaction, the merchant pays an interchange fee to the card issuer. In credit card transactions, merchants also pay a processing fee to an intermediary acquiring bank.

Fintech caused a major change in payments with the development of digital wallets accessible through a website or mobile device, including smart watches. Digital wallets make it possible to integrate multiple accounts, make payments, and transfer funds through a single, consolidated interface. PayPal is a leading global provider of such services and enables its users to make payments using their credit cards or bank accounts online or with their mobile app. More recent developments include Google Wallet and Apple Pay. Individual merchants such as Starbucks, Dunkin' Donuts, and Walmart have also developed their own mobile payment apps that compete with mobile wallets.

Platforms built on top of bank and other existing electronic networks have also been developed to enable online payments as an alternative to cash, checks, or wire transfers. Dwolla, for example, provides a network that allows users to establish an account and then transfer funds among each other, and it only charges 25 cents if the amount is over $10. Venmo, a platform owned by PayPal, lets users transfer bank and debit card payments for free and is integrated with Facebook accounts. Social media platforms, such as Facebook and Snapchat, also introduced features in 2015 enabling their users to transfer payments. In addition to peer-to-peer payments, fintech is also improving international currency exchange. Companies like TransferWise and CurrencyFair offer cheaper exchange rates than are traditionally available by matching buyers and sellers of different currencies together directly, taking bank currency exchangers out of the equation altogether.

Fintech has also enabled electronic payments to be made without using traditional banking and card networks. PayNearMe allows individuals to pay their utility, rent, and other bills with cash at locations such as 7-Eleven by converting the cash payment into an electronic form acceptable to service providers.[17] In addition, Vodafone's M-Pesa has radically altered the payments landscape in countries such as Kenya by linking payments and fund transfers to mobile phone accounts to enable electronic payments without a bank account.[18] Cryptocurrencies such as bitcoin enable users to transfer units of digital currency without using any bank or centralized entity and for minimal cost. For example, the bitcoin exchange and wallet provider Coinbase does not itself charge for transferring or making payments with bitcoin.

Mobile payments made with digital wallets employ other technologies, including near-field communications or a location-based system that becomes responsive within the proximity of a particular merchant. When using a smart phone to make a payment, the mobile wallet itself may require that an additional PIN be entered.

Fintech has also made it significantly easier for merchants to accept electronic payments instead of cash. Portable point-of-sale systems such as Square allow retailers to accept credit and debit cards through a smart phone or other mobile device. Other companies such as Stripe make it easier for online merchants to accept credit card payments by offering a simplified platform and fee structure for a wide variety of local and international cards.

An important outcome of fintech payments developments is greater consumer data security. Outside of North America, credit card payments are processed using the Europay, MasterCard, and Visa (EMV) standard that uses a PIN and enhanced encryption with a microchip embedded into the card to reduce fraud. The EMV standard also allows a contact-free payment "tap" with a credit card that transmits less information than a standard credit card transaction and creates a unique card verification code for each transaction. In October 2015, US card issuers and merchants began to implement the EMV standard. The adoption of EMV is an example of private law developments that protect consumers without governmental regulation. Merchants have an incentive to upgrade to EMV or else they will be liable for certain types of fraudulent charges.

Mobile payments are also increasingly using the security advancement known as tokenization. Tokenization replaces a traditional sixteen-digit credit card number by creating a unique, random number and expiration date for every transaction. The benefit of tokenization is that it enables sensitive information to be hidden from, and never stored by, a merchant or others involved in processing payment transactions. Unlike encryption, sensitive data is never passed along to third parties. Apple Pay, for example, uses tokenization to avoid storing sensitive credit card information on a user's iPhone, Apple's servers, or with the merchant.[19] Biometric technologies, such as fingerprint-based identification systems, are also increasingly being integrated into payments systems to reduce fraud. Overall, these and other technologies indicate that the market for consumer payments security is functioning well and improving.

Mobile and other forms of fintech payments typically use or expand the functionality of traditional regulated intermediaries, such as card networks and banks, and are accordingly subject to a wide variety of regulations. These include mandates regarding information retention, disclosure, and acquisition; substantive prohibitions on how and to whom payments may be made; and provisions that limit consumer liability. The primary purpose of these requirements is to prevent the use of funds in illicit activities and to protect consumers.

Fintech payment providers that transmit or exchange money are subject to a wide variety of anti–money laundering laws, including criminal statutes.

Statutes such as the Bank Secrecy Act (BSA) impose recordkeeping and report-ing requirements, customer information-gathering ("know your customer") requirements, and the implementation of anti–money laundering programs. Payment providers must also comply with Treasury Department rules that prohibit being involved with payments to sanctioned persons, countries, or entities. In addition, the Gramm-Leach-Bliley Act and regulations of the Federal Trade Commission (FTC) subject institutions and companies to rules that require them to protect consumers' confidential information. Money transmitters are also generally subject to state-level money transmission stat-utes. Some states, such as New York, have specific licensing requirements for digital currency businesses.[20]

Electronic funds transfers between accounts at financial institutions are governed by the Electronic Fund Transfer Act (EFTA) and Regulation E. These laws limit consumer liability to $500 and require institutions to dis-close information about financial charges. Credit card and other types of consumer credit are governed by the Truth in Lending Act (TILA) and Regulation Z. These rules require card issuers to provide continuous disclo-sure to credit card users, provide procedures for resolving errors and fraud, and generally limit consumer liability for fraud to $50. In 2010, the Dodd-Frank Wall Street Reform and Consumer Protection Act gave the CFPB authority over implementing EFTA and TILA regulation, among several other stat-utes.[21] The CFPB has broad authority to regulate consumer financial prod-ucts, which includes the authority to prohibit unfair, deceptive, or abusive acts or practices.[22] Although telephone carrier–based billing systems are not widely used in the United States, the FTC requires carriers to disclose infor-mation about mobile payments charged directly to a user's phone bill.[23]

In general, the regulatory framework applicable to consumer payments has enabled a wide range of innovation to emerge while protecting consumers from fraud and abuse. Regulators have also promoted innovation by gather-ing data and information about the changing nature of the payments market before enacting new rules. For example, the Federal Reserve Banks of Boston and Atlanta established the Mobile Payments Industry Workgroup in January 2010 to bring together regulators and other stakeholders to study and make recommendations on improving the US payment system. Notably, none of the Workgroup's publications identified any market failures warranting addi-tional regulation.

In some cases, however, the existing regulatory framework and agency actions undermine payment innovations or hurt consumers and companies. For example, laws prohibiting money laundering likely make banks overly cautious about compliance risks and cause them to not provide financial services to underserved communities because they are perceived as being too risky.[24] Cryptocurrencies such as bitcoin are another case in point. Although bitcoin's underlying blockchain technology enables users to transfer value globally, bitcoin exchanges, electronic storage wallets, and other intermediaries are generally required to register with and be licensed by the federal government and also in numerous states and thereby are subject to redundant regulation regarding anti–money laundering, consumer protection, and other areas. A second problem is scope. Decentralized cryptocurrency networks operate in ways that do not fit traditional regulatory categories. For example, bitcoin wallets that require the consent of multiple parties to initiate a transfer likely do not fit within traditional regulatory categories of "money transmitter" or "custodian" yet may be subject to regulation nonetheless. Likewise, cryptocurrencies may also be used to record transactions or enable nonfinancial software applications yet may be subject to money transmitter regulation, despite being used for nonfinancial purposes. A final issue is regulating on the basis of unrealistic harms and without regard to marketplace developments that reduce traditional consumer protection concerns. For example, cryptocurrency networks provide a permanent and publicly verifiable record of transactions. In addition, technologies that require multiple parties to approve a transaction (multisignature) or confirm that a firm has sufficient funds (proof-of-reserve) provide market-based protections to consumers against fraud and insolvency.[25] For such reasons, the potential application of CFPB prepaid card regulation to cryptocurrency intermediaries not involved in a payment transaction seems unnecessary.

FUNDRAISING AND ACCESS TO CAPITAL

Fintech is dramatically increasing the accessibility of capital. This is especially true for individuals and small companies—segments of the public that continually have problems borrowing money or finding investors. A basic way that fintech is increasing access to capital is by making the loan application process less of a hassle. Potential borrowers may now apply for mortgages and other loans with their smart phones and receive funds in minutes.

For companies, online platforms are also making it easier to raise capital by selling their invoices and receivables.[26]

The development of online fundraising platforms is how fintech has fundamentally broadened access to capital. Rewards-based crowdfunding platforms that aggregate small amounts of money in return for public recognition or a payment-in-kind have opened up new vistas of capital for new businesses, art projects, and social causes. The well-known crowdfunding platform Kickstarter has raised more than $2.5 billion in funds since its founding in 2009.[27] These platforms are regulated at the federal level by the FTC.

Online platforms have also increased access to capital from investors and lenders seeking a return on capital. Equity crowdfunding platforms allow investors with small amounts of capital to share in the profits of enterprises. The platforms may play a relatively passive role in allocating capital and grouping investors or take an active role by vetting companies, taking board seats, and providing mentorship. Equity crowdfunding platforms make it much easier for private companies to raise capital by giving them direct access to investors instead of having to rely on professionals or informal networks that are typically very costly and may take years to establish.

Congress took a significant step in the direction of enabling online equity crowdfunding platforms by passing the Jumpstart Our Business Startups Act of 2012 (the JOBS Act). Title III of the JOBS Act permits online crowdfunding portals to serve as intermediaries for fundraising by providing legal certainty that they may operate as matchmakers between firms and sophisticated investors without necessarily being subject to broker-dealer regulation that would make it too costly to operate.[28] AngelList is a prominent example of such a portal.

Going further, Title III of the JOBS Act permitted private companies for the first time to raise funds selling their securities to the public and not just wealthy investors who meet the legal definition of accredited investor. The purpose of the Title III crowdfunding rules is to enable new companies to raise small amounts of funds from numerous investors without costly registration and compliance requirements. In any twelve-month period, the rules permit a company to raise up to $1 million and limit investors to investing no more than (1) the greater of $2,000 or 5 percent of annual income or net worth, if annual income or net worth is below $100,000, or (2) 10 percent of the lesser of annual income or net worth up to a total of $100,000, if both annual income and net worth are $100,000 or above.[29] Online crowdfunding portals are permitted to curate the companies that list on their platforms and take equity stakes in them on similar terms as other investors.

Online "marketplace lending" platforms connect borrowers to investors. Investors provide funding to borrowers by purchasing loans or notes representing fractional interests in loans, or through securitization. For example, investors may purchase three- to five-year notes backed by the payments of numerous diverse borrowers that are often disclosed on a loan-level basis.[30] Institutional investors make up most of the purchasers of such notes in the United States, and banks often play a role in marketplace lending by originating the loan and selling it to the online platform.[31] The loans usually range in size from $1,000 to $35,000 and may include refinancing and consolidation. The platforms often use a wide variety of traditional and nontraditional criteria to assess a borrower's risk, such as FICO scores, data from social media and seller channels, or banking and merchant processing data. Marketplace lenders may also use large sets of data and machine-learning algorithms in making loan decisions to borrowers, as well as qualitative factors such as endorsements and community affiliations. As of 2015 approximately $12 billion in marketplace loans had been issued.[32]

In addition to making more funds available for loans in the first place, marketplace lending has several important benefits for borrowers. First, loans from online platforms are generally cheaper.[33] This is because marketplace lenders are not encumbered by inefficiencies of traditional banking that stem from mismanagement, the costs of maintaining a branch infrastructure, overhead, and regulatory capital requirements. Second, obtaining a marketplace-funded loan is more streamlined and faster than obtaining a traditional bank loan and often a more manageable form of credit. Unlike credit cards, marketplace loans tend to be fully amortizing with fixed interest rates. Third, marketplace lenders may be willing to lend to individuals and companies otherwise unable to obtain a loan or refinancing due to the lenders' use of innovative underwriting practices and access to capital market funding.

The practice of marketplace lending is subject to wide-ranging regulation. Any notes issued by marketplace lenders are subject to securities laws. In addition, marketplace lenders that extend consumer credit are subject to federal and state laws, including TILA, FTC, and CFPB prohibitions on unfair and deceptive practices, fair lending rules, and federal Bank Secrecy Act anti–money laundering and know-your-customer regulations. On March 7, 2016, the CFPB issued an alert to educate borrowers about the risks of marketplace loans.[34] Other bodies of law that may apply to marketplace lending include state usury laws, vendor management programs, and the Fair Debt Collection Practices Act. Industry-led initiatives such as the Small Business Borrowers' Bill of Rights also provide protections for companies that may lack the financial acumen of sophisticated borrowers.[35] Although the increasing use of data and algorithms to automate lending decisions potentially raises unique concerns— about violating fair lending and disparate impact regulations, predatory lending, and confusing consumers about why they were (or were not) approved for a loan—the same legal protections still apply. Nonetheless, the use of data and algorithms may be an area in which regulators need to increase their focus.

Despite a new regulatory regime enabling crowdfunding, and the explosion in marketplace lending, regulators can also take steps to ensure further growth in both.

Crowdfunding regulations subject companies and investors to overly restrictive or burdensome rules. The crowdfunding investment limit should be raised from $1 million to $5 million to permit companies to adequately capitalize themselves through crowdfunding without having to resort to other methods of finance. Crowdfunding portals are prohibited from making any investment recommendations or having their directors and officers take equity positions in the companies listed on their platforms. These restrictions prevent crowdfunding platforms from providing potentially valuable information regarding the quality of investments they offer. They likewise may prevent platforms from listing higher quality companies due to insiders having a direct stake in their success. The restrictions should be relaxed. Conflicts of interest that arise from such activities can likely be addressed with proper mandated disclosures.

In addition, crowdfunding regulations likely require too much ongoing reporting for certain startups. The rules require that startups publicly file a new form anytime a material update takes place. However, given how often startups make significant changes to their businesses, it seems that filing a new form each time may be overly burdensome and not meaningful to investors. This is because such changes are often short-lived and not related to the long-term success of the startup, despite potentially meeting the legal definition of materiality. The SEC should also permit single-purpose funds to crowdfund and invest as a single shareholder. Single-purpose funds could help startups avoid amassing too many investors to be attractive to subsequent investors. To prevent crowdfunding from being unattractive to startups with plans of growing large, Congress or the SEC should exempt crowdfunding startups from being required to go public if they have more than $25 million in assets and 500 nonaccredited shareholders.

A crowdfunding regulatory regime that strikes a better balance between investor protection and innovation is the substantially less restrictive approach of the UK's Financial Conduct Authority.[36] In contrast to the SEC regime, the UK regime does not impose numerous specific disclosure or periodic reporting requirements on crowdfunding companies, but rather requires disclosure sufficient for investors to make informed decisions.[37] UK crowdfunding portals vet which startups are permitted to use their platform and impose their own disclosure requirements based on the requirements' anticipated costs and benefits as well as demand from investors. Despite the lighter touch of the UK approach, the UK equity crowdfunding market raised approximately £332 million in 2015 without significant fraud.[38] Based on the UK experience, it seems that crowdfunding portals can develop investor protection practices without wide-ranging regulation as is the case in the United States.

Marketplace lending would also likely be able to bring more benefits to borrowers with a more streamlined regulatory framework. This could be accomplished through the establishment of a new federal charter for marketplace lenders. The charter would subject the lenders to consumer protection rules and rules designed to limit their systemic risks, while removing the redundancies and operational efficiencies that result from the current patchwork of rules.[39] Currently, to operate legally, marketplace lenders must either obtain a license in each state in which they operate or partner with a federally chartered bank that is already permitted to operate nationally. Neither of these arrangements is optimal. The costs of state-by-state licensing likely outweigh its benefits. In addition, partnering with a national bank may undermine innovation and competition. Marketplace lenders may be constrained by a bank's organizational inertia and its traditional approach to regulatory compliance. Limited opportunities to partner with banks and the costs of doing so may dissuade additional marketplace lenders from entering the market. Like any relatively new and growing industry, marketplace lending can also likely be improved through greater standardization and transparency, as well as broader partnerships and access to data that improves borrower decision-making.[40] To the extent regulators mandate or facilitate the development of such improvements, the principles identified earlier in this chapter should be followed.

CONCLUSION

The delivery of financial services is undergoing a process of increasing change that benefits society by reducing costs and increasing accessibility. Robo-advisers have brought reduced fees and more transparency to retail investors. Payments technology has made it easier, faster, and cheaper for more consumers and merchants to enjoy the benefits of electronic payments. Online equity crowdfunding and marketplace lending platforms are opening up significant sources of capital to individuals and small businesses. While the US financial regulatory framework has largely enabled these fintech innovations to grow, in certain areas such as equity crowdfunding regulation needs to be less restrictive.

NOTES

1. Irrera, "FN Fintech Focus."
2. "Pulse of Fintech, 2015 in Review," 11.
3. Emmerson, "3 Trends Driving FinTech," cites this Gartner estimate.
4. Financial Conduct Authority, "Regulatory Sandbox," 5–7.
5. CFPB, "CFPB Finalizes Policy."
6. Ibid.
7. Financial Conduct Authority, "Regulatory Sandbox," retrieved May 26, 2016, https://innovate.fca.org.uk/innovation-hub/regulatory-sandbox.
8. Kiernan, "Credit Card and Debit Card Fraud Statistics."
9. Thierer, *Permissionless Innovation*, 63–65.
10. Ripken, "Dangers and Drawbacks of the Disclosure Antidote," 139, 160–90; Ben-Shahar and Schneider, *More than You Wanted to Know*.
11. Brummer and Gorfine, "FinTech," 6–14.
12. Office of the Comptroller of the Currency, "Supporting Responsible Innovation," 6.
13. Regan, "Robo Advisers to Run $2 Trillion."
14. Bruno, "E-Trade to Unveil Global Trading Platform."
15. Investment Advisers Act of 1940 (Advisers Act), 15 U.S.C. §§ 80b-1-80b-21 (2012); US Securities and Exchange Commission, "Study on Investment Advisers and Broker-Dealers," 2011, 22; Prohibition of Fraud by Advisers to Certain Pooled Investment Vehicles, 72 Fed. Reg. (August 9, 2007): 44756, 44759. Advisers Act, Rule 206(4)-7.
16. SEC, "Investor Alert."
17. "7-Eleven and PayNearMe."
18. "M-Money Channel Distribution Case."
19. First Data Corporation, "First Data Enables Industry Payment."

20. N.Y. Comp. Codes R. & Regs. tit. 23, Part 200.

21. These statutes consist of the Equal Credit Opportunity Act, the Fair Credit Reporting Act, the Fair Debt Collection Practices Act, the Home Mortgage Disclosure Act, the Real Estate Settlement Procedures Act, the Secure and Fair Enforcement for Mortgage Licensing Act, and the Truth in Lending Act.

22. See Dodd-Frank §§ 1002, 1031, and 1036(a), codified at 12 U.S.C. §§ 5481, 5531, and 5536(a).

23. FDIC, "Mobile Payments."

24. Lowery and Ramachandran, "Unintended Consequences of Anti–Money Laundering Policies."

25. Valkenburgh, "Comments to the Consumer Financial Protection Bureau," 8–11.

26. Cuesta et al., "Crowdfunding in 360°," 10.

27. Kickstarter.

28. Jumpstart Our Business Startups Act of 2012, Pub. L. No. 112-106, 126 Stat. 313-315 (2012).

29. SEC, "Regulation Crowdfunding."

30. "Peer Pressure," 1.

31. Cuesta et al., "Crowdfunding in 360°," 9.

32. Brainard, "Community Banks."

33. "Lending Club's Response to Marketplace Lending RFI," 1.

34. CFPB, "Understanding Online Marketplace Lending."

35. Small Business Borrowers' Bill of Rights.

36. "Global Crowdfunding Market."

37. Financial Conduct Authority, *Review of the Regulatory Regime*, 6–9; "Financing the New Innovation Economy," 19–21.

38. Zhang et al., "Pushing Boundaries," 13, 33.

39. Knight and Warden, "Re: Public Input," 10–11.

40. US Department of the Treasury, "Opportunities and Challenges," 28–33.

REFERENCES

Ben-Shahar, Omri, and Carl E. Schneider. *More than You Wanted to Know: The Failure of Mandated Disclosure*. Princeton, NJ: Princeton University Press, 2014.

Brainard, Lael. "Community Banks, Small Business Credit, and Online Lending." Speech at the Community Banking in the 21st Century, Third Annual Community Banking Research and Policy Conference, St. Louis, MO, September 30, 2015.

Brummer, Chris, and Daniel Gorfine. "FinTech: Building a 21st-Century Regulator's Toolkit." Working Paper, Milken Institute, Washington, DC, October 21, 2014.

Bruno, Joe Bel. "E-Trade to Unveil Global Trading Platform." *USA Today,* February 20, 2007. http://usatoday30.usatoday.com/tech/news/2007-02-20-etrade-global_x.htm.

Bureau of Consumer Financial Protection (CFPB). "CFPB Finalizes Policy to Facilitate Consumer-Friendly Innovation." February 18, 2016. http://www.consumerfinance.gov/about-us/news room/cfpb-finalizes-policy-to-facilitate-consumer-friendly-innovation/.

———. "Understanding Online Marketplace Lending." Consumer Bulletin, March 2016. http://files .consumerfinance.gov/f/201603_cfpb_understanding-online-marketplace-lending.pdf.

Cuesta, Carmen, Santiago Fernández de Lis, Irene Roibas, Ana Rubio, Macarena Ruesta, David Tuesta, and Pablo Urbiola. "Crowdfunding in 360º: Alternative Financing for the Digital Era." BBVA Research, January 30, 2015. https://www.bbvaresearch.com/wp-content/uploads /2015/02/Crowdfunding_Watch.pdf.

Emmerson, Louis. "3 Trends Driving FinTech Investment in 2015." Symbid, June 12, 2015. http:// blog.symbid.com/2015/trends/3-trends-driving-fintech-investment-2015/.

Federal Deposit Insurance Corporation (FDIC). "Mobile Payments: An Evolving Landscape." Supervisory Insights 9, no. 2 (2012): 3–11.

Financial Conduct Authority. A Review of the Regulatory Regime for Crowdfunding and the Promotion of Non-readily Realisable Securities by Other Media. February 2015.

———. "Regulatory Sandbox." November 10, 2015. https://www.fca.org.uk/publications /documents/regulatory-sandbox.

"Financing the New Innovation Economy: Making Investment Crowdfunding Work Better for Startups and Investors, Engine Advocacy." White Paper, Engine Advocacy, San Francisco, October 2015.

First Data Corporation. "First Data Enables Industry Payment Innovation with Apple Pay." Atlanta, GA, September 11, 2014.

"Global Crowdfunding Market Now Worth 30 Billion." Consultancy.uk, September 14, 2015. http://www.consultancy.uk/news/2593/global-crowdfunding-market-now-worth-30-billion.

Irrera, Anna. "FN Fintech Focus: Disruptors' $4trn Fortune." Financial News, March 20, 2015. http://thetally.efinancialnews.com/2015/03/fn-fintech-focus-much-finance-incumbents -stand-lose-disruptors/.

Kickstarter. Retrieved August 16, 2016. https://www.kickstarter.com/help/stats?ref=hello.

Kiernan, John. "Credit Card and Debit Card Fraud Statistics." CardHub. Retrieved May 26, 2016. http://www.cardhub.com/edu/credit-debit-card-fraud-statistics/.

Knight, Brian R., and Staci Warden. "Re: Public Input on Expanding Access to Credit through Marketplace Lending." Public Interest Comment, Milken Institute, Washington, DC, September 28, 2015.

"Lending Club's Response to Marketplace Lending RFI." Public Interest Comment, Lending Club, San Francisco, September 30, 2015.

Lowery, Clay, and Vijaya Ramachandran. "Unintended Consequences of Anti–Money Laundering Policies for Poor Countries." CGD Working Group Report, Center for Global Development, Washington, DC, 2015.

"M-Money Channel Distribution Case—Kenya." Case Study, International Finance Corporation, March 2009. http://www.ifc.org/wps/wcm/connect/4e64a80049585fd9a13ab519583b6d16 /tool+6.7.+case+study+-+m-pesa+kenya+.pdf?mod=ajperes.

Office of the Comptroller of the Currency. "Supporting Responsible Innovation in the Federal Banking System: An OCC Perspective." March 2016.

"Peer Pressure: How Peer-to-Peer Lending Platforms Are Transforming the Consumer Lending Industry." PricewaterhouseCoopers, February 2015. http://www.pwccn.com/home/eng/peer_to_peer_feb2015.html.

"The Pulse of Fintech, 2015 in Review: Global Analysis of Fintech Venture Funding." KPMG and CB Insights, March 9, 2016.

Regan, Michael P. "Robo Advisers to Run $2 Trillion by 2020 If This Model Is Right." *Bloomberg Business*, June 18, 2015. http://www.bloomberg.com/news/articles/2015-06-18/robo-advisers-to-run-2-trillion-by-2020-if-this-model-is-right.

Ripken, Susanna Kim. "The Dangers and Drawbacks of the Disclosure Antidote toward a More Substantive Approach to Securities Regulation." *Baylor Law Review* 58, no. 1 (2006): 139–204.

"7-Eleven and PayNearMe Introduce the First Mobile Bill Payment Center for Cash Users." PRNewswire, September 22, 2015. http://www.prnewswire.com/news-releases/7-eleven-and-paynearme-introduce-the-first-mobile-bill-payment-center-for-cash-users-300141975.html.

Small Business Borrowers' Bill of Rights. Responsible Business Lending Coalition. Retrieved May 26, 2016. http://www.responsiblebusinesslending.org/.

Thierer, Adam. *Permissionless Innovation: The Continuing Case for Comprehensive Technological Freedom.* Arlington, VA: Mercatus Center at George Mason University, 2014, Kindle edition.

US Department of the Treasury. "Opportunities and Challenges in Online Marketplace Lending." May 10, 2016.

US Securities and Exchange Commission. "Investor Alert: Automated Investment Tools." May 8, 2015. http://www.sec.gov/oiea/investor-alerts-bulletins/autolistingtoolshtm.html.

———. "Regulation Crowdfunding: A Small Entity Compliance Guide for Issuers." May 13, 2016. https://www.sec.gov/info/smallbus/secg/rccomplianceguide-051316.htm.

———. "Study on Investment Advisers and Broker-Dealers."

US Securities and Exchange Commission Staff. "Study on Investment Advisers and Broker-Dealers." US Securities and Exchange Commission, January 2011. https://www.sec.gov/news/studies/2011/913studyfinal.pdf.

Valkenburgh, Peter Van. "Comments to the Consumer Financial Protection Bureau on Proposed Rules Relating to Prepaid Accounts." Public Interest Comment, Coin Center, Washington, DC, March 23, 2015.

Zhang, Bryan, Peter Baeck, Tania Ziegler, Jonathan Bone and Kieran Garvey. "Pushing Boundaries: The 2015 UK Alternative Finance Industry Report." Cambridge Centre for Alternative Finance at University of Cambridge Judge Business School and Nesta, February 2016.

CHAPTER 16
Ending the Specter of a Federal Corporate Law

J. W. VERRET*

Antonin Scalia Law School, George Mason University

For most of US history, corporation law, or the law governing the interaction between investors and the companies in which they invest, was a function of state law. State corporate law governed the duties that company directors owed to their investors, established the powers of investors to select new directors and managers, and maintained authority for fundamental business decisions in the board of directors. State corporate codes have evolved in the intervening years, increasingly allowing investors and companies to design alternative arrangements to the default provisions contained in these old codes. Steady incursions by federal law into discrete pieces of state corporate law have begun to slowly erode this system, however, and threaten to inhibit innovation in corporate governance at the state level.

In 1933 and 1934, the US Congress passed laws requiring disclosure of financial information to investors in widely traded firms, but left the working parts of state corporate law largely intact. For the first thirty years after the US Securities and Exchange Commission (SEC) was established, it was clearly understood that state law governed traditionally state corporate law matters, such as the duties that boards owed to shareholders or the permitted structural makeup of a

*This chapter is based in part on J. W. Verret, "Uber-ized Corporate Law: Toward a 21st Century Corporate Governance for Crowdfunding and App-Based Investor Communications," *Journal of Corporation Law* 41 (Summer 2016): 927–69.

company and the way its directors and officers were selected. In 1945, for example, the SEC made clear that the propriety of shareholder proposals at annual company meetings would be determined pursuant to state law.[1]

The détente began to change in 1968 when the Williams Act gave the SEC authority to go beyond merely disclosure-based regulation and actually empowered the SEC to regulate the process whereby public companies were taken over by new buyers. In the 1970s, then SEC Chairman William Cary proposed an express federal corporate law that entirely preempted state corporate law when he urged that "a pygmy among the 50 states prescribes, interprets, and indeed denigrates national corporate policy."[2]

Bill Cary's express suggestion never happened, but a slow advance of federal incursions into state corporate law continued, culminating with an explosive enlargement of the federal footprint in state corporate law in financial reform legislation in 2002 and 2010. The Dodd-Frank Wall Street Reform and Consumer Protection Act (Dodd-Frank), for example, included a variety of corporate governance reforms that were in large part entirely unrelated to the financial crisis of 2008. For example, one of them required companies to disclose their use of minerals mined in the Democratic Republic of the Congo. Another required a nonbinding vote by shareholders, which carries no practical consequences, on CEO pay. Still another required companies to disclose the ratio of their CEO's pay to that of the average worker, a suggestion made some ten years earlier by a labor-funded group as a way to increase union leverage in negotiations.[3] Many of the suggested reforms had been proposed long before 2008, yet were included in what was perceived as must-pass financial reform legislation in order to cater to the powerful special interest groups that had long supported those proposals.

As much as the corporate governance reforms of 2008 were misguided, they were the result of many years of regulation by the federal government that has slowly eroded the role of states in creating corporate law. That process began with rules adopted in response to the Enron and WorldCom scandals in 2001 and 2002, embodied in the Sarbanes-Oxley Act that now determines the qualifications for service on company boards of directors. Oddly, the corporate governance rules regarding independence that were codified in 2002 and 2003 largely reflected attributes of the Enron board of directors.[4]

Much of existing corporate law scholarship has been divided into two competing camps. One urges that states "race to the top" and seek to balance the rights of shareholders and the obligations of directors by adopting laws that maximize shareholder value. That side of the discussion tends to argue that the market for publicly traded stock will discipline any excesses by the state that cater to corporate insiders at shareholders' expense. The opposing camp urges that corporate insiders will distort the race into a "race to the bottom" in which the state that designs corporate governance codes that allow insiders to exploit shareholders and destroy firm value will attract the most new incorporators. The latter camp typically urges as an alternative a federal incorporation regime broadly, and also urges discrete preemptions of state law by a more enlightened federal regulator.

This chapter urges that over the last five decades, the race has been distorted by the presence of federal preemption. The supposed race is not much of a race at all. Federal incursions into state law have themselves garnered significant market power to the currently dominant state for public incorporations, Delaware. Proponents of the "race to the bottom" theory have the causal link backwards. Federal preemption of discrete areas of corporate law is not the answer to market failures in the market for corporate law, federal preemption is in fact causing market failures. Federal incursions do this in part by inhibiting innovations, like an arbitration-based corporate code, which could challenge Delaware's dominance in corporate law by challenging one of the principal competitive attributes of Delaware in its predictable court system. As such, a rollback of the federal footprint is the best way to reinvigorate the chartering race in corporate law.

This chapter argues that first and foremost, this federal overlay in corporate governance must be stripped away. Alternately, at a minimum the existing federal corporate governance rule book should at least become part of an optional opt-in regime and thereby allow a firm's shareholders to determine whether the federal arrangement is best for their particular firm. But arguing for removal of current federal encroachments on state corporate law contained in Sarbanes-Oxley and Dodd-Frank is just the beginning. This chapter goes on to explore how other existing federal laws can be molded to empower the states to compete with each other in corporate law. A number of institutional changes will be needed to develop the foundations necessary to facilitate innovation and economic growth in state corporate law.

Dodd-Frank, legislation built on an improper understanding of the factors leading to the 2008 financial crisis, ultimately threatens the competition and flexibility required for consumer benefits created via innovation. Specifically, Title IX, Subsection G, of Dodd-Frank continues the trend of centralizing corporate law by consolidating regulatory power over corporate governance in the federal government, thus preempting the ability of states to be competitive in chartering. State chartering may be competitive within the modes of governance permitted by the federal overlay.[5] This chapter's examination of a range of innovations that would be clearly helpful in experimental environments, like crowdfunding, will demonstrate that the federal footprint in corporate law stifles the chartering race by inhibiting innovation.

Business entity law has been around since the establishment of the firm and has remained an important contributing factor to the economic systems that develop and utilize them. Corporate law was key to building the Roman aqueducts and critical to the Industrial Revolution. The advent and public embrace of innovative business models like Kickstarter's crowdfunding approach and Uber's sharing-economy structure demonstrate demand for a more flexible approach toward corporate governance. With each unique business model comes the necessitation of an equally unique corporate structure. However, the mere fact that the economics of new-age firms suggest a demand for flexible innovation in corporate governance does not mean that states are in a position to make that innovation available.

For example, Stephen Bainbridge at the UCLA School of Law and M. Todd Henderson of the University of Chicago Law School recently designed a novel approach to the structure of boards of directors in which other business entities can themselves serve as members of the board, which would allow board member companies to economize on scale and scope, have more directed compensation and liability incentives than the current model, better expose the market for board membership to market forces, and provide reputational constraints for repeat player board member firms.[6] Bainbridge and Henderson note that federal rules that would prevent their idea were not necessarily even designed to prevent entity membership on the board, but the references to natural persons in the federal rules effectively preclude their innovation from being implemented.[7] Moving forward, a competitive model for the production of corporate law will be critical to make the most of technological advances that are reducing the cost of individual interaction. In this chapter I suggest that the reinvigoration of state law federalism can serve to support such a competitive model.

CORPORATE FEDERALISM UNDER THE THREAT OF FEDERAL PREEMPTION

The corporate codes that govern business entities have been the lynchpin of America's economic development since the start of the industrial age. Business entities with separate existence, able to protect their shareholders from liability for corporate actions, were essential to facilitate the first large-scale industrial investments in the late nineteenth and early twentieth centuries. States competed to offer increasingly accommodative corporate codes, and eventually Delaware became a dominant player in that race by allowing companies to own stock in other companies—something its chief competitor, New Jersey, prohibited until the middle of the twentieth century.

This competitive state system, in which states compete to attract out-of-state entrepreneurs to form corporations in their state, has also been beneficial to shareholders. A study found that firms incorporated in Delaware, the current winner of the incorporation race, experience an increase in shareholder value at the initial public offering (IPO) stage over other firms solely by virtue of being incorporated in Delaware.[8]

Roberta Romano of Yale Law School has described this state system as allowing states to serve as laboratories in which new corporate governance arrangements can be invented and measured against offerings from competing states. While not every state actively competes in this arena, smaller-population states like Delaware have been eager to compete for incorporation fees from newly formed companies.

A more recent innovation in business entity law has been the widespread use of limited liability companies, or LLCs, which have a greater degree of flexibility in designing the range of fiduciary obligations that boards and CEOs owe to their shareholders. While that degree of flexibility is greater than the flexibility afforded CEOs and boards of corporations, it remains somewhat limited. Delaware still maintains an obligation of "good faith and fair dealing" that shareholders are not permitted to opt out of in favor of contractually specified obligations. The late Professor Larry Ribstein also notes a number of cases in which Delaware courts have struggled to uphold the Delaware legislature's intent to promote freedom of contract in LLC agreements.

While Delaware competes to maintain its advantage in new business entity formation, Jonathan Macey of the Yale Law School and Geoffrey Miller of the New York University School of Law suggest that the state may enjoy an extent of market power that allows it to also maximize the litigation fees enjoyed by Delaware law firms that help to craft Delaware's code.[9] That would certainly explain Delaware's reaction in 2015 to a court ruling that companies are allowed to adopt bylaws that force losing plaintiffs to pay a company's legal fees in shareholder actions. The Delaware bar, fearing a loss in litigation business, immediately moved to change the Delaware code to reverse the Delaware Supreme Court's ruling and prohibit such "loser pays" bylaws.[10]

Many of Delaware's critics suggest that it does not actually actively compete for business entity formation any longer, and that the idea of state competition in business entity formation is largely a myth at this point. They argue that Delaware has a hundred years of precedent behind it, and as such its advantage is insurmountable for new states that might attempt to compete with Delaware by improving on its code. For example, if another state wanted to take Delaware's code, improve on it, and thereby compete with Delaware, it would find the Delaware code filled with nebulous concepts like "good faith" obligations and a "duty of care" and "duty of loyalty" that have slowly been defined over a hundred years and thousands of pages of precedent. States may feel Delaware's body of precedent is an insurmountable obstacle in trying to make their own codes work.

Supporters of Dodd-Frank's corporate governance reforms latched on to that argument and urged that Delaware failed investors by not adopting corporate governance reforms they favored. Ann Yerger of the Council of Institutional Investors testified with respect to the proxy access rule included in Dodd-Frank that "the States have failed investors too long, Delaware in particular, and it really only acted when it had to. And I think it is important that the SEC take action on this important reform."[11] Relative to other states in the incorporation race, it is not clear that Delaware is failing shareholders. For example, as noted earlier, companies incorporated in Delaware enjoy a premium in their average market value compared to non-Delaware companies at the time they go public. Relative to the range of options for shareholders that could be observed in a more competitive chartering environment free of a federal footprint, which stamps out more competitive innovations, Yerger may well be right. But relaxing federal incursions into state law is the answer to the problem.

Delaware's critics may certainly have a point that Delaware imperfectly competes in the race to charter new businesses and to innovate in corporate governance. Those critics, however, have made the wrong diagnosis. Federal preemption of state corporate law, and the specter of future federal preemption, discourages other states from challenging Delaware. The state laboratories described by Romano do not really work if the innovators must work under the threat that their innovations may be destroyed by federal action. Indeed, Professor Mark Roe argues that Delaware is uniquely adept among the states at responding to the specter of federal preemption with narrowly tailored changes that outmaneuver some of the goals of blunt federal legislation.[12]

The threat of federal action has important consequences for arbitration as a means to invigorate state competition. The market power that Delaware enjoys in the chartering race could be sidestepped with an entirely new corporate governance system designed to be enforced in an entirely different way. Rather than litigating nebulous "fiduciary duties" in court, like the current model most states use and which was inspired by Delaware, an arbitration-based system could design duties through contract, and rather than relying on judges in states without Delaware's judicial expertise, it could rely on industry veterans specializing in arbitration of complaints. Such an approach would allow other states to break Delaware's market power and shake the very foundations of American corporate law.

And yet, the SEC has strongly discouraged firms going public from requiring that investors arbitrate claims against the company. This restriction should be expected to apply to crowdfunded firms as well. The SEC has refused to approve the offering documents of firms including arbitration in their offering documents, despite the fact that the Federal Arbitration Act provides investors with such a right. This is but one example of how federal preemption of state corporate law actually impedes state competition and thereby provides an advantage to the currently dominant state of Delaware.

Some protection of federalism, and therefore the states' ability to compete via governance innovation, is supposed to be offered via the internal affairs doctrine, a rule of construction created by judges that applies both in interpretation of federal statutes and an interstate choice of law rule. The doctrine holds that the "internal affairs" of corporations, or the contractual relationship between shareholders, directors, and officers of corporations, should be determined pursuant to the laws of the state of incorporation.[13] While many states respect the doctrine, New York and California abandon it in the context of companies not traded on a national securities exchange.[14] And while some federal court interpretations of the securities laws demonstrate respect for the internal affairs doctrine,[15] others do not. At times, Congress will either explicitly preempt matters covered by the internal affairs doctrine through statute or the SEC will infringe on the matters within the internal affairs doctrine through administrative action.

The internal affairs doctrine has been a vital component in sustaining interstate chartering competition. This doctrine has been one by which federal judges, in interpreting the federal securities laws, have tended to read the securities laws as not intending to preempt state law unless such intent is clear from the statute. This doctrine also has been used by state judges to give mutual respect to each other's corporate law (e.g., a shareholder in a Delaware corporation, suing in California, has traditionally seen the claim determined pursuant to Delaware law). And yet the internal affairs doctrine has begun to come apart at the seams, further threatening to limit competition in the state system. This is true both insofar as discrete incursions into state law are occurring at the federal level, and also with respect to states that have refused to fully give deference to the laws of a company's state of incorporation when suits or administrative action are brought in other states.

While the internal affairs doctrine has at some points limited the SEC from undertaking to preempt state law, it has not always served as a binding constraint on the SEC's use of discretionary power to preempt state corporate law. Further, California and New York have adopted statutes that ignore the internal affairs doctrine for companies with a large number of shareholders in their states.

The mere existence of a threat of federal preemption can dissuade states from pursuing corporate innovation. This chilling effect on innovation is not new. Delaware judges William Chandler and Leo Strine previously expressed the frustration of state corporate innovators regarding the prospect of federal preemption when they noted in response to Sarbanes-Oxley, "What's next? A ban on going private transactions? Or on options-based compensation of executives? Or on interested transactions?"[16] This manifestation of concern is not contained to existing innovations, either. The incompatibility and lack of clarity inherent to one-size-fits-all regulation results in a restriction on competition, as it discourages states from deviating from the status quo.

The Sarbanes-Oxley Act, for example, set mandatory requirements for independence of certain committees, mandatory CEO certification of financial systems, and a prohibition on loans to corporate officers. The footprint of preemption is probably wider than originally intended by the drafters of the statute: if, for example, some method of governing firms is stricter than the board-centric model that was in vogue during the passage of Sarbanes-Oxley, states would be precluded from developing it because Sarbanes-Oxley entrenches a board-centric approach.

To this point, Professors Kobayashi and Ribstein note that one prerequisite for a quality sorting model, or interstate competition, to be effective is that "jurisdictions are free to select any set of laws they desire."[17] However, Roe's extensive analysis of the extent to which federal law preempts state corporate law demonstrates the constraints on a full Tiebout model in the corporate federalism context. Roe defines the problem of the federal overhang succinctly:

> Federal authorities can, and do, confine state competition. They have made rules—such as vast parts of the securities laws—that are functionally part of America's corporate law. They could do more, were they so inclined. In nearly every decade of the twentieth century, the decade's major corporate law issue either went federal or federal authorities threatened to take it over—from early twentieth century merger policy, to the 1930s securities laws, to the 1950s proxy fights, to the 1960s Williams Act, to the 1970s going-private transactions. Even if the states never adjust to the federal presence, Washington is a player in American corporate governance.[18]

Roe's conclusion: "Because Delaware players can never be oblivious to the possibility of being displaced, we have never had, and we never could have, a full state-to-state race in corporate law."[19] While Roe is correct that the federal overhang inhibits competition, he overstates the case, particularly with respect to the prospect of significantly enhancing interstate competition through self-enforcing limits on the federal overhang.

Roe notes that federal preemption breaching the internal affairs doctrine frequently occurs both through statute and through the SEC's discretionary authority.[20] Roe generally points to sources of federal preemption such as the SEC, the Congress, federal courts interpreting securities law cases (the existing internal affairs doctrine notwithstanding), and the national exchanges.[21] Romano notes that the SEC typically strongly pressures the national exchanges to adopt uniform corporate governance provisions.[22]

Roe goes on to state that "Presidents Roosevelt, Taft and Wilson each sought mandatory federal incorporation."[23] Each of those attempts failed, however, suggesting that full-scale nationalization of corporate law is constrained by interest group dynamics. Macey described in 1990 that dynamic as one in which "Congress can amass significant political support by refraining from preempting state law in this area. The fact that Congress has not enacted a national corporate law indicates that deference to the states is in fact its political-support-maximizing solution."[24] Though large-scale incursion into state law did not occur, Congress did find discrete incursions helpful, as for instance with the Williams Act's regulation of takeovers. And at times the SEC used authority delegated to it to undertake preemptive actions under its own initiative. Furthermore, since the time of Macey's exploration, a number of large-scale federal incursions into discrete pieces of state corporate law have occurred, usually during times of national attention to corporate governance scandals or crisis.

But even the larger-scale incursions do not preempt completely. For example, proposals to mandate an independent board chairman and impose constraints on executive compensation were pared back in favor of optional approaches for public companies in Dodd-Frank. So while bulwarks against federal incursion can be sustained in part, they must also be built in advance of crisis-induced legislation. Reforms to strengthen additional states' interest in preventing future preemption, and making it difficult for the federal government to selectively preempt and instead leaving full-scale preemption as its only option, may fortify the bulwark against federal incursions into state corporate law.

Roe concludes that one of the earliest forms of preemption in the Securities Exchange Act of 1934 was preemption of shareholder voting disclosure and voting processes, stating, "The wide SEC regulation of proxies determines what goes into the proxy request to shareholders, what gets onto the ballot, who gets access to shareholder lists, and how a proxy fight . . . is waged. . . . Voting is probably the single most important internal corporate affair."[25]

Similarly, Michael Greve of the Antonin Scalia Law School at George Mason University and his co-author Ashley Parrish point out an increasing level of agency delegation by Congress and cite Dodd-Frank as an example.[26]

This delegation provides the SEC with an opportunity to expand the reach of its authority into traditionally state areas. If the internal affairs doctrine were codified and a procedure for states to challenge its violation were adopted, it would be harder for the SEC to unilaterally expand its reach through purely administrative preemption, even if Congress continues to practice excessive agency delegation.

This practice is no longer limited to the SEC, however, as other federal agencies are increasingly seeing preemption of state corporate law as a means to enhance their authority over the entities they regulate. Federal Reserve Board Governor Daniel Tarullo recently proposed the notion of a massive expansion of fiduciary duties for banks regulated by the Federal Reserve, arguing for a change in which:

> the fiduciary duties of the boards of regulated financial firms . . . reflect what I have characterized as regulatory objectives. Doing so might make the boards of financial firms responsive to the broader interests implicated by their risk-taking decisions even where regulatory and supervisory measures had not anticipated or addressed a particular issue. And, of course, the courts would thereby be available as another route for managing the divergence between private and social interests in risk taking.[27]

It was not clear whether Governor Tarullo was suggesting a change to state law or instead was suggesting a federal preemption of state fiduciary duties. At present, the fiduciary duties owed by banks to their shareholders with respect to chartered banks are a function of federal law that itself references state corporate law. It may have represented both: pressure on states to reform their fiduciary duty jurisprudence backed up by an implicit threat of federal preemption. The Roe thesis suggests Delaware may respond to that threat. Certainly this proposal was highly provocative and has not been directly adopted by the Federal Reserve. But it presents an extreme case of the threat of federal preemption. Governor Tarullo additionally suggested federal rules concerning executive compensation, management reporting systems, and board structure as additional corporate governance avenues that federal regulators might regulate.[28]

CORPORATE GOVERNANCE NEEDS OF CROWDFUNDED FIRMS: A MICROCOSM OF THE DAMAGE FEDERAL PREEMPTION CAN DO TO ECONOMIC GROWTH

One development in the capital markets world that promises to renew innovation in methods of business financing is a new regime of crowdfunding that has been facilitated by regulations at the SEC, adopted pursuant to the Jumpstart Our Business Startups (JOBS) Act of 2012, to allow very small and early-stage companies and investment projects to access public markets.[29] This new innovation will of necessity require a new corporate governance system designed for the unique needs of crowdfunding, but unfortunately the existing federal overhang in corporate law threatens to impede the promise of crowdfunding.

The regulatory regime for crowdfunding is relatively new. It remains to be seen whether crowdfunding will reshape startup financing. And if it does not, it also remains to be seen whether crowdfunding will be primarily held up by regulatory constraints that remain despite the JOBS Act. Crowdfunding is nevertheless a helpful microcosm for the experiment.

The questions at the heart of this chapter are simple: In the absence of federal preemption in corporate law, what range of alternative innovations would be possible? And in the absence of federal preemption, how much more competitive would the state system for creating corporate law become?[30]

Answering these questions also calls for a difficult thought experiment, because one must consider a world in which a range of institutional constraints in corporate law and financial markets that presently exist are eliminated, and consider a world in which the path dependencies in the law and the institutional design of the industry itself would disappear.

The environment best suited for this thought experiment is crowdfunding. It is presently at a nascent stage with respect to the regulatory regime that governs it. The financing mechanism also was allowed to grow, in a limited capacity, before the federal regulatory regime went online.[31] The institutional dynamics seen in that early precursor to crowdfunding afford sufficient data to begin the necessary thought experiment.

Crowdfunded firms are expected to be designed around a number of "quasi for-profit" models that will require legal duties and structures very different from those popular in previous models. Some crowdfunded firms, for example, are expected to specialize in funding drug research to find cures for ailments with small patient populations. Such a firm could face difficult choices in the tradeoff between searching out the most profitable drugs and maximizing the odds of finding a cure.

Indeed, one would expect that funders would go into the investment expecting the possibility that the firm might stretch the boundaries of traditional fiduciary obligations, or the residual obligation of good faith and fair dealing, in the initial search for a cure if necessary, but would subsequently seek to maximize profits obtained by successful research. Such a mixed-motive firm will of necessity require a corporate code that maximizes freedom of contract to define the obligations owed by a board to shareholders and one that permits use of arbitration rather than litigation to enforce any contractual duties.

It is already clear that crowdfunded firms, much like master limited partnerships (MLPs), are likely to utilize nontraditional monitoring to protect against fraud. A study by Wharton Professor Ethan Mollick on a platform similar to crowdfunding found that funders of most projects were highly involved and provided ideas from the design of consumer products to the development of business strategy.[32] That study also found that fraud detection was essentially "crowdsourced" with rapid detection of fraudulent projects through user commentary on platform blogs and comment sites.

A large community of users can maximize on the low costs of communication in the era of social networking to better police fraud.[33] This new model of corporate governance is vastly different from the current model, which is based on a theory developed by Berle and Means and premised on an assumption that small shareholders face insurmountable costs in communicating with each other and with directors of the firms they own.[34]

Some crowdfunded firms may find that shareholder participation is useful, although not necessarily through the rigid mandates established by federal law. Other firms may find shareholder participation harmful. Entertainment projects, like fan-based movie funding, have been particularly successful on crowdfunded platforms that predated the new crowdfunding regulatory regime. Those projects tend to center on a specific director or actor as a necessary element in the project and may therefore seek to limit the ability of shareholders to interfere in decisions by that individual. Thus old models of the fiduciary duties that companies owe to their shareholders will be largely outdated for this new model.

An explicit recognition of the right of investors and firms to choose arbitration to resolve claims against public companies, whether through SEC guidance or statutory reform of the Securities Act of 1933, is vital to assist the development of new publicly traded small businesses like those expected to evolve under crowdfunding. One reason arbitration is so important is that firms funded under crowdfunding will have unique designs vastly different from those seen in the publicly traded space thus far. Crowdfunded firms will be much smaller, will be publicly traded much earlier in the innovation life cycle than any firms previously seeking public capital, and will go public with the assumption that multiple rounds of future funding will be required.

The fact that the suggestions in this chapter are designed to facilitate crowd-funding will also serve to generate retail support from individual investors, in much the same way the ride-sharing app Uber has managed to generate strong retail support that has allowed it to successfully challenge the powerful lobby of incumbent taxi cabs. Crowdfunding, like Uber, is a service that directly challenges the incumbent methods of financing and whose most cogent threat is the regulatory barriers to entry supported by incumbent firms. And crowd-funding, like Uber, is poised to utilize technological improvements in the cost of communication that are popular among millennial consumers.[35]

While crowdfunding platforms may escape most of the requirements put into place by Dodd-Frank and Sarbanes-Oxley, those crowdfunded firms that hope to evolve and grow into larger public companies listed on exchanges may nonetheless feel compelled to abide by securities laws' strictures any-way. Furthermore, while crowdfunding is used as an example for how the fed-eral government encroaches on the states, that is merely a microcosm for the broader damage to innovation in the state-based corporate law system caused by federal preemption.

WHEN THE FEDERAL OVERLAY IS ROLLED BACK, INNOVATION SPROUTS: THE CASE OF PUBLICLY TRADED MASTER LIMITED PARTNERSHIPS

The governance of publicly traded master limited partnerships provides a small-scale case study in the adaptability and heterogeneity of businesses' organizational form. MLPs form a small subset of publicly traded companies in which the federal overlay has been moderately lifted by the exchanges. They were created pursuant to a tax exemption for energy companies that allows them to avoid entity-level taxation if they make regular distributions of earn-ings to investors. Looking more broadly to the MLPs that continue to operate using a limited partnership form, John Goodgame notes that as of 2012, there were eighty-seven energy-related MLPs traded on public markets.[36] While they have traditionally been organized as limited partnerships, more recently some of them have organized as LLCs.[37] These energy firm MLPs make up the vast majority of publicly traded alternative entities on US exchanges.

Under exchange listing rules, MLPs are not required to have a majority of independent directors, a nominating committee, or a compensation committee.[38] MLPs and other public companies are otherwise subject to the same set of federal securities laws.[39] Thus, with this relatively minor exception from the federal overlay, a wide diversity of governance arrangements has evolved.

Goodgame generally describes a great deal of heterogeneity in organizational form, as some MLPs provide for annual elections and some have staggered boards. Some MLPs have poison pills, others do not. Some choose default fiduciary duties, and some opt out of fiduciary duties. But they generally choose to opt out of rules favored in the public context as they have stronger contractual requirements to distribute all their earnings on a quarterly basis. That mandatory quarterly earnings disbursement in the partnership or LLC agreement essentially substitutes for the traditional monitoring mechanisms of corporate law, like fiduciary duty litigation or board committee oversight. And it is structurally a much stronger means of policing against fraud, as equity owners see hard cash flow every quarter (and the firm does not regularly take in large amounts of new capital such that a Ponzi scheme–type fraud would be possible). It is very difficult for these companies to mask losses.

MLPs further have a governance innovation similar in many ways to the organization board member proposal advanced by Bainbridge and Henderson (and referenced earlier in this chapter).[40] MLPs are typically controlled by a sponsoring general partnership, which reserves contractual control of the board of directors for itself by reserving a majority of board seats for individuals selected by the general partnership. Structural heterogeneity in governance tends to adapt to the particular needs of individual firms; those with more dependable and steady streams of cash flow tend to substitute for traditional governance arrangements earnings distribution and regular fundraising from capital markets as agency monitoring measures.[41]

One can readily think of other governance arrangements that could be useful for other types of firms, from crowdfunding to unique industries, which states could develop if freed from the overbroad federal footprint. One could imagine a different appraisal process tailored uniquely to handle the needs of biotech firms that lack cash flow for long periods. This limited innovation leads one to wonder what level of innovation may have been possible in the absence of the full federal overlay. At this point one can only guess the possibilities.

RECOMMENDATIONS
Repeal Federal Corporate Governance Mandates
The struggle of meshing the needs of new business models with rigid federal regulation prompts a larger consideration of the current state of interaction between states and the federal government in corporate law. This leads to the claim of this chapter that state competition is currently not robust enough to support novel corporate structures because states are hindered by an ever-expanding federal overlay of blanket regulation. Title IX of Dodd-Frank perpetuates this federalization of corporate law in the face of the internal affairs doctrine. As noted in the MLP case study, reducing regulation that results in the allowance of innovation can have an immediate beneficial effect in the form of firms' willingness to innovate. Revitalizing state federalism in pursuit of genuine competition, as opposed to the centralization purposes of Title IX's corporate governance provisions, would serve to incentivize states to create and promote innovative and more effective corporate law.

Codify the Internal Affairs Doctrine as a Binding Constraint on Federal Regulatory Agencies, with Express Standing for States to Challenge Federal Action
The internal affairs doctrine has helped to maintain a vibrant competition between the states in the development of corporation law. This has helped to develop a rich body of law that has made it possible for large-scale industrial development through the twentieth century. But the internal affairs doctrine is under siege from regulators who have preempted large swaths of corporate law, and other regulators who continually look to sidestep it. A clear and binding constraint on federal regulators will be necessary in order to allow corporation law to undergo a renaissance for a new and vibrant century of capital markets.

For a federalist system to survive, it must be self-enforcing. In other words, it must be able to survive future attempts to slowly erode the federalist system in corporate governance. The explicit standing of individual states to challenge violations of the internal affairs doctrine helps to create that self-enforcing character.

Give Statutory Recognition to Publicly Traded Companies' Right to Require Investor Arbitration

This chapter has demonstrated that permitting arbitration for shareholder claims against companies, whether under the federal securities laws or pursuant to state corporate law, is a vital component to reinvigorating interstate competition. It is also clear that many crowdfunded firms would benefit from an alternative corporate law model grounded in a more flexible and adaptable arbitration-based approach to adjudicating corporate disputes. The SEC should not prohibit arbitration for investor claims in any instance in which a state's corporate law permits it. Delaware appears to presently discourage an arbitration alternative, but under a more competitive system some state would likely design an alternative that more directly used arbitration as a means of resolving shareholder complaints.

Preempt Authority of State Attorneys General to Bring Investor Claims against Out-of-State Firms

Yet another threat to state chartering competition is in the form of state attorneys general who bring claims on behalf of investors in companies outside of their state. In particular, New York attorneys general have brought many claims under New York's overly broad Martin Act against companies incorporated outside of New York for claims between investors and companies that should be resolved pursuant to the other state's corporate code.

An analyst writing for *Legal Affairs* described former New York Attorney General Eliot Spitzer's use of the Martin Act as follows:

> To win a case, the AG doesn't have to prove that the defendant intended to defraud anyone, that a transaction took place, or that anyone actually was defrauded. Plus, when the prosecution is over, trial lawyers can gain access to the hoards of documents that the act has churned up and use them as the basis for civil suits.[42]

Limiting the authority of state attorneys general for investor fraud actions to companies incorporated in their home state will more faithfully respect the internal affairs doctrine and provide those attorneys general with an incentive to balance any desire to bring meritless litigation against out-of-state firms for political motivations.[43]

In the event state competition for corporate chartering becomes markedly more competitive as a result of the suggestions in this chapter, states may then be tempted to use the power of state attorneys general to engage in unfair competition with other states. Corporate governance practices that give other states a competitive advantage in the chartering race may be deemed "unfair" under a nebulous statute like the Martin Act.

Out-of-state attorneys general could then threaten innovations in other jurisdictions that are otherwise beneficial to shareholders. If instead state attorneys general are limited in their authority to bring investor fraud claims against entities incorporated in their own states, then they will be better incentivized to consider the collateral consequences of any abuse of their authority.

Out-of-state attorneys general have no incentive to consider the collateral consequences of their actions on the broader investing public. One might imagine, for example, the New York attorney general forcing companies as part of settlement agreements to regularly require that all members of the board be independent of the company, thereby discouraging other states from beneficial innovations in the design of boards of directors to leverage the expertise of nonindependent directors.

This is a critical distinction to appreciate in discussions about federal preemption. When states create law, as through the creation of a corporate code, and when states internalize much of the impact of their lawmaking, as through chartering fees, a competitive race is possible and principles of federalism apply. But in the use of state attorney general power, states create law in the use of enforcement actions. They craft new law through enforcement settlements, and the institutional actors with the power to craft that law have no balancing force to discourage abuse of their power.

If a New York attorney general oversteps and presses initiatives that destroy shareholder value, his influence and political standing will be unaffected. Shareholders and incorporators cannot choose to avoid the law effectively created by New York in this way; they cannot choose corporate law created by enforcement action the way they can choose statutory corporate law by selecting a particular state of incorporation. All publicly traded companies have many of their trades routed through the various exchanges that operate in the jurisdiction of the New York attorney general.

The recommendation offered here will encourage a more federalism-based approach to the use of this executive authority. State attorneys general would be more sensitive to the impact of their decisions if the rate of incorporation in their home state were linked to the enforcement environment they provide. Furthermore, any under-enforcement by an attorney general that left shareholders exposed to fraud would result in a discount to the traded value of firms incorporated in that state.

Thus this suggestion creates an institutional environment in which state enforcement actions premised on investor claims are more balanced and responsive to the costs of over- or under-enforcement relative to legitimate shareholder fraud claims.

CONCLUSION

When the SEC was created in the 1930s, the state-based system of corporate law was kept in place. That system had helped to facilitate the accumulation of wealth necessary for large-scale capital investments during the Industrial Revolution. When SEC Chairman William Cary suggested in 1970 that a federal corporate law be adopted, the suggestion was largely ignored. Even in the wake of the Enron scandal and, later, the 2008 financial crisis, the federal response did not include a wholesale preemption of state corporation law. This indicates an enduring, centuries-long respect at the federal level for the vital role of the states as sources of corporation law.

The slow preemption of discrete pieces of state corporate law has, however, taken its toll on the state-based corporate law system. The discrete preemptions have a much larger impact on the state system than the sum of their parts, as they discourage innovation in corporate governance and impede state competition to create new legal and contractual regimes to govern the relationships between investors of capital and managers of capital.

At each major turn in human history, corporate law has served as a foundation for mankind's forward progress. In ancient Babylonia, a version of partnership law helped farmers band together for mutual investments in farming infrastructure. A more sophisticated form of corporate law developed to facilitate Roman-era investments in large capital projects like the aqueducts. America's first major evolution in corporate law facilitated the Industrial Revolution, and the next spurt of ingenious innovations helped America's post–WWII economic boom.

Looking forward, an entirely new era in which investors are likely to interact with their investments in an increasingly low-cost, app-based environment is possible. Crowdfunding in particular promises to allow small-dollar investors to invest in very early stage ventures like never before. Innovation's promise will be lost, however, if the federal overlay in corporate law does not stand aside to allow renewed competition and innovation in the state-based corporate law system.

NOTES

1. See Gallagher and Cook, "Shareholder Proposals."

2. "Triumph of the Pygmy State."

3. Piwowar, "Dissenting Statement."

4. See generally Romano, "Sarbanes-Oxley Act."

5. Roughly half of all publicly traded companies are incorporated in Delaware. Romano describes Delaware's dominance of the corporate chartering market as a feature, not a bug, of a successful race to the top. Bilateral investments by both users of corporate law and by Delaware in the production of corporate law may make it difficult for another small state to compete with Delaware, but at the same time those bilateral investments serve to enhance the quality of Delaware's code. She describes it as "development of transaction-specific human capital [which] establishes what Oliver Williamson terms a 'mutual reliance relation' creating a reciprocal vulnerability on both sides of the charter market that joins the parties together in a cooperative long-term relationship." See Romano, "Law as a Product," 225–26.

6. Bainbridge and Henderson, "Boards-R-Us."

7. Ibid., 1100.

8. Daines, "Does Delaware Law Improve Firm Value?"

9. See Macey and Miller, "Toward an Interest Group Theory."

10. Verret, "Uber-ized Corporate Law," 964.

11. Yerger, Testimony before the Senate Subcommittee.

12. Roe, "Corporate Shareholder's Vote," 9.

13. For a possible definition of the internal affairs doctrine from the Restatement (Second) Conflict of Laws, see "Internal Affairs Doctrine."

14. "Internal Affairs Doctrine."

15. Edgar v. MITE Corp., 457 U.S. 624, 645 (1981).

16. Chandler and Strine, "New Federalism," 953, 974.

17. Ribstein and Kobayashi, "Economics of Federalism," 3.

18. Roe, "Delaware's Politics," 2498. While Roe overstates the case by describing Delaware as thus a "monopoly," he nevertheless accurately sketches Delaware's relationship to the federal government. See Roe, "Delaware's Politics." In "Delaware and Washington as Corporate Lawmakers," 10–11, Roe goes on to describe the ways in which the federal government can and has preempted state corporate law:

   "Washington makes corporate law. From 1933 to 2002, that is, from the passage of the securities laws to the passage of Sarbanes-Oxley, Washington has made rules governing the voting of stock and the solicitation of proxies to elect directors. It has made the main rules governing insider trading, stock buybacks, how institutional investors can interact in corporate governance, the structure of key board committees, board composition (how independent some board members must be), how far states could go in making merger law, how attentive institutional investors must be in voting their proxies, what business issues and transactional information public firms must disclose (which often affect the structure and duties of insiders and managers to shareholders in a myriad of transactions), the rules on dual class common stock recapitalizations, the duties and liabilities of gatekeepers like accountants and lawyers, and more. Even when the SEC cannot, or does not, make the substantive rule, its capacity to force disclosure of numbers and transactions can turn a spotlight onto those transactions and numbers, thereby affecting whether or not they happen."

19. Roe, "Delaware's Competition," 592.

20. Ibid., 597.

21. Ibid., 598–99.

22. Romano, "States as a Laboratory," 209, 220.

23. Roe, "Delaware's Competition," 601.

24. Macey, "Federal Deference to Local Regulators," 279.

25. Roe, "Delaware's Competition," 611.

26. Greve and Parrish, "Administrative Law without Congress," 501, 505.

27. Tarullo, Speech at the Association of American Law Schools.

28. Ibid., 7.

29. A corollary regime of state-based crowdfunding has also sprung up (though the state version requires that investors be circumscribed within a particular state or geographic area).

30. Note that this chapter considers the damaging effects of preemption of corporate governance rules. Preemption of state securities regulations of out-of-state offerings, as was necessary in the crowdfunding context, is subject to a different set of institutional incentives in which states do not internalize the effect of their regulations on out-of-state offerings. This costly effect at the state level is similar to that analyzed below in the attorney general context.

31. Crowdfunders were allowed to raise money by offering benefits like advanced purchases or participation in the project, but prohibited from selling actual stock. For more detail on this question, see Verret, "Uber-ized Corporate Law."

32. Mollick, "Dynamics of Crowdfunding."

33. Agrawal, Ajay K., Christian Catalini, and Avi Goldfarb. "Some Simple Economics of Crowdfunding." NBER Working Paper 19133, National Bureau of Economic Research, Cambridge, MA, June 2013.

34. See Berle and Means, *Modern Corporation and Private Property.*

35. For additional discussion about how crowdfunding bears similarity to Uber, see Verret, "Uber-ized Corporate Law."

36. Goodgame, "New Developments," 81, 83.

37. Ibid., 84.

38. Ibid., 98.

39. Ibid.

40. Bainbridge and Henderson, "Boards-R-Us."

41. Goodgame, "Master Limited Partnership Governance," 471, 480.

42. Thompson, "Sword of Spitzer."

43. For an extended argument about how many of Eliot Spitzer's prosecutions under the Martin Act were based on questionable assertions of fact and politically motivated, see Greve, "Federalism's Frontier," 93. See also Greve, "Business, the States," 895.

REFERENCES

Agrawal, Ajay K., Christian Catalini, and Avi Goldfarb. "Some Simple Economics of Crowdfunding." NBER Working Paper 19133, National Bureau of Economic Research, Cambridge, MA, June 2013.

Bainbridge, Stephen M., and M. Todd Henderson. "Boards-R-Us: Reconceptualizing Corporate Boards." *Stanford Law Review* 66, no. 5 (May 2014): 1051–120.

Berle, Adolph, and Gardiner Means. *The Modern Corporation and Private Property.* New York: MacMillan, 1933.

Chandler, William B., and Leo E. Strine Jr. "The New Federalism of the American Corporate Governance System." *University of Pennsylvania Law Review* 152 (2003): 953–1006.

Daines, Robert. "Does Delaware Law Improve Firm Value?" *Journal of Financial Economics* 62, no. 3 (2001): 525–58.

Gallagher, Daniel M., and John C. Cook. "Shareholder Proposals: An Exit Strategy for the SEC." Critical Legal Issues Working Paper 193, Washington Legal Foundation, Washington, DC, September 2015.

Goodgame, John. "Master Limited Partnership Governance." *Business Lawyer* 60, no. 2 (2005): 471–506.

———. "New Developments in Master Limited Partnership Governance." *Business Lawyer* 68, no. 1 (2012): 81–101.

Greve, Michael S. "Business, the States, and Federalism's Political Economy." *Harvard Journal of Law and Public Policy* 25, no. 3 (2002): 895–929.

———. "Federalism's Frontier." *Texas Review of Law and Policy* 7, no. 1 (2002): 93–126.

Greve, Michael S., and Ashley C. Parrish. "Administrative Law without Congress." *George Mason Law Review* 22, no. 3 (2015): 501–47.

"The Internal Affairs Doctrine: Theoretical Justifications and Tentative Explanations for Its Continued Primacy." *Harvard Law Review* 115, no. 5 (2002): 1480–501.

Macey, Jonathan R. "Federal Deference to Local Regulators and the Economic Theory of Regulation: Toward a Public Choice Explanation of Federalism." *Virginia Law Review* 76, (1990): 279–91.

Macey, Jonathan, and Geoffrey Miller. "Toward an Interest Group Theory of Delaware Corporate Law." *Texas Law Review* 65, no. 3 (1987): 469–524.

Mollick, Ethan. "The Dynamics of Crowdfunding: An Exploratory Study," *Journal of Business Venturing* 29, no. 1 (2014): 1–16.

Piwowar, Michael S. "Dissenting Statement at Open Meeting on Pay Ratio Disclosure." Public Statement, US Securities and Exchange Commission, August 5, 2015.

Ribstein, Larry E., and Bruce H. Kobayashi. "The Economics of Federalism." George Mason Law and Economics Research Paper No. 06-15, 2006.

Roe, Mark J. "Delaware's Competition." *Harvard Law Review* 117, no. 2 (2003): 588–644.

———. "Delaware's Politics," *Harvard Law Review* 118, no. 8 (2005): 2491–543.

———. "Delaware and Washington as Corporate Lawmakers." *Delaware Journal of Corporate Law* 34, no. 1 (2009): 1–33.

———. "The Corporate Shareholder's Vote and Its Political Economy, in Delaware and in Washington." *Harvard Business Law Review* 2, no. 1 (2012): 1–38.

Romano, Roberta. "Law as a Product: Some Pieces of the Incorporation Puzzle." *Journal of Law, Economics, and Organization* 1, no. 2 (1985): 225–83.

———. "The Sarbanes-Oxley Act and the Making of Quack Corporate Governance." Faculty Scholarship Series Paper 1919, Yale Law School, New Haven, CT, 2005.

———. "The States as a Laboratory: Legal Innovation and State Competition for Corporate Charters." *Yale Journal on Regulation* 23, no. 2 (2006): 209–47.

Tarullo, Daniel K. Speech at the Association of American Law Schools 2014 Midyear Meeting, June 9, 2014.

Thompson, Nicholas. "The Sword of Spitzer." *Legal Affairs*, May–June 2004. http://www.legalaffairs.org/issues/May-June-2004/feature_thompson_mayjun04.msp.

"Triumph of the Pygmy State." *Economist*, October 23, 2003. http://www.economist.com/node/2155765.

Verret, J. W. "Uber-ized Corporate Law: Toward a 21st Century Corporate Governance for Crowdfunding and App-Based Investor Communications." *Journal of Corporation Law* 41, no. 4 (2016): 927–69.

Yerger, Ann. Testimony before the Subcommittee on Securities, Insurance, and Investment of the Senate Committee on Banking, Housing, and Urban Affairs, Hearing on "Protecting Shareholders and Enhancing Public Confidence by Improving Corporate Governance," July 29, 2009.

PART 6

IMPROVING THE REGULATORY PROCESS

CHAPTER 17
Is Regulatory Impact Analysis of Financial Regulations Possible?

JERRY ELLIG AND VERA SOLIMAN
Mercatus Center at George Mason University

D uring the past several years, a vigorous debate has raged in the courts, the US Congress, and academia about the proper role of economic analysis in financial regulation. At first glance, this seems to be a strange topic for debate. Most actors in financial markets are highly motivated by monetary values, financial market data are widely available, and the economics profession has a long history of studying banking and finance.[1] Therefore, economic analysis of financial regulation should be easier and less controversial than economic analysis of some other forms of regulation, such as environmental or health and safety regulation. Nevertheless, skeptics abound, arguing that the unique nature of financial markets means that the analysis is either impossible or at least must be conducted much differently than analysis of economic, health, safety, and security regulations.[2]

No well-executed analysis of a complex economic topic is easy, nor is it perfect. But reasonably good regulatory impact analysis of financial regulations is possible, and it yields useful information for decision makers. In this chapter, we outline the basic elements of regulatory impact analysis, suggest the standards a good regulatory impact analysis should meet, and employ quantitative data from the Mercatus Center's Regulatory Report Card (Report Card) to assess the current quality of analysis for financial regulations issued by executive branch agencies. We also include an extensive case study of the regulatory impact analysis accompanying a financial regulation proposed by the Department of Housing and Urban Development (HUD) in 2008 to revise mandatory disclosures for residential real estate transactions. The case study demonstrates that HUD did a reasonably good job on what is arguably the most difficult aspect of regulatory impact analysis: analyzing the underlying problem the regulation is intended to solve and quantifying the benefits of the regulation. The Report Card data and our case study both suggest that regulatory impact analysis of financial regulations is no more difficult than for other types of regulations.

WHAT IS REGULATORY IMPACT ANALYSIS?

For more than three decades, presidents of both political parties have instructed executive branch agencies to conduct regulatory impact analysis when issuing significant regulations.[3] Some independent agencies are required by law to assess the economic effects of their regulations or "consider" the benefits and costs when they make decisions about regulations.[4] Executive orders and laws requiring economic analysis of regulations reflect a bipartisan consensus that the analysis should inform, but not dictate, regulatory decisions. The purpose of the analysis is to ensure that regulators base their decisions on knowledge of the likely consequences of regulations, "rather than on dogmas, intuitions, hunches, or interest group pressures."[5]

A thorough regulatory impact analysis should do at least four things:

1. **Assess the nature and significance of the problem the agency is trying to solve.** Assessment of the problem is the first principle of regulation listed in President Clinton's Executive Order 12866, which has governed regulatory analysis by executive branch agencies since 1993.[6] It is also the logical starting point for regulatory impact analysis.[7] If the agency has not identified the root cause of the problem it is trying to solve, it has no basis for claiming that the regulation will create benefits (by solving the problem) and little guidance for developing effective alternative solutions. Unfortunately, assessment of the problem is the aspect of regulatory impact analysis that agencies perform most poorly.[8] Often agencies merely cite the statute authorizing the regulation, assert a

problem exists without providing evidence, or claim the problem exists in spite of evidence to the contrary.[9]

If there is no significant problem, or if the problem is likely to shrink or disappear in the future in the absence of new regulation, then it is wasteful to regulate. Public and private resources could be better devoted to other priorities. If a significant problem exists and is expected to persist, regulators are unlikely to devise an effective solution unless they identify the problem's root cause or causes. Even if regulators get lucky and devise an effective solution without identifying the problem's root cause, the regulation is likely to be over broad, covering entities that are not a significant source of the problem.

Regulations address three types of problems: market failures, government failures, and overriding social needs. Remedying the first two types of failures improves economic efficiency: it allows markets or government to produce the mix of goods and services that consumers value most. The third type of problem, an overriding social need, usually involves some aspect of public health, fairness, or justice that may or may not have an explicit efficiency rationale.[10]

Analysis of the problem should include a clear, coherent theory of why the problem exists and what caused it. For financial markets, theories of potential market or government failures abound. Equity holders in financial firms may have incentives to take on excessive risks, since they receive the profits from successful investments but can shift the losses to bondholders (through bankruptcy) or taxpayers (through deposit insurance or bailouts). Government policies intended to expand consumers' access to credit can encourage excessive borrowing. Information asymmetries between lenders and borrowers create opportunities for deception and fraud, but mandated disclosures may backfire if they are poorly crafted or overload consumers with information. Incentive structures may not perfectly align the interests of agents, like corporate managers or investment advisers, with the interests of investors.[11]

The analysis should include evidence demonstrating that the problem is significant and widespread. In other words, the evidence should be systematic and generalizable, not just anecdotes about the behavior of a few bad actors.[12]

2. **Identify a wide variety of alternative solutions.** Executive Order 12866 indicates that agencies should consider a variety of alternative solutions to the problem identified, including performance standards, economic incentives, provision of information, modification of existing regulations or laws, and the alternative of not regulating.[13] The guidance document from the Office of Management and Budget (OMB) for regulatory impact analysis, *Circular A-4*, provides a broader list of alternatives, such as fees, bonds, insurance, changes in liability rules, definition or redefinition of property rights, and information provision or disclosure.[14] Regulatory scholars suggest additional alternatives that can be effective in some situations, such as requiring firms to analyze and plan for potential hazards or risks, or voluntary standards adopted at the behest of customers or suppliers.[15] Or the regulator might consider a "nudge" strategy to require individuals or businesses to explicitly consider certain types of information before making a decision, but refrain from compelling any particular decision.[16] Finally, alternatives can also consist of variations on the same basic regulatory approach, such as setting standards at different levels or making a larger or smaller number of entities subject to the regulation.[17]

A thorough regulatory impact analysis can include alternatives outside the scope of current law. OMB guidance indicates that agencies should include such alternatives if legislative constraints prevent them from adopting the most effective approach.[18] Such information is useful to Congress if it considers disapproving the regulation under the Congressional Review Act or rewriting the law that authorized the regulation.

None of this means that a regulatory impact analysis must identify and assess every alternative imaginable. That would be an impossible standard for any agency to satisfy. But prominent alternatives that have been discussed in the scholarly literature, considered in the broader policy debate about the problem, or identified by agency staff as a result of their own expertise on the subject matter should be considered for inclusion in the regulatory impact analysis.

3. **Define the benefits the agency seeks to achieve in terms of ultimate outcomes that affect citizens' quality of life, and assess each alternative's ability to achieve those outcomes.** The analysis should specify

the ultimate outcomes that benefit citizens—not just inputs, activities, or processes.[19] For financial regulations, examples of outcomes could include improved returns to investors, reduced costs to borrowers, reduced administration and compliance costs, or reduced risk of a financial crisis (and thus a reduction in the expected costs of financial crises). Improved compliance, successful enforcement actions, and increased bank capital are inputs or activities, not outcomes.

The analysis should include a theory explaining how each alternative is expected to produce the desired outcomes, along with evidence that the theory is actually correct. As with analysis of the problem, the evidence that the regulation is likely to produce benefits should be systematic and generalizable.

Wherever possible, each type of outcome for each alternative should be quantified and converted into monetary terms to facilitate comparison with other outcomes and with costs. The analysis should also forthrightly acknowledge and assess uncertainties associated with the estimates: "Rather than abandon the attempt to quantify costs and benefits, I think it would be better for the structures guiding cost-benefit analysis to simply reflect the statistician's dictum: every number should have a band of uncertainty associated with it."[20]

The benefits of each major requirement should be estimated separately. This practice helps decision makers understand which provisions produce most of the benefits, and it allows them to compare the benefits of each provision with its costs. Scholarly research finds that the cases in which regulatory impact analysis has most clearly influenced decisions are usually cases in which regulators achieved significant increases in benefits or reduction in costs by altering regulations on the margins.[21]

4. **Identify and measure costs.** In mainstream economic theory, the term "cost" means "opportunity cost"—the value of benefits forgone because one course of action was chosen over another course of action.[22] The social costs of a regulation are the good things that regulated entities, consumers, and other stakeholders must sacrifice to receive the benefits the regulation produces. Just like benefits, costs may involve far more than monetary expenditures. Costs include the value of time people spend complying with the regulation and the value consumers forgo

when they cut back their purchases of a good or service in response to regulation-induced price increases or quality reductions. Costs include the value of projects or innovations forgone because businesses or other regulated entities must devote time, attention, and money to regulatory compliance. Posner and Weyl illustrate this point in their assessment of the regulatory impact analysis for a 2008 regulation on bank capital adequacy issued by the Office of the Comptroller of the Currency: "[W]hile it did quantify the trivial administrative costs to banks of implementing the regulations, it ignored the much larger opportunity costs."[23]

It is a common impression that costs of regulation are usually easier to estimate than benefits because costs are merely money spent by regulated entities, whereas benefits often involve things that are difficult to place monetary values on, such as clean air, the existence of endangered species, or the reduced risk of a future financial crisis.[24] This belief confuses monetary outlays with social opportunity costs. Correct estimation of the social cost of a regulation can require assessments of cause-and-effect relationships and monetary valuation challenges that are every bit as difficult as those involved in estimating benefits.

Where possible, the costs of each alternative should be quantified and converted into monetary terms to facilitate comparison with benefits and with the costs of other alternatives. The cost of each major requirement should be estimated separately. This practice helps decision makers understand which provisions produce most of the costs, and it allows them to compare the costs of each provision with its benefits.

Without evidence-based analysis of the systemic problem and the benefits and costs of alternatives, regulatory decisions are more likely to be based on hopes, intentions, and wishful thinking rather than reality.

WHAT STANDARDS SHOULD THE ANALYSIS MEET?

An academic debate has raged for several years over whether it is possible to conduct a reliable, "quantified" benefit-cost analysis of financial regulations. (Typically, commentators use the term "quantified" as a synonym for "monetized," even though some benefits or costs might be quantified even if they are not monetized.) Skeptics contend that financial agencies should not be expected to quantify or monetize all (or even most) relevant benefits and costs, because some of them are extremely difficult or even impossible to quantify or monetize given the current state of data and analytical techniques. Financial regulations pose special challenges because finance affects many other markets, estimating the effects of regulations requires predicting human behavior rather than the behavior of chemical compounds or machines, and there are fewer stable, predictable relationships in finance than in the physical sciences.[25] Given these difficulties, the skeptics call for "qualitative" or "pragmatic" analysis that considers the pros and cons of a proposed regulation but does not demand quantification of benefits and costs. One prominent skeptic characterizes all analyses with partial quantification as "guesstimates" that camouflage agency judgments, apparently leaving nonquantified benefit-cost analysis as the only intellectually honest option.[26]

Defenders of benefit-cost analysis counter that estimating benefits and costs of financial regulations should be easier than estimating benefits and costs of some other types of regulations, since financial markets involve money and there is a great deal of financial market transaction data available.[27] They also point out that, in practice, regulatory agencies are generally not held to the impossible standard of precisely quantifying every imaginable benefit and cost of a regulation. Instead, agencies are expected to do the best they can to quantify and monetize benefits and costs given the current state of data and analytical techniques.[28] Monetization of all benefits and costs with complete certainty is rarely possible, but some degree of quantification is usually possible.[29] When there are ranges of uncertainty associated with numerical values, analysts should identify those ranges and explain reasons for choosing some values over others.[30] When significant benefits or costs are not quantified, techniques such as break-even analysis can be used to assess how plausible it is that benefits may exceed costs.[31] A key virtue of this "quantify where possible" approach is that it forces agencies to be more explicit about the sizes and probabilities of effects that they are considering anyway, at least implicitly.[32]

We agree with the critics that regulatory agencies should not be expected to perform analysis that is impossible—or not currently possible. But we also agree with the defenders that the current practice of quantifying benefits and costs when possible is "the basic kind of analysis one would expect of an economic regulatory agency."[33] The key to resolving the debate is a principle enunciated in Executive Order 12866: "Each agency shall base its decisions on the best reasonably obtainable scientific, technical, economic, and other information concerning the need for, and consequences of, the regulation."[34] This principle reflects the commonsense idea that regulatory agencies should not be expected to do the impossible but should be expected to use the best analytical information obtainable—including the best obtainable information that would help them to quantify and monetize benefits and costs.

This principle also implies that if the agency considers factors that are not quantified and/or monetized, it should nevertheless use the best reasonably obtainable information about those factors. In other words, if nonmonetized values play a major role in the decision, the agency has a responsibility, in its regulatory impact analysis, to define those values, present evidence that they matter to citizens, present evidence that the regulation will significantly advance those values, and assess how alternative proposals would affect those values. The fact that the agency cites something other than benefits or costs as the reason for its decision does not mean that good intentions can take the place of evidence. Nonquantified values, fairness, and distributive impacts should be discussed thoughtfully, with citations to the best available relevant research and evidence.

The wording of this principle holds an additional implication that has not been discussed in the US debate over quantification of the benefits and costs of financial regulations. The executive order states that agencies should use the best reasonably obtainable information not just about the consequences (benefits and costs) of the regulation, but also "concerning the need for" the regulation. A regulatory impact analysis assesses the need for regulation by assessing the nature, significance, and root cause of a systemic problem. Two financial economists at the UK's former financial regulator—Financial Services Authority—have noted that "cost-benefit analysis (CBA) is a practical and rigorous means of identifying, targeting, and checking the impacts of regulatory measures on the underlying causes of ills with which regulators need to deal, those causes being the market failures that in turn may justify regulatory intervention."[35] A regulatory impact analysis also assesses the need for the particular regulation the agency proposes by developing alternatives, assessing their consequences against the baseline of no regulatory change, and comparing these consequences with the likely consequences of the proposed regulation. Thus, the assessment of the systemic problem and alternatives should also use the best reasonably obtainable scientific, technical, economic, and other information.

EVALUATION OF REGULATORY IMPACT ANALYSIS
OF FINANCIAL REGULATIONS

Unfortunately, most regulatory impact analyses (RIAs) produced by executive branch agencies fail to live up to the standards articulated in Executive Order 12866. The most recent data on this topic come from the Mercatus Center's Regulatory Report Card project.

The Report Card qualitatively assessed the quality and use of regulatory analysis for proposed, economically significant, prescriptive regulations issued by executive branch agencies from 2008 through 2013.[36] The assessment criteria include the four key elements of regulatory impact analysis described previously: analysis of the problem, alternatives, benefits, and costs. The scoring methodology is a middle ground between "checklist" systems for scoring regulatory analysis[37] and in-depth qualitative case studies.[38] Expert reviewers trained in the evaluation method assign each regulatory analysis a Likert scale (0–5) score. For each criterion, the evaluators assign a score ranging from 0 (no useful content) to 5 (comprehensive analysis with potential best practices). The scores are ordinal, not cardinal, and so we caution the reader to interpret these numerical comparisons the same way one would interpret student test scores. An analysis that earns twice as many points as another one is clearly better, but not necessarily twice as good.

A 2012 article in the peer-reviewed journal *Risk Analysis* describes the Report Card's methodology and first year's results; we refer readers to that article for a more detailed description.[39] Several articles using Report Card data have been published in scholarly journals.[40] Statistical tests show that the method has produced consistent results from scorers trained in the evaluation method.[41] Report Card findings on the quality of agency regulatory analysis are generally consistent with the results of prior researchers' quantitative and qualitative evaluations of RIAs.[42]

The Report Card results offer some hopeful signs for those who believe that decisions about financial regulations should be heavily informed by economic analysis. First, the data suggest that economic analysis of financial regulations is no more difficult than economic analysis of other types of regulations. Second, although no regulatory impact analysis of a financial regulation is consistently excellent, some parts of some regulatory impact analyses provide examples of reasonably good analytical practices.

The Report Card project evaluated eight financial regulations between 2008 and 2011, listed in table 1. (No economically significant financial regulations

471

Table 1. Financial Regulations Evaluated in the Mercatus Center's Regulatory Report Card Project, 2008–2011

Rule Name	Proposing Agency	Year Proposed	Regulatory Identifier Number
Real Estate Settlement Procedures Act	Department of Housing and Urban Development, Office of the Assistant Secretary for Housing	2008	2502-AI61
Class Exemption for Provision of Investment Advice, Proposed Rule	Department of Labor, Employee Benefits Security Administration	2008	1210-AB13
Fiduciary Requirements for Disclosure in Participant-Directed Plans	Department of Labor, Employee Benefits Security Administration	2008	1210-AB07
Notice of Class Exemption for Provision of Investment Advice	Department of Labor, Employee Benefits Security Administration	2008	1210-ZA14
Standardized Risk-Based Capital Rules (Basel II)	Department of the Treasury, Office of the Comptroller of the Currency and Office of Thrift Supervision; Board of Governors of the Federal Reserve System; Federal Deposit Insurance Corporation	2008	1557-AD07
Definition of "Fiduciary"	Department of Labor, Employee Benefits Security Administration	2010	1210-AB32
Prohibited Transaction Exemption for Provision of Investment Advice	Department of Labor, Employee Benefit Security Administration	2010	1210-AB35
Credit Risk Retention— Definition of Qualified Residential Mortgage	Department of the Treasury, Office of the Comptroller of the Currency; Board of Governors of the Federal Reserve System; Federal Deposit Insurance Corporation	2011	2501-AD53

Source: www.mercatus.org/reportcard.

were proposed by executive branch agencies in 2012 and 2013.) The topics covered by these regulations include bank capital adequacy requirements, the form and content of disclosures to mortgage borrowers, regulation of financial advisers, and a definition that determines when a loan securitizer must retain some of the credit risk (aka "skin in the game") from the mortgages it securitizes. Many financial regulations are issued by independent agencies, such as the US Securities and Exchange Commission, the US Commodity Futures Trading Commission, and the Bureau of Consumer Financial Protection. Regulation issued solely by independent agencies are not included in the Report Card because they are not subject to Executive Order 12866. Nevertheless, the financial regulations issued by executive branch agencies touch on many of the same kinds of prudential, consumer protection, and investor protection issues that the independent financial regulators deal with.

Figure 1 compares the Report Card scores for financial and nonfinancial regulations on the four major elements of regulatory impact analysis for 2008 through 2011, the time period when the financial regulations were proposed. Average scores for both types of regulations are quite similar.[43] The small differences between scores are not statistically significant; in other words, the differences could be due to random chance rather than any real differences in the quality or use of analysis.[44] Figure 1 clearly contradicts the claim that there is something unique about financial regulations that makes regulatory impact analysis more difficult than for other regulations. It is more consistent with Posner and Weyl's claim that "CBA [cost-benefit analysis] is at least as well suited to financial regulation as to other forms of regulation."[45]

Financial regulations evaluated in the Report Card share another similarity with nonfinancial regulations: no regulation offers an example of consistently good analysis on all of the criteria. Few financial regulations received a score of 5 on any of the four criteria, which would indicate complete analysis with one or more "best practices" that other agencies could learn from.[46] A score of 4 indicates that the analysis contains a reasonably thorough assessment of most aspects of the topic or an example of at least one "best practice." No regulation achieved a score of 4 on all four criteria.

One regulation, however—HUD's Real Estate Settlement Procedures Act (RESPA) regulation—received a score of 4 on the criterion that most often stymies all agencies: analysis of the problem. And the RIA clearly demonstrates how the benefits of the regulation flow from solving the problem. We examine

Figure 1. Comparison of Regulatory Report Card Scores for Financial and Nonfinancial Regulations, 2008–2011

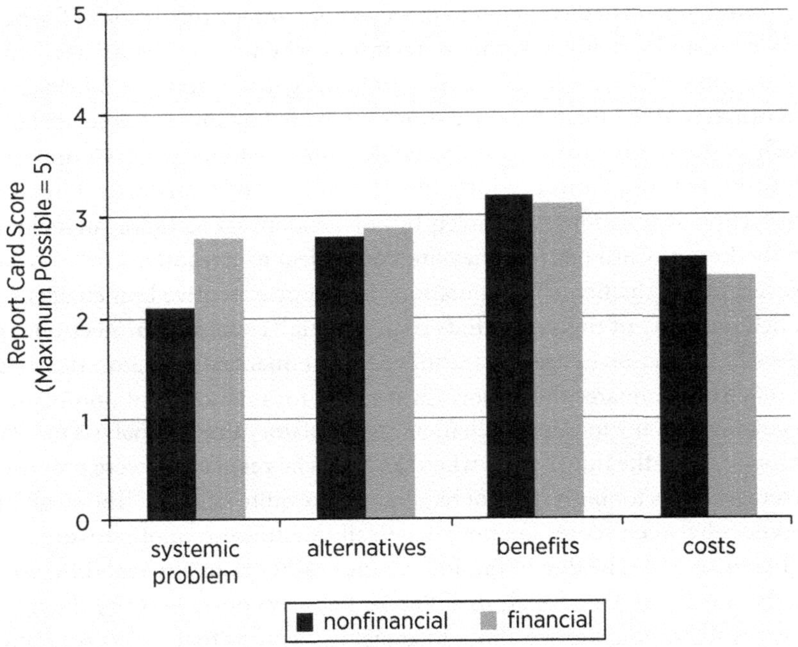

Source: Authors' calculations based on data available at www.mercatus.org/reportcards.

this part of HUD's analysis in greater detail to show how it is eminently possible to perform these crucial first steps of an RIA reasonably well, even for a financial regulation.

HUD'S RESPA REGULATORY IMPACT ANALYSIS: A CASE STUDY

Congress passed RESPA in 1974 to help consumers become better shoppers for settlement services and to eliminate kickbacks and referral fees. Since the passage of RESPA, HUD has adopted numerous regulations. One regulation, proposed in 2008, would have revised the good faith estimate (GFE) of closing costs, revised the HUD-1 form consumers receive at closing to make it track more closely with the proposed new GFE, and added a "closing script" to the revised HUD-1. The proposed GFE revision was accompanied by extensive analysis assessing the underlying problem HUD sought to solve and suggesting how the new regulation could create benefits for consumers.

Theory of the Problem

The department argues that the system for originating and closing mortgages is unnecessarily complex, makes it hard for many borrowers to identify the cheapest loan, and thus allows mortgage originators to impose higher costs on borrowers who cannot identify the cheapest loan.[47] Higher costs for borrowers create an obvious distributional issue that Congress was concerned about, but higher costs can also create economic inefficiency by prompting some potential borrowers to forgo home ownership or refinancing of an existing mortgage.

A key reason for consumer confusion was that the then-current GFE disclosures did not present costs and fees in an understandable way. Previous regulations under RESPA simply required increased disclosure of information on the GFE form, which the RIA acknowledges did little to help alleviate consumer confusion.[48] Confusion is especially likely when the loan involves a yield spread premium (YSP). A yield spread premium is a payment the lender makes to the mortgage originator because the loan carries an above-market interest rate. In theory, a YSP allows the borrower to reduce up-front closing costs in exchange for paying a higher interest rate. But if the GFE disclosures are not clear, consumers may not understand the tradeoffs and may have difficulty comparing loans from different lenders with different terms.

Evidence of the Problem

The RIA cites several studies to support the claim that asymmetric information or consumer confusion lead to higher settlement costs.

Woodward Study. One study, conducted for HUD by Susan E. Woodward and the Urban Institute,[49] used data from a national sample of 7,560 thirty-year, fixed-rate home purchase loans, insured by the Federal Housing Administration (FHA), that closed in May and June of 2001. Woodward's assessment included several findings that support HUD's theory:

- 495 of the 7,560 loans studied were no-cost loans. These are loans for which the YSP covered all lender and broker closing costs. Borrowers choosing no-cost loans simplified their shopping problem by shopping on rate alone, and they saved $1,200 compared to other borrowers.[50]

- Borrowers from direct lenders who received counseling from a third party saved $306 compared to borrowers who declined counseling or received counseling from the lender. This suggests that if a better disclosure could go part of the way in providing what counseling provides, borrowers could find better deals.[51]

- Borrowers with only a high school education paid higher settlement charges than buyers with a college education.[52] The differentials are large by any metric.[53] The difference amounts to nearly $1,090 for all loans classified as "nonsubsidized" and almost $1,271 for nonsubsidized loans with an interest rate above 7 percent.[54] This observation implies that better disclosures can fill a gap in the knowledge of borrowers who do not have the benefit of more (formal) education.[55] While all FHA loans are subsidized in the sense that that they carry lower interest rates because FHA guarantees them, in this study "subsidized" loans are those that have contributions to closing costs or down payments by state or local programs, interest rates at or below 6 percent, or interest rates off the one-eighth tick that is standard in the FHA market.[56]

Urban Institute Study. The Urban Institute also conducted an analysis of 5,926 nonsubsidized FHA loans drawn from the 7,560 loans in the Woodward study.[57] As table 2 shows, there is significant variation in closing costs. The ratio of what the 75th percentile pays to what the 25th percentile pays is 1.7 for total closing costs, 2.0 for total loan charges, 2.4 for the YSP, 2.9 for direct loan fees, 1.7 for title charges, and 1.6 for other third-party charges.[58] The variation is still substantial when the charges are calculated as a percentage of the loan amount. The ratio of what the 75th percentile pays as a percentage of the loan to what the 25th percentile pays is 1.8 for total loan charges, 2.1 for the YSP, and 2.4 for direct loan fees.[59]

From these results HUD concludes that half of the borrowers pay loan charges equal to or greater than 3.2 percent of the loan amount; one-quarter

Table 2. Distribution of Categories of Closing Costs

Series	5th Percentile	25th Percentile	50th Percentile (median)	75th Percentile	95th Percentile
Total closing cost	$2,663	$4,045	$5,334	$6,889	$10,183
Total loan charges	$1,104	$2,310	$3,392	$4,714	$7,394
Yield spread premium (indirect) loan fee	$250	$1,249	$2,041	$3,016	$4,658
Direct loan fee	$21	$683	$1,387	$2,008	$3,696
Total title charges	$666	$953	$1,267	$1,652	$2,407
Total other third-party charges	$293	$469	$574	$744	$1,097

Source: Department of Housing and Urban Development (HUD), Office of the Assistant Secretary for Housing, "Real Estate Settlement Procedures Act (RESPA): Simplification and Improvement of the Process of Obtaining Home Mortgages and Reducing Consumer Costs," Regulatory Impact Analysis (March 14, 2008): 6-22 at table 2-2 (reproducing Signe-Mary McKernan, Doug Wissoker, and William Margrabe, "Descriptive Analysis of FHA Loan Closing Costs, Prepared for the Department of Housing and Urban Development," Urban Institute, May 9, 2007, exhibit 11).

pay loan charges of at least 4.2 percent of the loan amount; and 5 percent pay loan charges of at least 6.2 percent of the loan amount. The variation is similar for title charges and other third-party charges. Half of the borrowers pay total closing costs equal to or greater than 5.1 percent of the loan amount; one-quarter pay closing costs of at least 6.4 percent of the loan amount; and 5 percent pay closing costs of at least 8.9 percent of the loan amount.[60]

Root Cause of the Problem: Misleading Mandated Disclosures

HUD made extensive use of a Federal Trade Commission (FTC) study on mortgage disclosure, as well as its own tests of alternative GFE disclosures.[61] These studies revealed that substantial percentages of borrowers could not identify important loan costs using then-current GFE disclosures, but some simple revisions could substantially improve consumer understanding.

The FTC conducted thirty-six in-depth interviews with recent mortgage customers and tested current and proposed disclosure language with more than 800 mortgage customers.[62] The interviews revealed that many respondents could not understand the disclosures on their own and asked the loan originators or closing agents to explain them.[63] Many did not understand the various itemized fees on the GFE form, such as the discount fee,[64] annual percentage rate (APR), amount financed, and the finance charge disclosure, or they could not determine how the individual fees related to the total.[65]

The quantitative consumer tests were conducted with two different loan-cost scenarios—one with relatively simple loans and the other with more complex loans that included features such as optional credit insurance, interest-only monthly payments that did not include escrow for taxes and insurance, a large balloon payment, and prepayment penalties.[66] Table 3 shows that

Table 3. Percentage of Respondents Viewing the Current Disclosure Forms Who Could Not Correctly Identify Various Loan Costs

Loan Cost	Percentage of Current-Form Respondents
APR amount	20
Settlement charges amount	23
Interest rate amount	32
Whether loan amount included financed settlement charges	33
Which loan was less expensive	37
Loan amount	51
Presence of prepayment penalty for refinance in two years	68
Presence of charges for optional credit insurance	74
Reason why the interest rate and APR sometimes differ	79
Property tax and homeowner's insurance cost amount	84
Total up-front charges amount	87
Prepayment penalty amount	95
Balloon payment (presence and amount)	30
Monthly payment (including whether it included taxes and insurance)	21
Cash due at closing amount	20

Source: James M. Lacko and Janis K. Pappalardo, "Improving Consumer Mortgage Disclosures: An Empirical Assessment of Current and Prototype Disclosure Forms," Staff Report, Federal Trade Commission (Washington, DC: Bureau of Economics, June 2007), 79.

Table 4. Improvements Provided by the Prototype Disclosure Form in the Percentage of Respondents Correctly Identifying Various Loan Costs

Loan Cost	Percentage Point Improvement
APR amount	16
Settlement charges amount	15
Interest rate amount	12
Whether loan amount included financed settlement charges	9
Which loan was less expensive	13
Loan amount	37
Presence of prepayment penalty for refinance in two years	24
Presence of charge for option credit insurance	43
Reason why the interest rate and APR sometimes differ	21
Property tax and homeowner's insurance cost amount	62
Total up-front charges amount	66
Prepayment penalty amount	53

Source: Lacko and Pappalardo, "Improving Consumer Mortgage Disclosures," 80.

substantial percentages of consumers could not correctly identify important information such as the total settlement charges, total up-front charges, the loan amount, optional charges, or which loan was less expensive.

The FTC also found that a revised GFE significantly increased consumer understanding. FTC researchers designed a three-page prototype disclosure form that summarized all key loan costs on the first page and provided additional detail on the second and third pages.[67] Table 4 reveals that the prototype form substantially increased the proportion of consumers who could correctly identify most major costs using the form, regardless of whether the loan was prime or subprime. As table 5 shows, much larger percentages of consumers correctly identified loan costs using the prototype form.

HUD also conducted multiple rounds of tests of alternative disclosures. Many of the questions HUD asked consumers were either identical to or closely analogous to those used in the FTC's survey. Table 6 reveals that

Table 5. Percentage of Questions Answered Correctly with Current and Prototype Disclosure Forms

Loan Scenario and Borrower Type N (Current Forms/ Prototype)	Percentage of Questions Answered Correctly		Difference between Forms (Prototype– Current)	
	Current Forms	Prototype Forms	Percentage Point Difference	Percentage Change
Both loans combined				
All borrowers (411/408)	60.8	79.7	19.0**	31.3
Prime borrowers (204/211)	62.0	80.6	18.6**	30.0
Subprime borrowers (207/197)	59.6	78.8	19.2**	32.2
Simple purchase loan				
All borrowers (205/201)	65.9	81.9	16.0**	24.3
Prime borrowers (100/102)	67.0	82.6	15.6**	23.3
Subprime borrowers (105/99)	65.0	81.2	16.2**	24.9
Complex refinance loan				
All borrowers (206/207)	55.7	77.7	22.0**	39.5
Prime borrowers (104/109)	57.2	78.8	21.6**	37.8
Subprime borrowers (102/98)	54.0	76.4	22.4**	41.5

Source: Lacko and Pappalardo, "Improving Consumer Mortgage Disclosures," 70.

** Indicates significance at the 1 percent level.

HUD's results confirm the FTC's conclusion: revised GFEs could substantially improve consumer understanding of key costs.[68] The first two rounds of HUD testing involved new disclosures. The first round determined whether consumers more easily understand a form containing a summary of settlement costs on the first page of the GFE or a form with total settlement costs disclosed after full disclosure of the mortgage details. The GFE form that included the summary of costs on the first page was preferred, and so it was used in the second round of testing. Round two tested a crosswalk from the GFE to the HUD-1 with participants, varying the order of presentation.[69] The FTC tested current disclosures[70] and an alternative disclosure. HUD tested two new disclosures; the RIA includes the results of these studies in a format similar to the one shown in table 6.

Table 6. Percentage of Respondents Who Could Not Correctly Identify Loan Costs, Terms, and Conditions

	Current Required Disclosures (Tested in FTC Study) (%)	Redesigned Disclosures		
		Alternative Tested in FTC Study (%)	Alternative Tested in Round 1 HUD Study (%)	Alternative Tested in Round 2 HUD Study (%)
APR	20	5	n/a	n/a
Amount of cash due at closing	20	17	n/a	n/a
Monthly payment	21	10	5	0
Settlement charges	23	8	9	3
Presence of balloon payment	30	30	7	10
Interest rate	32	20	7	0
Finance settlement charges	33	24	n/a	n/a
Less expensive of two loans	37	24	27	14
Loan amount	51	13		
Presence of a prepayment penalty	68	44	9	3
Presence of charges for optional credit insurance	74	30	n/a	n/a
Reason why the interest rate and APR sometimes differ	79	59	n/a	n/a
Property tax and homeowner's insurance amount	84	21	n/a	n/a
Total up-front cost	87	22	n/a	n/a
Prepayment penalty amount	95	42	n/a	n/a

Source: HUD, "Real Estate Settlement Procedures Act (RESPA)," 2-61.

Note: HUD marked cells as n/a when "the methodology of those surveys was different enough to preclude direct one-to-one comparison" with the FTC results. Ibid., 2-60.

Outcomes

The RIA identified the desired outcome of this rule as decreased settlement costs, which would make home ownership more affordable for consumers. Decreased settlement cost is clearly an outcome of great interest to consumers. In economic terms, the reduction in settlement cost is a transfer to consumers. The cost reduction may lead to an improvement in economic efficiency if more consumers buy homes or refinance existing loans as a result.[71]

481

To test the theory that more straightforward disclosures could increase consumer understanding of loan and mortgage offers, and that this understanding could reduce consumer costs, HUD engaged a contractor to conduct six rounds of consumer surveys that tested revised GFE forms. Various rounds of testing occurred from 2002 through 2007.

In the first two rounds of testing, consumers were asked to compare two loan offers using information from a redesigned GFE. In the first round of testing the revised GFE, 73 percent of people could identify the less costly loan. After further revision, round two increased this proportion to 90 percent. The third round of testing evaluated consumer understanding of a GFE with an alternative presentation of discount points (i.e., the amount of money a consumer pays up-front to decrease the interest rate) and the yield spread premium. Under this GFE format, 93 percent of the participants correctly identified the cheaper loan.[72]

Both the FTC and HUD undertook consumer tests to determine whether disclosure of the yield spread premium had any effect on a consumer's ability to accurately compare the cost of different loans.[73] Both agencies created information for a broker loan that was cheaper than a loan from a lender. The FTC tested several versions of GFE information with and without disclosure

Table 7. Identification and Selection of Broker Loan as Cheaper Loan with and without YSP Disclosure

	FTC Testing		HUD Testing: Round 4	
	When YSP Is Disclosed	When YSP Is Not Disclosed	YSP Disclosed	YSP Not Disclosed
% Correctly selecting broker loan as cheaper	72	90	83	92
% Incorrectly identifying lender loan as cheaper	17	4	8	1
% Who would choose broker loan	70	85	72	88
% Who would choose lender loan	16	3	11	1

Source: HUD, "Real Estate Settlement Procedures Act (RESPA)," 3-40.

of the YSP. HUD tested one version of the GFE with and without a YSP disclosure. Table 7 shows the results. In both sets of tests, a higher percentage of consumers identified and chose the cheaper loan when the YSP was not disclosed. The difference was narrower for HUD's version of the GFE. In HUD's test, 83 percent of consumers identified the cheaper loan when the YSP was disclosed, compared to 72 percent in the FTC's test.

The FTC concluded that the disclosure of the YSP impaired the ability of borrowers to comparison-shop and that disclosure of the YSP introduced bias in the selection process that favored lenders over brokers.[74]

The fifth round of HUD testing sought to verify that consumers' choices were the result of their understanding and not of a bias for or against a broker or a lender. All loan options included a YSP disclosure, but sometimes the broker loan was cheaper, sometimes the lender loan was cheaper, and sometimes the loans cost the same.[75] More than 90 percent of participants identified the cheapest loan, regardless of whether the broker loan or the lender loan was cheaper or the loans cost the same. A final round of testing included changes in the language on time frames and compensation to lenders, changes in the title, government recording and transfer charges, and an expansion of disclosed loan terms to alert the borrower to potentially unfavorable changes in their obligations.[76]

Following these tests, the department expressed great confidence that the simpler and more straightforward presentation of information in the proposed GFE form would improve the ability of the consumer to shop, compare offers, and identify the cheapest loan.[77]

Quantitative Estimates of Outcomes

Multiple studies have estimated the typical percentage of the yield spread premium that accrues to the borrower to offset closing costs. Empirical studies have also demonstrated that consumers pay lower fees when they seek loans that require simpler shopping strategies.[78] Since more informative disclosures are expected to make it easier for consumers to shop, the RIA assumes that improved disclosures will increase the percentage of the YSP that offsets borrower closing costs, generating savings for borrowers. The RIA offers a primary estimate that improved disclosures will reduce origination fees by 14 percent, saving borrowers $5.88 billion. It estimates an additional $2.47 billion in savings on third-party fees that are partially due to improved disclosures and partially due to other aspects of the regulation that we have not considered here.[79] (Unfortunately, the sizes of these effects are not broken out separately.) The RIA accurately labels these savings as transfers from loan originators and service providers to borrowers, not social benefits.[80] A separate analysis quantifies the portion of the transfers that comes from small businesses.[81] Another section presents extensive discussion of how the regulation would affect the competitive positions of various types of lenders, mortgage originators, and third-party service providers.[82]

The RIA notes that there is substantial uncertainty about the size of the likely consumer savings because the regulation could lead to substantial changes in mortgage markets.[83] Rather than using this as an excuse to avoid quantification, the RIA quite properly performs a sensitivity analysis to see how the results change when key input parameters change. The sensitivity analysis shows how the size of the transfers changes under several alternative calculation methods. It also shows how the results change under different assumptions about the size of origination charges as a percentage of the loan value, different levels of third-party fees, different volumes of mortgage origination, different percentages of consumer savings from improved disclosures, and different percentages of transactions accounted for by small businesses.[84] Alternative assumed input values are usually based on ranges of findings implied by studies or data sources, not just arbitrary assumptions.

The regulation generates an improvement in economic efficiency and social benefits if the savings that borrowers achieve as a result of more accurate disclosures prompt more people to become homeowners. Multiple studies find that insufficient cash to pay up-front closing costs is a significant barrier to home ownership, and they estimate the effect on home ownership of cash grants to pay closing costs. Since consumer savings from more effective shopping also reduce up-front costs, the RIA uses the results of the cash grant studies to estimate how the consumer savings from the regulation would affect home ownership. It estimates that the savings from the regulation could lead 100,000 to 400,000 renters to become homeowners.[85] It also estimates that the cost savings would generate between 500,000 and 3 million additional refinancings, since refinancing becomes more attractive to more homeowners when the up-front cost falls.[86]

CONCLUSION

The available evidence suggests that economic analysis of financial regulations needs substantial improvement. But the evidence also suggests that there is no reason financial regulations are inherently more difficult to analyze. In fact, the regulatory impact analysis for HUD's RESPA disclosure regulation demonstrates that even for the step in the analysis that most agencies neglect—analysis of the problem the regulation seeks to solve—it is possible to do quite good analysis for a financial regulation.

Skeptics concerned with the current state of data and analytical techniques, which they regard as an obstacle to the quantification of all (or even most) benefits and costs of financial regulation, should find reassurance in HUD's RESPA RIA. While it is true that financial regulation addresses problems that are different from the problems addressed by health, safety, or environmental regulation, success or failure can still be understood using numbers and units of measurement like percentages and dollar values. To assess the need for the regulation, the RIA utilized studies that measured the percentage of consumers who correctly understood loan costs and other terms after reading the current mandated disclosures and several possible alternatives. HUD found that the existing mandated disclosures confused consumers and enabled mortgage originators to impose higher costs on consumers (the Woodward study and FTC study).

Estimating the improvement in consumer understanding expected to flow from clearer disclosures was the first step in estimating the expected benefits of the regulation. The RIA then proceeded to estimate potential savings to consumers, accompanied by a sensitivity analysis that accounted for substantial uncertainties. The department determined that the asymmetric information problem could be mitigated by revising and simplifying mortgage cost disclosures, which would help consumers choose the lowest cost loan (FTC study, HUD study, comparison of results in RIA). The RIA also relied on studies that tested alternative disclosure forms, which helped to identify the sources of consumer confusion and identify ways to improve the disclosures (HUD study).

HUD certainly did not let a lack of available data restrict the analysis contained in this RIA. In fact, the Woodward study prepared for HUD and discussed extensively throughout the RIA itself, states that "[HUD] is responsible for writing the regulations for and enforcing RESPA, but has, until this study, lacked any data with which it might assess its effectiveness."[87] In other words, upon realizing a need for data, the agency commissioned research from outside scholars with expertise in consumer shopping behavior in the mortgage market and amassed a body of research to consult in the future.

The former administrator of the Office of Information and Regulatory Affairs (OIRA), Cass Sunstein, in an article describing his experience with OIRA review of RIAs, noted that "the most difficult problems appeared quite rarely, and when they did, there were generally standardized methods of handling them."[88] Our research suggests that Sunstein's statement is as true of financial regulation as it is of other types of regulation. The appropriate course of action, therefore, is to undertake regulatory impact analysis for financial regulations with the expectation that we will learn much more by trying than by cataloging problems that prevent perfect analysis.

NOTES

1. Posner and Weyl, "Cost-Benefit Analysis of Financial Regulations."

2. See, for example, Coates, "Cost-Benefit Analysis of Financial Regulations"; Gordon, "Empty Call for Benefit-Cost Analysis"; Cochrane, "Challenges for Cost-Benefit Analysis."

3. Exec. Order 12044, 43 Fed. Reg. (March 24, 1978): 12661; Exec. Order 12291, 46 Fed. Reg. (February 19, 1981): 13193; Exec. Order 12866, 58 Fed. Reg. (October 4, 1993): 51735; Exec. Order 13563, 76 Fed. Reg. (January 21, 2011): 3821.

4. Copeland, "Economic Analysis and Independent Regulatory Agencies"; and Peirce, "Economic Analysis."

5. Sunstein, "Financial Regulation and Cost-Benefit Analysis."

6. Exec. Order 12866, §1(b)(1).

7. Williams and Thompson, "Integrated Analysis," 1617.

8. Ellig, "Improving Regulatory Impact Analysis," 4.

9. Ellig, Broughel, and Bell, "Regulating Real Problems."

10. McLaughlin, Ellig, and Shamoun, "Regulatory Reform in Florida."

11. Posner and Weyl, "Benefit-Cost Paradigms."

12. Muris, "Rules without Reason."

13. Exec. Order 12866, §§ 1(a), 1(b)(2), 1(b)(3), 1(b)(8).

14. OMB, Circular A-4, 8–9.

15. Coglianese and Lazer, "Management-Based Regulation"; Prakash and Potoski, "Racing to the Bottom?"

16. Thaler and Sunstein, *Nudge*.

17. OMB, *Circular A-4*, 8.

18. Ibid., 17.

19. Ibid., 12.

20. Cochrane, "Challenges for Cost-Benefit Analysis," S99.

21. Hahn and Tetlock, "Has Economic Analysis Improved Regulatory Decisions?"

22. The Mercatus Center has developed a survey instrument called the Regulatory Cost Calculator that agencies and stakeholders can use to gather more accurate information about opportunity costs. See http://mercatus.org/publication/regulatory-cost-calculator.

23. Posner and Weyl, "Benefit-Cost Paradigms," S17.

24. See, for example, Senate Committee on the Budget, "Hearing," 45.

25. Coates, "Cost-Benefit Analysis of Financial Regulations," 999–1003; Gordon, "Empty Call for Benefit-Cost Analysis," S358–60.

26. Coates, "Cost-Benefit Analysis of Financial Regulation," 891–92.

27. Posner and Weyl, "Cost-Benefit Analysis of Financial Regulations," 247.

28. Cass Sunstein, former administrator of the Office of Information and Regulatory Affairs (OIRA), offers numerous stylized examples. See Sunstein, "Real World of Cost-Benefit Analysis." This argument is made in the specific context of financial regulation by Rose and Walker, "Importance of Cost-Benefit Analysis," 17–18.

29. Alfon and Andrews, "Cost-Benefit Analysis in Financial Regulation," 344.

30. Posner and Weyl, "Cost-Benefit Analysis of Financial Regulations," 258.

31. Sunstein, "Real World of Cost-Benefit Analysis," provides several examples.

32. Posner and Weyl, "Cost-Benefit Analysis of Financial Regulations," 257.

33. Manne, "Will the SEC's New Embrace?," 22.

34. Exec. Order 12866 §1(b)(7).

35. Alfon and Andrews, "Cost-Benefit Analysis of Financial Regulation," 339–40.

36. "Economically significant" regulations have a material adverse effect on the economy or have an annual effect on the economy of $100 million or more. "Prescriptive" regulations are what most people think of when they think of regulations: they mandate or prohibit certain activities. This is distinct from budget regulations, which implement federal spending programs or revenue collection measures. The Report Card methodology is explained in Ellig and McLaughlin, "Quality and Use of Regulatory Analysis." An explanation of the scoring method and all score data for the Mercatus Regulatory Report Card are available at http://mercatus.org/reportcard.

37. Fraas and Lutter, "Challenges of Improving the Economic Analysis"; Hahn et al., "Assessing Regulatory Impact Analyses"; Hahn and Dudley, "How Well Does the Government?"; Hahn and Litan, "Counting Regulatory Benefits and Costs."

38. Harrington, Heinzerling, and Morgenstern, *Reforming Regulatory Impact Analysis*; Morgenstern, *Economic Analyses at EPA*; McGarity, *Reinventing Rationality*.

39. Ellig and McLaughlin, "Quality and Use of Regulatory Analysis."

40. Ellig, McLaughlin, and Morrall, "Continuity, Change, and Priorities"; Ellig and Conover, "Presidential Priorities."

41. An evaluation of inter-rater reliability is available at http://mercatus.org/reportcard.

42. Ellig, "Comprehensive Regulatory Impact Analysis," 5–6.

43. Results are substantially the same when comparing median scores. Median scores for financial regulations on each of the four criteria are either equal to or slightly higher than median scores for nonfinancial regulations.

44. A t-test found that none of the differences are significant at even the 10 percent level; that is, there is a greater than 10 percent likelihood that the differences are due to random chance. The conventional cutoff point in economics for judging whether a difference is "statistically significant" is a 5 percent or lower likelihood that the difference is due to random chance. Three of the Labor Department regulations on exemptions for provision of investment advice are closely related; two utilize the same RIA, and the third modified some assumptions in the initial RIA. Differences in average scores are still not statistically significant when this RIA is included in the average only once.

45. Posner and Weyl, "Cost-Benefit Analysis of Financial Regulations," 262.

46. In this context, the term "best practices" means the best practices the Report Card evaluators have seen while evaluating regulatory impact analyses for economically significant regulations.

47. HUD, "Real Estate Settlement Procedures Act (RESPA)," 6-20.

48. Ibid., 6-5: "The current GFE is typically comprised of a long list of charges, as today's rules do not prescribe a standard form and consolidated categories. Such a long list of individual charges can be overwhelming, often confuses consumers, and seems to provide little useful information for consumer shopping. The current GFE certainly does not inform consumers what the major costs are so that they can effectively shop and compare mortgage offers among different loan originators. The current GFE does not explain how the borrower can use the document to shop and compare loans. Also, the GFE fails to make clear the relationship between the closing costs and the interest rate on a loan, notwithstanding that many mortgage loans originated today adjust up-front closing costs due at settlement, either up or down, depending on whether the interest rate on the loan is below or above 'par.' Finally, current rules do not assure that the 'good faith estimate' is a reliable estimate of final settlement costs. As a result, under today's rules, the estimated costs on GFEs may be unreliable or incomplete, and final charges at settlement may include significant increases in items that were estimated on the GFE, as well as additional fees, which can add to the consumer's ultimate closing costs."

49. Woodward, "Study of Closing Costs." The report lists a date of 2008 because the study was not presented in public until then. It is listed in RIA references as Urban Institute, "A Study of Closing Costs for FHA Mortgages," prepared for Department of Housing and Urban Development Office of Policy Development and Research by Susan E. Woodward, November 29, 2007b; and also referred to as "The HUD/FHA Study of Mortgage Closing Costs: Preliminary Report" in chapter 2 of the RIA and Urban Institute (2007b), 37–41.

50. HUD, "Real Estate Settlement Procedures Act," 2-43.

51. Ibid.

52. Ibid., 2-51. The HUD study used the average educational attainment of the adults in the borrower's census tract as a measure of education level because actual individual education levels are not known. The differences are calculated from regression analyses that control for the following borrower characteristics: loan amount, credit scores, income, whether borrowers were counseled and by whom, metropolitan area incomes, and borrower race, etc.

53. Ibid., 2-50.

54. Ibid.

55. Ibid., 2-42.

56. Woodward, "Study of Closing Costs," 22 (also mentioned in RIA, chap. 2, 42n52).

57. McKernan, Wissoker, and Margrabe, "Descriptive Analysis of FHA Loan Closing Costs." According to the RIA, this study was conducted for internal use only (see the RIA references list, 17). The RIA refers to this study by two different short forms "Urban Institute 2007a" and "Urban Institute (2008)."

58. HUD, "Real Estate Settlement Procedures Act," 6-21.

59. Ibid., 6-22, including table.

60. Ibid., 6-21.

61. Lacko and Pappalardo, "Improving Consumer Mortgage Disclosures." Also referred to as "the FTC study."

62. Lacko and Pappalardo, "Improving Consumer Mortgage Disclosures," ES-3: "The current disclosure forms consisted of the Truth-in-Lending Act ('TILA') statement that is required for closed-end, fixed-rate residential mortgages under TILA, and the Good Faith Estimate of Settlement Costs ('GFE') required under the Real Estate Settlement Procedures Act ('RESPA')."

63. Lacko and Pappalardo, "Improving Consumer Mortgage Disclosures," 31.

64. Ibid., 34: "The discount fee denotes a charge on the borrower in exchange for a lower interest rate than would otherwise be charged on the loan. The term 'discount' refers to the lowered interest rate, not lowered fees. The discount fee is one of the required itemized settlement charges that must be disclosed in the GFE, if such a charge is included in the loan . . . roughly a third of the respondents misunderstood the term to indicate a discount received by the borrower, rather than a charge paid, and believed that the settlement fees were being discounted by the stated amount. . . ."

65. Lacko and Pappalardo, "Improving Consumer Mortgage Disclosures," 31–37.

66. The results of twenty-five questions (or combinations of questions) were analyzed to assess the ability of respondents to understand and use the disclosure forms. Twenty-one questions were used in the simple-loan scenario because some of the loan terms were not present in these loans.

67. Lacko and Pappalardo, "Improving Consumer Mortgage Disclosures," 11.

68. HUD, "Real Estate Settlement Procedures Act," 2-60.

69. Ibid., 3-35n21.

70. Ibid., 2-60: "Since no standardized good faith estimate (GFE) form exists, a form similar to many currently in use was created specifically for this purpose; both the FTC and the Department believe that the instrument is representative of mainstream practices."

71. Ibid., 3-120. Of course, not every policy that incentivizes renters to become homeowners represents an improvement in economic efficiency. Improved disclosures that give consumers more accurate information about the cost of loans, however, reduce transaction costs and hence improve efficiency.

72. Ibid., 3-37, 3-39. According to the department, while this technique identifies how well participants use the GFE form as a stand-alone document in a testing situation, consumers using these forms in actual situations may perform even better because a loan originator and local consumer groups that focus on lending issues would be able to answer borrower ques-

tions about the information on the forms and improve the borrower's understanding of the form. The department notes that because none of these sources were available during the testing, the results should be viewed as underestimates of how much the new forms will help consumers who are actually obtaining financing to purchase a home or refinance an existing loan.

73. Ibid., 3-39 (this is actually referring to Lacko and Pappalardo, "Effect of Mortgage Broker Compensation Disclosures").

74. Ibid., 3-41.

75. Ibid., 2-43, 3-42.

76. Ibid., 3-45.

77. Ibid., 3-47.

78. Ibid., 3-92–93.

79. Ibid., 3-98.

80. Ibid., 3-103.

81. Ibid., 3-104–8.

82. Ibid., 3-131–51.

83. Ibid., 3-87.

84. Ibid., 3-108–15.

85. Ibid., 3-121–23.

86. Ibid., 3-123–24.

87. Woodward, "Study of Closing Costs," viii.

88. Sunstein, "Real World of Cost-Benefit Analysis," 4.

REFERENCES

Alfon, Isaac, and Peter Andrews. "Cost-Benefit Analysis in Financial Regulation: How to Do It and How It Adds Value." *Journal of Financial Regulation and Compliance* 7, no. 4 (1999): 339–52.

Coates, John C., IV. "Cost-Benefit Analysis of Financial Regulations: Case Studies and Implications." *Yale Law Journal* 124, no. 4 (January–February 2015): 882–1011.

Cochrane, John H. "Challenges for Cost-Benefit Analysis of Financial Regulation." *Journal of Legal Studies* 43 (2014): S63–S105.

Coglianese, Cary, and David Lazer. "Management-based Regulation: Prescribing Private Management to Achieve Public Goals." *Law and Society Review* 37, no. 4 (December 2003): 691–730.

Copeland, Curtis W. "Economic Analysis and Independent Regulatory Agencies." Report prepared for the Administrative Conference of the United States, April 30, 2013.

Department of Housing and Urban Development (HUD), Office of the Assistant Secretary for Housing. "Real Estate Settlement Procedures Act (RESPA): Simplification and Improvement of the Process of Obtaining Home Mortgages and Reducing Consumer Costs." Regulatory Impact Analysis, March 14, 2008.

Ellig, Jerry. "Improving Regulatory Impact Analysis through Process Reform." Testimony before the US Congress Joint Economic Committee, June 26, 2013.

———. "Comprehensive Regulatory Impact Analysis: The Cornerstone of Regulatory Reform." Testimony before the Senate Committee on Homeland Security and Government Affairs, February 25, 2015.

Ellig, Jerry, James Broughel, and Spencer Bell. "Regulating Real Problems: The First Principle of Regulatory Impact Analysis." Mercatus on Policy, Mercatus Center at George Mason University, Arlington, VA, March 2016.

Ellig, Jerry, and Christopher J. Conover. "Presidential Priorities, Congressional Control, and the Quality of Regulatory Impact Analysis: An Application to Health Care and Homeland Security." *Public Choice* 161 (2014): 305–20.

Ellig, Jerry, and Patrick A. McLaughlin. "The Quality and Use of Regulatory Analysis in 2008," *Risk Analysis* 32 (2012): 855–80.

Ellig, Jerry, Patrick A. McLaughlin, and John F. Morrall III. "Continuity, Change, and Priorities: The Quality and Use of Regulatory Analysis across U.S. Administrations." *Regulation & Governance* 7 (2013): 153–73.

Fraas, Art, and Randall Lutter. "The Challenges of Improving the Economic Analysis of Pending Regulations: The Experience of OMB Circular A-4." *Annual Review of Resource Economics* 3, no. 1 (2011): 71–85

Gordon, Jeffrey N. "The Empty Call for Benefit-Cost Analysis in Financial Regulation." *Journal of Legal Studies* 43, no. S2 (June 2014): S351–78.

Hahn, Robert W., Jason Burnett, Yee-Ho I. Chan, Elizabeth Mader, and Petrea Moyle. "Assessing Regulatory Impact Analyses: The Failure of Agencies to Comply with Executive Order 12,866." *Harvard Journal of Law and Public Policy* 23, no. 3 (2001): 859–71.

Hahn, Robert W., and Patrick Dudley. "How Well Does the Government Do Cost–Benefit Analysis?" *Review of Environmental Economics and Policy* 1, no. 2 (2007): 192–211.

Hahn, Robert W., and Robert Litan. "Counting Regulatory Benefits and Costs: Lessons for the U.S. and Europe." *Journal of International Economic Law* 8, no. 2 (2005): 473–508.

Hahn, Robert W., and Paul C. Tetlock. "Has Economic Analysis Improved Regulatory Decisions?" *Journal of Economic Perspectives* 22, no. 1 (Winter 2008): 67–84.

Harrington, Winston, Lisa Heinzerling, and Richard D. Morgenstern, eds. *Reforming Regulatory Impact Analysis*. Washington, DC: Resources for the Future, 2009.

Lacko, James M., and Janis K. Pappalardo. "The Effect of Mortgage Broker Compensation Disclosures on Consumers and Competition: A Controlled Experiment." Bureau of Economics Staff Report, Federal Trade Commission, 2004.

———. "Improving Consumer Mortgage Disclosures: An Empirical Assessment of Current and Prototype Disclosure Forms." Staff Report, Federal Trade Commission, Bureau of Economics, Washington, DC, June 2007.

Manne, Henry G. "Will the SEC's New Embrace of Cost-Benefit Analysis Be a Watershed Moment?" *Regulation* (Summer 2012): 20–25.

McGarity, Thomas O. *Reinventing Rationality: The Role of Regulatory Analysis in the Federal Bureaucracy*. New York: Cambridge University Press, 1991.

McKernan, Signe-Mary, Doug Wissoker, and William Margrabe. "Descriptive Analysis of FHA Loan Closing Costs." Urban Institute for US Department of Housing and Urban Development, Washington, DC, May 9, 2007.

McLaughlin, Patrick A., Jerry Ellig, and Dima Yazji Shamoun. "Regulatory Reform in Florida: An Opportunity for Greater Competitiveness and Economic Efficiency." *Florida State University Business Review* 13, no. 1 (Spring 2014): 110–15.

Morgenstern, Richard D. *Economic Analyses at EPA: Assessing Regulatory Impact.* Washington, DC: Resources for the Future, 1997.

Muris, Timothy J. "Rules without Reason." *Regulation* (September–October 1982): 20–26.

Peirce, Hester. "Economic Analysis by Federal Financial Regulators." *Journal of Law, Economics, and Policy* 9, no. 4 (2013): 569–613.

Posner, Eric A., and E. Glen Weyl. "Benefit-Cost Paradigms in Financial Regulation." *Journal of Legal Studies* 43, no. S2 (June 2014): S16–S25.

———. "Cost-Benefit Analysis of Financial Regulations: A Response to Criticisms." *Yale Law Journal Forum* (January 22, 2015): 246–62.

Prakash, Aseem, and Matthew Potoski. "Racing to the Bottom? Trade, Environmental Governance, and ISO 14001." *American Journal of Political Science* 50, no. 2 (April 2006): 350–64.

Rose, Paul, and Christopher Walker. "The Importance of Cost-Benefit Analysis in Financial Regulation." Report for the US Chamber of Commerce, March 2013.

Senate Committee on the Budget. "Hearing: Moving to a Stronger Economy with a Regulatory Budget." Transcript, December 4, 2015.

Sunstein, Cass R. "Financial Regulation and Cost-Benefit Analysis." *Yale Law Journal* 124 (January 22, 2015): 263. http://www.yalelawjournal.org/pdf/SunsteinPDF_4nf1d4ar.pdf.

———. "The Real World of Cost-Benefit Analysis: Thirty-Six Questions (and Almost as Many Answers)." *Columbia Law Review* 114 (2015): 168–212.

Thaler, Richard H., and Cass R. Sunstein. *Nudge: Improving Decisions about Health, Welfare, and Happiness.* New Haven, CT: Yale University Press, 2008.

Williams, Richard A., and Kimberly M. Thompson. "Integrated Analysis: Combining Risk and Economic Assessments while Preserving the Separation of Powers." *Risk Analysis* 24, no. 6 (2004): 1613–23.

Woodward, Susan E. "A Study of Closing Costs for FHA Mortgages." Urban Institute for US Department of Housing and Urban Development, Office of Policy Development and Research, Washington, DC, May 2008.

ABOUT THE CONTRIBUTORS

Holly A. Bell is an associate professor of business and economics at the University of Alaska Anchorage and a contributing scholar with the Cato Institute and the Mercatus Center at George Mason University. Her areas of expertise include high-frequency trading, financial markets, risk management, and financial regulations. She holds a BA in economics and foreign policy from the University of Memphis, an MBA from the University of South Dakota, and a doctorate in business administration from George Fox University.

Harold A. Black is a professor emeritus of financial institutions, at the University of Tennessee, Knoxville. He lectures, consults, and publishes extensively in the areas of financial institutions and the monetary system. He previously served as a director and chairman of the Nashville Branch of the Federal Reserve Bank of Atlanta. A native of Atlanta, Georgia, Black received his undergraduate degree from the University of Georgia and his MA and PhD degrees from Ohio State University.

David R. Burton is a senior fellow in economic policy at The Heritage Foundation. His research focuses on tax matters, securities law, entrepreneurship, financial privacy, and regulatory and administrative law issues. Previously, Burton was general counsel at the National Small Business Association and was chief financial officer and general counsel of the start-up Alliance for Retirement Prosperity. For fifteen years, Burton was a partner in the Argus Group, a Virginia-based law, public policy, and government relations firm. Burton received a JD from the University of Maryland School of Law and a BA in economics from the University of Chicago.

Jerry Ellig is a senior research fellow at the Mercatus Center at George Mason University and a former assistant professor of economics at George Mason University. He specializes in federal regulatory process, economic regulation, and telecommunications regulation. Previously, he was deputy director and acting director of the Office of Policy Planning at the Federal Trade Commission. He also served as senior economist for the Joint Economic Committee of the US Congress. Ellig holds a BA in economics from Xavier

University and he received his MA and PhD in economics from George Mason University.

Hon. Daniel M. Gallagher is president of Patomak Global Partners, LLC. From November 2011 to October 2015, he served as a commissioner of the US Securities and Exchange Commission (SEC). During his tenure, he focused on initiatives aimed at strengthening the capital markets and encouraging small business capital formation. Before being appointed commissioner, Gallagher served on the staff of the SEC in several capacities and spent a number of years in the private sector. Gallagher received his BA in English from Georgetown University and his JD from the Catholic University of America.

Hon. J. Christopher Giancarlo is a commissioner of the US Commodity Futures Trading Commission. Before entering public service, Giancarlo served as the executive vice president of GFI Group Inc., a financial services firm. Before joining GFI, Giancarlo was executive vice president and US Legal Counsel of Fenics Software and was a corporate partner in the New York law firm of Brown Raysman Millstein Felder & Steiner. He has testified five times before Congress and has written and spoken extensively on public policy, legal, and other matters involving technology and financial markets. Giancarlo received his BA in government from Skidmore College and his JD from the Vanderbilt University School of Law.

Thomas L. Hogan is a committee staff member in the US Senate and is currently on leave from Troy University where he is an assistant professor of finance at the Johnson Center for Political Economy. Previously, he was an assistant professor of economics at West Texas A&M University. He has worked for Merrill Lynch's commodity trading group, as a derivatives trader for investment funds in the United States and Europe, and as a consultant to the World Bank. Hogan received his PhD in economics from George Mason University and both his BBA and MBA from the University of Texas at Austin.

Kristine Johnson is a committee staff member in the US Senate and is an alumna of the Mercatus Center MA Fellowship at George Mason University.

Her research focuses on the regulation of financial markets. Johnson earned her MA in economics from George Mason University and her BA from Towson University in international studies.

Garett Jones is a senior scholar and BB&T Professor for the Study of Capitalism at the Mercatus Center at George Mason University and an associate professor of economics at George Mason University. He specializes in macroeconomics, monetary economics, and the microfoundations of economic growth. He is the author of *Hive Mind: How Your Nation's IQ Matters So Much More Than Your Own*, published by Stanford University Press. Jones received his BA in history from Brigham Young University, his MPA from Cornell, his MA in political science from the University of California at Berkeley, and his PhD in economics from the University of California at San Diego.

James M. Kilts is a partner at Centerview Capital, an operationally oriented private equity firm focused on the US consumer middle- and upper-middle market. Mr. Kilts has also served as vice chairman of the board at Procter & Gamble Company; chairman of the board, CEO, and president at The Gillette Company; president and CEO at Nabisco; head of the $27 billion Worldwide Food group (Kraft Foods) of Philip Morris Companies; and president of Kraft and Oscar Mayer. Mr. Kilts began his career with the General Foods Corporation. A graduate of Knox College in Galesburg, Illinois, Mr. Kilts earned his MBA from the University of Chicago. He serves on the board of trustees at both schools and on multiple corporate boards of directors. Mr. Kilts is also a member of the advisory council for the University of Chicago Booth School of Business and the board of overseers of Weill Cornell Medical College.

Arnold Kling is an affiliated senior scholar at the Mercatus Center at George Mason University. Previously, Kling served as a senior economist at Freddie Mac and a staff economist on the Board of Governors of the Federal Reserve System. He testified before Congress on the collapse of Fannie Mae and Freddie Mac. He started Homefair, one of the first commercial websites on the Internet. He specializes in housing finance policy, financial institutions, macroeconomics, and the inside workings of America's federal financial institutions. Kling has authored and coauthored a number of books, including *Specialization and Trade: A Re-introduction to Economics*, published by Cato in 2016, and

From Poverty to Prosperity: Intangible Assets, Hidden Liabilities and the Lasting Triumph Over Scarcity, published by Encounter Books in 2009. Kling obtained his BS in economics from Swarthmore College and his PhD in economics from the Massachusetts Institute of Technology.

Benjamin Klutsey is the program manager for the Financial Markets Working Group and the Program on Monetary Policy at the Mercatus Center at George Mason University. Klutsey was previously with the Institute of International Finance, where he served as policy assistant analyzing international financial regulations related to liquidity risk management and risk governance. He received his MA in international commerce and policy from George Mason University and his BA in government and philosophy from Lawrence University.

William J. Luther is an assistant professor of economics at Kenyon College, adjunct scholar with the Cato Institute's Center for Monetary and Financial Alternatives, and a fellow with the Atlas Network's Sound Money Project. His research focuses primarily on questions of currency acceptance and the role governments play in determining commonly accepted media of exchange. He earned his MA and PhD in economics at George Mason University and his BA in economics at Capital University.

Stephen Matteo Miller is a senior research fellow at the Mercatus Center at George Mason University. Before joining the Mercatus Center, he was a visiting assistant professor at Bryn Mawr College. Miller also spent several years as a consultant at the World Bank and seven years teaching macroeconomics and financial economics at Monash University in Melbourne, Australia. His research focuses on the origins, effects, and resolution of market crashes and financial crises. Miller earned his BA and PhD in economics from George Mason University.

Thomas W. Miller Jr. is a professor of finance and the inaugural holder of the Jack R. Lee Chair in Financial Institutions and Consumer Finance at Mississippi State University and a visiting scholar with the Mercatus Center at George Mason University. He has held positions at Saint Louis University, Washington University in St. Louis, and the University of Missouri and has taught in Italy and France. Professor Miller has won numerous teaching and research awards. He earned his BS and MS in economics from Montana State University and his PhD in finance from the University of Washington.

Hester Peirce is a senior research fellow and director of the Financial Markets Working Group at the Mercatus Center at George Mason University. Before joining the Mercatus Center, she served as a senior counsel to the Republican staff on the Senate Committee on Banking, Housing, and Urban Affairs. Before that, she served as counsel to Commissioner Paul S. Atkins at the US Securities and Exchange Commission and as a staff attorney in the Division of Investment Management at the US Securities and Exchange Commission. She earned her BA in economics from Case Western Reserve University and her JD from Yale Law School.

Houman B. Shadab is a professor of law and codirector at the Center for Business and Financial Law at New York Law School and also serves as the editor-in-chief of the *Journal of Taxation and Regulation of Financial Institutions*. Before joining New York Law School's faculty, Shadab was a senior research fellow at the Mercatus Center at George Mason University. His research focuses on financial technology, smart contracts, hedge funds, derivatives, commercial transactions, and blockchains. Shadab received his JD from the University of Southern California School of Law and BA from the University of California at Berkeley.

Vera Soliman is a research assistant at the Mercatus Center at George Mason University. She attended the University of Connecticut where she earned a BA in economics.

Edward Stringham is Davis Professor of Economic Organizations and Innovation at Trinity College. He is president of the Society for the Development of Austrian Economics, former president of the Association of Private Enterprise Education, editor of the *Journal of Private Enterprise*, editor of two books, and author of more than sixty journal articles, book chapters, and policy studies. Stringham authored *Private Governance: Creating Order in Economic and Social Life*, published by Oxford University Press in 2015. His research examines the efficacy of self-governance versus central planning and how self-governance provides order in instances where government enforcement cannot. Stringham earned his BA in economics from College of the Holy Cross and his PhD in economics from George Mason University.

J. W. Verret is an associate professor at the Antonin Scalia Law School at George Mason University and a senior scholar at the Mercatus Center at George Mason University. In 2013, he took leave for two years to serve as the chief economist and senior counsel for the US House Committee on Financial Services. His primary research interests include corporate governance, securities regulation, and executive compensation. Verret received his BS in financial accounting from Louisiana State University, his MA in public policy from the Harvard Kennedy School of Government, and his JD from Harvard Law School.

Peter J. Wallison holds the Arthur F. Burns Chair in Financial Policy Studies and is codirector of the American Enterprise Institute's program on Financial Policy Studies. Wallison has held a number of government positions, including general counsel of the US Treasury Department, where he had a significant role in the development of the Reagan administration's proposals for the deregulation of the financial services industry, and White House counsel to President Ronald Reagan. He is the author of the 2015 book *Hidden in Plain Sight: What Really Caused the World's Worst Financial Crisis and Why It Could Happen Again*, published by Encounter Books. Wallison earned his BA from Harvard College and his LLB from Harvard Law School.

Todd J. Zywicki is George Mason University Foundation Professor and executive director of the Law & Economics Center at the Antonin Scalia Law School at George Mason University, senior scholar of the Mercatus Center at George Mason University, and former director of the Office of Policy Planning at the US Federal Trade Commission. He has testified on numerous occasions before the US Congress and is a frequent commentator in the print and broadcast media on issues of consumer credit and consumer bankruptcy. Zywicki coauthored *Consumer Credit and the American Economy*, published by Oxford University Press in 2014. Zywicki holds an AB from Dartmouth College, a JD from the University of Virginia, and an MA in economics from Clemson University.

INDEX

Page numbers in *italics* indicate figures and tables.

risk management
  CCPs, 183, 187–188, 209–210nn75–78
  clearing mandate, 186–187
  DCOs, 210n80
  international standards, 183–184
  OTC derivatives regulation, 186–187,
    196–201
  regulatory conflicts of interest, 191–195
  role of derivatives in, 181
risk tolerance, 285, 286
risk-weighted assets, 19, 21, 37, 44, 123
Robert Thompson, 282
Roberts, Russ, 4, 118
Robinhood (robo-adviser), 423
Robinson, Kenneth J., 70
robo-advisers, 423
Roe, Mark J., 185, 443, 445, 446, 447, 457n18
Rolnick, Arthur J., 79
Romano, Roberta, 227, 282, 441, 443, 446,
  456n5
Rome, ancient, 229, 440, 455–456
Roosevelt, Franklin, 63, 86n13
Rose, Paul, 487n28
Royal Bank of Canada, 262
Royal Exchange (England), 232
Rundle, James, 210n82
Russell Sage Foundation, 360, 361, 371–372,
  377, 381n64
Russia, federal deposit insurance, 68
Russo, Daniela, 217n148

Saar, Gideon, 254
safe harbors, 419
Sage, Margaret Olivia, 360
Saltz, Ira, 64
Saltzman, Paul, 214n123, 216n141
Saluzzi, Joseph, 257
Samolyk, Katherine, 359, 380n31, 381n55
"sandboxes" (experimental initiatives), 419
Sanders, Bernie, 262
S&L Crisis. See Savings and Loan (S&L)
  Crisis
S&Ls. See savings and loans
Sarao, Navinder Singh, 268
Sarbanes-Oxley Act (2002)
  corporate governance, 438, 439, 444–445
  emerging growth companies, 279
  flawed implementation, 227
  public company compliance costs, 294
  rationale behind, 226
  reporting requirements, 279
Sargent, Thomas, 85n4
savings accounts, 44–45

Savings and Loan (S&L) Crisis
  aftermath, 14
  banking crisis, 38–39
  book-value accounting, 23–24
  causes, 63, 64–65, 102
  Maryland, 77
  mortgage lending, 14
  Ohio, 77
  total cost of, 65
savings and loans (S&Ls)
  charter value, 28
  deregulation, 82
Scheinkman, Jose, 344
Schnabl, Philipp, 29–30
Schooling Latter, Edwin, 177n86
Schumer, Charles, 227, 333, 401–402
Schumer Box, 333
SCI (Systems Compliance and Integrity),
  258–259, 267
Scott, Hal S., 102, 192, 217n149
SDR. See swap data repository
SDs. See swap dealers
SEC. See Securities and Exchange Commission
Secure and Fair Enforcement for Mortgage
  Licensing Act, 434n21
securities. See offering and disclosure reform
Securities Act (1933)
  amendments, 306n126
  audit requirements, 293
  crowdfunding, 450
  exemptions, 278, 298n6
  policy proposals, 290, 293
  registration requirements, 277–278
  Regulation A, 289
Securities Acts Amendments (1964), 288
securities and derivatives markets, regulating,
  137–315
  broker-dealer regulation, 137–154
  clearinghouses, 180–224
  Dodd-Frank swaps trading regulatory
    framework, 155–179
  exchanges as regulators, 225–252
  offering and disclosure reform, 277–315
  OTC derivatives regulation, 180–224
  proprietary algorithmic trading, 253–276
  state laws, 457n30
Securities and Exchange Commission (SEC)
  automated investment advisers, regulation
    of, 424
  Automated Review Policy, 258–259
  bitcoin regulation, 392
  broker-dealer regulation, 137–154
  CCP regulation, 180–224

6153401